M000250505

Embedded Microprocessor Systems Design:

An Introduction
Using the Intel 80C188EB

Kenneth L. Short

Prentice Hall
Upper Saddle River, New Jersey 07458

Library of Congress Cataloging-in-Publication Data

    Embedded microprocessor systems design : an introduction using the
Intel 80C188EB / Kenneth L. Short.
             p.   cm.
    Includes bibliographical references and index.
    ISBN 0-13-249467-1
      1. Embedded computer systems--Design and construction. 2. Intel
microprocessors.   I. Title.
TK7895.E42S48 1998
004.2'1--DC21   98-9722

Publisher: Tom Robbins
Production Editor: Joan Eurell
Editor-in-Chief: Marcia Horton
Managing Editor: Bayani Mendoza deLeon
Vice President of Production and Manufacturing: David W. Riccardi
Cover Designer: Bruce Kenselaar
Manufacturing Manager: Trudy Pisciotti
Manufacturing Buyer: Donna Sullivan
Editorial Assistant: Nancy Garcia
Compositor/Art Management: RDD Consultants, Inc.
Art Director: Jayne Conte

©1998 by Prentice-Hall, Inc.
Simon & Schuster / A Viacom Company
Upper Saddle River, NJ 07458

All rights reserved. No part of this book may be reproduced, in any form or by any means, without permission in writing from the publisher.

The author and publisher of this book have used their best efforts in preparing this book. These efforts include the development, research, and testing of the theories and programs to determine their effectiveness. The author and publisher make no warranty of any kind, expressed or implied, with regard to these programs or the documentation contained in this book. The author and publisher shall not be liable in any event for incidental or consequential damages in connection with, or arising out of, the furnishing, performance, or use of these programs.

Printed in the United States of America

10 9 8 7 6 5 4 3 2 1

ISBN 0-13-249467-1

Prentice Hall International (UK) Limited, *London*
Prentice Hall of Australia Pty. Limited, *Sydney*
Prentice Hall of Canada, Inc., *Toronto*
Prentice Hall Hispanoamericana, S.A., *Mexico*
Prentice Hall of India Private Limited, *New Delhi*
Prentice Hall of Japan, Inc., *Tokyo*
Simon & Schuster Asia Pte. Limited, *Singapore*
Editora Prentice Hall do Brasil, Ltda., *Rio de Janeiro*

*This book is dedicated to my
friend and father, Robert F. Short.*

CONTENTS

Preface   xi

CHAPTER 1 Introduction   1
1.1   Microprocessors and Embedded Systems   3
1.2   Diverse Applications   5
1.3   Common System Structure and Operation   9
1.4   Embedded System Design   11
1.5   The 80C188EB Microprocessor and the 80x86 Family   16
1.6   Organization of this Text   20
1.7   Summary   22

CHAPTER 2 Register View of a Simple Microprocessor System   23
2.1   Memory Cells   24
2.2   Storage Registers   27
2.3   Data Transfer Between Registers   31
2.4   Register View of a Memory Subsystem   35
2.5   Register View of I/O Subsystems   36
2.6   Operational Registers   38
2.7   Register View of a Simple Microprocessor   39
2.8   Register View of a System's Operation   43
2.9   Summary   46
2.10 Problems   47

CHAPTER 3 Register View of 80C188EB Systems   51
3.1   80C188EB CPU Subsystem   52
3.2   Memory Subsystem   55
3.3   I/O Subsystems   57
3.4   80C188EB Modular Core CPU   59
3.5   Memory Segmentation and the BIU's Segment Registers   62
3.6   The EU and its Registers   70
3.7   Programmer's Register View of an 80C188EB System   71
3.8   The 80C186EB Microprocessor   72
3.9   Summary   72
3.10 Problems   73

CHAPTER 4 Assembly Language and Assemblers   77
4.1   Machine Language Instructions   78
4.2   Assembly Language Instructions   80
4.3   Simple Programs Structured as Sequential Tasks   84
4.4   ASM86 Assembly Language and Assemblers   88
4.5   Relocatable Program Modules and Location   91

4.6   Embedded Assemblers Versus DOS Assemblers   93
4.7   Intel's ASM86 Assembler and Utilities   94
4.8   Assembly Language Programs that Run Under DOS   100
4.9   Borland's TASM Assembler and Paradigm's LOCATE   102
4.10   ROMable DOS and DOS Emulators   106
4.11   Summary   107
4.12   Problems   108

CHAPTER 5 Debugging Tools   **111**
5.1   Debugger Fundamentals   112
5.2   Debugging Tools Overview   116
5.3   Borland's Turbo Debugger   124
5.4   Intel's RISM (Remote) Monitor   129
5.5   PromICE ROM Emulator   129
5.6   Paradigm DEBUG/RT Remote Debugger   130
5.7   CodeTAP Target Access Probe   133
5.8   Intel EV80C186EB Evaluation Board   135
5.9   Observing Instruction and Program Execution   136
5.10   Summary   139
5.11   Problems   140

CHAPTER 6 Data Transfer, Data Allocation, and Addressing Modes   **141**
6.1   Data Transfer and Addressing Modes   142
6.2   I/O Port Addressing   145
6.3   Register Addressing   148
6.4   Immediate Addressing   148
6.5   Allocating RAM for Data Variables   150
6.6   Memory Addressing Modes   157
6.7   Structures   164
6.8   Addressability and Segment Overrides   167
6.9   Allocating ROM for Data Constants   167
6.10   Address Object Transfers   170
6.11   80C186EB Data Transfer Considerations   172
6.12   Summary   173
6.13   Problems   173

CHAPTER 7 Bit Manipulation, Branching, and Looping   **179**
7.1   Flags Register   180
7.2   Logical Instructions   182
7.3   Shifts and Rotates   185
7.4   Unconditional Jumps   188
7.5   Conditional Jumps   194
7.6   Looping and Iteration Control   199
7.7   Conditional Task Execution   202
7.8   Repeated String Instructions   206
7.9   Records   209
7.10   Summary   211
7.11   Problems   212

CHAPTER 8 The Stack, Procedures, and Modular Software   217

8.1   The Stack   218
8.2   80C188EB Stack Allocation and Operation   220
8.3   Procedures   224
8.4   Procedures in a Single Module Program   232
8.5   Parameter Passing   234
8.6   Modular Software Design Using Procedures   244
8.7   Procedure Sequencing Using a Finite State Machine   247
8.8   Testing and Debugging Procedures   252
8.9   Summary   253
8.10 Problems   253

CHAPTER 9 Arithmetic Operands and Arithmetic   257

9.1   Numeric Operand Representations   258
9.2   Unsigned Binary Arithmetic   259
9.3   Signed Binary Arithmetic   264
9.4   Unpacked BCD Arithmetic   269
9.5   Packed BCD Arithmetic   272
9.6   Binary/BCD Conversions   273
9.7   Summary   273
9.8   Problems   276

CHAPTER 10 80C188EB CPU Subsystems   281

10.1   CPU Subsystems   282
10.2   The 80C188EB Microprocessor   285
10.3   System Clock, Reset, and Bus Cycles   287
10.4   Address/Data Bus Demultiplexing   296
10.5   A Fully Buffered 80C188EB CPU Subsystem   299
10.6   Logic Family Compatibility, Loading, and Buffering   302
10.7   A Minimum Component Complete System   309
10.8   Single and Multi-Board Systems   311
10.9   Peripheral Control Block (PCB)   315
10.10 The 80C186EB Microprocessor   319
10.11 Summary   320
10.12 Problems   321

CHAPTER 11 Memory Subsystems   325

11.1   Memory Subsystems   326
11.2   Logical Structure and Operation of Memory ICs   328
11.3   Static Random Access Memory, SRAM   333
11.4   Erasable Programmable Read Only Memory (EPROM)   337
11.5   Flash Memory   339
11.6   Memory Subsystem Design   349
11.7   80C188EB Memory Subsystem Design   351
11.8   80C186EB Memory Subsystem Design   353
11.9   Memory Address Decoding   356
11.10 The 80C188EB's Chip-Select Unit   358
11.11 SSI and MSI External Address Decoders   364
11.12 PLD External Address Decoders   366
11.13 Summary   374
11.14 Problems   374

CHAPTER 12 Basic I/O Subsystems   **377**

12.1   Basic I/O Ports   378
12.2   MSI I/O Ports   384
12.3   I/O Ports on Microprocessor Compatible ICs and Device Controllers   387
12.4   I/O Port Address Decoding   388
12.5   PLD External I/O Address Decoders   392
12.6   SSI and MSI External I/O Address Decoders   394
12.7   Conditional I/O   397
12.8   The 80C188EB Input/Output Unit   401
12.9   Interfacing I/O Ports to an 80C186EB   408
12.10 82C55A Programmable LSI I/O Ports   409
12.11 Summary   415
12.12 Problems   416

CHAPTER 13 Timing   **419**

13.1   Timing Constraints and System Architecture   420
13.2   Instruction Execution Time   420
13.3   Wait States   423
13.4   Memory IC Timing Parameters   425
13.5   Memory Subsystem Timing Compatibility Calculations   429
13.6   I/O Timing Considerations   441
13.7   80C188EB Timer/Counter Unit   442
13.8   82C54 Programmable Interval Timer/Counter   453
13.9   Real-Time Clocks   456
13.10 Watchdog Timers   459
13.11 Summary   459
13.12 Problems   460

CHAPTER 14 Interrupts and Exceptions   **463**

14.1   Fundamental Interrupt Concepts   464
14.2   80C188EB Interrupts and Interrupt Processing Sequence   467
14.3   Interrupt Vector Table   470
14.4   80C188EB Hardware Interrupts   473
14.5   80C188EB Interrupt Control Unit   480
14.6   Interrupt Service Routines   491
14.7   Interrupt Driven Systems   496
14.8   Software Interrupts and Exceptions   497
14.9   Interrupt Priority and Latency   500
14.10 82C59A Priority Interrupt Controller   503
14.11 Debugging Hardware Interrupts   506
14.12 Summary   507
14.13 Problems   508

CHAPTER 15 Data Entry and Display   **511**

15.1   User Data Entry   512
15.2   Mechanical Switches   512
15.3   Keypads and Keyboards   525
15.4   Optical Shaft Encoders   532
15.5   Displays   540

15.6   LED Displays   541
15.7   Multiplexed Eight-Digit LED Display Driver   547
15.8   Liquid Crystal Display (LCD) Modules   549
15.9   Vacuum Fluorescent Display (VFD) Modules   562
15.10 Summary   563
15.11 Problems   563

CHAPTER 16 Serial I/O Subsystems   **567**
16.1   Serial Data Transfer   568
16.2   Universal Asynchronous Receiver/Transmitters (UARTs)   573
16.3   The 80C188EB's Serial Communications Unit, SCU   576
16.4   SCU Asynchronous Serial Transfers   577
16.5   Circular Memory Buffers   585
16.6   RS-232 and Other Serial Communications Interfaces   586
16.7   Flow Control   592
16.8   "PC Type" UARTs   594
16.9   SCU Asynchronous Serial Transfer for Multiprocessor Systems   598
16.10 Synchronous Serial Data Transfer   601
16.11 Clocked Synchronous Transfers Using the SCU   602
16.12 Summary   603
16.13 Problems   604

CHAPTER 17 Analog Data and Analog Output Subsystems   **607**
17.1   Analog Data and Analog I/O Subsystems   608
17.2   Digital-to-Analog Converters (DACs)   610
17.3   DAC to System Bus Interface   618
17.4   Basic DAC Circuits   624
17.5   Loading and Impedance Considerations   627
17.6   Operational Amplifiers   630
17.7   Analog Demultiplexers   633
17.8   Track-Holds   636
17.9   Digital Potentiometers   640
17.10 Summary   642
17.11 Problems   643

CHAPTER 18 Analog Input Subsystems   **647**
18.1   Analog Data Acquisition   648
18.2   Input Transducers   649
18.3   Analog Input Signal Conditioning   651
18.4   Track-holds for Analog to Digital Conversion   657
18.5   Analog-to-Digital Converters (ADCs)   658
18.6   Direct Conversion Techniques   662
18.7   Indirect Conversion Techniques   668
18.8   Analog Multiplexers   672
18.9   Multichannel Data Acquisition System   675
18.10 Summary   677
18.11 Problems   678

CHAPTER 19 High Data Rate I/O   **681**
   19.1 Programmed I/O and Interrupt Driven I/O Data Transfer Rates   682
   19.2 Hardware FIFO Buffers   684
   19.3 DMA Transfers   689
   19.4 The 80C188EB's Support for DMA and Multiple Bus Masters   692
   19.5 82C37A DMA Controller   693
   19.6 80C18xEx Family Members with On-Chip DMA   695
   19.7 Summary   703
   19.8 Problems   704

CHAPTER 20 Multi-Module and Multi-Language Programs   **705**
   20.1 Multi-Module Programs   706
   20.2 Linking Multiple Modules   709
   20.3 Managing Multi-module Programs with a Make Utility   713
   20.4 Segment Groups   717
   20.5 Mixed Language Programs   719
   20.6 Memory Models   721
   20.7 Interfacing C and Assembly Language Modules   722
   20.8 Simplified Segment Directives   732
   20.9 Startup Code   734
   20.10 Summary   735

Appendix A: ASCII Codes   **739**

Appendix B: Some Useful URLs   **741**

Appendix C: Instruction Set Descriptions   **743**

Appendix D: Instruction Set Opcodes and Clock Cycles   **791**

Bibliography   **801**

Index   **809**

PREFACE

Embedded systems continue their pervasive expansion as a means of implementation of all manner of electronic systems and of an enormous variety of systems, products, and services not primarily perceived as electronic. For computer engineering, electrical engineering, and computer science students and practitioners the need to understand the capabilities, design, and operation of embedded systems is imperative.

Purpose

The purpose of this book is to provide the reader with the fundamental hardware and software concepts needed for the design of embedded systems. The emphasis is on hardware design at the chip level and software design at the assembly language level. These concepts are illustrated using practical design examples based on Intel's popular 80C188EB microprocessor.

Intended Audience

The reader is expected to have a basic knowledge of digital logic design and to be familiar with software programming using a high-level language. No prior knowledge of assembly language programming nor of microprocessor system design is assumed.

Organization of the book

Chapters 1 through 3 provide an overview of embedded systems hardware and adequate detail to support the software design and assembly language programming concepts presented in Chapters 4 through 9.

The focus returns to hardware in greater detail in Chapters 10 through 12. Chapters 13 through 19 deal with concepts where the software and hardware are tightly coupled and where opportunities for trading off hardware for software to implement various functions abound. Finally Chapter 20 focuses exclusively on software. More information on the organization of this book is given in Section 1.6 of Chapter 1.

Course Partitioning

There is more than enough material in the text for a two semester course and a variety of ways courses can be structured based on this text. At Stony Brook University the material in this text is used in a two semester lecture and laboratory course taken by undergraduate computer engineering, electrical engineering, and computer science students. Each semester course consists of three hours of lecture and three hours of laboratory each week. The first semester covers Chapters 1 through 9 and selected material from Chapters 10, 11 and 12 needed to implement designs in the laboratory. Chapters 10 through 20 are covered in the second semester.

A draft version of this text was used in classes by Professor Donald Dietmeyer at the University of Wisconsin-Madison campus, and by Professor Valdemar Finanger at the Sor-Trondelag College in Trondheim, Norway.

Acknowledgments

A number of people contributed to making this book possible and I would like to acknowledge their contributions and support. A very special and heartfelt thanks to Scott Campbell and Scott Tierno who read through numerous early drafts of the entire text and provided valuable suggestions for improving the accuracy and clarity of the presentation. John Murray provided valuable constructive criticism on the analog chapters. My students in ESE380 and ESE381 Introduction to Embedded Microprocessor Systems Design I and II at Stony Brook University also contributed directly and indirectly through their questions, comments, suggestions, and criticism.

Donald Dietmeyer of the University of Wisconsin-Madison generously provided feedback and suggestions based upon his use of the draft text in his classes at Madison. Valdemar Finanger at Sor-Trondelag College also provided helpful comments.

While I have attempted to correct any errors and address all the issues raised by reviewers, some errors may still remain. For these I am completely responsible. I would appreciate hearing from any reader who finds any errors or who has suggestions for improvements in the text. I can be contacted by email at kshort@ccmail.sunysb.edu.

Thanks to my publisher Tom Robbins at Prentice Hall for his patience and support. Also thanks to the production editor Joan Eurell for her efforts to produce this book under significant time constraints. Appreciation is due to Rodney Sauer of RDD Consultants for his perseverance in formatting and to Donna Sullivan at Prentice Hall for her help in making sure the necessary and ongoing paperwork was completed.

Finally, I am grateful to Howie Bertan for providing me numerous opportunities over the years to design embedded systems for industrial applications and for many insightful conversations.

1

INTRODUCTION

1.1   Microprocessors and Embedded Systems

1.2   Diverse Applications

1.3   Common System Structure and Operation

1.4   Embedded System Design

1.5   The 80C188EB Microprocessor and the 80x86 Family

1.6   Organization of this Text

1.7   Summary

Microprocessors find extensive use as fundamental components in modern electronic systems. Continued increases in their performance and capabilities, along with reductions in their cost, have resulted in fundamental changes in the way electronic systems are designed. Often, it is more economical to structure an electronic system's design around a microprocessor than to use any other design approach. When an electronic system incorporates a microprocessor, additional system features can usually be added with only a marginal increase in software development cost.

Electronic systems based on a microprocessor and designed for a specific application are called embedded systems. An embedded system can range in complexity from rather trivial to exceedingly complex. Embedded systems control everything from the blinking lights in athletic shoes to flight control systems for high performance military aircraft.

Use of microprocessors in electronic systems is prevalent and can be expected to increase substantially in the future. Fig. 1.0-1 shows the number of microprocessors and microcontrollers shipped worldwide from 1985 through 1995, and includes projected shipments through the year 2000. Fig. 1.0-2 gives the actual and projected dollar values of these shipments. As this figure indicates, microprocessors and microcontrollers alone are a multibillion dollar business. The total dollar value of the systems built with them is much greater.

A thorough understanding of, if not an expertise in, microprocessor-based electronic system design is essential for all electrical and computer engineers. Microprocessor-based systems are flexible, versatile, efficient, and allow complex designs to be completed quickly and at relatively low cost. A thorough understanding of embedded systems provides a

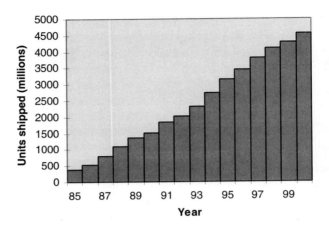

Figure 1.0-1   Unit microprocessor and microcontroller shipments worldwide from 1985 through 1995. Shipments from 1996 through the year 2000 are projections. (From data provided by Jack Quinn, Micrologic Research.)

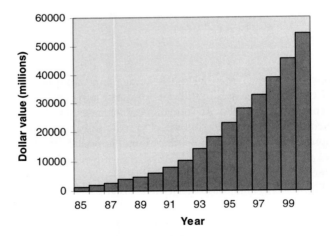

Figure 1.0-2   Dollar value of microprocessor and microcontroller shipments worldwide from 1985 through 1995. Shipments from 1996 through the year 2000 are projections. (From data provided by Jack Quinn, Micrologic Research.)

greater understanding of all microprocessor-based systems. A fundamental knowledge of this area is also becoming increasingly important in many other technical disciplines, such as mechanical, aerospace, and biomedical engineering.

1.1   Microprocessors and Embedded Systems

A **microprocessor** is an integrated circuit (IC) implementation of the **central processing unit** (**CPU**) of a computer. As a consequence, a microprocessor is often simply referred to as a CPU, and that portion of a system that contains the microprocessor is referred to as the CPU subsystem. Different microprocessors vary widely in power, complexity, and cost. Microprocessors range from devices with a few thousand transistors and costing less than a dollar each to devices with more than 5.5 million transistors that cost more than one thousand dollars each.

Input, output, and memory subsystems must be combined with a CPU subsystem to form a complete computer (Fig. 1.1-1). These subsystems are interconnected by the **system bus**.

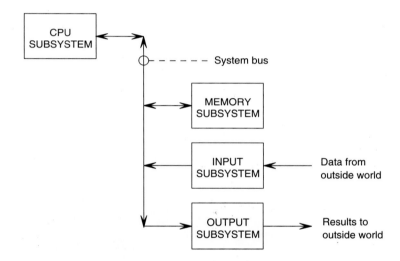

Figure 1.1-1   Subsystems that comprise a microcomputer system.

The **input subsystem** accepts data to be processed from the outside world. The **output subsystem** transfers the results of the processing to the outside world. While Fig. 1.1-1 shows a single input and a single output subsystem, a typical embedded system has several input and output subsystems. Input and output subsystems are often referred to collectively as I/O subsystems or I/O peripherals. The term **peripheral** is frequently used for I/O devices connected to the system bus and controlled by the microprocessor.

The **memory subsystem** stores the instructions that control the operation of the system. These instructions comprise the **program** that the system executes. The memory also stores several kinds of data: data that has been input and not yet processed, intermediate results from processing, and final results that are waiting to be output.

It is important to realize that the subsystems in Fig. 1.1-1 represent how a system is subdivided functionally. The physical subdivision of a system, in terms of ICs or printed circuit boards, may be different. A single IC or printed circuit board may provide multiple functions, such as both memory and input/output (I/O).

A **microcomputer** is a complete computer implemented using a microprocessor as the primary CPU subsystem component. A typical microcomputer is constructed using numerous integrated circuits. However, simple microcomputers can be integrated onto a single IC. A **single-chip microcomputer** is a single IC that includes a microprocessor and a limited amount of memory and I/O.

A **microcontroller** IC includes a microprocessor and I/O subsystems, but it may not include a memory subsystem. If not included, the memory subsystem must be added externally. Microcontrollers usually include I/O subsystems, such as: timers, analog-to-digital converters, and serial communications channels. The I/O subsystems of a given microcontroller are optimized for specific classes of applications.

The actual lines of distinction between microprocessor, microcontroller, and single-chip microprocessor are often blurred. When intended for use specifically in embedded systems, the terms embedded microprocessor and embedded microcontroller are also used.

An **embedded system** is a microcomputer system whose hardware and software are specially designed and optimized to solve a single problem efficiently. Typically, an embedded system continually interacts with its environment to monitor or control some process. Its hardware is often custom designed from the IC component level using the minimal circuitry required for the particular application. Alternatively, the hardware can be designed from the board level, using a commercial off-the-shelf single-board microcomputer (Fig. 1.1-2). A simple embedded system consists of a microprocessor, memory, a few I/O peripherals, and a dedicated application program permanently stored in its memory.

Figure 1.1-2   A single board microcomputer for embedded applications. (Courtesy of Micro/sys, Inc.)

The term embedded refers to the fact that the microcomputer is enclosed or embedded in a larger system and its existence as a microcomputer may not be apparent. A nontechnical user of an embedded system may not be aware that he or she is using a computer system. In some homes, the average non-computer user uses as many as ten or more embedded systems each day. The microcomputers embedded in these systems control household appliances, such as: televisions, VCRs, clothes washers, dryers, food processors, thermostats, alarm systems, exercise equipment, lawn sprinklers, and cordless telephones. Even a general purpose personal computer (PC) contains embedded microcomputers in its keyboard, monitor, and peripheral devices. These embedded microcomputers are in addition to the main CPU in the PC.

A single automobile may contain as many as one hundred embedded microprocessors and microcontrollers that control such things as: engine ignition, transmission shifting, power steering, antilock braking, traction control, and security.

Embedded systems are usually characterized by their need for special I/O devices. When a single board microcomputer is used, additional I/O boards are purchased or designed to meet an application's unique I/O requirements.

Unlike a PC, embedded systems are not programmed by the end user. An embedded system's application program is an integral part of the system and usually must execute without the services of an operating system. Thus, the application program must include software to control and interact with the system's peripheral devices at the most detailed, or lowest, hardware level.

Many embedded systems are real-time systems. A **real-time system** must respond, within a constrained time interval, to external events by executing the task associated with each event. Real-time systems can be characterized as soft or hard. If a **soft real-time system** does not meet its time constraints, the system's performance is simply degraded, but if a **hard real-time system** does not meet its time constraints, it fails. This failure results in possibly catastrophic consequences.

A complex embedded system may utilize an operating system to support the execution of its application program. When an operating system is used, it is most likely a real-time operating system. A **real-time operating system** (**RTOS**) is an operating system designed and optimized to handle the strict time constraints associated with events in real-time applications. In a complex real-time application, use of a RTOS can simplify software development.

Since embedded systems are our focus, the word **system,** when used alone in this text, means an embedded system.

1.2   Diverse Applications

Embedded systems provide an ideal solution to many diverse problems. A glance at advertisements for all kinds of products—consumer, commercial, industrial, and medical—tout the capabilities bestowed upon the product via the inclusion of a microprocessor. A few representative products containing microprocessors are listed in Table 1.2-1. Many of these products can be economically realized only as embedded systems.

The following examples consider a few embedded systems in greater detail.

Table 1.2-1   Some representative embedded systems.

Burglar alarm system	Microwave oven
Cellular phone	Lawn sprinkler system
Digital camera	Bathroom scale
Exercise bike	Computer modem
Blood pressure monitior	Global Positioning System receiver

1.2.1   VISA SuperSmart Card

The **VISA SuperSmart Card** is a high-technology credit card. An early prototype of this card is shown in Fig. 1.2-1. It looks like a typical credit card with the addition of a keyboard and display on its back. This card can be interfaced to terminals and other equipment via contacts located above the word VISA. The SuperSmart Card not only performs the functions of a traditional credit card, it also keeps track of running balances in several accounts, in whatever currency is desired. It can convert from the currency of one country to that of another.

Figure 1.2-1   An early prototype of a VISA SuperSmart Card. (Courtesy of VISA International.)

In addition to its four-function calculator, the card has a real-time clock/calendar and several notepad sections. The notepad sections can be used to store telephone, passport, and other important numbers. When used to purchase airline tickets, the airline reservation system can automatically load the customer's itinerary into one of the card's notepads, for later reference.

The SuperSmart Card can function as a prepayment card, an "electronic purse," to pay for the use of copy machines, fast food, or admission to events. The card's balance can be updated electronically through an Automated Teller Machine (ATM). The card holder can also update the balance using information obtained from a monthly statement or over the phone. This information includes an amount, an expiration date, and a cryptographic code that must be entered through the card's keypad.

When making a purchase, the card processes verification and purchase authorization directly. The card checks the purchase amount against the balance stored in the card and provides the sales clerk, or a machine, with a purchase authorization number. This eliminates the telecommunications costs involved in obtaining an authorization number when using a conventional credit card.

1.2.2   Symbol Technologies Bar Code Symbol Scanner

Among their many uses, bar code symbols are printed on products or their packaging for identification. Information is encoded in the bar code symbol's pattern of bars (dark areas) and spaces (light areas) (Fig. 1.2-2). Different encoding schemes are used by various industries. Figure 1.2-3 shows a model **LS8120 bar code symbol scanner** designed and manufactured by Symbol Technologies. This handheld scanner decodes bar code symbols and outputs the sequence of numbers and/or characters that are encoded in the symbol.

To decode a symbol, the operator aims the scanner at the symbol and presses the trigger switch. The scanner emits a laser light beam that sweeps across the symbol. A photodiode in the scanner detects the intensity of the reflected light. The analog output from the photodiode is electronically converted to a serial digital signal. This signal is decoded by the microprocessor to obtain the encoded sequence of numbers and/or characters. The decoded information is transmitted to other equipment through a cable attached to the scanner's handle.

In decoding the symbol, the scanner's microprocessor must determine the relative widths of the bars and spaces as well as the beginning and end of the symbol. It must identify the type of code being scanned as well as the actual information encoded. If the decoding is successful, the scanner generates an audible beep and transmits the decoded information.

A scanner is often connected to a point of sale terminal. Information from the scanner is used by the point of sale terminal, or by a larger computer to which the point of sale terminal is connected, to identify the product scanned and determine its price. This price is added to the total cost of the items being purchased. Inventory and ordering information in the larger computer are simultaneously updated.

Figure 1.2-2   Bar code symbols. (Courtesy of Symbol Technologies, Inc.)

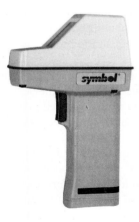

Figure 1.2-3   LS8120 bar code symbol scanner. (Courtesy of Symbol Technologies, Inc.)

1.3   Common System Structure and Operation

As was shown in Fig. 1.1-1, a microcomputer's subsystems are interconnected by its system bus. The system bus provides electrical connections that allow data to be transferred between subsystems. The system bus is subdivided by function into address, data, and control buses (Fig. 1.3-1). The microprocessor uses the address bus to specify a particular storage location in memory or in I/O to, or from, which data is transferred. The microprocessor uses signals on the control bus to control the transfer of data on the data bus. A fourth bus, not shown, is used to distribute power to the subsystems.

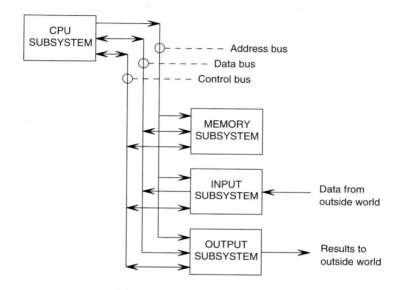

Figure 1.3-1   Constituent buses of the system bus.

A microprocessor controls the overall system operation by executing a program consisting of instructions stored in the memory subsystem. When a system is first powered up, the microprocessor addresses a predefined location in memory and reads (fetches) an instruction from that location. The microprocessor then executes the instruction, by carrying out the operation(s) specified by the instruction. When the execution of an instruction is complete, the microprocessor addresses the next instruction in sequence and fetches and executes it. The microprocessor continues this process indefinitely, or until either it executes an instruction telling it to halt (stop) or the system's power is turned off.

The specific instructions that a microprocessor can execute comprise its **instruction set**. An instruction set includes instructions that: input data, transfer data between the microprocessor and memory, process data using arithmetic or logical operations, and output data. Also included in the instruction set are branch instructions that can cause the next instruction to be fetched from a nonsequential memory location. Whether or not a branch is taken can be conditioned on the result of a previous arithmetic or logical operation. Conditional branching gives an embedded system its ability to respond differently to different values of input data or computational results.

While the systems described in Section 1.2 are quite dissimilar in function, they share the common structure of Fig. 1.1-1. Table 1.3-1 characterizes the details of those systems in the context of the structure of Fig. 1.1-1.

Table 1.3-1(a)   Subsystem details for VISA SuperSmart Card.[a]

Microprocessor	Memory	Inputs	Outputs
8-bit	$16K \times 8$ ROM	20-key keypad	16-character dot matrix
	$8K \times 8$ RAM	Asynchronous serial	Asynchronous serial

a. All CMOS. Powered by 2 paper-lithium 3V batteries with 3 years average life. Standard credit card functions plus: four function calculator, real-time clock, note pads, tracks balances in several accounts, accounts kept in currency of choice, currency conversion, prepayment card. Programmed in assembly language. Manufacturing cost approximately $20.

Table 1.3-1(b)   Subsystem details for Symbol Scanner.[a]

Microprocessor	Memory	Inputs	Outputs
8-bit 80C31	$32K \times 8$ CMOS PROM	Trigger switch	Indicator LED
	$8K \times 8$ CMOS RAM	Photodiode	Beep tone
	64×16 EEPROM		RS232 serial
			Laser beam

a. Visible solid state laser diode, 780 nm, 36 scans per second. Decodes UPC/EAN, Codabar, Interleaved 2 of 5, Code 128, Discrete 2 of 5 and Code 93. Serial communications at 300 Baud to 19.2 K Baud.

Table 1.3-1(c)   A general purpose microcomputer.

Microprocessor	Memory	Inputs	Outputs
Pentium II	$64K \times 8$ Flash EPROM	Keyboard	Video monitor
	64Mb DRAM	Mouse	Speaker
	$512K \times 8$ Cache	Floppy disk	Floppy disk
	6.4GB Hard Disk	CD ROM/DVD ROM	
		Serial Ports	Serial ports
			Parallel port

The SuperSmart Card (Table 1.3-1(a)) contains an 8-bit microprocessor, 16 Kbytes (16,384 bytes) of memory for its program, and 8 Kbytes of memory for data. It uses CMOS technology for low power consumption. Its operator input device is a 20-key keypad and its display is a 16-character liquid-crystal display. A serial data channel permits communications with equipment that accepts the card.

The Symbol Technologies LS8120 symbol scanner (Table 1.3-1(b)) contains an 8-bit microprocessor, 32 Kbytes of program memory, 8 Kbytes of data memory, and a special 64-word memory for parameters. CMOS technology is also used in this system for low power consumption. The operator input is the trigger switch. The photodiode that detects reflected light is an analog input device. Output to the operator consists of a buzzer, which indicates when a successful decode has occurred. Another output device, a serial communications channel, allows decoded information to be transmitted to a point of sale terminal or other equipment to which the scanner is connected. The laser beam emitted by the scanner's laser diode is also an output.

These two embedded systems can be contrasted to a personal computer, which also shares the structure of Fig. 1.1-1. However, a PC's design is optimized to allow it to execute a multitude of different application programs efficiently. Therefore, a PC provides as much memory as economically possible and supports standard types of I/O devices.

The general purpose microcomputer (Table 1.3-1(c)) uses an Intel Pentium II microprocessor operating at 300 MHz. The system board has a primary memory capacity of from 64 Mbytes to 384 Mbytes. Secondary memory is supported by an on-board floppy disk drive controller that supports two drives and a hard disk controller that supports up to four drives. Additional secondary memory is provided by a CD-ROM/DVD ROM drive. Connections to external devices are provided by two serial ports, one parallel port, a mouse port, a keyboard port and connector for a video monitor. Seven expansion slots are provided.

1.4   Embedded System Design

In addition to having a common fundamental structure, embedded systems also share a common development cycle. A **development cycle** model for an embedded system represents the process by which the system is created, Fig. 1.4-1. The development cycle represents an engineering approach that is essential for maximizing the likelihood of producing an effective, reliable, and maintainable system.

Each development cycle phase is identified by a block with its dominant activity indicated inside. The primary outcome of each phase is shown as the block's output. Each outcome is represented by documentation that describes the system at that stage of development. Producing accurate and complete documentation of the results from each phase of development and for the final system is extremely important. The same development cycle is applicable whether a system is designed by a single person or a team. Understanding the development cycle's phases and completing them in a methodical fashion is critical to successful system design.

Figure 1.4-1 is, of necessity, an idealization of a typical system development cycle. The figure shows the phases occurring separately or in parallel, but only once, and in the ideal sequence. In reality, information developed, problems encountered, and decisions made during one phase can cause that phase to interact with preceding and succeeding phases. This may require that a previous phase be reentered. As a result, the entire process is somewhat iterative, rather than strictly sequential. The phases are briefly defined in the paragraphs that follow.

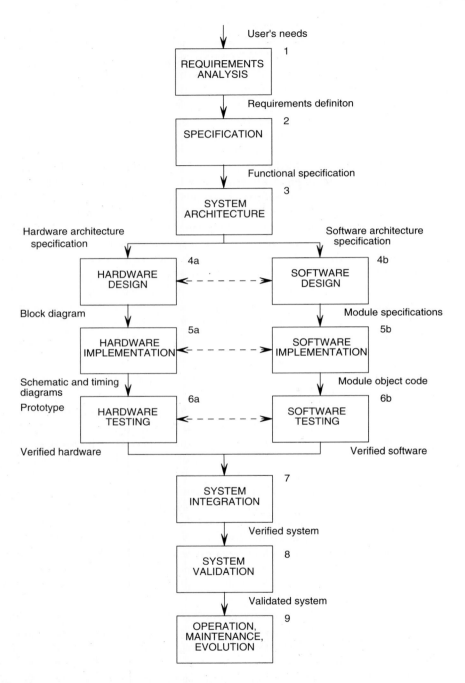

Figure 1.4-1   Embedded system development cycle.

Requirements Analysis. Requirements analysis involves a detailed examination of the end user's needs—the problem to be solved. The end user's, or customer's, needs are studied to determine what the user wants or needs the system to do. This requirement is defined from the user's point of view, and without any reference to possible solutions. Some nontechnical matters that may also be part of the requirements analysis are the determination of the overall schedule and budget. The results of the analysis are documented in a **requirements definition**.

Specification. Based on the requirements definition, the essential functions of, and operational constraints for, the system are determined. Functional specifications define system features that can be directly tested. In addition to required functions, goals and objectives are also specified. What the system should do is determined, but not how it will be done. The user interface to the system is also defined. The desired functions and user interface are clearly documented in a **functional specification**.

System Architecture. From the functional specification, the overall architecture or framework of the system is developed in a top down fashion. First the major functional elements and their relationships are determined. An objective is to define the functional elements so that the interactions among them are limited, resulting in a modular structure. Each functional element is first described independently of its implementation in either hardware or software.

The major functional elements are then partitioned into hardware subsystems and software modules and the interfaces between them are defined. This involves making **hardware/software tradeoff** implementation decisions that are critical to the system's performance and cost. These decisions reflect what portion of each subfunction is implemented primarily in hardware and what portion is implemented primarily in software.

The system architecture is documented as a hardware and a software architecture specification. Selection of essential algorithms and data representations are part of the software architecture specification.

With separate hardware and software architecture specifications, it is possible for the system's development to be split into separate, and possibly concurrent, hardware and software phases, as indicated by the split in the diagram.

Hardware Design. During the hardware design phase, hardware subfunctions are specified generically, and the interfaces between the hardware subsystems are defined. Hardware subsystem interfaces, as well as interfaces to the outside world, may be custom designed or follow one of the many accepted industry standards. Included in these interface specifications are each signal's name and its function and characteristics. These results are described by a document that includes hierarchical **hardware block diagrams** of the system.

Hardware Implementation. IC technologies are selected. The microprocessor, memory, and peripheral ICs are chosen and their interconnection to implement the subfunctions is specified. Timing analysis is performed. Detailed analog and digital circuit design is carried out. **Schematic diagrams** and **timing diagrams** document the implementation. A hardware prototype is constructed.

Hardware Testing. Test procedures are developed, and the hardware subsystems are independently tested to determine whether their functional specifications and timing constraints are met.

Software Design. The overall structure and execution flow of the software is defined in terms of software modules and their interaction. A microprocessor and language independent statement of how the individual software modules interact to implement the system's functions is developed. The procedures that comprise each of the modules are defined. Module specifications are produced that define each software module's hierarchy and function and its interface to and interaction with other modules.

Software Implementation. Detailed algorithms and data structures are developed. Software modules are designed to be reusable in other applications, even though the system being designed is application specific. The software modules are written in one or more programming languages. The actual writing of a module's instructions is referred to as **coding**. Software modules are independently assembled or compiled and syntactical errors are detected and corrected.

Software Testing. Test data is developed and the procedures that comprise each module are tested individually, typically by using simulation or emulation. After individually testing each module's procedures, the modules are linked together in stages to form incrementally the complete program. The program is tested at each incremental stage.

System Integration. If the preceding software and hardware phases were performed separately, the results of these efforts must now be merged. The system software and prototype hardware are integrated and tested. Problems in the interaction or interfaces between subsystems are detected and corrected.

System Validation. Deficiencies or invalid assumptions in the requirements analysis and specification phases may have resulted in an inadequate or inaccurate functional specification. The system is tested to determine whether it actually meets the user's needs, in contrast to meeting simply the functional specification. Problems that are the result of errors in earlier development phases are detected and corrected.

Operation, Maintenance, and Evolution. Errors detected after the system is put into service are corrected. The system is modified to meet new needs and is enhanced by adding new features. Customer support is provided including continued correction of errors.

A development cycle model like that of Fig. 1.4-1 is often referred to as the **life cycle model** because it describes the existence of the system from initial concept (birth) to obsolescence (death). A narrow view of system design considers only phases three, four, and five as design. In this view, phases one and two are considered analysis; phases six, seven, and eight are considered as testing; and phase nine is considered maintenance. This narrow view tends to result in less successful designs. It is advantageous to consider the entire development cycle as design.

While each phase in the model is of critical importance to a successful design, the emphasis in this text is on phases four through six because the concepts and techniques associated with these phases must be well understood before the other phases can be mastered. Hardware and software phases four through six are interrelated and, as a result, are often carried out in parallel.

1.4.1   Hardware Design

Aspects of the hardware and software design phases and selection of a microprocessor are elaborated on in this and the following two subsections.

Hardware design and implementation may involve design at any or all of the following levels:

1. component
2. printed circuit board
3. system

Some systems are designed entirely at the component level. At this level of design, you must select and specify the interconnection of discrete ICs. This step is typical for small embedded systems consisting of only one or a few printed circuit boards.

The hardware for other systems may be implemented at the board level. At this level, you select commercially available printed circuit boards that provide the required subsystems. These boards are combined by plugging them into a **backplane** that carries the system bus connections. The backplane and bus signals may correspond to one of numerous bus standards. These bus standards are independent of a specific microprocessor. If a subsystem function is not commercially available, then it is necessary for you to design, from the component level, a board that provides the required function and is compatible with the system bus.

At the system level, hardware is purchased as a complete, or essentially complete, system. If the complete system hardware cannot be purchased, it may still be necessary to design one or more special function circuit boards, compatible with the system bus, to complete the system.

Successful hardware design at the component and board levels requires that you have a thorough understanding of logic and circuit design principles and an understanding of the function and operation of commonly used ICs. The design of a board for use at the system level requires an understanding of bus interface design and the details of the particular system bus used.

1.4.2   Software Design

Software design and implementation can be carried out at any of several language levels:

1. assembly language
2. high-level language
3. mixed assembly and high-level

In addition, your program must be written to be executed either independently of or under the control of an operating system.

Programming in assembly language requires a detailed understanding of the chosen microprocessor's architecture and the register structure of the entire system. Most low to moderate complexity embedded systems are implemented in assembly language.

Programming in a high-level language does not require a detailed knowledge of the architecture of the microprocessor that executes the program. However, it requires a compiler that produces output specifically for the chosen microprocessor, as well as a detailed knowledge of the input and output subsystems.

A mixed assembly and high-level language program has some modules that are written in assembly language and some that are written in one or more high-level languages. These modules are linked together to form the complete program. In addition to a knowledge of both the assembly language and high-level languages used, writing mixed-language programs requires a detailed knowledge of how the specific compiler passes data to, and gets results from, procedures or subroutines.

The primary focus of this text with regard to hardware design and implementation is at the component level, and with regard to software design and implementation is at the assembly language level. Once you understand system design at these lowest hardware and software levels, it is easy to implement systems at higher levels.

1.4.3   Microprocessor Selection

Selection of a microprocessor for an embedded system design usually involves criteria significantly different from that used for selection of a microprocessor for a PC. When selecting a microprocessor for a PC, the preference is usually the most powerful microprocessor that can be afforded.

Selection of a microprocessor for use in an embedded system involves selecting a microprocessor that has the appropriate power required for the application. In terms of performance requirements for most low-level and mid-level applications, numerous microprocessors are available to choose from, including 4-, 8-, 16-, and 32-bit microprocessors.

Other significant considerations in microprocessor selection are related to cost, not performance. Cost considerations go far beyond the cost of the microprocessor itself. Other factors that impact cost include availability and cost of compatible peripheral and support ICs, availability and cost of software and hardware development tools, and the cost of learning a new microprocessor's architecture, assembly language, and development tools. Often the microprocessor's component cost is overshadowed by these and other related cost considerations.

1.5   The 80C188EB Microprocessor and the 80x86 Family

The microprocessor selected as the instructional example for this text is Intel's 80C188EB, which became commercially available in 1990. Before considering some of the factors that make the 80C188EB an ideal choice as both an instructional example and for a wide range of embedded system applications, we need first to consider its origins.

Intel's very popular **80x86 microprocessor family** includes the 8086, 8088, 80186, 80188, 80286, 80386, 80486, and Pentium microprocessors. These microprocessors' data bus widths range from 8 to 32 bits. Table 1.5-1 provides information about selected family members.

Table 1.5-1   Some 80x86 microprocessor family members.

Microprocessor	8086	8088	80188	80286	80386	80486	80C 188EB	Pentium Pro
Date of Intro.	1978	1979	1982	1984	1985	1989	1990	1995
Address bus (bits)	20	20	20	24	32	32	20	32
Address space (bytes)	1M^a	1M	1M	16M	4G^b	4G	1M	4G
Data bus (bits)	16	8	8	16	32	32	8	64
Register size (bits)	16	16	16	16	32	32	16	32
Transistors (millions)	0.029	0.029		0.134	0.275	1.18		5.5
Package pins	40	40	68	68	132	168	80, 84	273
Original technology	MOS	MOS	MOS	CMOS	CMOS	CMOS	CMOS	CMOS

a. M (Mega) = 2^{20} = 1,048,576
b. G (Giga) = 2^{30} = 1,073,741,824

The first microprocessors in this family were the **8086**, introduced in 1978, and the **8088**, introduced in 1979. These two microprocessors are essentially identical, except that the 8086 has a 16-bit data bus and the 8088 has an 8-bit data bus. The 8088 is probably best known as the microprocessor used in the original IBM PC and XT microcomputers. The 8086 was used in early IBM PS2 models and in many early PC clones.

For moderately complex 8086/8088 systems, as many as a dozen or more support ICs are typically required. In 1982 Intel introduced the **80186/80188** microprocessors, which consisted of an enhanced 8086/8088 and six commonly used peripherals integrated together on a single chip. Integration of peripherals on-chip with the microprocessor reduces the size, cost, and complexity of the resulting system while increasing its reliability. The 80186 and 80188 differ from each other primarily in data bus width: the 80186 has a 16-bit data bus and the 80188 has an 8-bit data bus. The 80186/80188 instruction set is a superset of that of the 8086/8088, adding seven new instructions and enhancing three existing instructions.

In the same year that the 80186 and 80188 were introduced, Intel also introduced the **80286** microprocessor. The 80186 and 80286 were targeted for different categories of applications. The 80286 was designed for personal computers and was used in the IBM PC/AT.

Over the years, the 80186/80188 continued to evolve. In 1987 CMOS versions, the 80C186 and 80C188 were introduced. However, the biggest change came in 1990 when the first in a series of 80C186/80C188 microprocessors with an E suffix was introduced. These microprocessors were specifically optimized for embedded applications.

The CPU of the 80C186/80C188 was redesigned as a stand alone **modular core CPU** that could be connected to on-chip peripherals through an internal bus. The on-chip peripherals of the 80C186/80C188 were redesigned to be compatible with this new internal bus. The purpose of this redesign was to allow the creation of application specific microprocessors containing unique sets of on-chip peripherals optimized for particular application areas.

1.5.1   The 80C186EB and 80C188EB Microprocessors

The first two microprocessors to use the 80C186 modular core CPU were the **80C186EB** and **80C188EB**. These microprocessors contain a different set of on-chip peripherals than do their 80C186/80C188 predecessors (Table 1.5-2). Four more modular core family members were introduced in 1991, the 80C186EA/80C188EA, and 80C186EC/80C188EC. Each uses the same modular CPU core but has a different set of on-chip peripherals. All of these microprocessors maintain full code compatibility with the original 80186/80188.

Table 1.5-2   Integrated peripheral differences for 80C18xEx microprocessors[a].

Device	Input Levels	DMA Channels	WDT[b]	ChipSelect Pins	I/O Pins	Serial I/O
80186[c] 80188	TTL	2	No	13	0	0
80C186EA 80C188EA	CMOS	2	No	13	0	0
80C186EB 80C188EB	CMOS	0	No	10	16	2
80C186EC 80C188EC	CMOS	4	Yes	10	22	3

a. All devices have CMOS input levels, integrated clock generator, 3 counter timers, interrupt controller, referesh control unit, and power down options and are available in 5V and 3V versions.
b. Watchdog timer
c. 80186/80188 are MOS devices with TTL input levels and are included for comparison.

The 80C188EB integrates the following peripherals with its modular core CPU: Power Management Unit, Serial Communications Unit, Input/Output Port Unit, Chip Select Unit, Refresh Control Unit, Interrupt Control Unit, and Timer/Counter Unit (Fig. 1.5-1). Use of an 80C188EB significantly reduces the number of ICs needed in those designs that require the integrated peripherals it provides. This results in more economical and reliable designs. The 80C188EB's features are suitable to a wide range of applications including instruments, data acquisition systems, controllers, and portable equipment.

In terms of Fig. 1.1-1, the 80C188EB alone provides both CPU subsystem and I/O subsystem functions. In some applications the 80C188EB's integrated Input/Output Port Unit and other peripherals may provide all of the I/O capability needed. In these cases, separate external I/O subsystems would not be utilized.

One advantage in choosing an 80C188EB for design or for instructional purposes is its software compatibility with other 80x86 family microprocessors. Software written for the 8086/8088 is upward compatible with the other microprocessors in the 80x86 family; that is, it can run on any of these microprocessors. Intel has stated that compatibility between the 8086/8088 and future microprocessors in this family will be maintained. This

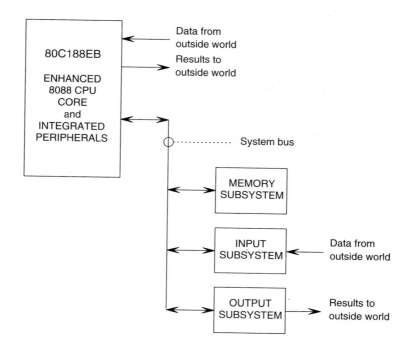

Figure 1.5-1   80C188EB based microprocessor and external memory and input/output subsystems.

ensures that most, if not all, of the investment in learning the software and hardware of the 80C188EB can be carried forward to future generations of the 80x86 family.

The existing base of software written for the 80x86 family is larger than that written for any other microprocessor family. This provides you with a wealth of prewritten software. Programming an 80C186Ex/80C188Ex system is essentially the same as programming an 8086 system.

Software can be developed for the 80x86 family on a PC. In addition there are more hardware and software development tools and operating systems available for the 80x86 architecture than there are for any other architectures.

Although the 80C188EB is primarily referred to in this text, what is stated about the 80C188EB also generally applies to the 80C186EB. Where there are minor differences, they are explained. When the 80C186EB's differences are significant, they are detailed in separate sections. Thus, this text provides coverage of both of these microprocessors.

The 80C188EB's 8-bit data bus makes it possible to build powerful, yet economical, embedded systems using this microprocessor. The smaller size of the 80C188EB's data bus simplifies the layout and reduces the area of printed circuit boards. In many applications, use of an 80C188EB with its smaller data bus does not significantly limit system performance, when compared to using an 80C186EB. When used for instructional purposes, the 80C188EB's 8-bit data bus has the advantage that it simplifies the construction of prototype systems. Learning the 80C188EB is a natural starting point for understanding the other, more complex microprocessors in the 80x86 family.

1.6   Organization of this Text

As previously stated, successful system design requires that you have expertise in many areas, including hardware design, software design, and system synthesis. The purpose of this text is to present the fundamental concepts upon which this expertise is developed. It is assumed that you have a basic knowledge of digital logic design at the gate and flip-flop level and some experience programming a general purpose computer in a high-level language. This chapter's bibliography, located at the end of this text, lists some texts that provide the prerequisite knowledge of digital logic design. Prior experience with assembly language programming is not necessary.

The subsystems of Fig. 1.1-1 contain various types of registers. Considering a system's architecture in terms of its registers is fundamental to understanding its underlying structure and operation. This register view provides a foundation for understanding a system's hardware and software architectural design. Chapter 2 defines the type of registers in a system and provides a description of a simple generic system's structure and operation in terms of its registers.

The register structure of a system using an 80C188EB microprocessor is described in Chapter 3. The chapter discusses the architecture and operation of the 80C188EB's modular core CPU and the basic structure of memory and I/O subsystems used with an 80C188EB. The 80C188EB views its memory as consisting of blocks or segments. This concept of segmentation is explained. The register structure of the 80C188EB's integrated peripherals is introduced in this chapter, but the integrated peripherals themselves are not considered in detail until the later half of this text.

Assembly language programs deal with operations and data at the register level. Chapter 4 gives an overview of assembly language programming and explains how an assembler, linker, and locator are used to convert an assembly language source program into machine code bit patterns that can be loaded into a system's memory and executed.

In the software development process, some means of testing programs and identifying their logical errors is necessary. Chapter 5 introduces various debugging tools useful for this purpose. These tools are introduced early because they are also very useful for learning the basic operation of the 80C188EB's instruction set.

Assembly language programs implement their tasks by transferring data between registers in the microprocessor and in the memory and I/O subsystems, and transforming data in registers within the microprocessor. Chapter 6 presents data transfer instructions and the memory addressing modes that are used to select a specific memory register as either the source or destination for a transfer.

Transformation of data takes place in the microprocessor and is accomplished by the microprocessor's arithmetic and logic unit. Transformations are either logical or arithmetic. Chapter 7 examines instructions that implement logical transformations as well as the flags register and branch instructions. Branch instructions modify a program's execution flow based on the results from the execution of logical or arithmetic instructions.

As more complex programs are designed, they must be organized to make their complexity manageable. Implementing software functions as procedures or subroutines is the first step in organizing software in a modular fashion. Procedures, and the last-in first-out stack storage structure required to support their use, are the topic of Chapter 8.

Various methods of representing arithmetic operands in binary and binary coded decimal and the arithmetic instructions that operate on them are given in Chapter 9.

In Chapter 10, the focus shifts back to hardware. Chapter 10 covers the details of the structure, design, and operation of 80C188EB and 80C186EB CPU subsystems. Issues from bus cycles to the design of minimum component and multi-board systems are presented.

Memory ICs and memory subsystem design are considered in Chapter 11, which also covers address decoding using either the 80C188EB's integrated Chip Select Unit, discrete MSI circuits, or programmable logic devices, PLDs.

Parallel I/O subsystems and serial I/O subsystems are presented separately. Chapter 12 deals with basic parallel I/O and discusses the 80C188EB's Input/Output Port Unit and the implementation of parallel I/O subsystems using MSI circuits and programmable LSI circuits.

A variety of software and hardware timing considerations are collected together in Chapter 13. The determination of instruction execution time is considered first. The chapter then discusses hardware timing analysis, an important practical consideration in designing memory and I/O subsystems so that they are compatible with the CPU subsystem's timing. Measuring and generating precise time intervals are also important in embedded systems design. Implementing these operations using either software or hardware counter/timers are compared. Three programmable counter/timers are provided by the 80C188EB's Counter/Timer Unit. Additional programmable counter timers can be provided by using external counter/timer ICs. For measuring relatively long time intervals, clock calendar ICs are presented.

The response of a microprocessor to a peripheral device's need to transfer data to the microprocessor can be made more efficient if the peripheral device directly signals the microprocessor when it has data ready. This is accomplished using interrupts, as described in Chapter 14.

An operator interacts with a system through data entry and display peripherals. Chapter 15 covers some of the most common of these: switches, keypads, LEDs, and LCDs.

Chapter 16 considers serial I/O subsystems implemented using either the integrated serial ports of the 80C188EB's Serial Communications Unit or an external Universal Asynchronous Receiver/Transmitter, UART, IC.

Data from a physical process that a system monitors or controls usually originates as an analog output from a transducer. Peripheral devices that convert digital data to analog data are covered in Chapter 17. Chapter 18 introduces devices that convert analog data to digital data, so that the data can be processed by a microprocessor.

Some peripheral devices need to transfer data at very high speeds. Dealing with high speed data transfers is accomplished by using FIFOs to buffer data or by allowing a peripheral device to directly transfer data to or from memory with no intervention by the microprocessor. Chapter 19 presents these techniques.

Programs are organized in a modular fashion for ease of development and maintenance. Use of procedures is one step toward achieving modularity. Modularity is further enhanced by developing a program as separate modules, or files, that are assembled independently and then linked together to form a complete program. Individual modules may be written in assembly language or in a high-level language. Modules written in a high-level language are compiled and the output from their compilation is then linked (combined) with the output from the assembly of assembly language modules to form the complete program. These concepts are introduced in Chapter 20.

1.7 Summary

Microprocessors are key components in a vast range of electronic systems designed today. These embedded systems have become ubiquitous. As a result, every electronic or computer engineer should be familiar with the fundamentals of the operation and design of embedded systems.

While the range of embedded systems applications is extremely diverse, there is a common structure that these systems share. This common structure can be used as the basis upon which to develop an understanding of the operation and design of these systems. Learning embedded system design concepts at the lowest level—component level for hardware and assembly level for software—gives you the foundation needed to build a clear understanding of hardware and software principles of embedded system design.

Because of its core 80x86 architecture and integrated peripherals, this text uses the 80C188EB microprocessor as its instructional example.

2

REGISTER VIEW OF A SIMPLE MICROPROCESSOR SYSTEM

2.1   Memory Cells

2.2   Storage Registers

2.3   Data Transfer Between Registers

2.4   Register View of a Memory Subsystem

2.5   Register View of I/O Subsystems

2.6   Operational Registers

2.7   Register View of a Simple Microprocessor

2.8   Register View of a System's Operation

2.9   Summary

Registers are one of the most fundamental system components. There are three basic operations that take place on data in a system. All of these operations involve registers. Data is stored in registers, transferred between registers, and transformed in operational registers. Thus, the structure and operation of a system can be visualized in terms of its registers. This "register view" aids in both the analysis and design of a system's hardware and software.

In this chapter, register concepts are reviewed starting with memory cells and simple registers. Next, the architecture and operation of memory, I/O, and CPU subsystems are described in terms of their registers. Finally, the operation of a simple system is described in terms of data transfers between its registers and data transformations in its operational registers. An understanding of the structure and operation of this simple system, from a register viewpoint, provides the foundation for mastering the operational details of practical systems, including 80C188EB systems. This chapter also presents terminology and signal naming conventions used throughout this text.

2.1   Memory Cells

Registers are comprised of memory cells. A **memory cell**, or **cell**, stores one bit of data. A **bit** is a binary digit that has a value of either 0 or 1. A memory cell has two stable states to represent these two values. Each cell includes provisions to place it in either state and to determine its present state. In Fig. 2.1-1, a cell is conceptually represented as a box with its stored bit value indicated inside.

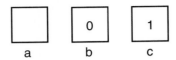

Figure 2.1-1   Conceptual representations of a memory cell: (a) with stored value not indicated; (b) with a 0 stored; (c) with a 1 stored.

Figure 2.1-2 is a more detailed representation, showing the cell's data line, write enable input, and output enable input. A **data line** is a transfer path that can carry a single bit of data at any given time. However, the data line cannot store the bit value it transfers. The value transferred, 0 or 1, appears on the data line only as long as some other device, not yet discussed, causes it to appear. The device causing a value to appear on the data line is said to **drive** the line with that value. When no device is driving the data line, the data line has the value Z. For now, the value Z simply means that no data exists on the data line.

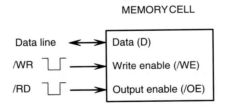

Figure 2.1-2   Memory cell and its connections.

2.1.1   Signal Naming Conventions

Before going further, a few comments on signal naming conventions and use of the terms "asserted" and "unasserted," "deasserted," or "negated" may be helpful. Control signals and status signals in systems have names associated with them. A signal's name denotes the action controlled or the status indicated by the signal. Each signal name has an **active level**. A signal is **active high** if the operation or state it denotes occurs or exists when the signal is high, or 1 (the positive logic convention is used throughout this text). Conversely, a signal is **active low** if the operation or state it denotes occurs or exists when the signal is low, or 0.

A signal is said to be **asserted** when it is at its active level, and **unasserted, deasserted,** or **negated** when it is not at its active level.

The active level of a signal is usually specified as part of its name by some naming convention. One convention is to use a forward slash, /, as the first character in the name for signals that are active low, and to omit the slash for signals that are active high. For example, /WR denotes an active low signal. When this signal is active, /WR = 0, it is said to be asserted and its associated operation, a write, occurs or is in the process of occurring. When it is inactive, /WR = 1, it is said to be unasserted, and its associated operation does not occur, or is not occurring.

/WR = 1 is spoken as "WR bar equals one," because the / is simply an alternative representation of the overbar used above a signal name to represent an active low signal (e.g., $\overline{WR}$). This alternative representation is used for typographical convenience. Accordingly, if /WR is the input to an inverter, the inverter's output is //WR, or simply WR.

2.1.2   Writing (Storing) Data

A cell can store data that is driven on its data line by some other device. The process of storing data in a cell is called a **write** operation. To write a cell, data is first driven on the data line, then a **write strobe**, a pulse, is generated on the cell's **write enable input, /WE.** The write strobe is denoted as **/WR.** The occurrence of a write strobe causes a copy of the data on the data line to be stored in the cell. After the /WR strobe terminates, the device can stop driving the data line.

Generating a write strobe when there is no valid data on the data line is not an acceptable operation, because the resultant state, 0 or 1, of the cell cannot be predicted. There is no valid data on the data line when either the data line equals Z or when the data line is changing from 0 to 1, or vice versa.

A one bit cell can be constructed from a D-type flip-flop and a three-state buffer as shown in Fig. 2.1-3. This depiction of a memory cell is used to clarify some of the concepts mentioned earlier and to introduce timing considerations for writing or reading a cell.

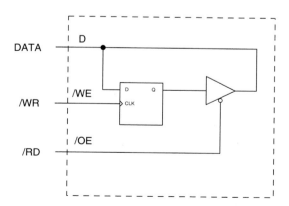

Figure 2.1-3   Logic representation of a memory cell constructed from a D flip-flop and a three-state buffer.

The flip-flop provides the cell's memory capability. There are three connections to the flip-flop: data input (D), data output (Q), and clock input (CLK). The value stored in the flip-flop is always available at its Q output.

Connections to the cell are labeled D, /WE, and /OE. The D connection carries both input data and output data, but not simultaneously. Because it transfers data in either direction, D is a **bidirectional** connection. The other two connections are used to control the operation of the cell. /WE, the write enable input, is used to control writing the cell. /OE, the output enable input, is used to enable the three-state buffer. When not enabled, the three-state buffer isolates Q from D.

To write the cell, data is applied to the DATA line then a /WR strobe is generated. The timing diagrams in Figs. 2.1-4(a) and 2.1-4(b) show a 1 and a 0, respectively, being written into the cell. The dashed horizontal lines for DATA, midway between the 0 and 1 logic levels, indicate when the DATA input has the value Z. For the physical implementation in Fig. 2.1-3, data is actually stored in the flip-flop on the positive edge of /WR (the 0 to 1 transition) since the flip-flop depicted is positive-edge triggered.

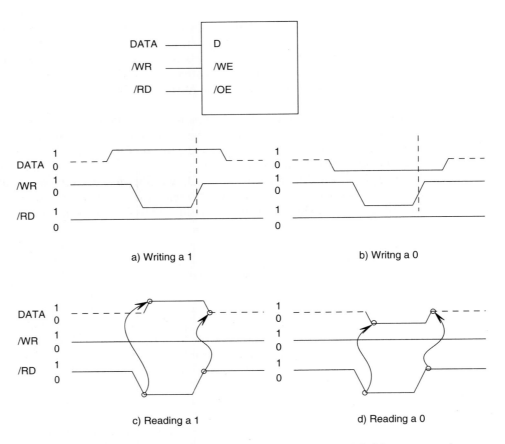

Figure 2.1-4   Writing and reading a memory cell: in (a) and (b) an external source drives the data line: in (c) and (d) the memory cell drives the data line.

To guarantee proper operation of the flip-flop, the data must be stable for a specified time before the positive edge of /WR occurs (**setup time** specification) and must remain stable for a specified time after this edge (**hold time** specification). The timing diagrams of Fig. 2.1-4 reflect these requirements in a qualitative way.

During write operations, the output enable input, /OE, must be held in its unasserted state, logic 1.

2.1.3   Reading Data

A **read** operation makes a copy of the value stored in a memory cell available on the data line. A read operation requires the occurrence of a read strobe on the **output enable input** (**/OE**) of the cell. The memory cell drives the data line with its stored value, during the **read strobe (/RD)**.

To read the memory cell, a /RD strobe is applied at the cell's /OE input and the DATA line is monitored. Asserting /RD turns on the three-state buffer connected from the flip-flop's Q output to its D input, Fig. 2.1-3. This allows the value at Q to drive the DATA line, but only while /RD is asserted. Figures 2.1-4(c) and 2.1-4(d) show the reading of a 1 and a 0, respectively, from the cell. The arrows in Figs. 2.1-4(c) and (d) are used to indicate **causality**. In Fig. 2.1-4(c) a 0 level for /RD causes the cell to drive DATA to the logic level stored in the cell, in this case a logic 1. A 1 level for /RD causes DATA to be in the **high-impedance state** (**Z state**). During a read operation, the write enable input must be held in its unasserted state, logic 1.

Because the same data line is used for both input to and output from the cell, write and read operations must not be attempted at the same time. When both the write and output enable inputs are unasserted, no operation occurs.

Additional requirements, beyond the relative sequence of actions just described, must be met to successfully write or read a cell. These requirements relate to signal voltage levels and detailed timing constraints that are considered in Chapters 10 and 11.

2.2   Storage Registers

A **storage register**, or **register**, is a group of memory cells that have a common write enable input and a common output enable input. But each cell has its own individual data line. The number of cells in the register defines its **width**. A register with n cells is referred to as an **n-bit register**. Figure 2.2-1 shows an n-bit register constructed using D-type flip-flops and three-state buffers.

Several conceptual representations of an 8-bit register are shown in Fig. 2.2-2. For identification, individual bits in a register are numbered from the right, from 0 to $n-1$. A write or read strobe operates on all n bits simultaneously. These n bits, taken together, are referred to generically as a **word** of data. A 4-bit word is often called a **nibble** and an 8-bit word a **byte**. Other common word sizes are 16, 32, and 64 bits.

The bits stored in a register can be represented as a binary number. A more succinct representation uses an octal or hexadecimal number. Figure 2.2-3 shows the contents of a register expressed in binary, octal, and hexadecimal. Suffixes B, Q, and H are used to indi-

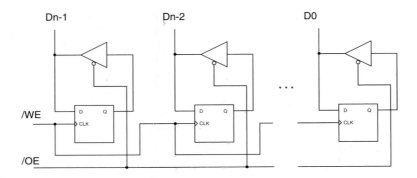

Figure 2.2-1   *n* bit register.

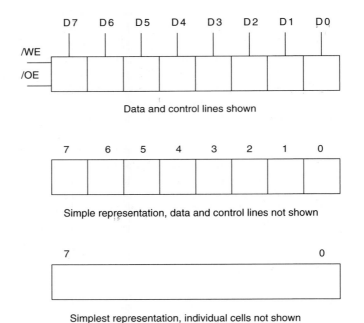

Figure 2.2-2   Conceptual representations of an 8-bit register.

cate a representation's base. Another commonly used convention for indicating a hexadecimal number is to prefix the number with 0x and not use a suffix. Thus, 0xb6 represents the hexadecimal number B6.

7	6	5	4	3	2	1	0
1	0	1	1	0	1	1	0

10110110B Binary representation

266Q Octal representation

B6H Hexadecimal representation

0xb6 Another hexadecimal representation

Figure 2.2-3   Representations of register contents in different bases.

2.2.1   Register Files

To store several words of data, multiple registers are combined to form a **register file** or **memory**. A conceptual representation of a register file is shown in Fig. 2.2-4. The registers share a common set of data lines, a single write enable input, and a single output enable input. For simplicity, the figure omits the internal routing of data and control lines to the individual registers.

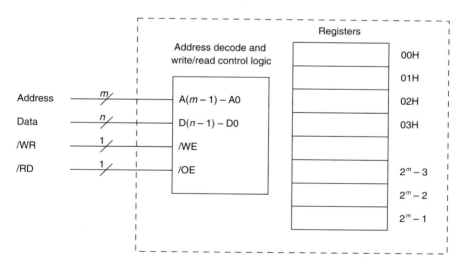

Figure 2.2-4   Representation of a register file.

Data is written to (or read from) a single register at a time. The n data lines are represented by a single line. A slash, (/), labeled with an n across a line indicates that the single line actually represents n lines.

To select a specific register to be written or read, each register has a unique **address**. This requires that the register file have a set of address inputs. With m address inputs, any one of 2^m registers can be uniquely selected. Address decoding logic is included in the register file to route a write strobe or read strobe to only the addressed register. Address values, like data values, are expressed in binary, octal, or hexadecimal numbers.

The sequence of steps to write a register in a register file is:

1. The register's address is placed on the address lines.
2. The data to be written is placed on the data lines.
3. A write strobe is generated.

To read a register in a register file:

1. The register's address is placed on the address lines.
2. A read strobe is generated.
3. The register's contents are obtained from the data lines during the read strobe.

Larger register files are simply called memories. A memory with 2^m registers, each n-bits wide, is called a $2^m \times n$ memory, and referred to as a "2^m by n memory." For example, with $m = 8$ and $n = 4$, the memory is a 256×4 memory. The total number of bits in a memory is its **bit capacity**. A 256×4 memory has a bit capacity of 1024 bits.

Memories with a large number of words (registers) are common. For memories with 2^{10} (1,024) or more words, the number of words is expressed as a multiple of 1,024. Because base two numbers are used in computing, the suffix K (kilo) is used to represent 2^{10} or 1024. In other areas of engineering, kilo is used to represent 1000, as in kHz for 1000 Hz. An upper case K is used for 1024 to distinguish its value from that of lower case k (for 1000).

A 4096×8 memory, a 4 kilobyte memory, is denoted as a $4K \times 8$ memory or 4 Kbyte memory. For larger memories where the number of words is a multiple of 2^{20} (1,048,576) words, the suffix M (mega) is used to represent 2^{20}. A memory containing 2^{22} bytes is a $4M \times 8$ or 4 Mbyte memory. G (giga) is used as a suffix in describing very large memories with a number of words that is a multiple of 2^{30} (1,073,741,824).

A block diagram of a memory represented as a subsystem is shown in Fig. 2.2-5. The address and control lines are inputs to the subsystem. The data lines are shown with double arrows, indicating they are bidirectional, serving as inputs during write operations and as outputs during read operations.

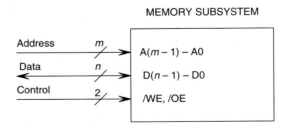

Figure 2.2-5   Memory subsystem block diagram.

2.3   Data Transfer Between Registers

A data transfer involves a **source register**, or **source**, from which data is read, and a **destination register**, or **destination**, to which data is written. In the previous section, writing data to, or reading data from, a single register or a register file was discussed without regard to the source of the data written or the destination of the data read.

A data transfer is actually a copy operation. Data is copied from the source register to the destination register. After the "transfer," both source and destination registers contain identical values. The source and destination must be connected by a data bus. Since there are a large number of possible source and destination pairs in a system, it is impractical to connect each register pair with its own dedicated data bus. Therefore, a single **shared data bus** is used. The shared data bus is the common pathway used to transfer data between registers.

Figure 2.3-1 shows an interconnection of several 1-bit registers. On the right side of the figure are four registers. The first two, with addresses 0 and 1, can be considered as a two word by one bit (2×1) memory. These two registers can receive data from and transfer data to the shared data line, which represents a 1-bit data "bus."

The third register on the right, register 2, must be written by some as yet unspecified external device. This allows the system to input data from the outside world. The external device provides data at the D input of register 2 and provides the clock signal to write the data. Data written into register 2 can later be read onto the data bus. A register used in this fashion is called an input port.

The fourth register on the right, register 3, can only receive data from the data bus. The output buffer of this register is not connected to the data bus. Instead, it provides a way to transfer data to the outside world. A register used in this fashion is called an output port. Note that in this example, the three-state buffer associated with the output port is always enabled.

Any of the four registers on the right can be selected by an address on the two bit address bus, A1–A0. An address is generated by the block on the lower left labeled "timing and control." The timing and control block also generates the /WR and /RD strobes. The address on the address bus is decoded by the two 1-out-of-4 decoders on the right. One of the decoders, the read decoder, is enabled by /RD. When /RD is asserted, this decoder asserts one of its outputs, either /RD0, /RD1, /RD2, or /RD3. The output asserted depends on the address on the address bus. Output /RD3 is not connected to any component in the circuit.

The other decoder, the write decoder, is enabled by /WR. When /WR is asserted, this decoder asserts either /WR0, /WR1, /WR2, or /WR3, depending on the address on the address bus. Output /WR2 is not connected to any component in the circuit. The timing and control block never asserts /RD and /WR simultaneously.

Register X, on the left side of the data bus, is directly controlled by the timing and control block. This register is analogous to a register in a microprocessor.

Consider the operation of inputting data to the system and storing it in memory. To get data from the outside world via the input port, register 2, and transfer it to the memory, register 0, data is input by the timing and control section putting the value 2 on the address bus and generating a read strobe. This action asserts /RD2, enabling the three-state buffer connected to register 2. With this three-state buffer enabled, data from the outside

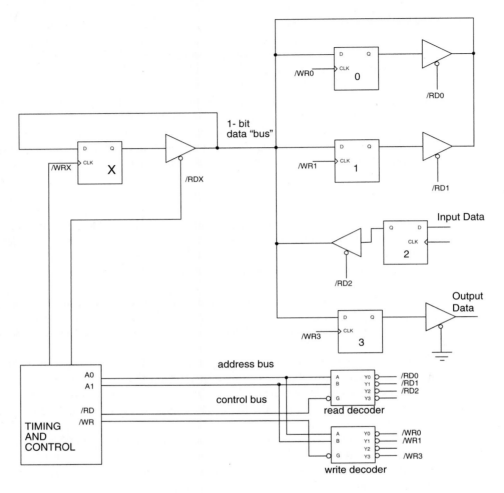

Figure 2.3-1   Interconnection of 1-bit registers with address decoding and control.

world is driven onto the data bus. Since there is only a single address bus, and it is currently being used to address the source register, the input data can only be transferred to register X. While it holds /RD asserted, the timing and control block must generate a /WRX strobe to write the data into register X.

The next operation performed by the timing and control block is to transfer the data now in register X to register 0. The write operation to register 0 is performed when the timing and control block addresses register 0 by placing 0 on the address bus. It then causes register X to drive the data bus by asserting /RDX. Next, the timing and control block generates a /WR strobe. As a result, the write address decoder generates a /WR0 strobe. The data driven on the data bus by register X is stored in register 0.

In terms of data transfer, Fig. 2.3-1 demonstrates an important constraint that occurs in a microprocessor system. The address and data bus structure in Fig. 2.3-1 constrains all transfers to involve register X as either the source or destination. This constraint results because the address bus can only address one of the registers on the right at a time. For example, as a result of this constraint, to transfer data from register 1 to register 3 requires two transfers, the first from register 1 to register X, followed by a transfer from register X to register 3.

Figure 2.3-1 also illustrates the general principal that each data transfer involves only one source register and one destination register. Three-state output buffers physically connect register outputs to the shared data bus. However, only one source register is allowed to place data on or to drive the data bus at any time. Thus, only one source register's three-state buffer is ever enabled. The three-state buffers of all other source registers must be disabled.

If two registers with their three-state outputs connected to the data bus were to have their output buffers enabled simultaneously, **bus contention** would result. If one of the enabled buffers tries to drive the data bus to logic 1 and the other enabled buffer tries to drive it to logic 0, excessive current through the buffers results. Excessive buffer current can effect the life of an IC or destroy it immediately. At the least, this condition produces invalid data on the bus. It can also produce power supply spikes that can cause the loss of data stored in other registers.

The address decoding logic in Fig. 2.3-1 is designed to eliminate the possibility of bus contention. When a read operation takes place, the read decoder uses the address on the address bus to select only a single register to be enabled. The address decoding logic also insures that the addressed register drives the data bus only while /RD is asserted. **Proper design of address decoding logic to prevent bus contention is an extremely important consideration!**

In Fig. 2.3-1, 1-out-of-4 decoders are used for address decoding. Figure 2.3-2 gives the function table for a 1-out-of-4 decoder. The decoder has an enable input, /G, select inputs B and A, and four outputs, /Y0, /Y1, /Y2, and /Y3. When its enable input is unasserted, all of the decoder's outputs are forced to 1, independently of the value at its select inputs.

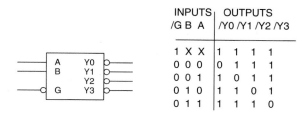

INPUTS	OUTPUTS			
/G B A	/Y0	/Y1	/Y2	/Y3
1 X X	1	1	1	1
0 0 0	0	1	1	1
0 0 1	1	0	1	1
0 1 0	1	1	0	1
0 1 1	1	1	1	0

Figure 2.3-2   A 1-out-of-4 decoder: (a) logic symbol; (b) truth table.

Note that this decoder does not have three-state outputs and that the purpose of its enable input is functionally different from the enable input of a three-state buffer. When the decoder is not enabled, all of its outputs are logic 1. When the decoder is enabled, only its output selected by inputs B and A is 0, and all other outputs are 1s. For example, if B = 1 and A = 0, then only output /Y2 is 0 when /G is asserted.

Returning to Fig. 2.3-1, three outputs from the read decoder are connected to the control inputs of three of the three-state buffers to select which register's three-state buffer is enabled. As long as /RD is unasserted all output buffers are disabled and the data bus is in its high-impedance (Z) state. When /RD is asserted, the three-state buffer selected by A1 and A0 is enabled. The fourth three-state buffer is used to drive an output device and is hardwired such that it is always enabled.

For write operations, the write decoder uses address bits A1 and A0 to select the register to be written. The control strobe, /WR, enables the decoder's output, causing a write strobe only at the addressed destination register.

The timing diagram of Fig. 2.3-3 shows the relative timing relationship required between the read and write strobes. Two data transfers are shown, the first from register 1 to register X. The next transfer is from register X to register 3. The elapsed time for each transfer defines a **bus cycle**. To meet the destination register's setup and hold timing requirements, the read strobe must cause the data to be on the data bus for a sufficient time before and after the trailing edge of the write strobe. To meet this requirement in the first bus cycle, /RD is wider than and centered around /WRX. Accordingly, in the second bus cycle, /RDX is wider than and centered around /WR.

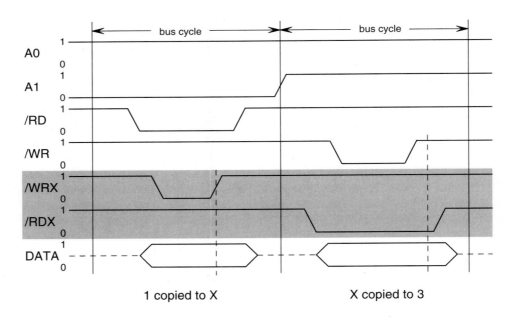

Figure 2.3-3   Timing relationships for data transfers.

As stated, to prevent bus contention the address decoder enables only one three-state buffer for a given address. Bus contention is further avoided by separating the intervals within a bus cycle during which the data bus is driven by intervals when no source drives the data bus. This separation is accomplished by the timing and control section generating read strobes that are narrower than and centered in the bus cycle. The data bus is in the high-impedance state during the undriven intervals. For example, in Fig. 2.3-3 there is an interval at the end of the first bus cycle when /RD is no longer asserted and an interval at the beginning of the second bus cycle before /RDX is asserted.

2.4   Register View of a Memory Subsystem

In this section, memory is considered in the context of an embedded system. The memory subsystem in Fig. 1.1-1 is directly addressable by the system's microprocessor. It can be viewed as a collection of addressable storage registers as described in Section 2.2. Registers in the memory subsystem are usually referred to as **memory locations** or simply locations. The memory subsystem's address, data, and control lines are connected to the system bus. The width of the memory's registers corresponds to the number of bits, or width, of the microprocessor's data bus. The maximum number of registers that can be addressed, or equivalently the maximum number of words in the memory, is limited by the number of address bits provided by the microprocessor's address bus.

There are two principal generic classes of memory, RAM and ROM. Read-write memory, most often referred to as RAM, can be written and read while the system is in operation. Memory in this class is used for temporary storage of data. The data stored may have been obtained from an input device and is awaiting processing, or it may be the intermediate results of computations, or it may be data that has been processed and is being stored until it can be output. RAM is usually **volatile**, meaning that when power to the memory is turned-off, the stored data is lost.

Read Only Memory (ROM) is nonvolatile. Data is written to ROM only once. Writing a ROM occurs before the system is placed in operation. When the system is in operation, a ROM can only be read. The permanent nature of its stored data makes ROM ideal for storing an embedded system's program. Whenever the system is powered on, it simply starts executing its program from ROM.

The generic terms RAM and ROM are used in this text to represent the entire classes of memory that have the previously defined class characteristics. Specific types of RAM, such as SRAM and DRAM, and specific types of ROM, such as masked ROM, EPROM, and Flash, are presented in Chapter 11.

General purpose microcomputers, such as a PC, use ROM to store a program called the Read Only Memory–Basic Input/Output System (**ROM-BIOS**). This name is derived from the fact that the ROM-BIOS contains software routines that control the detailed hardware operation of the system's basic input and output devices, such as keyboard and display. At power on, the ROM-BIOS first performs a self test of the system's hardware to determine whether it is operating properly. Next, this program initializes the I/O devices, and loads the operating system from disk into the system's RAM. After this process, the computer is ready for use.

The actual number of registers in a system's memory subsystem, and what portion is RAM and what portion is ROM, is a function of the application. For general purpose PCs, the objective is usually to provide as much RAM as economically possible, thereby allowing the system to efficiently run the widest range of programs. In contrast, for embedded systems the objective is to provide only the RAM and ROM required for a specific application, to minimize memory cost.

For example, the Intel 8051, a single-chip microcomputer often used in simple control applications, has only 4K bytes of ROM and 128 bytes of RAM and can transfer 8 bits of data at a time. In contrast, the Intel 80486 microprocessor, used in personal computers has 32 address bits and can directly address as much as 2^{32} or 4 Gbytes of memory. The data bus of the 80486 is 32 bits wide, hence 4 bytes, or 32 bits of data, can be transferred to or from memory in one bus cycle.

The actual amount of memory existing in a particular system is often less than the maximum the microprocessor is capable of directly addressing. A memory map is used to graphically represent the total memory space that the microprocessor can address. This map is labeled to show the address ranges that correspond to memory that actually exists in the system, and the type of that memory, RAM or ROM. A memory map for a memory subsystem of a microprocessor that has a 16-bit address bus and an 8-bit data bus is shown in Fig. 2.4-1. The application requires 8K of ROM to hold the program and 2K of RAM for data. The address boundaries for the ROM and RAM areas are indicated by hexadecimal numbers.

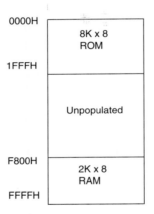

Figure 2.4-1   Memory map for a microprocessor with a 16-bit address bus and 8-bit data bus where the memory contains 8K × 8 of ROM and 2K × 8 of RAM.

2.5   Register View of I/O Subsystems

Input and output subsystems are also viewed in terms of their registers. Input registers are unique in that their inputs are connected to the outside world. Correspondingly, output registers are unique in that their outputs are connected to the outside world.

A simpler variant of the previously presented memory cell is used for input and output registers. Figure 2.5-1 shows a memory cell with **separate I/O**, separate input and output data lines. This circuit is a slight modification of that of Fig. 2.1-3. There is no connection from the output back to the data input.

An input register is written by an input device, Fig. 2.5-2. The input device drives data on the DATA IN lines of the input register and then generates a strobe to write the data into the register. The DATA OUT lines of the register are connected to the system data

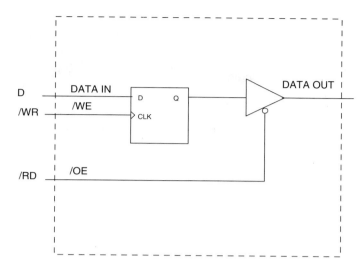

Figure 2.5-1   Logic representation of a memory cell with separate input and output.

bus through three-state buffers. Data stored in an input register appears on the system data bus only during a bus cycle where the microprocessor is addressing the input register and only for the duration of /RD. This operation is called an **I/O read** to distinguish it from a memory read. Since the input register provides the data a port or gateway from the input device to the system data bus, it is referred to as an **input port**.

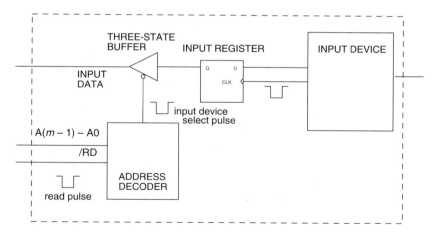

Figure 2.5-2   Input subsystem.

Several input devices typically exist in an application and each has one or more associated input registers. Each input register must be uniquely addressable. The address decoder in Fig. 2.5-2 passes the /RD strobe through to enable the three-state buffer if, and only if, the address at the decoder's address input corresponds to the address assigned to the input port. The strobe that appears at the address decoder's output is called an **input device select pulse**. In summary, input registers, or input ports, are addressable registers that can only be read by the microprocessor. Their function is to allow data to be brought into the system from the outside world.

To transfer data on the system data bus to an output device, an output register is required. The type of cells in an output register are the same as in Fig. 2.5-1. However, in this case the register's data inputs are connected to the system data bus and its outputs are connected to an output device (Fig. 2.5-3). An output register, also referred to as an **output port**, allows data to be made available to the outside world. The strobe that is generated at the address decoder's output in response to the appropriate address and /WR strobe is called an **output device select pulse**. The three-state buffer in the figure is hardwired so that it is always enabled. In some cases the buffer's enable input is controlled by the output device.

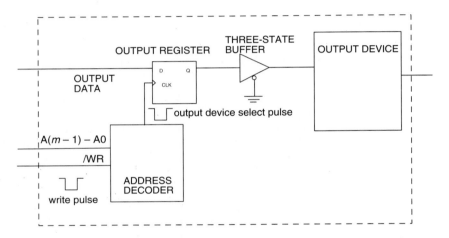

Figure 2.5-3   Output subsystem.

2.6   Operational Registers

All the registers previously considered are storage registers. Data in a **storage register** can be modified only by writing a new data value to the register. In contrast, **operational registers** can also modify their stored data by performing some arithmetic or logical data transformation. This capability is provided by logic connected to the register's cells. Shift registers and counters are common examples of operational registers that are available as MSI circuits.

The most powerful operational register in a simple microprocessor is the accumulator register. The **accumulator** is associated with the Arithmetic and Logic Unit, ALU, Fig. 2.6-1. The ALU performs all of the microprocessor's data transformations. Control signals to the ALU, from the microprocessor's timing and control unit, specify which operation is to be performed.

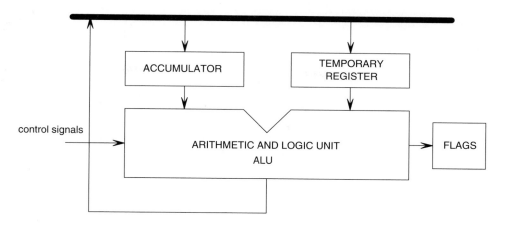

Figure 2.6-1   A microprocessor's accumulator register and associated ALU form an operational register.

The accumulator register and temporary register are both simple storage registers. However, their outputs provide the inputs to the ALU. In its simplest form, the ALU is a combinational circuit that performs logic operations (e.g. complement, AND, OR, and XOR) and arithmetic operations (e.g. addition and subtraction) on its inputs and provides the result at its output. The result of the operation is written to the accumulator, replacing the accumulator's original operand. Thus, an accumulator is considered an operational register capable of transforming its contents using any of the operations that can be performed by the ALU.

The width of the accumulator, in bits, typically defines the **microprocessor's wordlength**. A microprocessor with an 8-bit accumulator is characterized as an 8-bit microprocessor.

2.7   Register View of a Simple Microprocessor

A microprocessor's architecture and operation can be viewed in terms of its registers. Figure 2.7-1 is a block diagram of a very simple microprocessor showing its registers and major functional units. The microprocessor's registers are interconnected by an internal data bus. This internal bus is distinct from but connects to the system bus. Internal control signals used to accomplish internal data transfers are not shown. A microprocessor's **architecture** is distinguished by:

1. The specific storage and operational registers it contains
2. The data transfers that can occur among these registers
3. The kinds of operations that can be performed on data in its operational registers.

The architecture of Fig. 2.7-1 will be used to illustrate the basic operation of a simple microprocessor. This microprocessor has a 16-bit address bus and an 8-bit data bus.

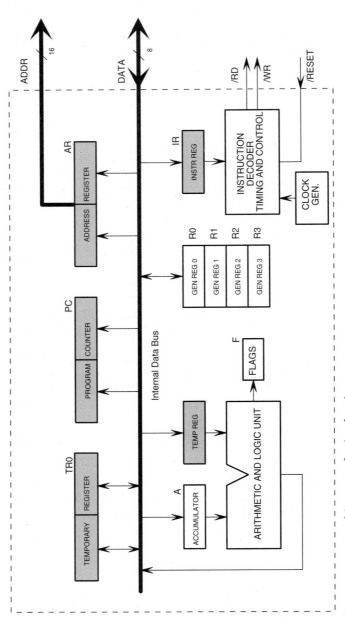

Figure 2.7-1   Architecture of a simple microprocessor.

A microprocessor is a clocked sequential machine. Its timing and control section directs the operations it carries out. The control section of a simple microprocessor causes repetitive **fetch-execute cycles** to occur. The microprocessor first fetches (transfers) an instruction from memory to registers in the microprocessor and executes the instruction. It then fetches and executes the next instruction in memory.

These fetch and execute cycles are repeated indefinitely unless an instruction to halt operation is executed or power to the microprocessor is turned off. Even during times when you don't have anything useful for the microprocessor to do, it still fetches and executes instructions.

A single instruction may be from one to several bytes in length. If an instruction is longer than the data bus is wide, the instruction fetch involves several data transfers (bus cycles) to copy the entire instruction from memory to the microprocessor. Our simple example microprocessor has an 8-bit data bus. Thus, to fetch an instruction, there has to be one data transfer for each byte of the instruction.

The execution of some instructions may also require one or more transfers of data between the microprocessor and memory or I/O. Each data byte transferred requires a bus cycle.

In this simple microprocessor, a register called the **program counter (PC)**, contains the memory address of the first byte of the next instruction to be fetched or the address of the next byte of a multibyte instruction that is currently being fetched. When this microprocessor is powered on or is reset, its control section sets the PC's value to the predefined starting address of 0000H. Thus, the first instruction to be executed is fetched from the first address in memory, address 0000H.

The control section causes several actions that together fetch an instruction. First, the contents of PC are transferred to the address register. The **address register's** function is to hold the address of the memory or I/O location being referenced during a bus cycle. The outputs of the address register drive the address bus lines. During the bus cycle, the PC's contents are incremented so that the PC contains the memory address of the next instruction byte in sequence. Since its contents are incremented by the control section, PC is a simple operational register. Incrementing is the only operation that can be performed on PC, other than its being written.

With an address on the address bus, the control section generates a memory read strobe to transfer the first byte of the instruction at the addressed memory location to the microprocessor's **instruction register (IR)**. This first byte, the instruction's **operation code** or **opcode**, identifies the instruction's size and function. The contents of the instruction register are input to the instruction decoder. The instruction decoder decodes the opcode to determine what the control section must do to complete the fetching of the instruction and to execute the instruction.

If the instruction consists of more than one byte, the PC's contents are again transferred to the address register to provide the address of the next byte of the instruction. After the address is transferred to the address register, PC is incremented to the address of the next byte. This process continues until an entire instruction has been transferred to registers in the microprocessor. The value in PC after an entire instruction is transferred is always the address of the first byte of the next instruction to be fetched.

Any additional instruction bytes beyond the opcode contain either an operand or the memory address of an operand. The control section determines from the opcode into which of the microprocessor's registers the additional bytes of the instruction should be placed. For example, the temporary register TR0 is used to hold additional bytes of some instructions.

Only after all bytes of an instruction are transferred into the microprocessor can the instruction be executed. Execution of an instruction entails performing the operations specified by the instruction's opcode. Instruction operations include:

1. Transferring data from memory or an input port to the microprocessor.
2. Carrying out a logical or arithmetic operation on data in a register in the microprocessor.
3. Transferring the contents of one of the microprocessor's registers to memory or an output port.

Logical and arithmetic operations involve the accumulator register, A. The accumulator takes its name from the fact that it typically receives or accumulates the results of logical and arithmetic operations. **Unary operations**, such as increment or complement, involve a single operand. The instruction assumes the single operand is already in the accumulator, placed there by a previous instruction. The result of the operation is left in the accumulator, replacing the original operand.

Binary operations involve two operands. One of the operands is assumed to be in the accumulator and the other is specified by the instruction to be in either a microprocessor register or a memory location. A copy of the second operand is automatically transferred to the Temp register before the binary operation is performed. The result of the binary operation is left in the accumulator.

The **flag register** contains bits that indicate characteristics of the result of unary or binary operations. For example, one bit in the flag register is the carry flag. This flag is set if an operation, such as addition, results in a carry out of the most significant bit of the result.

Once an instruction's execution is complete, the control unit transfers the contents of PC, which is the address of the first byte of the next instruction to be fetched and executed, to the address register. The control unit then fetches and executes the next instruction. This repetitive sequence of actions results in instructions normally being taken from consecutive addresses in memory and executed.

The fetching of instructions from consecutive memory addresses can be altered by the execution of a branch instruction. A branch instruction's execution causes PC to be loaded with a new, nonconsecutive memory address that is contained in the branch instruction. When this nonconsecutive address is loaded into PC, it automatically becomes the address of the next instruction to be fetched and executed.

Additional registers in a microprocessor improve its performance. For example, the general purpose storage registers (R0, R1, R2, and R3) in Fig. 2.7-1 are used to store intermediate results thus saving the time that would be required to transfer these results to memory and later retrieve them for further processing. More complex microprocessors have additional storage registers and operational registers to enhance their performance.

2.8   Register View of a System's Operation

From the previous discussions, it is clear that an entire system can be viewed in terms of its registers. All of the system's registers are either storage registers or operational registers. The operation of the system can be described in terms of storage of data in registers, transfers of data between registers, and transformations of data in operational registers. The data transferred or transformed may be interpreted as either data to be processed, instructions, or address values. The register view of a system is not only useful for developing a conceptual understanding of the system, but also for performing hardware and software design.

A microprocessor's instruction set specifies what transfers between registers (microprocessor registers, memory registers, and I/O registers) and what transformations on data in the microprocessor's registers are possible with the microprocessor's architecture. The instruction set specifies only the register transfers and transformations that are directly controlled by instructions and are the objective of the instruction execution. Table 2.8-1 gives the instruction set for the simple microprocessor. The instructions are divided into the following groups: data transfer, logic, execution flow, arithmetic, and processor control. The first column of the table lists each instruction and its function.

From a programming point of view, only the accumulator register, flag register, and general registers (R0, R1, R2, and R3) in Fig. 2.7-1 can be directly manipulated by instructions. Therefore, these are the only registers of concern when writing an assembly language program. Considering only these registers leads to a simpler register view of the microprocessor called the "programmer's register view." The programmer's register view of the simple microprocessor is illustrated in Fig. 2.8-1. Only three bits in the flags register are defined. These bits correspond to the zero flag, Z; the sign flag, S; and the carry flag, C.

The programmer's register view of the entire system adds to the microprocessor's registers the registers in memory and I/O ports, Fig. 2.8-2.

The assembly language form of each instruction is given in column two of Table 2.8-1. Only the symbols for the registers that make up the programmer's view of the microprocessor can be used as operands in the assembly language instructions. For example, to transfer the contents of register R0 to A, you would use the move (MOV) instruction. This instruction is written in assembly language as:

```
MOV      A,R0
```

The second operand in the MOV instruction is always the source register and the first operand is always the destination. This fact is ascertained from the register transfer expression for the MOV instruction in column three of the table.

```
(r1) <- (r2)
```

This register transfer expression indicates that the instruction copies the contents of the register specified as the second operand to the register specified as the first operand. **Register transfer expressions** describe the function of each instruction in terms of the data transfer or logical or arithmetic operation that is the instruction's objective.

Ultimately, each of the microprocessor's instructions must be represented as a binary value. This is the only representation that can be stored in memory and fetched and decoded (understood) by the microprocessor. The binary encoding of the simple micro-

Table 2.8-1   Instruction set for simple microprocessor.

	Instruction	Assembly Language	Register Transfer	Instruction Bit Patterns
Data Transfer	move register	MOV r1,r2	$(r1) \leftarrow (r2)$	`01DDDSSS`
	move from memory	MOV r1,addr16	$(r1) \leftarrow (addr16)$	`01DDD110` `Low Addr` `High Addr`
	move to memory	MOV addr16,r1	$(addr16) \leftarrow (r)$	`01110SSS` `Low Addr` `High Addr`
	move immediate	MVI r,immed8	$(r) \leftarrow (byte2)$	`00DDD110` `Data`
Logic	complement accumulator	CMA	$(A) \leftarrow (\overline{A})$	`0010111`
	AND register	AND r	$(A) \leftarrow (A) \wedge (r)$	`10100SSS`
	OR register	OR r	$(A) \leftarrow (A) \vee (r)$	`10110SSS`
Execution Flow	unconditional jump	JMP addr16	$(PC) \leftarrow byte3 \cdot byte2$	`11000011` `Low Addr` `High Addr`
	conditional jump	J<cond> addr16	if <cond> = 1 then $(PC) \leftarrow byte3 \cdot byte2$	`11CCC010` `Low Addr` `High Addr`
Arithmetic	add register with carry	ADD r	$(A) \leftarrow (A) + (r) + (C)$	`10000SSS`
Processor Control	clear carry	CLC	$(C) \leftarrow 0$	`00110111`
	stop executing instructions	HLT		`01110110`

r: A, R0, R1, R2, R3 (where A = 111, R0= 000, R1 = 001, R2 = 010, and R3 = 011)
addr16: 16-bit address contained in the 2nd (low byte) and 3rd (high byte) of the instruction.
immed8: 8-bit constant contained in the 2nd byte of the instruction.
flags for conditional jumps: Z, zero; S, sign; C, carry
arithmetic and logic instructions alter flags

Figure 2.8-1   Programmer's view of the simple microprocessor.

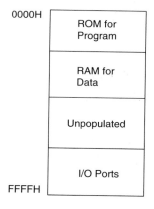

Figure 2.8-2   Programmer's view of memory and I/O for the simple microprocessor.

processor's instructions is given in column four of Table 2.8-1. The five registers that exist in the programmer's view can be distinguished using only three bits. The source register is encoded by the three bit code SSS and the destination register is encoded by the three bit code DDD. The specific assignment of codes to registers is given at the bottom of Table 2.8-1. For example, the instruction MOV A,R0 would be encoded as 01111000, where DDD = 111 and SSS = 000.

To input data from an input port requires a Move from Memory instruction. As can be seen from Fig. 2.8-2, an input port appears to the simple microprocessor as a memory register that can only be read. If the register at address FFFEH is actually an input port, its contents can be copied to register A with the instruction

        MOV   A,0FFFFH

This instruction requires three bytes when encoded in binary. The first byte is the opcode that specifies that this instruction moves data from memory to the destination register DDD. For register A, DDD = 111 and the opcode byte is 01111110 or 7EH. The second and third bytes comprise a 16-bit address, which in this example is the address of the input port. The second byte of the instruction is the low byte of the port address, FEH. The third instruction byte is the high byte of the port address, FFH. Appending these two bytes gives the memory address FFFEH. Therefore, the contents of memory location FFFEH are moved to the accumulator.

Looking at the register transfer expression for the Add Register with Carry instruction, ADC,

$$(A) <- (A) + (r) + (C)$$

we see that this instruction adds the contents of register A, the contents of the register specified as the operand r, and the contents of the carry flag, C. The result of this addition is left in register A. In assembly language form, only one of this instruction's operands is specified explicitly. The other two operands, A and C, are implied.

If you wanted to add the contents of registers A and R2, you would have to use two instructions:

```
CLC
ADC     R2
```

Since ADC is the only addition instruction in the instruction set, and it always adds in the carry, the carry must first be cleared. The Clear Carry, CLC, instruction clears the carry.

To fetch and execute an instruction, the timing and control section automatically manipulates other registers in the microprocessor, such as the program counter, temporary registers, address register, and instruction register. Some of these transfers and transformations, called micro-operations, involve registers that are not part of the programmer's view of the microprocessor and are not of concern when you write a program for the microprocessor. But they are of great concern to the designers of the microprocessor.

2.9   Summary

No matter how complex a system's task, it is ultimately accomplished by a sequence of transfers of data between registers and transformations of data in operational registers.

The memory subsystem consists of two classes of storage registers, RAM and ROM. RAM is used to store the program's variables. RAM is also used to temporarily store data that has been input but not yet processed, and to store data that has been processed but not yet output. During normal operation of the system, RAM is both written and read.

ROM is used to store the application program and data constants. During normal operation of a system, ROM is only read. Usually, the ROM is written only once when the system is constructed.

The input subsystem consists of storage registers that are written by an input device and read by the microprocessor. The output subsystem consists of storage registers that are written by the microprocessor and "read" by an output device.

The microprocessor in the CPU subsystem contains both operational and storage registers. Operational registers are able to modify their own contents. One of the simplest operational registers is the program counter, PC. PC is automatically incremented to point to the next instruction byte in memory. The most powerful operational register is the accumulator register, which is associated with the microprocessor's ALU. Data in the accumulator can be modified either logically or arithmetically. When an operation that modifies data involves two operands, one operand is in the accumulator and the other is in another register. The operation's result is left in the accumulator.

2.10   Problems

1. If the memory cell of Fig. 2.1-3 is constructed using a 74HC74 flip-flop and a 74HC125 three-state buffer, what other connections would have to be made for the circuit to operate properly? You may need to consult a data sheet for these parts to answer this question.

2. When each of the signals below has the logic level specified, is the signal asserted or unasserted? Is the signal active or inactive?

   a. /BUSY = 1

   b. /WR = 0

   c. RDY = 0

   d. EOC = 1

3. One signal naming convention uses two names separated by a / to label a single signal to indicate one of two possible states or conditions, for example, IO/M. Following this convention, the function denoted by the name preceding the / is active or asserted when the signal is 1 and the function denoted by the name following the / is asserted when the signal is 0. For each of the signals below and the given logic value, determine which function is active.

   a. IO/M = 0

   b. UP/DOWN = 1

   c. READY/BUSY = 0

   d. NEG/POS = 1

4. Draw the logic diagram of a 2-bit register with common I/O. The register is to be constructed from positive edge-triggered D-type flip-flops and three-state buffers with active-low enables. If this register is clocked with a negative pulse, will the input data be latched on the leading or trailing edge of the pulse?

5. Draw a schematic diagram for a 2-bit register constructed from 74HC74 D-type flip-flops and 74HC125 three-state buffers. Unlike the logic diagram of problem 3, a schematic diagram must contain all the information required to actually wire the circuit. This means inclusion of pin numbers and package designators, power and ground connections and proper termination of unused inputs.

6. Given the following register contents represented in binary, determine their octal, hexadecimal, and decimal representations.

   a. 10110101

   b. 01011111

   c. 1100101000011001

   d. 0100110101100000

7. Express the following hexadecimal numbers in binary and decimal.

   a. F0

   b. 3C

   c. 20A4

   d. B1E6

8. Convert the following decimal numbers to binary and hexadecimal.

   a. 174

   b. 56

   c. 482

   d. 255

9. Determine the bit capacity of the following memories.

   a. 1024×8

   b. 256×4

   c. $16K \times 8$

   d. $2K \times 16$

10. Restate the following memory configurations using the K suffix.

   a. $2^{14} \times 8$

   b. $2^{17} \times 8$

   c. 8192×8

   d. 12288×8

11. For each of the following memory structures rewrite the representation using the appropriate prefix; K, M, or G. Also state the bit capacity of the memory structure. How many address lines are necessary to address a register in each structure?

   a. 2048×4

   b. 16384×8

   c. 65536×8

   d. $1,048,576 \times 8$

12. List the sequence of steps required to write data into a memory. List the sequence of steps to read data from a memory. When reading data from a memory what determines when and how long the data is available on the data lines?

13. For the 1-out-of-4 decoder of Fig. 2.3-2 draw a logic diagram of an implementation of the decoder that uses only NAND gates and inverters.

14. Two one bit source registers, S1 and S2, are to be connected to a one bit destination register via a unidirectional one bit data bus. The source and destination registers are all 74HC74 D-type positive edge-triggered flip-flops. Two pulsers (pulse generators)

are provided, one that generates /WR and one that generates /RD. Using as few other logic devices as is necessary, draw a logic diagram of the circuit showing the connection of the source register's outputs and destination register's inputs to the bus. The circuit should include all the other logic needed so the output from either source can be transferred to the destination without bus contention. The pulsers are to be simply shown as blocks.

15. Draw a block diagram of a 4×1 memory with common I/O. The block diagram should show all inputs and outputs properly labeled.

16. Using D-type flip-flops, three-state buffers with active-low enables, and 1-out-of-4 decoders with active-low outputs and a single active-low enable, draw the logic diagram for the implementation of the memory in problem 15.

17. A 74HC574 IC is an octal D-type edge triggered flip-flop with three-state outputs. This IC contains eight positive edge triggered D-type flip-flops. It has eight data inputs and eight data outputs, a single clock input (CLK) and a single output control (/OC). /OC controls the three-state buffer associated with each output. A 74HC139 is a dual 1-out-of-4 decoder. Each decoder in the 74HC139 has a single active-low enable input. Draw a block diagram of a 4×8 RAM constructed using these devices and as few other logic gates as required. Your block diagram must show all the inputs and outputs for each device. Data lines can be shown as buses.

18. A microprocessor generates a 14-bit address. Draw a memory map of its address space with boundaries specified in hexadecimal. A 4K ROM is located in the memory address space starting at the lowest address. A 2K RAM is located in the memory address space ending at the highest possible address. Show these memory ranges in the address map with their boundaries also labeled (in hexadecimal).

19. How does the simple microprocessor know whether an address is actually the address of a memory register, an input register, or an output register? How would you know whether an address is the address of a memory register, an input register, or an output register?

20. By examining Fig. 2.5-2 and 2.5-3 develop a concise statement explaining the difference between the circuitry of an input subsystem and an output subsystem.

21. For the microprocessor of Fig. 2.7-1, list the registers that are simple storage registers. List the registers that are operational registers.

22. For the simple microprocessor described in Section 2.7, PC was incremented during some bus cycles and was not incremented during others. Explain under what conditions PC is incremented during a bus cycle and under what conditions it is not.

23. The first instruction in a program executed on the simple PC clears register A. This is accomplished using the "move immediate" instruction (MVI A,0). This is a two byte instruction. The first byte is the opcode (3EH) and the second byte is the constant (0 in this case) that is to be loaded into A. List, in the proper order and starting from reset, all internal and external transfers and transformations required to fetch and

execute this instruction. For each transfer give the source and destination and the data value transferred.

24. The PC of the simple microprocessor, Fig. 2.7-1, has the value 021AH at the beginning of an instruction cycle. In memory, starting at address 021AH, are three bytes (77H, 76H, 10H) which make up the move to memory instruction, MOV 1076H,A. For each of the bus cycles which comprise the instruction cycle for this instruction, list the source and destination registers and their contents. Also list the value of PC at the end of each bus cycle.

25. What information does a microprocessor's instruction set give you about its architecture?

26. For each of these simple microprocessor instructions write the instruction's bit pattern in hexadecimal.

    a. MOV R1,A

    b. AND R2

    c. ADD R3

    d. MVI A,49

27. The following sequence of instructions is a program. List, in hexadecimal, the byte values that would be stored in memory if this program starts at memory address 0000H.

```
MOV     A,0FFFEH
CMA
MOV     0FFFFH,A
JMP     0000H
```

CHAPTER 3

REGISTER VIEW OF 80C188EB SYSTEMS

3.1   80C188EB CPU Subsystem

3.2   Memory Subsystem

3.3   I/O Subsystems

3.4   80C188EB Modular Core CPU

3.5   Memory Segmentation and The BIU's Segment Registers

3.6   The EU and its Registers

3.7   Programmer's Register View of an 80C188EB System

3.8   80C186EB Microprocessor

3.9   Summary

As discussed in Chapter 2, it is advantageous to visualize a system in terms of its registers. This is true when analyzing an existing system or designing a new system. Since the programmer's register view of a system considers only those registers that can be directly manipulated by instructions, this is the view of the hardware that is used for software design.

This chapter provides an overview of the register structure and operation of 80C188EB systems, and is organized according to the constituent subsystems: CPU, memory, input, and output. Each subsystem is briefly considered from a register viewpoint. The objective of this chapter is to provide only the system hardware prerequisites for the in-depth discussions of software development provided in Chapters 4 through 9. Detailed hardware design of these subsystems is presented in Chapters 10 through 19.

The 80C188EB microprocessor is used in a wide range of systems, from small uniprocessor (single microprocessor) minimal-memory designs to multiprocessor systems with 1M byte of memory for each microprocessor. Since our interest is in fundamental concepts, the focus of this text is on uniprocessor systems.

3.1   80C188EB CPU Subsystem

A conceptual division of an 80C188EB system into subsystems is shown in Fig. 3.1-1. Each subsystem is delineated by function. An actual implementation may physically combine some memory, input, or output functions on the same IC or the same printed circuit board.

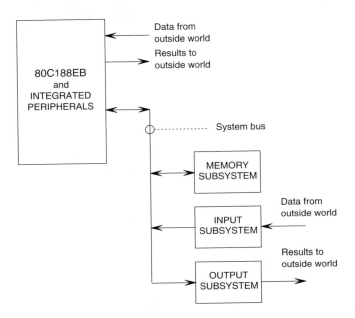

Figure 3.1-1   80C188EB based system composed of CPU subsystem and external memory and input/output subsystems.

This figure differs slightly from the microcomputer system representation in Fig. 1.1-1. In that representation, all input and output connections are through input and output subsystems that connect to the system bus. However, the 80C188EB includes integrated I/O peripherals on the same chip as the microprocessor (Fig. 3.1-2). Pin connections to these integrated peripherals allow data to be directly transferred between the CPU subsystem and the outside world. Figure 3.1-1 shows connections, not present in Fig. 1.1-1, from the CPU subsystem directly to the outside world. Other connections, primarily control connections, may exist between the integrated peripherals and the memory, input, and output subsystems. These connections are not shown in Fig. 3.1-1 and are not of interest until the later half of this text.

A closer look at the 80C188EB CPU subsystem's bus reveals a 20-bit unidirectional address bus, denoted A19–A0; an 8-bit bidirectional data bus, denoted D7–D0; and a control bus, which may utilize as many as 12 signals (Fig. 3.1-3). With respect to the CPU subsystem, some control signals are outputs and others are inputs. A simple system can operate with as few as three control signals: /S2, /RD, and /WR. These are the only control signals of interest in this chapter. These three signals are all outputs (from the CPU subsystem).

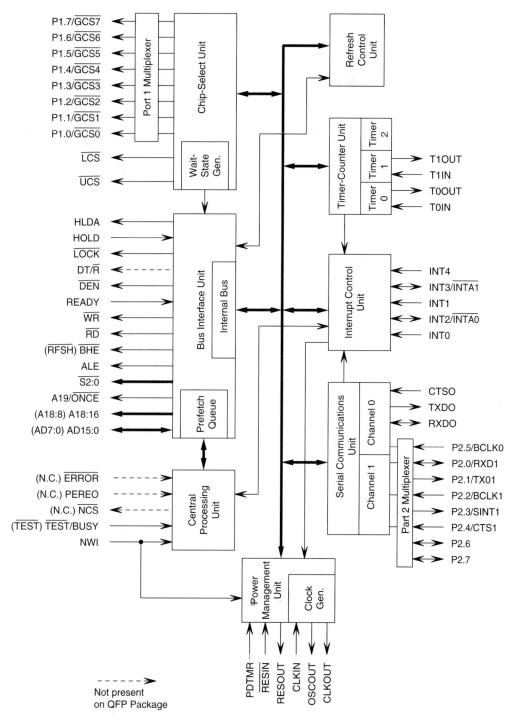

Figure 3.1-2   80C188EB/80C186EB block diagram. (Courtesy of Intel Corp.)

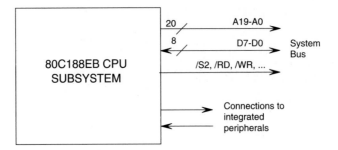

Figure 3.1-3   80C188EB CPU subsystem and its connections to the system bus and to its integrated peripherals.

An 80C188EB CPU subsystem typically requires some support ICs in addition to the 80C188EB. The number of support ICs required varies depending upon factors such as the overall functionality and bus drive required for an application.

A simple CPU subsystem implementation is shown in Fig. 3.1-4. Three ICs are used, an 80C188EB and two octal (8-bit) positive level-triggered latches. The latches are necessary to demultiplex the address and data bus signals. Demultiplexing address and data bus signals are discussed in detail in Section 10.4.

As Fig. 3.1-4 shows, and as is generally true, the ultimate source and destination of system bus signals is the microprocessor. As a result, the microprocessor selected for a design dictates the number of address bits and data bits, and the number and nature of the control signals that comprise the system bus.

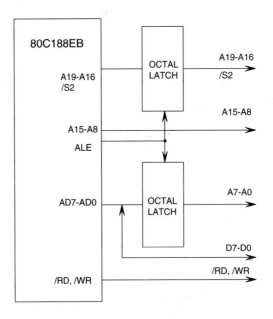

Figure 3.1-4   Block diagram of a simple 80C188EB CPU subsystem.

3.2   Memory Subsystem

The memory subsystem connects to the system bus via A19–A0, D7–D0, /S2, /RD, and /WR (Fig. 3.2-1). During a bus cycle, the 80C188EB uses **/S2** to indicate to external hardware whether the address it is generating is for memory or I/O. When a memory address is being generated, /S2 is 1. For an I/O address, /S2 is 0. The memory location or I/O register addressed is read or written in response to a /RD or /WR strobe from the 80C188EB. The data read or written is transferred over the data bus.

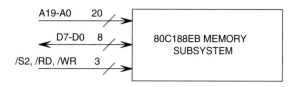

Figure 3.2-1   80C188EB memory subsystem.

With 20 address bits, an 80C188EB is capable of uniquely addressing 2^{20} memory locations. Each location is an 8-bit register. Thus, the memory address space is 1M bytes or 1,048,576 bytes in length. Figure 3.2-2 shows a **memory map** for the 80C188EB's memory address space. The addresses indicated are those that appear on the address bus and to which the memory responds. The 20-bit address that appears on the address bus is called the **physical address**.

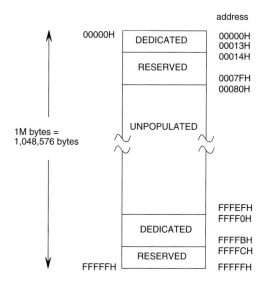

Figure 3.2-2   80C188EB memory map.

In Fig. 3.2-2 the lowest physical address, 00000H, is shown at the top of the memory map, and the highest, FFFFFH, is shown at the bottom. This convention of drawing a memory map with its lowest address at the top is followed throughout this book. Some literature follows the opposite convention, which places the highest address at the top. To avoid confusion when viewing figures in other literature, be careful to first determine which convention is being used.

There are restrictions on the use of two areas in the memory address space. One restricted area is in the extreme low address range and the other is in the extreme high address range of Fig. 3.2-2. One portion of each area is dedicated to specific microprocessor functions and the other portion is reserved, by Intel, to maintain compatibility with future hardware and software products. The area in low memory from 00000H to 0007FH (128 bytes) is used for interrupt processing. The high memory area from FFFF0H to FFFFFH (16 bytes) is used for system reset processing. These constraints and how these areas are used are discussed in detail in later chapters.

The amount of memory that physically exists in a particular system, and which portions are RAM and which are ROM, is a function of the application's requirements. In simple systems, only two relatively small areas of memory may need to be implemented, RAM starting at address 00000H and ROM ending at address FFFFFH. Starting RAM at the lowest address and ending ROM at the highest address in the memory address space of an 80C188EB system is the opposite of what was the case for the simple microprocessor of Chapter 2. You will discover in Section 3.5.4 the reason for this difference.

Figure 3.2-3 shows a memory map for an application that requires no more than 2K × 8 of RAM and 8K × 8 of ROM. Since a 2K × 8 RAM IC and an 8K × 8 ROM IC are the smallest sizes readily available, this memory configuration is likely to be used even in very simple systems that require substantially less RAM and ROM. That portion of the memory

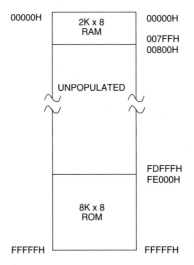

Figure 3.2-3   Memory map for an application that requires no more than 8K × 8 ROM and 2K × 8 RAM.

address space where no memory exists in a particular system is referred to as being **unpopulated**.

3.3 I/O Subsystems

Unlike Chapter 2's simple microprocessor, the 80C188EB provides separate address spaces for input and output. An 80C188EB can address a 64K-byte input space and a 64K-byte output space that are separate from its memory address space. The input address space and output address space are jointly referred to as the **isolated I/O space**, or simply, **I/O space**. Address bits A19–A16 are always 0H when ports in the I/O space are being read or written. Since A19–A16 are always 0H, they are ignored by the I/O subsystem. Accordingly, isolated I/O subsystems connect to the system bus using A15–A0, D7–D0, /S2, /RD, and /WR (Fig. 3.3-1).

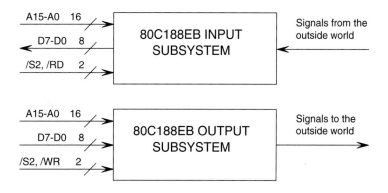

Figure 3.3-1   80C188EB external input and output subsystems.

Maps for the I/O address space are shown in Fig. 3.3-2. Since there are two distinct I/O spaces, one for input and one for output, two separate maps are shown. A register in the input map is selected when /S2 is 0 and /RD is asserted during a bus cycle. A register in the output map is selected when /S2 is 0 and /WR is asserted during a bus cycle. As a result of the separation of the I/O space, based on whether /RD or /WR is asserted, it is possible to have an input and an output port with the same address, but which are physically distinct entities.

Just as there are areas in the memory space that are reserved, there are also reserved areas in the I/O space. When an 80C186EB is used, ports 00F8H through 00FFH are reserved for communication with an 80C187 numerics processor extension. The 80C187 numeric processor extension cannot be used with an 80C188EB.

3.3.1   Peripheral Control Block (PCB)

Each of the 80C188EB's integrated peripherals has its own set of registers. These registers are used to configure the peripheral, provide status information, and transfer data to/from the peripheral. Each integrated peripheral's registers are physically located in the periph-

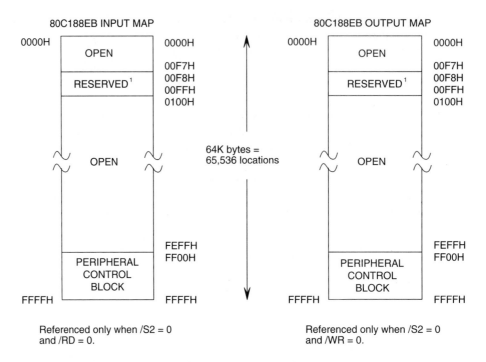

Figure 3.3-2   80C188EB Input and Output Maps.

eral. However, for addressing purposes, the registers of all the different integrated peripherals are addressed as members of a single logical block of 256 contiguous bytes (128 word
registers) called the **Peripheral Control Block (PCB)**. Some of the 128 word registers in
the PCB are unassigned. Unassigned registers in the PCB must be treated as reserved and
not written or read.

   When an 80C188EB is reset, the PCB's base address is FF00H. Thus, after reset, the
PCB occupies the last 256 bytes in the I/O space, FF00H to FFFFH as shown in Fig. 3.3-2.
Unless there are external I/O devices with addresses in this range, the PCB is left in its
default position.

   One of the registers in the PCB is the relocation register, RELREG. This register has
an offset of 00A8H from the PCB's base address, equivalent to address FFA8H after reset.
Your program can use RELREG to relocate (move) the PCB to any 256 byte boundary in
either the I/O or memory space. The PCB is discussed in detail in Chapter 10.

3.3.2   Integrated Input/Output Unit

One of the 80C188EB's integrated peripheral units is the Input/Output Unit. The I/O Unit
provides two general purpose 8-bit I/O ports, Port 1 and Port 2. Each port is multiplexed
to pins shared with other integrated peripherals. You have the choice of configuring these

pins for use as I/O ports or as their other peripheral functions. When your program configures these pins as ports, the CPU subsystem is able to directly provide I/O capability. In some limited applications, the availability of these ports can eliminate the need for the external I/O subsystems shown in Fig. 3.1-1. However, if your application needs to use the more powerful integrated peripherals that share pins with the integrated I/O ports, then external I/O subsystems are required.

Port 1 is an output only port whose pins are multiplexed with general purpose chip select signals from the integrated Chip Select Unit. These shared pins are configured by your program during initialization so that the port/peripheral multiplexer selects either an output-port signal or a chip-select signal to be available at each pin.

Port 2 consists of four input, two output, and two open drain bidirectional pins. The four input and two output pins are multiplexed with signals from the Serial Communications Unit, SCU. The two bidirectional pins are not multiplexed.

Port 1 and Port 2 have their own sets of four registers in the 80C188EB's peripheral control block; a Control Register ($P n$CON), a Direction Register ($P n$DIR), a Latch Register ($P n$LTCH), and a Pin Register ($P n$PIN). Only the low byte of each register is used. One bit in the low byte of each register is associated with each pin. The purpose of these registers is covered in detail in Section 12.8.

For simplicity, examples involving I/O ports that appear in this text prior to Chapter 12 use only ports in external I/O subsystems.

3.3.3   Memory Mapped I/O

Like Chapter 2's simple microprocessor, I/O ports can also be placed in the memory address space. I/O ports located in the memory address space are called **memory mapped I/O**. Memory mapped input ports appear to the 80C188EB as memory locations that can only be read. Memory mapped output ports appear as memory locations that can only be written. Whether an external I/O port appears in either the memory or I/O space is a function of how the port's address decoder is designed to respond to /S2. If the port's address decoder selects the port when /S2 is 0, then the port is in the I/O space. If the port's address decoder selects the port when /S2 is 1, then the port is in the memory space. Advantages and disadvantages of isolated I/O compared to memory mapped I/O, along with I/O port address decoding, are presented in Chapter 12.

3.4   80C188EB Modular Core CPU

The 80C188EB microprocessor consists of a modular core CPU and integrated peripherals (Fig. 3.1-2). The modular core CPU has the same basic architecture as that of 8086/8088 microprocessors and has full instruction code compatibility with 80186/80188 microprocessors. Because of hardware enhancements, most instructions execute faster on an 80C188EB than on an 8088 operating at the same clock speed. If you already know the 8086/8088's architecture, then you are familiar with the 80C188EB modular core CPU architecture.

Chapter 2's simple microprocessor has a single control unit. This control unit continually alternates between performing an instruction fetch and executing the instruction it has just fetched. First, the control unit causes the actions required to completely fetch an instruction from memory. Then, it causes the actions required to execute that same instruction. Only after an instruction's execution is complete can the control unit fetch the next instruction.

Use of a single control unit results in the system's bus being unused or idle during those periods of time when the execution of an instruction involves only operations internal to the microprocessor. Conversely, once an instruction's execution is complete, the execution portion of the microprocessor's hardware is idle while the next instruction is fetched. Thus, with a single control unit, the simple microprocessor's operation is inefficient, because either the system's bus is idle or the microprocessor's arithmetic and logic unit is idle.

The 80C188EB is designed to significantly reduce this inefficiency. Its modular core CPU is internally divided into two independent processing units, the Bus Interface Unit and the Execution Unit (Fig. 3.4-1). The Bus Interface Unit handles the transfer of instructions and data over the system bus, and the Execution Unit handles the execution of instructions. Each unit has its own control section. Both control sections operate from the same system clock. Working in parallel, these two units can run a program faster than if a single control unit were used.

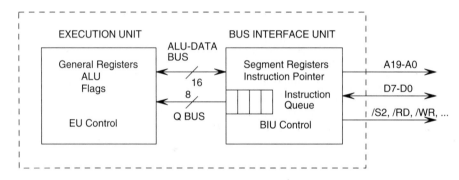

Figure 3.4-1   80C188EB microprocessor's EU and BIU.

3.4.1   Bus Interface Unit (BIU)

All data transfers between registers in the 80C188EB and memory or I/O are handled by the **Bus Interface Unit (BIU)**. The BIU generates the 80C188EB's system bus signals. Data transfers are of two general types—instruction transfers and operand transfers. An instruction transfer copies an instruction byte from memory to the 80C188EB's instruction queue. An operand transfer copies data between memory or I/O and an 80C188EB register. Operand transfers are not only used to read operands but also to write results. To accomplish either type of transfer, the BIU generates a 20-bit physical address to select a memory location or I/O port and generates a /RD or /WR control strobe to control the transfer.

The Execution Unit has no direct connection to the system bus and must rely on the BIU for its instructions and operands. The BIU performs an operand transfer only when requested to do so by the Execution Unit. The BIU transfers the requested operand to or from the EU on the 80C188EB's internal **ALU-Data Bus** (Fig. 3.4-1). When not transferring an operand, the BIU fetches instruction bytes from memory and places them in its four byte **instruction prefetch queue** or **pipeline**.

3.4.2   Execution Unit, EU

The **Execution Unit (EU)**, takes instructions from the BIU's instruction prefetch queue via the internal **Q Bus** (Fig. 3.4-1) and executes them. When an instruction's execution requires that an operand be read from memory or an input port, the EU transfers the operand's 16-bit address offset to the BIU. The BIU uses this 16-bit address offset in creating the operand's 20-bit physical address. The BIU then reads the operand and passes it to the EU. The next section explains how the BIU generates a 20-bit physical address using a 16-bit address offset from the EU.

When an instruction's execution requires that an operand be written to either memory or an output port, the EU transfers the operand along with its 16-bit address offset to the BIU. The BIU then writes the operand to the memory location or output port, as required.

3.4.3   Overlapped Instruction Fetch and Execution

The separate BIU and EU allow instruction fetch and execution to be overlapped. Overlapping fetch and execution results in more instructions being executed per unit time. The BIU can fetch an instruction while the EU executes a previously fetched instruction. When, as part of the current instruction's execution, the EU requests an operand transfer, the BIU gives this request priority over fetching instruction bytes.

If the instruction queue is not full and the EU is not currently requesting an operand transfer, the BIU **prefetches** the next instruction byte. At any given time, the instruction prefetch queue may vary between the extremes of being empty or being full. 80C188EB instructions are from one to six bytes long. Thus, the queue may contain no instructions, a portion of a multibyte instruction, or as many as four complete one byte instructions. The number of instructions in the queue at any particular time varies.

Usually, when the EU completes the execution of an instruction, the next instruction to be executed is already available in the instruction queue for execution. When this is the case, no time is lost in waiting for the next instruction to be fetched.

The speedup normally achieved by prefetching instructions is briefly lost when the EU executes a branch instruction. In this situation, the next instruction to be executed is not the next instruction available in the queue. The instructions that remain in the queue are no longer of use and the queue is flushed. The EU must wait while the BIU fetches the first byte of the instruction at the branch location. During this brief period, the 80C188EB's operation is like that of the simple microprocessor in that it must wait for the next instruction to be fetched. After fetching the instruction at the branch address, the BIU continues by sequentially prefetching instructions bytes that follow the instruction at the branch address. At this point, the fetch time again becomes transparent.

3.5   Memory Segmentation and the BIU's Segment Registers

The 80C188EB has a **segmented memory address space**. This simply means that your programs view the 80C188EB's 1,048,567 byte memory address space as being logically divided into blocks of bytes (Fig. 3.5-1). These blocks are called segments. A **segment** is a separately addressable logical unit of memory that can be up to 64K bytes long. The actual size of a particular logical segment, up to its 64K limit, is defined by the application.

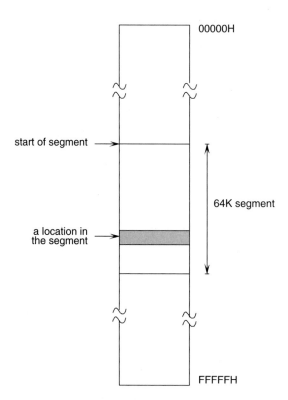

Figure 3.5-1   A location in a segment in the 80C188EB address space.

To access a location, your program must specify the location's logical address. A location's **logical address** is comprised of two parts, its segment address and its offset address. The **segment address** identifies the start of the segment in memory. The **offset address** specifies the distance, in bytes, from the segment's start to the location of interest (Fig. 3.5-2). Your program must place the location's segment address in a segment register prior to accessing the location. The location's offset address can come from an instruction, another register, or be computed by the EU. The BIU combines the logical segment address and logical offset address to produce the physical address on the system address bus. The 80C188EB's segment and offset addresses are 16-bit values. Its physical address is a 20-bit value.

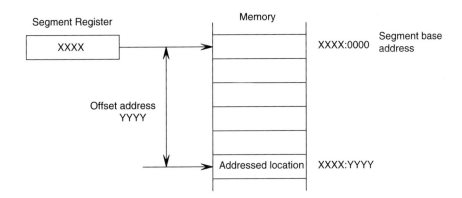

Figure 3.5-2   Use of a segment register and an offset to determine the physical address of a byte in memory.

There are hardware and software advantages to microprocessor architectures that use segmented addressing. One hardware advantage is that the segment and offset address values manipulated internally by the microprocessor are not as large as the physical address generated on the external address bus. This allows the registers in the microprocessor used to manipulate the segment and offset addresses to be smaller than the physical address.

As stated, 80C188EB segment and offset addresses are 16-bit values. Therefore, only 16-bit registers and data paths are required inside the 80C188EB. In fact, all registers in an 80C188EB, excluding the 8-bit wide queue, are 16-bit registers (Fig. 3.5-3). The 80C188EB's ALU is designed to perform 16-bit arithmetic. Thus, address offsets computed by the EU are 16 bits in length. The 80C188EB's internal ALU/data bus is also 16-bits wide. Restricting registers and internal data paths to 16 bits results in an IC with a smaller area, which reduces IC production costs.

Segmented addressing has a similar impact on the software. Separate instructions in your program deal with a location's smaller logical segment address and logical offset address. As long as your program is accessing locations in the same block, only the offset addresses change. So, usually your program must only manipulate offset addresses. This reduces the number of bytes required in instructions and programs. As a result, your programs execute faster because fewer instruction bytes need to be fetched. Your programs also require less memory for storage, resulting in reduced hardware costs.

For a small program, the number of locations in one segment is sufficient. Therefore, the segment register only needs to be loaded once, at the start of the program, and does not need to be changed subsequently.

For larger programs, more than one segment is required. When locations in another segment must be accessed, an instruction in your program must first change the value in the segment register. Once this change is made, your program can now access any locations

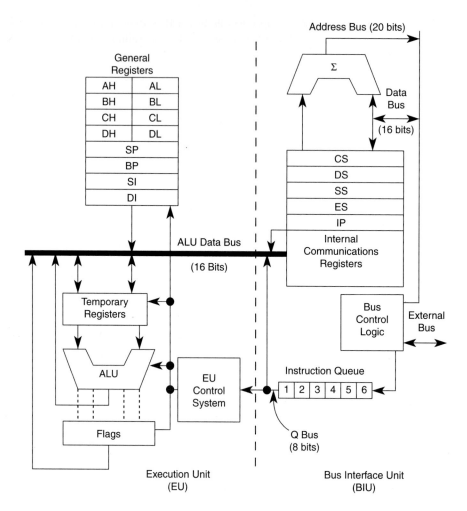

Figure 3.5-3   80C186EB/80C188EB modular core simplified block diagram. For the
                80C188EB the instruction queue is only 4 bytes long. (Courtesy of Intel
                Corp.)

in this segment by using only the locations' offset addresses. Even in large programs,
changing from one segment to another and the corresponding required change in the segment register's value, need be made only infrequently.

3.5.1   Address Relocation

The physical address that the BIU puts on the address bus is 20-bits long. To generate a 20-
bit physical address, the BIU automatically performs an operation called **address relocation**. Address relocation combines a logical 16-bit segment address with a logical 16-bit
offset address to create a 20-bit physical address.

A 16-bit segment register holds the segment address. This segment register provides the most significant 16-bits of the 20-bit physical **segment start address** that specifies the start of a segment (Fig. 3.5-1). The least significant four bits of the 20-bit segment start address are always 0H. The segment register is said to "point" to the beginning of the segment.

The position of a byte within a segment is defined by its offset address. The offset address is the distance in bytes from the start of the segment to the location of interest. A 16-bit offset restricts any memory location that it specifies to be within 64K bytes of the segment's start. Consequently, the maximum length of a segment is 64K bytes.

The BIU automatically generates the 20-bit physical address by adding the 16-bit offset address to the 20-bit segment start address. The BIU first creates the 20-bit segment start address by appending four 0's to the right side of the 16-bit segment address. The 16-bit offset is then added to the 20-bit segment start address.

Address relocation is equivalent to shifting the 16-bit segment address four bits to the left (multiplying it by 16) and adding to this shifted value the 16-bit offset address. The actual process is performed by a dedicated 16-bit adder in the BIU (Fig. 3.5-4). The least significant four bits of the resulting 20-bit physical address are simply the least significant four bits of the offset. The most significant 16-bits of the 20-bit physical address are the sum of the 16-bit segment address and the most significant 12-bits of the offset. Any carry out of bit 19 is discarded.

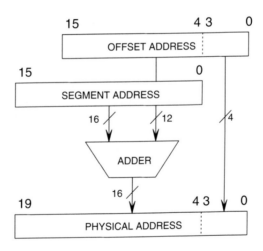

Figure 3.5-4   Address relocation; generating a 20-bit physical address by adding an offset address to a segment address that has been shifted left four places.

For example, consider a memory location with a segment address of FC00H and an offset of 1024H. Appending 0H to the segment address gives the segment start address of

FC000H. Adding the offset address to the segment start address gives the physical address
FD024H.

$$
\begin{array}{lll}
& \text{FC000H} & \text{segment start address} \\
+ & \underline{\text{1024H}} & \underline{\text{offset address}} \\
& \text{FD024H} & \text{physical address}
\end{array}
$$

The physical address which results from combining a particular segment address and
offset, as described above, is denoted by writing the segment and offset values separated by
a colon. For example, FC00:1024 represents FD024H. Writing a physical address in this
manner clearly shows its segment and offset components.

3.5.2   The Four Segment Registers

Instead of a single segment register, the 80C188EB's BIU has four. They are the: **Code Segment (CS), Data Segment (DS), Stack Segment (SS),** and **Extra** data **Segment (ES)** registers. These register names correspond to the typical division of system memory into
segments according to use. One segment of memory holds the program's instructions, or
code. Another segment holds the program's variables, or data. The extra segment provides
an additional segment for data. A special last-in-first-out memory structure, called a stack,
is implemented in the stack segment. The stack is necessary to support the use of subroutines, or procedures, in a program. Using multiple segment registers allows simple memory partitioning and aids in modular programming.

Since there are only four segment registers and the maximum length of a segment is
64K bytes, a maximum of only 256K bytes of the 1M byte memory address space is directly
addressable at any given time. This maximum is achieved when none of the four segments
overlap (Fig. 3.5-5). However, there is no restriction on the placement of segments; they
can be contiguous, disjoint, or overlapping.

Memory locations encompassed within the segments defined by the values in the
segment registers are said to be **currently addressable**. A location that lies outside all of the
segments defined by the four segment registers, is not currently addressable. To address a
location that is not currently addressable, an instruction must first load the appropriate
segment register with the segment address of the location. A subsequent instruction provides the location's offset address and accesses the location.

The segment register and the source of the offset used to generate a particular 20-bit
address are a function of the type of memory reference used. The allowed combinations of
segment registers and offset address sources, as a function of the type of memory reference,
are summarized in Table 3.5-1. The **default segment register** is the segment register automatically used by the 80C188EB for a particular type of memory reference. Instead of the
default register, the 80C188EB will use an alternate segment register if you include a special
segment override prefix as part of the instruction. The segment override prefix specifies
which of the alternate segment register is to be used.

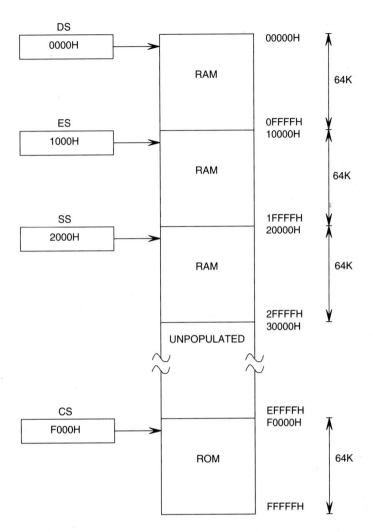

Figure 3.5-5   One possible non-overlapping assignment of segment addresses.

3.5.3   Offset Address Sources

For instruction fetches, the offset address always comes from the 16-bit **Instruction Pointer** register (**IP**), Table 3.5-1. IP is similar to the program counter register, PC, of the simple microprocessor of Chapter 2. However, there are two important differences. First, in the simple microprocessor, PC contained the physical address of the next instruction to be fetched and executed. In contrast, IP contains only part of the address, the offset within the code segment, not the full physical address, of the next instruction byte to be fetched. To generate the physical address, the BIU automatically adds IP to the code segment start address that corresponds to the segment address in CS. The physical address created in this

Table 3.5-1　Segment register and offset sources.

Type of Memory Reference	Default Segment Register	Alternate Segment Register	Offset
Instruction Fetch	CS	None	IP
Data Variable (except following)	DS	CS, ES, SS	Effective Address
BP Used as Base Register	SS	CS, DS, ES	Effective Address
String Source	DS	CS, ES, SS	SI
String Destination	ES	None	DI
Stack Operation	SS	None	SP

way is denoted CS:IP. For example, if CS is 0800H and IP is 0123H, then CS:IP is 0800:0123H and the corresponding physical address is 08123H.

The second difference is that while the physical address derived from IP is the address of the next instruction to be fetched, this instruction is not necessarily the next instruction to be executed. Other instructions typically precede this one in the queue and must be executed first.

For memory operand references (excluding references made by string instructions), the 16-bit offset address is computed by the EU. The EU computes the offset based on the instruction's addressing mode and passes this offset to the BIU.

The offset calculated by the EU is called the **effective address** (**EA**). The effective address is, in general, the result of the addition of the contents of one or two EU registers and a constant value, called the instruction's **displacement**, contained in the instruction. Which EU registers are added together in computing the effective address is a function of the memory addressing mode used by the instruction. Memory addressing modes are discussed in detail in Chapter 6.

The BIU normally combines the effective address with the contents of register DS to compute the physical address of data, row two of Table 3.5-1. Thus, the use of DS in forming a physical address is implied for most memory references to data. To cause the BIU to use an alternate segment register, an explicit segment override prefix, written as part of the instruction, is used.

Data can also be stored in the stack. This is commonly done in passing parameters to procedures. Register BP is used to point to data in the stack. When BP is used in a memory reference instruction, the default segment register is SS, the stack segment register, rather than DS. Methods for accessing data on the stack using BP are detailed in Chapter 8.

References to data strings, such as arrays or character strings, can be made with instructions that use a string addressing mode. String instructions can move data from one memory location to another. The implied (default) segment register for the source memory location is DS and for the destination location is ES.

For operations that put data onto the stack or take data from the stack, the offset address comes from the EU's 16-bit **Stack Pointer register** (**SP**). This offset is used with SS to form the physical address of the location in the stack. The 80C188EB automatically alters the value in SP during stack operations. This automatic alteration insures that SP always points to the top of the stack as data is written to or read from the stack.

3.5.4   Initializing Segment Registers

When the 80C188EB is reset, its segment registers are automatically initialized as follows:

CS = FFFFH
DS = 0000H
ES = 0000H
SS = 0000H

In addition, IP is initialized to 0000H and the Flags register to F000H. The contents of all the other 80C188EB registers are undefined.

With CS and IP automatically initialized to FFFFH and 0000H, respectively, the first instruction is always fetched from physical address FFFF0H (CS:IP = FFFFH:0000H). Your program code must be stored in ROM. Since the first instruction is fetched from location FFFF0H, this address must be in an area in the system memory populated by ROM. Therefore, for a simple 80C188EB system, ROM is placed in the address space so that it ends at the end of the address space. This insures that address FFFF0H is in ROM since this address is only 16 bytes from the end of the memory address space.

RAM, for a simple 80C188EB system, is placed in the memory address space starting at address 00000H. Your program's variables (data) and stack are located in RAM.

The instruction at location FFFF0H is normally a jump instruction to the start of your program (Fig. 3.5-6). This instruction is often referred to as the **bootstrap instruction**. Execution of the bootstrap instruction loads CS and IP with the values contained in the instruction. These values correspond to the starting address of your program.

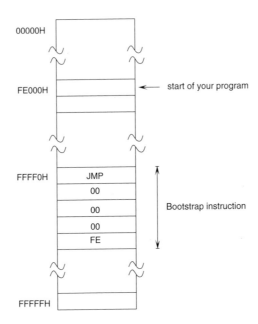

Figure 3.5-6   Bootstrap instruction, a FAR jump located at FFFF0H, jumps to the start of your program.

The bootstrap instruction loads CS with the segment address corresponding to the start of your program. This takes care of loading CS. You must place instructions at the beginning of your program to load DS, ES, and SS with appropriate values so that these segment registers point to the beginning of the appropriate segments in your system's memory. In simple applications, the segment registers can be initialized and then forgotten. In contrast, complex applications may require relatively infrequent changes in segment register values as your program executes.

3.6   The EU and its Registers

As shown in Fig. 3.5-3, the Execution Unit contains eight 16-bit **general purpose registers** and the Flags register. For descriptive purposes, these eight registers are divided into two groups: data registers, and pointer and index registers. These registers are briefly introduced in this section. They are covered in detail in later chapters as their use by various instructions is considered.

The **data registers** are the four general purpose registers, **AX, BX, CX,** and **DX**. These registers are unique in that each can be used interchangeably as either a 16-bit register or as two independent 8-bit registers. For example, when used as a single 16-bit register AX is simply referenced as AX. When used as two separate 8-bit registers, the high byte of AX is referenced as AH and the low byte as AL. This referencing convention applies to all four registers in the data group.

Data registers have general usage in logical and arithmetic operations. In addition, these registers serve special functions when certain instructions are performed. For example, AL is always the destination register for input instructions from 8-bit input ports. Sometimes the use of a register in an instruction is implicit. Implicit use of registers allows very compact instruction encoding, since one or more of the registers involved in an operation need not be explicitly specified in the instruction. For example, CX is used to hold the iteration count for the LOOP instruction.

The **pointer registers, Base Pointer, BP**, and **Stack Pointer, SP,** are primarily used for operations involving the stack. The **index registers, Source Index, SI,** and **Destination Index, DI,** are used primarily for operations on strings. The pointer and index registers can also be used in most logical and arithmetic operations.

The 16-bit **Arithmetic and Logic Unit, ALU,** is also located in the EU. The ALU manipulates the contents of general purpose registers and other instruction operands and asserts the status and control flags. Registers and data paths in the ALU are all 16-bits wide. As stated, the EU obtains instruction bytes from the BIU's instruction queue. When an instruction's execution requires access to memory or I/O to obtain or store data, the EU tells the BIU to access the data. To do this the EU must pass to the BIU the operand's offset or effective address. The EU uses the ALU in the automatic computation of effective addresses. All effective addresses manipulated by the EU are 16-bits wide.

Status flags and control flags are bits contained in the **flags register (F)**, also called the **processor status word (PSW)**. Only nine of the 16-bits in this register are used. Six status flags reflect various properties of the results of logical or arithmetic operations carried out by the EU. Three control flags control specific 80C188EB modes of operation.

After reset, the contents of the EU's general registers are undefined. As a result, your program cannot assume these registers contain 0000H (or any other value) and must load appropriate values into any of these registers before using them in a logical or arithmetic operation.

3.7 Programmer's Register View of an 80C188EB System

Register views of a system that provide different levels of detail are useful. For example, for hardware analysis or design, knowledge of the detailed characteristics of all the registers in a system and their interconnection paths is required. Conversely, for the purpose of analyzing or writing programs in assembly language, a simpler register view, the **programmer's view** or **programmer's model,** is important.

A programmers's register view of the 80C188EB's modular core is shown in Fig. 3.7-1. In this view, only registers that can be directly manipulated by 80C188EB instructions are shown. These fourteen 16-bit registers are labeled with their mnemonics and a word or phrase that indicates their function. General purpose registers can be used interchangeably in logical or arithmetic operations. However, their names reflect how they are specifically used by some instructions.

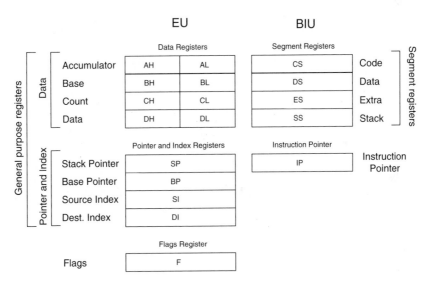

Figure 3.7-1   Programmer's register view of the 80C188EB's fourteen 16-bit registers.

Registers that cannot be directly manipulated by instructions are omitted from the programmer's register view. For example, registers that comprise the instruction prefetch queue are not shown. Also, the data paths that allow the transfer of data are not a part of this view. The interconnections of various registers by internal data paths is implied by the data transfers realizable by the instruction set. A register's operational nature is also defined by the instruction set.

This register view of an 80C188EB's modular core CPU is used extensively in the chapters in this text that focus on software.

The complete register view of an entire 80C188EB system must also include the registers in the memory and I/O subsystems. The registers in the memory subsystem are defined by the memory map. This map must show the types of memory actually provided in the memory subsystem and their address ranges. The register view of the I/O subsystem is defined by the I/O address map and documentation that provides the name and function of each register. Assuming that the Peripheral Control Block is left in the I/O space, the PCB register map and definitions of all of its registers would be part of the I/O register view. If the PCB is relocated to the memory address space, then it is included in the memory map.

3.8   The 80C186EB Microprocessor

The 80C186EB and 80C188EB microprocessors have identical EUs. As a result, they are software compatible. Code written for an 80C188EB can be executed on an 80C186EB without modification, and vice versa.

The major differences between the two microprocessors are their data bus widths and instruction queue lengths. The 80C186EB has a 16-bit data bus, in contrast to the 80C188EB's 8-bit data bus. The 80C186EB has a 6 byte instruction queue, in contrast to the 80C188EB's 4 byte instruction queue. These differences are confined to the BIUs, which though functionally identical, differ in their implementations to accommodate the bus width and queue length differences.

In most applications, the 80C186EB's 16-bit data bus gives it a speed advantage since it can transfer 16 bits of data per bus cycle. In applications that manipulate 8-bit data quantities extensively, or that are computation bound, the 80C188EB can approach 90% of the 80C186EB's processing throughput.

Data bus width differences lead to significant differences in the details of memory and I/O subsystems hardware design. The 80C188EB, with its 8-bit data bus, allows you to take advantage of the extensive variety of 8-bit peripheral devices available. Also, designing the 8-bit data interfaces of memory and I/O to the 80C188EB is simpler. And you still have the power of a microprocessor with a 16-bit internal architecture. Details of the hardware differences between the 80C186EB and 80C188EB are discussed in Chapters 10, 11, and 12.

3.9   Summary

An 80C188EB CPU subsystem provides fourteen 16-bit registers in the 80C188EB's modular core CPU. Some of these registers are in the Execution Unit (EU) and the others are in the Bus Interface Unit (BIU). The EU contains general purpose registers that are used in logical and arithmetic operations on data and in computing the effective addresses for memory operands.

The BIU contains the segment registers and the instruction pointer (IP). The segment registers are used to hold the segment addresses that specify the starting addresses for each of the four kinds of segments into which memory is divided. This division of memory corresponds to the common division of a program into: code, data, extra data, and stack.

The physical address of a location in any of these segments is automatically computed by the BIU. The BIU uses the appropriate segment register and the location's offset in the segment for this computation.

Register IP is used to provide the offset of the next instruction byte to be fetched. This offset is with respect to the code segment, so the BIU automatically uses address relocation to combine CS and IP to generate the physical address of the next instruction byte to be fetched.

The registers in the CPU subsystem are the same for any 80C188EB or 80C186EB subsystem. Thus, once the functions and use of these registers are understood, the register structure of the CPU subsystem of any 80C188EB or 80C186EB system is known.

It is possible for the memory subsystem to contain as many as 1,048,576 byte registers. Fortunately, these registers are simple storage registers. Some of these registers (RAM) can be written and read. The others (ROM) can only be read. The system's memory map specifies exactly how much memory actually exists in a specific system and which areas of it are RAM and which are ROM. Once the memory map is known, no other information about the memory subsystem is needed in terms of a programmer's register view.

The part of systems register view that differs most dramatically from one system to another is that of the input and output subsystems. The number and nature of these registers is the direct result of the peripheral ICs and devices selected for a specific application. Register maps for I/O are subdivided in terms of specific I/O subsystems. The address and function of each of these registers must be known.

3.10   Problems

1. How does the block diagram for an 80C188EB system in Fig. 3.1-1 differ from the microcomputer block diagram in Fig. 1.1-1?

2. What are the widths of (how many bits comprise) an 80188EB's address bus and its data bus? Are these buses unidirectional or bidirectional? How large is an 80188EB's memory address space and how does its size relate to the widths of its address and data buses?

3. What is the function of each of the control signals /S2, /RD, and /WR? Indicate which of these signals can be considered similar to an address signal and which can be considered timing signals. Explain why.

4. The address 008A2 appears on an 80C188EB's address bus. List the names and the values of the system bus signals sufficient to indicate that this address is that of:

   a. a memory location

   b. an input port

   c. an output port

5. An 80C188EB system application requires 8 K bytes of SRAM and 256 K bytes of EPROM. The SRAM starts at address 00000H and the EPROM ends at address FFFFFH. The SRAM devices to be used are 4K × 4 and the EPROM devices are 128K × 8. Draw a memory map of the system showing each device's boundaries in hexadecimal.

6. An application requires 32K × 8 of SRAM starting at location 00000H and 64K × 8 of EPROM ending at location FFFFFH. The SRAM is to be implemented using mem-

ory ICs that are 8K × 8. The EPROM is to be implemented with 32K × 8 memory ICs. Draw the memory map of the system and label all device boundaries with their hexadecimal addresses.

7. An 80C188EB memory subsystem consists of two 2K × 8 RAM ICs and one 8K × 8 ROM IC. The first RAM is placed in the memory address space starting at the lowest address. The second RAM is placed so there is a 4K × 8 gap (unused area) between the end of the first RAM and the beginning of the second RAM. The 8K × 8 ROM is placed so that the last location in the ROM corresponds to the last location in the memory space. Draw the memory map and indicate, in hexadecimal, the physical addresses of all RAM and ROM boundaries.

8. A memory subsystem for an 80C188EB contains 4K × 8 of RAM and 64K × 8 of ROM. The RAM is implemented by two 2K × 8 SRAMs with common I/O. The control inputs to the SRAM are /WE, /OE, and /CS. The ROM is implemented by two 32K × 8 EPROMs. The control inputs to the EPROMs are /CE and /OE. The SRAM starts at address 00000H and the EPROM ends at address FFFFFH. Draw a map of the memory subsystem showing the address boundaries for each memory IC. Draw two logic symbols, one to represent the SRAM and a second to represent the EPROM. Label each symbol's inputs and outputs. Using the logic symbols created, draw a block diagram of the memory subsystem and its connection to the system bus. Show any required decoders as a single block. Label all inputs and outputs to the address decoder(s). Each decoder output must also be labeled with the Boolean function that it implements.

9. How large is the 80C188EB's I/O space? Which of the system address bus bits are used in addressing ports in the I/O space? What is the value of the unused address bits during a bus cycle that addresses a port in the I/O space?

10. How do subsystems determine if an address on the address bus is for memory or isolated I/O? Why aren't addresses A19–A16 included as inputs to isolated I/O subsystems?

11. Explain how it is possible for an input port and an output port to have the same address yet be two distinct entities. How does the system distinguish between them?

12. Draw the logic diagram of a byte input port that inputs the states of eight switches. Use a 74HCT541 octal three-state buffer and any other necessary components. The 74HCT541 has two active-low enables. The eight switches are SPST maintained switches. The port is to be located at address 1000H in the I/O space of an 80C188EB system. Represent the address decoder as a single block. Label all the decoder's inputs and outputs. Write the Boolean equation for the decoder's output.

13. Redo problem 12, but now the input port is to be memory mapped. The port's address is still 1000H.

14. Draw the logic diagram of a byte output port that drives eight light emitting diodes (LEDs). Use a 74HC574 octal D-type edge triggered flip-flop with three-state outputs. The three-state outputs of the 74HC574 are controlled by its output control, /OC, input. Use 330 ohm current limiting resistors and assume that the 74HC574's outputs have sufficient current drive for the LEDs. The output port is to be located at address 2000H in the I/O space of an 80C188EB system. Represent the address decoder as a single block. Label all of the decoder's inputs and its output. Write the Boolean equation for the decoder's output.

15. What is the PCB? How large is it and where is it located immediately after an 80C188EB is reset?

16. Name the 80C188EB modular core's two functional units and describe the primary functions of each. What is the advantage gained by the use of two functional units as opposed to the single control unit used in earlier microprocessors. Under what conditions is this advantage briefly lost?

17. List and explain three significant architectural differences between the simple microprocessor architecture of Section 2.7 and the CPU modular core architecture of the 80C188EB.

18. What are the advantages to you as a designer in using the 80C188EB because its modular core has the same architecture as the 8086/8088 microprocessors?

19. Why is segmentation used in the 80C188EB architecture? List the mnemonics for the 80C188EB's segment registers. What is the maximum number of memory bytes that can be currently addressable? Write the equation which specifies how a physical address is "computed" by the BIU from a segment address and an offset.

20. Draw a diagram of the logic in an 80C188EB which accomplishes address relocation. Write the equation that specifies the function implemented by this logic. Is this logic part of the EU or the BIU? Provide a written explanation of what this logic does and why it is done in this fashion.

21. For each of the following segment and offset address combinations, compute the corresponding physical address. Carry out the computation in a manner that reflects the computation implemented by the hardware of Fig. 3.5-4.

segment address	offset address
a. 40A5	3C5D
b. F800	034C
c. C0F0	FEF0
d. FF00	A41B

22. Given the following register contents:

    CS = F000H   DS = 40CCH   ES = 1F9DH   SS = C9F0H
    IP = 8AC7H   SP = A0A0H

    compute the physical address corresponding to:

    a. CS:IP
    b. SS:SP
    c. DS:4A02H
    d. ES:0FAB0H
    e. DS:0F0DH

23. Assume that the contents of an 80C188EB's segment registers are as follows:

    CS = F531
    DS = 02CE

SS = 4777

ES = A094

List in hexadecimal the range of physical addresses that are currently addressable (addressable without changing the contents of any of the segment registers).

24. Assume DS has been loaded with 0040H and ES has been loaded with 0080H. Four memory locations and their offsets from the start of the ES segment are as follows:

Loc1	014F
Loc2	0A20
Loc3	BC00
Loc4	FC01

If each of the corresponding physical locations is to be addressed using DS, what are the required offsets?

25. Given the following segment register values: CS = F800H, DS = 0040H, and SS = 0800H, find the value of the offsets needed to:

a. address a byte variable at physical address 02214H

b. address a byte variable at physical address 07E00H

c. address a byte variable at physical address 01372H

d. fetch an instruction byte at physical address FE001H

e. transfer a byte from the stack at physical address 0FFFEH

26. What are the similarities and distinctions between the program counter, PC, of the simple example microprocessor and the instruction pointer, IP, of the 80C188EB? What aspect(s) of the 80C188EB's architecture causes the distinctions?

27. Given below are the physical addresses and memory contents for a portion of an 80C188EB system's memory prior to reset. List in order the first four bytes that are entered into the 80C188EB's instruction queue after reset.

FFFFD	54
FFFFE	3A
FFFFF	CC
FFFF0	B1
FFFF1	18
FFFF2	90
FFFF3	67
FFFF4	A4

28. What criteria determines whether a register in a microprocessor is included in the programmer's register view of a microprocessor?

29. List the registers in the programmer's register view of an 80C188EB that are in the EU and list those in the BIU. Which of these registers are involved in logical and arithmetic operations?

30. List the advantages and disadvantages of using an 80C188EB instead of an 80C186EB in a system.

CHAPTER 4

ASSEMBLY LANGUAGE AND ASSEMBLERS

4.1   Machine Language Instructions

4.2   Assembly Language Instructions

4.3   Simple Programs Structured as Sequential Tasks

4.4   ASM86 Assembly Language and its Assemblers

4.5   Relocatable Program Modules and Location

4.6   Embedded Assemblers Versus DOS Assemblers

4.7   Intel's ASM86 Assembler

4.8   Assembly Language Programs that Run Under DOS

4.9   Borland's TASM Assembler and Paradigm's LOCATE

4.10   ROMable DOS and DOS Emulators

4.11   Summary

You can write an embedded system program in a high-level language like C, C++, Pascal, or BASIC, or in assembly language, a low-level language. Still another approach is to write portions of your program in a high-level language and other portions in assembly language.

Using a high-level language eliminates the need for detailed knowledge of the selected microprocessor's architecture, because instructions in a high-level language express their operations independently of a particular microprocessor's architecture.

In contrast, instructions in an assembly language program make direct reference to the registers of a particular microprocessor to accomplish their operations. As a result, you must know the microprocessor's architecture in order to write an assembly language program. Assembly language's primary advantage is that its instructions deal directly with a microprocessor at the lowest and most direct level. Accordingly, it is possible for you to write programs that obtain the maximum performance from the microprocessor.

Programs for small embedded systems are typically written in assembly language. For medium and larger sized systems, at least some portions of a program are usually written in assembly language. In order to develop a comprehensive understanding of embedded system design, the emphasis in this text is on assembly language programming. Once assembly language programming is understood, moving to a high-level language is relatively easy.

Your ultimate objective during software development for an embedded system is the creation of a pattern of 1s and 0s that when placed in the ROM in your embedded system causes the system to carry out its specified function. After describing machine and assembly language programming, this chapter presents the tools and processes needed to go from creating an assembly language program source file, using an editor, to entering the desired pattern of 1s and 0s into a ROM.

An assembly language program must be translated to binary code (1s and 0s) before it can be loaded into ROM and executed. A program in its absolute binary code form is referred to as ROMable. ROMable code can be placed in a system's ROM and executed without the need for an operating system. The translation process requires the use of several programs called utilities or tools. The first step in the translation process is performed by the assembler. The other utilities used, in sequence, are a linker, locator, and an object-to-hex translator.

Tools for 80C188EB software development fall into two general categories, embedded tools and DOS tools. Embedded tools are specifically designed for developing programs for embedded systems. Using these tools, you can directly generate ROMable code.

DOS tools are designed for creating programs that execute under the DOS operating system. Because of their widespread use in developing PC software, DOS tools have the advantage of lower cost. However, these tools do not directly generate ROMable code. Fortunately, special locators are available that are used with DOS tools to generate ROMable code.

For large programs, inclusion of DOS or a DOS emulator may be justified. Inclusion of DOS allows the use of DOS tools without the need for a special locator. If the system does not have a disk, the version of DOS used must itself be ROMable. Commercial ROMable versions of DOS are available. To varying degrees, they provide the functions normally provided by a PC DOS. Inclusion of a commercial version of DOS in a system can add 15 to 40 Kbytes or more of code to your software, and may also require the payment of royalties. As a result, this approach is not emphasized in this text.

4.1   Machine Language Instructions

Your program's instructions must be stored in the memory subsystem to be executed. Thus, they must be in binary form. Instructions in binary form are called **machine language** or **machine code**.

When a microprocessor is designed, its designers must devise a scheme for the binary **encoding** of each instruction. Each instruction's binary encoding must specify the operation to be performed and either the operands' values or their addresses. The microprocessor designers' objective is to create an efficient encoding scheme where instructions are encoded using as few bytes as possible. An efficient instruction encoding means that you can write programs that require fewer bytes, less memory, and less execution time because fewer instruction bytes must be fetched.

The encoding scheme for the 80C188EB's more than three hundred machine language instructions is fairly complex. Instructions range from one to six bytes in length. Different instructions use different encoding formats depending on the instruction's operation and type of operands. One byte instructions generally operate on a single register or a flag. The single instruction byte provides the opcode and identifies the flag or register operated on.

Some of the longest multibyte instructions follow the format in Fig. 4.1-1. The first byte is the opcode, which specifies the instruction's operation. The second byte contains mode and register bit fields to identify either two registers as operands, or one register and the memory addressing mode used for addressing a memory operand.

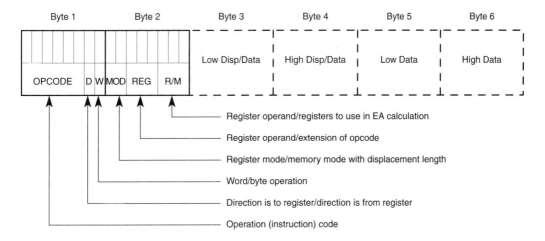

Figure 4.1-1   A typical 80C188EB multibyte machine language instruction format. (Courtesy of Intel Corp.).

The remaining instruction bytes hold one or two constants. A constant in an instruction is either an actual operand value (immediate data) or a displacement value used in computing an operand's offset address. Both types of constants may be contained in a single instruction. When this is the case, the third and fourth bytes of the instruction are the displacement, and the fifth and sixth bytes are the immediate data. Details of 80C188EB instruction encodings are given in Appendix D.

Instruction encoding is mentioned here to give you some idea of the complexity involved in the encoding scheme. When designing a system, you typically do not need a detailed knowledge of instruction encoding, since you are not going to write your program in machine language. However, if you are debugging a system by monitoring system bus activity or by examination of memory contents, you will need to understand the 80C188EB's instruction encodings.

4.2   Assembly Language Instructions

Writing and reading programs in machine language is extremely difficult. For this reason, instructions are represented in a more convenient form called **assembly language**. Each assembly language instruction uses an **instruction mnemonic** to represent its operation. An instruction mnemonic is simply a word or abbreviation that makes it easy for you to remember what an instruction does.

Because of the use of general purpose mnemonics, each machine language instruction does not necessarily have its own unique mnemonic. A single general purpose instruction mnemonic represents one of several similar but distinct machine instructions. For example, the mnemonic MOV is used to represent any one of twenty eight different machine language instructions, all of which move (transfer) data. MOV has the general form:

mov *destination, source*

The destination and source operands define which one of the 28 different kinds of data transfers is intended. Consider the following three instructions:

```
mov ax,cx                    ;move contents of register CX to AX
mov bl,72h                   ;move the constant 72h to register BL
mov value,al                 ;move contents of register AL to the
                             ;memory location with the name VALUE
```

These instructions all use the MOV mnemonic. Attributes of each instruction's operands provide the information that the assembler needs to generate the machine language instruction corresponding to a specific type of move instruction.

In terms of assembly language mnemonics, the over 300 80C188EB machine instructions are represented by only about 118 different mnemonics. For example, the instructions above are all different machine language instructions that use the same mnemonic, MOV.

4.2.1   Categories of Assembly Language Instructions

From this point on, when discussing either individual instructions or entire programs, use of the term register is specifically limited to a register in the 80C188EB. Registers in memory are simply referred to as memory locations or memory. Registers in I/O ports or peripheral ICs are referred to as ports.

To facilitate learning the instruction set, instructions are grouped into categories by function. Table 4.2-1 lists a subset of 80C188EB instructions divided into five categories: data transfer, arithmetic, logic, execution flow, and processor control. This subset of instructions is adequate for producing useful, though perhaps not particularly efficient, programs.

Instructions in the data transfer category either input data, output data, transfer data between two registers, or transfer data between a memory location and a register. Instructions in the arithmetic and logic categories carry out computations. Execution flow instructions can change the order of execution by branching to nonsequential locations in your program. By using execution flow instructions, your program is not limited to exe-

Table 4.2-1   A limited subset of 80C188EB instructions.

Catagory	Instruction	Function
Data Transfer	IN *accumulator*, DX	input from port pointed to by DX
	OUT DX,*accumulator*	output to port pointed to by DX
	MOV *destination,source*	copy from source to destination
Arithmetic	ADC *destination,source*	add with carry
Logic	AND *destination,source*	logical AND
	OR *destination,source*	logical OR
	NOT *destination*	one's complement
Execution Flow	JMP *target*	jump
	JZ *short-label*	jump if result is zero
	JNZ *short-label*	jump if result is not zero
	CALL *target*	call a procedure
	RET	return from a procedure
Processor Control	STC	set carry
	CLC	clear carry

cuting the same exact sequence of instructions every time it is run. Processor control instructions allow the state of the 80C188EB to be directly controlled.

4.2.2   Assembly Language Instruction Syntax

80C188EB assembly language instructions have the following general syntax:

[label:]   [prefix] mnemonic [operand [,operand[,operand]]] [;comment]

Brackets indicate that the enclosed item is optional. A **label** is an optional identifier, used by other instructions to refer to the place in the program marked by the label. Equivalently, a label identifies the address in memory where an instruction begins and is said to point to the instruction it labels. Instruction labels always end with a colon. In the instruction:

start: mov dx,SWITCHES   ;load DX with input port address

start is a label that symbolically represents the address in memory where the instruction mov dx,SWITCHES is located.

An instruction prefix modifies the operation of the instruction it prefixes. You will not encounter instructions with prefixes until Chapter 7. The instruction mnemonic specifies the operation the instruction performs. A mnemonic is always required for an instruction. In the previous example, the instruction mnemonic is MOV.

The operand field specifies the object(s) on which an instruction operates. Depending on the instruction, there may be none, one, two, or three operands. Only one instruction, IMUL, allows three operands, so the appearance of three operands in an instruction is not common.

An **operand** is the object or data item that is operated on. An assembly language instruction operand can be the data itself or an address that specifies where the data is stored. An operand may be a constant, register, variable, or label. For instructions with two operands, the first operand is the destination and the second is the source. The operation is carried out on the source and destination operands. The result is stored in the destination. In the previous example, the destination operand is the register DX and the source operand is a constant. This constant is represented by the symbol SWITCHES.

A comment is an optional note used to document or clarify a program's operation. A nonblank line in a program need not include an instruction (mnemonic). It can consist of a label alone or a comment alone.

4.2.3   A Simple Program

A very simple program is shown in both its machine language and its assembly language forms in Fig. 4.2-1. This program inputs a byte of data and places it in register AL, complements the contents of AL, then outputs the complemented data. The input data is read from eight switches, and the output data is displayed on eight light emitting diodes (LEDs). When this program is executed, this sequence of operations is repeated indefinitely. The effect of this program is relatively clear from reading the assembly language listing. However, the assembly language form is less easily understood if its comments are removed. In contrast, reading the machine language representation doesn't provide you with any clue as to what the program does!

Machine Language			Assembly Language		
BA0080	main:	mov	dx,SWITCHES	;load port address of switches
EC		in	al,dx	;read switch port
F6D0		not	al	;complement data read
BA0080		mov	dx,LEDS	;load port address of LEDs
EE		out	dx,al	;output complement of input data
EBF4		jmp	main	;do it all over again

Figure 4.2-1   Machine language and assembly language representations of a simple program.

The program's task is to display the position of eight mechanical switches. The input and output subsystems are shown in Fig. 4.2-2. The input device is a bank of eight single-pole single-throw (SPST) mechanical switches. The position of each switch is converted to a logic level by a pull-up resistor connected to +5 V. When a switch is open, its logic level is 1. When closed, its logic level is 0. The input port is a 74HC541 octal noninverting three-state buffer. The input address decoder, which controls the enabling of the octal buffer, is shown in block form. This address decoder controls the octal buffer's outputs by conditionally routing the /RD strobe to the 74HC541's enable inputs. The three-state buffer is enabled only when A15–A0 = 8000H, /S2 is 0, and /RD is asserted.

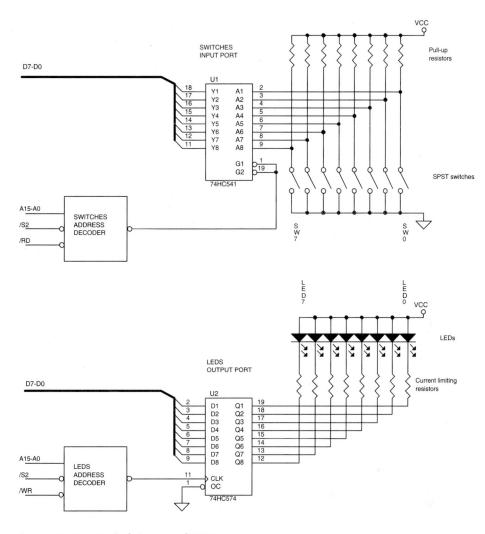

Figure 4.2-2   Switch input and LEDs output ports.

The output device is an array of LEDs controlled by the output port. The output port is a 74HC574 octal D-type edge-triggered flip-flop. An output port bit must be logic 0 to turn on its associated LED. Complementing the input data before it is output results in a switch that is in the open (logic 1) position causing its associated LED to light. The output port's address decoder, which routes the /WR strobe to the CLK input of the 74HC574, is shown in block form. Data on the data bus is written to the 74HC574 only when A15–A0 = 8000H, /S2 is 0, and a 0 to 1 transition of /WR occurs. The 0 to 1 transition of /WR is the trailing edge of the active-low /WR strobe.

Let's reexamine the program of Fig. 4.2-1 in greater detail. Together, the first two instructions input a byte of data from the input port and place it in the 80C188EB's AL register. The first instruction places the input port's address in register DX. The symbols chosen to represent the port addresses indicate the kind of device connected to the port. SWITCHES is the symbol chosen to represent the input port's address, which is 8000H. The second instruction actually transfers the data. **IN** is the mnemonic for the *input* instruction. This particular form of IN inputs a data byte from the port whose address is in DX (the port pointed to by DX) and places the byte in register AL.

The third instruction, **NOT**, complements (changes each bit to its opposite value) the contents of AL.

The next two instructions output the contents of AL to the port LEDS. The first instruction loads the output port's address into DX. Then, the **OUT** instruction outputs the contents of AL to the port pointed to by DX.

The last instruction jumps back to the beginning of the program. This instruction makes the program an infinite loop. The label main has been used to identify the address of the first instruction in the program. main is used as an operand in the *jump* instruction (**JMP**) to identify the next instruction to be executed. The jump instruction causes the program's execution flow to be transferred back to the first instruction. This causes the program's fixed sequence of instructions to be repeated indefinitely.

This program can be considered to perform a single simple task. A more complex program would consist of many tasks carried out in an appropriate sequence to achieve a more complex overall task.

4.3   Simple Programs Structured as Sequential Tasks

The overall function that a system implements can be subdivided into subfunctions or tasks. A **task** is an element of work carried out by the system. Each task must be executed at a particular time and in a particular sequence for a system to accomplish its overall purpose. Associated with each task is both the hardware and software necessary for its accomplishment. At this point, our emphasis is on software for tasks.

A program's execution flow must insure that tasks are carried out at the right time and in the right sequence. At the conceptual level, execution flow and the structure that controls it are independent of whether a program is written in machine language, assembly language, a high-level language, or a combination of several languages. The structure must be appropriate to the program's overall function. Determination of the structure for a program's execution flow is an important consideration.

The simplest execution flow structure involves each task being executed one after another in a fixed sequence. In embedded systems, this sequential execution of tasks is usually repeated indefinitely in an infinite loop, as in the last example.

The overall function of the program in Fig. 4.2-1 could be stated as "Display the switch positions on the LEDs." This is accomplished by three tasks:

1. Determine the switch positions.
2. Process the switch position data to obtain control bits that can be used to control the LEDs.
3. Output the control bits to turn each LED either ON or OFF.

In this simple example, each task is implemented by one or two instructions and the sequence of execution is controlled by the order in which the instructions physically appear in the program. The jump instruction at the end of the program is thought of as controlling the program's execution flow, rather than implementing a task. This jump causes the sequence of tasks to be repeated indefinitely.

A slightly more complex example of a system whose program is structured as a sequence of tasks is the simple temperature measurement system of Fig. 4.3-1. This system measures and displays ambient air temperatures in the range from 0 to 99 degrees Fahrenheit. It has a single byte input port and a single byte output port.

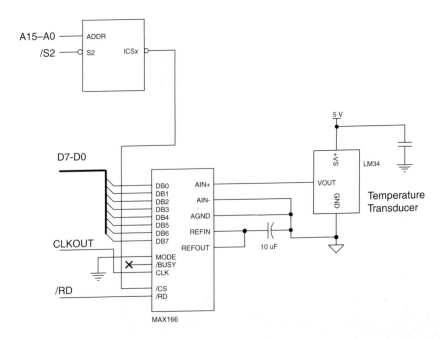

Figure 4.3-1   (a) Simple temperature measurement system—temperature transducer input subsystem.

The input device consists of a National Semiconductor LM34 Fahrenheit Temperature Sensor and a MAXIM MAX166 8-bit analog-to-digital converter, ADC. The temperature sensor provides an output voltage proportional to the temperature in degrees Fahrenheit. The scale factor for the LM34 is +10.0 mV/degree.

The 8-bit ADC is designed to convert input voltages that range from 0 V to 2.46 V and produce a binary output that ranges from 0 to 255. Thus, a change in the ADC's input of 9.609 mV (2460 mV/256) produces a one bit change in the ADC's output. To obtain a binary value that directly represents the temperature in degrees Fahrenheit, the ADC's output value must be scaled.

The ADC is operated in a mode where it continually carries out conversions. If the converter's output is read while a conversion is in progress, the result provided is simply

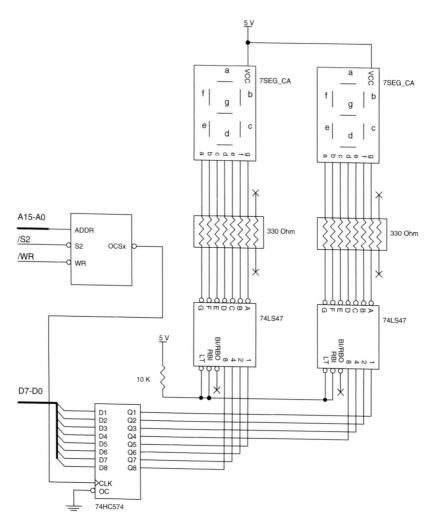

Figure 4.3-1   (b) Simple temperature measurement subsystem—seven segment display output subsytem.

that from the previously completed conversion. To read the converter, its /CS and /RD inputs are asserted simultaneously, enabling the converter's three-state outputs.

The output port is a 74HC574 octal D-type edge-triggered flip-flop. The output device consists of two 74LS47A BCD-to-seven-segment decoder drivers and two seven segment LED displays. Each decoder driver takes as its input a 4-bit binary code representing a decimal digit. The decoder driver converts the 4-bit binary code into the seven output bits required to turn ON or OFF the individual segments of a seven-segment LED display.

The most significant 4-bits of the output port are inputs to the decoder driver for the most significant decimal digit. The least significant 4-bits are inputs to the decoder driver for the least significant digit.

In a typical program, anywhere from a few to a few hundred instructions may be required to implement a single task. Tasks should be defined so that they are logically coherent subfunctions of limited complexity. This results in a program that is modular, easy to understand, and to modify.

For this example, the tasks are:

1. Input the ADC's binary output.
2. Scale the ADC's output value so that 1-bit corresponds to 1 degree.
3. Convert the scaled result to packed BCD (two BCD digits in one byte).
4. Output the packed BCD number to the output port.

The required program is given in Fig. 4.3-2. The first and last tasks are each implemented by two instructions. The second task requires five instructions, and the third task requires four. The effect of each instruction is not important at this point. This example illustrates that a simple but useful system can be implemented by sequential tasks, each comprised of one or more instructions.

In this simple program, each task is always executed immediately after the task that precedes it. In a more complex program, each task may not necessarily be executed during each pass through the program.

```
;get binary ADC result

main:   mov     dx,A_TO_D
        in      al,dx

;scale binary data from ADC
        mov     ah,0
        mov     cx,9609
        mul     cx
        mov     cx,10000
        div     cx

;convert scaled binary result to packed BCD
        mov     cl,10
        div     cl
        rol     al,4
        or      al,ah

;display temperature
        mov     dx,SSLEDS
        out     dx,al

;repeat the program's execution indefinitely
        jmp     main
```

Figure 4.3-2   Temperature measurement and display program consisting of four tasks.

There are many ways to control, either by software or hardware, if and when a specific task is executed. Various software approaches to organizing and controlling the sequencing of tasks are introduced in Chapters 7 and 8. An approach that lets external hardware devices control when tasks are executed is discussed in Chapter 14.

The simple hardware of Fig. 4.2-2 can be used to test the program written for the more complex hardware of Fig. 4.3-1. Both systems contain a single byte input port and a single byte output port. The switches of the input port of Fig. 4.2-2 can be used to simulate the input from the ADC. The result, computed by the program and output to the eight LEDs, can be observed to verify that it is the appropriate packed BCD value corresponding to the simulated temperature.

4.4   ASM86 Assembly Language and Assemblers

An assembly language program cannot be directly loaded into a system's memory and executed. The assembly language program must first be translated to machine language. In theory, this translation can be accomplished by hand, using information in Appendix D. In practice, this translation is carried out automatically by an assembler program.

An **assembler** program, or assembler, translates an assembly language program into its machine language equivalent. A particular assembler translates assembly language programs written for a specific microprocessor, or family of microprocessors. The assembly language program that you write and input to the assembler is called the **source program**, or simply the source.

The source exists as an unformatted ASCII text file that you create using a text editor or word processor. The source is written to adhere to the syntax defined for the assembly language. An assembly language's syntax defines the mnemonics used to represent each machine language instruction and how data may be represented symbolically. The machine language output produced by an assembler is called **object code,** since it is the object of the translation. This output is a binary data file.

The term **target** is often used to describe the microprocessor or embedded system for which some design process or action is carried out. Assemblers that execute on the same type of microprocessor as that used in the **target system** are called **native assemblers**. Other assemblers, called **cross assemblers,** run on a computer that uses a microprocessor different from the **target microprocessor.**

An assembly language program consists of **statements,** each of which is usually a single line in the program. There are two kinds of statements.

One kind is an assembly language **instruction statement**, or simply an instruction. Each assembly language instruction statement is translated by the assembler into a single machine language instruction. The time during which the assembler translates the program is called **assembly time**. The machine code generated can later be executed by the target microprocessor. The time during which the target microprocessor executes the machine code is called **run time**.

The other kind of statement that appears in a program is a directive statement, or directive. A **directive** is not translated into machine code. You use directives in your program to tell the assembler how to translate the program's instructions. Operations specified by directives are carried out by the assembler at assembly time.

The original assembly language for 8086 and 8088 microprocessors is Intel's ASM86 assembly language. This language was later expanded to include the additional instructions of the 80186 and 80188 microprocessors. Assembly languages for the 80186/80188 family from other companies typically use the same ASM86 mnemonics and syntax for instructions. However, each assembler has its own set of directives. While some directives and their mnemonics are common for most assemblers, others are unique.

The assembly language program of Fig. 4.2-1 is not a complete ASM86 source program. It is rewritten in Fig. 4.4-1 as a complete ASM86 program. The first line in the program, $MOD186, is an assembler control, a type of directive. Assembler controls define assembly conditions and can be specified on the command line or in the file. This particular control tells the assembler to accept the additional instructions of the 80186 instruction set. By default, the assembler recognizes only the instructions of the 8086 instruction set, and would generate errors when assembling a program that uses any of the extended instructions.

```
$MOD186
          name        iorel           ;name of module

SWITCHES              equ 8000h       ;assign input port address
LEDS                  equ 8000h;      assign output port address

assume    cs:code                     ;address assumed to be in CS

code      segment     'ROM'           ;code segment starts here

main:     mov         dx,SWITCHES     ;load port address of switches
          in          al,dx           ;read switch port
          not         al              ;complement data read
          mov         dx,LEDS         ;load port address of LEDs
          out         dx,al           ;output complement of input data
          jmp         main            ;do it all over again

code      ends                        ;code segment ends here

          end         main            ;end of source file
```

Figure 4.4-1   The assembly language program of Figure 4.2-1 rewritten as a complete ASM86 source program.

The four statements preceding the six instructions of the original program are directives. The **NAME** directive provides a name for the object module (file) produced by the assembler. This module name is included in the object file. It is not a filename, and may be different from the name of the file that contains the source program.

The two equate directives (**EQU**s) assign values to the symbols SWITCHES and LEDS. The **ASSUME** directive defines the addressability of the code segment and is discussed in Chapter 6. A **logical segment** in a program is a connected unit of code or data. Instructions in a logical segment operate relative to the same segment address. The **SEGMENT** directive and its accompanying **ENDS** directive identify all instructions that exist between them as belonging to the same logical segment. In this example, the logical segment is named code. The object code produced by instructions in this logical segment eventually become the bit patterns that are placed in the physical code segment in memory. Finally, the **END** directive tells the assembler where the program's statements end. The assembler ignores any text after an end directive.

When a source file is assembled, two output files are generated, a list file and a relocatable object file. The **list file** can be printed and lists the original assembly language program, the resulting object code, any assembly error messages, and other useful information. The list file from assembling the source program in Fig. 4.4-1 is given in Fig. 4.4-2.

```
8086/87/88/186 MACRO ASSEMBLER    IOREL
PAGE   1


DOS 6.20 (038-N) 8086/87/88/186 MACRO ASSEMBLER V3.1 ASSEMBLY OF MODULE IOREL
OBJECT MODULE PLACED IN A:IOREL.OBJ
ASSEMBLER INVOKED BY:  C:\INTEL86\ASM86.EXE A:IOREL.ASM


LOC OBJ        LINE          SOURCE


               1 +1          $MOD186
               2                    name    iorel            ;name of module
               3
8000           4             SWITCHES        equ 8000h        ;assign input port address
8000           5             LEDS            equ 8000h        ;assign output port address
               6
               7             assume cs:code                  ;address assumed to be in CS
               8
----           9             code    segment 'ROM'           ;code segment starts here
               10
0000 BA0080    11            main:   mov     dx,SWITCHES      ;load port address of switches
0003 EC        12                    in      al,dx            ;read switch port
0004 F6D0      13                    not     al               ;complement data read
0006 BA0080    14                    mov     dx,LEDS          ;load port address of LEDs
0009 EE        15                    out     dx,al            ;output complement of input data
000A EBF4      16                    jmp     main             ;do it all over again
               17
----           18            code    ends                    ;code segment ends here
               19
               20                    end     main             ;end of source file


ASSEMBLY COMPLETE, NO ERRORS FOUND
```

Figure 4.4-2   List file from assembling the program of Figure 4.4-1 using Intel's ASM86 assembler.

In the list file, the hexadecimal values under the column labelled LOC are the offset addresses from the segment base address to the beginning of each instruction. The object code for the instructions appears under the column labeled OBJ. For example, the instruction mov dx,SWITCHES is assembled into the three bytes BAH, 00H, and 80H. Byte BAH has offset address 0000H, byte 00H has offset 0001H, and byte 80H has offset 0002H. The instruction out dx, al assembles into the single byte EEH with offset address 0009H.

The relocatable object file contains an intermediate and typically incomplete form of the binary machine code. Because this file is not an ASCII file, it cannot be printed. Because it is incomplete, it cannot be loaded into ROM and executed. Providing the missing information in the relocatable object file is the topic of the next section.

This brief overview of an ASM86 assembly language source program illustrates that ASM programs consist of both the instructions that are executed by the microprocessor at run time, and directives that provide information needed by the assembler at assembly time.

4.5   Relocatable Program Modules and Location

A **module** is a functional unit of code and data separately created, edited, assembled, and tested. A module may contain one or more segments. At the source code level, a source module is the same as a source file. Small programs, like the previous example, consist of a single module. Large programs consist of many modules that are combined or linked together.

At the time when a source program is being written, the final locations in physical memory of the object code and data that will be produced are either not known or not of interest. This is because most programs consist of a number of source modules that are assembled separately and linked later to form the complete program. Also, it is desirable to create source modules in such a way that they can be reused in other programs or applications. Thus, at the time a module is written and assembled, not having to specify its actual final location in memory is advantageous.

A logical segment in a program may be **relocatable** in the sense that you do not specify its final location in memory until you locate it, or **absolute** in the sense that you assign the segment's location when you write the source program.

A **relocatable object module** is an object module where the location of the object code is specified relative to a symbolic segment address to which no actual value has yet been assigned. An assembler that can generate this type of object module as an output is called a **relocatable assembler** (Fig. 4.5-1).

The source program of Fig. 4.4-1 does not specify where the CODE segment will physically exist in memory and is, therefore, a relocatable source module.

Specification of the starting address of the program in the END statement makes this relocatable source module a **main module**. Every program must have one, and only one, main module. Since this program consists of a single module, this module must be the main module.

After each module of a multi-module program is separately assembled, the resulting object modules are linked together to form the complete program. Linking is accomplished by the **linker** program. If any object file in a group of object files that are to be linked together is relocatable, the composite object file that results from the linking is also relocatable.

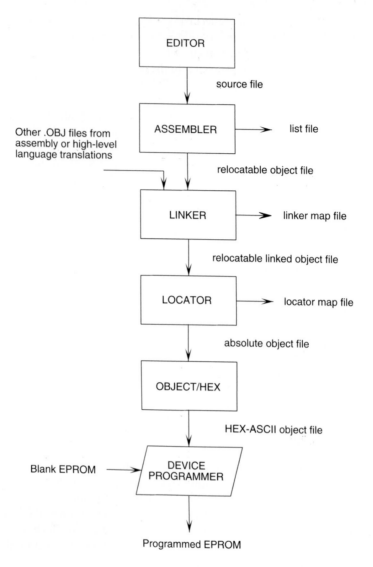

Figure 4.5-1   Generic steps to create an EPROM containing the object code produced
                by a relocatable assembler.

For a multi-language program, each source module is translated to an object module using the appropriate translator (assembler or compiler). To be linked, the translators must produce object files that have the same object module format. If the object modules produced do not follow the same format, a special linker that is able to convert different object module formats to a common format for linkage must be used.

Relocatable object modules can also be placed in special files called **libraries**. Libraries provide a convenient means of collecting groups of related object modules together so individual modules in the group can be automatically included in a program by the linker. An object file normally contains a single object module, whereas a library file can contain a number of object modules.

Creating a large program as a collection of interacting modules simplifies program design and development. The object modules that are combined may not all have resulted from the translation of assembly language source modules. Some may be the result of translating high-level language source modules such as C or Pascal. Creating a program by combining several modules also allows each module to be developed by a different person, thereby permitting parallel software development. Initially, our focus is limited to single module assembly language programs. Multi-module and multi-language programs are the topic of Chapter 20.

A relocatable object module is incomplete and is not executable. All the symbolic address references in a relocatable module must be converted to physical memory addresses corresponding to where the object code will be placed in the system's memory. These physical addresses are placed in the object code by a locator program and the result is an **absolute object module**.

A **locator** program accepts a relocatable object module and control expressions as input. You use the control expressions to specify the physical addresses where the various segments in the module are to be located in memory. The locator produces an absolute object module as an output, which is complete and executable.

4.6 Embedded Assemblers Versus DOS Assemblers

There are numerous assemblers available for the 80186/80188 family. Most accept the ASM86 assembly language instruction statement syntax. Most also accept ASM86 directive statements, although some have their own alternative set of directives that accomplish the same purposes. All such assemblers are referred to in this text as ASM86 compatible assemblers.

ASM86 compatible assemblers fall into one of two broad categories: embedded assemblers and DOS assemblers. **Embedded assemblers** are designed specifically for assembling programs for embedded systems. These assemblers, along with their associated linker and locator programs, generate absolute object code that can be loaded into ROM on the target system and executed. Embedded assemblers make no assumptions about the hardware environment of the target system, other than the type of microprocessor used.

DOS assemblers are designed for assembling programs that are to be executed on a PC under control of a disk operating system such as MS DOS, PC DOS, or DR DOS. Because the user base for PC assemblers is so large, several low-cost, high-quality assemblers and software development tools are available for the PC.

Linking the object modules produced by a DOS assembler creates a relocatable file with an EXE extension. This file consists of two parts, a relocation header and the actual relocatable object code. When an EXE program is executed on a PC, the loader in DOS uses information in the relocation header to load the object code in the system's RAM. The loader decides where it will load the object code in memory. After loading the object code, the loader places the appropriate segment address values into the microprocessor's segment registers. In summary, an EXE file is designed to be loaded into RAM by an operating system's loader. After loading the object code, the operating system's loader initializes the segment registers then the program is executed.

In contrast, in an embedded system, the object code is loaded into ROM ICs when the system is built. The program is executed from the ROM without the aid of an operating system. Because there is no operating system, an EXE file cannot simply be programmed into ROM and executed. A special locator must be used to convert an EXE file to an absolute object file that can be loaded into and executed from ROM.

Sections 4.7 and 4.9 describe two popular assemblers for the 80x86 family. An overview is given of the steps necessary to use these assemblers to generate object code that can be loaded in a system's ROM and executed. The first assembler discussed is Intel's ASM86 assembler, which is an embedded assembler. The second is Borland's TASM assembler, which is a DOS assembler.

4.7   Intel's ASM86 Assembler and Utilities

ASM86 is the name used for Intel's assembly language and for its assembler. The ASM86 Assembler generates object code for 8086, 8088, 80186, and 80188 microprocessors. As previously stated, the 8088 and 8086 have identical instruction sets. The 8086/8088 instruction set is upward compatible with the 80186/80188 instruction set. The 80186/80188 instruction set contains all of the 8086 instructions plus seven additional instructions. Several of the original 8086/8088 instructions are expanded in the 80C186EB/80C188EB instruction set to allow the use of immediate operands.

The steps to assemble, link, and locate a program using Intel's ASM86 assembler and its associated utilities are given in Fig. 4.7-1. Filename extensions shown are the defaults used by Intel's tools.

Figure 4.7-1 is drawn to emphasize that the objective in embedded systems software development is to produce the HEX-ASCII file (filename.HEX) that is used to program the system's ROM. Using the IOREL program from Fig. 4.4-1 as an example, the program is first created and saved as the source file IOREL.ASM. IOREL.ASM is then assembled by invoking the ASM86 assembler at the operating system prompt with the command:

```
asm86 iorel.asm
```

The list file, IOREL.LST, from this assembly was shown in Fig. 4.4-2.

If a source program contains syntax errors, those errors are specified in the list file. **Errors** are fatal, and the object code, if it is produced, cannot be linked. Warnings may also be generated. In the case of **warnings,** the object code can usually be linked, but may or may not execute correctly.

The relocatable object module (file) that results from the assembly is IOREL.OBJ. It contains binary object code and cannot be viewed with an editor.

Creating and modifying libraries is accomplished using Intel's **LIB86** library manager. Commercial libraries are available for many commonly used algorithms such as floating point arithmetic, trigonometric functions, data conversion, and I/O.

Intel's linker, **LINK86**, can combine several object modules, including object modules that reside in library files, into a single object module. Even though IOREL consists of

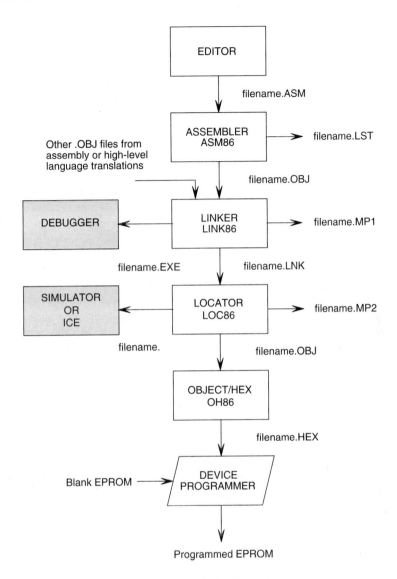

Figure 4.7-1   Steps to assemble, link, and locate files using Intel's tools.

a single module, it must still be processed by the linker. For this example, the input to the linker is a single relocatable object file. The command is

    link86 iorel.obj

Unless otherwise specified, the relocatable object module from the link operation has, by default, the filename of the first file in the list of files linked and has the extension LNK. The output IOREL.LNK is a binary file. Since IOREL.OBJ was relocatable, IOREL.LNK is also relocatable. If you've had some experience with writing assembly language programs for a PC, it is important to note that unlike a DOS linker, the output of this linker is not a relocatable executable (EXE) file. LINK86's output cannot be executed on a PC.

To create the absolute object file that can be loaded into ROM and executed, the relocatable module IOREL.LNK must be located. To locate IOREL.LNK, the physical location in memory where the object code should begin must be specified as an input to the locator. The locator generates an absolute object module as its output.

Assume the program is to be placed in an 8K × 8 EPROM. An EPROM is a type of ROM whose contents are programmed by the user. EPROMs are covered in Chapter 11. The 8K × 8 EPROM is positioned in the memory address space so that its last location corresponds to the last location in the memory address space. Since the EPROM ends at address FFFFFH and is 8K bytes long, it must start at address FE000H. The starting address of the EPROM can be expressed as segment address FE00H and offset address 0000H, or FE00:0000H. The command for Intel's locator, **LOC86**, to create the absolute object module from IOREL.LNK is:

```
loc86 iorel.lnk addresses(segments(code(fe000h))) bootstrap
```

The **ADDRESSES** control in the LOC86 command specifies that the logical segment CODE is to be located starting at the physical address FE000H. In general, the process of associating two pieces of information is called **binding**. The ADDRESSES control in this example binds the symbol CODE to the physical address FE000H.

After being reset, the 80C188EB always fetches its first instruction from memory location FFFF0H. You must make sure that a bootstrap instruction that jumps to the start of your program exists at this address. The **BOOTSTRAP** control in the command line causes LOC86 to automatically insert a JMP FAR PTR MAIN instruction into the absolute object code at location FFFF0H. The locator knows which of the program's instruction is to be executed first because the assembler placed that instruction's label, which was specified in the END directive, into the relocatable object module.

As described in Section 3.5.4, execution of a JMP FAR PTR instruction loads CS and IP with new values. In this example, CS is loaded with FE00H and IP with 0000H. These new values, CS:IP = FE00:0000 = FE000H, cause the next instruction to be fetched from memory location FE000H. This is the location of the instruction mov dx,SWITCHES in the IOREL program. This is actually the second instruction executed after reset. The first instruction executed is the bootstrap instruction.

By default, the absolute object module that results from LOC86's operation has the name of the file on which the locator operated but has no extension. In this example, the absolute object module is IOREL.

The locator also generates a printable text file called a **map file.** This file is so named because it lists addresses that provide a map of the locations assigned to each segment. Listed are the start and end addresses and length of each segment located. The map file has the extension MP2. You view this file to confirm that your program was located as desired. The map file IOREL.MP2 is given in Fig. 4.7-2.

Three segment names are listed in IOREL.MP2. ??SEG is a default segment automatically created by the assembler to contain any code or data in the source program that does not lie within a segment defined in the source program. In IOREL.ASM, there is no code or data outside of a defined segment. Therefore, the length of ??SEG is zero. The segment

```
DOS 6.20 (038-N) 8086 LOCATER, V2.5

INPUT FILE: A:IOREL.LNK
OUTPUT FILE: A:IOREL
CONTROLS SPECIFIED IN INVOCATION COMMAND:
  ADDRESSES(SEGMENTS(CODE(FE000H)))
  BOOTSTRAP


DATE: 01/20/97  TIME: 20:45:17
WARNING 63:  SS AND SP REGISTERS NOT INITIALIZED
WARNING 64:  DS REGISTER NOT INITIALIZED


MEMORY MAP OF MODULE IOREL


MODULE START ADDRESS  PARAGRAPH = FE00H  OFFSET = 0000H
SEGMENT MAP


START    STOP      LENGTH    ALIGN    NAME        CLASS       OVERLAY


00200H   00200H    0000H      G                ??SEG
FE000H   FE00BH    000CH      G                CODE        ROM
FFFF0H   FFFF4H    0005H      A                (ABSOLUTE)
```

Figure 4.7-2   Map file IOREL.MP2 generated from locating IOREL.LNK.

code starts, as specified, at location FE000H and is 12 (000CH) bytes long. These 12 bytes comprise the program's six instructions. The last segment has no name. It is an absolute segment that contains the five byte long jmp far ptr main instruction. Recall that this instruction was automatically inserted into the program's object code by the locator, in response to the BOOTSTRAP switch in the locator's command line.

When an application program is executed by an embedded system that does not have an operating system, the segment registers must be initialized by instructions in the program. These instructions load the segment registers with values that correspond to the physical location of the segments in memory.

In this example, only a code segment exists in the program, so only CS must be initialized. Execution of the jmp far ptr main instruction loads CS and IP with the values contained in the instruction. Thus, CS is initialized by the bootstrap instruction. This is the normal method for initializing CS.

Typical programs also include segments for data, extra data, and stack. If your program uses these segments, you must include instructions at the beginning of the program to load DS, ES, and SS.

4.7.1   Generating a HEX-ASCII File for Device Programming

An **object-hex translator** translates an absolute object file into a format appropriate for serial transfer from a computer to a device programmer. The device programmer loads the object code into an EPROM or some other type of programmable nonvolatile memory.

Intel's **OH86** object-hex translator translates an absolute object file to a HEX-ASCII object file. **HEX-ASCII** coding represents a single byte of data as two separate hexadecimal digits. Each hexadecimal digit is then individually encoded as an ASCII character. This encoding requires one byte for each hexadecimal digit. Since a HEX-ASCII file is an ASCII text file, it can be easily printed or serially transmitted. The output obtained from translating the absolute object code file IOREL to the HEX-ASCII file IOREL.HEX using the command:

        oh86 iorel.

is shown in Fig. 4.7-3. Each line is a record, and there are four different record types: extended address, data, start address, and end of file.

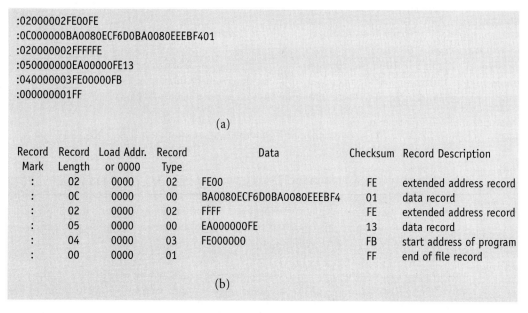

```
:02000002FE00FE
:0C000000BA0080ECF6D0BA0080EEEBF401
:020000002FFFFFFE
:050000000EA00000FE13
:040000003FE00000FB
:000000001FF
```

(a)

Record Mark	Record Length	Load Addr. or 0000	Record Type	Data	Checksum	Record Description
:	02	0000	02	FE00	FE	extended address record
:	0C	0000	00	BA0080ECF6D0BA0080EEEBF4	01	data record
:	02	0000	02	FFFF	FE	extended address record
:	05	0000	00	EA000000FE	13	data record
:	04	0000	03	FE000000	FB	start address of program
:	00	0000	01		FF	end of file record

(b)

Figure 4.7-3   HEX-ASCII file: (a) IOREL.HEX, from processing the absolute file IOREL using Intel's OH86 object to hex translator; (b) annotated HEX-ASCII file.

Each record consists of several fields and starts with a colon. Counting the colon as the first ASCII character, the 8th and 9th ASCII characters in a record indicate the record's type. For example, 02 in the record type field indicates an extended address record, and 00 indicates a data record.

The 2nd and 3rd characters give the record length. The record length specifies the number of bytes of binary data that follow the record type field. The actual number of characters is twice the number of bytes indicated by the record length, since it takes two ASCII characters, in HEX-ASCII representation, to represent one binary data byte.

Each record ends with a checksum field. The **checksum** is computed by first converting each pair of HEX-ASCII digits to a byte, starting with the record length bytes up to and including the last byte of the data field. These bytes are then added together. Finally, the two's complement of the least significant byte of the sum is taken. This two's complement result is the checksum byte.

When a HEX-ASCII file is transmitted to a device programmer, the device programmer uses the checksum to verify the integrity of the transmitted data. If all the characters in a record, excluding the record mark but including the checksum, are converted to binary and added, the result (modulo 256) should be 00H. If this is the case, the probability that an error occurred in the transmission will be low. If it is not, it indicates that an error did occur in the transmission.

Returning to Fig. 4.7-3, the first record in IOREL.HEX is an extended address record that specifies the segment address as FE00H. This value of segment address remains valid until another extended address record is encountered. The second record is a data record that specifies a load address (offset from the segment base address) of 0000H. The data record also contains 12 bytes (24 HEX-ASCII characters) of data. This data, which is the HEX-ASCII representation of the program's object code, is to be loaded at the address that has its segment value specified in the extended address record, and its offset specified as the data record's load address, FE00:0000H.

The third record is another extended address record. It specifies a new segment base address, FFFFH. This is the segment address for the bootstrap instruction contained in the fourth record.

The fifth record is a start address record. The start address record is used to specify the start address for object code that is loaded into the memory of a microcomputer by an operating system. An operating system would cause the program's execution to begin at this start address. The start address is CS:IP = FE00:0000. The last record is the end of file record which marks the end of the file.

Once the HEX-ASCII file has been transferred to the device programmer, an EPROM can be placed in a socket on the device programmer and programmed. The EPROM can then be removed from the programmer and placed in the system prototype. When the prototype is powered on, the program executes.

Unfortunately, your prototype may not work as desired. This failure may be the result of errors in your program or prototype hardware, or both. The prototype must be debugged to identify the source of errors. Once identified, all software and hardware errors must be corrected. Methods to efficiently identify software and hardware errors are essential. In the initial testing stages, programming a new EPROM each time an error is found would be very time consuming. Fortunately, more efficient methods exist.

Simulators, native debuggers, monitors, remote debuggers, ROM emulators, target access probes and in-circuit emulators are the principal tools used for detecting logic errors in software. The branches to the left in Fig. 4.7-1 show that the located object code can be input to one of these debugging tools to allow you to debug the software. An in-circuit emulator (ICE) is also very useful for detecting hardware errors during system development. If you know your system well, the other tools can also be used to perform a limited degree of hardware debugging. Debugging tools are discussed in the next chapter.

4.8   Assembly Language Programs that Run Under DOS

The previous programs are intended to be run on an embedded system as stand-alone programs, without the need for an operating system.

Many programs written to be run on PCs are also written in ASM86. You might think these programs can also be directly run on an 80C188EB embedded system. Unfortunately, this is not true. Application programs written for a PC are not written to be run as stand-alone programs, and they are not loaded into, and run from, ROM.

PC's use their disk operating system, DOS, to provide an interface between your program and the PC's hardware. One purpose of DOS is to provide a standard set of prewritten functions that allow your programs to take advantage of the hardware capabilities of the PC, without you having to deal with the low level details of the PC's hardware. Programs written to be run on a PC typically use, and therefore require the existence of, these DOS functions.

These functions are referred to as DOS system's services and are stored on disk. A portion of DOS, the resident portion, is loaded into RAM at system power up. Other portions of DOS are transient and are loaded into RAM only when needed. A program can cause a DOS system service function to be executed by first loading specific microprocessor registers with appropriate parameter values then executing a software interrupt instruction.

Other lower level functions are provided by the Basic Input/Output System, **BIOS**. These functions are stored in the PC's BIOS ROM. Like DOS functions, BIOS functions can be invoked using a software interrupt. Many DOS functions may in turn invoke BIOS functions to carry out their operations.

At power on, the first instruction executed is, as always, taken from location FFFF:0000H. In a PC, this location is in the BIOS ROM and contains a jump to the beginning of the BIOS ROM routines (Fig. 4.8-1). A series of Power-On Self Test (POST), routines in the BIOS are then executed. These routines test various system components such as RAM, disk drives, and the keyboard to see if they are connected and operating.

Next, the ROM bootstrap initialization procedure is executed. After carrying out hardware and software initialization, the ROM bootstrap routine reads the disk bootstrap code from the first sector of the boot disk. The disk bootstrap code is loaded into RAM and control is passed to this code. The disk bootstrap code then loads the files IO.SYS and MSDOS.SYS. Control is then passed to IO.SYS. After several programs are automatically executed, the command processor, COMMAND.COM is loaded and the DOS prompt appears. At this point, a typical memory map for a system running DOS is as shown in Fig. 4.8-1.

An application program run under DOS is loaded by DOS from disk when the program's name is typed at the command prompt (C:>). The application program is loaded into the Transient Program Area (user memory area) of the PC's RAM. After loading, DOS transfers control to the first instruction in the application program. When the application program's execution is complete, it transfers control back to DOS.

Many popular assemblers, such as Borland's Turbo Assembler, TASM, and Microsoft's Macro Assembler, MASM, produce object code to be executed under DOS. These assemblers generate relocatable object code output. The linkers provided with these assemblers generate an executable program file called an EXE program, which is load-time

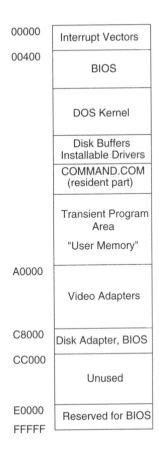

00000	Interrupt Vectors
00400	BIOS
	DOS Kernel
	Disk Buffers Installable Drivers
	COMMAND.COM (resident part)
	Transient Program Area "User Memory"
A0000	Video Adapters
C8000	Disk Adapter, BIOS
CC000	Unused
E0000	Reserved for BIOS
FFFFF	

Figure 4.8-1   Memory map for a DOS system with 1M bytes RAM.

locatable. A **load-time locatable** program is one that can be loaded into RAM at run-time by DOS's loader. The load-time locatable program is placed in memory at locations determined by DOS's loader.

In addition to the object code for the instructions that are to be executed, EXE program files contain a header that provides information used by the DOS EXEC function to load and execute the program. The decision as to where the code will be loaded into memory is made by the DOS EXEC function when it loads the program. Since the program is designed to be loaded into RAM, and executed under the control of DOS, an EXE file cannot be directly translated to HEX, loaded into ROM, and executed in an embedded system that does not also execute DOS or a DOS emulator.

Fortunately, there are special locator programs that can translate an EXE program file into a program that is **ROMable**. Such a locator can convert an EXE program into a form that can be loaded into ROM and executed without DOS. An example of such a program is Paradigm Systems' LOCATE.

4.9   Borland's TASM Assembler and Paradigm's LOCATE

Borland's Turbo Assembler (TASM) generates relocatable executable code for the entire 80x86 family from the 8086 to the Pentium Pro and also for other compatible microprocessors. TASM accepts assembly language programs that conform to ASM86's syntax. TASM also accepts either the directives used by Intel's ASM86 Assembler or its own alternate set of directives. The alternative directives are particularly useful when creating multilanguage programs using Borland's C.

The steps for creating absolute object code in HEX-ASCII form for loading into ROM, using Borland's TASM and its associated utilities, are given in Fig. 4.9-1. These steps are similar to those used for Intel's ASM86 Assembler.

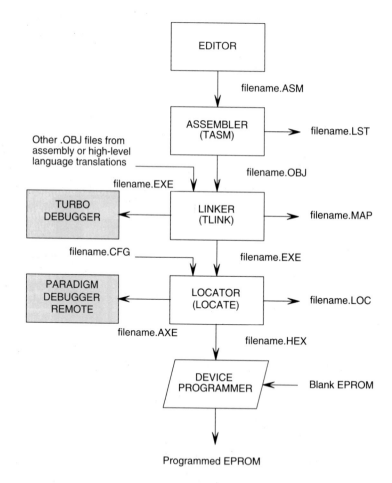

Figure 4.9-1   Steps to assemble, link, and locate files using Borland's TASM and Paradigm's LOCATE.

Before the source file IOREL.ASM, in Fig. 4.4-1, can be assembled using TASM, the $MOD186 assembler control must be changed to .186, which is the equivalent control for TASM. The command to invoke TASM is:

    tasm /l iorel.asm

Execution of this command from the system prompt causes TASM to assemble IOREL.ASM and generate the output file IOREL.OBJ. Command line parameters, called **switches** or **options**, let you control the behavior of the assembler and the information it outputs. The command line switch /l causes a list file, IOREL.LST, to be generated (Fig. 4.9-2).

The list file generated by TASM provides essentially the same information as the list file generated using ASM86 (Fig. 4.4-2). There are minor differences in how the object code is presented in the two list files. The ASM86 listing shows the bytes of each instruction in the exact order they will be stored in memory. The TASM listing presents the two bytes of a 16-bit constant with the high byte first, so its actual value is clear. For example, notice how the constant 8000H, which is the value of the symbol SWITCHES, in the first instruction is listed as 0080H in the ASM86 listing and as 8000H in the TASM listing. In the object code files from either assembler, this value is stored low byte first, as 0080H. This represents the actual storage order for a 16-bit constant for the 80C188EB.

Using switches, many other command line options are available for both TASM and ASM86. The switch symbols used for similar options differ for TASM and ASM86. There is a default case for each option, which causes the option to either be in effect or not, if the switch is not specified in the command line. For example, for TASM, the default is to not generate a list file. The /l switch must be specified if a list file is desired. In contrast, with ASM86, the default is to generate a list file. The command line option, NOLIST, must be used if no list file is desired.

TASM allows you to put frequently used options into a configuration file in the current directory. This eliminates the need for you to remember to type a string of options each time you run the assembler. The name of the configuration file must be TASM.CFG. TASM looks for the file and processes the options in the file before processing any related option in the command line. Options in the command line override any in the configuration file.

The object file resulting from assembly by TASM must then be processed by Borland's Turbo Linker (TLINK), which converts the OBJ file to an EXE file. The EXE file can only be executed on a system running DOS.

The linker command,

    tlink iorel.obj

produces the relocatable executable file IOREL.EXE.

4.9.1   Paradigm's LOCATE Locator

The relocatable executable file, IOREL.EXE, requires a DOS loader or an equivalent utility to properly load it into memory for execution. The DOS loader automatically locates the file's object code when it loads the program for execution.

Turbo Assembler Version 4.0   Page 1
iorel.asm

```
 1                      .186
 2                               name      iorel           ;name of module
 3
 4    =8000      SWITCHES            equ 8000h      ;assign input port address
 5    =8000      LEDS                equ 8000h      ;assign output port address
 6
 7             assume   cs:code                    ;address assumed to be in CS
 8
 9    0000      code      segment    'ROM'          ;code segment starts here
10
11    0000 BA 8000 main:   mov      dx,SWITCHES   ;load port address of switches
12    0003 EC            in       al,dx          ;read switch port
13    0004 F6 D0         not      al             ;complement data read
14    0006 BA 8000       mov      dx,LEDS        ;load port address of LEDs
15    0009 EE            out      dx,al          ;output complement of input data
16    000A EB F4         jmp      main           ;do it all over again
17
18    000C      code      ends                    ;code segment ends here
19
20                       end      main           ;end of source file
```

Turbo Assembler Version 4.0   Page 2 Symbol
Table

Symbol Name	Type	Value	Cref (defined at #)
??DATE	Text	"08/30/96"	
??FILENAME	Text	"iorel "	
??TIME	Text	"14:29:56"	
??VERSION	Number	0400	
@CPU	Text	0103H	#1
@CURSEG	Text	CODE	#9
@FILENAME	Text	IOREL	
@WORDSIZE	Text	2	#1 #9
LEDS	Number	8000	#5 14
MAIN	Near	CODE:0000	#11 16 20
SWITCHES	Number	8000	#4 11

Groups & Segments	Bit	Size	Align	Combine	Class	Cref (defined at #)
CODE	16	000C	Para	none	ROM	7 #9

Figure 4.9-2   List file from assembling the program of Fig. 4.4-1 using Borland's Turbo Assembler, TASM.

For a system without DOS, the EXE file must be located to convert it to an absolute object file that corresponds to the target system's memory map. The resulting absolute object code can then be loaded into the target's EPROM and executed on the prototype. One method of accomplishing the location of an EXE file is to use **Paradigm's LOCATE** program.

Like Intel's LOC86, the input to LOCATE is the output of a linker. However, the output of TLINK is an EXE file, which LOCATE accepts as input. For LOC86, you provide segment address information in the locator's invocation command line. With Paradigm's LOCATE, segment address information is provided in a separate locator configuration file. This configuration file, which is automatically read by LOCATE, has the same filename as the EXE file, but has the extension CFG. A simple configuration file, IOREL.CFG, used to locate IOREL.EXE, is given in Fig. 4.9-3.

```
//      iorel.cfg

hexfile  intel86       //Intel extended hex for programming EPROMs
listfile segments regions symbols publics    //for documentation
cputype I80C188EB   //for Intel 80C188EB microprocessor
initcode reset

//definition of the target system's address space
map    0x00000 to 0xfdfff as reserved//unpopulated
map    0xfe000 to 0xfffff as rdonly   //ROM

class   ROM = 0xfe00 //code segment at 0fe000h
output ROM
```

Figure 4.9-3   Configuration file IOREL.CFG used with Paradigm's LOCATE to locate the relocatable executable file IOREL.EXE.

With the EXE and CFG files as input, LOCATE generates an absolute object code output file. Normally this file is in Paradigm's own format and has the extension AXE. LOCATE can simultaneously produce an object code file in Intel's HEX-ASCII format for downloading to a device programmer. This file has the extension HEX.

The configuration file consists of directives to LOCATE describing the organization of your target system's memory and indicating the format for the output files.

The first line of IOREL.CFG is a comment line. LOCATE treats everything from the // until the end of the line as a comment. The second two lines specify the format for the absolute object file and the HEX-ASCII file that are generated. The LISTFILE directive tells LOCATE what information to include in the list file. The list file has the extension LOC, and can be viewed to see if the object code has been located as desired. The CPU-TYPE directive specifies which microprocessor will execute the located code.

The INITCODE RESET directive has the same effect as the bootstrap switch has for LOC86. This directive causes the locator to automatically place the code for a jmp far ptr main instruction into the object code at physical address FFFF0H. As a result, the bootstrap instruction gets programmed into the target ROM along with the program's object code.

The MAP directive assigns access attributes to the various areas of the memory address space. These attributes are used by the locator to verify that reserved regions of the address space are vacant.

Rather than using the segment name, LOCATE uses the classname segment attribute specified in the SEGMENT directive to bind a physical address to a segment. LOCATE's CLASS directive assigns a physical address to the segment CODE in terms of its classname, in this case "ROM." The OUTPUT directive specifies which classes are to be included in the output files specified in the ABSFILE and HEXFILE directives.

The HEX-ASCII file generated by TASM is shown in Fig. 4.9-4. The HEX-ASCII files generated by ASM86 and TASM are exactly the same with the exception of line 5, which is the start address record used by an operating system. When the HEX-ASCII file is downloaded to a device programmer to program an EPROM, the programmer ignores this record. Accordingly, the code programmed into an EPROM and its location in memory are exactly the same regardless of which HEX file is used.

```
:02000002FE00FE
:0C000000BA0080ECF6D0BA0080EEEBF401
:02000002FFFFFE
:05000000EA000080FF92
:04000003FFFF0000FB
:00000001FF
```

Figure 4.9-4   HEX-ASCII file generated by Paradigm's LOCATE from the file IOREL.EXE.

The command for Paradigm's LOCATE is:

```
locate iorel.exe
```

4.10   ROMable DOS and DOS Emulators

An alternative approach that allows you to use DOS tools without using a special locator is to include a ROMable version of DOS in your system. ROMable versions of DOS provide varying degrees of DOS functionality. At the limited end of the range are clones that provide only enough DOS functionality to allow simple EXE programs to be run. At the other end of the range are full implementations of DOS that can be placed in ROM.

Some single board 80C188EB systems provide DOS emulator software that allows an EXE program to be placed in ROM and executed without the EXE program first being translated to a "ROMable" version using a special locator. A DOS emulator may execute your program in one of two ways. In one approach your program's data segment and stack are copied to RAM by the DOS emulator program, but your code is executed from ROM.

In the second approach, the code, data, and stack are all copied to RAM then executed from RAM.

ROMable DOS versions that have extensive DOS functionality usually provide the DOS kernel as a linkable object module library. Source code is provided for configuration files so they can be configured to match the system's hardware. Also provided are the command processor (COMMAND.COM), basic device drivers, and the ROM BIOS. The configuration files are modified as necessary, then the modules are all linked together to form the ROMable DOS system.

Utilities are also provided that allow a collection of files to be translated to a binary image that looks the way files would look on a disk. This binary image is placed in ROM and the result is a ROM disk. DOS can load programs from the ROM disk for execution. This eliminates the need for a floppy or hard disk in the system.

One of the drawbacks to using ROMable DOS and DOS emulators is that they require a substantial amount of additional memory. Additional ROM must be provided to support the inclusion of a ROMable version of DOS or a DOS emulator. In addition to the ROM, RAM must be provided for your program if your ROMable version of DOS copies your program to RAM for execution. The amount of memory required depends on the amount of DOS functionality provided. Another drawback is that most versions of DOS for PCs are not designed for real-time applications. A typical PC version of DOS is a disk-oriented, single-user, non-multitasking, and non-reentrant operating system. In complex embedded systems, a real-time, multitasking, preemptive operating system is required.

4.11   Summary

A microprocessor can only execute a program that is in its native machine language. The machine language's binary code must be in the memory subsystem to be executable.

Instead of writing programs in machine language, they are written in the more convenient forms of assembly language or a high-level language. These source programs are then translated to machine language by an assembler or compiler, respectively.

The assembly language for the 80C188EB is called ASM86. A number of assemblers are available that translate an ASM86 source program to object code. These assemblers fall into one of two broad categories, embedded assemblers and DOS assemblers. Embedded assemblers are designed to assemble programs to be directly run on an embedded system without the aid of an operating system.

DOS assemblers are designed to translate assembly language programs to EXE files that can be run on a PC with a DOS operating system. A special locator is required to convert the load-time locatable output of a DOS assembler to absolute object code. The absolute object code can then be loaded into ROM and run without the aid of DOS.

Most programs in this book use a common subset of the language elements shared by most ASM86 assemblers (ASM86, TASM, and MASM) and can be assembled on any of these assemblers with, at most, some minor substitutions of directives. The assembly language programs in the remainder of this text were assembled using TASM.

4.12   Problems

1. Are the assembly language instruction set and the machine language instruction set the same?

2. Use the Instruction Set Mnemonic Encoding Matrix of Appendix D-4 to verify that there actually are 28 different machine instructions corresponding to the general purpose MOV mnemonic. How many different machine instructions are there corresponding to each of the following general purpose assembler directives: IN, ADC, OR, and JMP?

3. Using the Instruction Set Descriptions in Appendix C-4, list all the MOV instruction variations in terms of destination of and source for the transfer. How many bytes long is the shortest MOV instruction? How many bytes is the longest MOV?

4. Since each assembly language instruction translates to a single machine language instruction, how is it possible that the more than 300 80C188EB machine language instructions can be represented by only approximately 100 assembly language instruction mnemonics?

5. For each assembly language instruction in Fig. 4.2-1 identify its label, prefix, mnemonic, destination operand, source operand, and comment.

6. Examine the machine code for the IN instruction in Fig. 4.2-1 and, using the Machine Instruction Decoding Guide of Appendix D-3, determine which particular input instruction has been assembled.

7. How is it possible, operationally and in terms of the circuit's logic, that the input port and output port in Fig. 4.2-2 can have the same address?

8. If the 74HC541 noninverting three-state buffer in Fig. 4.2-2 is changed to a 74HC540 inverting buffer, how must the program of Fig. 4.2-1 be changed so that the system still accomplishes its original function?

9. If the SWITCHES address decoder in Fig. 4.2-2 were redesigned so that it enabled the three-state buffer when A15–A0 = C040H, /S2 = 0, and /RD = 0, how must the machine code for the program of Fig. 4.2-1 be changed for the system to continue to function properly?

10. If the third instruction in the program of Fig. 4.2-1 is given the label again and the label in the jump instruction is changed from main to again what will the program do when it is run? What pattern will appear on the LEDs each time the OUT instruction is executed.?

11. If the ADC in Fig. 4.3-1 were replaced with an 8-bit ADC with an input range of 0 V to 2.55 V, how should the program of Fig. 4.3-2 be modified to achieve its original purpose?

12. Use your editor to create the source file of Fig. 4.4-1. Use your assembler to assemble the source file. Print the list file created.

13. With the help of Table 4.2-1, describe what the following program does. Add comments to document the program's operation. Define the program's operation as a sequence of five tasks. Specify each task's purpose.

```
main:   clc
        mov     dx,augend
        in      al,dx
        mov     bl,al
        mov     dx,addend
        mov     al,dx
        adc     al,bl
        mov     dx,sum
        out     dx,al
        jmp     main
```

14. Using Fig. 4.4-1 as a model, add the directives required to make the program in problem 13 a complete ASM86 program. Give the program the name SUMPORTS. For the input ports use addresses 8000H and 8001H. For the output port use address 8000H. Create a source file PROB4_12.ASM. Assemble the source file and print the list file.

15. In an embededed system, why must the modules that make up the program be located?

16. What are some of the advantages of relocatable program modules?

17. Assembly language is a low-level language. Why would you choose to design an entire program or some modules of a multimodule program in assembly language?

18. Link and locate the object file from problem 13, so that the absolute object code starts at address FE000H. Generate the ASCII-HEX file for programming the absolute object code into a ROM IC. If you are using TASM and Paradigm's LOCATE, the file IOREL.CFG in Fig. 4.9-3 can be renamed SUMPORTS.CFG and used as the configuration file for LOCATE.

19. Compare the HEX-ASCII file from problem 18 with the list file from problem 14. Identify the object code bytes for the program and the object code for the bootstrap instruction. Identify each of the record types. Verify from the HEX-ASCII listing that the program and bootstrap instruction start at the desired addresses.

20. Including a ROMable DOS increases the hardware overhead of an embedded design. What are the advantages of a ROMable DOS that might offset these increased costs?

5.1   Debugger Fundamentals

5.2   Debugging Tools Overview

5.3   Borland's Turbo Debugger

5.4   Intel's (Remote) RISM Monitor

5.5   Paradigm DEBUG/RT Remote Debugger

5.6   PromICE ROM Emulator

5.7   Code Tap Target Access Probe

5.8   Intel Evaluation Board EV80C186EB

5.9   Summary

Simulators, native debuggers, monitors, remote debuggers, target access probes, and in-circuit emulators are all tools used for debugging. Each provides you with the capability to interactively control, examine, and modify the execution of your program. With these capabilities, you can detect and locate your program's logical errors. All these different tools are loosely referred to as debuggers and are similar in use. However, they differ considerably in their implementations and capabilities.

Using a debugger, you can interactively control the execution of your program. You can execute a single instruction or a small portion of your program then stop program execution. This allows you to examine the effect of each instruction or each portion of your program on your system's registers, memory, and I/O ports. The use of good debugging tools is imperative in system development because more time is usually spent on debugging than is spent on designing and coding a program.

While the primary use of a debugging tools is to detect and locate errors in software and hardware, a debugger is also an excellent aid for learning the operation of a microprocessor and the effects of its instructions. For this reason, debuggers are introduced in this chapter, before the 80C188EB's instruction set is presented in detail. Use of one of the debuggers presented in this chapter, in combination with the study of this text, will be extremely helpful in mastering the 80C188EB's instruction set and understanding the details of how your programs execute.

Section 5.1 of this chapter discusses basic operations common to all debuggers. Section 5.2 gives a brief overview of each of the different kinds of debuggers available. Each of the Sections 5.3 through 5.7 discusses a specific example of one of the debuggers appropriate for an 80C188EB system. After reading Sections 5.1 and 5.2, you may wish to skip Sections 5.3 through 5.8 for now, and return to them after reading subsequent chapters. Or, if you have one of the specific debuggers detailed in these sections, you may wish to read that particular section before continuing.

5.1   Debugger Fundamentals

A **bug** is an error in a system's hardware or software. The process of detecting errors is called **testing**. The subsequent process of locating and correcting errors is called **debugging**. For hardware errors, the debugging process is more often referred to as **trouble shooting**.

Software errors may be errors in syntax or logic. A **syntax error** is a violation of one of the grammatical rules of the particular programming language. Syntax errors are detected and located by the assembler when you assemble your program, so syntax errors are fairly easy to correct.

A **logic error** is an error that causes your program to malfunction or produce incorrect results when it executes. **Software testing** is carried out to detect whether logic errors exist in a program. This type of testing involves inputting data and examining the corresponding program outputs to determine whether the program produces correct results. One of the most critical aspects of this process is the careful selection of a set of input data values that adequately test your program. You must know, prior to testing, exactly what input values you should use for testing and what the corresponding output values should be. While debuggers are interactive, casually picking input values and observing output values while you run a test is not an effective testing method.

Logic errors may be subtle or catastrophic. Catastrophic errors make their presence obvious and thus are easy to detect. Subtle logic errors may be very difficult to detect. For either type of logic error, locating the error's source may be a challenge. Once the source is found, the error's correction is usually relatively easy. Debugging tools are used to pinpoint the location of a logic error's source.

Later chapters discuss the modular development of programs. Large programs are written, tested, and debugged as coherent pieces. Modular development allows you to concentrate on testing and debugging each simpler piece, rather than trying to test and debug an entire program at once.

5.1.1   Basic Debugger Operation

Sometimes debuggers are referred to as either **software debuggers** or **hardware debuggers**. These terms refer to the design of the debugger rather than what they are used to debug. A software debugger is a tool that is primarily a program (software) used to debug both software and hardware. A hardware debugger is a tool that includes special hardware that connects to your system's prototype and is used to debug both software and hardware.

A hardware debugger typically has its own software. This software may be as, or more, complex than the software of a software debugger.

Both software and hardware debuggers are usually hosted on a general purpose or a dedicated computer. Usually a PC is used. When operating the debugger, you input commands from a keyboard or mouse and observe results on the computer's monitor. The debugger typically uses a graphical user interface (GUI) to present information on the monitor.

The operation of an interactive debugging tool alternates between two modes, command and execution. When first invoked, a debugging tool is in its command mode. During a debugging session, control is alternated back and forth between the command and execution modes. In **command mode**, you enter commands to examine the current status of the microprocessor system and to control the subsequent execution of your program. You examine the current state of your system by using commands that display the contents of the microprocessor's registers, memory locations, and I/O ports.

Debuggers include commands that allow you to specify conditions that will cause your program's execution to be stopped. When execution stops, the debugger returns to the command mode. Once back in the command mode, you can use other commands to examine the system's state at the current point in your program's execution.

When your program is executing, the debugger is in **execution mode**. The lowest level of execution control is to execute a single instruction at a time. The execution of a single instruction can cause the contents of a register, memory location, or I/O port to change. After each instruction is executed, you can view the contents of the registers, memory locations, and I/O ports involved.

Whether used for debugging or for learning a microprocessor's instruction set, there are some basic capabilities required of, and common to, most debugging tools. A generic set of fundamental debugger commands is listed in Table 5.1-1.

The first command in Table 5.1-1 is the **load command.** This command loads your program's object code into memory for debugging. Once the object code is loaded, the

Table 5.1-1   A generic minimum set of debugging commands.

Command	Function
load	Loads object code file
step	Execute an instruction
breakpoint	Specify location to stop program execution
go	Start execution of program
display register	Display microprocessor register contents
display memory	Display the contents of a memory location
display output port	Display the data output to a port
set register	Set the value of the contents of a register
set memory	Set the value of the contents of a memory location
set input port	Set the value to be input to a port

address at which execution should begin must be specified. Also, some means of stopping execution and transferring control back to command mode must be established.

When a program is loaded, the system usually expects to start execution at a default address, typically the first instruction in your program. Since there are debugger commands that allow you to change the value in any register, one method of establishing a different starting address is to simply change CS and IP to the desired starting address values.

For testing a short instruction sequence, the **step command** is used. This command allows one or a specified number of instructions to be executed before control returns to the command mode. Executing one instruction at a time is called **single-stepping**. After an instruction is single-stepped, control is returned to the command mode. Once in the command mode, you can use a **display command** to inspect or change the value of any registers, memory locations, or ports that are of interest.

When an instruction that outputs data to a port is executed, a debugger must either provide a command that allows the output value to be displayed, or must allow the actual port to be written. When an instruction that inputs data from a port is executed, the debugging tool must allow you to specify the value to be input, or must actually read the input port hardware.

Figure 5.1-1 shows the display of a debugger running the program IOREL from Chapter 4. The instructions are being single stepped. The IN instruction has just been stepped and AL has received the value 5AH from the input port.

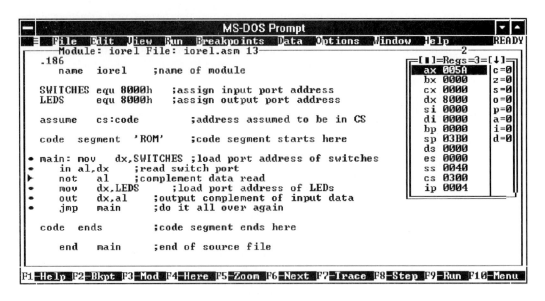

Figure 5.1-1   Display from a debugger running the program IOREL.

When long programs are debugged, it is still necessary to be able to examine the program's operation in detail, but only after execution has reached a desired point. This is accomplished using a **breakpoint command**. A **breakpoint** is a controlled way to force a program to stop its execution. A program can be executed at full speed until it hits a breakpoint. The simplest type of breakpoint stops execution when a particular point (instruction) in your program is reached. An **execution breakpoint** stops execution and returns control to the command mode, immediately **before** the instruction at the breakpoint location is executed.

After you set a breakpoint, to provide a means of stopping your program's execution, you can use the **go command** to cause execution to begin. The debugger enters its execution mode and executes the program. When the breakpointed instruction is reached, your program stops and the debugger enters its command mode. You can then single step the program from the breakpoint's location. Typically, a number of breakpoints can be set simultaneously. Execution stops when any one of the breakpoints is encountered. You can resume execution of your program, with the execution of the breakpointed instruction, by using the step command.

While a breakpoint causes your program to stop execution, for most types of debuggers, the microprocessor, which executes both your program and the debugger program, actually continues executing at full speed. However, after a breakpoint, when the debugger is in the command mode, the microprocessor is executing instructions from the debugger, not from your program. These instructions allow the debugger to respond to the commands you enter.

Most debugging tools use a windowed environment as the user interface, as shown in Fig. 5.1-1. With this type of environment, commands are typed into a command window or selected with a mouse click. Other windows display the next instructions to be executed, the contents of the registers, and the contents of memory locations corresponding to selected variables.

5.1.2   Symbolic Debugging

A debugger with **symbolic debugging** capability allows you to use the symbols used for addresses and data values in your source program to refer to addresses and data values during debugging.

For a debugger to support symbolic debugging, it must be provided with debug information that associates each symbol in the source program with the address or constant value that the symbol represents. The assembler must be instructed to include this symbol, or debug, information in the object code module(s) it produces. The linker must also be instructed to include the debug information in the EXE file that it produces. For example, for Turbo Assembler and Turbo Linker to produce an EXE file with debugging information, the switches /zi and /v must be used, respectively.

```
tasm /zi filename.asm      ;/zi includes debug info in OBJ file

tlink /v filename.obj      ;/v includes debug info in EXE file
```

The /zi switch causes the assembler to include debug information in the OBJ file it produces. The /v switch causes the linker to include debug information in the EXE file produces.

5.2   Debugging Tools Overview

Simulators, debuggers, monitors, remote debuggers, target access probes, in-circuit emulators, and logic analyzers all provide the basic debugging capabilities listed in Table 5.1-1, but in different ways and with significant differences in additional features and cost. Depending on the complexity of the system being designed, a single debugging tool may be adequate for all the design phases. However, certain tools are more effective during particular phases. Therefore, more than one debugging tool may be used for the same project. This section provides a brief overview of the various debugging tools and discusses their differences. Each of the remaining chapter sections considers in greater detail one version of these tools specifically for the 80C188EB.

To appreciate the differences among these tools, assume that the ultimate objective of the design process is to create a fully operational production prototype of your system. A **prototype** is a working model used for testing and design refinement. A **production prototype** is constructed using only those components that will be used in the production version of the system. In a production prototype, IC components are mounted on the printed circuits board(s) that are to be used for production. The production prototype has your program contained in ROM and includes, or has connections to, all of its I/O devices (Fig. 5.2-1).

Figure 5.2-1   Photograph of a production prototype of an embedded system.

The production prototype operates standalone at full speed, and meets all of its real-time requirements. Prototypes leading up to the production prototype may contain extra ICs, hardware, and software that are used only for development purposes. Such intermediate prototypes may be implemented in different ways. Simple designs can be bread-boarded, while more complex designs may have their components interconnected by wire wrapping. Some designs may require only an off-the-shelf single board computer.

The most common types of debugging tools are described in the following sections.

5.2.1   Simulators

A **simulator** is a program that runs on a general purpose **host** computer or microcomputer (Fig. 5.2-2). The simulator simulates the effect of your program running on the production prototype. Inputs to the simulator are your program's object code file and interactive commands that you issue to control the simulation. The microprocessor in the host computer and the simulated microprocessor, your target microprocessor, may be different. For example, a simulator running on a SUN workstation might simulate an 80C188EB. The simulator program simulates the 80C188EB's registers, the memory subsystem, and the I/O subsystem, using only the host computer's memory. To simulate execution by the 80C188EB of a single instruction from your program, the host computer must execute numerous instructions from its own instruction set.

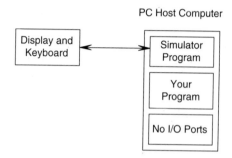

Figure 5.2-2   Representation of a simulator.

A simulator does not use a hardware prototype. As a result, the actual interaction of your program with the production prototype's I/O devices cannot be tested. When the execution of an input instruction is simulated, the simulator prompts you to type in the data expected from the input port. When an output instruction's execution is simulated, the simulator displays the value output on the host's display.

One of a simulator's advantages is that it allows you to debug your program's logic without the need for any prototype hardware. As a result, it is an ideal tool when it is necessary to start debugging your program before the hardware prototype is available. Usually, a significant portion of your program's basic logic and algorithms can be tested without a prototype. A simulator is often the most convenient debugging tool for learning a particular microprocessor's instructions and basic operation.

There are two areas where a simulator cannot support effective testing of a system: real-time operation and software interaction with complex I/O devices. Real-time operation requires full speed operation of the prototype system. Verifying that your program can execute various tasks as quickly as is required is very difficult with most simulators. In general, a simulator can only provide you with a rough approximation of a task's execution time.

Simulating the interaction of your program with complex I/O devices ranges from difficult to impossible with most simulators. Either the simulator must provide software to model the I/O device or you must write this software. If the simulation model created for an I/O device is not accurate, the resulting overall simulation of your system cannot be accurate.

Simulators are more readily available for 8-bit microprocessors and microcontrollers than for more complex 16-bit and 32-bit microprocessors. This is due primarily to the fact that it is easier to simulate the simpler 8-bit architectures. Simulators are most appropriate when the debugger's host computer contains a microprocessor that is not compatible with the simulated microprocessor. Because PCs are readily available, they are commonly used as the host for software development for 80C188EB systems. As a result of the 80C188EB's software compatibility with the microprocessors used in PCs, use of one of the other kinds of debuggers is more appropriate than use of a simulator for debugging an 80C188EB system.

5.2.2   Native Debuggers

Native debuggers, often simply called debuggers, also allow the logic design of your program to be debugged without a hardware prototype (Fig. 5.2-3). However, a **native debugger** must run on a host microcomputer whose instruction set is identical to, or is upward compatible with, that of your target microprocessor. This is necessary because your program executes directly on the host PC's microprocessor, under the control of the debugger. For example, a native debugger for the 80C188EB might be run on a Pentium PC.

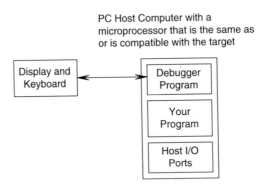

Figure 5.2-3   Representation of a native debugger.

Native debuggers are primarily designed for debugging programs that are to be ultimately run on the same or compatible general purpose microcomputer as the one on which they are debugged. In effect, native debuggers are not specifically designed for debugging embedded systems. A native debugger's biggest drawback, when used for embedded systems design, lies in its handling of I/O.

When your program, being run by a native debugger, executes an output instruction, the host microcomputer attempts to output the data to the addressed port. If a port with this same address happens to exist in the host PC, the host PC's port is actually written. If the host uses this port for its own operation, it may crash. Even if the port does not exist in the host, there is still a problem. The debugger does not directly display the value written to the port.

The converse problem exists when an input instruction in your program is executed. If a port with the same address happens to exist in the host PC, it is read. Your program's reading of an input port can also cause problems. Inadvertently reading an input port that is one of the PC host's status registers may cause status bits to be automatically cleared. This will interfere with the host's operation. Even if there is not a conflict with a host input port's address, there is no direct way for you to specify the value to be input to your program when it executes an input instruction.

You can set a breakpoint on an output instruction to allow the 80C188EB register (AX or AL) used for output to be examined to determine the data value that will be output. A breakpoint can also be set after an input instruction to allow the contents of the 80C188EB register that would normally receive the input (AX or AL) to be changed to the desired input value. A convenient method for setting breakpoints at all IN and OUT instructions in your program is presented in Section 5.4.

Even with these work-arounds for handling input and output instructions, native debuggers are still best suited for testing those portions of your program that don't use extensive I/O operations.

5.2.3   Resident Monitors

A **monitor** is a program that runs on your hardware prototype and controls your program's execution on the prototype (Fig. 5.2-4). Because the monitor exists in the prototype's ROM, it is often called a **resident monitor.** The prototype must contain additional ROM, beyond that needed for your program, to store the monitor. The prototype must also contain additional RAM for use by the monitor. The simplest monitors require that the prototype have a keypad and a simple display for you to interact with the monitor. With this type of monitor no host PC is required.

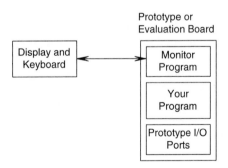

Figure 5.2-4   Representation of a monitor.

Another approach is for the prototype to contain a serial communications channel. A CRT or a PC is then connected to the prototype's serial channel to serve as an input and display device for the monitor. Using the CRT, you can type in the HEX-ASCII object code for your program. Using a PC, you can use a file transfer to transfer your object code to the prototype. The monitor loads your object code into the prototype's RAM for debugging. You use the monitor to control the execution of your program and to display your prototype's state.

A disadvantage of a monitor is that your prototype must include the additional hardware resources necessary to support the monitor. An advantage is that the application program runs on the prototype, so it can interact at full speed with the actual I/O devices in, or connected to, the prototype.

Another disadvantage of a monitor is that it may use some of the microprocessor's capabilities, such as an interrupt input, for its own needs. Any microprocessor capabilities required by the monitor are not available for use by your program.

Microprocessor IC manufacturers often provide evaluation boards for their microprocessors. These evaluation boards are single board microcomputers that include the microprocessor, ROM, RAM, limited I/O, and a monitor program. These boards are used to evaluate the microprocessor. They can also be used to build simple prototypes by adding application specific I/O devices.

5.2.4   Remote Debugger

A **remote debugger** combines the best features of the last two approaches and requires both a host computer and a prototype (Fig. 5.2-5). A remote debugger consists of two programs, a debugger program and a remote monitor program. These two programs work together to provide the tool's debugging capability. The debugger runs on the host, and the remote monitor runs on the prototype. The prototype contains RAM for use by the remote monitor, a serial communications channel, and the remote monitor in ROM. The remote monitor program on the prototype communicates over the serial channel with the debugger program running on the PC host.

You use the debugger program to download your program's object code file to the remote monitor on the prototype. The remote monitor stores your program in the prototype's RAM. You enter commands to the debugger via the host PC. The debugger translates these commands into the lower level commands that the remote monitor understands. The debugger transfers the lower level commands over the serial link to the remote monitor. The remote monitor executes these commands and sends the results back to the debugger. The debugger formats the received results for display then displays them.

A remote debugger has the advantages of allowing you to easily load large programs into the prototype from disk. A remote debugger also provides a powerful set of debugging commands along with a comprehensive display of the contents of the prototype microprocessor's registers, and the prototype's memory and I/O ports.

5.2.5   ROM Emulator

A ROM emulator is a hardware debugger that eliminates the hardware overhead required by a remote debugger. The ROM emulator plugs into the socket for the prototype's ROM (Fig. 5.2-6). RAM in the ROM emulator emulates the prototype's ROM and is used to hold

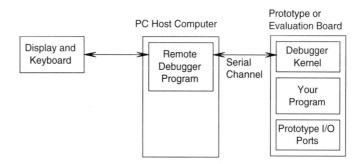

Figure 5.2-5   Representation of a remote debugger.

your program. The ROM emulator provides its own serial channel to allow both your program and the remote debugger to be downloaded from the PC host. Thus, use of a ROM emulator eliminates the requirement that your prototype contain additional ROM for the remote debugger, additional RAM to hold your program, and an extra serial channel.

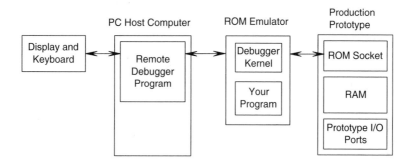

Figure 5.2-6   Representation of a ROM emulator.

5.2.6   Target Access Probe

Like a ROM emulator, a **target access probe** does not require the prototype to provide any additional hardware resources (ROM, RAM, or serial port) for its own operation, nor does it preclude the use of any of the microprocessor's capabilities. Unlike the ROM emulator, a target access probe plugs into the prototype's microprocessor socket instead of its ROM socket. The target access probe includes a hardware module that contains its own microprocessor and additional logic to allow the access probe to gain control of your prototype. This module has one cable with a plug or intercept pod that plugs into the prototype's microprocessor socket and another cable that plugs into the host computer's serial port (Fig. 5.2-7). A target access probe provides more debugging features than a ROM emulator.

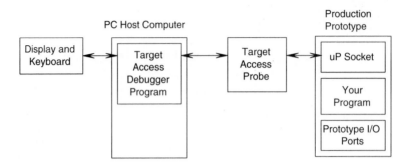

Figure 5.2-7   Representation of a target access probe.

5.2.7   In-Circuit Emulation

The most powerful, and correspondingly most expensive, debugging tool is an **In-Circuit Emulator** system (**ICE**). An ICE is a hardware debugger that can be used to debug both software and hardware. An ICE is often the tool of choice when it is time to integrate your software and prototype hardware. An ICE consists of one or more hardware systems and related software. The ICE is connected by a cable to the host computer's serial port or to a special hardware board that plugs into the host computer's bus (Fig. 5.2-8). A second cable from the emulator has a plug that plugs into the microprocessor socket on the prototype. The emulator contains its own microprocessor, which is identical to, or a special bond-out version of, the target microprocessor.

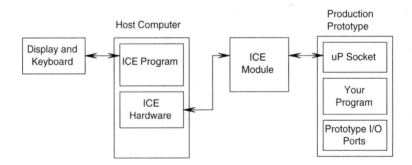

Figure 5.2-8   Representation of an in-circuit emulator.

A **bond-out chip** is a special version of a microprocessor that has additional internal connections to the microprocessor IC brought out. Bond-outs allow these additional internal signals to be used in monitoring and controlling the microprocessor's execution of your program. When using a bond-out chip, the ICE can usually monitor every aspect of the microprocessor's operation.

Some emulators have a mode of operation called **ONCE**, for **ON Circuit Emulation**. This mode is used for systems where the microprocessor is soldered to the prototype's printed circuit board. However, the microprocessor must be designed to support this function. A special adapter clamps onto the microprocessor from above and provides connections between the emulator and all the microprocessor's pins. The clamp drives a pin on the microprocessor into a special state just before and immediately after the reset pulse. When this condition exists, the microprocessor's outputs are totally disabled, effectively disconnecting the microprocessor from the system. This places the microprocessor in the ONCE mode. The emulator then drives the system using the microprocessor's pins. The 80C188EB supports the ONCE mode.

ICE systems can be used in all phases of software and hardware development. During the initial phases, when there is no prototype hardware, you can use the ICE to debug your program. When operated in this manner, the ICE uses its own microprocessor and uses its own **overlay memory** to serve in place of the prototype's ROM and RAM. Thus, in this mode the emulator functions very much like the debuggers previously described.

When the hardware prototype is partially constructed, the ICE's probe is plugged into the prototype's microprocessor socket. The ICE's probe usually contains buffers to protect its circuitry from electrical problems in the prototype. The ICE system can then be used to run hardware checks of the prototype's memory and I/O.

An ICE's ability to monitor bus activity in the prototype is very helpful for hardware trouble shooting during a prototype's development. As construction of the memory and I/O portions of a prototype is completed, you can command the ICE to use memory and I/O from the prototype, rather than its overlay memory, for execution of your program.

Other powerful features of an ICE include trace memory and event monitoring.

Table 5.2-1 summarizes the debugging tools discussed. Once you start to use any one of these tools, the distinctions between them will become much clearer.

Table 5.2-1   Debugging tools feature comparison.

	Prototype Hdwe. Required	Real-Time	Inherently Accurate	Interacts with Actual I/O	Cost	Symbolic Debugging	Prototype Requires Additional Hdwe.	Real-time Bus Cycle Trace	Uses Target uP Resources	Difficult to Debug Interrupts
Simulator	none	no	no	no	mod.	yes	no	no	no	yes
Native Debugger	none	no	yes	no	low	yes	no	no	no	yes
Monitor	yes	yes	yes	yes	low	no	no	yes	yes	yes
Remote Debugger	yes	yes	yes	yes	mod.	yes	no	yes	yes	yes
ROM Emulator	no	yes	yes	yes	mod.	yes	no	no	no	yes
Target Access Probe	yes	yes	yes	yes	high	yes	yes	no	no	no
In-Circuit Emulator	no	yes	yes	yes	high	yes	yes	no	no	no

5.3   Borland's Turbo Debugger

Borland's Turbo Debugger is designed for debugging assembly language programs assembled using TASM. Turbo Debugger can also be used to debug programs written in a high-level language and compiled with one of Borland's compilers. Versions of Turbo Debugger that run under DOS or Windows on a PC are available.

Turbo Debugger can be operated as a remote debugger using an appropriate remote kernel in your prototype's ROM. However, the discussion in this section concerns operating Turbo Debugger as a native debugger on a PC with no prototype. This use of Turbo Debugger is ideal for learning the operation of assembly language programs. This approach also makes it possible to test major portions of your program when a prototype is not available. This situation often occurs in industry when a prototype is being constructed in parallel with software development under a tight time schedule. This situation also occurs in a university when a student must develop a program outside of a laboratory environment, prior to loading and running the program on a prototype in the laboratory.

Turbo Debugger is a source level debugger that provides a comprehensive set of debugging features. Mouse driven use of menus, multiple windows, dialog boxes, and on-line context-sensitive help provide a fast and easy-to-use interactive debugging environment.

Turbo Debugger can be invoked from the DOS command line. Turbo Debugger can also be invoked from within Borland's **Integrated Development Environment (IDE),** which Borland includes with its high-level language compilers. The IDE provides an integrated editor, compiler, assembler, and linker. This discussion of Turbo Debugger uses command line invocation of Turbo Debugger from a DOS prompt.

5.3.1   Preparing a Program for Turbo Debugger

The design flow for debugging a program using Turbo Debugger is illustrated in Fig. 5.3-1. The normal method of preparing a program for Turbo Debugger requires that the program be assembled using TASM and linked using TLINK. The assembler and linker must be invoked with the appropriate switches so that full debug information is included in the OBJ and EXE files produced.

The following sequence of commands assembles and links the program IOREL.ASM and invokes Turbo Debugger.

```
tasm      /c /l /zi iorel.asm
tlink     /s /v iorel.obj
td        iorel.exe
```

To see a listing of the full complement of switch options available with either TASM or TLINK you can simple type the utilities name at the DOS prompt with no parameters.

```
tasm
tlink
```

Upon entering Turbo Debugger with the CPU window selected, the screen is as shown in Fig. 5.3-2. In the code pane, the top left area of the screen, the physical address of

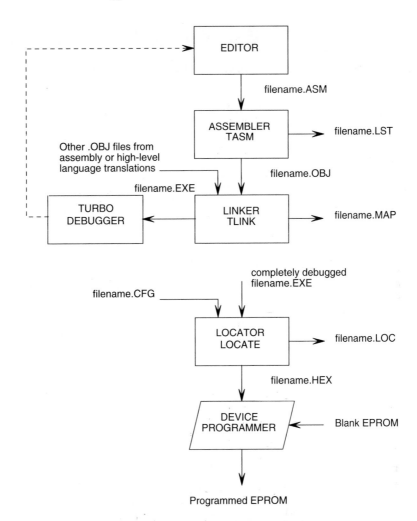

Figure 5.3-1   Steps to assemble, link, and debug a program using Borland's TASM, TLINK, and Turbo Debugger. After debugging is completed, the EXE file must be located for the target's memory configuration using Paradigm's LOCATE.

each machine instruction is listed followed by the instruction's object code. To the right of the object code, and preceded by a diamond symbol, is the assembly language representation of each instruction along with the comments from the source file. The debugger has also disassembled into instructions the contents of several memory locations past the twelve needed to store the program. These locations contain random values, are not part of the program, and will not be executed. Each instruction that is actually part of the program is preceded by a diamond symbol.

The program can be single stepped by clicking on F8-Step in the function bar at the bottom of the window. The arrow symbol to the left of the object code for the first instruc-

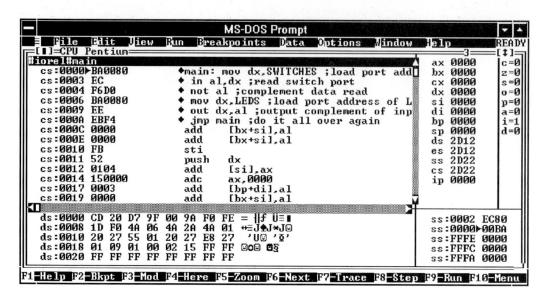

Figure 5.3-2   Turbo Debugger's CPU window with IOREL.EXE loaded.

tion, indicates this instruction will be executed next. As soon as the IN instruction is executed, you encounter the previously discussed (Section 5.2) I/O problems inherent with native debuggers. The first of these problems is that of adversely effecting the PC host by reading or writing one of its I/O ports. The second is the difficulty you encounter in specifying what data value is read from an input port or observing what data value is written to an output port.

For this simple program, you can avoid part of the first problem by making sure the port addresses in your program are not the same as any of the PC host's port addresses. If a port address in the prototype and the host are the same, then for debugging purposes, you must change the port address in your program to one that does not conflict. You must then assemble, link, and debug your program using the nonconflicting port addresses.

The second problem is dealt with as follows. After an IN instruction is single stepped, you must change the value in AL to the value you want from the port pointed to by DX. This is accomplished by clicking on register AX in the register pane and typing in a new value for the low byte of AX. The register pane is in the top right of the CPU window.

There is also a simple way to observe what value is output to an output port. Immediately before the OUT instruction is executed, you examine the values in AL and DX to determine what value is output and to which port.

Once debugging is complete, you must change to the actual prototype addresses any port addresses that were modified because of host address conflicts. Use of symbolic port addresses in the body of a program and EQU directives at the beginning of a program simplify the process of changing addresses. To obtain ROMable code, after changing port address values to those of the prototype, you must repeat the assembly and linking process then locate the linker's output. The location procedure is illustrated in the bottom half of Fig. 5.3-1.

The approach just described is adequate only if you know what I/O port addresses exist in your host, and you are satisfied with single stepping as your only method of program execution. In debugging large programs, you only want to single step through small portions of your program beginning where you expect a bug resides. To get to these points, you want to execute the preceding portions of your program in their entirety and at the debugger's maximum execution speed. However, you still need to stop at every IN and OUT instruction to provide the correct input or to examine the output. This can be accomplished using Turbo Debugger's breakpoint feature to place a breakpoint at every input and output instruction, but this approach is tedious.

The I/O instructions we have previously encountered are the variable port addressing versions of the IN and OUT instructions. For these versions of IN and OUT, a simpler approach to handling I/O instructions during debugging is available. Macros can be used to cause each I/O instruction to be automatically replaced with a breakpoint at assembly time. To accomplish this, you use the macros defined in Figure. 5.3-3 and placed in the file TDEBUG.INC. You must place an **INCLUDE** directive specifying the TDEBUG.INC file, INCLUDE TDEBUG.INC, at the beginning of your program's code segment.

```
; macro tdebug = replaces variable addressing IN and OUT
; instructions with INT 3 instruction.

ifdef tdebug
in macro a, b
int 03h
endm
out macro a, b
int 03h
endm
endif
```

Figure 5.3-3   Macro definitions in file TDEBUG.INC. These macros replace IN and OUT instructions that use variable addressing with INT 03H instructions to cause breakpoints in Turbo Debugger.

A **macro** is a name that defines a set of instructions that are substituted for the macro name wherever the macro appears in the original program. The substitution takes place when the assembler expands the macro before assembling the resulting program.

The macros in Fig. 5.3-3 are conditionally defined, so that the macro is not expanded by the assembler unless the symbol TDEBUG is defined. The symbol TDEBUG is defined by the /d*symbol* assembler switch. The required sequence of commands is:

```
tasm     /dtdebug /c /l /zi iorel.asm
tlink    /s /v iorel.obj
td       iorel.exe
```

The first macro in Fig. 5.3-3,

```
in macro a,b
int 03h
endm
```

instructs the assembler to replace any occurrence of the text IN followed by any two parameters with the text INT 03H. The assembler finds each occurrence of a text string consisting of IN followed by a space and any two parameters and then replaces it with the text string INT 03H. Therefore, the instruction

```
in        al,dx
```

is replaced by

```
int       03h
```

The second macro tells the assembler to replace OUT A,B with INT 03H. The assembler performs these macro expansions before assembling the resulting program.

This process was carried out for a version of the program IOREL.ASM modified to include the INCLUDE TDEBUG.INC statement at the beginning of the code segment. The result is shown in the screen of Fig. 5.3-4. The object code for the int 03h instruction is CCH. The object code bytes for the in al,dx and out dx,al instructions have been replaced by CCH.

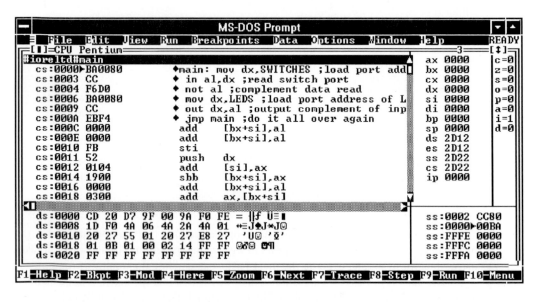

Figure 5.3-4   Turbo Debugger CPU window with IN and OUT instructions replaced by INT 03H using the macro TDEBUG.INC.

int 03h is the one byte long interrupt instruction used to create a breakpoint. When you set a breakpoint using Turbo Debugger's breakpoint feature, Turbo Debugger temporarily replaces the first byte of the instruction, where you want the breakpoint placed, with int 03h. When your program is run and an int 03h instruction is encountered, execution of your program by Turbo Debugger is stopped and Turbo Debugger is placed in the command mode. At this point, you can examine or change the values in any of the registers then continue by either single stepping or running the program from that point.

When the program is run at full speed, the program's execution stops at the breakpoint for the IN instruction. The IN instruction has not been executed. You can now single step the IN instruction causing it to be executed. Then, you can select AX in the register pane and change its value to the value you want from the input port. Only the low byte of AX, corresponding to AL, should be changed. If you then run the program full speed, it will stop at the OUT instruction. You can examine the value of AL (low byte of AX) and DX to determine what value will be output and to what port when OUT is executed.

5.4   Intel's RISM (Remote) Monitor

An example of a simple remote monitor, one resident on the prototype, is Intel's RISM monitor. This monitor is designed for use with Intel's evaluation board for the 80C186EB/80C188EB. The approach used with RISM is to have a small monitor on the prototype, which communicates with a larger monitor program running on a PC host. RISM is approximately 300 bytes long. The monitor running on the PC host is Intel's Embedded Controller Monitor, ECM. ECM executes basic program loading and debug commands that you enter through a character user interface. ECM converts the commands you enter to primitive commands that it sends over the serial link to the prototype. RISM executes these primitive commands and sends requested data values back to the PC host. ECM then formats this data for display.

ECM will only accept files in Intel's absolute object file format, OMF86. This is the file format that results from processing a source file with ASM86, LINK86, and LOC86. Borland's TASM and TLINK coupled with Paradigm's LOCATE can also generate absolute object file output in the OMF86 format. The output from source files assembled and linked with TASM and TLINK must be located with LOCATE. The locator configuration file must contain the directive ABSFILE OMF86 to obtain the appropriate output file format.

As a remote monitor, RISM has the advantage over a native debugger of allowing your program to read and write the actual I/O ports interfaced to the evaluation board. However, RISM has two disadvantages. One is its character user interface. The other disadvantage is that it requires a serial port for its operation.

5.5   PromICE ROM Emulator

The ROM emulator described in this section has the advantage of allowing your program to execute on your prototype and allowing the use of a graphical user interface. This ROM emulator also has the advantage of not requiring that the prototype provide a serial port for its use.

A ROM emulator replaces the prototype's ROM during software development. The ROM emulator has ribbon cables and a connector that plugs into the prototype's ROM. A second cable connects to the serial port of the PC host. The ROM emulator contains a UART that allows it to communicate with the PC host. The host can download your program's object code to the ROM emulator. Your program can then be executed on the prototype. When the prototype's microprocessor fetches an instruction from its ROM, the instruction is actually taken from the ROM emulator's RAM. The emulator's RAM emulates the prototype's ROM. When a ROM emulator is used in this manner, your program can be executed on the prototype, but no debugging capability is provided.

Another way to use a ROM emulator is to combine it with a software debugger. This approach is useful when your prototype does not have a spare serial port or enough ROM and RAM to support a remote monitor's needs.

For example, Grammar Engines Inc. makes a ROM Emulator called PromICE. PromICE's Analysis Interface provides a "virtual UART" for communications between the prototype and a PC host through PromICE. This allows the use of a remote debugger without using the prototypes's serial port or other target resources. This approach is ideal when the prototype does not have enough RAM or does not have a serial port to support the remote monitor.

Paradigm's DEBUG/RT Remote Debugger, which is described further in the next section, can be used with PromICE. There are two basic ways to use Paradigm DEBUG/RT with PromICE. In one approach, PDREMOTE/ROM is burned into EPROM on the prototype and PromICE provides the RAM to hold your program code and data for debugging.

In the other approach, PDREMOTE/ROM is downloaded to PromICE. When Paradigm DEBUG executes, it loads your program code and data into RAM in PromICE. With either approach, you must connect a write line from the prototype to the PromICE. This is necessary so that the prototype's microprocessor can write your program's data segment, which resides in PromICE. The LOCATE configuration file must also be modified to reflect the relocation of your program during debugging.

5.6   Paradigm DEBUG/RT Remote Debugger

Paradigm Systems makes a series of debuggers for the 80x86 microprocessor family called Paradigm DEBUG. These products are enhanced versions of Turbo Debugger specifically developed for debugging embedded systems applications. Since they are based on Turbo Debugger, their user interface is an extension of Turbo Debugger's user interface. Paradigm DEBUG can be used to debug programs created using Borland, Microsoft, Intel, and Watcom assemblers and compilers. This debugger is run under DOS or a DOS window in Windows or Windows NT.

Different versions of Paradigm DEBUG are available for different processors in the 80x86 family and for different development hardware. Some versions operate from a PC host with a serial connection to a remote monitor in your prototype. Others operate with target access probes or in-circuit emulators.

Paradigm DEBUG/RT-186EB is the version of Paradigm's debugger designed for debugging programs written for the 80C186/188EB. DEBUG/RT-186EB operates with a remote monitor that resides in your prototype's system ROM. DEBUG/RT-186EB has features in addition to those of Turbo Debugger. For instance, DEBUG/RT-186EB has a window that directly displays and allows you to modify the on-chip peripheral registers in the PCB.

The remote monitor supplied with Paradigm DEBUG/RT-186EB is called PDREMOTE/ROM. This small monitor requires approximately 5K of ROM and 1K of RAM from your prototype. PDREMOTE/ROM comes preconfigured on some evaluation boards if you purchase the board as part of a development package that includes Paradigm DEBUG/RT. It is also available preconfigured for a number of single board microcomputers designed for use in embedded systems.

If you want to debug a program running on a prototype of your own, you must customize PDREMOTE/ROM. Portions of PDREMOTE/ROM are supplied in source code for this purpose. The only system dependent components in PDREMOTE/ROM are the drivers for the serial communications and interrupt controllers. Prebuilt serial drivers are provided for the most common serial communications devices. These drivers are the only parts of the code that you must modify for your prototype. After modifying PDREMOTE/ROM you compile and locate it then burn it into EPROM.

The PDREMOTE/ROM monitor residing on the prototype services requests from Paradigm DEBUG/RT running on a PC. PDREMOTE/ROM uses the remote debugging capabilities of Paradigm DEBUG/RT to allow you to execute your program on your prototype. Paradigm DEBUG/RT and PDREMOTE/ROM working together allow you to load your program into your prototype's RAM. This requires that your prototype include additional RAM above that required when the program is fully debugged and loaded into ROM. To successfully debug a program using a remote monitor requires that the CPU, memory, and serial I/O portions of your hardware must be working properly.

5.6.1   Preparing a Program for Paradigm DEBUG/RT

This subsection describes how to prepare a program for debugging using DEBUG/RT. This is the procedure that you would follow if you had an evaluation board or single board computer that was supplied with a preconfigured version of the PDREMOTE/ROM monitor. This same process applies if you have built your own prototype and configured the PDREMOTE/ROM monitor for your prototype. In addition, this process is essentially the same when preparing your program to be debugged using versions DEBUG/RT designed for use with the ROM emulator of Section 5.6 or the target access probe of Section 5.7.

To use Paradigm DEBUG/RT with Borland and Microsoft language products you must locate the EXE file produced by these products using Paradigm's LOCATE. To use Paradigm DEBUG/RT with Intel's development tools, you must have a copy of the Paradigm OMFCVT utility that converts object code in Intel OMF-86 format to the format used by Paradigm DEBUG/RT. The design flow for creating a program and debugging it using Borland's TASM and Paradigm DEBUG/RT is illustrated in Fig. 5.6-1. The program is assembled with TASM and linked with TLINK. The assembler and linker must be invoked with appropriate switches so the full debug information is included in the OBJ files produced. The linked OBJ files are located using Paradigm's LOCATE. The output from Paradigm's LOCATE is a file in absolute executable format, AXE.

The following sequence of commands assembles and links the program IOREL.ASM and then invokes Paradigm Debugger.

```
tasm     /c /l /zi iorel.asm
tlink    /s /v iorel.obj
```

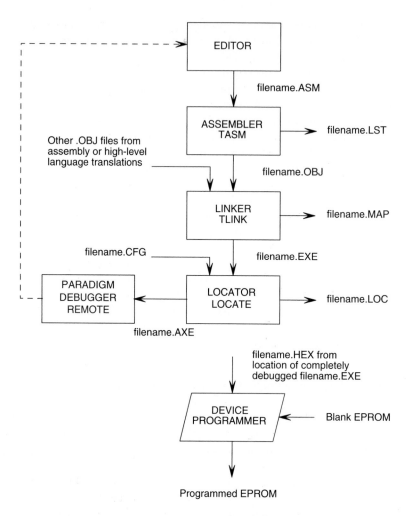

Figure 5.6-1   Steps to assemble, link, and debug a program using Borland's TASM, TLINK and Paradigm DEBUG/RT.

```
locate -ciorel.cfg iorel.exe
pdrt186            iorel.axe
```

The configuration file, iorel.cfg, in Fig. 5.6-2 includes additional locator directives required for Paradigm DEBUG/RT. The class directive must map your program's code to your prototype's RAM, not its ROM.

Upon entering Paradigm DEBUG/RT, the screen is as shown in Fig. 5.6-3. This screen is nearly identical to that of Turbo Debugger. However, there are additional items in some of the menus that support Paradigm DEBUG/RT's added features.

When the IN instruction is executed, the actual input port of your prototype is read. When the OUT instruction is executed, data is actually output to the output port of your prototype.

```
//      iorel.cfg
absfile   axe86        //required for Paradigm Debugger
hexfile   intel86      //Intel extended hex for programming EPROMs
listfile segments regions symbols publics    //for documentation
cputype I80C188EB   //for Intel 80C188EB microprocessor

//definition of the target system's address space
map      0x00000 to 0x02fff as reserved    //unpopulated
map      0x03000 to 0x07fff as rdonly      //ROM
map      0x08000 to 0xfffff as reserved    //unpopulated

class    ROM = 0x0300//code segment at 30000h
output   ROM
```

Figure 5.6-2   Modified configuration file IOREL.CFG for use with Paradigm's LOCATE
to locate the relocatable executable file IOREL.EXE. Directives have been
added to support debugging using Paradigm DEBUG/RT and to locate
the CODE segment temporarily in the prototype's RAM.

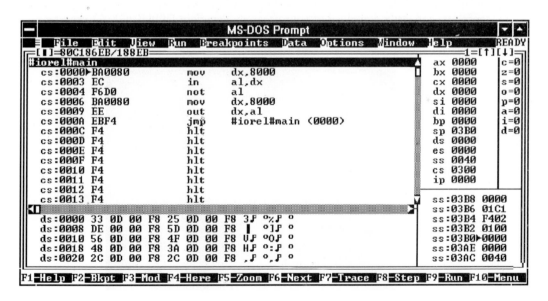

Figure 5.6-3   Paradigm DEBUG/RT CPU window with IOREL.AXE loaded.

5.7   CodeTAP Target Access Probe

One of the drawbacks of a resident monitor or a remote debugger is its use of your prototype's resources, such as memory, I/O, a serial port, and an interrupt. This requires that the
prototype include additional RAM to hold your program during development as well as

the RAM needed for the monitor or remote kernel's operation. Additional ROM is required to hold the monitor or remote debugger code. A monitor's need for a serial port may require the addition of a serial port to your prototype, if both serial ports on the 80C188EB are used by your program. Also, your program cannot use the same interrupt used by the debugger for serial communications with the PC host. Other more subtle problems that result from the use of interrupts to support communication between the monitor or remote kernel are discussed in Chapter 14.

Target access probes and in-circuit emulators eliminate the need to use any of your prototype resources.

Applied Microsystems Corporation makes a target access probe for the 80C188EB and 80C186EB called CodeTAP-XA C186EB. CodeTAP-XA is used with a version of Paradigm Debugger called Paradigm DEBUG/CT-XA. This version of Paradigm DEBUG provides full support for CodeTAP's hardware. The basic user interface for this version of Paradigm DEBUG is the same as for the DEBUG/RT version, and by extension, Turbo Debugger. Additional menu items and commands support the additional features provided by CodeTAP's hardware.

The CodeTAP-XA probe is a small module that contains Intel's special bondout version of the 80C186EB/80C188EB, overlay memory, and a special custom ASIC. CodeTAP-XA connects to a PC host via either the host's serial port or a special high speed serial adapter card (Fig. 5.7-1). Use of the high speed serial adapter card provides quicker response and faster download of your program. Paradigm DEBUG/CT-XA executes on a PC host.

Figure 5.7-1   Code TAP-XA target access probe. (Courtesy of Applied Microsystems Corporation.)

You connect CodeTAP-XA to your prototype by removing the 80C188EB from the prototype and plugging the CodeTAP-XA module in its place. The bondout 80C186EB/80C188EB in the CodeTAP-XA physically replaces the 80C188EB in the prototype.

Program preparation is the same as for Paradigm DEBUG/RT; the EXE file produced by the linker must be located using Paradigm's LOCATE.

The program to be executed can be loaded into RAM in the prototype or into the CodeTAP-XA's overlay memory. Using debugger commands, the overlay memory can be mapped to replace specific address spaces in your prototype. CodeTAP-XA is available with either 256K or 1M bytes of overlay memory. If overlay memory is used, no RAM from your prototype is required. Using overlay memory, none of your prototype's resources are required to support the debugger. CodeTAP is then completely transparent to the prototype.

Your program is executed at the speed determined by the prototype's crystal. Therefore, execution is real-time.

Some other features of CodeTAP-XA are the availability of hardware breakpoints in addition to software breakpoints, $4K \times 64$ bits of bus cycle trace history, and trigger input output capability.

Hardware breakpoints do not consume any prototype resources. These multilevel hardware breakpoints are also more powerful than software breakpoints. Custom hardware in the CodeTAP-XA is used to evaluate and trigger breakpoints. Hardware breakpoints can be further qualified by the type of bus cycle, the data value transferred, and a passcount that specifies how many times the breakpoint conditions must be met before execution is stopped. When conditions occur that match the breakpoint conditions, execution stops. Hardware breakpoints can even be set over code in the prototype's ROM. This allows debugging code that was previously programmed into ROM. Setting breakpoints over code in ROM cannot be accomplished using software breakpoints because of the necessity for the debugger to replace the first byte of the breakpointed instructions with the INT3 instruction.

CodeTAP-XA's $4K \times 64$ bits of bus cycle trace history allows you to capture and record in real-time the execution history of your program without stopping execution. This is particularly helpful in some real-time systems where you need to know the execution path that gets you to the breakpoint, but you cannot single step the program because of real-time constraints. Four trace display modes are provided. These modes allow you to display trace information on bus cycles, assembly language instructions executed, C-source level instructions, or mixed C and assembler instructions.

5.8   Intel EV80C186EB Evaluation Board

Microprocessor manufacturers often make evaluation boards for each of their microprocessors. These boards are designed to allow you to evaluate the hardware and software performance of a microprocessor prior to deciding on its use in a design. Evaluation boards are excellent vehicles for learning a microprocessor's operation and for quickly breadboarding simple systems.

The EV80C186EB board is capable of supporting either the 80C186EB or 80C188EB microprocessor. The board is delivered with a 16 MHz 80C186EB, 32 Kbytes of EPROM that contain the RISM186 monitor described in Section 5.4, 32 Kbytes of SRAM, and 512 Kbytes of DRAM. When configured for an 80C188EB only 256 Kbytes of DRAM is available. A 72 pin expansion connector makes available the buffered system bus and connections to one of the timer/counters, Port1 pins 1.0 to 1.3, and two interrupts. A separate 16-pin header provides connections to the two integrated serial channels. An 82510 UART is used to provide the serial interface to a host PC.

Your program can be executed and debugged using the Embedded Control Monitor (ECM) executing on a PC host and communicating with the resident RISM monitor. The RISM monitor resides in an EPROM located in the last 32 Kbytes of the address space. Your program can be loaded into the user portion of the SRAM or into DRAM.

If you wish to use Paradigm's DEBUG/RT with the EV80C186 board you can obtain the DK80C186EB design kit that includes both products.

5.9   Observing Instruction and Program Execution

The reason for this chapter's early introduction of debuggers, before detailed consideration of individual 80C188EB instructions, is so you can make use of a debugger as an instructional aid. You can use a debugger in this manner to:

1. Clarify your understanding of the basic operation of the 80C188EB microprocessor.
2. Determine the effect of execution of a particular instruction.
3. Visualize the execution flow of a program.

Paradigm DEBUG/RT remote debugger was chosen to illustrate how a debugger can be used for these purposes. The descriptions presented apply in general to other versions of Paradigm DEBUG and to Turbo Debugger. The focus in this section is on using a debugger to observe the basic operation of an 80C188EB microprocessor and the effect of executing individual instructions.

It is not the primary purpose of this text to focus on either debugging or the operation of Paradigm DEBUG/RT. However, the use of a debugger is so fundamental to developing software that a few chapters include a section that presents the use of DEBUG/RT within the context of the chapter's focus. Therefore a brief overview of DEBUG/RT follows.

A program must first be prepared for debugging by following the procedure described in Section 5.5. DEBUG/RT can then be invoked and your program loaded. For example, you load the program IOREL with the command:

```
pdrt186    iorel.axe
```

When the debugger is entered, a menu bar appears across the top of the display. Multiple windows can be open at a time on the display. The View menu allows you to select which windows are displayed (Fig. 5.1-1). There are two display configurations of interest now:

1. The Module and Registers windows together.
2. The CPU window alone.

A display with the Module and Registers windows both open is shown in Fig. 5.1-1. This display configuration has the advantage of being relatively uncluttered. The Module window displays the program to be debugged and the Registers window displays the 80C188EB's registers and flags.

In the upper right hand corner of the display, the activity monitor shows the word READY. This indicates that the debugger is in the READY state (command mode) and you can enter commands. The other state is the RUNNING state (execution mode), which indicates your program is executing.

The Function-key menu bar at the bottom of the display allows you to use a function key or mouse click to immediately select a command to be executed from a small subset of the debugger's commands. Other commands can be executed by selecting them from either one of the menu bar's drop down menus or a pop up local menu, obtained by clicking the right mouse button.

An arrow appears in the Module window to the left of the instruction to be executed next. To single step an instruction, press the F8 function key or click on Step in the Function-key menu bar. After an instruction is single stepped, the value displayed for a register in the Registers window will have changed if the instruction's execution modifies the register's contents. Changed registers are highlighted, so it is easy for you to quickly determine which registers values have changed.

For example, execution of the first instruction in the program, MOV DX, SWITCHES, causes the contents of registers DX and IP to change. We expect DX to change, since it is the destination of the MOV instruction. IP changes because it is the instruction pointer. The debugger uses CS:IP to indicate the address of the next instruction to be executed, rather than the next instruction to be fetched. The effect of the instruction queue is not shown in the debugger display.

Another way to single-step an instruction is to use Function-key F7 or click Trace. For our current purposes, the distinction between Step and Trace is unimportant. Thus, either one can be used for single stepping.

Each time an instruction is single stepped, the debugger always returns to the READY state. There are a number of ways other than single stepping to execute your program. Some of the other ways require you to force the program to stop running if no breakpoints have been previously set. When your program is running, you can force the debugger to return to the READY state by pressing and holding the control key then pressing the break key, Ctrl-Break.

An interesting way of executing your program is to select Animate from the Run drop down menu, Run|Animate. After you select Run|Animate you are prompted for a time delay in tenths of a second. This is the time the debugger will delay between the execution of each instruction. As a result, you can cause your program to execute in slow motion. You can watch the register's values change as your program runs. To stop your program, use Ctrl-Break.

You can execute your program full speed by pressing Function-key F9 or clicking Run in the Function-key menu bar. To stop your program's execution use Ctrl-Break.

The other display configuration of interest now is the CPU window (Fig. 5.6-3). The two panes of current interest in this window are the Code pane, at the top left of the window, and the Register pane, to its right. These two panes were discussed in Section 5.6. As can be seen, the CPU window gives much more detail than the Module and Register windows combined. In particular, each instruction's location in memory and its object code is displayed.

Some windows and panes have local menus. These pop-up menus are displayed by a right click of the mouse.

One command in the Code pane's local menu is the I/O command. Selecting this command menu pops up a submenu with four commands, In Byte, Out Byte, In Word, and Out Word (Fig. 5.9-1). These commands allow you to directly read or write ports in your prototype system without executing your program. This is a convenient way to check the hardware of simple input and output ports for proper operation.

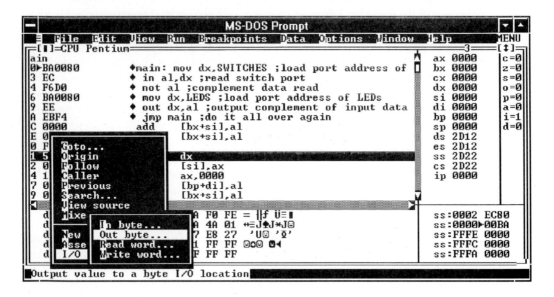

Figure 5.9-1   Using the Out Byte command from the I/O command submenu of the Code panel's local menu.

Figure 5.9-2 shows the prompt that results from selecting Out Byte. The port address and byte value to be output have been entered. When OK is clicked, the port will be written.

The In Byte Command prompts you for the port address. After you enter the address, the port address and its contents are displayed in decimal and hexadecimal.

Out Word and In Word commands operate on word ports in a manner similar to their byte counterparts.

As this brief introduction shows, you can observe the effect of executing a single instruction or sequence of instructions by single stepping. If, after reading an instruction's description in the instruction summary, you still have a question about some aspect of what it does, single step the instruction in a program and see for yourself.

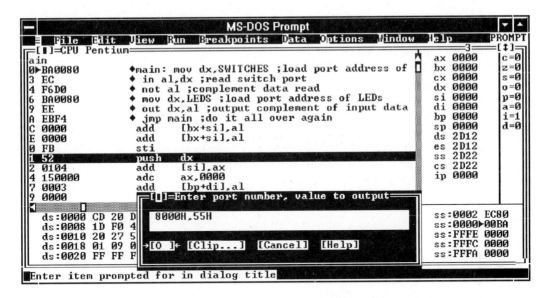

Figure 5.9-2   Execution of an Out Byte command prompts you to indicate the output port's address and the data to be output.

5.10   Summary

Successful software development for all but the simplest programs requires the use of effective debugging tools.

A wide range of debuggers are available and some representative debuggers were described in this chapter. Almost any debugger with a graphical user interface makes an excellent tool for learning the 80C188EB's instructions. Short programs can be single stepped to observe the operation of individual instructions and the program's overall operation. For a larger program, an execution breakpoint can be used to allow your program to execute at full speed until it reaches a predetermined point in your program. From that point you can single step your program to observe the details of its operation.

The debuggers described differ most in terms of their ability to interact with a hardware prototype. The extent of interaction ranges from none to essentially complete interaction and determines the kinds of problems that can be debugged.

At one end of the range, a simulator cannot provide any interaction with your prototype. As a result, you can debug basic program logic and algorithms with a simulator, but you cannot debug problems associated with your program's interaction with complex I/O devices or with its meeting real-time constraints.

At the other end of the range, an ICE provides complete interaction with your prototype. In addition, an ICE does not require your prototype to provide any extra hardware to support its operation, nor does it require any of your microprocessor's capabilities to support its operation.

In between these two extremes is a variety of debuggers that provide different degrees of prototype interaction. These debuggers offer a compromise between cost and real-time interaction with a prototype.

Efficient design of an embedded system requires tools whose capabilities are appropriate for the complexity of the system to be designed. Of the various software and hardware tools you will use, using a debugger with the appropriate capability for your design will have the most impact on your success. Of course, there is another limit on the capability of any debugger, your understanding and ability to make use of the capabilities the debugger does provide. Most debuggers require a significant investment of your time to be able to use them to their fullest extent. This investment on your part will provide substantial returns.

5.11   Problems

1. Explain the distinction between testing and debugging a program.
2. Explain the distinction between syntax errors and logical errors. How is each type of these errors detected and located?
3. What are the two primary modes of a debugger? What is the purpose of each mode?
4. Why does a debugger stop your program's execution just before executing the instruction at the location of a breakpoint, rather than just after the breakpointed instruction's execution.

DATA TRANSFER, DATA ALLOCATION, AND ADDRESSING MODES

6.1   Data Transfer and Addressing Modes

6.2   I/O Port Addressing

6.3   Register Addressing

6.4   Immediate Addressing

6.5   Allocating RAM for Data Variables

6.6   Memory Addressing Modes

6.7   Structures

6.8   Addressability and Segment Overrides

6.9   Allocating ROM for Data Constants

6.10   Address Object Transfers

6.11   80C186EB Data Transfer Considerations

6.12   Summary

One of the fundamental operations in a system is data transfer. The 80C188EB's instruction set has a variety of instructions for this purpose. Instructions are provided that transfer data between an I/O port and an 80C188EB register, between two 80C188EB registers, between an 80C188EB register and a memory location, between an I/O port and a memory location, and between two memory locations.

Another fundamental system operation is data storage. One or more memory locations must be assigned for each variable in your program. Related data elements should be collected together and stored in memory in an organized fashion, or structure. The variety of instructions available for transferring data between an 80C188EB and memory is particularly rich. These memory reference instructions provide numerous ways to specify the address of a memory location. Optimal design of an application's data structures and appropriate choices of the instructions used to access data in these structures results in a more efficient program.

While data is usually stored in the data or extra segments, it can also be stored in the code or stack segments. Segment override instructions allow access to data stored in segments other than the data segment.

In this chapter, the 80C188EB's data transfer instructions are presented based on the subsystem to, or from, which data is transferred. Separate sections are devoted to transferring data to and from I/O ports, 80C188EB registers, and memory. Instructions that load 80C188EB registers or memory with constant values are also described in a separate section. Other sections of this chapter describe how RAM is allocated for variables and more complex data structures. Allocating and initializing ROM for storing tables of data is also described.

6.1   Data Transfer and Addressing Modes

In this section it is advantageous to briefly return to the generic use of the term register, as used in Chapter 2. During a single bus cycle data is transferred from a source register to a destination register. One of these registers, either the source or destination, is an 80C188EB register. The other register is either an 80C188EB register, a memory location, or an I/O port. For the purposes of this discussion, 80C188EB registers are called **internal registers**. Memory locations or I/O ports are called **external registers** (external to the 80C188EB).

In general, a source register can either be an input port, an 80C188EB register, or a memory location. A destination register can either be an output port, an 80C188EB register, or a memory location. A single bus cycle can transfer a data byte between any source and destination register pair as long as one of the two is an internal register and the other is an external register. Accordingly, there are instructions that can transfer a data byte from an input port to an 80C188EB register, from one 80C188EB register to another, or from an 80C188EB register to an output port in one bus cycle.

By using two bus cycles, a single instruction can transfer a data byte from memory to memory, from an input port to memory, or from memory to an output port. Each of the bus cycles still involves an internal register and an external register. The only transfer that is not possible with a single instruction is from an input port to an output port.

Transfers of data words involving each of the previous source and destination pairs are also possible. However, for the 80C188EB, these word transfers require one additional bus cycle for each word transferred between an internal and external register.

6.1.1   Logical Versus Physical Addresses

Every register, whether internal or external, has two kinds of addresses, a logical address and a physical address. Programs use logical addresses. The system hardware uses physical addresses.

A **logical address** is a name or symbol used to represent a register. These are the types of addresses that appear in an assembly language instruction. For example, AL is the logical address of a particular 8-bit 80C188EB register. SWITCHES is a logical input port address that was used in several examples. If a variable named maximum were used in a program, maximum would be the logical address of the memory location used to hold the variable's value. Using logical addresses for memory locations allows you to develop a program without having prior knowledge of precisely where the program will be located in the system's memory.

A **physical address** is the actual address used by a system's hardware to identify and access a register. Every register has a unique physical address in the address space in which it exists. For example, an input port has a unique address in the input address space. An 80C188EB register has a unique address in the internal address space of the 80C188EB's architecture. A memory location has a unique address in the memory address space.

Our focus in this chapter is on data transfer instructions and how these instructions are written in assembly language programs. Accordingly, we are interested in logical addresses. The logical address of an 80C188EB general register is its name, for example, AX, or AL. In contrast, the physical address of an 80C188EB general register consists of a 3-bit value preassigned by Intel. This 3-bit address, used in conjunction with the W bit field in the instruction's machine language encoding, uniquely identifies the register.

The logical address of an I/O port is the name that represents the register that holds the value input from, or output to, the port. In contrast, the physical address of an I/O port is a 20-bit value that appears on the system bus to uniquely identify the port. The most significant 4 bits of this physical address are always 0H. The least significant 16-bits of the port's address are represented in the program by its logical address.

The logical address of a memory location is actually comprised of two parts, a logical segment address and a logical offset address. An instruction usually specifies only the location's logical offset address. Its segment address is implied from the instruction's addressing mode. In contrast, the physical address of a memory location is the 20-bit value that appears on the system bus to uniquely identify the location. In forming the physical address, the BIU normally uses the contents of the default segment register for the segment address. However, you can write a memory reference instruction in a form that tells the BIU to use an alternate segment register in forming the physical address.

A logical address in an instruction must be translated to its corresponding physical address before the instruction can be executed. For an 80C188EB register or an I/O port, this translation takes place during assembly time. For a memory location, part of the address translation may take place during the assembly and location times, and part may occur at execution time. For some addressing modes, a memory location's offset address is calculated by the EU at execution time. The BIU then combines this offset address with the segment address to form the 20-bit physical address.

6.1.2   Addressing Modes

The term **operand addressing mode,** or **addressing mode,** refers to the method used by an instruction to specify the address of an internal or external register that contains the operand of interest. The objective of some instructions is to transfer data between an internal register (one in the 80C188EB) and some "other register." The "other register" may also be internal, or it may be external (a port or memory location). For these instructions the 80C188EB's addressing modes are named based on how the other register is addressed. Table 6.1-1 lists the 80C188EB addressing modes where the other register is not a memory location.

Table 6.1-1   80C188EB non-memory operand addressing modes.

Addressing Mode	Operand Located in	Instruction Operand Format (for "other register")	Default Segment Register
Fixed Port	port pointed to by address in instruction	port name	none
Variable Port	port pointed to by register DX	DX	none
Register	80C188EB register specified	register	none
Immediate	instruction itself	constant value	none

With fixed port and variable port addressing, the "other register" is an I/O port. The operand is read from or written to this port. The port's address is either contained in the instruction (fixed port addressing) or in register DX (variable port addressing). Port addressing is covered in detail in the next section.

In register addressing, the operand is in an internal register specified by the instruction. Register addressing is the subject of Section 6.3.

Immediate addressing is used to transfer a constant value contained in the instruction, to a register. For this addressing mode, it may not be obvious that the constant is transferred from a register. This will be clarified in Section 6.4.

There are several 80C188EB addressing modes where the "other register" is a memory location. These are called memory addressing modes. Memory addressing modes are discussed in detail in Section 6.6.

The data transfer instructions presented in this chapter are summarized in Table 6.1-2.

Table 6.1-2   Data transfer instructions introduced in this chapter.[a]

Mnemonic	Operands	Function
IN	acc,port[b]	input byte or word
OUT	port,acc	output byte or word
INS	dst_s,port	input byte or word string
OUTS	port,src_s	output byte or word string
MOV	dst,src	move byte or word
XCHG	dst,src	exchange byte or word
MOVS	dst_s,src_s	move string byte or word
LODS	src_s	load string byte or word
STOS	dst_s	store string byte or word
XLAT	translate_tble	translate AL

a. No flags are modified by the execution of these instructions.

b. Abbreviations: acc = accumulator, dst = destination, src = source, src_s = source string, and dst_s = destination string.

We will now return to the more restrictive use of the word register, where register, when used alone, implies a register in the 80C188EB. Registers in memory will again simply be referred to as memory locations and I/O registers referred to as I/O ports. It is often convenient to refer to data based on where it is stored. The terms used are: port data, register data, and memory data.

6.2   I/O Port Addressing

Ports in the I/O address space are accessed using **I/O port addressing**. There are three I/O port addressing modes: fixed, variable, and string. The most commonly used I/O instructions, *input*, **IN**, and *output*, **OUT**, use either fixed or variable port addressing. They have the general form:

        in   *acc, port*
        out   *port, acc*

Both the IN and OUT instructions must use AX, the 16-bit accumulator, for word transfers or AL, the 8-bit accumulator, for byte transfers. These restrictions make the machine language encoding for IN and OUT instructions more compact and efficient.

Generation of a physical address for I/O is a special case. Since the I/O space is only 64K bytes long, only the least significant 16 address bits need be specified ($2^{16} = 64K$). As a result, address bits A19–A16 are always 0H. Thus, the 80C188EB does not need nor use a segment register for isolated I/O.

6.2.1   Fixed Port Addressing

With **fixed port addressing** only the least significant eight address bits are specified by the I/O instruction. The most significant twelve address bits are all zeros. As a result, an address specified using fixed port addressing can only range from 00000H through 000FFH. This means that only the first 256 input and first 256 output ports in the I/O space can be addressed. One advantage of this addressing mode is the simplicity of the I/O instruction. The machine language encoding is only two bytes. Another advantage is simpler port address decoders, since they have to decode fewer address inputs. The forms for these instructions are:

        in   al,*port*   ;input from a byte port
        in   ax,*port*   ;input from a word port
        out   *port*,al   ;output to a byte port
        out   *port*,ax   ;output to a word port

where *port* is the 8-bit port address. A **byte port** is an 8 bit data port. A **word port** is a 16 bit data port.

The following instruction sequence contains examples of fixed port addressing of byte ports.

```
in      al,SWITCHES        ;input from a byte port
not     al
out     LEDS,al            ;output to a byte port
```

Here the port addresses, SWITCHES and LEDS, are logical addresses and must be assigned values using EQU directives.

Word ports are designed so the port address used in an instruction is the address of the least significant byte of the port's word. The most significant byte has the next higher address (Fig. 6.2-1). When an instruction accesses a word port, the 80C188EB requires two

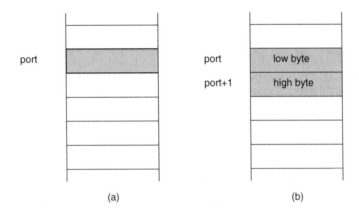

(a)   (b)

Figure 6.2-1   Byte and word ports in the isolated I/O space: (a) byte port; (b) word port.

bus cycles to transfer the word. The 80C188EB accesses the low byte during the first bus cycle using the address specified in the instruction. The high byte is accessed during the second bus cycle. The BIU automatically increments the address used in the first bus cycle for use in the second bus cycle. For example:

```
in      ax,SWITCHES        ;AL receives byte at port address SWITCHES
                           ;AH receives byte at address SWITCHES + 1
```

6.2.2   Variable Port Addressing

Variable port addressing allows you to specify a full 16-bit port address. Any one of the 64K possible input or 64K possible output ports can be accessed (2^{16} = 64K). You must load the 16-bit port address into DX prior to the I/O instruction. The forms for variable port I/O instructions are:

```
in      al,dx              ;input a byte from a byte port pointed to by DX
in      ax,dx              ;input a byte from a word port pointed to by DX
```

```
out      dx,al               ;output a word to a byte port pointed to by DX
out      dx,ax               ;output a word to a word port pointed to by DX
```

The operand notation here is very misleading since it is not the contents of DX that are being transferred. DX contains the port address. The contents of the port whose address is in DX are transferred. You simply have to remember that for IN and OUT instructions that have DX as an operand, DX contains the address of, or points to, the port.

Variable port addressing was used in the program of Fig. 4.4-1:

```
mov      dx,SWITCHES         ; DX <- address of byte input port
in       al,dx               ; AL <- byte value from port
not      al
mov      dx,LEDS             ; DX <- address of byte output port
out      dx,al               ; output port LEDS <- contents of AL
```

In each case, the port's address is loaded into DX prior to the I/O instruction, so DX pointed to the desired port.

Variable port addressing has two important advantages over fixed port addressing. One is that any port in the I/O space can be accessed. Fixed port addressing can only access the first 256 ports. The other advantage is that variable port addressing allows the port address to be computed or modified during program execution. For example, a program loop can be written that reads or writes several contiguous ports by simply incrementing DX during each pass through the loop.

6.2.3   String Port Addressing

The *in string* (**INS**) instruction transfers data from the input port pointed to by DX to the memory location pointed to by ES:DI. *Out string* (**OUTS**) transfers data from the memory location pointed to by DS:SI to the output port pointed to by DX. The port can be a byte or word port. Suffixes B and W are used with INS and OUTS to indicate whether the port is a byte or word, respectively.

The registers that hold the source and destination addresses must be loaded prior to execution of an INS or OUTS instruction. For example, the following instruction sequence inputs data from byte port SWITCHES and stores it in memory location sw_image.

```
mov      es,seg sw_image     ;load segment address of memory loc.
mov      di,offset sw_image  ;load offset addr. of memory loc.
mov      dx,SWITCHES         ;load address of input port
insb                         ;transfer byte from port to memory
```

The actual transfer of the byte from the input port to memory is accomplished by the single instruction INSB. However, execution of this instruction takes two bus cycles. In the first bus cycle, the byte is input from the port to a temporary register in the 80C188EB. In the second bus cycle, the byte is transferred from the temporary register to the memory location. Thus, the constraint that a single bus cycle always transfers data between an internal and external register still holds.

The true power of string instructions will not be obvious until repeated string instructions are described in Section 7.8.

6.3   Register Addressing

Instructions that use **register addressing** transfer data from one 80C188EB register to another. For example:

```
mov ax,bx          ;move (copy) the contents of BX to AX
```

This instruction copies the contents of register BX to register AX. The *move* instruction mnemonic, **MOV,** actually specifies a copy operation. After execution of this instruction, both registers contain the value originally in the source. The operation is referred to simply as "move BX to AX," where it is understood that the contents of BX are copied to AX. Source and destination registers for MOV instructions must be the same length.

Because it takes only four bits to distinguish between the small number of registers in the 80C188EB, machine instructions for register to register transfers are only two bytes in length. These instructions execute in a very short time since no external bus cycles are needed for their execution.

The *exchange* (**XCHG**) instruction also accomplishes a register to register transfer. However, XCHG swaps, or exchanges, the contents of its operand registers. For example,

```
xchg      ax,bx          ;swap the contents of AX with BX
```

swaps the contents of AX with those of BX. To accomplish this without the XCHG instruction, requires three instructions:

```
mov cx,ax        ;save ax in another register
mov ax,bx        ;move bx to ax
mov bx,cx        ;move cx to bx
```

6.4   Immediate Addressing

With **immediate addressing**, the data to be transferred is contained in the machine code of the instruction that transfers the data. Since this data must be placed in the machine code during assembly, it is a constant value and can only be the source in a transfer. Consider the assembly language instruction:

```
mov       al,37
```

The source is the immediate data, 37 decimal, and the destination is register AL. The assembler translates this instruction into two bytes of machine code, B0H and 25H. The first byte is the opcode and the second byte, 25H, is the hexadecimal equivalent of 37. The transfer actually takes place in two steps. The data in the instruction is transferred from memory to the 80C188EB's instruction queue when the MOV instruction is fetched by the BIU. When the EU decodes and executes the instruction, it obtains the data from the instruction queue (a register) and writes it to AL.

Immediate addressing allows specification of an 8- or 16-bit constant value. This value can be specified as an unsigned or signed number. The assembler sign-extends immediate values to fill all 8 or 16 bits in the instruction. For the previous example, the assembler sign extends 0100101B (+37) to provide the 8-bit value 00100101B. If the constant value specified in the instruction were −37, then the assembler would sign-extend the two's-complement representation of −37, 1011011B, to 11011011B to provide 8-bits. Two's complement number representation is discussed in Chapter 9.

In an assembly language statement, a number can be written in either binary, octal, decimal or hexadecimal notation. A suffix is used to indicate the base. Binary numbers must have a B suffix, octal numbers an O or Q suffix, and hexadecimal numbers an H suffix. When hexadecimal numbers appear in a program they must begin with one of the digits 0 through 9. If the first digit of a hexadecimal number is A through F, then it must be preceded with a zero so the assembler can distinguish it from text. Decimal numbers do not require a suffix, although a D suffix is optional. When no suffix is used, the default decimal base is assumed.

There are numerous ways an immediate value can be specified. A symbol that has been assigned a value can be used. For example:

```
const equ 37
...
mov al,const
```

An ASCII character can be used to represent its constant value. These constants are called **string constants** and consist of one or two characters enclosed in single quotes. For example:

```
mov al, 'a'              ;move 61h (ASCII 'a') to al
mov cx, 'AB'             ;mov 4142h (ASCII 'A'= 41h, 'B'=42h) to cx
```

6.4.1   Expressions and their Arithmetic Operators

Expressions make assembly language programs easier to write and to understand. The assembler has a number of **expression operators** that can be used with *constant* operands to form expressions (Table 6.4-1). All expressions are evaluated to constant values by the assembler and are included in the assembled code. Expressions using these operators can appear in instructions wherever a constant value is acceptable.

Given that CONST has been equated to 37, the instruction,

```
mov     al, 2*CONST
```

causes the assembler to create the object code for a move immediate instruction with 74 as its immediate value. The assembler can evaluate the expression 2 * CONST because all operands in the expression are constants and their values are known to the assembler. The expression 2 * CONST is evaluated by the assembler at assembly time to create the instruction's object code. This expression does not cause a multiplication to be performed by the 80C188EB at run time.

The instruction,

```
mov al, ((2*CONST) shl 1)/3
```

moves 31H, or 49, into AL. Again, it is important to keep in mind that the operators in Table 6.4-1 are assembler operators. They are evaluated by the assembler at assembly time. The mnemonic SHL is used to represent both an assembler expression operator and the

Table 6.4-1   Assembler expression operators.

	Operation	Operator	Operand Syntax	Result
Arithmetic	High byte isolation	HIGH	HIGH operand	high byte of operand
	Low byte isolation	LOW	LOW operand	low byte of operand
	Shift right	SHR	operand SHR count	bitwise shift count places
	Shift left	SHL	operand SHL count	bitwise shift count places
	Multiplication	*	operand * operand	product
	Division	/	operand / operand	quotient
	Modulo division	MOD	operand MOD operand	remainder
	Addition	+	operand + operand	sum
	Subtraction	-	operand – operand	difference
Logical	logical AND	AND	operand ANDoperand	logical AND
	logical OR	OR	operand OR operand	logical OR
	logical XOR	XOR	operand XOR operand	logical XOR
	logical NOT	NOT	NOT operand	complement
Relational	equal	EQ	operand EQ operand	all 1s if relation is TRUE, otherwise all 0s
	less than or equal	LE	operand LE operand	
	less than	LT	operand LT operand	
	greater than or equal	GE	operand GE operand	
	greater than	GT	operand GT operand	
	not equal	NE	operand NE operand	

80C188EB's shift logical left instruction! In this example, it should be clear that SHL is used as an assembler expression operator and is evaluated by the assembler at assembly time. In contrast, MOV is executed by the 80C188EB at run time. Other expression operator names that are also names of assembly language mnemonics are: SHR, NOT, AND, OR, and XOR.

Keep in mind when writing assembly language expressions that the operands, even if expressed as names, must all be constants.

6.5   Allocating RAM for Data Variables

80C188EB instructions can operate directly on one of three elementary data items: bytes, words, and double-words. A byte is eight bits. A **word** is 16 bits, or two consecutive bytes. A **double-word** is 32 bits, or two consecutive words. Two more complex data items are introduced later, structures in Section 6.7 and records in Section 7.9.

The **type** of a data item is its size in bytes, and its size determines the range of values it can be assigned. The assembler associates a type with every variable, so it can generate the correct object code for each instruction that accesses a variable.

Words are stored in memory with their low byte in the lower address of the two locations used. For double-words the low word is stored in the lower two addresses of the four used. Figure 6.5-1 illustrates the convention for storing bytes, words and double-words in memory.

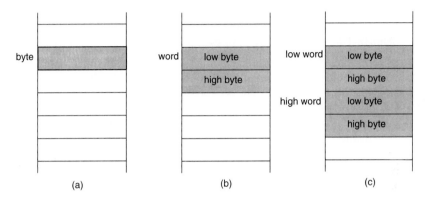

Figure 6.5-1   Storage of elementary data types in memory: (a) byte; (b) word; (c) double word.

A byte's location in memory is specified by its segment:offset address pair. The offset of a data item is the distance in bytes from the beginning of the logical segment in which the data item is defined to the first byte of the data item.

6.5.1   Simple Variables and Arrays

You must assign or allocate the locations in memory for each data item used in your program. During its execution, your program can change the value of a data item stored in RAM. Data items in RAM that are given symbolic names when they are allocated are called **named variables,** or **variables**. In essence, a variable is a named location in memory whose contents can be changed by your program.

Allocating memory and assigning variable names to locations are accomplished using **data allocation directives,** also known as **data definition directives**. To allocate memory for a data item, you must specify its size and location. Data allocation directives are placed inside a data segment. The data segment is assigned to RAM when the program is located.

Like a code segment, a data segment is created using a SEGMENT/ENDS directive. For example, the following directives define a logical segment with the name DATA and allocate four data items, all of which are variables:

```
data      segment
          byt1 db ?          ;allocate a byte
          wrd1 dw ?          ;allocate a word
          dwrd1 dd ?         ;allocate a double-word
          byt2 db ?          ;allocate a byte
data      ends
```

Data allocation directives use the mnemonics **DB**, **DW**, and **DD**, for **define byte**, **define word**, and **define double-word**, respectively. These mnemonics specify the data item's type (its size in bytes). In the previous example, variable byt1 is of type byte, wrd1 is of type word, and dwrd1 is of type double-word. The offset of byt1 is 0, the offset of wrd1 is 1, and the offset of dwrd1 is 3. The ? means that the initial value (contents) of the memory location(s) allocated is unspecified.

A variable's segment address is simply the name of the logical segment in which it is defined. Thus, the full address of byt1 is data:byt1, or equivalently data:0. The address of dwrd1 is data:dwrd1, or data:3. At the time a program is being written, the actual value of data (the segment address) is not important. This value is not specified until the program is located. Specification of a value for data during location of the program's object code binds the logical segment data to a physical segment.

All data items have three attributes: type, segment, and offset. Type and offset have been defined previously. The **segment attribute** is the name of the segment in which a data item is defined and is the data item's segment address. These three attributes of a data item simply specify its size (type attribute) and location in memory (segment attribute and offset attribute).

The general forms of the data allocation directives for bytes, words, and double-words are, respectively:

[var_name] db   [initval1, initval2, ...]
[var_name] dw   [initval1, initval2, ...]
[var_name] dd   [initval1, initval2, ...]

A data allocation directive's *init* field is used to specify the number of bytes, words, or double-words to be allocated and, optionally, their initial values. The notation *[initval1, initval2, ...]* indicates that a comma separated list of values can be specified. These values can be provided as numbers or expressions. A question mark (?) is used in the *init* field to indicate an uninitialized value.

If initial values for data items are specified, the assembler includes these values as initialization records in the object code file it generates. For a system that has an operating system, the operating system's loader can respond to data initialization records in the object code file and set each variable to its initial value when the loader loads the program for execution. However, in an embedded system that does not have an operating system, the object code is loaded by programming it into a ROM device. In this case, "loading" the program takes place on a device programmer when the ROM is programmed.

When an embedded system is powered-up, all RAM values are random. Variables can only be initialized by the execution of instructions in your program. Therefore, instructions in your program must copy the initial values from ROM to RAM.

Since the programs in this text do not use an operating system, they do not use data allocation directives to initialize variables. Initializing variables in systems that use a high-level language without an operating system is covered in Chapter 20.

Identifiers are used to name user-defined objects, such as variables, in a program. For example, byt1 is an identifier that allows the first byte allocated in the previous data segment to be referenced symbolically. An identifier:

1. Must begin with a letter or one of the following three special characters: ?, @, and _.

2. May contain only letters, digits, or the three special characters.

3. Cannot be a reserved word.

All characters in an identifier in excess of the first 31 are ignored by the assembler. The underscore is often used to join separate words into a single identifier. **Reserved words** are predefined words that have special meaning in assembly language. Included in the list of reserved words are all the instruction, directive, and register mnemonics. Reserved words cannot be used as variable names.

6.5.2   Arrays and Strings

Elementary data types can be collected or arranged together to create **data structures**. One of the simplest data structures is an **array**. An array consists of related elements that are all of the same type. A specific element in an array is denoted by its index. Its index indicates an element's position in the array. If a byte array containing four elements is given the name array, then the elements in the array are, in order: array[0], array[1], array[2], and array[3]. The following statement allocates storage for the array:

```
array           db ?,?,?,?           ;array is not a reserved word
                                     ;it is merely a convenient identifier
```

A special construct, **DUP**, can be used to allocate an area of memory with a repeated value or repeated list of values. Its form is:

repeatval dup *(val[,...])*

For example, the previous data allocation statement is more concisely written as:

```
array           db 4 dup (?)
```

6.5.3   A Simple Program with a Data Segment

The source file for a program IOAVE.ASM is given in Fig. 6.5-2. This program contains both a code segment and a data segment. The program continuously outputs the average of the last four data values input from a byte port. The computed output is correct only when the average is less than 64, because the sum is stored as an 8-bit value. To compute the running average of the last four input values, these values are stored as variables. The storage locations, dt0, dtm1, dtm2, and dtm3, used for this purpose are allocated in the segment data.

A segment register points to a segment in memory. The assume directive tells the assembler what segment in memory is referenced by a particular segment register. In this case the assembler is told that CS will be loaded with the segment value for (point to) code and that DS will be loaded with the segment value for data. The ASSUME directive only promises the assembler that the segment registers will be loaded with specific values. It does not actually load any values into any registers. Instructions in your program must do this.

When the 80C188EB is reset, a jmp far ptr start bootstrap instruction at physical address FFFF0H loads CS with the segment attribute (segment address) of start, which is code, and

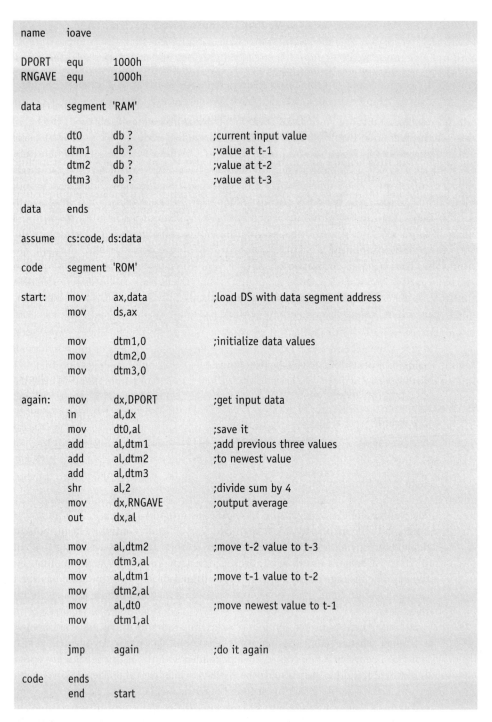

```
name     ioave

DPORT    equ      1000h
RNGAVE   equ      1000h

data     segment  'RAM'

         dt0      db ?            ;current input value
         dtm1     db ?            ;value at t-1
         dtm2     db ?            ;value at t-2
         dtm3     db ?            ;value at t-3

data     ends

assume   cs:code, ds:data

code     segment  'ROM'

start:   mov      ax,data         ;load DS with data segment address
         mov      ds,ax

         mov      dtm1,0          ;initialize data values
         mov      dtm2,0
         mov      dtm3,0

again:   mov      dx,DPORT        ;get input data
         in       al,dx
         mov      dt0,al          ;save it
         add      al,dtm1         ;add previous three values
         add      al,dtm2         ;to newest value
         add      al,dtm3
         shr      al,2            ;divide sum by 4
         mov      dx,RNGAVE       ;output average
         out      dx,al

         mov      al,dtm2         ;move t-2 value to t-3
         mov      dtm3,al
         mov      al,dtm1         ;move t-1 value to t-2
         mov      dtm2,al
         mov      al,dt0          ;move newest value to t-1
         mov      dtm1,al

         jmp      again           ;do it again

code     ends
         end      start
```

Figure 6.5-2   Program with a data segment that computes the running average of the last four values read from input port DPORT and outputs the result to port RNGAVE.

loads IP with the offset of start, which is 0. As a result, the first of the ASSUME's promises, that CS will contain the value of code, is met by execution of the bootstrap instruction.

To keep the second promise, DS must be loaded with the value for data. The first instruction in the program loads AX with the value of data. The next instruction moves this value to DS. The 80C188EB does not allow the destination of a move immediate instruction to be a segment register. Thus, two instructions are required to initialize DS with the constant data. At this point in the program, all segment registers to be used by the program have been properly initialized.

After assembly of this program, the actual segment address value for data is undefined. The segment address for code, which must be placed in the bootstrap instruction, is also undefined. The actual segment address values are specified when the object file is located.

To compute the average value, the three previous values stored in memory, variables dtm1, dtm2, and dtm3, are added to the new input value. However, the initial values of these variables are random. Therefore, they must be initialized the first time through the program. The next three instructions initialize dtm1, dtm2, and dtm3 to zero.

With all initializations complete, the program inputs a data byte from input port DPORT. The three data values dtm1, dtm2, and dtm3, are then added to the value most recently input. The sum of the four values is now in AL. This value must be divided by four to get the average. This division is accomplished by shifting the value in AL two positions to the right. Shifting a binary value right one position is equivalent to dividing it by two. The result is then output to port RNGAVE.

Inputting a new data byte from DPORT, to compute a new average, corresponds to the next sampling time. In preparation for the next sampling time, the existing data must be shifted back one sample time.

The next six move instructions transfer the value in dtm2 to dtm3, the value in dtm1 to dtm2, and the value in dt0 to dtm1. In this process, the oldest of the last four data values, dtm3, is discarded, and the most recent three are retained in preparation for the next computation. The jump instruction then transfers program control to the instruction with the label again, and a new computation begins.

If this program were run at full speed, the input device providing data to port DPORT must be ready with the next input value each time the IN instruction is executed. Running this program on the hardware of Chapter 4, where the input port consists of a set of manual switches and the output port consists of LEDs, would always cause the output to appear to be the same as the last input. This happens because of the rapid speed at which the data is input. However, if the program is run on this same hardware, but single stepped under the control of a debugger, it would be seen that the output is actually the average of the last four input values. If the input port was driven by an 8-bit analog-to-digital converter and the output port was the input to an 8-bit digital-to-analog converter, the system would act as a low pass filter.

6.5.4   Selecting Variable Names

Well-chosen names for variables make a program easier to read, understand, and maintain. A variable's name should be meaningful, clearly indicating what the variable represents in the context of the application. A good variable name is descriptive and easy to remember.

It should be distinctive, so it cannot be easily confused with other variables in the program. Names for different variables should be clearly unique. Names that are similar or differ in only a few characters should be avoided.

With most assemblers, a variable's name can be any length, but only a limited number of characters, usually the first 31, are used by the assembler. Longer names tend to be more descriptive than shorter names. However, they require more typing. Names that are too short usually don't convey enough information. You must make a reasonable comprise with regard to name length.

One way to name a variable is to have the name state in a few concatenated words what the variable represents. For example, a variable that represents the temperature of an engine cylinder might be named:

cylindertemperature

To make names that are constructed from several words more readable, an underscore can be used to separate each word:

cylinder_temperature

Another method of distinguishing between the constituent words is to capitalize the first letter of each:

CylinderTemperature

With this method the distinction is clear in the source file, but this distinction may not be carried over to list files if the assembler is not case sensitive.

The length of variable names can be shortened by various techniques including removing all nonleading vowels. For example:

cylndr_tmprtr

Another approach is to simply truncate each word after a few characters:

cyl_temp

Whatever technique you use to shorten a variable's name, the shortened name should be easy to decipher. If not, another choice of name should be made. For example:

exhaust_gas_temperature

would be shortened to:

exhst_gs_tmprtr

using the first technique, but a better choice is probably:

exhst_gas_temp

Use of a consistent convention to create variable names makes programs easier to read.

Short variable names that consist of standard or conventional abbreviations accepted in a particular field are often appropriate. For example, EGT is the common abbreviation for exhaust gas temperature. However, it is not always appropriate to assume that a reader of your program is familiar with the terminology of the application area.

All variables, and particularly short variable names, should be defined by an appropriate comment when they are allocated. If there are units of measurement associated with the variable, they should be specified in the definition.

```
cyl_temp        db      ?           ;Cylinder temperature (in Fahrenheit)
```

If space is limited, the definition can precede the allocation directive. The two should then be separated from the rest of the text by white space:

```
;Engine cylinder temperature (in degrees Fahrenheit)
cyl_temp        db      ?
```

6.6   Memory Addressing Modes

As previously discussed, a memory address consists of a segment address and an offset address combined as a segment:offset pair. A variable's segment address must be in one of the segment registers before the variable can be accessed. Which segment register the 80C188EB should use to access a variable can be specified explicitly. For example:

```
mov     ds:dtm1,0
```

loads 0 into the variable dtm1 in the segment pointed to by DS. For variables, the default segment register is the Data Segment register, DS. This follows from the fact that variables are usually contained in the data segment. As a result, the previous instruction can be simplified to:

```
mov     dtm1,0
```

In this case, the BIU automatically uses DS in generating the physical address.

It is possible to specify use of a segment register other than the default. This is accomplished by using a segment override in the instruction. Segment overrides are discussed in Section 6.8. For now, it is assumed that all variables are contained in the data segment and that the data segment's address is in DS. If the name of the data segment were data, then the segment address is loaded into DS by the sequence:

```
mov     ax,data
mov     ds,ax
```

The EU must provide a variable's offset to the BIU. The BIU combines the two components of the logical address, the contents of the appropriate segment register and the offset, to create the 20-bit physical address. An instruction usually specifies only the offset, or how it is calculated. The segment value is automatically obtained from the default segment register. The offset is calculated by the EU and is called the effective address. The **effective address** (**EA**) is an unsigned 16-bit number that specifies the distance, in bytes, from the beginning of the segment that contains the operand to the least significant byte of the operand.

There are a number of ways that the EU can compute an effective address. Each way comprises a different memory addressing mode (Table 6.6-1). The memory addressing modes are: direct, register indirect, based, indexed, based indexed, and string. Certain addressing modes are more efficient than others for accessing particular types of data

Table 6.6-1   80C188EB memory operand addressing modes.

Addressing Mode	Operand Located in	Instruction Operand Format[a] (for other register)	Default Segment Register
Direct	memory location pointed to by address contained in instruction	displacement	DS
Register Indirect	memory location pointed to by address contained in specified register	[BX] [BP] [DI] [SI]	DS SS DS DS
Indexed	memory location pointed to by sum of index register and immediate data contained in instruction	displacement[SI] displacement[DI]	DS DS
Based	memory location pointed to by sum of base register and immediate data contained in instruction	displacement [BX] displacement [BP]	DS SS
Based Indexed	memory location pointed to by sum of base register contents and index register contents and possibly immediate data contained in the instruction	displacement[b][BX][SI][c] displacement[BX][DI] displacement[BP][SI] displacement[BP][DI]	DS DS SS SS
String	source is memory location pointed to by register SI and destination is memory location pointed to by register DI	none required[d]	DS (source) ES (destination)

a. Entries in this column also reprsent the components summed to create the effective address.
b. The displacement is optional for based indexed addressing.
c. [BX][SI] is the same as [BX+SI].
d. The offset for the source is contained in SI and the destination offset is contained in DI.

structures. The third column of the table shows how to denote a memory operand using each addressing mode. This column also indicates the components that are summed to create the effective address for each mode.

In general, an effective address is the sum (modulo 2^{16}) of the contents of an instruction's displacement field, a base register, and an index register. Thus:

$$EA = [displacement] + [\ BX \mid BP\ ] + [\ SI \mid DI\ ]$$

The items enclosed in square brackets are optional. A vertical line indicates that only one of the items separated by the vertical line can be chosen. The displacement is either an 8-bit or 16-bit number.

An instruction may sum from one to three of the terms. The assembler determines from an instruction's form which terms are to be added. This information is encoded in the mode field of the second byte of the machine instruction (Fig. 4.1-1). At execution time, the EU examines the instruction's mode field to determine which addressing mode to use, then computes the EA. The time required for the EU to compute the EA is a significant factor in an instruction's execution time.

It is important to realize that these addressing modes can be used in all instructions that reference a memory operand, not just data transfer instructions. This includes instructions that implement logical and arithmetic operations and have a memory location as one operand. Use the Instruction Set Summary in Appendix C to verify that a specific instruction can reference a memory operand.

6.6.1   Direct Addressing

Direct addressing is used to access simple variables. A direct address is simply a variable's offset in its memory segment. The EA is completely contained in the displacement field of the machine instruction. In an assembly language instruction, the operand can simply be a variable name. In such a case, the displacement is the offset attribute of the variable. Variable names used in the following examples are defined in the segment data in Fig. 6.6-1. The third memory byte allocated (offset 2) is not, in the strict sense, a variable because it does not have a name.

```
data    segment
        bvar1  db ?              ;byte variable at offset 0
        bvar2  db?               ;byte variable at offset 1
               db ?              ;byte with no name at offset 2
        wvar1  dw ?              :word variable at offset 3
        wvar2  dw ?              :word variable at offset 5
        array  db 4 dup (?)      ;4 byte array, at offset 7
        help   db 'help'         ;ASCII character sequence, at offset B
        bvar3  db ?              ;byte variable at offset F

data    ends
```

Figure 6.6-1   Allocation of memory for variables in a data segment.

The examples that follow assume DS has been initialized to data.

```
mov     bvar2,cl
mov     bvar2+1,al
mov     dx,wvar1
mov     array[2],6
```

The first instruction copies the contents of register CL to the memory variable bvar2. The second instruction copies the contents of AL to the byte following bvar2. The third instruction copies a word from word variable wvar1 to DX. The last instruction loads 6 into the third element (index 2) of the byte array, array.

The assembler creates a displacement for the first instruction equal to the offset of bvar2. For the second instruction, the assembler generates a displacement one higher than bvar2. In the last instruction, the displacement is equal to the offset of array plus 2.

6.6.2   Register Indirect Addressing

In **register indirect addressing** the contents of a base or index register, BX, BP, SI, or DI, holds the EA. The register used is said to "point to" the target memory location. Using this addressing mode, one instruction in a loop can operate on many different variables if the value in the base or index register is modified appropriately on each pass through the loop. The assembler encodes in a field of the second byte of the machine language instruction which base or index register is to be used.

In assembly language form, the base or index register used is placed in square brackets, [ ]. The assembler interprets a bracketed reference to BX, BP, SI, or DI to mean that the contents of the register is to be used in constructing the operand's address. **When BP is used, the default segment register is SS, not DS.**

Before a register indirect instruction is executed, the register used for indirection must be loaded with the offset of the target memory location. The value returning assembler operator **OFFSET,** is used to obtain the offset of a variable. The following instruction sequence:

```
mov       bx,offset bvar2
mov       [bx],cl
```

copies the contents of CL to bvar2. The first instruction is a move immediate instruction. The constant placed in this instruction by the assembler is the offset of bvar2. When the instruction is executed, the offset of bvar2 is moved into BX. The second instruction moves the contents of CL to the memory location whose offset is in BX (memory location "pointed to" by BX).

Each element in an array named array can be initialized to zero by putting 0 into AL and the OFFSET of array into BX

```
mov       al,0
mov       bx,offset array
```

then including the following instructions in a loop that is executed four times:

```
mov       [bx],al
inc       bx
```

The last two instructions copy the contents of AL to the memory location pointed to by BX, then increment BX to point to the memory location to be written on the next pass through the loop.

It might seem more efficient to replace the above instruction with

```
mov       [bx],0
```

removing the necessity to move a 0 into AL prior to the loop. However, this instruction presents the assembler with a dilemma. This type of memory reference is called an **anonymous**

reference because it contains no variable name from which the assembler can determine a type attribute. Should the assembler create the object code for an instruction that moves 00H to the memory *byte* pointed to by BX, or should it create object code to move 0000H to the memory *word* pointed to by BX? To resolve this dilemma, ASM86 provides the pointer operator, **PTR**, to let you define the type for a memory reference. PTR has the form:

> *type* ptr   *name*

where type is the type being specified. Name can be a variable, label, address expression or integer representing an offset. To write 00H into the byte pointed to by BX, the correct instruction is:

> mov   byte ptr [bx],0

In contrast, to write 0000H to the word pointed to by BX, the instruction is:

> mov   word ptr [bx],0

In addition to the OFFSET and PTR operators, the assembler has several other operators used with operands, Table 6.6-2. Most operators, like OFFSET, return one of the attribute values of a variable or a label. Others, like PTR, override an attribute of a variable or a label for a particular reference. These operators are explained further as the need arises.

Table 6.6-2   Some ASM86 assembler attribute operators.

	Operation	Operator	Syntax[a]	Result
Value Returning	segment	SEG	SEG varlab	segment address
	offset	OFFSET	OFFSET varlab	offset address
	type	TYPE	TYPE varlab	number of bytes
	size	SIZE	SIZE varlab	total number of bytes[b]
	length	LENGTH	LENGTH varlab	number of data units
Overriding	pointer	PTR	type PTR name	specify type
	short	SHORT	SHORT label	specify distance
	segment override	CS	CS:varlab	use segment register CS
	segment override	DS	DS:varlab	use segment register DS
	segment override	SS	SS:varlab	use segment register SS
	segment override	ES	ES:varlab	use segment register ES

a. varlab = variable or label
b. SIZE = LENGTH * TYPE

6.6.3   Indexed Addressing

The EA for **indexed addressing** is the sum of a displacement and the contents of either index register, SI or DI. The assembly language instruction has either SI or DI, in brackets, along with the displacement. The displacement may be written as a variable name, a number, or both. The concatenation of a variable name and/or a number and a register in brackets implies addition. The assembler puts the sum of the variable's offset and the number, if one is specified, in the instructions's displacement field. The number specified can be a signed 8- or 16-bit value. When executing the instruction, the 80C188EB adds the contents of the register to the displacement contained in the instruction to get the operand's offset. Indexed addressing is often used to address elements in an array.

The following instructions copy the contents of DL to the third element of a byte array:

```
mov      si,2
mov      array[si],dl                    ;location (ARRAY + 2) <- contents of DL
```

Since every element in an array is composed of the same number of bytes, simple arithmetic operations on the contents of an index register can provide access to any array element. When an index is altered for an array of word elements, it must be altered by 2 for consecutive elements. Though indexed addressing typically uses SI or DI, BX or BP can also be used.

6.6.4   Based Addressing

In **based addressing,** the EA is the sum of a displacement and the contents of either base register BX or BP. Though based addressing typically uses BX or BP, SI or DI can also be used. When BP is specified, the default segment register is SS, not DS. Using BP is a convenient way to access data on the stack, and this technique is discussed in Chapter 8. An assembly language instruction using based addressing has BX or BP in brackets along with a displacement. Some examples follow.

```
;Copy the contents of AL to the byte with offset 2 from DATA
        mov      bx,1
        mov      bvar2[bx],al

;Another way to accomplish the same thing
        mov      bx,offset bvar2
        mov      [bx]+1,al
```

Based addressing may at first seem identical to indexed addressing, except that BX or BP is used instead of SI or DI. However, there is an important difference in how these addressing modes are typically used when working with arrays and structures.

Indexed addressing is typically used to access elements of an array. The instruction's displacement (the array's name) corresponds to the offset from the start of the segment to the start of the array. SI or DI, holds the distance from the start of the array to the specific element (the index of a specific array element). SI or DI is modified to select different elements in the array. The displacement remains fixed (Fig. 6.6-2(a)).

A structure is a collection of related variables of different types. Based addressing is often used to access an element in a structure. BX or BP holds the offset from the start of the segment to the structure. The displacement corresponds to the fixed distance from the start of the structure to a particular element (Fig. 6.6-2(b)). To reference the same element in a different copy of the structure, BX or BP is modified to select the desired copy, and the displacement (structure element's name) remains fixed. Structures are discussed further in Section 6.7.

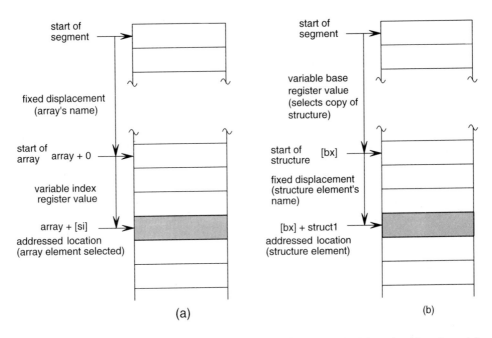

Figure 6.6-2   The difference between indexed addressing and based addressing: (a) indexed addressing of an element in an array; (b) based addressing of an element in a structure.

6.6.5   Based Indexed Addressing

Based indexed addressing sums an optional displacement with the contents of a base register and an index register to produce the EA. If the instruction specifies BP as the base register, the default segment register is SS.

6.6.6   String Addressing

A **string** is a data structure consisting of a sequence of elements. These elements are often the codes for human-readable characters. String instructions can be used to transfer data between two memory locations, the accumulator and a memory location, or a port and a memory location. String addressing differs considerably from the previous memory addressing modes. **String addressing** uses DS as the default segment register for a source memory location and SI to hold the source's offset. ES is used as the segment register for a destination memory location and DI holds the destination's offset. Assuming DS and ES have both been loaded with the same segment address, data, the following instructions copy the first byte of help to the first byte of array (Fig. 6.6-1).

```
mov    si,offset help
mov    di,offset array
movs   array,help
```

Move string (**MOVS**), like the other string instructions, is a generic primitive. Operands are used only to indicate to the assembler whether a byte or word is to be moved. The assembler uses the operands' types to determine whether to assemble an instruction that transfers a byte or a word. The source address is always DS:SI and the destination address is always ES:DI. In the MOVS instruction above, the assembler can tell from the type of array (or help) that a byte transfer is required. The MOVS primitive only transfers a single byte, the first byte of the array help.

An alternate way of specifying whether a byte or word is to be moved is to use a B or W suffix with MOVS, giving MOVSB or MOVSW respectively. When a suffix is used, no operands are allowed.

```
mov     si,offset help
mov     di,offset array
movsb
```

While a MOVS instruction can transfer data from one memory location to another, each data byte transferred actually requires two bus cycles. The first bus cycle transfers a byte from the source memory location to a temporary register in the 80C188EB. This temporary register is not one of the registers shown in the programmer's model of the 80C188EB, so no data in an 80C188EB register is destroyed. The second cycle transfers the byte from the 80C188EB's temporary register to the destination memory location. Thus, each transfer of a byte during a bus cycle always involves one internal (80C188EB) register as either the source or the destination.

Load string (**LODS**) transfers a byte or word addressed by DS:SI to either register AL or AX. *Store string* (**STOS**) transfers a byte or word from either AL or AX to the location addressed by ES:DI.

The in string (INS) and out string (OUTS) instructions were introduced in Section 6.2. INS transfers data from the input port pointed to by DX to the memory byte or word pointed to by ES:DI. OUTS transfers data from the memory byte or word pointed to by DS:SI to the output port pointed to by DX.

Execution of a string primitive automatically increments or decrements SI and/or DI after the byte or word is transferred. If the direction flag, DF, is 0, the index registers are incremented. If DF is 1, they are decremented. If a byte were transferred, the increment or decrement is by one. If a word were transferred, the index register(s) would be incremented or decremented by two. This makes looping to reference subsequent bytes or words convenient. The real power of string addressing is realized when string primitives are used with a repeat prefix (REP) to cause string operations to repeat. Using REP makes it convenient to copy all elements of a string from one place in memory to another, to input a string to memory, or to output a string to a port. Repeated string operations are discussed in Section 7.8.

6.7   Structures

A **structure** is a collection of related data items each with its own name and type. Structures are useful when it is desirable to associate data in logical groups. A **structure tem-**

plate names each data item and specifies its type and position in the structure. A **STRUC/ENDS** directive pair is used to define a structure's template.

Data allocation directives are used inside the STRUC/ENDS pair to define the structure's data items. However, when used inside STRUC/ENDS, data allocation directives do not actually allocate any storage.

For example, if a collection of weather variables are of interest, the following structure template could be defined:

```
weather struc
      temp db ?
      humidity db ?
      pressure dw ?
      wnd_spd db ?
weather ends
```

This structure template has four fields. Three are bytes and one is a word. The data allocation directives within STRUC/ENDS do not allocate any memory; they simply define the offset and type for each field name. A field name defined in a structure definition has no segment attribute and its offset attribute is measured from the start of the structure, not the start of a segment. The type of each field is as specified by its data allocation directive.

The definition of the weather data structure defines a new data type called weather with a type attribute equal to the total number of bytes in the definition. The size of a structure is also equal to the total number of bytes in the structure. Since a structure represents a single data item, its length, as indicated by the LENGTH operator, is always equal to one.

After a structure is defined, it is still necessary to allocate memory for any instance of the structure. One method of actually allocating storage is to define a variable with a number of bytes equal to the total number of bytes in the structure. Memory can be allocated for two structures to store the high and low values of the weather variables as follows:

```
high_val        db 5 dup(?)
low_val         db 5 dup(?)
```

When memory is actually allocated for a structure, the name of the structure is a variable whose segment attribute is the current segment, and whose offset is the distance from the beginning of the segment in which it is allocated to the start of the structure.

An alternate method of accomplishing the previous memory allocation uses the name of the data structure:

```
high_val        weather <>
low_val         weather <>
```

In this case, the assembler uses the type attribute of the previously defined structure, weather, to determine the number of bytes to allocate to high_val and to low_val.

It is possible to indicate an initial value for fields in the structure template. These initial values can sometimes be overridden during the allocation. The override values are placed inside the angle brackets. However, as was the case with variables, we will not initialize structure fields during allocation of memory for the structure. The empty angle brackets above indicate that no initialization values are to be overridden. Angle brackets are required when the allocation uses the structure name even if no fields are initialized.

The instructions:

```
mov     high_val.temp,92
mov     low_val.temp,34
```

set the variable temp in the data structure high_val to 92 degrees and set temp in the data structure low_val to 34 degrees. In the first instruction, high_val selects the structure and temp selects the field within the structure. Direct addressing is used here to access the memory location. For memory addressing, the **period operator** "." is just another form of the plus operator. The instruction's displacement, generated by the assembler, is the sum of the offset of high_val and the offset of temp. Use of the period operator makes clear that a structure field is being accessed.

An alternate instruction sequence that accomplishes the previous assignments using based addressing is:

```
mov     bx,offset high_val
mov     [bx].temp,92
mov     bx,offset low_val
mov     [bx].temp,34
```

Arrays and structures can be combined to create even more complex data structures. Each element in an array can be a structure, or one or more elements in a structure can be an array. For example, assume that 240 measurements of the weather variables are to be made over a 24 hour period and saved. An array of structures, meas, could be created where each element in the array is a structure that follows the weather structure template. The statement to allocate memory for the array of structures is:

```
meas     weather 240 dup(<>)
```

If the measured values were read from ports, the following sequence of instructions would load a set of measured values into an array element, a structure in this case. Assume that DI points to the element (structure) to be loaded.

```
in      al,m_temp
mov     meas[di].temp,al
in      al,m_hum
mov     meas[di].humidity,al
in      ax,m_press
mov     meas[di].pressure,ax
in      al,m_wnd_spd
mov     meas[di].wnd_spd,al
add     di,type meas
```

The last instruction uses the TYPE attribute operator to add 5 to DI. This sequence of instructions could be placed inside a loop that is executed each time a set of measurements is made.

With STRUC/ENDS it is easy to create a structure. The structure definition provides data typing for fields within the structure and is easy to change if it becomes necessary to change the size of a field.

6.8   Addressability and Segment Overrides

For an instruction to reference a variable, the variable must be addressable. A variable is **addressable** only if its segment address is in an appropriate segment register. Instructions in your program must load a segment register with an operand's segment address before any references are made to the operand.

When assembling a source file, the assembler generates object code for a single segment at a time. Within a given segment, the assembler only needs to keep track of the offset of an object, regardless of whether the object is code or data.

You use the ASSUME directive to tell the assembler which segment's address will be in each of the segment registers at run time. The ASSUME serves several purposes. First, it reminds you what will be addressable at run time. Second, it provides the assembler with information it needs to check whether the code or data referenced is addressable. And, third, it provides information the assembler needs to automatically insert a segment override if a variable's segment address is not in the default segment register but is in one of the alternate segment registers.

The assembler checks each memory reference for addressability based on information in an ASSUME directive. Remember, ASSUME itself does not load any segment registers; they must be loaded by instructions in your program. The assembler determines the segment attributes of all variables and labels in your program. When checking for addressability, the assembler checks whether an ASSUME states that the variable's segment address will be in one of the segment registers.

If an ASSUME states that the variable's segment address will be in the default segment register for the type of memory reference, then everything is fine. If not, the assembler checks whether an ASSUME promises that the variable's segment address will be in one of the allowed alternate segment registers (Table 3.5-1). If the segment address is promised to be in one of the alternate segment registers, the assembler inserts a segment override byte in the object code immediately preceding the memory reference instruction. The **segment override** byte tells the 80C188EB to form the physical address using the segment register specified by the override byte, rather than the default segment register.

If no ASSUME statement promises the variable's segment address is in either the default or one of the alternate segment registers, then the variable is unaddressable and the assembler generates an error.

6.9   Allocating ROM for Data Constants

A constant value can be transferred to a register using immediate addressing, as discussed in Section 6.4. The constant value is contained in one or two bytes of the immediate instruction. But, named data items of constant value are also needed during a program's execution, and these are called **constants**. Two common uses of constants are to provide strings of constant data and tables of constant data.

Data allocation directives with initial values are used to specify the constants. These directives are placed in the code segment of a program, not the data segment. The locator is used to place the code segment in ROM. The following data allocation directives define constants in a code segment.

```
DIGITS          db 0,1,2,3,4,5,6,7,8,9
MODE            db 4
LIMITS          dw 100, 2345h
CHECKER         db      5 dup (55h,0aah)
```

These directives allocate 25 bytes of memory. The first directive allocates 10 bytes, with the first byte equal to 0, the second to 1, and so on. DIGITS is the name of the first byte. Assuming the data allocation directives above are placed at the very beginning of the code segment, the offset of DIGITS is 0. DIGITS is also the name of the 10 element array containing digits 0 through 9. MODE is a byte with the value four. The offset of MODE is 10. LIMITS is a word array with element values 100 and 2345H. The last directive allocates a ten byte array, named CHECKER, with the elements in the array alternating between 55H and AAH.

6.9.1   String Constants

An ASCII string of alphanumeric characters can be allocated and initialized using the DB directive with the character string in single quotes. DB is the only data allocation directive that can be used to initialize bytes to ASCII values. For example, the message "system ready" is stored as the string SIGNON, by the following directive:

```
SIGNON          db 'system ready'
```

This directive allocates 12 bytes. The ASCII representation for the letter "s" is 73H and is stored in location SIGNON. The ASCII representation for "y" is 79H and is stored in location SIGNON + 1, and so on.

Instructions that transfer an ASCII string from one place in memory to another or between memory and an I/O port, need to determine where the string ends. One way to accomplish this is to terminate the string with a **termination character** that would not normally appear in a string. A commonly used termination character is the ASCII null character, 00H. Strings terminated in this fashion are called **ASCIIZ strings**. The previous string can be formed as an ASCIIZ string as follows:

```
SIGNON          db 'system ready', 00h
```

A program that transfers bytes from SIGNON can check each byte transferred to see if it is equal to 00H. As soon as this is the case, the transfer is complete.

6.9.2   Constant Tables and Table Lookup

Tables are used extensively when it is easier to look up rather than compute the value of a function. The program in Fig. 6.9-1 uses a **table lookup** technique to convert a BCD digit to the pattern required to display the digit on a seven-segment LED display. Individual segments of the display are controlled by bits of the output port to which the display is connected. This program can be used to replace the hardware function of the 74LS47s in Fig. 4.3-1 by an equivalent software function. This is another example of the common occurrence of trading off hardware for software. The cost of this tradeoff is slower operation.

The table contains constants placed in ROM in the final system. For this reason, the table is defined in the segment CODE. When assembling the instruction,

```
mov       al,lkup_tbl[si]
```

the assembler knows that lkup_tbl has the segment attribute code. Since lkup_tbl is not in the segment pointed to by DS, the assembler knows it must generate a segment override byte. In Fig. 6.9-1, the first byte of this instruction's object code, 2E, is the segment override byte. This byte tells the 80C188EB to use CS to calculate the physical address of the source rather than the default segment register, DS. The segment override byte is an instruction prefix. An **instruction prefix** alters the operation of the instruction it precedes. It is not a separate instruction and effects only the instruction that it immediately precedes.

```
 1                                name bcdsvn
 2
 3         =3000                   bcd   equ   3000h
 4         =3000                   leds  equ   3000h
 5
 6                                 assume  cs:code
 7
 8  0000                           code  segment
 9                                       ;define table entries
10  0000 01 4F 12 06 4C 24 60+ lkup_tbl   db   01h,4fh,12h,06h,4ch,24h,60h,0fh,00h,0ch
11        0F 00 0C
12  000A BA 3000                   start: mov  dx,bcd    ;get bcd code
13  000D EC                               in   al,dx
14  000E B4 00                             mov  ah,0  ;zero AH
15  0010 8B F0                             mov  si,ax  ;use bcd code as index into table
16  0012 2E: 8A 840000r                    mov  al,lkup_tbl[si] ;get table entry
17  0017 BA 3000                           mov  dx,leds
18  001A EE                                out  dx,al    ;output pattern to seven segment LED
19  001B EB ED                             jmp  start
20  001D                           code  ends
21                                       end  start
```

Figure 6.9-1   List file for a table lookup program for BCD to seven segment conversion.

A segment override can be explicitly specified. For example, the instruction:

```
mov       al,[bx]
```

causes a physical address to be calculated using the contents of DS for the segment address and the contents of BX for the offset. DS is used by default for this addressing mode. But if the location to be referenced were in the segment pointed to by ES, instead of by DS (the value placed in BX is the offset of the memory location from ES), the override of the default segment would have to be specified explicitly:

```
mov     al,es:[bx]
```

Explicit specification of the segment override is necessary because there is no variable name in the instruction,

```
mov     al,[bx]
```

so, the assembler is unable to check for addressability or automatically determine that a segment override is needed.

You can use an explicit segment override prefix to make most memory reference instructions access any segment you chose. Any alternate segment register allowable for the type of memory reference (Table 3.5-1) can be specified by the segment override.

Table Lookup using XLAT

Table lookup operations are so common that an instruction *translate_table* (**XLAT**) is provided for this specific purpose. To use XLAT, the table's base address is placed in BX and the desired entry's table index is placed in AL. When XLAT is executed, it adds the contents of AL to BX and uses the result as the effective address of the table entry. The byte at this address is copied into AL and BX is left unchanged. Since a byte register, AL, originally holds the index into the table, the table's length is limited to 256 bytes. A version of the BCD to seven-segment program using XLAT is given in Fig. 6.9-2.

6.10 Address Object Transfers

Three instructions are specifically for transferring address pointers to registers (Table 6.10-1). These address object instructions each transfer the address of a variable, rather than the value of the variable. LEA is used to transfer a 16-bit pointer prior to accessing a memory location in a current segment. LDS and LES are used to transfer 32-bit pointers from memory to the 80C188EB prior to accessing memory locations not in a current segment.

The *load effective address* (**LEA**) instruction transfers the effective address of its source operand to a 16-bit general register. This instruction is useful for setting up a pointer register for register indirect addressing. In previous examples, the OFFSET operator has been used to load a register with a memory location's offset. However, the OFFSET operator can only provide the offset of a simple variable, or an offset that is a constant displacement from a simple variable. OFFSET will not work for a case like:

```
mov     bx, offset subtable[si]              ;invalid operation
```

because the desired offset is a function of the contents of SI, which is not known at assembly time. However,

```
lea     bx,subtable[si]
```

```
 1                         name    xbcdsvn
 2
 3      =3000              bcd     equ     3000h
 4      =3000              leds    equ     3000h
 5
 6                         assume  cs:code
 7
 8   0000                  code    segment
 9                                 ;define table entries
10   0000  01 4F 12 06 4C 2460+  lkup_tbl  db    01h,4fh,12h,06h,4ch,24h,60h,0fh,00h,0ch
11   0F 00 0C
12   000A  BB 0000r  start:  mov     bx,offset lkup_tbl    ;BX points to base of table
13   000D  BA 3000   again:  mov     dx,bcd
14   0010  EC                in      al,dx              ;get bcd code
15   0011  2E: D7            xlat    lkup_tbl           ;lookup table entry
16   0013  BA 3000           mov     dx,leds
17   0016  EE               out     dx,al              ;output pattern to seven segment LED
18   0017  EB F4            jmp     again
19   0019            code    ends
20                          end     start
```

Figure 6.9-2   List file for a table lookup program using XLAT instruction.

Table 6.10-1   Address object transfer instructions.[a]

Mnemonic	Operands	Function
LEA	dst,src	load effective address
LDS	dst,src	load double word pointer using DS
LES	dst,src	load double word pointer using ES

a. No flags are modified by the execution of these instructions.

gives the correct offset, which is the sum of the offset of subtable and the contents of SI. LEA computes the source operand's effective address at run time and loads it into the destination.

Since LEA carries out an addition to compute an effective address, it can also be used as an arithmetic instruction. Using based indexed addressing, three values can be summed by a single LEA instruction. For example,

```
lea     ax, [bx][si]43
```

sums the contents of the registers BX and SI and the constant 43 and leaves the result in AX. Accomplishing the equivalent task requires three instructions.

The instruction *load pointer using DS* (**LDS**) transfers a 32-bit pointer from a double word in memory. The low word of the double word, the offset address, is transferred to the destination register, which must be a 16-bit general register. The high word, the segment address, is transferred to DS. *Load pointer using ES* (**LES**) is similar in operation, except the high word is transferred to ES.

Since string instructions assume that the source and destination strings are in the current DS and ES segments respectively, LDS and LES are useful for setting up 32-bit pointers to strings in segments other than those currently pointed to by DS and ES. When this situation occurs, the destination specified for LDS is SI and for LES is DI. For example, assume that srcarray and dstarray are each double words in memory allocated as:

```
srcarray          dd ?
dstarray          dd ?
```

and memory location srcarray has been loaded with a 32-bit pointer to the starting address of an array and dstarray has been loaded with a 32-bit pointer to the starting address of a second array, then execution of the instruction sequence:

```
lds       si,srcarray
les       di,dstarray
movsb
```

loads the pointers and transfers the first byte of the first array to the first byte of the second array.

6.11   80C186EB Data Transfer Considerations

The preceding discussions of data transfers apply equally well to programs written for the 80C186EB. Any program written for an 80C188EB will execute properly on an 80C186EB. However, the speed at which a program executes on an 80C186EB can be improved if it is written to take advantage of the 80C186EB's 16-bit data bus.

To take advantage of the 80C186EB's 16-bit data bus, the alignment of data in a data segment must be considered. The 80C186EB can transfer an entire word in a single bus cycle but only if the word is aligned. Otherwise, two bus cycles are required. An aligned word is a word stored in memory starting at an even address. Transfer of an unaligned word takes the 80C186EB two bus cycles. The reason for this is discussed in Chapter 11. However, knowing this is the case, word data should be aligned in programs written for an 80C186EB.

An **EVEN** directive placed in front of a data allocation statement for words forces the words to be aligned. For example, the following allocation,

```
                  even
word_array        dw        100 dup (?)
```

in a data segment forces word_array to start at an even address, regardless of any allocations that may precede it in the segment. If necessary, the assembler inserts a NOP (90H) in front of word_array to force its starting address to be even.

6.12   Summary

The 80C188EB's instruction set provides numerous data transfer instructions. With these instructions, you can accomplish the fundamental operation of data transfer between an I/O port and the 80C188EB, between an I/O port and a memory location, between 80C188EB registers, between a memory location and a register, and between two memory locations. Proper choice of the instruction to use for a particular transfer lets you create the most efficient program. This efficiency can be in terms of program length, program speed, or both.

Your program must allocate memory locations for variables and constants. Data allocation directives are used to allocate memory for data items that are bytes, words, double words, arrays, structures, or records. Records are discussed in the next chapter.

Variables are normally allocated in a data segment pointed to by DS. In embedded systems, the initial values of these variables are not specified. If a variable must have an initial value, then this value must be initialized by an instruction in your program. To allow the values of variables to be modified, the data segment containing variables must be placed in RAM when the program is located.

Instructions that transfer data to or from a memory location can use any one of several addressing modes to form the memory location's address. These memory addressing modes are: direct, register indirect, indexed, based, based indexed and string.

Constants are normally allocated in a code segment pointed to by CS. The initial value of a constant is specified in the data allocation directive that reserves memory for the constant.

With an understanding of the data transfer instructions presented in this chapter, you will be able to write programs that efficiently transfer data. Using the data allocation directives, you will be able to write programs that efficiently provide storage for variables and constants. Now you have the ability to program two of a system's fundamental operations, data storage and data transfer. Chapters 7 and 9 present instructions that will allow you to accomplish the third fundamental operation, data transformation.

6.13   Problems

1. List all the source to destination transfers possible in an 80C188EB system in terms of the following operands: immediate data, register, memory location, input port, and output port.

2. What is the difference between a logical address and a physical address? Where are logical addresses used and where are physical addresses used? How and when is a logical address translated to a physical address?

3. What is an addressing mode? Do both registers in a data transfer instruction have an address?

4. Name the 80C188EB addressing modes available for accessing ports in isolated I/O space. What range of physical addresses is appropriate for each of these addressing modes? What are the constraints on the destinations for input transfers and on the sources for output transfers?

5. Write an instruction, or short sequence of instructions, that performs each of the following data transfers:

 a. Output AL to the byte port LEDS. Assume LEDS has been equated to 10H.

 b. Output AX to the word port LEDS. Assume LEDS has been equated to 10H.

 c. Output AL to the byte port LEDS. Assume LEDS has been equated to 1000H.

 d. Output AX to the word port LEDS. Assume LEDS has been equated to 1000H.

6. Assume that I_PORT has been equated to 2000H and 0_PORT has also been equated to 2000H. For each sequence below, initially AX = 2C0AH, BX = 45B7H, and the contents of I_PORT is 73D1H. In each case, specify the contents of AX, BX, input port registers 2000H and 2001H and output port registers 2000H and 2001H after execution of the instruction sequence.

 a. mov   dx,I_PORT
    in   ax,dx
 b. mov   dx,I_PORT
    in   al,dx
 c. mov   dx,0_PORT
    out   dx,al
 d. mov   dx,0_PORT
    out   dx,ax
 e. mov   dx,0_PORT
    mov   al,bl
    out   dx,ax

7. Given a word port in I/O space with the name WPORT and the statement WPORT EQU 80H, write example instruction sequences, using every possible I/O port addressing mode to implement an input operation from this port. Give the name of each addressing mode along with its example. List one advantage for the use of each addressing mode.

8. Write an example instruction sequence that uses the OUTSB instruction to transfer a word from memory location control_wd to port CNTRL_PORT.

9. For each of the following instructions assume the initial register contents are: AX = 10C2H, BX = 5AB4H, CX = C176H, DX = 99A0H, and SI = 49ADH. Give the contents of each register that has data transferred to it by the instruction or sequence of instructions:

 a. mov   cx,bx
 b. xchg   dx,cx
 c. mov   si,ax
 d. mov   bx,ax
    mov   ax,bx

10. Write an instruction, or short sequence of instructions, that performs each of the following data transfers. Assume that each port's name has be equated to an address less than 100H.

 a. Output to byte port CONTROL the contents of register BH.

b. Input to AH from the port pointed to by DX.

c. Input from word port LEVEL to CX.

d. Output CL to the byte port pointed to by DX.

e. Input the contents of word port SETPOINT to AX.

11. For each of the following cases, write an instruction that uses immediate addressing to load the constant specified in decimal using the base specified.

a. load CX with 65,535 specified in hexadecimal.

b. load BL with 139 specified in binary.

c. load AH with 241 specified in octal.

d. load DX with 39,904 specified in decimal.

12. Specify the value transferred to the destination register by each of the following instructions.

a. mov   cl,27 shr 2
b. mov   cx,237h + 0A2Bh
c. mov   al,27 mod 4
d. mov   bx,not 01100101b

13. Create a data segment called data that allocates memory for all the following variables: a byte variable key, a word variable TOTAL, an array meas consisting of eight words, and a double-word variable pointer. All these variables are to be uninitialized.

14. In a system that does not have an operating system, why aren't variables allocated with initial values?

15. What type of data objects would be allocated with initial values in a system without an operating system? In which segment would these objects be allocated?

16. List the three attributes of each of the following variables.

```
data      segment
abc             db ?
xyz             db ?
result          dw ?
buff            db 8 dup (?)
lngptr          dd ?
omega           db ?
data ends
```

17. For the following data segment:

```
data      segment
          x       db ?
          y       db ?
          z       dw ?
          line    db 20 dup (?)
          max     dw ?
          min     dw ?
data ends
```

list the three attributes of each of the variables.

18. List the attributes of each of the following variables.

```
data segment
        alpha      dw 4 dup (?)
        bravo      db ?
        charlie    db 2 dup (?)
        delta      dw 3 dup (?)
        echo              db ?
    data ends
```

19. Write the general formula that expresses the possible constituents of an 80C188EB effective address (EA) for memory accesses. List the names of all of the memory addressing modes and for each mode specify the particular formula for EA that applies.

20. Write an instruction, or sequence of as few instructions as possible, that perform the following data transfers using the addressing mode specified. The variables are as defined in problem 17.

    a. Transfer a byte from CL to X using direct addressing.

    b. Transfer a byte from AH to the second byte in the array line using direct addressing.

    c. Transfer a word from max to min using direct addressing.

    d. Transfer a word from DX to max by register indirect addressing using BX.

    e. Transfer the constant 45 to Y by register indirect addressing using SI.

21. Write a single instruction, or as few instructions as necessary, to carry out the following specified data transfers. If an addressing mode is specified, use that mode.

    a. CL to bravo using register indirect addressing.

    b. echo to bravo using direct addressing.

    c. move AL to charlie and AH to charlie + 1 using direct addressing.

    d. fill the array delta with a value that is twice the offset of echo. Use the LOOP instruction.

    e. data from the word port INDATA to the third element in the array alpha.

22. Given the following register contents:

    CS = FF00H   AX = 3487H   SP = 0400H   IP = 045CH
    DS = 1000H   BX = CD01H   BP = 3089H
    ES = 8000H   CX = 1111H   SI = EEC0H
    SS = A000H   DX = 5A5AH   DI = 7788H

    for each of the following instructions, specify the physical memory location(s) written or read, the number of bytes of data transferred, and the memory addressing mode used. If the instruction is not a legitimate instruction so indicate.

    a. mov bx,cx

    b. mov byte ptr [bx],dl

    c. mov [bx][di][7],al

    d. mov dx,[bp]+4

    e. mov word ptr [di],4

23. Given the following register contents:

$$CS = 0000H \quad AX = 238CH \quad SP = 4000H \quad IP = 0311H$$
$$DS = 1000H \quad BX = 0004H \quad BP = 0700H$$
$$ES = 2000H \quad CX = 10F0H \quad SI = 0007H$$
$$SS = 3000H \quad DX = 55AAH \quad DI = 001FH$$

and data allocation:

```
data      segment
          x1      dw ?
          buff    db 8 dup (?)
          segptr  dd ?
          temp            db ?
          rec             db 80 dup(?)
data      ends
```

for each of the instructions below, specify the effective address, the physical memory location referenced, the number of bytes of data transferred, and the addressing mode used. If the instruction specified is not a legitimate instruction so indicate.

    a. mov ax,buff[si]

    b. mov cx,segptr+2

    c. mov [bp],x1

    d. mov cl,bl

    e. mov rec[bx][di],dx

24. A system has eight contiguous input ports and eight contiguous output ports. All the ports are byte ports. Write a complete ASM86 program that reads the input ports in sequence and transfers the data read to an array in memory called inbuff. The program then outputs the data in the array to the output ports. This sequence is to repeat indefinitely. The address of the first of the eight input ports is 40H and the address of the first of the eight output ports is 10H. Use as few instructions as possible.

25. Why does a memory to memory transfer implemented by a single string instruction, not violate the constraint that, at the physical level, an 80C188EB register is involved in every data transfer?

26. The function $Y = X^2 - X$ is to be determined by a table lookup, where X is the index into the table and Y is the value of the table entry for an index of X. Assume that X is always less than or equal to 10.

    a. List the value of the table entry for each index value.

    b. Write a **complete program** to continuously input a byte from port X, compute the function $Y = X^2 - X$, and output the result to port Y. Write this program as an

ASM86 program using a table lookup to "compute" Y. The addresses of both ports X and Y are 1000H.

27. Write a program that inputs a binary value n which ranges from 0 to 7 and outputs 2^n in binary. The output value is to be generated using a table lookup. The binary input n is obtained from bits 2 – 0 of byte port EXP and the result is to be output to byte port NUM. Both ports are in the isolated I/O space and both have the address 00H. The program is to repeat indefinitely.

BIT MANIPULATION, BRANCHING, AND LOOPING

7.1   Flags Register

7.2   Logical Instructions

7.3   Shifts and Rotates

7.4   Unconditional Jumps

7.5   Conditional Jumps

7.6   Looping and Iteration Control

7.7   Conditional Task Execution

7.8   Repeated String Instructions

7.9   Records

7.10   Summary

The simple programs presented in Chapter 4 consisted of a collection of tasks that are executed in sequence. The sequential execution of these tasks continued indefinitely.

More complex programs also consist of a collection of tasks. However, these programs cannot effectively accomplish their overall functions by executing the same sequence of tasks over and over. A complex program must be capable of determining, based on input data values, the results of prior logical or arithmetic operations, or external events, which task to perform next. This decision making capability allows a program to execute each task as needed. Without this capability, any program is limited to repeatedly executing exactly the same sequence of tasks.

Conditional jump instructions allow a program to change its execution flow based on the state, set or clear, of one or more status flags. By changing its execution flow, a program controls which task is executed next. The status flags are bits in the 80C188EB's Flags register. These status flag bits are set or cleared automatically to reflect characteristics of the result produced by a logical or arithmetic instruction.

Logical instructions manipulate data bits. Characteristics of the results produced by logical instructions are recorded in the 80C188EB's flags register. Using logical instructions in your program, you can set or clear status flags to indicate the occurrence of a particular input data value or external event. Conditional jump instructions are then used to test these flag bits and, based on the test results, possibly change the execution flow of the program, determining which task is executed next.

By changing the execution flow back to a previous instruction, a program loop can be constructed. This loop repeats the same task multiple times. By altering one or more parameters each time through the loop, substantial processing capability is achieved. A loop can be exited after a predetermined number of iterations or after a specific event occurs.

This chapter describes the flags register and the logical instructions that can cause its status bits to be set or cleared. Conditional jump instructions that alter execution flow, based on the states of the flags, are then presented. Techniques for using these instructions to provide looping and for conditional task execution are also described. Using these techniques you will be able to create powerful programs.

7.1 Flags Register

In general a **flag** is a marker used to indicate or record a condition. We will encounter different types of flags in the various subsystems of an embedded system. The flags of interest here are bits in the 80C188EB's **Processor Status Word**, PSW (Fig. 7.1-1). PSW is a 16-bit register located in the EU. This register is also known as the **Flags, F**, register.

The Flags register contains both status and control flags. The six **status flags, AF, CF, OF, PF, SF**, and **ZF**, indicate specific characteristics of the result produced by a logical or arithmetic operation. The three **control flags, DF, IF**, and **TF**, control or alter the 80C188EB's mode of operation. The remaining seven Flags register bits are not used.

The purpose of the control flag, DF, and the instructions that set and clear it are covered in Section 7.8. Control flags IF and TF are covered in Chapter 14. Only the status flags are of interest here.

Conditional jump instructions can alter a program's execution flow based on the states, set (flag = 1) or cleared (flag = 0), of specific status flags. The states of these status flags are, in turn, the direct or indirect result of a previous instruction's execution. Some instructions affect the flags, others do not. An instruction's effect, if any, on each status flag depends on the specific instruction and its operands. The data transfer instructions of Chapter 6 have no effect on any of the flags. In contrast, logical or arithmetic instructions alter the flags to reflect various properties of the result they produce. The status flags not only indicate characteristics of the result, but provide information about relationships between the instruction's operand values.

All status flags can be modified indirectly, as a side effect of the execution of various instructions. The **carry flag** (CF) is the only status flag that can be directly set or cleared. The *set carry* (**STC**) and *clear carry* (**CLC**) instructions accomplish these purposes (Table 7.1-1). The flag columns on the right side of Table 7.1-1 indicate how each flag is affected. CF can also be complemented (toggled) by the *complement carry flag* (**CMC**) instruction.

Immediately after the 80C188EB is reset, the Flags register has the value F000H.

Register Name: Processor Status Word
Register Mnemonic: PSW (FLAGS)
Register Function: Posts CPU status information.

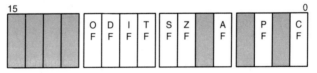

A1035-0A

Bit Mnemonic	Bit Name	Reset State	Function
OF	Overflow Flag	0	If OF is set, an arithmetic overflow has occurred.
DF	Direction Flag	0	If DF is set, string instructions are processed high address to low address. If DF is clear, strings are processed low address to high address.
IF	Interrupt Enable Flag	0	If IF is set, the CPU recognizes maskable interrupt requests. If IF is clear, maskable interrupts are ignored.
TF	Trap Flag	0	If TF is set, the processor enters single-step mode.
SF	Sign Flag	0	If SF is set, the high-order bit of the result of an operation is 1, indicating it is negative.
ZF	Zero Flag	0	If ZF is set, the result of an operation is zero.
AF	Auxiliary Flag	0	If AF is set, there has been a carry from the low nibble to the high or a borrow from the high nibble to the low nibble of an 8-bit quantity. Used in BCD operations.
PF	Parity Flag	0	If PF is set, the result of an operation has even parity.
CF	Carry Flag	0	If CF is set, there has been a carry out of, or a borrow into, the high-order bit of the result of an instruction.

NOTE: Reserved register bits are shown with gray shading. Reserved bits must be written to a logic zero to ensure compatibility with future Intel products.

Figure 7.1-1   80C188EB's Processor Status Word (PSW), or Flags, register. (Courtesy of Intel Corp.)

Table 7.1-1   Instructions that operate directly on the carry flag.[a]

Mnemonic	Operands	Function	O	D	I	T	S	Z	A	P	C
STC	none	Set carry flag	–	–	–	–	–	–	–	–	1
CLC	none	Clear carry flag	–	–	–	–	–	–	–	–	0
CMC	none	Complement carry flag	–	–	–	–	–	–	–	–	✓

a. Flag key
   – flag is not altered
   ✓ flag reflects result
   0 flag is cleared
   1 flag is set
   ? flag is undefined
   r flag is restored from previously saved value

7.2   Logical Instructions

Logic operations implemented in hardware using NOT, AND, OR, and XOR gates are defined in Tables 7.2-1, 2, 3, and 4. These hardware operations have software counterparts in the *logical NOT*, **NOT**; *logical AND*, **AND**; *logical OR*, **OR**; and *exclusive OR*, **XOR,** instructions (Table 7.2-5). These instructions allow individual bits in a byte or word to be manipulated as defined by the basic logic operations.

   NOT operates on a single byte or word operand and complements all the operand's bits. NOT has no effect on the flags.

Table 7.2-1   NOT logic operation.

X	NOT X
0	1
1	0

Table 7.2-2   AND logic operation.

X	Y	X AND Y
0	0	0
0	1	0
1	0	0
1	1	1

Table 7.2-3   OR logic operation.

X	Y	X OR Y
0	0	0
0	1	1
1	0	1
1	1	1

Table 7.2-4   XOR logic operation.

X	Y	X XOR Y
0	0	0
0	1	1
1	0	1
1	1	0

Table 7.2-5   Logical instructions.

Mnemonic	Operands	Function	O	D	I	T	S	Z	A	P	C
NOT	dst	Logical complement	–	–	–	–	–	–	–	–	–
AND	dst,src	Logical AND	0	–	–	–	✓	✓	?	✓	0
OR	dst,src	Logical OR	0	–	–	–	✓	✓	?	✓	0
XOR	dst,src	Logical exclusive OR	0	–	–	–	✓	✓	?	✓	0
TEST	dst,src	Non-destructive AND	0	–	–	–	✓	✓	?	✓	0

AND, OR, and XOR instructions have two operands. These instructions have the general form:

mnemonic   destination, source

The operation specified by the mnemonic is carried out on the *destination* and *source* operands and the result is stored in the *destination*.

AND, OR, and XOR are **bitwise operations**. They operate on the corresponding bits of their operands. The PF, SF, and ZF flags reflect the result of the operation based on each flag's function as defined in Fig. 7.1-1. CF and OF are always cleared and AF is undefined. Until you are certain of the effect of each instruction on the flags, it is advisable to consult the tables that appear in the chapters or the Instruction Set Descriptions in Appendix C.

Each logical operation is often used for specific purposes, like clearing, setting, or complementing bits in a byte or word. Some of the most common uses are explained in the following subsections.

7.2.1   Clearing Bits using AND

The AND instruction is often used with a constant source operand to force designated bits in a byte or word to 0s. This operation is referred to as **masking**. The constant that designates which bits are to be forced to 0s, is referred to as a **mask**. For an AND operation, bits in a mask that are 0, force the corresponding bits in the result to 0. Bits in a mask that are 1, leave the corresponding bits in the result the same as in the original destination operand. The effect of masking is like that of a filter that passes the destination operand's bits corresponding to the 1's positions in the mask and blocks (forces to 0) the bits corresponding to the 0's positions in the mask.

A common application of using masking is in converting an ASCII character to BCD. An ASCII character that represents a decimal digit is a byte with its most significant 4 bits equal to 3H and least significant 4 bits equal to the binary equivalent of the decimal digit (Appendix A). For example, the ASCII code for the decimal digit 5 is encoded as 35H. Conversion of an ASCII character in AL to binary is accomplished by the single instruction:

```
and     al,0fh              ;mask out most significant 4 bits of AL
```

or equivalently:

```
and     al,00001111b
```

The effect of the AND instruction when AL contains the ASCII character 39H, which represents the digit 9, is:

AL =	0011 1001
mask =	0000 1111
AND result (in AL)=	0000 1001

The result, left in AL, is binary 9.

The mask could also be in a register or memory location as for example:

```
and     al,ah              ;where AH contains 0Fh
```

or

```
        and     al,maskval          ;where location MASKVAL contains 0FH
```

AND is also used with a mask to isolate a selected bit in an operand so the bit's value can be tested. The mask must have 1 in the bit position to be tested, and all other bits must be 0s. Execution of the AND causes the zero flag (ZF) to be set, if the bit being tested is a 0, and clears ZF if the bit tested is a 1. In this use, the AND instruction is normally followed by a conditional jump instruction that jumps based on the value of ZF. For example, the jump if zero instruction, JZ, jumps to the specified destination if ZF = 1, or, equivalently, if the bit tested is 0.

As an example, assume that when bit 4 of input port ADC_STATUS is set, the analog-to-digital converter, ADC, associated with the port is idle. This bit can be thought of as a status bit that reflects the status of the ADC. If bit 4 is 0, an analog-to-digital conversion is in progress. If bit 4 is 1, any previous conversion is complete and the converter is idle. The following instruction sequence waits in a loop until the ADC completes a conversion in progress.

```
        mov     dx,ADC_STATUS       ;put ADC_STATUS's address into DX
busy:   in      al,dx               ;input byte from port ADC_STATUS
        and     al,00010000b        ;clear all bits except bit 4
        jz      busy                ;if bit 4 is 0, jump to BUSY
        ...
```

7.2.2   Setting Bits with OR

The OR instruction is often used with a mask to force designated bits in a byte or word to 1s. For example, converting a byte containing a binary number in the range 0 to 9 to its equivalent ASCII representation simply requires forcing the most significant 4 bits of the byte to be 3H. If a binary number from 0 to 9 is in AL, it can be converted to ASCII by the single instruction:

```
        or      al,30h
```

The effect of this instruction when AL is originally 5 is:

```
        AL =                        0000 0101
        mask =                      0011 0000
        OR result (in AL) =         0011 0101
```

35H is the ASCII representation for decimal 5.

7.2.3   Complementing Bits with XOR

In addition to determining the XOR of two values, the XOR instruction is often used with a mask to complement designated bits in a byte or word. Bit positions in the mask that are 1 cause the corresponding bit values in the result to be the complement of those in the original destination operand. Bits in a mask that are 0 cause the corresponding bits in the result to have the same value as in the original destination operand.

Since any value XORed with itself is 0, XOR is a convenient and commonly used way to clear a register. For example, to clear AH use:

      xor   ah,ah

Since the NOT instruction has no effect on the flags, to complement an operand and have the flags reflect the characteristics of the result, the operand can be XORed with all 1s. To complement AL and affect the flags use:

      xor   al,0ffh

7.3 Shifts and Rotates

Two kinds of instructions shift the bits in a register or memory location, shift instructions and rotate instructions (Table 7.3-1). The contents of an 8- or 16-bit register or memory location can be shifted left or right. The number of bit positions the bits are shifted can be fixed or variable. Rotate instructions perform left or right rotates of a fixed or variable number of bit positions. Shift and rotate instructions have two operands. The destination operand, which is the register or memory location whose contents are shifted or rotated, and the count, which is the number of bit positions to shift or rotate the bits. The general form for these instructions is:

    mnemonic   *destination, count*

Table 7.3-1   Shift and rotate instructions.

Mnemonic	Operands	Function	O	D	I	T	S	Z	A	P	C
SHL	dst,count[a]	Shift logical left	✓	–	–	–	✓	✓	?	✓	✓
SAL	dst,count	Shift arithmetic left	✓	–	–	–	✓	✓	?	✓	✓
SHR	dst,count	Shift logical right	✓	–	–	–	✓	✓	?	✓	✓
SAR	dst,count	Shift arithmetic right	✓	–	–	–	✓	✓	?	✓	✓
ROL	dst,count	Rotate left	✓	–	–	–	–	–	–	–	✓
ROR	dst,count	Rotate right	✓	–	–	–	–	–	–	–	✓
RCL	dst,count	Rotate left through carry	✓	–	–	–	–	–	–	–	✓
RCR	dst,count	Rotate right through carry	✓	–	–	–	–	–	–	–	✓

a. Count is either a constant or CL. When count is a 1, OF is set if the shift causes the sign bit's value to change. For a multibit shift, CF is cleared. When CL is used for count, CL retains its original value after the instruction is executed.

The count can be either a constant value or it can be the contents of register CL. For shifts, the 80C188EB ANDs the count with the value 1FH before shifting, limiting these instructions to shifts of no more than 31 bit positions.

For variable shifts (rotates), the number of bit positions shifted (rotated) is specified by the contents of CL. Use of register CL allows the shift (rotate) count to be computed during program execution.

For the special case when count is the constant 1, OF is set if the shift (rotate) causes the sign bit to change. This is useful when the contents of the register or memory location being shifted is interpreted as a two's complement number. When count is CL, OF is cleared. The only status flag, other than OF, affected by the rotate instructions is CF. In contrast, the shift instructions affect all the status flags.

7.3.1   Shift Instructions

Shift instructions are classified as either logical or arithmetic. **Logical shift** instructions are used to shift non-numbers or unsigned numbers. **Arithmetic shifts** are used to shift signed numbers. Therefore, arithmetic shifts must preserve the sign bit. For a logical shift of one bit position, each bit is shifted one position in the specified direction. A 0 is shifted in, and the bit shifted out goes into CF. For example, for each bit position shifted, the *shift logical left* (**SHL**) instruction, shifts a 0 into the least significant bit and shifts the most significant bit into CF (Fig. 7.3-1).

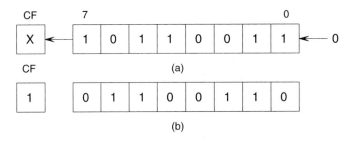

Figure 7.3-1   Effect of shift logical left, SHL, instruction on an 8-bit register: (a) before shift; (b) after shift.

Like all shift and rotate instructions, there are two forms of SHL. One form shifts the bits a constant number of bit positions. The other form shifts the bits a variable number of bit positions. CL is used to hold the count for variable shifts. The contents of CL are unchanged after execution of a shift. Either of the following instruction sequences shifts the contents of AX two positions to the left:

```
        shl     ax,2                ;shift ax left 2 bit positions
```

or:

```
        mov     cl,2                ;load shift count
        shl     ax,cl               ;shift ax left cl bit positions
```

In the latter case, CL is loaded with the shift count. Execution of SHL leaves the contents of AX shifted two bit positions to the left with the two least significant bit positions filled with 0s. However, CL still has the value 2 after SHL has been executed.

If the contents of a register were interpreted as an unsigned binary number, each logical left shift multiplies the number by two, as long as the result fits (can be represented correctly in the destination register). The 80C188EB accomplishes multiplication by powers of two more quickly using SHL than using its MULT instruction.

The *shift logical right* (**SHR**), instruction is similar to SHL, except for the shift direction. For each bit position shifted, a 0 is shifted into the most significant bit and the least significant bit is shifted into CF. For register contents interpreted as unsigned binary integers, each logical right shift divides the register's contents by two. SHR is illustrated in Fig. 7.3-2(b), which summarizes all the shift instructions.

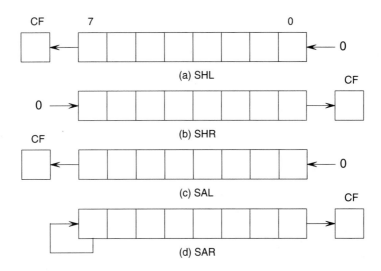

Figure 7.3-2   Logical shift instructions operating on 8-bit registers: (a)shift logical left, SHL; (b) shift logical right, SHR; (c) shift arithmetic left, SAL; (d) shift arithmetic right, SAR.

Arithmetic shifts are necessary for operands interpreted as two's complement numbers. Two's complement representation is used in the 80C188EB for signed numbers and is covered in Chapter 9. Arithmetic shifts are designed to preserve the sign of the operand. An arithmetic left shift multiplies its operand by two, as long as the result fits in the destination. The instruction that accomplishes this is *shift arithmetic left* (**SAL**, Fig. 7.3-2(c)). It turns out that no special actions are required to preserve the sign for a left arithmetic shift. As a result, assembly of the SHL and SAL instructions generate the same object code.

Because they generate the same object code, SHL and SAL are mnemonic synonyms. Mnemonic synonyms allow you to select the mnemonic that best reflects the purpose of the instruction in the context of your program.

To preserve the sign for an arithmetic right shift, the most significant bit of the operand must retain its original value after the shift. The *shift arithmetic right* (**SAR**) instruction copies the most significant bit back to the most significant bit position, in addition to shifting it to the right, for each bit position shifted, (Fig. 7.3-2(d)).

7.3.2   Rotate Instructions

Rotate instructions implement circular shifts as shown in Fig. 7.3-3. With *rotate left* (**ROL**) the most significant bit's value is rotated back into the least significant bit position as well as shifted into CF (Fig. 7.3-3(a)). For *rotate right* (**ROR**), the least significant bit's value is rotated around to the most significant bit position as well as shifted into CF (Fig. 7.3-2(b)). ROL and ROR implement either 8-bit or 16-bit rotates, depending on the operand's size.

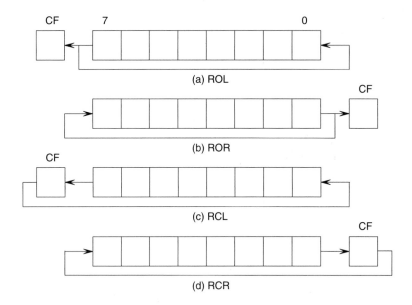

Figure 7.3-3   Logical rotate instructions operating on 8-bit registers: (a) rotate left, ROL; (b) rotate right, ROR; (c) rotate through carry left, RCL; (d) rotate through carry right, RCR.

A simple example demonstrating the use of a rotate is to swap the high and low nibbles of AL:

```
rol     al,4     ;swap high and low nibbles of AL
```

Rotate through carry left (**RCL**) and *rotate through carry right* (**RCR**) instructions treat CF as either the most significant or least significant bit, respectively, of the operand (Fig. 7.3-3(c) and (d)). These instructions rotate either 9-bits or 17-bits, depending on whether the operand is a byte or word, respectively.

7.4   Unconditional Jumps

In the previous programs, instructions were executed in a fixed sequence. Each instruction was executed immediately after execution of the instruction that preceded it in the program, until the last instruction in the program was executed. This corresponds to fetching instructions from consecutive memory locations. The last instruction in each program was a jump that caused either the entire program, or a portion of it, to repeat indefinitely. The jump accomplished this by causing an instruction other than the next consecutive instruction in memory to be executed.

This kind of jump instruction is an unconditional jump. Whenever an **unconditional jump** is executed, execution flow is transferred to the specified target memory location. The next instruction to be executed is fetched from that location. In contrast, a **conditional jump** instruction changes the execution flow only if certain conditions, associated with one or more status flags or with the contents of CX, are met. Neither kind of jump instruction alters any flags.

An unconditional jump instruction has the form:

jmp   *target*

where *target* specifies the memory location from which the next instruction is fetched or, equivalently, to which execution flow is transferred. *Target* is either a label representing the address, or is a register or memory location that contains the address, to which execution flow is transferred.

Most often, the target address is a label. A **label** defines the address of an instruction by giving a name to the instruction's location in memory. One method of specifying a label is to place the label name followed by a colon in the label field of the target instruction. For example,

main: mov   dx,SWITCHES

defines main as a label for the instruction mov dx,switches. Like variables, labels have three attributes. Two of these attributes, segment and offset, are the same as for variables. In Fig. 4.4-2, the label main has the segment attribute code and has an offset of 0 from the beginning of the code segment.

The type attributes for a label are different than those for a variable. There are only two possibilities, NEAR and FAR. A **NEAR** label can be accessed by a jump instruction in the same segment as the label. A **FAR** label can be accessed by a jump instruction in any segment. A jump to a target in the same segment is called an **intrasegment jump**. A jump to a target in a different segment is called an **intersegment jump**.

To transfer execution flow to a target, the 80C188EB makes CS equal to the target's segment address and IP equal to the target's offset address. If the target is a NEAR label, only IP must be changed. The BIU then reinitializes the instruction queue and fetches the next instruction using the new CS:IP value, thus implementing the transfer of execution flow.

7.4.1   Direct Addressing of a Target

A target can be specified using either direct or indirect addressing. With direct addressing, the target's address is contained in the instruction. With indirect addressing the target's address is contained in either a register or memory location referenced by the instruction. All jump instructions in previous programs were direct jumps.

Intrasegment Direct Jump

In an intrasegment JMP, the number of bytes required to specify the target's address depends on the distance from the JMP instruction to the target. Since the target is in the same segment as the JMP, CS does not need to be changed. All that is required is to provide a new value for IP. Thus, at most, a 16-bit displacement in the instruction is sufficient.

A 16-bit displacement in a jump instruction is not the target's actual offset. Instead, it is the **relative displacement** (distance in bytes) of the target from the first instruction byte following the JMP (Fig. 7.4-1). Since the direction can be forward or backward, the displacement can be positive or negative and is expressed in two's complement form.

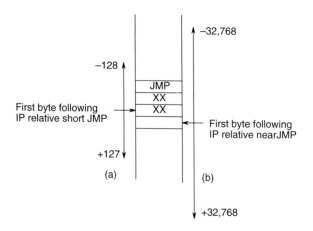

Figure 7.4-1   Ranges for an instruction pointer, IP, relative JMP; (a) short JMP; (b) near JMP.

To generate the new IP value for an intrasegment jump, the EU first automatically modifies IP to have the value of the offset of the first byte following the JMP instruction. Modification of IP, before adding the displacement, is necessary to compensate for the fact that, due to the instruction queue, IP holds the offset address of the next instruction to be *fetched*, not necessarily the next instruction to be *executed*.

The EU adds the modified IP to the relative displacement contained in the instruction. The sum is the actual offset of the target. Computing a new IP by adding a relative displacement to the modified IP is called **instruction pointer relative addressing**. The assembler does the work of determining the relative displacement needed in the instruction. With a 16-bit displacement, the resulting JMP machine instruction consists of three bytes, one for the opcode and two for the displacement.

A 16-bit displacement restricts the target to be located in memory within +32,767 or −32,768 bytes of the first byte of the instruction following the JMP. However, this range is sufficient to allow the JMP's target to be anywhere within the segment containing the JMP, since a segment can only contain a maximum of 2^{16} bytes and a segment wraps around.

Segment wrap around means that starting from one location (a given offset) in a segment, if you cannot reach a target location in the segment that has a larger offset by adding a displacement of from 0 to +32,767 to the starting offset, then you can reach the target location by adding a negative displacement from −1 to −32,768 to the starting offset. The same argument holds going from a starting location to a target location with a less positive offset.

For example, assume that the starting location's offset (adjusted IP) is 001AH and that the target location's offset (target IP) is FFE2H. Going forward, the distance from 001AH to FFE2H (FFE2H − 001AH) is FFC8H bytes. If FFC8H is interpreted as an unsigned number, the displacement would have to be 65,480, which is larger than 32,767. At first, it might seem that you can't reach the target with a 16-bit displacement. However, the 16-bit displacement is interpreted as a signed 2's complement number. Interpreted as a signed two's complement number, FFC8H is equal to −56, which is in the allowed range for the displacement. Instead of going forward to reach the target, we go backwards in the wrapped around segment (Fig. 7.4-2).

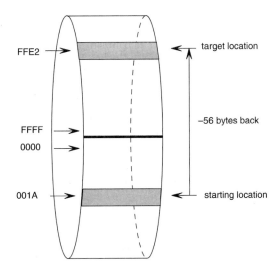

Figure 7.4-2   Representation of a segment with its ends wrappedaround so that the first location and last location are adjacent.

Short Jumps

If the assembler determines that the target is within −128 to +127 bytes from the first byte following the JMP, it automatically produces a shorter, two byte jump instruction that has only an 8-bit relative displacement. The EU always sign extends an 8-bit displacement before adding it to the modified IP.

For a **backward reference**, one where the target precedes the JMP instruction in the program, it is easy for the assembler to determine whether the target is within −128 bytes from the first byte following the JMP. For example, in Fig. 4.4-2, the jmp main instruction that transfers execution flow to the instruction with the label main. main is twelve bytes back (−12 relative displacement) from the first byte following jmp. Therefore, jmp main is assembled into object code as EBF4H. EB is the opcode for a short intrasegment direct jump. F4 is the 8-bit relative displacement and is the two's complement representation of

−12. The offset of the first byte following jmp main in the code segment is 12. Therefore, the modified IP is 12. When the relative displacement is added to the modified IP (12 + (−12)) the result is 0, which is the offset of the label main.

For forward references, the assembler assumes that a 16-bit relative displacement is required unless told otherwise by the **SHORT** assembler operator (Table 6.6-2):

jmp   short *target*

When the assembler sees the SHORT operator, it allocates only one byte for the relative displacement.

This operator was obviously named after the author, as was the famous electric circuit that bears his name. In fact, the author's namesake electric circuit is extensively used by students and professionals (often unwittingly and without acknowledgment) when they are developing systems.

Intersegment Direct Jump

An intersegment jump can jump to a target in a different segment, Therefore, an intersegment jump requires new values for both CS and IP. Intersegment direct jumps are not relative. These five byte machine instructions contain the target's actual segment and offset addresses. The first byte is the opcode. The second and third bytes are the target's offset and the fourth and fifth bytes are the target's segment address.

When the assembler encounters a direct JMP instruction, it automatically determines whether to assemble a NEAR or FAR jump machine instruction based on whether the target's label is in the same segment or not. The assembler can be forced to assemble a FAR jump by using the **FAR PTR** assembler operator (Table 6.6-2):

jmp far ptr target

7.4.2   Indirect Addressing of a Target

Intrasegment Indirect Jump

Intrasegment indirect jumps reference a 16-bit register or memory location that contains the actual new value for IP, rather than a displacement. Indirect addressing allows your program to compute the target address during its execution. This provides greater programming flexibility. For example, the program template in Fig. 7.4-3 allows any one of four tasks to be executed depending on a task number corresponding to the two least significant bits of a byte read from an input port. Each task is represented by a NOP instruction and is followed by a JMP that causes the program to repeat. In an actual program, each NOP would be replaced by instructions that implement the corresponding task.

The indirect jump transfers execution flow to a specific task by obtaining the task's offset address from a jump table. A **jump table** is a table of addresses. Each address is the offset of the associated task. Entries in the jump table are produced using a DW directive. ***When a label appears in the list for a DW directive, the label is replaced by the value of its offset address.*** Since only a new offset is provided, and not a new segment address, the target must be within the current segment.

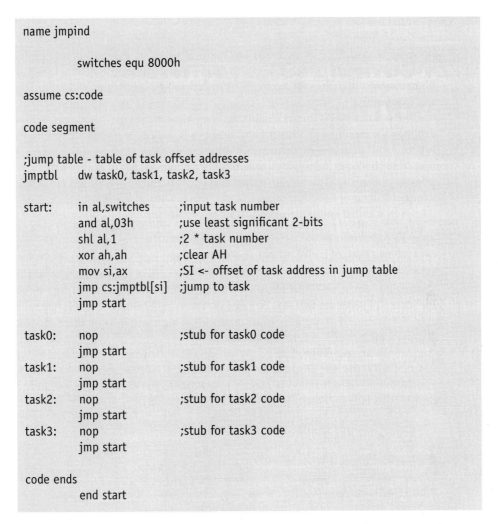

```
name jmpind

        switches equ 8000h

assume cs:code

code segment

;jump table - table of task offset addresses
jmptbl     dw task0, task1, task2, task3

start:     in al,switches        ;input task number
           and al,03h            ;use least significant 2-bits
           shl al,1              ;2 * task number
           xor ah,ah             ;clear AH
           mov si,ax             ;SI <- offset of task address in jump table
           jmp cs:jmptbl[si]     ;jump to task
           jmp start

task0:     nop                   ;stub for task0 code
           jmp start
task1:     nop                   ;stub for task1 code
           jmp start
task2:     nop                   ;stub for task2 code
           jmp start
task3:     nop                   ;stub for task3 code
           jmp start

code ends
           end start
```

Figure 7.4-3   Using an indirect jump and jump table to repeatedly execute a task.

Intersegment Indirect Jump

An intersegment indirect jump can only use a double word memory location as its operand. This memory location holds the address to which execution flow will be transferred. This memory location's low word holds the target's offset address and its high word holds the target's segment address. Entries in a jump table for intersegment jumps can be created by placing the targets' labels in the list of a DD directive. *When a label appears in the list for a DD directive, the label is replaced by its offset and segment addresses.*

7.5   Conditional Jumps

As stated in this chapter's introduction, a critical aspect of any useful program is its ability to make decisions that determine which task(s) should be executed next. Using an indirect jump instruction in the manner outlined in the previous section provides a limited form of this capability.

The 80C188EB's conditional jump instructions provide a powerful means of controlling task execution as a function of input data, logical or arithmetic results, or external events. A conditional jump instruction jumps to its target if its conditions are met. Otherwise, execution continues with the instruction following the jump instruction. The conditions tested are related to the status flags' states, and, for one special instruction, to whether CX is 0.

Conditional jump instructions have the form:

j<X> short-label

where <X> represents a one to three letter mnemonic for the required condition(s). *Short-label* is a label within −128 to +127 bytes of the instruction following the conditional jump instruction. The conditional jump instructions and required states of the status flags for each jump to occur are listed in Table 7.5-1. There are 17 unique conditional jumps. However, the assembler recognizes some conditional jumps by two or three mnemonic synonyms, resulting in 31 different mnemonics.

A conditional jump must be preceded by an instruction that causes the flags to have the required states that dictate if the change in execution flow should take place. For example, the following instruction sequence inputs data from port INDATA if, and only if, bit 7 of port PSTATUS is 1:

```
        mov     dx,PSTATUS      ;input from port status
        in      al,dx
        and     al,10000000b    ;force bits 6 through 0 of AL to 0
        jz      noinput         ;jump if all the bits of AL are 0
        mov     dx,INDATA       ;input data from port INDATA
        in      al,dx

        ...
noinput: ...
```

The first two instructions read a byte from port PSTATUS and place it in AL. Then AND is used with the mask 10000000B to force bits 6 through 0 of AL to 0s. Bit 7 is left unaltered. If bit 7 were originally a 0, then after the AND is executed, AL = 00H and ZF is set. If bit 7 were originally a 1, then AL = 80H and ZF is cleared. The ZF flag is tested by the conditional jump instruction JZ. If ZF is 1, JZ branches to the label noinput, and the second input instruction is skipped.

Some caution is necessary when using JZ to branch based on the ZF flag. *You must remember that when a result is 0, the ZF flag is 1. When a result is not zero, the ZF flag is 0.*

Since the most significant bit of an operand is defined as its sign bit, and the JNS instruction jumps if flag SF is 0, it might seem that an alternative and shorter sequence to accomplish the previous task is:

```
        mov     dx,PSTATUS      ;input from port status
        in      al,dx
```

Table 7.5-1   Jump instructions.

Mnemonic	Jump if condition	Flags for condition
JA/JNBE	above[a]/not below nor equal	(CF OR ZF) = 0
JAE/JNB	above or equal/not below	CF = 0
JB/JNAE	below/not above nor equal	CF = 1
JBE/JNA	below or equal/not above	(CF OR ZF) = 1
JC	carry	CF = 1
JCXZ	jump if CX equal 0	CX = 0
JE/JZ	equal/zero	ZF = 1
JB/JNLE	greater[b]/not less nor equal	((SF XOR OF) OR ZF) = 0
JGE/JNL	greater or equal/not less	(SF XOR OF) = 0
JL/JNGE	less/not greater or equal	(SF XOR OF) = 1
JLE/JNG	less or equal/not greater	((SF XOR OF) OR ZF) = 1
JMP	unconditional	none
JNC	no carry	CF = 0
JNE/JNZ	not equal/not zero	ZF = 0
JNO	not overflow	OF = 0
JNP/JPO	not parity/parity odd	PF = 0
JNS	not sign	SF = 0
JO	overflow	OF = 1
JP/JPE	parity/parity equal	PF = 1
JS	sign	SF = 1

a. "Above" and "below" refer to the relationship between unsigned numbers.
b. "Greater" and "less" refer to the relationship between twos complement numbers.

```
XX        jns      noinput           ;jump if bit 7 of AL is 0 XX
          mov      dx,INDATA
          in       al,dx
          ...
noinput: ...
```

However, this instruction sequence does not accomplish the intended objective. The jump is conditioned on the state of the sign flag. However, execution of an IN instruction has no effect on the flags. Thus, a change in execution flow caused by the conditional jump in previous instruction sequence has nothing to do with the value of bit 7 of PSTATUS! This example illustrates two important points. One is that the IN instruction, like all data transfer instructions, has no effect on the flags. So, the state of the flags after execution of IN does not reflect the value of the input data. The second point is that a conditional jump instruction should normally follow the instruction that alters the flags to test the condition. Sometimes it is necessary to have other instructions between the instruction that alters the flags and its associated conditional jump instruction. If this is the case, care must be taken to insure that none of the intervening instructions affect the flags to be tested.

The previous instruction sequence can be modified to achieve proper operation:

```
mov     dx,PSTATUS        ;input port status
in      al,dx

or      al,al             ;make flags reflect contents of AL
jns     noinput           ;jump if bit 7 of al is 0

...
```

The OR instruction is inserted to alter the flags based on the contents of AL. Since ORing any value with itself does not alter the original value, the contents of AL are not modified, but the flags are affected.

7.5.1   Conditional Data Transfer, Polling, or Handshaking

Testing a status flag associated with an input port is commonly used to synchronize a microprocessor with an input device. The status bit indicates when new data has been placed in the input port by its input device. This method of synchronization is called **conditional data transfer, polling**, or, **handshaking**. Figure 7.5-1 shows hardware designed so that when the input device loads data into the port, it simultaneously sets the status flag. The hardware is designed so that reading the input port also simultaneously clears the status flag.

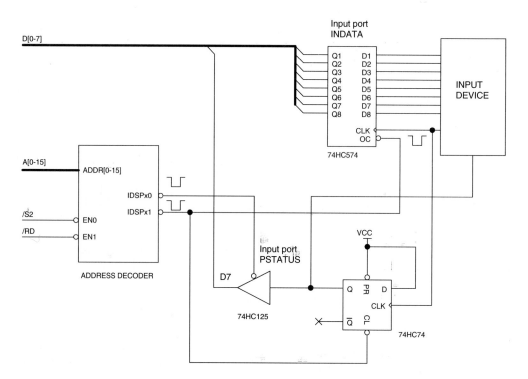

Figure 7.5-1   Conditional transfer of data from an input port.

The following sequence causes the 80C188EB to wait in a loop for the input device to load new data into the input port (INDATA) before it reads the data.

```
            mov     dx,PSTATUS              ;input port status
waitlp:     in      al,dx
            or      al,al                   ;update flags based on AL
            jns     waitlp                  ;jump back if bit 7 of al is 0
            mov     dx,INDATA               ;input new data
            in      al,dx
            ...
```

It is important to note here that the only function of input port PSTATUS is to provide a flag bit that indicates when the input device has loaded new data into the input port INDATA.

Often, it is desirable to test several bits of an operand one at a time then jump to a different target depending on which bit is set. Use of an AND instruction with a mask would cause the original operand to be replaced by the result, destroying the operand's original value. This makes it impossible to test any of the other bits in the original operand.

This problem is solved by using the *test instruction*, **TEST**. TEST performs a logical AND of its operands, but does not transfer the result to the destination. Thus, the original operand value is unaltered. TEST does, however, alter the flags in the same way that AND does. For example:

```
            mov     dx,PSTATUS
            in      al,dx                   ;input from port status
            test    al,10000000b            ;clear ZF if bit 7 of al is 1
            jnz     bit7set                 ;jump to bit7 set if ZF is 0
            test    al,01000000b            ;clear ZF if bit 6 of al is 1
            jnz     bit6set                 ;jump to bit6set if ZF is 0
            ...
bit7set:    ...
            ...
bit6set:    ...
```

When AND, OR, XOR, and TEST are used to establish status flag values for conditional jumps, the jump is dependent on the logical relationship between the operands. Interestingly, the NOT instruction, although it is a logical instruction, has no effect on any flags. Therefore, NOT can't be used to establish flag values for conditional jumps.

7.5.2   Arithmetic Relationships

If an arithmetic relationship between operands is to be the basis for a change in execution flow, the instruction used to establish the flags' values must be arithmetic, such as ADD or SUB. When comparisons between two arithmetic operands are to be made, an important consideration is whether the operands are interpreted as unsigned or signed numbers.

Since signed numbers are represented in two's complement form, the flags' states when reflecting arithmetic relationships are different for signed and unsigned numbers. As a consequence, the instruction set provides different conditional jump instructions for unsigned and signed numbers. The distinction is apparent from the instruction's mnemonics. If A or B (for above or below) appears in the mnemonic, the instruction applies to unsigned numbers. If G or L (for greater or less) appears in the mnemonic, the instruction applies to signed numbers. For example, to jump if the unsigned operand in AL is larger than the unsigned operand in BL, the following sequence is used:

```
        sub     al,bl     ;place (AL - BL) in AL, alter flags
        ja      larger    ;jump if AL was larger than BL
        ...

larger:

        ...
```

However, if the operands are signed numbers and you wish to jump if AL is larger than BL, the conditional jump JG must be used. For example:

```
        sub     al,bl     ;place (AL - BL) in AL, alter flags
        jg      larger    ;jump if al was larger (more positive)
        ...

larger:

        ...
```

In each of the previous cases, the SUB instruction is used to modify the flags. SUB replaces the operand in AL with the computed difference. Alternatively, the *compare instruction* (**CMP**) allows arithmetic comparisons without altering the destination operand. The function of CMP is the same as SUB, except the difference is not placed in the destination. In effect, the destination's value is not altered. With CMP, an operand can be compared with several values, in turn, without destroying the operand's original value.

Conditional jump instructions can jump to targets no further than +127 or −128 bytes from the byte following the jump instruction. To jump farther, a conditional jump instruction must be combined with an unconditional jump. The conditional jump is used to jump around (skip) the unconditional jump. For example, to jump to a NEAR label, larger, when the unsigned integer in AL is larger than the unsigned integer in BL, and where the label larger is more than 127 bytes away, use:

```
        cmp     al,bl     ;compute (AL - BL) to alter flags
        jbe     notlrgr   ;jump if below or equal
        jmp     larger    ;jump if above
notlrgr: ...

        ...
larger:  ...
```

This technique is sometimes referred to as **double jumping.** Note that when double jumping is required, the conditional jump instruction's condition is the complement of what it would be if the target were a short distance away and the conditional jump was made directly.

7.6   Looping and Iteration Control

A conditional jump that jumps back to a preceding instruction creates a loop. This allows a task placed inside the loop to be repeated. Looping can be terminated after a predetermined number of passes through the loop or when a particular event occurs. The wait loop in the previous section is an example of the latter case, looping continued until a status bit from the port PSTATUS was set.

When coding loops that are terminated after a predetermined number of passes, it is very important that the loop is properly initialized so that the correct number of passes occur. To execute a loop a predetermined number of times requires a **loop control variable**. You must initialize this variable before the loop is entered. The loop control variable is modified on each pass. A conditional jump at the bottom of the loop tests the loop control variable. If the loop control variable has not reached its limit (usually 0), a jump back to the beginning of the loop occurs. The following sequence reads data from four input ports, with addresses 2000H to 2003H, and stores the data in the array pdata:

```
        mov     dx,2000h          ;address of first input port
        mov     bx,offset pdata   ;offset of first array element
        mov     cx,4              ;number of ports to be read
rdport: in      al,dx             ;read port
        mov     [bx],al           ;store in pdata array
        inc     dx                ;point to next port
        inc     bx                ;point to next array element
        dec     cx                ;dec loop control variable
        jnz     rdport            ;loop if cx is not 0
```

The first two move instructions initialize pointers to the port and to the start of the memory array. The third instruction initializes the loop control variable CX. Instead of CX, a different general register or a memory location could have been used. After a byte is input from a port and stored in memory, the pointers and loop control variable must be modified. The *increment* (**INC**) instruction increments its operand by one and *decrement* (**DEC**) decrements its operand by one (Table 7.6-1). Both instructions modify AF, OF, PF, SF, and ZF, but neither affects CF. The conditional jump instruction tests ZF and loops if ZF is 0 (CX not equal 0).

Table 7.6-1   Increment, decrement, and compare instructions.

Mnemonic	Operands	Function	O	D	I	T	S	Z	A	P	C
INC	dst	Increment by 1	✓	–	–	–	✓	✓	✓	✓	–
DEC	dst	Decrement by 1	✓	–	–	–	✓	✓	✓	✓	–
CMP	dst,src	Compare (dst-src)	✓	–	–	–	✓	✓	✓	✓	–

Since the condition to be tested is whether CX is zero, DEC CX immediately precedes JNZ. This insures that ZF reflects the result of decrementing CX when JNZ executes.

Looping is such a common operation that a *loop* (**LOOP**), instruction is provided (Table 7.6-2). LOOP combines the actions of the DEC and JNZ, in that order, into a single instruction. LOOP has the form:

loop   *short-label*

Table 7.6-2   Loop instructions.

Mnemonic	Operands	Function	O	D	I	T	S	Z	A	P	C
LOOP	short_label	Loop	–	–	–	–	–	–	–	–	–
LOOPE	short_label	Loop if equal	–	–	–	–	–	–	–	–	–
LOOPZ	short_label	Loop is zero									
LOOPNE	short_label	Loop if not equal	–	–	–	–	–	–	–	–	–
LOOPZ	short_label	Loop if not zero									

LOOP can only use CX as the loop control variable. For this reason, CX is sometimes referred to as the "count" register because it holds the count for several different repetitive instructions. LOOP does not alter any flags, but decrements CX. Using LOOP, the previous sequence becomes:

```
        mov     dx,2000h        ;address of first port
        mov     bx,offset pdata ;offset of first array element
        mov     cx,4            ;number of ports to be read
rdport: in      al,dx           ;read port whose address is in dx
        mov     [bx],al         ;store in element bx of pdata array
        inc     dx              ;point to next port
        inc     bx              ;point to next array element
        loop    rdport          ;decrement loop control variable
                                ;and loop if cx is not 0
```

Two other loop instructions are used when a loop must also terminate if some other condition occurs before CX becomes zero. Each of these two instructions is known by either of two mnemonic synonyms. *Loop while equal* (**LOOPE**) is also known as *loop while zero* (**LOOPZ**). Each time this instruction is executed, CX is decremented. After CX is decremented, if ZF is 1 and CX is not 0, the transfer of execution flow to the target occurs. This instruction allows either of two conditions to cause the loop to be exited and execution continue with the instruction following the LOOPE instruction. Either ZF is 0 or CX is 0.

The following example uses LOOPE. An EPROM is an erasable and reprogrammable nonvolatile memory IC. A device programmer needs to verify that an EPROM is erased before it starts to program the device. Assuming that the device programmer is itself an 80C188EB system. The EPROM that is to be programmed is plugged into a socket on the device programmer. This action places the EPROM in the 80C188EB's memory address space. A task that verifies the EPROM is erased must transfer execution to either of two targets: erased, if the EPROM is erased, or nerased, if not. If the EPROM is not erased, the address of the first unerased memory location must be provided to the nerased task. Each byte in an erased EPROM has the value FFH. The following sequence of instructions accomplishes the task for EPROMs of no more than 64 Kbytes.

```
          mov     cx,length eprom
          mov     di,0ffffh         ;load (0000h - 1) into DI
erased?:  inc     di                ;increment index into EPROM
          cmp     eprom[di],0ffh    ;compare EPROM byte with 0ffh
          loope   erased?           ;loop if byte = 0ffh and CX not = 0
          jz      erased            ;if ZF = 1, EPROM is erased

nerased:  ...                       ;target for EPROM that is not erased


          ...
erased:   ...                       ;target for erased EPROM
```

Indexed addressing is used to reference the EPROM. DI is initialized as the index register. The index value for the first location in the EPROM is 0. However, because DI is incremented before each comparison, it is initialized to 0FFFFH. DI must be incremented before CMP, not after. Otherwise, when LOOPE checks ZF, the value of ZF would reflect the result from the INC, not the result from the CMP.

When the loop is exited, it is necessary to determine whether the exit occurred because a byte that was not FFH was encountered or because the entire EPROM was checked and all bytes were FFH. If ZF is still 1 when the loop is exited, then the EPROM is erased. JZ checks for this condition. If the EPROM is not erased, DI contains the address of the first unerased memory location.

Another form of the loop instruction is *loop while not equal* (**LOOPNE**) also known as *loop while not zero* (**LOOPNZ**). LOOPNE requires that ZF is a 1 or CX is 0 in order to exit the loop.

Typically, the loop control variable's initial value specifies how many times the task inside the loop should be executed. For a value of 0, the intent is to execute the task 0 times. But, loop instructions decrement CX before testing. Thus, initializing CX to 0 causes 65,536 loops to occur, instead of 0 loops. To avoid this problem, the *jump if CX is zero* (**JCXZ**), instruction can be used to test CX for 0 before entering the loop. If CX is 0, then the loop is skipped.

Loops are often used to implement imprecise timing delays. A delay of approximately one millisecond is implemented on an 80C188EB operated at 8 MHz by the following sequence:

```
          mov     cx,500
one_msec: loop    one_msec
```

Delays of integer multiples of this time period are easily achievable. The following instruction sequence delays for *n* multiples of the previous delay:

```
          mov     bx,n              ;want n multiples of delay
          or      bx,bx             ;check for 0 delay specified
          jz      skip              ;jump if 0 delay
delay:    mov     cx,500            ;delay 1 millisecond
one_msec: loop    one_msec
```

```
          dec    bx              ;if bx is not 0
          jnz    delay           ;delay another millisecond
skip:            ...
```

This instruction sequence uses two loops, an inner loop and outer loop, and two loop control variables, CX and BX. Each time the inner loop control variable CX is decremented to 0, the outer loop control variable, BX, is decremented by 1. If BX is not 0, as determined by JNZ, the inner loop is reinitialized and reentered.

7.7   Conditional Task Execution

Conditional jumps and the LOOP instruction allow implementation of a full set of basic program execution flow logical structures, such as:

1. SEQUENCE
2. IF/ELSE
3. SWITCH
4. WHILE
5. DO-WHILE

These structures can be combined to implement any algorithm. In **structured programming**, these structures are constrained to have a single entry point and a single exit point. The syntax of many high-level languages directly support these, or equivalent, program structures. When the single entry/single exit constraint is applied to assembly language implementations of these structures, the resulting instruction sequences are often slightly longer than if the constraint is not met. However, use of a structured approach leads to programs that are easier to understand, document, and maintain.

7.7.1   SEQUENCE

A **SEQUENCE** structure consists of tasks executed in a fixed sequence (Fig. 7.7-1). Circles are used to represent entry and exit points. Rectangles represent a task or process. Execution is transferred to a task, the task is performed, and execution is transferred out. Tasks can vary in complexity from a single instruction to an entire program. A nontrivial task is itself constructed using combinations of the basic program logical structures. Often, each task is implemented by a procedure to produce a program with an even greater degree of modularity. Procedures are introduced in the next chapter.

7.7.2   IF/ELSE

The **IF/ELSE** structure allows a decision to made as to which of two tasks is executed (Fig. 7.7-2). An **IF** structure is a variation of IF/ELSE, where one of the tasks is a null task. The IF structure allows for the conditional task execution. A diamond shaped symbol represents a decision element. Execution is transferred into the decision element, a decision is made to follow one of two execution paths based on some condition. The task in the path chosen is executed.

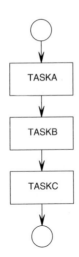

Figure 7.7-1   Sequence structure.

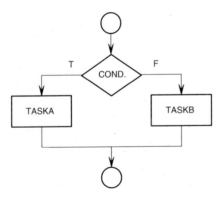

Figure 7.7-2   If /Else structure.

A decision element represents the instructions that test the condition and implement the appropriate branch. The condition tested is ultimately reflected in the value of flags and the test is of the flags' value. The one exception is when JCXZ is used. This instruction tests for CX = 0.

As an example of the typical situation where a flag is tested, suppose memory variable mode contains a bit pattern that specifies the mode of operation of a system, or in effect, whether certain tasks should be skipped. If bit 0 of mode is a 1, taska is to be executed. Otherwise, it is skipped. The instructions to implement this IF are:

```
entry:      test    mode,01h        ;is bit 0 of mode = 1?
            jz      skip
taska:      ...                     ;yes
            ...
skip:       ...                     ;no
```

7.7.3　SWITCH

The **SWITCH** structure (Fig. 7.7-3) selects a single task to be executed out of several choices. This structure can be implemented using an indirect jump instruction. With this approach, instructions that comprise the decision element use the operand on which the decision is based to derive an index into a jump table. The jump table contains the offset for the start of each task. The offset corresponding to the selected task is obtained from the table and the indirect jump is executed. The program of Fig. 7.4-2 implements a SWITCH structure.

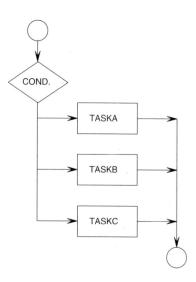

Figure 7.7-3　　　Switch structure.

7.7.4　WHILE

There are two basic logical structures associated with program looping: WHILE and DO-WHILE. These structures differ in whether the task is executed before or after the condition is tested.

　　　The **WHILE** structure tests a condition prior to the possible execution of a task (Fig. 7.7-4(a)). It is possible to enter and leave the WHILE structure, but never execute the task. Suppose it is necessary to input ten bytes of data from the port INDATA, and store them in the memory buffer inbuff. If inputting one byte from the port and storing it in memory is considered a task, then this task needs to be repeated 10 times to accomplish the desired function. The following instructions implement the function as a WHILE structure:

```
              mov     cx,11                           ;(times to execute task) + 1
              mov     bx,offset inbuff
              mov     dx,indata

check:        dec     cx                              ;decision
              jz      exit
```

```
input:              in      al,dx                           ;task
                    mov     [bx],al
                    inc     bx
                    jmp     check
exit:               ...
```

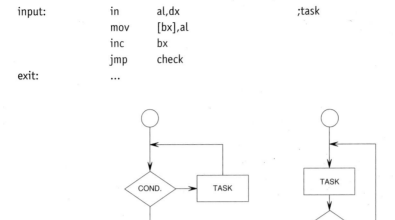

(a)   (b)

Figure 7.7-4   Loop structures: (a) WHILE structure; (b) DO WHILE structure.

The entry point for this WHILE is the label check and the exit point is the label exit. The first three instructions carry out initialization and are not a part of the WHILE structure. These instructions constitute an additional task that is in sequence with the WHILE structure.

Because a WHILE structure makes the test prior to execution of the task, the loop control variable is set to $n + 1$ to achieve n executions of the task. A WHILE structure is sometimes called **count-then-execute**.

7.7.5   DO WHILE

In the **DO-WHILE** structure (Fig. 7.7-4(b)) the task is executed before the condition is tested. Thus, whenever this structure is entered, the task is always executed at least once. The following instructions implement the previous example using a DO-WHILE structure:

```
                    mov     cx,10               ;number of times to execute the task
                    mov     bx,offset inbuff
                    mov     dx,indata
input:              in      al,dx               ;task
                    mov     [bx],al
                    inc     bx
                    loop    input               ;decision
exit:               ...
```

The entry point of the DO-WHILE is the label INPUT and the exit point is the label EXIT. The decision is made by the LOOP instruction, which first decrements CX then tests for CX = 0. The task is executed before the decision is made. Therefore, the task is always executed at least once whenever the structure is entered. A DO-WHILE structure is sometimes called **execute-then-count.** The first three instructions carry out initialization and are not a part of the DO-WHILE structure. These instructions constitute an additional task in sequence with the DO-WHILE structure.

In the previous looping examples, the number of transitions through the loop is fixed and known prior to loop execution. Both the DO-WHILE and the WHILE structures can be used to loop an indeterminate number of times based on the occurrence or nonoccurrence of some event. For example, bytes can be input from a port and stored in a memory buffer until a specific byte is input. In the example that follows, the task continues to be executed until the byte 0DH is input and stored:

```
            mov     bx,offset inbuff
            mov     dx,indata
input:      in      al,dx                    ;task
            mov     [bx],al
            inc     bx
            cmp     al,0dh
            jnz     input                    ;decision
exit:       ...
```

7.8   Repeated String Instructions

String instruction primitives for data transfer: INS, OUTS, MOVS, STOS, and LODS, were introduced in Chapter 6. String instruction primitives for data scanning are introduced in this section. The repeat prefixes (Table 7.8-1) used to repeat string operations are also introduced in this section.

All string instruction primitives use DS:SI as the pointer to the source operand and ES:DI as the pointer to the destination operand. All string instruction primitives also increment or decrement SI, DI, or both, after a data transfer or scan operation is completed. Whether SI and DI are incremented or decremented, depends on the value of the **direction flag (DF,** Fig. 7.8-1). If DF is 0, the index registers are incremented. If DF is 1, they are decremented. DF is set using the *set direction* (**STD**) instruction and cleared using the *clear direction flag* (**CLD**) instruction.

The real power of string instructions is realized when they are used repetitively to process data in a string, buffer, array, or similar data structure. While a string primitive can be repeated by placing the primitive inside a loop, repetition is achieved more efficiently using a repeat prefix.

The *repeat prefix* (**REP**) is not an instruction. It is an instruction prefix that modifies the operation of the string primitive it precedes. REP tests CX. If CX is not 0, CX is decremented and the string primitive is then executed (Fig. 7.8-1). This process continues until CX is 0. REP can only be used to prefix string instruction primitives.

Table 7.8-1   String instructions for data scanning and repeat instruction prefixes.

Mnemonic	Operands	Function	O	D	I	T	S	Z	A	P	C
STD	none	Set direction flag	–	1	–	–	–	–	–	–	–
CLD	none	Clear direction flag	–	0	–	–	–	–	–	–	–
SCAS	dst_s	Scan string	✓	–	–	–	✓	✓	✓	✓	✓
CMPS	dst_s	Compare string	✓	–	–	–	✓	✓	✓	✓	✓
REP	none	Repeat string operation	–	–	–	–	–	–	–	–	–
REPE	none	Repeat string operation while equal	–	–	–	–	–	–	–	–	–
REPZ		Repeat string operation while zero									
REPNE	none	Repeat string operation while not equal	–	–	–	–	–	–	–	–	–
REPNZ		Repeat string operation while not zero									

For example, to copy the contents of one buffer to another:

```
cld                               ;SI and DI are to be incremented

mov     ax,seg buff1              ;load segment address of BUFF1
mov     ds,ax
mov     si,offset buff1          ;point DS:SI to source

mov     ax,seg buff2              ;load segment address of BUFF2
mov     es,ax
mov     di,offset buff2         ;point ES:DI to destination

mov     cx,length buff1          ;load repetition counter
rep     movs    buff2,buff1     ;xfer (DS:SI) to (ES:DI)
```

The first instruction clears the direction control flag (DF), which causes SI and DI to be incremented each time the string primitive is executed.

The next six instructions set up the pointers DS:SI and ES:DI. The SEG operator is used to load the segment addresses of the buffers into DS and ES. The buffers' offsets are loaded using the OFFSET operator. The length operator is used to load CX with the number of data items in the source buffer. Since CX is loaded with the number of data items in the source buffer, the last instruction copies the entire buffer. If CX were initially 0, the repeated instruction executes zero times. That is, it does nothing.

The MOVS instruction is the nonexplicit version of MOVS. The assembler determines from the type attributes of the MOVS instruction's operands whether the opcode for a MOVSB or a MOVSW should be generated. MOVSB moves a byte and MOVSW moves a word. Thus, the previous example works regardless of whether the elements in the buffer are bytes or words.

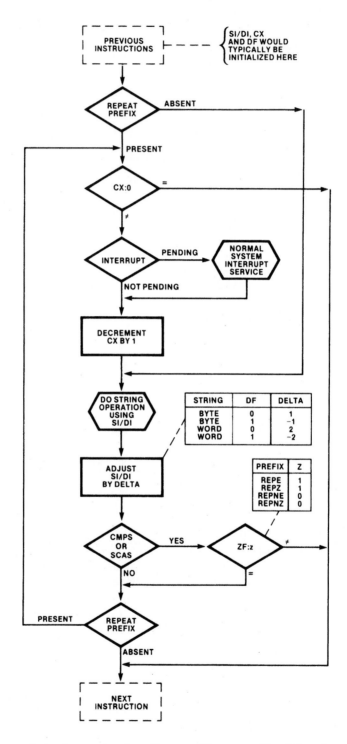

Figure 7.8-1   String instruction flow diagram. (Courtesy of Intel Corp.)

By using just a single MOVSW instruction with CX initially 32,768, all the bytes in the segment pointed to by DS can be moved to the segment pointed to by ES!

The *scan string* (**SCAS**) and *compare string* (**CMPS**) instructions are for scanning and comparing blocks of memory. SCAS compares the accumulator to an area of memory pointed to by ES:DI. For example, SCASB subtracts the byte pointed to by ES:DI from AL, AL – (ES:DI), to set the flags.

CMPS compares two memory locations, either bytes or words. For CMPS, the flags are set based on the results of the computation (DS:SI) – (ES:DI).

It is important to note that both SCAS and CMPS set the flags as the result of a subtraction, similar to the CMP instruction. However, there is an important difference. CMP computes *(destination – source)*, and CMPS, CMPSB, and CMPSW computes *(source – destination)*.

When prefixed by *repeat while equal* (**REPE**) either SCAS or CMPS can perform a comparison until either CX becomes 0 or a not equal comparison occurs. When prefixed by *repeat while not equal* (**REPNE**) either instruction can perform a comparison until either CX is 0 or an equal comparison occurs. SCAS and CMPS are the only string instructions that affect flags. The flags are altered to reflect the comparisons. String instructions never alter any flags to reflect changes to the index registers or to CX.

As an example of the use of SCAS, the code from Section 7.6 is rewritten using SCASB. The objective is to find the first byte in an EPROM that is not equal to 0FFH.

```
            cld                                     ;increment DI during scan
            mov     di,offset eprom                 ;set ES:DI to point to eprom
            mov     ax,seg eprom
            mov     es,ax
            mov     cx,length eprom                 ;number of bytes in eprom
            mov     al,0ffh                         ;pattern to check for a match
            repe    scasb                           ;scan while ES:DI = AL, and CX not 0
            jz      erased                          ;either CX = 0 or ES:DI != AL
            ...
nonerased:
            dec     di                              ;must decrement DI to point back to
            ...                                     ;first non erased location in eprom
erased:
            ...
                                                    ;all locations of eprom = 0ffh
```

Since the appropriate index register(s) is always incremented or decremented each time a string instruction is executed, it is necessary to decrement DI for the nonerased condition, so that DI points back to the first memory location not equal to 0FFH.

7.9   Records

The record directive allows you to symbolically define individual bits and strings of bits within a byte or word. This allows you to construct **bit encoded data structures**. Use of records provides efficient storage of data, while at the same time improving a program's readability. Each named bit string within a record is called a **field**. Bit field definitions of records can be used to generate masks to isolate bits or can be used to generate shift counts to right-justify a bit field.

Records must be defined using the **RECORD** directive, and then memory must be allocated to store instances of the record. The record directive specifies a template that defines the field names and sizes within a record. The record directive has the form:

name   RECORD *field-name:exp [= initval] [,...]*

For example, consider an application that involves the serial transfer of data. Format characteristics for the serial transfer, such as the baud rate, number of stop bits, use of a parity bit, and whether the parity bit, if used, should be odd or even, are read from an input port and stored in memory. This allows these parameters to be set on the input port's switches before the system is powered on. The program reads this port and stores the bits read in memory as a record. A record definition for this information might be defined as follows:

serial_io   record   baud:4,stop:1,parity:1,even:1

This record consists of 7-bits, 4 for baud rate, and one each for stop, parity, and even parity. While this directive defines the bit fields of the record and their names, it does not allocate memory for any instances of the record. As is the case for a structure, defining a record does not allocate storage. A **record definition** is simply a template that tells the assembler the name and location of each bit field within a byte or word. Allocation of memory is accomplished using the record name in a data allocation directive, for example:

channel1   serial_io   <>

This data allocation directive allocates memory for the variable channel1, which is a record with its fields defined by the record directive for serial_io. A record is either 8- or 16-bits in size depending on how many bits are required by the record's definition. If the total number of bits in all the fields of a record is 8 or fewer, a byte is allocated. Since the record serial_io requires 7-bits, the assembler allocates a byte of memory for channel1. When the number of bits defined in the record is less than a byte or a word, the assembler right justifies the fields.

The smallest data item that the 80C188EB can directly manipulate is a byte. But, the assembler provides three special operators that can be used to access bit fields in records (Table 7.9-1). The **MASK operator** defines a mask that has 1s in the positions that correspond to the bits assigned to the specified field and 0s in all other bit positions. This operator is used in an AND or TEST instruction to isolate a field. For example, the following instruction sequence jumps to a memory location that has instructions to set up the parity if the parity bit field is 1:

```
mov     al,channel1
test    al,mask parity          ;TEST AL with the value 00000010B
jnz     set_up_parity
```

The **shift count operator** does not have an explicit name. When a field name of a record is used as an operand, the assembler replaces the field name with the number of bit positions a record must be shifted to right justify the specified field. The shift count operator can be used to load CL with a shift count so that the SHR instruction can be used to

Table 7.9-1   Assembler record specific operators.

Operator	Operation	Syntax	Explanation
MASK	mask	MASK record-field	Creates a byte or word with 1s in the bit positions associated with the specified field
none	shift count	field name is used as an operand	Returns a number equal to the number of bits the record must be shifted to the right to right justify the field
WIDTH	width	WIDTH record WIDTH record-field	Returns number of bits in record Returns number of bits in record field

right justify the field. Assume that the baud field is used as the index into a table to look up a load value corresponding to the desired baud rate. The following instruction sequence leaves the value in the baud field right justified in AL, so that it can be used as an index for the table lookup:

```
mov     al,channel1              ;loads AL with CHANNEL1
and     al,mask baud             ;ANDs AL with 01111000B
shr     al,baud                  ;shifts AL right 3 bit positions
```

The **WIDTH operator** returns the number of bits in a record or record field.

7.10   Summary

The 80C188EB's logical instructions allow you to perform the basic logic operations of NOT, AND, OR, and XOR on byte and word operands. Additional bit manipulations can be performed using shift and rotate instructions. Characteristics of the result produced by a logical operation are indicated by the status flags AF, CF, OF, PF, SF, and ZF.

A conditional jump instruction changes a program's execution flow based on whether specific status flags are set or cleared. If the conditional jump instruction's conditions are met, execution flow precedes from the instruction at the specified target location. If the conditions are not met, execution flow continues with the instruction following the conditional jump.

Using a logical instruction and a conditional jump instruction makes possible the implementation of a full set of basic program execution flow logical structures. These logical structures are used to control execution flow and, consequently, the order in which tasks are executed. With these structures, task execution can be conditioned on input data, the results from a logical or arithmetic operation, or an external event.

Looping allows a task to be repeated a fixed or variable number of times. To repeat a loop a fixed number of times, a loop control variable is decremented each time through the loop and a conditional jump instruction is used to test the loop control variable. If the loop control variable is not zero, the conditional jump instruction jumps back to the beginning of the loop. If the loop control variable is zero, the loop is exited. The decrement and jump if zero operations can be implemented by a single LOOP instruction. The LOOP instruction uses the contents of CX as its loop control variable.

Looping a variable number of times requires testing for the occurrence of a specific event each time through the loop. This event is typically associated with the occurrence of a particular data value. The event may be external or internal. For external events, the data value tested is input through a port. For an internal event, the data value tested is the contents of a register or memory location. If a register's contents are tested, then some instruction in the loop modifies the register's contents each time through the loop. The same can be done for a memory location. Another approach involving memory locations is to scan sequential locations looking for a specific data value. In this approach, a memory pointer is incremented (or decremented) each time through the loop.

The REP prefix allows your program to have a string primitive loop on, or repeat, itself. CX is used as the loop control variable. In addition to the MOVS string primitive, a scan string (SCAS) and a compare string (CMPS) are also available. With SCAS you can compare AL or AX with a sequence of consecutive memory locations containing bytes or words, respectively.

Records provide a convenient means of naming bits and fields of bits in a byte or word, so these bits can be manipulated by name.

7.11   Problems

1. List the mnemonics and their meanings for each of the 80C188EB's six status flags and three control flags.

2. Which status flags can be directly set or cleared, and by which instructions?

3. What is the value, in hexadecimal, of the 16-bit PSW register immediately after an 80C188EB is reset? What are the values of each of the individual flags after reset?

4. For each of the following instructions, assume the same initial conditions: AL = 0A5H and DL = 4CH. Give the contents of AL, DL, and all the status flags after each instruction is executed. Use a dash symbol (-) to indicate flag values that are not modified by an instruction's execution.

   a. not dl

   b. and dl,al

   c. xor dl,dl

   d. or   al,dl

   e. stc

5. Concisely describe the effect of each of the following instructions, acting individually.

   a. xor ah,ah

   b. not dx

   c. xor al,80h

   d. or   al,80h

   e. and cl,0fh

6. Write an instruction sequence that clears bits 0, 6, and 7, and sets bits 2 and 3 of register AL.

7. Write an instruction sequence that toggles the most significant and least significant bits of AH while leaving the other bits unchanged.

8. Write a program that continually performs the following operations. The program inputs data from two byte input ports, PORT0 and PORT1. If the least significant four bits of PORT0 are identical to the most significant four bits of PORT1, then bit 6 of the output port MATCH is to be set. Otherwise, this bit is cleared. All other bits of port MATCH are to be 0. The port addresses are: PORT0 = 8000H, PORT1 = 8001H, and MATCH = 8000H.

9. Write a program that continually inputs data from the byte port INDATA and then outputs this data to either PORT0, PORT1, PORT2, or PORT3. The port to which the data is output is specified by bits 1 and 0 of the byte input port SELECT. The other bits of SELECT are used for other purposes and their logic values are unknown. Whenever bits 1 and 0 of port SELECT are changed, the port to which the data is output should immediately change. The ports addresses are: INDATA = 8000H, SELECT = 8001H, PORT0 = 8000H, PORT1 = 8001H, PORT2 = 8002H, and PORT3 = 8003H.

10. Write a program that outputs to PORTC a bit pattern that is the same as the bit pattern obtained from PORTA, except that those bits from PORTA that are in positions that are 1s in the bit pattern obtained from PORTB are complemented. In other words, those bits of PORTB that are 1s require that the corresponding bits from PORTA be complemented, before being output to PORTC. The program should continue to carry out this operation indefinitely. All three ports are bytes in the I/O space. The port address are PORTA = 8000H, PORTB = 8001H, and PORTC = 8002H.

11. An 8-bit output port, RBPORT (C000H), has a readback capability that allows the port's actual output value to be read in through an input port with the same address as the output port. Write a sequence of instructions that uses this readback capability to set bits 7 and 5 and clear bit 1 of the output port, while leaving the remainder of the output port's bits unchanged.

12. Draw a block diagram of the output port with readback capability described in problem 11 and its interface to an 80C188EB system bus. The output port's bits are to be constantly enabled. Assume that the address of the port is 8000H. Show the address decoder for the port as a single block and label all of its inputs. Write the Boolean equations for the device select pulses generated by the address decoder. For the other blocks use as few SSI and MSI circuits as possible. Label the function and device number for each of these ICs.

13. Using the following initial register values for each case: AX = 0B517H, BX = 0C7A2H, CL = 4 and CF = 0, specify the result after each instruction is executed.

   a. shl   ax,3
   b. shl   al,cl
   c. sal   al,cl
   d. shr   bh,1
   e. sar   bl,2

14. Using the following initial register values for each case: AX = 0B517H, BX = 0C7A2H, CL = 4 and CF = 0, specify the result after each instruction is executed.

   a. rol   ax,3
   b. rcl   ax,3
   c. ror   bh,cl
   d. rcr   bl,7
   e. rcr   ah,cl

15. Write a sequence of instructions that uses shifts to multiply an unsigned integer in AL by 2^n, where n is the value in BL. Assume that n is less than or equal to 8. The result is left in AX.

16. Assuming that AL initially contains C4H in each of the cases below,

   a. shr al,3
   b. sar al,3

   what is the value in AL, in hexadecimal, after each instruction is executed? If in (a) the content of AL were interpreted as an unsigned integer, what is the unsigned integer's decimal value before and after the instruction is executed? If in (b) the contents of AL were interpreted as a two's complement number, what is the number's value before and after the instruction is executed? What is the common effect of the two instructions?

17. What effect do jump instructions and data transfer instructions have in common with regard to the status flags?

18. What are the three kinds of attributes for a label? How does a label's attributes differ from those of a variable?

19. What registers are changed for an intrasegment jump? What registers are changed for an intersegment jump?

20. Why is the value of IP modified before it is used in the computation of the target address for an intrasegment direct jump?

21. What type of jump instruction is the bootstrap instruction and why is it of this type?

22. The program in Fig. 4.4-1 continually inputs bytes of data from the port SWITCHES, complements each byte, and outputs it to the port LEDS. Both the input and output transfers are unconditional. Write a program that implements the same task, except that the input of a byte from SWITCHES is conditioned on a momentary contact switch being pressed. Pressing this momentary contact switch sets bit 6 of the port STATUS. Also draw a logic diagram of the hardware required. Represent the address decoding logic as a block with all inputs and outputs labeled. The address of port STATUS is one greater than that of port SWITCHES.

23. A simple system has a 16-key keypad to select the next task that the system does. When a task is complete, the system reads input port KEYPAD and tests bit 7 to determine if a new task is to be done. If bit 7 is a 1, a new task is to be done and the task's number is contained in the least significant 4 bits of the byte that was input from KEYPAD. Modify the program in Fig. 7.4-2 to do this.

24. A system has 16 input ports (addresses 00H–0FH) and 16 output ports (addresses 00H–0FH). These are byte ports that are used to route data. Each time the XFER flag (bit 6 of port STATUS) is set, a byte of data is to be input from one of the input ports and output to one of the output ports. This process is to continue indefinitely. The input and output ports for a particular transfer are specified by data from the input port ROUTE. The least significant 4 bits of ROUTE specify the source port and the most significant 4 bits specify the destination port. Write a program that accomplishes this task. The port STATUS has address 10H and the port ROUTE has address 11H. Reading the port STATUS causes the hardware to clear all the port's bits.

25. A system is able to implement any of four tasks selected by an operator. The least significant four bits of byte port TASKN specify which of the four possible tasks is to be carried out. If bit 0 is set, task 0 is carried out. If bit 1 is set, task 1 is carried out, and so on, similar to Fig. 7.4-2. Each of these bits is controlled by its own momentary contact switch. A BUSY LED indicates when the system is busy doing a task. The BUSY LED is controlled by bit 0 of port ANNUN. The operator is only allowed to press one task switch at a time, and then only if the BUSY LED is not lighted. Pressing a task switch sets the DOTASK bit, bit 6 of the port STATUS. When this bit is set, the program is to execute the selected task. Draw a block diagram of the port hardware. Address decoding logic can be represented as a single block. Each output of this block must be labeled with the Boolean equation that it implements. Port STATUS has address 00H, port TASKN address 01H, and port ANNUN address 00H. Write the program. When no task switch is pressed, the program simply waits. Each task is to be represented by a NOP instruction.

26. Given the following data allocation:

```
data     segment          'RAM'
         bin       db      10 dup (?)
data     ends
```

write a program that uses the LOOP instruction to initialize each element of the array bin to zero.

27. Write a program that continually checks to see if any one or more of the bits from four byte input ports is 0. If this is the case, bit 7 of byte output port ALARM is to be set, if this is not the case, bit 7 is cleared. The four input ports occupy consecutive locations starting at address 04H. The address of port ALARM is also 04H.

28. Write a program that conditionally inputs ten words of data from the word port SOURCE then outputs these 10 words in reverse order to the word port REVERSED. This process is repeated indefinitely. The input of each byte from the port SOURCE is to be conditioned on bit 7 of the byte port READY being set. The output of each byte to port REVERSED is to be conditioned on bit 6 of port READY being set. The port addresses are: READY = 00H, SOURCE = 01H, and REVERSED = 00H.

29. The LOOP instruction takes 16 states each time it loops back to its target and 6 states when it does not loop back and terminates. Using this information:

    a. Compute the initial value of the loop control variable needed to achieve a 10 ms delay with a LOOP instruction that loops to itself. Assume that the 80C188EB's crystal frequency is 16 MHz. Show the complete computation.

    b. Write a sequence of instructions that uses the 10 ms delay from part (a) inside of another loop to create a 1 second delay. Compute the initial value of the outer loop's loop control variable. In the computation of the outer loop's initial loop control variable, disregard the additional delay introduced by the execution of the instructions in the outer loop.

30. An application contains an array of eight byte input ports. The name of the first port in the array is SENSORS. This port has the address 8000H in the I/O space. The remaining seven ports consecutively follow the first. Two eight byte memory arrays, sen_n and sen_o, are declared in the data segment.

    a. One of the tasks that the application must accomplish is to read the eight input ports and store the values in the memory buffer called sen_n. Write a sequence of instructions that accomplishes this task.

    b. Write a sequence of instructions that copies the contents of the byte memory array sen_n to the byte memory array sen_o.

    c. Write a sequence of instructions, that does not include string instructions, that compares the contents of the two memory buffers sen_n and sen_o, and if they are not identical, sets bit 7 of the byte output port MOTION. If they are the same, bit 7 of MOTION is to be cleared. MOTION's address is 0C000H.

31. A byte output port, DOUT, provides output data to an output device. Draw a logic diagram for this output port and its interface to an 80C188EB system bus. This port is in the 80C188EB's I/O space. Data transfer to this output port must be conditional. An external hardware flag must be included that indicates to the 80C188EB when the output port can accept the next data byte. This same flag indicates to the output device when there is new data in the output port for the output device to process. The 80C188EB inputs the flag bit as bit 3 of byte port STATUS. Assume that when this bit is 0, the microprocessor can output another byte to the output port. In your logic diagram, show the address decoder as a block. The address decoder should implement exhaustive decoding. Label all of the address decoder's inputs and outputs.

32. A system has eight contiguous byte input ports and eight contiguous byte output ports. Using string instructions and the REP prefix, write a complete program that reads all the input ports in sequence and transfers the data read to an array in memory called inbuff. The program then outputs the data in the array to the output ports. The first element in the array is output to the first output port. The second element in the array is output to the second output port and so on. This process is repeated indefinitely. The address of the first of the eight input ports is 40H, the address of the first of the eight output ports is 10H. Use as few instructions as possible.

8

THE STACK, PROCEDURES, AND MODULAR SOFTWARE

8.1   The Stack

8.2   80C188EB Stack Allocation and Operation

8.3   Procedures

8.4   Procedures in a Single Module Program

8.5   Parameter Passing

8.6   Modular Software Design using Procedures

8.7   Procedure Sequencing Using a Finite State Machine

8.8   Testing and Debugging Procedures

8.9   Summary

Procedures are an important programming language feature. Use of procedures reduces program size, enhances program modularity, aids code reuse, and facilitates the formulation of the software architecture.

A procedure is a named sequence of instructions that performs a single task. The instructions that comprise a procedure appear at only one point in a source program. However, these instructions can be caused to execute from any point in the program by calling the procedure. After the instructions in the procedure have completed execution, execution flow automatically continues from the point in the program where the procedure was called. Because the instructions that comprise a procedure appear at only one point in a program, but can be executed from any point in the program, the program's size is reduced. This reduces the amount of memory required to store a program.

Procedures allow software to be designed and coded in a modular fashion. All the details of accomplishing a task can be hidden within a procedure. This makes the overall structure and operation of a complex program easier to understand. Procedures can be tested and debugged individually, then included in the complete program.

Well designed and documented procedures can be used in programs other than the one for which they were originally written. Procedures can be written to have wide applicability by using parameters to increase their generality. When a procedure is executed, specific parameter values are passed to the procedure. These values tailor the procedure for each specific instance of its execution.

A program's architecture might consist of a main program that contains calls to procedures. The procedures must be called in an appropriate sequence so the program's tasks are carried out as required.

One very flexible method of sequencing task execution (procedure calls) as a function of the system's inputs is to use a table driven finite state sequential machine. This machine provides a software architecture that is suitable for many different applications. Inputs to the system cause the machine to change state. Based on its present state and input, the machine changes to a new state and calls the appropriate procedure. A table driven finite state machine is easily modifiable when a system's requirements change.

Before transferring execution flow to a procedure, the call instruction stores the address of the instruction following the call. This return address is stored in a special memory structure called a stack. A return instruction at the end of the procedure causes the return address to be retrieved from the stack. The return address is then used to fetch the instruction that follows the call.

Programs can also use the stack to pass parameters to a procedure and to store any local variables the procedure requires. Our study of procedures begins with the stack that is required to support their use.

8.1 The Stack

A **stack** is a memory structure that can hold a fixed maximum number of bytes. The only means of putting data into or removing data from a stack is via the stack's top register. Thus, a stack is a last-in first-out (**LIFO**) memory structure. The last data item written to a stack is the first data item that can be read from the stack.

8.1.1 The Stack Concept

Before considering how a stack is implemented and operates in an 80C188EB system, some fundamental concepts regarding stacks must be introduced. Conceptually, a stack can be thought of as several registers stacked one on top of the other (Fig. 8.1-1). The number of registers determines the **stack's length**. The top register is termed, appropriately, the top of the stack, and is the only register in the stack that can be written or read.

A **push** operation writes data to the top register of the stack. The data written is said to have been "pushed" onto the stack. Since only the top register can be accessed, any subsequent word pushed onto the stack must be stored in the top register. Thus, the data previously in the top register must automatically be shifted down to the next register by a push operation. As each additional data word is pushed onto the stack, all previously stored data in the stack is shifted down one register.

A **pop** operation reads a word of data from the top of the stack. When a word is popped from the stack, it is read from the top register and all other words in the stack are automatically shifted up one register. Since only the top stack register can be read by a pop

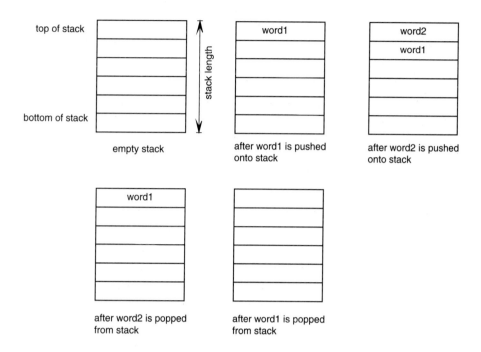

Figure 8.1-1   Conceptual representation of a stack of length 6.

operation, data can only be read from the stack in the reverse order from which it was written.

If an *n* word stack is initially empty, and *n* words are pushed onto the stack without any intervening pop operations, the stack will be full. If an additional word is subsequently pushed onto the stack, the first word that was pushed onto the empty stack is forced out of the bottom register and lost.

Whenever the total number of pop operations equals the total number of push operations, the stack is considered to be "empty." The term "empty" is used to indicate that there is no data available in the stack.

Some early microprocessors implemented their stacks as a special hardware structure on the microprocessor chip. The need to provide large stacks eventually made this approach impractical.

8.1.2   Stacks Implemented in Standard Memory

Instead of a special hardware structure, a stack can be implemented using an area reserved in ordinary RAM. This is accomplished by designing the microprocessor to automatically manipulate a special internal **stack pointer** register. This register acts as a pointer to the location in RAM that is to be considered the top of the stack. Logic within the microprocessor automatically manipulates the stack pointer's contents in response to instructions that push data onto or pop data off of the stack. By automatically manipulating the stack pointer, the microprocessor creates a stack in ordinary RAM.

8.2 80C188EB Stack Allocation and Operation

In an 80C188EB system, the stack segment register (SS) points to the base of the memory segment reserved for the stack (Fig. 8.2-1). The memory location within this segment that represents the top of the stack is pointed to by the stack pointer register (SP). Thus, the address of the top of the stack, at any instant, is SS:SP. In response to push and pop operations, the 80C188EB automatically modifies the value in SP to create the effect of a stack in the reserved memory. Thus, the actual physical address of the top of the stack changes. In effect, the position of the top of the stack moves in memory. The address of the top of the stack decreases as words are placed on the stack and increases as they are removed.

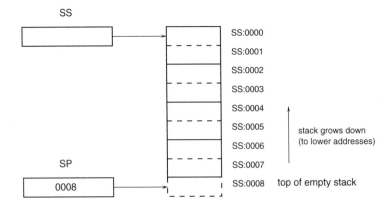

Figure 8.2-1   An empty 80C188EB stack of length 4 words, shown as a stack of bytes.

Memory for the stack is reserved in a separate logical segment. The following directives allocate the four word stack shown in Fig. 8.2-1:

```
stack     segment 'STKRAM'
          dw 4 dup (?)
tos       label word
stack     ends
```

The name stack has been used to name the stack segment to make its purpose clear. However, TASM defines stack as a reserved word and will generate a warning during assembly. If you wish to avoid this warning, you can use another name. The **LABEL** directive specifies a name and type for the current location of assembly. However, unlike a data allocation directive, LABEL does not allocate memory. LABEL has the general form:

name   label *type*

In the preceding example, LABEL assigns the name TOS to the first word following the four words allocated for the stack. As a result, TOS has an offset attribute of 8, type attribute word, and segment attribute STACK. The label TOS is created so it can be used in the program to initialize SP.

Before you can allow any instructions that use the stack to be executed, you must initialize both SS and SP. Instructions that initialize SS and SP must be preceded by an ASSUME statement that includes SS. For example:

```
assume          ss:stack
```

The following instructions initialize the stack:

```
mov       ax,stack          ;initialize SS with segment name
mov       ss,ax
mov       sp,offset tos     ;SP points to top of empty stack
```

Immediately following initialization, the stack is empty. When the stack is empty, the stack pointer actually points to the first word following the end of the memory area reserved for the stack. This location constitutes the top of the empty stack. In Fig. 8.2-1, the physical address of the top of the empty stack is SS:0008H. The address of the top of the stack when it is full is SS:0000H.

Some instructions, like PUSH and POP, are used to directly manipulate the stack. Others, like CALL and RET, use the stack indirectly to carry out other objectives (Table 8.2-1).

Table 8.2-1   Instructions that use the stack.

Mnemonic	Operands	Function	O	D	I	T	S	Z	A	P	C
PUSH	src	push a word onto stack	–	–	–	–	–	–	–	–	–
PUSHA	none	push general regs. onto stack	–	–	–	–	–	–	–	–	–
POP	dst	pop a word from stack	–	–	–	–	–	–	–	–	–
POPA	none	pop general regs. from stack	–	–	–	–	–	–	–	–	–
PUSHF	none	push flags onto stack	–	–	–	–	–	–	–	–	–
POPF	none	pop flags from stack	✓	✓	✓	✓	✓	✓	✓	✓	✓
CALL	target	call a procedure	–	–	–	–	–	–	–	–	–
RET	opt.-pop-val	return from procedure	–	–	–	–	–	–	–	–	–
ENTER	locals,levels	procedure entry	–	–	–	–	–	–	–	–	–
LEAVE	none	leave	–	–	–	–	–	–	–	–	–

Only word data can be transferred to or from the 80C188EB's stack. The *push word onto stack* (**PUSH**) instruction pushes a word onto the stack. The source of the data can be a word register, a memory word, or immediate data. Execution of a PUSH causes SP to be decremented. The high byte of the word is then written to the stack location pointed to by SP. SP is then decremented again, and the low byte of the word is written to the new stack location pointed to by SP. Thus, a word pushed onto an empty stack is written to the last two bytes in the memory area allocated for the stack.

Figure 8.2-2 represents the 80C188EB's word oriented stack implemented in a byte-wide memory. After execution of a single PUSH, SP has a value two less than its prior value. A series of PUSHes writes data into successively lower memory addresses. In other words, pushing data onto the stack causes the stack to "grow" toward successively lower memory addresses.

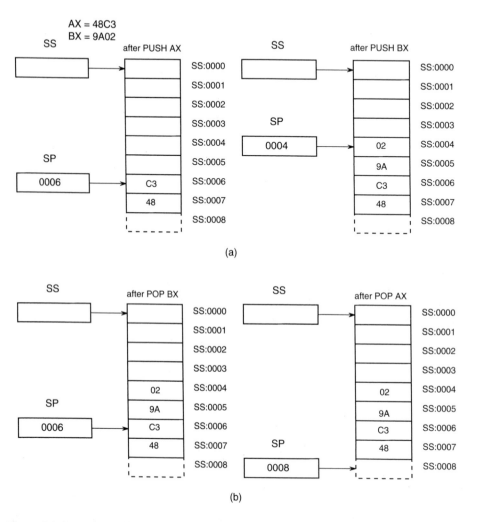

Figure 8.2-2   An 80C188EB stack: (a) after execution of pushes; (b) after execution of pops.

A *pop word from stack* (**POP**) instruction reads a word from the top of the stack and transfers it to a word register or memory word. When a POP is executed, the byte pointed to by SP is transferred to the low byte of the destination. SP is incremented, then the byte now pointed to by SP is transferred to the high byte of the destination. Finally, SP is again incremented. When a POP's execution is complete, SP's value is two greater than its value prior to the POP.

PUSHes and POPs are complementary and should be paired. For example, the sequence of pushes in Fig. 8.2-2(a) that temporarily store AX and BX on the stack, are paired with an equal number of pops (Fig. 8.2-2(b)) that restore the values of AX and BX from the stack.

```
push    ax
push    bx
pop     bx
pop     ax
```

When pushes and pops are used to temporarily save and restore registers, the pops must occur in the reverse order of the pushes for the registers to be properly restored. When stack operations are properly paired, **balanced**, the value of SP will be the same, after the sequence of push and pop operations, as it was before. After the balanced sequence of pushes and pops in Fig. 8.2-2, the data pushed onto the stack is still present in memory even though the stack is considered "empty." Subsequent push operations will overwrite this data.

PUSH and POP can also be used to copy the contents of one segment register to another. For example,

```
push    ds
pop     es
```

copies the contents of DS to ES. This instruction sequence is very useful, since direct transfers from one segment register to another, such as mov es,ds, are not permitted. We often want to make ES equal to DS before carrying out a string transfer where both the source and destination are in the same segment.

The contents of the flags register can be saved on the stack using the *push flags onto stack* (**PUSHF**) instruction. The *pop flags off stack* (**POPF**) instruction pops a word off the top of the stack and copies the nine flag bits of this word to the flags register.

The *push all* (**PUSHA**) instruction pushes all the general registers onto the stack. The order in which these registers are pushed is AX, CX, DX, BX, SP, BP, SI, and DI. The SP value pushed is the value of SP before the first register is pushed. The *pop all* (**POPA**) instruction pops all the values from the stack to the general registers, except for SP. The value of SP popped from the stack is discarded.

Instructions such as PUSH and POP automatically modify SP in the appropriate manner. However, SP is a general register and, therefore, can also be modified directly, using instructions such as MOV, INC, and DEC. But, the purpose of SP is to maintain the stack! Accordingly, SP should be initialized to the offset of the top of the empty stack at the beginning of a program. Once initialized, instructions should not use SP for any non-stack purposes. To do otherwise is extremely risky.

One reason you should not directly manipulate SP is that the stack is also used to store return addresses for interrupt service procedures. If enabled, an interrupt can occur at any time. If SP has been temporarily changed and an interrupt occurs, the interrupt return address is written to whatever location corresponds to SP's current value. In an actual system, there may not even be RAM at this location. As a result, the return address is lost and your program fails!

Since all operations on the stack are word operations, a more concise stack representation, one that groups the stack's bytes as words, is often used (Fig. 8.2-3).

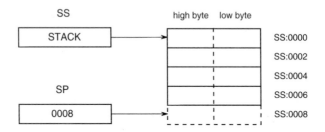

Figure 8.2-3   Stack from Fig. 8.2-1 drawn as a word stack.

8.3   Procedures

A **procedure**, or **subroutine**, is a named sequence of instructions. These instructions exist at only one point in your program. But, you can cause these instructions to be executed at any point in your program by placing the *call a procedure* (**CALL**) instruction at that point. When called, execution flow is transferred to the procedure (Fig. 8.3-1). The procedure's instructions are then executed. The last instruction executed in the procedure is a *return from a procedure* (**RET**) instruction. RET causes execution flow to be transferred back to, and continue with, the instruction that follows the CALL instruction. When a program has more than one CALL instruction to the same procedure, execution flow always continues with the instruction following the CALL that invoked the procedure.

In your program, the instructions that comprise a procedure are delineated by enclosing them in a **PROC/ENDP** directive pair as follows:

```
name        proc  [type]
            ...   ;instructions comprising the procedure's body
name        endp
```

For example, a procedure named scale that scales the value in AL by 0.9609 appears in a program as:

```
scale           proc
        mov     ah,0
        mov     cx,9609
        mul     cx
        mov     cx,10000
        div     cx
        ret
scale           endp
```

In addition to delineating the procedure's instructions or body, the PROC/ENDP directive pair serves several other purposes. PROC defines a label that is the entry point, or

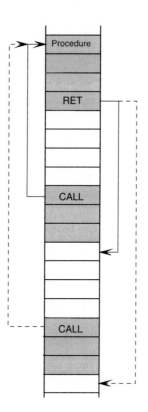

Figure 8.3-1   Procedure calls and returns. The return address always returns execution
flow to the instruction following the call that caused the procedure's execution.

name, of the procedure. This label is associated with the first instruction in the procedure's
body. This is the name used by any CALL instruction that invokes the procedure. The
label's segment attribute is the segment in which it is defined. The label's offset attribute is
equal to the distance in bytes from the beginning of its segment to the procedure's first
instruction.

A procedure's type is either NEAR or FAR. A **NEAR procedure** can only be called
from within the segment containing the procedure. A **FAR procedure** can be called from
any segment. If a procedure's type is not specified in the PROC directive, it defaults to
NEAR. The assembler uses a procedure's type to determine whether to generate a near or
far version of the CALL instruction.

ENDP defines the end of the procedure that was started by the PROC directive with
the same name.

A version of the program in Fig. 4.3-2, rewritten to use procedures, is shown in Fig.
8.3-2. The task of scaling the binary input from the ADC is carried out by the procedure
scale. The task of converting the scaled binary value to packed BCD is carried out by the
procedure bin_2_pbcd. These two procedures are placed in the beginning of the
segment code.

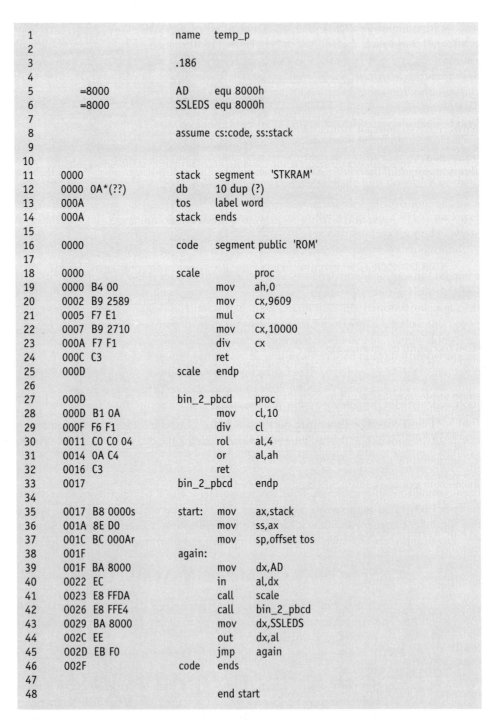

```
 1                              name    temp_p
 2
 3                              .186
 4
 5      =8000                   AD      equ 8000h
 6      =8000                   SSLEDS  equ 8000h
 7
 8                              assume  cs:code, ss:stack
 9
10
11      0000                    stack   segment    'STKRAM'
12      0000  0A*(??)           db      10 dup (?)
13      000A                    tos     label word
14      000A                    stack   ends
15
16      0000                    code    segment public  'ROM'
17
18      0000                    scale           proc
19      0000  B4 00                     mov     ah,0
20      0002  B9 2589                   mov     cx,9609
21      0005  F7 E1                     mul     cx
22      0007  B9 2710                   mov     cx,10000
23      000A  F7 F1                     div     cx
24      000C  C3                        ret
25      000D                    scale           endp
26
27      000D                    bin_2_pbcd      proc
28      000D  B1 0A                     mov     cl,10
29      000F  F6 F1                     div     cl
30      0011  C0 C0 04                  rol     al,4
31      0014  0A C4                     or      al,ah
32      0016  C3                        ret
33      0017                    bin_2_pbcd      endp
34
35      0017  B8 0000s         start:   mov     ax,stack
36      001A  8E D0                     mov     ss,ax
37      001C  BC 000Ar                  mov     sp,offset tos
38      001F                    again:
39      001F  BA 8000                   mov     dx,AD
40      0022  EC                        in      al,dx
41      0023  E8 FFDA                   call    scale
42      0026  E8 FFE4                   call    bin_2_pbcd
43      0029  BA 8000                   mov     dx,SSLEDS
44      002C  EE                        out     dx,al
45      002D  EB F0                     jmp     again
46      002F                    code    ends
47
48                              end start
```

Figure 8.3-2   Listing of the program of Fig. 4.3-2 rewritten to use procedures.

```
Turbo Assembler Version 4.0    11/14/96 07:52:01   Page 2
Symbol Table
```

Symbol Name	Type	Value	Cref (defined at #)		
??DATE	Text	"11/14/96"			
??FILENAME	Text	"temp_p"			
??TIME	Text	"07:52:01"			
??VERSION	Number	0400			
@CPU	Text	0103H	#3		
@CURSEG	Text	CODE	#11	#16	
@FILENAME	Text	TEMP_P			
@WORDSIZE	Text	2	#3	#11	#16
AD	Number	8000	#5	39	
AGAIN	Near	CODE:001F	#38	45	
BIN_2_PBCD	Near	CODE:000D	#27	42	
SCALE	Near	CODE:0000	#18	41	
SSLEDS	Number	8000	#6	43	
START	Near	CODE:0017	#35	48	
TOS	Word	STK:000A	#13	37	

Groups & Segments	Bit	Size	Align	Combine	Class	Cref (defined at #)	
CODE	16	002F	Para	Public	ROM	8	#16
STACK	16	000A	Para	none	STKRAM	8	#11 35

Figure 8.3-2   Listing of the program of Fig. 4.3-2 rewritten to use procedures.
(Continued.)

Though they appear at the beginning of the program, the procedures are not actually executed until the CALL instructions that use their names are executed. As always, the first instruction executed in the program is the instruction whose label is specified by the END directive. The label in this program's END directive is START. Thus, the instruction with the label START is the first to be executed. This instruction, together with the two instructions that follow it, initialize the stack.

For this simple example, it may seem that the use of procedures has made the program longer and more complex. The fact that procedures normally reduce a program's length is not demonstrated by this example, because the need to call the same procedure from multiple locations does not arise.

8.3.1   Calling a Procedure

A call instruction has the form:

    call   *target*

where target identifies the label of the procedure being called. Two CALL instructions appear in the program of Fig. 8.3-2:

```
call        scale

call        bin_2_pbcd
```

When a CALL instruction is executed, it does the following:

1. Saves the return address, by pushing it onto the stack.
2. Transfers execution to the first instruction in the procedure.

These two operations are equivalent to a "PUSH" of the return address, followed by a "JMP" to the procedure.

When the procedure's execution is complete, the **return address,** pushed onto the stack by the call instruction, is used to return execution flow to the instruction following the CALL. In this chapter, the focus is on **intrasegment CALLs**. These are CALLs to NEAR procedures, procedures in the same segment as the CALL. Since the target is in the same segment, the return address is completely specified by the offset of the instruction following the CALL. Therefore, an intrasegment call pushes onto the stack only the offset address of the instruction following the CALL.

A slight complication arises because of the 80C188EB's instruction queue. At the time the CALL instruction is executed, IP actually contains the offset of the next instruction to be fetched into the queue. This offset is not necessarily that of the instruction following the CALL. As a consequence, the 80C188EB automatically modifies IP to be equal to the offset of the instruction following the CALL, before pushing the contents of IP onto the stack. This is the same type of modification that the 80C188EB had to perform to execute an instruction pointer relative direct jump in Chapter 7.

From Fig. 8.3-2, it can be seen that when the instruction call scale (line 41) is executed, the return address that it pushes onto the stack is 0026H, the offset of the next instruction (line 42). When the instruction call bin_2_pbcd (line 42) is executed, the return address it places on the stack is 0029H, the offset of the instruction on line 43.

The 80C188EB transfers execution flow to a NEAR procedure by putting the offset of the procedure's label into IP. This causes the next instruction fetched to be the first instruction in the procedure. The offset of the label scale is 0000H and the offset of the label bin_2_pbcd is 000DH.

There are two forms of intrasegment CALLs. They are distinguished by how the procedure label's offset is specified. The two forms are instruction pointer relative and indirect.

For instruction pointer relative, **IP relative calls,** the procedure's offset, the new IP value, is the sum of the modified old IP and a 16-bit displacement contained in the CALL instruction. This displacement is the distance in bytes from the first byte of the instruction following the CALL to the first byte of the first instruction in the procedure.

The 16-bit displacement restricts the target procedure to be located in memory within +32,767 or −32,768 bytes of the first byte of the instruction following the CALL. However, this range is sufficient to allow the target procedure to be anywhere within the segment containing the CALL, since a segment can only contain a maximum of 2^{16} bytes and a segment wraps around. Wrap around in instruction pointer relative addressing was discussed in Section 7.4 with regard to JMP instructions and is the same for CALL instructions.

In Fig. 8.3-2, the instruction call scale is assembled into the three bytes E8 FF DA. E8 is the opcode for an IP relative call. The call instruction's displacement is FFDAH. FFDAH is the two's complement representation of –0026H. The adjusted value of IP is 0026H, the offset of the instruction following call scale. When the call scale instruction is executed, the adjusted value of IP is pushed onto the stack as the return address. Then, to transfer execution, the adjusted IP value of +0026H is added to the instruction's displacement value of +FFDAH to get the new IP value, 0000H. This new IP value is the offset of the procedure scale.

$$
\begin{aligned}
\text{adjusted IP} &= \quad 0026\text{H} \\
+ \text{ displacement} &= \quad \text{FFDAH} \\
\hline
\text{new IP} &= \quad 0000\text{H}
\end{aligned}
$$

For **indirect calls**, the new value for IP is taken from a 16-bit register or memory word. This value is the actual offset of the procedure's label, not a displacement. For example, a delay procedure, named delay, can be called indirectly through BX:

```
mov     bx,offset delay
call    bx
```

Indirect calls are particularly useful when the procedure to be called is determined during runtime. For example, a system might execute one of several functions implemented by procedures, task0, task1,..., based on a function number, (0,1,...) input from a keypad. Fig. 8.3-3 shows the structure of a program that accomplishes this. ctable is a **call table**, a table of procedure addresses (offsets). If an index into the call table has been placed in DI, the call to the corresponding task is accomplished with an indirect call through the memory location. The addressed memory location holds the target procedure's offset address.

Intersegment calls are used to call procedures in segments other than the segment containing the CALL. For intersegment transfers, a new value is required for both CS and IP. Intersegment calls push a two word return address, consisting of the contents of CS followed by the modified contents of IP, onto the stack.

There are two forms of intersegment calls, direct and indirect. A **direct intersegment call** is a five byte instruction that contains the target segment and offset values as its last four bytes. An **indirect intersegment call** is a four byte instruction that specifies the offset address of a double-word memory location that contains the new values for CS and IP.

8.3.2   Returning from a Procedure

The last instruction executed in a procedure is a RET. RET causes program execution to return to the instruction following the CALL. RET accomplishes this by popping the return address from the stack and transferring execution to this address. Although it is the

```
ctable  dw task0,task1,task2,...        ;table of procedure addresses
        ...
task0   proc                      ;procedure to implement function 0
        ...
        ret
task0   endp


task1   proc                                ;procedure to implement function 1
        ...
        ret
task1   endp
        ...
        in      al,KEYPAD             ;input function number from keypad
        mov     ah,0
        shl     ax,1                 ;multiply by 2 to use as an index
        mov     di,ax
        call    cs:ctable[di]        ;indirect call to procedure
        .
```

Figure 8.3-3   Using a call table to indirectly call procedures.

last instruction executed, RET does not have to physically be the last instruction in the procedure, though this is usually the case. The *return instruction*, **RET,** has the form:

> ret   *optional-pop-value*

There are actually four different machine language instructions that the assembler can generate when it encounters a RET. However, all RETs generated between a particular PROC/ENDP pair are of the same type. The assembler generates an **intrasegment return** for all RET instructions contained within the PROC/ENDP directives of a NEAR procedure. An intrasegment RET pops a single word from the top of the stack and puts it in IP. RET can also add an *optional pop value* to SP. If a pop value is specified, the assembler generates a second machine language form of the intrasegment return instruction. The purpose of a pop-value is discussed in Section 8.5.

For RETs in FAR procedures, the assembler generates an intersegment return. An **intersegment return,** pops two words from the stack. The first word popped is placed in IP. The second word popped is placed in CS. There are also two machine language forms of intersegment returns, one form increments SP by a pop-value and the other does not.

8.3.3   Nested Procedures

One procedure can call another. This is referred to as **procedure nesting**. Fig. 8.3-4 illustrates this situation. Each call pushes a return address onto the stack. The **levels of nesting** increase by one each time one procedure calls another without a return instruction being executed. The number of levels of nesting is limited only by the size of the stack. Since the last procedure called is always the first that needs to be returned from, the LIFO nature of the stack insures that the return addresses are popped in the required order.

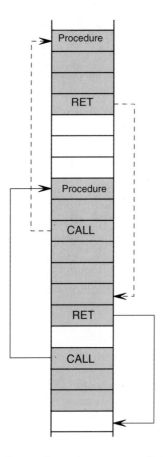

Figure 8.3-4   Nested procedure calls and returns. Call instructions shown are three bytes long. Return address always returns execution flow to the instruction following the call that caused the procedure's execution.

8.3.4   Saving Registers Used by a Procedure

A procedure usually needs to use some of the 80C188EB's general registers to carry out its task. Before a CALL is executed, these registers may hold information that is needed after the procedure is returned from. These registers' contents can be saved on the stack and then restored after the procedure has finished using them.

The most efficient way to do this is to have the procedure itself save and restore the registers. The first instructions in the procedure push the contents of the registers to be used by the procedure onto the stack, thus saving them. Immediately prior to the return from the procedure, the saved contents of the registers are popped from the stack, in reverse order. This restores the original register values. In the following example, instructions in the procedure modify AX, BX, and flags. These registers' contents are first saved on the stack, and later restored.

```
exmpl           proc
                push      ax          ;save registers used by procedure
                push      bx
                pushf

                ...                   ;instructions to carry out the procedure's
                ...                   ;task, these instruction modify AX,BX, and F
                popf                  ;restore registers
                pop       bx
                pop       ax
                ret                   ;return
exmpl           endp
```

The POPs must be in the reverse order of the PUSHes to properly restore the register's values. *If PUSHes and POPs in a procedure are not balanced, the word at the top of the stack when RET is executed will not be the desired return address, and execution will be transferred to some unintended location!*

8.4   Procedures in a Single Module Program

A program can be structured so each of its tasks is accomplished by a procedure. These procedures may, in turn, call other procedures. The main part of the program controls the order in which the procedures are called. The resulting program essentially consists of calls to procedures. Many of these calls are conditioned on the state of flags, that are set or cleared as a result of tests to determine whether a specific task should be executed.

A template for this form of a program is given in Fig. 8.4-1. Following the program's module NAME and EQU statements, are a data segment, stack segment, and code segment. The stack's size must be adequate for the application.

Unlike procedures in high-level languages, ASM86 procedures do not have restricted scope. An instruction sequence can "fall into" an embedded procedure. A program's procedures are placed at the beginning of the code segment to minimize the chance of accidental execution. Following the procedures are instructions that initialize the segment registers. These are the first instructions executed by the program, even though they are not the first instructions in the code segment.

If a procedure's execution is conditional, logical or arithmetic instructions are used to determine whether the conditions are met. Flags are set or cleared as a result of the execution of these instructions. A conditional jump instruction is then used to jump over the CALL if the conditions required for its execution are *not* met.

```
name        smwproc                    ;module name

_____       equ _____                  ;equates
_____       equ _____

data        segment 'RAM'              ;variable allocation
  .
  .
  .
data        ends

stack       segment 'STKRAM'           ;stack allocation
            dw __ dup (?)
tos         label word
stack       ends

assume cs:code, ds:data, ss:stack

code        segment 'ROM'              ;beginning of code segment

proc1       proc                       ;first procedure
  .
  .

            ret
proc1       endp

proc2       proc                       ;second procedure
  .
  .

            ret
proc2       endp

start:      mov ax,data                ;first instruction executed in program
            mov ds,ax                  ;initialize ds
            mov ax,stack               ;initialize ss
            mov ss,ax
            mov sp,offset tos          ;initialize tos
              .
              .
              .
code        ends
            end start
```

Figure 8.4-1   Template for a program that uses procedures.

8.5 Parameter Passing

Procedures perform their functions, or tasks, using well defined input data. This input data consists of:

1. data to configure a procedure for a specific instance of its execution, and
2. data to be transformed or processed by the procedure.

This input data is made available to a procedure in the form of **parameters** or **arguments**. A parameter can be either:

1. a copy of the actual data value, or
2. the address of the data value.

Parameters must be passed to a procedure by putting them in registers or memory locations where the procedure expects to find them. If a parameter is a copy of the actual data, the parameter is said to be **passed by value.** If a parameter is the address of the data, the parameter is said to be **passed by address** or **passed by reference**. The address of a data value is often referred to as a **pointer** to the data value.

You must write a sequence of instructions, preceding the call to a procedure, that places the procedure's parameters in the registers or memory locations where the procedure expects to find them. This sequence of instructions is referred to as the **calling sequence**. A procedure may be written to expect its parameters in any combination of the following places:

1. the 80C188EB's general purpose registers
2. memory variables
3. the stack

A procedure's **header** is a group of comments that document the procedure's function and specify how each parameter is passed. The header also indicates which registers or variables are modified by the procedure. A well written, documented, and tested procedure allows the details of its implementation to be of secondary concern to a user. A procedure's header should tell you all you need to know to use the procedure. It should not be necessary to read a procedure's instructions to understand what the procedure accomplishes.

In addition to providing information to another user, the header also relieves you of the need to reread, in detail, your own code later, when you can't remember exactly what the procedure that you wrote does. Some procedures in this text have abbreviated headers because the procedure's details are described in the text. However, in an actual program you should always provide complete headers.

Results computed by a procedure can be returned to the calling program using the same methods that are used to pass parameters.

8.5.1   Passing Parameters in General Purpose Registers

If an application requires a software delay of a specific duration, you could write a fixed delay procedure that provides the required delay. This procedure could then be called whenever a delay of its duration is required. If several delays of different durations were required in a single program, writing different fixed duration delay procedures would be inefficient.

Instead, a variable delay procedure can be written. The duration of the delay is specified by a parameter passed to the procedure each time the procedure is called. The variable delay procedure, vdelay (Fig. 8.5-1) can have its delay varied in 10 ms steps. This procedure can create delays ranging from approximately 10 ms to 10 minutes. The value in AX when vdelay is called determines its duration. This value is a parameter passed to vdelay. Because of the use of a parameter, vdelay can produce many different delays in a single application. Because it provides a variable delay, vdelay can also be reused, without modification, in other programs.

Since vdelay expects to find its parameters in AX, an instruction prior to its CALL must load AX with the number that represents the desired delay in multiples of 10 ms. This instruction comprises vdelay's calling sequence.

In general, it is good practice to have a procedure save and restore any registers it modifies that are not used to either pass parameters or return results. This makes the procedure reusable, without additional constraints.

Using general purpose registers for parameter passing is straightforward. But, since the number of general purpose registers is limited, this method is only useful when just a few parameters need to be passed.

8.5.2   Passing Parameters in Memory Variables

Variables in a data segment can be used to pass parameters. This method is advantageous in that, the number of parameters passed is not as limited as when using general purpose registers. A disadvantage of this method is that, if each parameter for every procedure uses a unique variable, the memory required can become large.

8.5.3   Using Pointers as Parameters

Registers or variables can be used to pass parameters that are pointers to (addresses of) data in memory. This method is particularly useful when the data is a structure consisting of a number of data items, such as an array, string, or list. The pointer simply points to the beginning, or starting address, of the structure. When the number of data items in the structure to be processed is not always the same, another parameter can be used to specify the number for each instance of the procedure's execution. For example, this allows the same procedure to process arrays of differing lengths.

The procedure max_r in Fig. 8.5-2 determines the maximum value in an array of unsigned binary words. The array's offset and length are passed using registers BX and CX, respectively. Instructions in the calling sequence load BX with the offset of the first word in the array and load CX with the length of the array. The parameter passed in BX, the array's offset, is a pointer. The procedure returns the maximum value in AX.

```
;******************************************************************
;
;NAME: VDELAY
;
;FUNCTION: Variable software delay
;
;CREATED:
;REVISED:
;
;ASSUMES: AX = delay time as a multiple of 10ms
;RETURNS: nothing
;MODIFIES: CX, AX, and F
;
;CALLS: nothing
;CALLED BY:
;
;DESCRIPTION: Variable software delay. Delay varies in 10 ms steps
; from 10 ms to 10.9 minutes. Delay as a multiple of 10 ms is passed
; in AX. AX = 1 provides approximately 10 ms delay for 80C188EB operated
; at 8 MHz. AX = 2 produces 20 ms delay etc. AX = 0 provides maximum
; delay. For 80C188EB clock speeds other that 8 MHz TENMSEC must be
; recomputed.
;
;
;******************************************************************


tenmsec        equ 5000

vdelay         proc

vdly0:         mov     cx,tenmsec
vdly1:         loop    vdly1
               dec     ax
               jnz     vdly0
               ret

vdelay         endp
```

Figure 8.5-1   Variable software delay procedure.

```
;*********************************************************************
;max_r
;
;illustrates the use of registers and pointers to pass paramters
;and a register to return a result from a procedure.
;the procedure max_r has two parameters passed to it in registers
;the length of an array and a pointer to the start of the array.
;after the procedure returns the maximum value will be in ax.
;*********************************************************************

name max_r

data            segment'    RAM'
                tmax        dw ?             ;maximum temperature
                tarray      dw 4 dup (?)     ;allocate array for temp
                pmax        dw ?             ;maximum pressure
                parray      dw 3 dup (?)     ;allocate array for pressure
data            ends

stack           segment
                dw 12 dup (?)                ;allocate stack
tos             label word
stack           ends

assume cs:code, ds:data, ss:stack

code   segment      'ROM'
;*********************************************************************
;name: max_r
;function: determines the maximum word in an array of unsigned binary words
;created: 11/4/90revised:
;assumes: cx=length of array,bx=pointer to array base
;returns: ax =maximum value
;modifies: ax,cx,si,f
;calls: none
;called by:
;description:
;*********************************************************************
```

Figure 8.5-2   A program that uses the procedure MAX_R to compute the maximum value in the arrays TARRAY and PARRAY.

```
max_r       proc
            mov     si,0                    ;initialize index into array
            mov     ax,0                    ;initialize ax to hold max value
max0:       cmp     ax,[bx][si]             ;compare current max with array element
            ja      max1                    ;jump if array element is smaller
            mov     ax,[bx][si]             ;else, copy array element to ax
max1:       inc     si                      ;increment array pointer
            inc     si
            loop    max0                    ;loop until end of array
            ret                             ;return and discard parameters from stack
max_r       endp

;start of main portion of program
start:      mov     ax,data                 ;load data segment register
            mov     ds,ax
            mov     ax,stack                ;load stack segment register
            mov     ss,ax
            mov     sp,offset tos           ;initialize top of stack
again:      mov     cx,length tarray        ;length of tarray in cx
            mov     bx,offset tarray        ;pointer to tarray in bx
            call    max_r                   ;compute max
            mov     tmax,ax                 ;store max
            mov     cx,length parray        ;length of parray in cx
            mov     bx,offset parray        ;pointer to parray in bx
            call    max_r                   ;compute max
            mov     pmax,ax
            jmp     again
code        ends
            end start
```

Figure 8.5-2   A program that uses the procedure MAX_R to compute the maximum value in the arrays TARRAY and PARRAY. (Continued.)

8.5.4   Passing Parameters Using the Stack

The stack can be used to pass parameters by having the calling sequence push the parameters onto the stack. At first it might seem that the procedure could simply pop the parameters from the stack. However, this approach is unwieldy because after the parameters have been pushed onto the stack, the call instruction pushes the return address onto the stack. As a result, the parameters are then beneath the return address. The called procedure would have to first pop the return address, and save it in a register or memory location. The procedure could then pop and process the parameters. Finally, the procedure must push the return address back onto the stack before it executes its RET. A more efficient method of using the stack to pass parameters is described in the next subsection.

8.5.5   Passing Parameters Using a Stack Frame

The preferred approach to using the stack to pass parameters still has the calling sequence push the parameters onto the stack. But, instead of popping them off, the procedure accesses them as memory locations. This approach involves the concept of a stack frame. A **stack frame** is an area of the stack used for passing parameters to a procedure. A stack frame can also be used by the procedure for storing temporary variables. Part of a stack frame is created by the calling sequence and the remainder is created by the procedure.

Accessing parameters and returning results in a stack frame uses BP as a frame pointer. A **frame pointer** points to a fixed reference point within the stack frame. The procedure accesses the parameters relative to this fixed reference point. This technique takes advantage of the fact that memory references that use BP, have SS as the default segment, not DS. Therefore, a reference relative to BP defaults to a location in the stack segment.

The calling sequence pushes the parameters onto the stack then calls the procedure. The first thing the procedure does is save BP by pushing it onto the stack. The procedure then copies SP to BP. BP now serves as the frame pointer, and parameters on the stack are referenced by their fixed displacement relative to BP (Fig. 8.5-3). Note that the offset from the frame pointer to the last parameter pushed by the calling sequence is +4 if the procedure called is a NEAR procedure. If the procedure called is a FAR procedure, the offset from the frame pointer, to the last parameter pushed, is +6.

Both the frame pointer and the stack pointer reference the stack. But, there is an important difference; the frame pointer references a fixed location in the stack. In contrast, the stack pointer is a moving reference to different locations in the stack. Whichever location is pointed to by the stack pointer is always the current top of the stack.

A variant of the max_r procedure, max_s (Fig. 8.5-4) illustrates passing parameters on the stack. The length of the array and offset address of the beginning of the array are passed to the procedure using the stack. The calling sequence first pushes the array's length, then the array's offset onto the stack. The CALL then pushes the return address onto the stack and transfers control to the procedure.

The first two instructions in the procedure push BP onto the stack then copy SP to BP. At this point, the stack is as shown in Fig. 8.5-5(a). BP now acts as the frame pointer. BP will continue to point to this same location in the stack during all accesses to this stack frame. The procedure then pushes the general purpose registers it will modify onto the stack before using them in determining the maximum value. The stack is then as shown in Fig. 8.5-5(b). The stack pointer points to successively lower addresses as registers are saved onto the stack. The frame pointer remains fixed.

To obtain the parameters from the stack, the procedure uses based addressing with BP as the base register. Since the default segment register for any addressing mode using BP is SS, the offset into the stack for the array's length parameter is [BP]+6. The offset for the array's offset parameter is [BP]+4. After the procedure determines the maximum value, it leaves this value in AX. The procedure then restores the 80C188EB's registers and returns.

The return instruction pops the return address off the stack. Then it increments SP by 4. This illustrates the use of a pop value with a RET to discard parameters passed to a procedure on the stack. In this case, the pop value is 4. Incrementing SP by 4 has the effect

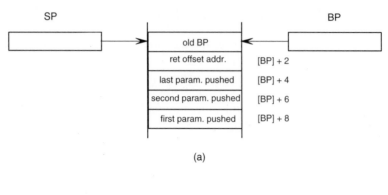

(a)

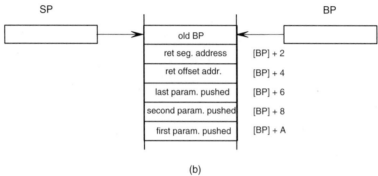

(b)

Figure 8.5-3   Stack frame after the procedure called has saved BP and then copied SP to BP: (a) procedure called is a NEAR procedure; (b) procedure called is a FAR procedure.

of discarding the two word parameters (4 bytes) pushed onto the stack by the calling sequence. SP's value is now what it was prior to the calling sequence.

Use of the stack to pass parameters allows reentrant procedures to be written. A **reentrant procedure** is one that can be called again while it is still in the process of executing due to a previous call. Reentering a procedure can be the result of: the procedure calling itself to execute a recursive algorithm; the procedure calling another procedure that, in turn, calls the first procedure; or the procedure being interrupted, and the interrupt service routine calling the procedure.

In order to be reentrant, all storage for parameters and any temporary storage needed by a procedure must use separate memory locations for each invocation of the procedure. If this condition is not met, parameters needed by an earlier procedure invocation will be corrupted by a later invocation, before the earlier invocation has completed processing its data. Passing parameters and returning results on the stack allows reentrancy to be achieved.

After a procedure copies SP to BP and pushes any registers it will modify, temporary storage for **local variables** can be allocated as a block on the top of the stack. This is accomplished by having an instruction in the procedure subtract a value equal to the desired

```
;****************************************************************
;sframe
;illustrates the use of a stack frame for passing parameters to a procedure.
;the procedure max_s has two parameters passed to it on the stack,
;the length of an array and a pointer to the start of the array.
;The maximum value will be in AX when the procedure returns.
;****************************************************************

        name sframe

data    segment
        tmax   dw ?              ;maximum temperature
        tarray dw 4 dup (?)      ;allocate array for temp
        pmax   dw ?              ;maximum pressure
        parray dw 3 dup (?)      ;allocate array for pressure
data    ends

stack   segment
        dw 12 dup (?) ;allocate stack
tos     label word
stack   ends

        assume cs:code, ds:data, ss:stack

code    segment

;****************************************************************
;name: max_s
;function:    determines the maximum word in an array of unsigned binary words
;created:
;revised:
;assumes:     calling sequence pushes length of array, then offset of array
;             onto stack
;returns:     maximum value in AX
;modifies:    AX
;calls:       none
;called by:
;description:
;****************************************************************
max_s   proc
        push bp                  ;save bp
```

Figure 8.5-4   A program that uses the procedure MAX_S to compute the maximum value in the arrays TARRAY and PARRAY. Parameters are passed to the procedure on the stack.

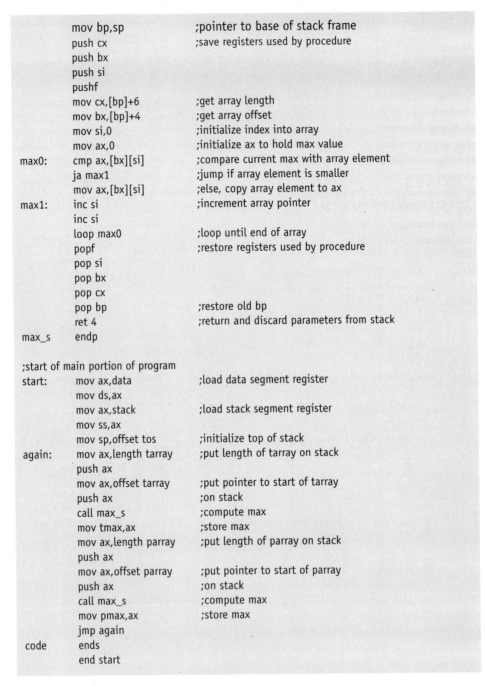

```
                mov bp,sp              ;pointer to base of stack frame
                push cx                ;save registers used by procedure
                push bx
                push si
                pushf
                mov cx,[bp]+6          ;get array length
                mov bx,[bp]+4          ;get array offset
                mov si,0               ;initialize index into array
                mov ax,0               ;initialize ax to hold max value
max0:           cmp ax,[bx][si]        ;compare current max with array element
                ja max1                ;jump if array element is smaller
                mov ax,[bx][si]        ;else, copy array element to ax
max1:           inc si                 ;increment array pointer
                inc si
                loop max0              ;loop until end of array
                popf                   ;restore registers used by procedure
                pop si
                pop bx
                pop cx
                pop bp                 ;restore old bp
                ret 4                  ;return and discard parameters from stack
max_s           endp

;start of main portion of program
start:          mov ax,data            ;load data segment register
                mov ds,ax
                mov ax,stack           ;load stack segment register
                mov ss,ax
                mov sp,offset tos      ;initialize top of stack
again:          mov ax,length tarray   ;put length of tarray on stack
                push ax
                mov ax,offset tarray   ;put pointer to start of tarray
                push ax                ;on stack
                call max_s             ;compute max
                mov tmax,ax            ;store max
                mov ax,length parray   ;put length of parray on stack
                push ax
                mov ax,offset parray   ;put pointer to start of parray
                push ax                ;on stack
                call max_s             ;compute max
                mov pmax,ax            ;store max
                jmp again
code            ends
                end start
```

Figure 8.5-4   A program that uses the procedure MAX_S to compute the maximum value in the arrays TARRAY and PARRAY. Parameters are passed to the procedure on the stack. (Continued.)

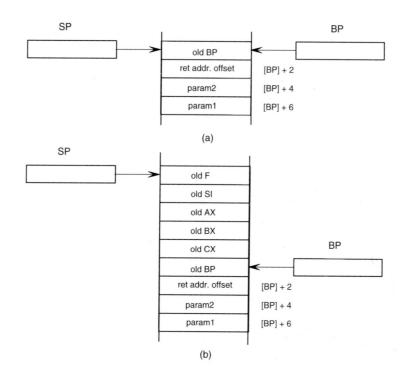

Figure 8.5-5   Stack frame for MAX procedure: (a) after MAX has saved BP; (b) after MAX has saved registers.

block size in bytes from SP. This moves SP down a number of bytes equal to the block size. The block of memory is now available to be used by the procedure to store local variables. The procedure accesses locations in this block using memory addressing relative to BP.

Local variables are located at negative displacements (lower addresses) relative to the location pointed to by the frame pointer (BP, Fig. 8.5-6). Parameters and the return address are located at positive displacements (higher addresses) relative to the frame pointer. When the procedure no longer needs the temporary storage, it deallocates it by adding a value equal to the memory block size to SP, or by copying BP to SP.

The 80C188EB provides an instruction that automatically creates a stack frame. The *procedure entry* (**ENTER**) instruction is primarily used by high-level languages compilers. The instruction has the form:

enter *locals, levels*

Of interest here is the form of this instruction with levels equal to 0. When this form of ENTER is used as the first instruction in a procedure, it first pushes BP onto the stack. Then, ENTER copies SP to BP. Finally, ENTER subtracts a value equal to locals from SP. Thus, locals specifies the number of bytes that the instruction will reserve for local variables. Therefore,

enter   locals,0

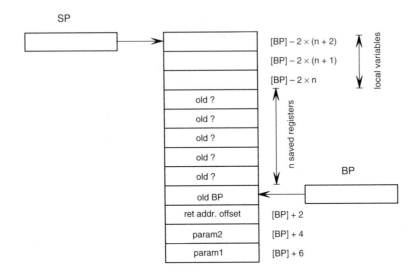

Figure 8.5-6   Creating storage for local variables in a stack frame.

is equivalent to

```
push            bp
mov             bp,sp
sub             sp,locals
```

A *leave* (**LEAVE**) instruction placed before the RET at the end of a procedure reverses the action of the most recent ENTER instruction. LEAVE copies the current value of BP to SP, thus collapsing the storage that was allocated in the stack frame for local variables by the ENTER. Then LEAVE pops the old BP from the stack. Thus, LEAVE is equivalent to:

```
mov      sp,bp
pop      bp
```

A RET instruction, with an appropriate pop value, then removes the parameters that were pushed onto the stack before the procedure was called.

Many examples of procedures using various parameter passing techniques are found throughout the remaining chapters. Use of a stack frame by a high-level language to pass parameters to an assembly language procedure is discussed in Chapter 20.

8.6   Modular Software Design Using Procedures

Tasks are typically implemented as procedures. This section describes how you should use tasks and their associated procedures to structure the overall architecture and design of your system's software.

Software design for nontrivial applications is accomplished by dividing or **decomposing** the system's overall functional specification into specifications for simpler, essentially independent, functions (Fig. 8.6-1). Each of these simpler functions is a task that the system must accomplish. If these tasks are executed in an appropriate order and within the necessary time constraints, the system's overall function is accomplished.

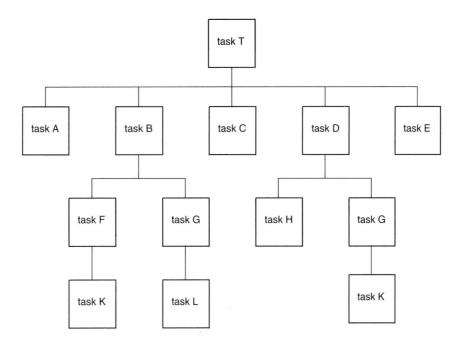

Figure 8.6-1   Decomposition of a software function into tasks.

Each task at the first level of decomposition can be further decomposed into simpler tasks with simpler specifications. The tasks into which a larger task is decomposed must, together, be sufficient to realize the larger task. Eventually during the decomposition process, a point is reached where each task is simple enough to code.

For decomposition to be effective, each task must be defined so that it is modular. **Modular tasks** have a high degree of independence from other tasks. This allows a task to be independently designed and tested based on its specification alone.

Decomposition must be carefully done, so that the division of the original problem produces tasks that are naturally or inherently modular. Often these divisions are obvious, as in the case of specifying a task whose function is to operate a specific I/O device.

Modularity also allows a task to be replaced, at some later time, by an equivalent task, an improved design that meets the same specification. Because modularity allows changes in a task's design, it makes both system development and maintenance easier. Maintenance is easier because changes can be isolated to the modification of one or a few specific tasks.

A modular task possesses the qualities of loose inter-task coupling and high internal cohesion. Coupling refers to how tasks are connected. **Loose inter-task coupling** means that a task is specified so that only a minimal amount of information must be passed between it and other tasks. **Cohesion** refers to the manner in which the elements within a task are related. High internal cohesion means that the elements within a task are tightly related or interdependent.

A modular task's specification and design are separate.

The **task's specification** consists of an interface specification and a behavioral specification. The **interface specification** defines the interface between this task and other tasks. This description includes: the name of the task, what information or data the task requires for its execution, and how the task's results are made available to other tasks.

The **behavioral specification** tells what the task does, but not how it is done. A task's behavioral specification is known to all the other tasks with which it interacts.

A **task's design** involves the details of how the task accomplishes its specified behavior. For a task to be modular, these implementation details must be hidden from other tasks. After the design and testing of an individual task are complete, its implementation details are of no further concern, as long as the task meets its specification. Since a task's implementation details are hidden, the design of other tasks cannot be dependent on these details. Consequently, a change in the details of one task's implementation does not invalidate the design of some other task. Each task's design is independent of the design details of any other task. This hiding of implementation information simplifies overall system design.

While modularity allows changes in the design of a task, it does not allow changes in a task's specification. If a task's specification changes, modularity is not sufficient to prevent these changes from requiring the specifications of other tasks to be changed.

Procedures were first introduced into programming languages to reduce memory requirements. However, procedures also provide a natural mechanism for the implementation of modular tasks (Fig. 8.6-2). A task's specification is documented in the header of the procedure that implements the task. The header describes the procedure's interface: how many parameters are passed to the procedure, how these parameters are passed, and how results are returned. If a procedure possesses the quality of being loosely coupled, its interface specification is simple to produce.

The header also describes the behavior of the procedure. If the procedure is highly cohesive, it is easy to summarize its behavior in its header.

A procedure's design, how the procedure actually accomplishes its task, does not need to be known for the procedure to be used by the main program or by another procedure. Initially, all that needs to be known is the procedure's behavior, so you can determine whether the procedure does the task you desire. If so, a knowledge of the procedure's interface is necessary so you can write a calling sequence to pass parameters to the procedure and write instructions to obtain the results from the procedure. Since this information is in the header, examination of the coding of the procedure is unnecessary. As a result, modular procedures readily lend themselves to reuse in other applications.

In Fig. 8.6-1, the same task may appear at more than one place in the lower levels of the hierarchy. This simply means that the same procedure is called by more than one task. Procedures along any particular branch are, in effect, nested.

Decomposing a specification into tasks and the design and coding of each task do not complete the software design. The execution of tasks at the first level of decomposition must be sequenced or scheduled so that each task executes in the proper order. In some systems, the main program (the top level task) simply calls procedures in the first level of

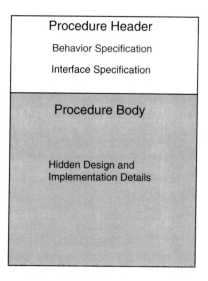

Figure 8.6-2   A procedure as the embodiment of a modular task.

the decomposition in the appropriate order. This is accomplished by branching around, or to, procedure calls using conditional jumps.

Other methods of sequencing the execution of tasks include: use of a finite state machine, interrupt driven sequencing, and the use of a real-time operating system. Use of a finite state machine for task sequencing is discussed in the next section. Interrupt driven task sequencing is discussed in Section 14.7.

8.7   Procedure Sequencing Using a Finite State Machine

Using a finite state machine to sequence tasks provides an excellent example of the use of procedures in structuring a program. The finite state machine implementation to be presented further illustrates some of the addressing modes from Chapters 6 and 7.

The state diagram of a simple Mealy model **finite state machine** (**FSM**) is shown in Fig. 8.7-1. Each circle represents one of the machine's states. When a new input arrives, a transition from the **present state** to the **next state** occurs. The state transition for each possible input is shown by a directed arc. Each arc is labeled with the input that causes the transition, and the output that results. The input and output pairs are separated by a slash (*input/output*).

An output can be a value or it can be an action that is taken. In either case, the output is generated by a procedure that implements a specific task. Accordingly, the state diagram in Fig. 8.7-1 is actually labeled with the task that generates the output, instead of the output itself.

Theoretically, the logic for any digital system can be implemented as a finite state machine. A simple example would be an alternate implementation of the application in Fig. 7.4-2. That application executed a specific task in response to each key pressed on a keypad.

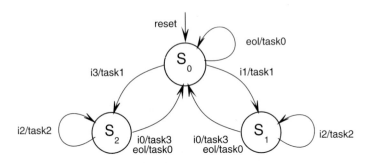

Figure 8.7-1   Finite state machine state diagram.

A similar, but more complex, type of application is a system that must respond to commands input from a keypad. Each command consists of a sequence of keypad inputs, rather than a single input. In this case, the state machine breaks the input string into substrings that are processed as a unit. This technique is called **parsing**. If the string is a valid command, the task associated with the command is executed.

A table driven procedure, fsm, that implements the finite state machine of Fig. 8.7-1 is shown in Fig. 8.7-2. The power of this table driven approach is that the fsm can be easily modified to implement any finite state machine. In a complete program, this fsm would be preceded by the procedures that implement the tasks that generate the state machine's outputs.

Immediately following the fsm procedure's header, the inputs to the machine are named and equated to binary encodings. The last input in this list, eol, is a pseudo input used to represent the end of the list. eol is equivalent to the set of all possible inputs not explicitly assigned to arcs emanating from a given present state.

Next, the function of the state machine is defined by a state table. The state table is the tabular equivalent of the fsm's state diagram. Starting with s0, the state table is divided into subtables. There is one subtable for each state. The subtable for a given state is searched when that state is the present state. Each subtable contains one or more copies of a data structure consisting of three elements: an input symbol, the next state corresponding to that input symbol, and the procedure (task) that should be executed. Each subtable is terminated by a data structure entry for the pseudo input, eol.

Each of the three elements that makes up a subtable data structure is a word. Use of a word to represent the input symbols allows as many as 65,536 different input symbols. Use of a word to represent the next state allows as many as 65,536 states to be realized. Use of a word to represent each task allows the task's actual offset to be used. This makes it simple to use an indirect call to execute a task's procedure.

The values for the three words in each structure are defined by DW directives. For example, the first row of the table is the first entry in the subtable for a present state of 0 (Fig. 8.7-1). This entry corresponds to an occurrence of an input of i1 while in state 0. For this case, the next state is specified as s1 and the output is task1. The second row corresponds to a present state of s0 and an input of i3. For this case, the next state is s2 and the output is task1.

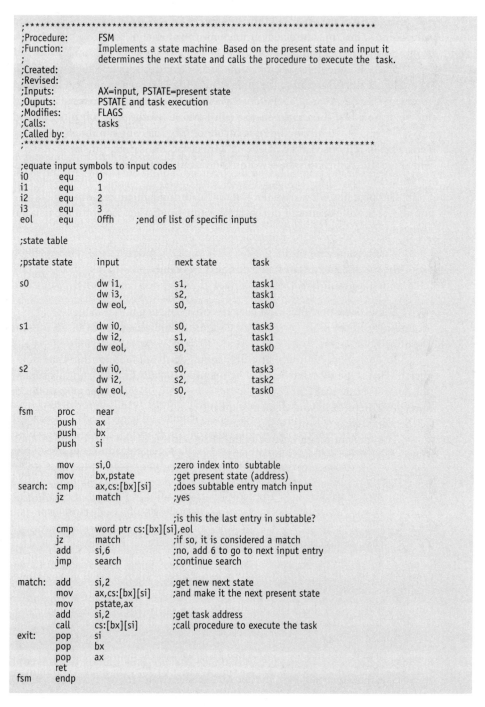

```
;****************************************************************
;Procedure:      FSM
;Function:       Implements a state machine  Based on the present state and input it
;                determines the next state and calls the procedure to execute the  task.
;
;Created:
;Revised:
;Inputs:         AX=input, PSTATE=present state
;Ouputs:         PSTATE and task execution
;Modifies:       FLAGS
;Calls:          tasks
;Called by:
;****************************************************************
;

;equate input symbols to input codes
i0       equ     0
i1       equ     1
i2       equ     2
i3       equ     3
eol      equ     0ffh       ;end of list of specific inputs

;state table

;pstate state    input           next state      task

s0               dw i1,          s1,             task1
                 dw i3,          s2,             task1
                 dw eol,         s0,             task0

s1               dw i0,          s0,             task3
                 dw i2,          s1,             task1
                 dw eol,         s0,             task0

s2               dw i0,          s0,             task3
                 dw i2,          s2,             task2
                 dw eol,         s0,             task0

fsm      proc    near
         push    ax
         push    bx
         push    si

         mov     si,0            ;zero index into  subtable
         mov     bx,pstate       ;get present state (address)
search:  cmp     ax,cs:[bx][si]  ;does subtable entry match input
         jz      match           ;yes

                                 ;is this the last entry in subtable?
         cmp     word ptr cs:[bx][si],eol
         jz      match           ;if so, it is considered a match
         add     si,6            ;no, add 6 to go to next input entry
         jmp     search          ;continue search

match:   add     si,2            ;get new next state
         mov     ax,cs:[bx][si]  ;and make it the next present state
         mov     pstate,ax
         add     si,2            ;get task address
         call    cs:[bx][si]     ;call procedure to execute the task
exit:    pop     si
         pop     bx
         pop     ax
         ret
fsm      endp
```

Figure 8.7-2   Table driven finite state machine implementation.

The third data structure in the subtable is for eol and marks the last data structure in subtable s0. Thus, in state s0, all inputs other than i1 and i3 cause a transition back to s0 and the output generated by task0.

When the assembler assembles the first line of this subtable, it generates three words. The value of the first word is the binary encoding EQUated to input i1. The second word represents s1. But, s1 is a label (an address) and the value the assembler always generates for a label in a DW directive list is the label's offset. So, the value of the second word is the offset address of the beginning of subtable s1. The last word in the first data structure is generated in response to the label task1. Label task1 is defined by task1's PROC directive. Therefore, the last of the three words generated, by the first DW, is the offset address of procedure task1.

The procedure fsm uses the state table to implement the state machine. When an input is received, the input's binary code is put in AX then fsm is called. fsm must do two things:

1. Change the value of the present state variable, pstate, to the value corresponding to the specified next state based on the input value.
2. Call the appropriate procedure (task).

A finite state machine must be placed in a specified initial state prior to its operation. Accordingly, in the main program pstate must be initialized to the offset of s0, making s0 the initial state.

To do its job, fsm must first determine which subtable of the state table it should search. This is the subtable denoted by the present state. fsm searches this subtable to find the data structure that corresponds to the current input. Once it has found this data structure, the structure's second element is the offset address of the next state. The third element of this data structure is the offset address of the task's procedure.

The value of pstate is actually the offset address of the start of the subtable that fsm must search. fsm uses based indexed addressing to search the table (Fig. 8.7-3). The search code is:

```
        mov     si,0                        ;zero subtable index
        mov     bx,pstate                   ;get present state (offset address)
search:
        cmp     ax,cs:[bx][si]              ;does subtable entry match input?
        jz      match                       ;yes

;no, then is this the last entry in subtable?
        cmp     word pointer cs:[bx][si],eol
        jz      match                       ;if so, it is considered a match
        add     si,6                        ;no, add 6 for next subtable entry
        jmp     search                      ;continue search
```

The third instruction in the above sequence compares the new input, in AX, with the input element in the data structure. If they are the same, control is transferred to match. If they are not the same, the input element in the data structure is compared with the symbol eol. If they are the same, this is the last data structure in the subtable, and is, by default, treated as a match.

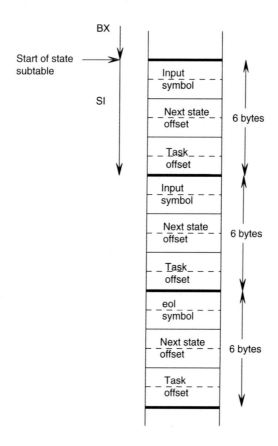

Figure 8.7-3   Subtable of state table associated with a single present state.

If the comparison with eol does not produce a match, then this is not the last data structure in the subtable. fsm must then continue to search the subtable. To continue the search, the index, si, must be increased by 6 to point to the next data structure.

When a match occurs, the next state value is copied from the data structure and made the new value of pstate. The task associated with the original present state and new input is then called:

```
match:
        add     si,2                    ;get new next state
        mov     ax,cs:[bx][si]          ;and make it the next present state
        mov     pstate,ax
        add     si,2                    ;get task address
        call    cs:[bx][si]             ;call procedure to execute the task
```

Two must be added to SI to point to the next state value. This next state value is copied from the table and becomes the new value of pstate. Two is again added to SI, so that SI points to the offset address of the task's procedure. An indirect call, using BX and SI for based indexed addressing, transfers execution to the procedure.

When the task's procedure returns execution to fsm, fsm restores the registers it saved and returns to the main program.

To implement a different finite state machine requires only that the state table be changed to correspond to the new machine's state diagram and that procedures for the new fsm's tasks be written.

8.8   Testing and Debugging Procedures

Because good procedures are modular, have high cohesion, and loose inter-task coupling, they can and should be tested and debugged independently. Furthermore, it is preferable to do this individual testing before including a procedure in a larger program.

One testing approach is to create a stub main program. This program calls only the procedure to be tested. If parameters are passed to the procedure in memory, your stub program must have a data segment that allocates the required memory. If your procedure uses memory for intermediate or final results, this memory must also be allocated. Your stub program must also allocate the stack in its stack segment.

The stub program's code segment includes the procedure to be tested. The first instructions in the program initialize the segment registers and stack pointer. These instructions are followed by the calling sequence and the procedure call. After the call instruction, the program can either jump back to the calling sequence or skip the calling sequence and jump directly back to the call instruction.

Simple procedures can be single stepped to verify their operation. Using Paradigm Debugger, the **Trace Into** command allows you to single step into your procedure. If you use the **Step Over** command to single step, the call instruction and the procedure it calls are executed together in one step. For the Step Over command, the debugger will not stop until the instruction following the call.

One thing you always want to check is that your procedure does not leave the stack pointer altered. Note the value of SP before executing the call instruction. When execution reaches the instruction following the call, compare the value of SP with the previously noted value. These values should be the same. If they are not, your procedure has failed to remove from the stack all the parameters that were passed on the stack by the calling sequence.

Paradigm Debugger's stack pane represents the stack as a word stack. It also shows the highest address of the stack at the top of the pane, not the bottom. This is opposite to the convention used for stack figures in this book.

When an assembly language procedure is called from other assembly language code, the procedure must clean up the stack, either by popping the parameters from the stack or by including a pop-value operand with the RET instruction. In contrast, as will be seen in Chapter 20, when an assembly language procedure is called from a C program, the procedure leaves the parameters on the stack when it returns. It is the C programs's responsibility to pop the parameters from the stack.

If, when you single step the RET instruction in your procedure, execution flow does not continue with the instruction following the CALL, then your procedure has executed an unbalanced number of PUSHes and POPs. This action leaves a value on the top of the stack, immediately before the RET is executed, that is not the return address pushed onto the stack by the CALL. As a result, execution continues at some unexpected location.

Once you have tested the basic execution flow of your procedure and its handling of the stack, you can test its operation against your set of input test data. If your stub program jumps back to the CALL, set an execution breakpoint on the CALL. When the break occurs, use the debugger's commands to modify registers, memory, or the stack, to establish the test parameter values that would have been provided by the calling sequence.

After a procedure has been thoroughly tested, you include it in your program. If you later suspect there is an error in a procedure, you can step through your main program using the Step Over command. This allows you to easily observe the parameter values before the execution of a procedure, and the results produced by the procedure, without single stepping through the procedure's instructions. If the results produced by the procedure are not correct, you can repeat the debugging process using the Trace Into command to single step through the procedure's instructions. At this point you should be able to locate any errors in the procedure.

8.9   Summary

Building a system's software architecture using procedures provides significant advantages. The size of your program is reduced because the code for a task that must be executed at several points in your program appears only once.

A procedure is designed to implement a single, well defined, and essentially independent task. Because of its modular nature and limited scope, a procedure is easier to comprehend and to code.

Well designed and well documented procedures can be reused in other programs. Reuse of procedures reduces the effort required in designing new systems based on the same or a compatible family of microprocessors. Over time you can create a library of procedures and have them available for your immediate use.

Once procedures are coded to implement a system's tasks, a method of properly sequencing the procedures' execution is necessary. A simple method is to use conditional jumps. You use a logical instruction to test a condition and then jump over the call instruction if a procedure should not be executed. Another more formal and more organized approach is to use a table driven state machine.

8.10   Problems

1. What does the acronym LIFO stand for and what unique properties does a LIFO memory structure have?

2. What is a push operation? What is a pop operation.?

3. For a simple conceptual stack, what happens if the number of push operations on the stack exceeds the stacks length? What happens if a pop operation is attempted on an empty stack?

4. What registers determine the address of the top of the stack in an 80C188EB system?

5. What does a LABEL directive do? How is a LABEL directive used in establishing the stack?

6. Write the directives that create a segment called stack and allocate a 64 byte stack. Include the definition of the symbol t_o_s, so this symbol can be used to establish the top of the empty stack. How many PUSH instructions can be executed, without any intervening POPs, before the area reserved for the stack is exceeded?

7. If the locator assigns a segment address of 0400H to the segment stack defined in problem 6, what will the physical address of the top of the stack be when it is empty? What will the physical address of the top of the stack be when it is full?

8. A stack can be allocated using the following directives:

```
stack            segment           'STKRAM'
                 dw 16 dup(?)
tos              dw ?
stack            ends
```

Is there any disadvantage in using a DW directive to define the name tos rather than a LABEL directive? How long is the stack in bytes? How many bytes of memory are allocated?

9. Given the following register contents,

AX = 04D2H, BX = 1A8CH, CX = 3302H, DX = 90CCH, SS = 0600H, SP = 0008H

an 8 byte long empty stack, and the following instruction sequence:

```
push     ax
push     bx
push     cx
push     dx
pop      ax
pop      bx
push     cx
```

draw a byte-wide memory map of the area reserved for the stack showing the contents of each memory location after the entire instruction sequence has been executed. Also, give the contents of each of the specified registers at that point.

10. Write a program that tests bit 0 of byte port STATUS and if this bit is set, inputs a byte of data from byte port indata. After 16 bytes of data have been input, the same 16 bytes are output in reverse order (the last byte input is the first byte output) to byte port REVERSED. The output of data to port REVERSED is unconditional. Your program must use the stack to store and reverse the order of the data. After 16 bytes are output the entire process is repeated indefinitely.

11. Of the three control flags DF, IF, and TF, only two, DF and IF, have instructions that directly set and clear the flags. Write an instruction sequence that uses the stack to set TF. Write a second instruction sequence that uses the stack to clear TF.

12. What is the purpose and use of the PROC/ENDP directive pair? How are the PROC and LABEL directives similar?

13. Explain the difference between a NEAR procedure and a FAR procedure. When a NEAR procedure is called, what does the CALL instruction push onto the stack? When a FAR procedure is called, what does the CALL instruction push onto the stack.

14. For the call bin_2_pbcd instruction in Fig. 8.3-2, what is this instruction's displacement? What is the offset of the instruction following this call (the adjusted IP)? Show that the sum of the adjusted offset and the displacement give the offset of the procedure being called. What type of call instruction is call bin_2_pbdc?

15. Modify the instructions in Fig. 8.3-3 to create a complete program. Assume that the function number is encoded in bits D1 and D0. Represent each procedure's body as a single NOP instruction. Assemble and simulate the program to verify its execution flow.

16. Write a procedure that outputs the contents of the flag register to the word output port FLAGS in the isolated I/O space.

17. Write a procedure that transfers the contents of a memory buffer to an output port. The elements in the buffer are words. Assume that output port WRDPRT is a word port and is always ready to accept the next element of data to be written. The calling sequence first pushes the buffer's offset from the beginning of the data segment onto the stack, followed by the number of elements in the buffer.

18. Write a procedure that fills a block of memory with a constant. The calling sequence first pushes the offset of the start of the block onto the stack followed by the block's length and the constant, then calls the procedure. Do not use string instructions to accomplish this task.

19. Write a procedure that compares two equal length blocks of memory to determine if they are identical. Both blocks are assumed to be in the segment pointed to by DS. The procedure is called with a pointer to one buffer in SI, a pointer to the other buffer in DI, and the buffer length in CX. If the blocks are identical, the procedure returns with CF = 0. If not, it returns with CF = 1 and offset of the first locations whose contents differ in SI an DI.

20. Write headers for the two procedures in Fig. 8.3-2.

21. Write a program that uses the procedure max_r, of Fig. 8.5-2, to find the maximum temperature in an array tarray. tarray is a byte array of 48 bytes. This value is to be output to the byte output port TMAX.

22. Repeat problem 21 but use procedure max_s of Fig. 8.5-4.

23. Rewrite the version of the max_r procedure in Fig. 8.5-2 so that no 80C188EB registers, except the register used to return the result, are left modified when the procedure returns.

24. Rewrite the version of the max_s procedure in Fig. 8.5-3 to be a FAR procedure.

25. Write a procedure that conditionally inputs data from a byte input port based on whether a data available flag in a second byte input port is set. If the data available flag is set when the procedure is called, the data byte is input to AL and the procedure returns. If the data available flag is not initially set, the procedure waits for up to (approximately) 10 ms for it to be set then returns. During the 10 ms period, the data available flag is constantly checked. The procedure is called with the address of

the status port in DX, the address of the data port in BX, and the bit position of the data available flag of the status port in AL. If the procedure returns with data, it sets the CF flag, otherwise it clears the CF flag. Use an EQU directive and a constant to allow the timeout period to be adjusted to achieve 10ms for different microprocessor clock speeds.

26. Write a procedure, PRNTB, which uses handshaking to output the contents of a 20 character buffer, charbuf, to the printer. To accomplish the handshaking, bit 0 or port PRINTRDY is checked. If this bit is 1, the printer is ready for the next character. Each character is stored in one byte. Assume that the printer port, named PRINTER, is a byte output port. The program which calls the procedure first loads BX with the off-set of the beginning of the memory buffer. The program is not returned from until all 20 characters in the buffer are printed.

27. Write a procedure, intrlv, that interleaves (alternates) the bits from two bytes to create a word. The two bytes are passed to the procedure in AH and AL. Bit 15 of the result is bit 7 from AH. Bit 14 of the result is bit 7 from AL. Bit 13 of the result is bit 6 from AH. Bit 12 of the result is bit 6 from AL and so on. The result is returned in AX. After the procedure returns, only AX should have been modified.

28. Prior to the call to a near procedure, the calling sequence pushes parameters X and Y, in that order, onto the stack. The procedure will access these two parameters relative to the frame pointer, BP. Assume the value of SP is 0100H just prior to the first push. Draw the stack frame as it would appear immediately after the frame pointer is loaded. Show the stack frame as a byte-wide memory. Label each location with its address and label its contents symbolically. What is the value of SP after the frame pointer is loaded?

29. Write a NEAR procedure, fill, that fills a block of memory in the current data seg-ment with a constant. The procedure's calling sequence first pushes the offset of the start of the block onto the stack, followed by the block's length, and the constant with which to fill the memory block. Use string instructions to implement the proce-dure's task. After the procedure returns, no registers should have been modified.

30. Draw a block diagram of the stack frame as it exists immediately after the call to the procedure in problem 29. Draw a second diagram that shows what the stack frame would look like if the procedure were a FAR procedure.

31. Draw a state diagram to represent the call table for Fig. 8.3-3. Assume that there are a total of four functions. Write the state table that would be used in Fig. 8.7-2 to imple-ment the state diagram.

ARITHMETIC OPERANDS AND ARITHMETIC

9.1   Numeric Operand Representations

9.2   Unsigned Binary Arithmetic

9.3   Signed Binary Arithmetic

9.4   Unpacked BCD Arithmetic

9.5   Packed BCD Arithmetic

9.6   Binary/BCD Conversions

9.7   Summary

How you choose to represent numeric data in your program is critical. Most programs require more that one numerical representation to handle the various types of data required in an application. Therefore, in addition to performing arithmetic computations on your chosen numeric representations or data types, it is also necessary to be able to convert from one representation to another. The number of bits used in each representation must also be carefully considered, so intermediate and final results can be stored without error.

The 80C188EB's arithmetic instructions and associated numeric operand representations are fairly limited in comparison to those of a high-level language. The 80C188EB's numeric representations consist of unsigned and signed binary integers and unsigned unpacked and packed binary coded decimal (BCD) integers. While limited, the 80C188EB's arithmetic instructions and operand types are sufficient for a wide range of embedded applications.

However, some applications require complex data types and correspondingly complex arithmetic operations on them. This may be necessary because the application's data values extend over a wide range, are nonintegral, or require that complex computations be carried out at high speed.

Either a software or hardware solution may be appropriate when more complex data types, or more powerful arithmetic operations, are necessary. Using a software approach, data types, such as fractional and floating point, can be defined. Procedures can be written for the addition, subtraction, multiplication, and division of these data types. Procedures can also be written to perform arithmetic functions, such as sine and square root, and to perform conversions between different data types. Alternatively, you may chose to use a commercial library of arithmetic procedures rather than write your own.

An alternative to performing floating point and other complex arithmetic computations in software is to use hardware in the form of a computational IC specifically designed to interface to a microprocessor. This kind of hardware approach may be necessary when very high speed computations are required. These ICs execute arithmetic operations on predefined data types. Such ICs include arithmetic processing units and numeric coprocessors. Arithmetic processing units (APUs) are essentially generic and can interface to most any microprocessor as a peripheral. Numeric coprocessors are designed to interface to a specific microprocessor and extend the microprocessor's instruction set.

The emphasis in this chapter is on numeric representations that can be directly operated on by 80C188EB instructions.

9.1   Numeric Operand Representations

The 80C188EB has arithmetic instructions that directly operate on four different number representations: unsigned binary integers, signed binary integers, unsigned unpacked BCD numbers, and unsigned packed BCD numbers (Fig. 9.1-1).

Unsigned binary operands represent positive integers. These operands are either bytes or words. Every bit in these operands is used to represent the magnitude of the number. A byte can represent unsigned values from 0 through 255. A word can represent unsigned values from 0 through 65,535.

Signed binary operands are represented in two's complement form. The most significant bit of these operands represents its sign. The remaining bits represent the number's magnitude. Signed binary operands are either bytes or words. A byte can represent signed numbers from −128 through +127. The positive range is one value smaller that the negative range because zero is represented as a positive number. A word can represent numbers from −32,768 through +32,767.

Binary Coded Decimal (BCD) formats represent decimal digits in binary. An unpacked BCD operand encodes a single BCD digit using only the least significant 4-bits (low nibble) of a byte. Since only the low nibble is used, an unpacked BCD byte represents a number that ranges from 0 through 9.

A packed BCD byte operand encodes two decimal digits in a single byte. The low nibble encodes the least significant digit. The most significant digit is encoded in the high nibble (most significant 4-bits). A packed BCD byte can represent values from 00 through 99.

The ranges of all these number representations can be extended by representing each value by multiple bytes or multiple words. Appropriate instruction sequences or procedures can be used to handle multibyte and multiword representations.

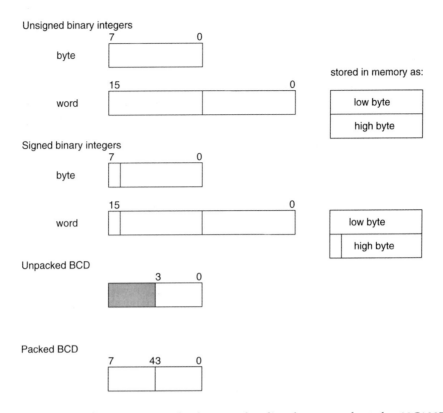

Figure 9.1-1   Arithmetic operands that can be directly operated on by 80C188EB instructions.

9.2   Unsigned Binary Arithmetic

Unsigned, or natural, binary is the simplest number representation. **Unsigned binary integers** can represent positive quantities only. All of an operand's bits are used to represent a number's magnitude. n-bit unsigned integers range in value from 0 through $2^n - 1$. Table 9.2-1 lists ranges for some common values of n.

Table 9.2-1   Range for common n-bit unsigned binary integers.

n	Range
8	0 to 255
16	0 to 65,535
32	0 to 4,294,967,295

An n-bit positive integer is written in positional notation as:

$$X = x_{n-1} x_{n-2} \ldots x_0$$

and its value in polynomial notation is:

$$V(X) = \sum_{i=0}^{n-1} x_i 2^i$$

The value of an n-bit integer equals the sum of the products of each bit, x_i, and the weight, 2^i, associated with the bit's position. For example, the 8-bit binary number

$$N_2 = 10110110$$

is equal to the decimal number

$$N_{10} = 1(2^7) + 0(2^6) + 1(2^5) + 1(2^4) + 0(2^3) + 1(2^2) + 1(2^1) + 0(2^0)$$

$$= 128 + 0 + 32 + 16 + 0 + 4 + 2 + 0$$

$$= 182$$

Subscripts, 2 and 10, on N indicate that the number is represented in base 2 (binary) or base 10 (decimal), respectively.

When two n-bit numbers are added, the sum can be as large as $2^{n+1} - 2$. For example, adding two byte operands can result in a sum as large as 510. A carry out of the sum's most significant bit occurs if the sum is greater than 255. Such a sum cannot be stored in a single byte. **Arithmetic overflow** occurs when a result is too large to be stored in the instruction's destination. The number of bytes used to represent a result in a particular application must be carefully chosen to avoid the possibility of overflow. Otherwise, the stored result will be incorrect.

Like all 80C188EB word data items, unsigned binary words are stored in memory with the least significant byte in the low address of the word. When integer quantities larger than a word need to be represented, multiple words are used to store a single value. Such operands are referred to as being **multiprecision**. Multiprecision operands are also stored in memory with the least significant byte in the lowest address. A 32-bit operand is stored in four consecutive bytes, or equivalently two consecutive words. A 64-bit operand requires eight consecutive bytes.

80C188EB arithmetic instructions that apply to unsigned binary operands are listed in Table 9.2-2. Operands for these instructions are either 8-bit or 16-bit. The 80C188EB can add to, or subtract from, 8-bit or 16-bit operands contained in any general purpose register or in memory. Multiplication and division are more restrictive, with one operand always in the accumulator, or the accumulator and its extension DX. The result of a multiplication or division is always left in either the accumulator, or the accumulator and DX.

9.2.1   Unsigned Binary Addition

Unsigned binary numbers are added using the *addition*, **ADD**, instruction:

add   *destination, source*

The destination and source operands are added and the result is placed in the destination.

Table 9.2-2   Arithmetic instructions for unsigned binary operands.

Mnemonic	Operands	Function	O	D	I	T	S	Z	A	P	C
ADD	dst,src	addition	✓	–	–	–	✓	✓	✓	✓	✓
ADC	dst,src	add with carry	✓	–	–	–	✓	✓	✓	✓	✓
INC	dst	increment by 1	✓	–	–	–	✓	✓	✓	✓	–
SUB	dst,src	subtraction	✓	–	–	–	✓	✓	✓	✓	✓
SBB	dst	subtract with borrow	✓	–	–	–	✓	✓	✓	✓	✓
DEC	dst	decrement by 1	✓	–	–	–	✓	✓	✓	✓	–
CMP	dst,src	compare	✓	–	–	–	✓	✓	✓	✓	✓
MUL	src	unsigned multiplication	✓	–	–	–	?	?	?	?	✓
DIV	src	unsigned division	?	–	–	–	?	?	?	?	?

To add operands larger than a word, *add with carry* (**ADC**) is used and multiple additions are required. The following sequence adds two 32-bit operands stored in memory as augend and addend and stores the sum back in augend.

```
        mov     ax,addend           ;add the least significant words
        add     augend,ax
        mov     ax,addend+2         ;add the most significant words
        adc     augend+2,ax
```

The second addition adds the carry, CF, resulting from the first addition to the most significant words of the two 32-bit operands. Larger operands simply require additional ADC operations. The instruction sequence that follows uses a loop to add two 64-bit operands.

```
        clc                         ;clear the carry
        mov     bx, offset addend   ;pointer to addend
        mov     di, offset augend   ;pointer to augend
        mov     cx,4                ;initialize loop control
mpadd:
        mov     ax,[bx]             ;move addend word to ax
        adc     [di],ax             ;add addend and augend,
        inc     bx                  ;increment addend pointer
        inc     bx
        inc     di                  ;increment augend pointer
        inc     di
        loop    mpadd               ;loop if not done
```

Increment (**INC**) adds one to its operand, but does not alter CF. This characteristic of INC is necessary in the previous instruction sequence to add 2 to each pointer. If add bx,2 were used instead, the value of CF used by ADC would not, as required, be the result of the previous addition.

INC and DEC are used for efficiently modifying memory pointers and counters. They use fewer machine code bytes and execute faster than the equivalent operations implemented using ADD or SUB. More importantly, INC and DEC do not alter CF.

By changing the value loaded into CX, operands consisting of a larger number of words can be added using the same instruction sequence.

9.2.2   Unsigned Binary Subtraction

Unsigned binary numbers are subtracted using the *subtraction* (**SUB**) instruction:

sub   *destination, source*

The source operand is subtracted from the destination operand and the difference is placed in the destination. Operands may be either bytes or words.

To subtract operands larger than a word, *subtract with borrow* (**SBB**) is used and multiple subtractions are required. The following sequence subtracts two 32-bit operands stored in minuend and subtra and stores the difference back in minuend.

```
mov    ax,subtra          ;subtract least significant words
sub    minuend,ax
mov    ax,subtra+2         ;subtract most significant words
sbb    minuend+2,ax
```

CF is set if a borrow occurs during a subtraction. Thus, for subtractions the carry flag functions as a **borrow flag**. The second subtraction subtracts the borrow, CF, resulting from the first subtraction, from the difference of the two most significant words of the 32-bit operands. Larger operands simply require additional SBB operations.

If the result of the final subtraction is negative, CF is set. This corresponds to an **arithmetic underflow** condition. The result is too small (it is negative) to be stored as an unsigned integer.

Other instructions that accomplish subtractions are CMP and DEC. *Decrement* (**DEC**) subtracts one from its operand, but does not alter CF. The *compare* (**CMP**) instruction was introduced in Chapter 7 as a means to modify flags based on the difference between two operands. It is similar to SUB, except the difference is not saved in the destination.

9.2.3   Unsigned Binary Multiplication

The *multiplication* (**MUL**) instruction performs an unsigned multiplication of the source operand and the accumulator. This instruction has the basic form:

mul   *source*

If source is a byte, then it is multiplied by the contents of AL and the double-length result is returned in AX (Fig. 9.2-1). Use of AL to hold the multiplicand and AX to hold the product is implied for the MUL instruction. Therefore, only the multiplier is specified as an instruction operand.

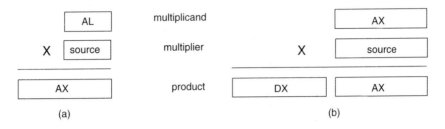

Figure 9.2-1   Implicit use of registers for unsigned multiplication using MUL: (a) byte source; (b) word source.

If source is a word, then it is multiplied by the contents of AX, and the double-length result is left in the **extended accumulator,** DX and AX. The most significant word of the result is in DX and the least significant is in AX. DX serves as the accumulator's, AX's, extension for multiplication and division operations involving words. Use of a pair of word registers to store a double-word is indicated using a colon notation, *most significant word:least significant word*. Or, in this case, DX:AX. It is important that you not confuse the use of a colon to denote concatenated register contents, with its use to denote a segmented address, as in *segment address:offset address*.

To multiply multiword operands, a procedure can be written that computes a series of cross products of words (or bytes), aligns, and adds them to get the product.

9.2.4   Unsigned Binary Division

Divide (**DIV**) divides an unsigned number in the accumulator by the source operand. It has the form:

    div   *source*

If the source operand (the divisor) is a byte, it is divided into the two-byte dividend assumed to be in AH and AL. The byte quotient is returned in AL and the byte remainder is returned in AH (Fig. 9.2-2). If the source operand is a word, it is divided into the two word dividend in DX:AX. The word quotient is returned in AX, and the word remainder is returned in DX.

Since DIV is designed for either a 16-bit dividend and 8-bit divisor or for a 32-bit dividend and 16-bit divisor, care must be taken to zero AH prior to division of an 8 bit dividend by an 8-bit divisor and to zero DX prior to the division of a 16-bit dividend by a 16-bit divisor.

If the quotient exceeds the capacity of its destination register (255 for a byte source and 65,535 for a word source), a divide error (type 0) interrupt is generated. For this situation, the quotient and remainder are undefined. This error is often incorrectly referred to as a divide by zero error. In fact, this error occurs not only for division by 0, but any time the dividend and divisor values are such that the quotient is too large for the destination. An interrupt is automatically generated when this error is detected. You must write an

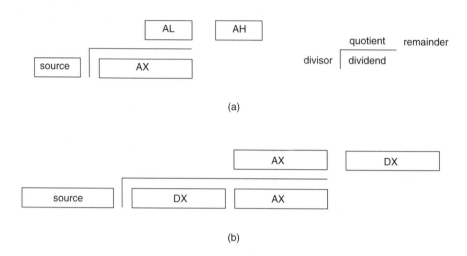

(a)

(b)

Figure 9.2-2   Implicit use of registers for unsigned division using DIV: (a) division of a word by a byte source; (b) division of a double word by a word source.

interrupt service procedure to handle this error condition in a manner appropriate for your application. Interrupts are discussed in Chapter 14.

DIV undoes what MUL did. MUL and DIV were designed so the double-length result of a multiplication can be used in a later division. An example of this occurred in the program of Fig. 4.3-2, where it was desired to multiply a byte value in AL by the fraction 0.9609. This was accomplished by multiplying the byte in AL by 9,609 then dividing it by 10,000:

```
mov    ah,0          ;clear ah
mov    cx,9609        ;load multiplier
mul    cx            ;multiply ax by cx
mov    cx,10000       ;divide dx:ax by cx
div    cx            ;al is now equal to original al * 0.9609
```

For multiplication and division you must be careful to place the operands in the correct registers or memory locations before the instructions execution. You must also be careful to obtain the results from the correct registers.

9.3   Signed Binary Arithmetic

Signed binary integers can represent positive and negative numbers. The 80C188EB uses the two's complement number system to represent signed numbers. In an n-bit **two's complement number**, the most significant bit is the sign bit. The **sign bit**, x_{n-1}, of a positive two's complement number is 0. The remaining $n-1$ bits represent the number's magnitude.

As a result, n-bit positive two's complement numbers can range from 0 to $+(2^{n-1} - 1)$. The value of an n-bit positive number is:

$$V(X) = \sum_{i=0}^{n-2} x_i 2^i$$

The sign bit of a negative number is 1. In the two's complement number system, negative numbers range from -1 to -2^{n-1} and have the value:

$$V(X) = -2^{n-1} + \sum_{i=0}^{n-2} x_i 2^i$$

Table 9.3-1 lists ranges for some common n-bit signed binary integers.

Table 9.3-1   Range for common n-bit signed binary integers.

n	Range
8	−128 to +127
16	−32,768 to +32,767
32	−2,147,483,648 to +2,147,483,647

Combining the two previous relationships gives an expression for the general case of both positive and negative numbers:

$$V(X) = -(x_{n-1} 2^{n-1}) + \sum_{i=0}^{n-2} x_i 2^i$$

The 8-bit two's complement representations of some signed numbers are given in Table 9.3-2. As the listing shows, the range of numbers is not symmetrical since there is one more negative integer than there are positive integers. This is a result of 0 being represented as a positive number.

9.3.1   Why Two's Complement?

The two's complement number system is used to represent signed numbers because it simplifies the ALU's hardware. Using the two's complement number system, subtraction can be accomplished using a binary adder and a complementor. No special subtractor hardware is required, resulting in a reduction in the ALU's complexity.

In the two's complement number system, negative numbers are represented as the two's complement of the corresponding positive number. The two's complement of the number X is defined as:

$$\text{two's complement of } X = \{X\} = 2^n - X$$

Table 9.3-2 Two's complement representation of some 8-bit signed numbers.

Weight	-2^7 -128	2^6 64	2^5 32	2^4 16	2^3 8	2^2 4	2^1 2	2^0 1	Decimal Equivalent
Signed Number	0	1	1	1	1	1	1	1	+127
	0	1	1	1	1	1	1	0	+126
	0	0	0	0	0	0	0	1	+1
	0	0	0	0	0	0	0	0	0
	1	1	1	1	1	1	1	1	–1
	1	1	1	1	1	1	1	0	–2
	1	0	0	0	0	0	0	1	–127
	1	0	0	0	0	0	0	0	–128

where n is the number of bits used to represent X. n is equal to the number of bits used to store X. This limitation is the key to the two's complement number system's usefulness.

If the two's complement of X is added to X:

$$\{X\} + X = (2^n - X) + X$$
$$= 2^n + 0$$

The result is 0 if the carry (2^n) is ignored. The carry is automatically ignored if the result is stored as an n-bit number. For example, if

$$X = 6_{10}$$
$$= 00000110_2$$

then the two's complement of X is:

$$\{X\} = 2^n - X$$
$$= 2^8 - 00000110_2$$
$$= 100000000_2 - 00000110_2$$
$$= 11111010_2$$

Adding X and its two's complement gives:

$$X = 00000110$$
$$\{X\} = 11111010$$
$$1\ 00000000$$

If the result of this 8-bit addition is stored in an 8-bit register, then the stored result is 0.

With the preceding example as a basis, it follows that the value A – B can be computed as A + (–B). Here –B is the two's complement of +B. If we can compute –B without using subtraction, then we can replace subtraction with addition of the two's complement, thereby eliminating the need for special subtractor hardware in the ALU.

Computing the two's complement of a number X without subtraction is easy because

$$\begin{aligned}
\{X\} &= 2^n - X \\
&= 1\,000...0 - (X_{n-1}X_{n-2}...X_0) \\
&= 111...1 + 1 - (X_{n-1}X_{n-2}...X_0) \\
&= 111...1 - (X_{n-1}X_{n-2}...X_0) + 1 \\
&= (1 - X_{n-1}, 1 - X_{n-2}, ...1 - X_0) + 1.
\end{aligned}$$

But since X_i is either 0 or 1

$$1 - X_i = \overline{X}_i$$

so $\{X\} = (\overline{X}_{n-1}, \overline{X}_{n-2}, ...\overline{X}_0) + 1.$

This value is easily computed by complementing each X_i and adding 1 to the result. Since the ALU must already include a complementor circuit for NOT logical operation and a binary adder, no subtractor circuitry is required.

Table 9.3-3 lists the 80C188EB instructions that apply specifically to signed binary numbers.

Table 9.3-3   Arithmetic instructions specifically for signed binary operands.

Mnemonic	Operands	Function	O	D	I	T	S	Z	A	P	C
NEG	dst	negate	–	–	–	–	–	–	✓	–	–
CBW	none	convert byte to word	?	–	–	–	?	?	✓	?	✓
CWD	none	convert word to double word	–	–	–	–	–	–	–	–	✓
IMUL	src	integer multiplication	✓	–	–	–	?	?	?	?	✓
IDIV	src	integer division	?	–	–	–	?	?	?	?	?

When a negative constant is specified in an instruction or directive, it is encoded in two's complement. For example, the instruction:

```
mov     al,-93
```

generates the object code B0A3H, where B0 is the opcode and A3H is the two's complement representation of –93.

The *negate* (**NEG**) instruction accomplishes the same result by subtracting its destination from 0. This instruction has the form:

neg   *destination*

Subtraction of the destination from 0 is accomplished by the hardware adding the two's complement of the destination to 0. Then the result is simply the two's complement of the destination.

If an attempt is made to negate a byte containing –128, or a word containing –32,768, the operand is left unchanged and the OF flag is set. This occurs since +128 and +32,768 cannot be represented by a signed byte or word, respectively.

9.3.2   Sign Extension

Before signed operands of different lengths can to be added or subtracted they must first be made the same length. For example, if a signed byte is to be added to a signed word, the signed byte must first be converted to a signed word. This conversion involves creating a high order byte with each bit equal to the sign bit of the low order (original) byte. This process is called **sign extension**. To sign extend a byte in AL to a word in AH:AL, the *convert byte to word* (**CBW**) instruction is used. To sign extend a word in AX to a double-word in DX:AX, *convert word to double-word* (**CWD**) is used.

9.3.3   Signed Binary Addition

Equal length numbers in two's complement representation can be added without consideration of their signs. The same instructions used to add unsigned binary numbers, ADD and ADC, correctly add signed binary numbers. The sum of two's complement operands is correct if it is within the allowed range for the destination. If an addition of two's complement operands results in a **signed overflow**, too large a positive number or too large a negative number, the OF flag is set.

The only difference in addition and subtraction of signed numbers compared to unsigned numbers, is that you must test OF rather that CF to determine if a result is out of range. The overflow flag can be tested after an addition by using a conditional jump instruction or the *interrupt on overflow* (INTO) instruction discussed in Chapter 13. INTO causes an interrupt if OF is set. You must write an interrupt service routine that appropriately handles the error for your specific application.

9.3.4   Signed Binary Subtraction

In a microprocessor, the ALU hardware subtracts two numbers by taking the two's complement of the subtrahend and adding it to the minuend. The sum is the correct difference, if it is in the allowable range for the size of the destination. This method for subtracting numbers is valid for both unsigned and signed binary numbers. Implementing subtraction this way eliminates the need for the ALU to have separate subtractor circuitry. The same instructions, SUB and SBB, used for unsigned subtraction are used to subtract signed numbers. Underflow is indicated by OF.

9.3.5   Signed Binary Multiplication

In contrast to addition and subtraction, the binary multiplication and division instructions that work for unsigned numbers *do not* give correct results for signed operands. A separate instruction, *integer multiply* (**IMUL**) is used for multiplying signed operands. One of its forms is :

     imul *source*

If source is a byte, it is multiplied by AL and the result is returned in AH:AL. If source is a word, it is multiplied by AX and the result is returned in DX:AX.

Another form of IMUL allows three operands to be used:

imul *destination, source, data*

This form allows an operand, the source, to be multiplied by an immediate operand, the data, and the result stored in the destination. Data can be an 8-bit or 16-bit constant. The source may be a register or memory location and the destination must be a general register. Only the lower 16-bits of the result are saved. This is the only 80C188EB instruction that has three operands.

9.3.6   Signed Binary Division

Signed binary division is accomplished using the *integer divide* (**IDIV**) instruction:

idiv   *source*

Source is the divisor. If source is a byte, the double-length dividend is assumed to be in AH:AL. The quotient is returned in AL, and the remainder in AH. If source is a word, the double-length dividend is assumed to be in DX:AX, the quotient is returned in AX, and the remainder in DX.

If the divisor is a byte and the dividend is a byte, then the dividend must be placed in AL and sign extended to a word using CBW. If the divisor is a word and the dividend is a word, then the dividend must be placed in AX and sign extended to a double-word using CWD.

For a byte source, a divide error (type 0) interrupt occurs if a positive quotient is larger than +127 or a negative quotient is less than −127. For a word source, a divide error interrupt occurs if a positive quotient is greater than +32,767 or a negative quotient is less than −32,767. Nonintegral quotients are truncated toward 0 to integers and the remainder has the same sign as the dividend.

9.4   Unpacked BCD Arithmetic

The **unpacked BCD** number representation encodes a single decimal digit in the low nibble of a byte. The high nibble is 0H. A single byte can represent a number that ranges from 0 (00H) through 9 (09H). A number larger than nine requires a multibyte representation.

There is a close correspondence between the unpacked BCD representation of a digit and its ASCII representation. The ASCII representation has the high nibble equal to 3H and the low nibble equal to the BCD code for the digit. A single ASCII character can represent numbers that range from 0 (30H) to 9 (39H).

An unpacked BCD number is easily converted to its ASCII equivalent by ORing it with 30H or by adding 30H. An ASCII number is easily converted to its unpacked BCD equivalent by ANDing it with 0FH or subtracting 30H.

There are no special 80C188EB instructions for directly adding, subtracting, multiplying, or dividing unpacked BCD operands. These operations are accomplished using the corresponding unsigned binary instructions in conjunction with the special adjust instructions in Table 9.4-1. An adjust instruction converts the result produced by the related unsigned binary arithmetic instruction to its valid unpacked BCD representation. The adjust instructions are referred to as ASCII adjust because ASCII is a common form of unpacked BCD. The adjust instructions presented in this section and in those in Section 9.5 are the only instructions that make use of the **auxiliary flag (AF)**.

Table 9.4-1   Arithmetic instructions specifically for signed binary operands.

Mnemonic	Operands	Function	O	D	I	T	S	Z	A	P	C
AAA	none	ASCII adjust for addition	?	–	–	–	?	?	✓	?	✓
AAS	none	ASCII adjust for subtraction	?	–	–	–	?	?	✓	?	✓
AAM	none	ASCII adjust for multiply	?	–	–	–	✓	✓	?	✓	?
AAD	none	ASCII adjust for division	?	–	–	–	✓	✓	?	✓	?

9.4.1   Unpacked BCD Addition

To add two unpacked BCD numbers, the numbers are added using either the ADD or ADC instruction with a destination of AL. Then, *ASCII adjust for addition* (**AAA**) is used to adjust the result in AL to a valid unpacked BCD number. For example, in the instruction sequence

```
xor     ah,ah           ;clear AH to receive carry
mov     al,09h          ;add two unpacked BCD numbers
add     al,04h
aaa                     ;adjust binary sum in AL to unpacked BCD
```

after the ADD instruction, AL is 0DH or 13 (00001101B) in binary, which is not a valid unpacked BCD number. After AAA, AH is 01H and AL is 03H. This is the valid unpacked BCD representation of the sum, and it requires two unpacked BCD bytes. It was necessary to use XOR to zero AH prior to the addition because the carry from the adjustment is added to AH.

To accomplish its adjustment, AAA adds 06H to AL if the low nibble of AL is greater than 9 or if AF is 1. Either of these conditions mean that the original sum was greater than 9 and must be adjusted. Adding 06H to the sum is the required adjustment for the low nibble because four bits can normally represent 16 distinct symbols and BCD has only 10 distinct symbols. If adjustment is required, AAA adds 1 to AH. Whether the adjustment is made or not, AAA zeros the high nibble of AL.

Because AAA examines only AF and the low nibble of AL, ASCII digits can be directly added and the result adjusted with AAA to give the correct unpacked BCD sum. AAA does not generate an ASCII result. Rather, it generates an unpacked BCD result that can easily be converted to ASCII. For example:

```
xor     ah,ah           ;clear AH to receive carry
mov     al,39h          ;add two ASCII numbers
add     al,34h

aaa                     ;adjust binary sum in AL
or      al,30h          ;convert low BCD digit to ASCII
or      ah,30h          ;convert high BCD digit to ASCII
```

9.4.2   Unpacked BCD Subtraction

ASCII adjust for subtraction (**AAS**) adjusts the result from a previous subtraction, using SUB or SBB, of two unpacked BCD operands. The subtraction's destination must have been AL. If the low nibble of AL is greater than 9 or if AF is 1, AAS subtracts 6 from the low nibble of AL and subtracts 1 from AH. The high nibble of AL is zeroed whether an adjustment is performed or not. For example:

```
mov     al,08h          ;subtract two unpacked BCD numbers
sub     al,03h

aas                     ;adjust binary difference in AL
                        ;to unpacked BCD
```

9.4.3   Unpacked BCD Multiplication

To multiply two unpacked BCD numbers, the numbers are multiplied using MULT. The product of the multiplication, which is in AL, is then corrected by using *ASCII adjust for multiply* (**AAM**). For example:

```
mov     al,02h          ;multiply two unpacked BCD numbers
mul     05h

aam                     ;adjust binary product in AL to
                        ;unpacked BCD quotient in AH
                        ;and unpacked BCD remainder in AL
```

AAM divides AL by ten. The quotient from this division is placed in AH and the remainder is placed in AL. AAM can be thought of as a special form of the DIV instruction which divides AL by ten. However, unlike the DIV instruction it places the quotient in AH and the remainder in AL, instead of vice versa. Before multiplying, the high nibbles of the unpacked BCD operands must be 0. Therefore, ASCII digits cannot be directly multiplied and the result adjusted with AAM.

9.4.4   Unpacked BCD Division

To divide a two digit unpacked BCD dividend by a single digit unpacked BCD divisor, the adjustment must be carried out before the division! First, the two digit dividend must be in AH and AL, with the most significant digit in AH. *ASCII adjust for division* (**AAD**) multiplies AH by ten and adds it to AL. This leaves the unsigned binary equivalent of the original two digit unpacked BCD number in AL and leaves AH = 00H. DIV is then used with the single digit divisor specified as the source. The unpacked BCD quotient is returned in AL and the unpacked BCD remainder is returned in AH.

```
mov     ah,upbcd_dvdndh     ;unpacked high dividend digit
mov     al,upbcd_dvdndl     ;unpacked low dividend digit
aad                         ;adjustment precedes division!
div     upbcd_dvsor         ;unpacked divisor
```

9.5   Packed BCD Arithmetic

Two decimal digits are packed into a single byte in the **packed BCD** number representation. The high nibble encodes the most significant BCD digit, and the low nibble encodes the least significant digit. For addition and subtraction of packed BCD digits, the usual unsigned addition and subtraction instructions are used, followed by special adjust instructions. No special adjust instructions are available to correct results generated using multiplication and division instructions. Therefore, for multiplication and division, you must write procedures to perform these operations.

80C188EB instructions specific to packed BCD arithmetic are listed in Table 9.5-1.

Table 9.5-1   Arithmetic instructions for packed BCD arithmetic.

Mnemonic	Operands	Function	O	D	I	T	S	Z	A	P	C
DAA	none	decimal adjust for addition	✓	–	–	–	✓	✓	✓	✓	✓
DAS	none	decimal adjust for subtraction	✓	–	–	–	✓	✓	✓	✓	✓

9.5.1   Packed BCD Addition

To add two valid packed BCD digits, they are first added using an ADD or ADC instruction with a destination of AL. The result in AL is then adjusted using *decimal adjust for addition* (**DAA**). DAA adjusts the sum from the addition by first examining the low nibble and if it is greater than 9 or if AF is 1, adds 06H to AL and sets AF. Then, if AL is greater than 9FH or if CF is 1, DAA adds 60H to AL and sets CF. The result after this process is the valid packed BCD sum.

9.5.2   Packed BCD Subtraction

Packed BCD subtraction is accomplished in a fashion similar to addition. The subtraction of two valid packed BCD digits, using SUB or SBB and having a destination of AL, is adjusted using the *decimal adjust for subtraction* (**DAS**) instruction.

9.5.3   Packed BCD Multiplication and Division

There is no instruction that can adjust the results of a multiplication of valid packed BCD operands to give a valid packed BCD result. The same is true for division of packed BCD operands. Multiplication or division can be accomplished by first converting the packed BCD operands to unsigned binary, multiplying or dividing the unsigned binary values using MUL or DIV, respectively, then converting the unsigned binary result to packed BCD. Procedures for converting packed BCD to unsigned binary and vice versa are provided in the next section.

9.6   Binary/BCD Conversions

One method of converting a BCD number to binary is based on the fact that a decimal number can be expressed as:

$$D = (.. ((d_{n-1}) \times 10 + d_{n-2}) \times 10 ...) \times 10 + d_1) \times 10 + d_0$$

An algorithm based on this expression starts with the most significant digit, d_{n-1}, multiplies it by 10, then adds the next-most significant digit. This result is multiplied by 10, and so on, until the least significant digit is added. The procedure in Fig. 9.6-1 converts a packed BCD word in AX into its binary equivalent, which is left in AX.

The previous expression for a decimal number also suggests how a binary number can be converted to decimal. If a binary number is divided by 10, the remainder is the least significant digit of the decimal equivalent of the binary number. Division by 10 of the quotient from the previous division gives the next-most significant digit of the decimal equivalent. This process is repeated until the quotient is less than or equal to 9. This last value determined is the most significant digit of the decimal equivalent.

A procedure that converts a binary word in AX into its packed BCD equivalent in DX:AX is given in Fig. 9.6-2

9.7   Summary

The 80C188EB provides arithmetic instructions that directly operate on four data types: unsigned binary, signed binary, unpacked BCD, and packed BCD. Unsigned binary and signed binary operands can be bytes or words. For these operand types, addition, subtraction, multiplication, and division instructions are provided.

Addition and subtraction are accomplished with the ADD, ADC, SUB, and SBB instructions. The ADD and SUB instructions add or subtract the operands but ignore the carry (or borrow). The ADC and SBB instructions include the carry in the addition or subtraction.

While the largest operand that can be directly operated on by these instructions is a word, larger operands are created by using multiple words to represent a single operand. Multiword operands can be added and subtracted by using the ADC or SBB instructions inside a loop. Each time through the loop, corresponding words of each operand are added or subtracted.

The MUL and DIV instructions multiply and divide, respectively, unsigned numbers. To multiply operands larger than words, or to use an operand larger than a word as a divisor, requires that you write a procedure that uses the basic arithmetic instructions to carry out the operation.

Signed binary numbers are represented in two's complement form. This representation reduces the logic required in the ALU because no special subtractor hardware is required. Subtraction is accomplished by taking the two's complement of the subtrahend and adding it to the minuend.

Addition and subtraction of signed numbers is accomplished using the same addition and subtraction instruction used for unsigned numbers. As long as the result is not too large or too small to be represented as a two's complement number using the number

```
;******************************************************************
;NAME:        BCDWBIN
;
;function:    Converts a packed BCD word to binary
;created:
;revised:
;assumes:     AX = BCD word
;returns:     AX = binary word
;modifies:
;calls:
;called by:
;
;DESCRIPTION:
;
;******************************************************************

bcdwbin proc
        push    bx      ;save registers
        push    cx
        push    dx
        push    bp
        push    di
        push    si
        pushf
        mov     bp,ax   ;BCD word in BP
        mov     bx,10   ;load multiplier
        xor     si,si   ;clear SI
        mov     di,3    ;digits to multiply by ten
nxtdig: mov     cx,4    ;digit bit counter
        xor     ax,ax   ;clear AX
shfdig: shl     bp,1
        rcl     ax,1
        loop    shfdig
        add     ax,si   ;add SI to new digit
        mul     bx      ;multiply by 10
        mov     si,ax
        dec     di
        jnz     nxtdig
        mov     cx,4
        xor     ax,ax
lsdig:  shl     bp,1    ;shift least significant digit is AX
        rcl     ax,1
        loop    lsdig
        add     ax,si
        popf            ;restore registers
        pop     si
        pop     di
        pop     bp
        pop     dx
        pop     cx
        pop     bx
        ret
bcdwbin endp
```

Figure 9.6-1   Procedure to convert a packed BCD word to binary.

```
;****************************************************************
;NAME:         BINWBCD
;
;function:     Converts a binary word to packed BCD
;created:
;revised:
;assumes:      AX = binary word
;returns:      DX:AX = packded BCD word, right justified
;modifies:     AX
;calls:
;called by:
;
;DESCRIPTION:
;
;****************************************************************

binwbcd proc
        push    bx      ;save registers
        push    cx
        push    bp
        push    di
        pushf
        xor     dx,dx   ;clear DX
        xor     bp,bp   ;clear BP
        mov     bx,10   ;load divisor
        mov     di,4    ;number of divisions by ten
nexdig: div     bx
        mov     cx,4    ;digit bit counter
shrdig: shr     dx,1    ;shift next least significant digit into BP
        rcr     bp,1
        loop    shrdig
        dec     di
        jnz     nexdig
        div     bx
        mov     ax,bp
        popf            ;restore registers
        pop     di
        pop     bp
        pop     cx
        pop     bx  .
        ret
binwbcd endp
```

Figure 9.6-2   Procedure to convert an unsigned binary word to packed BCD.

of bits of the destination, the result will be correct. When a signed byte is added to a word, the byte must be sign extended to 16-bits before the addition. When a word is added to a double word, the word must first be sign extended to a double word. Instructions are provided for these two operations.

Special instructions, IMUL and IDIV, are provided for multiplying and dividing signed numbers. These instructions are different from the instructions for multiplying and dividing unsigned numbers.

BCD number representations use 4-bits (one nibble) to represent a single decimal digit. The 80C188EB has instructions to operate on two kinds of BCD representations, unpacked BCD and packed BCD. Unpacked BCD uses the rightmost nibble in a byte to represent a single BCD digit. Unpacked BCD numbers are added and subtracted using the standard addition and subtraction instructions. However, after the addition or subtraction, the result must be adjusted to be a valid unpacked BCD number. The adjustment is accomplished by the ASCII adjust for addition and ASCII adjust for subtraction instructions, AAA and AAS, respectively. For multiplication and division, the AAM and AAD instructions are used to accomplish the adjustment. The AAD instruction is unique in that it is used before the DIV instruction, not after.

Packed BCD numbers encode two decimal digits in each byte. These numbers are added and subtracted using the regular addition and subtraction instructions. The result of an addition is adjusted afterwards using the DAA instruction. Subtractions are adjusted using DAS.

There are no instructions that can adjust the results from multiplying or dividing packed BCD numbers. Typically procedures are used to convert the packed BCD operands to unsigned binary, multiply or divide them as unsigned binary numbers, then use another procedure to convert the unsigned result to packed BCD.

9.8   Problems

Include a complete header for all procedures.

1. The 80C188EB provides arithmetic instructions that can directly operate on what kinds of number representations? For each of these representations, give the size of the representations in bytes that can be directly manipulated.

2. For each of the following unsigned binary numbers, compute its decimal value.

   a. 01101011
   b. 10111101
   c. 0100100111100001
   d. 1110001011001011

3. Write a NEAR procedure that adds two 32-bit unsigned binary operands stored in memory. Before the procedure is called, the calling sequence loads BX with the offset of the addend and DI with the offset of the augend. The procedure returns the computed sum in the memory locations previously occupied by the augend.

4. A NEAR procedure, sum, returns in registers DX:AX the sum of n unsigned binary words. The n values to be added are pushed onto the stack by the calling sequence followed by the value of n itself. Assume SS = 0100H and SP = 0040H. Draw the stack frame immediately after the CALL to the procedure has been executed. Assume that the calling sequence has pushed the required parameters onto the stack prior to

having sum add four values ($n = 4$). Indicate the physical address associated with each parameter on the stack. Write the procedure sum. Your procedure must use BP to reference the parameters. Note, your procedure must remove the parameters placed on the stack by the calling sequence. What is the maximum number of words your procedure can add without overflow?

5. An application requires a procedure that scales a word by returning a percentage (from 0 to 100%) of the word's value. The word to be scaled is passed to the procedure in AX and the percentage is passed in BL. The procedure in BL is an unsigned number between 0 and 100. The result is to be returned in AX. Write the procedure. The procedure must return with all registers, except AX, unaltered.

6. Write a procedure, adjust, that adjusts a measured value in the range 3 to 75 for offset and gain errors. The measured value is passed to the procedure in AL for offset and gain errors. The offset error is removed by subtracting 3 from the measured value. After the offset has been removed, the gain error is adjusted by multiplying the value by 0.875. The adjusted value is to be returned in AL.

7. Write a procedure that converts a temperature in Fahrenheit to its centigrade equivalent. The Fahrenheit temperature is stored as an unsigned binary number in the word variable fahrnht and the result is to be placed in the word variable cent. The Fahrenheit temperature is restricted to the range 32 degrees to 1000 degrees. The relationship between degrees Fahrenheit and centigrade is:

$$C = 5/9(F - 32)$$

8. Write a program that conditionally inputs unsigned integer data from the byte port meas, whenever bit 2 of the byte input port STATUS is set. The value input from meas is to be output to the byte port PEAK if its value is larger than each value previously input from meas since the last time the CLEAR bit, bit 7 of port STATUS, was set. Whenever the CLEAR bit is set, the process starts over with the assumption that the largest value is 0 and 0 is output to PEAK. Reading the port STATUS clears all of its bits. The port addresses are as follows: STATUS = 8000H, MEAS = 8001H, PEAK = 8000H.

9. Compute the decimal value of each of the following signed binary numbers.

   a. 01101011
   b. 10111101
   c. 0100100111100001
   d. 1110001011001011

10. For each of the following bit patterns, first compute its decimal value assuming it is interpreted as an unsigned binary number. Next compute its decimal value assuming it is interpreted as a signed binary number.

   a. 00111010
   b. 11001110
   c. 0110100111010011
   d. 1010110100010111

11. For each of the following signed binary numbers, compute its decimal value. Also
    compute the two's complement of each number. This is equivalent to negating the
    signed binary number. Verify that the addition of each number to its two's comple-
    ment gives a sum of 0.

    a. 10110110

    b. 01001011

    c. 11111111

    d. 01111110

12. For each of the following pairs of signed numbers in two's complement form, deter-
    mine if the first number is greater in magnitude that the second. Next determine if
    the first number is more positive that the second.

    a. 01110110   10001011
    b. 11110101   11010010
    c. 01100010   01000101
    d. 11001001   00001001

13. Assume that each of the following bytes is sign extended to a word using the CBW
    instruction. Write the resulting bit pattern in hexadecimal.

    a. 00101110

    b. 10001011

    c. 11111110

    d. 01111010

14. Add each of the following pairs of signed numbers. Assuming the sum is stored as a
    byte, what is its decimal value? For which cases, if any, does overflow occur?

    a. 11101010   01111010
    b. 10000100   01000101
    c. 01100001   01001101
    d. 00101110   11110101

15. For each of the following pairs of signed numbers, subtract the second number from
    the first, using the two's complement method to implement the subtraction. Assum-
    ing the result is stored as a byte, compute the decimal value of the difference. For
    which cases, if any, does underflow occur?

    a. 11100101   11110001
    b. 01000011   11111100
    c. 00001011   00010111
    d. 01101101   01101101

16. Write a sequence of instructions that add the signed binary bytes in AL and BL and
    stores the result as a word in the memory location wsum.

17. Write a sequence of instructions that multiplies the 8-bit number in AL by 9 for each of the following cases. Do not include instructions to test for overflow.

   a. The number in AL is unsigned binary and a multiply instruction is to be used.
   b. The number in AL is unsigned binary and a multiply instruction is not to be used.
   c. The number in AL is signed binary and a multiply instruction is to be used.
   d. The number in AL is signed binary and a multiply instruction is not to be used.

18. Write a sequence of instructions that divides the 16-bit number in AX by 4 for each of the following cases. Do not include instructions to test for overflow.

   a. The number in AX is unsigned binary and a divide instruction is to be used.
   b. The number in AX is unsigned binary and a divide instruction is not to be used.
   c. The number in AX is signed binary and a divide instruction is to be used.
   d. The number in AX is signed binary and a divide instruction is not to be used.

19. Write a procedure upbcd_add that adds two 4-digit unpacked BCD numbers. The procedure expects to find the augend in DX:AX and the addend in CX:BX. The procedure returns the sum in DX:AX. If there is a carry, CF is set.

20. Write a procedure upbcd_sub that subtracts two 4-digit unpacked BCD numbers. The procedure expects to find the minuend in DX:AX and the subtrahend in CX:BX. The procedure returns the difference in DX:AX. If there difference is negative, CF is set.

21. Write a procedure which inputs a four digit decimal number from a UART and returns the number as a binary value in AX. The procedure must check bit 7 of port UARTSTS for the availability of each ASCII digit. This bit is set when an ASCII digit has been received by the UART and is cleared automatically when the ASCII digit is read from port serin.

22. Write a procedure pbcd_add that adds two 4-digit packed BCD numbers. The procedure expects to find the augend in AX and the addend in BX. The procedure returns the sum in AX. If there is a carry, CF is set.

23. Write a procedure pbcd_sub that subtracts two 4-digit packed BCD numbers. The procedure expects to find the minuend in AX and the subtrahend in BX. The procedure returns the difference in DX:AX. If the difference is negative, CF is set.

10.1   CPU Subsystems

10.2   The 80C188EB Microprocessor

10.3   System Clock, Reset, and Bus Cycles

10.4   Address/Data Bus Demultiplexing

10.5   A Fully Buffered 80C188EB CPU Subsystem

10.6   Logic Family Compatibility, Loading, and Buffering

10.7   A Minimum-Component Complete System

10.8   Single and Multi-Board Systems

10.9   Peripheral Control Block (PCB)

10.10   The 80C186EB Microprocessor

10.11   Summary

When you develop a prototype system, the CPU subsystem is the first hardware to design and construct. The reliability and robustness of a system is constrained by the quality of the CPU subsystem's design. 80C188EB CPU subsystems can vary substantially in their complexity. To reduce costs, many CPU subsystems do not include the hardware necessary to support all of the 80C188EB's features. Only those features required by the specific application are supported.

This chapter focuses on the design of 80C188EB and 80C186EB CPU subsystems. The discussion refers primarily to the 80C188EB, but, with the exception of data bus width differences, is applicable to the 80C186EB as well. Section 10.10 describes the 80C186EB and 80C188EB differences in detail.

In this chapter, the design of a CPU subsystem is examined, starting from the 80C188EB and building outward to the system bus. After an overview of the 80C188EB's packaging and pinouts, options for generating the system clock and resetting the 80C188EB are presented.

80C188EB bus cycles are presented from the perspective of the system clock's timing. The 80C188EB multiplexes address and data signals on some of its pins. Methods for demultiplexing these signals to provide separate address and data bus signals are presented. You must also determine whether the 80C188EB's bus signals can drive the loads that will be connected to the system bus. If not, buffers are required to provide additional bus drive capability.

After considering conventional buffered CPU subsystem designs that are appropriate for moderate and large systems, the focus of the chapter shifts to two topics related to complete systems. One topic is a minimum component complete system, and the other is the placement of a system's components onto printed circuit boards.

The minimum component complete system presented stands in stark contrast to conventional buffered CPU subsystems. All of its functional subsystems, CPU, memory, input, and output are contained on two ICs: an 80C188EB microprocessor and a PSD311 Programmable Microperipheral with Memory.

In order to create a prototype or manufacture a system, ICs must be placed onto one or more printed circuit boards. This leads to a consideration of standard buses for multiboard systems. Use of a standard bus allows you to use commercial off-the-shelf printed circuit board subsystems to provide some, or all, of the subsystems required in an application.

10.1 CPU Subsystems

The **CPU subsystem** controls a system's overall operation. As stated in Chapter 2, a system's three fundamental operations are storage of data, transfer of data, and transformation of data. The CPU subsystem controls the transfer of data between the 80C188EB and I/O or memory. Arithmetic and logical operations that transform data are carried out in the CPU's key component, the 80C188EB microprocessor.

The CPU subsystem's design is primarily dictated by its data transfer role. To transfer data, the CPU subsystem generates and controls the system bus signals. The system bus consists of the address bus (A19–A0), data bus (D7–D0), and control bus (Fig. 10.1-1). Most of the CPU subsystem components, in addition to the 80C188EB, are needed to support the system bus.

Another set of external signals, not considered part of the system bus, allows direct connections to the 80C188EB's integrated peripherals (Fig. 10.1-1). These signals are considered in later chapters when the various integrated peripherals are presented.

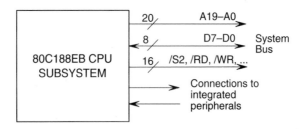

Figure 10.1-1   80C188EB CPU subsystem with its connections to the system bus and to its integrated peripherals.

10.1.1   Data Transfer on the System Bus

The minimum set of signals needed to control a transfer of data over the system data bus is /S2, /RD, and /WR. /RD and /WR control the direction and timing of data transfers. /S2 is actually a status signal that indicates whether I/O or memory is being addressed. Though it is a status signal, /S2 is used by external logic to select an address space. When /S2 is 1, memory is being addressed, when /S2 is 0, I/O is being addressed. Any external decoding logic that you design must include /S2 in its selection of either an I/O or memory device to participate in a transfer. Other signals that are part of the control bus, but are not needed for basic data transfer, are considered in later chapters.

The 80C188EB controls the transfer of data over the system bus in a series of steps. First, it generates an address and asserts the appropriate control signals to transfer data over the data bus to or from the addressed memory or I/O device. The sequence of actions that transfer data over the system bus constitutes a **bus cycle**. Read bus cycles transfer data *to* the 80C188EB and write bus cycles transfer data *from* the 80C188EB. A bus cycle is comprised of a number of time intervals called *T* states. Each *T* state is one period of the system clock. Thus, the time required for a bus cycle is a function of the frequency of the 80C188EB's system clock.

A read bus cycle transfers data from either an input port or a memory location to the 80C188EB. A read bus cycle timing diagram is given in Fig. 10.1-2. This diagram represents the timing of signals on the system bus. The timing of some signals on the system bus differs from their timing at the 80C188EB's pins. The reasons for these important differences are the focus of Section 10.4.

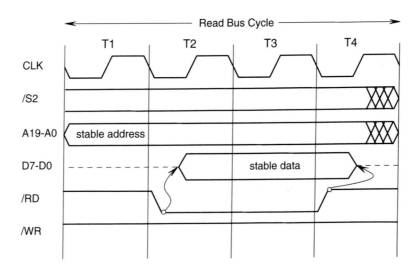

Figure 10.1-2   Read bus cycle timing diagram. Signals as they appear on the system bus, not at the 80C188EB's pins.

During a read bus cycle, the CPU subsystem:

1. Generates an address and asserts or unasserts /S2 to indicate whether the address is for an input port or a memory location.
2. Asserts /RD to signal the addressed port or memory location to drive data onto the data bus.
3. Latches the data on the data bus into one of the 80C188EB registers at the end of state T3.
4. Unasserts /RD.

The addressed input port or memory location drives the data bus only while /RD is asserted. When it is not being driven by the addressed I/O port or memory location, the data bus is in its high-impedance state. Notice that /WR remains unasserted for the duration of a read bus cycle.

A write bus cycle is shown in Fig. 10.1-3. To transfer data from the 80C188EB to an output port or memory location, the CPU subsystem:

1. Generates an address and asserts or unasserts /S2 to indicate whether the address is for an output port or a memory location.
2. Drives the data from the 80C188EB onto the data bus and asserts /WR.
3. Unasserts /WR.

The addressed output port or memory location must latch the data on the rising edge of /WR. This edge occurs when /WR is unasserted at the beginning of state T4. /RD remains unasserted for the duration of a write bus cycle.

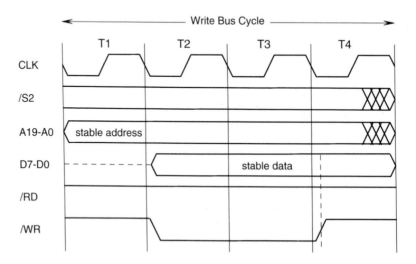

Figure 10.1-3   Write bus cycle timing diagram. Signals as they appear on the system bus, not at the 80C188EB's pins.

One of the primary objectives of CPU subsystem design is to generate the signals that comprise the system bus cycles of Figs. 10.1-2 and 10.1-3, from signals at the 80C188EB's pins. So, next we must take a closer look at the 80C188EB.

10.2   The 80C188EB Microprocessor

The peripheral functions included on an 80C188EB chip are a clock generator, two I/O ports, two serial communications channels, an interrupt controller, three timer/counters, chip select logic, refresh control, and a power management unit (Fig. 10.2-1). The registers in the integrated peripherals are introduced in Section 10.9 and discussed in detail in later chapters. The 80C188EB modular core is denoted as the Central Processing Unit and Bus Interface Unit in Fig. 10.2-1. What is labeled CPU in this figure is what we have referred to as the Execution Unit. Registers in the modular core and the modular core's basic architecture were discussed in Chapter 3.

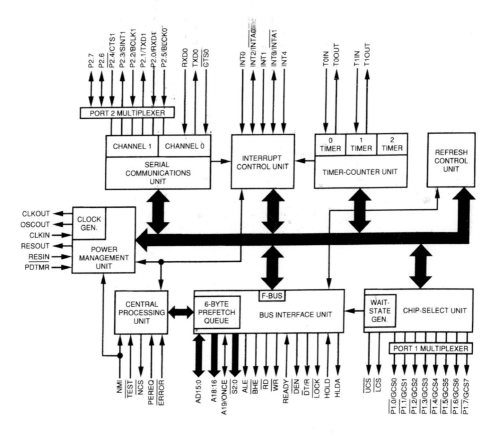

Figure 10.2-1   80C188EB block diagram. (Courtesy of Intel Corp.)

Inclusion of integrated peripherals on the same chip as the modular core requires numerous additional pins for signals to and from these peripherals. Several packaging options are available for the 80C188EB, including: an 84-pin Plastic Leaded Chip Carrier (PLCC), an 80-pin Quad Flat Pack (QFP), and an 80-pin Shrink Quad Flat Pack (SQFP). An 80C188EB logic symbol, with pin numbers corresponding to the PLCC package, is shown in Fig. 10.2-2. The pin numbers of signals for other packaging options are not the same.

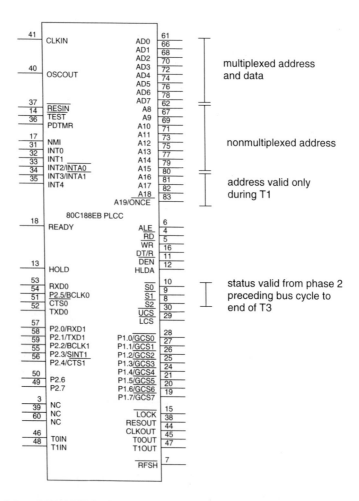

Figure 10.2-2   80C188EB logic symbol. Pin numbers are for PLCC package.

Since the number of pins available for any of the packages is limited, some of the 80C188EB's pins serve more than one purpose. There are two types of **multipurpose pins**. The first type is time-multiplexed. **Time-multiplexed** pins carry two different signals during different phases of the same bus cycle. For example, pin AD7 carries address bit A7 during the early part of a bus cycle. This same pin carries data bit D7 during the later part of the same bus cycle.

The second type of multipurpose pin is configured by your program to serve one of two possible purposes. For example, pin P1.7/GCS7 can be configured to be either output port bit P1.7 or general chip select signal GCS7. You configure this type of multipurpose pin at the beginning of your program. Once configured, a pin's configuration is usually not changed.

Power and ground connections must be made to multiple pins. For the PLCC package, four pins (1, 23, 42, and 64) must all be connected to +5 V (V_{CC}). The 80C188EB is specified to operate with V_{CC} from 4.5 V to 5.5 V. Six pins (2, 22, 43, 63, 65, and 84) must all be grounded (V_{SS}). Pins marked NC, no connection, must be left unconnected. The 80C188EB will not operate properly unless every one of its power pins is connected to V_{CC} and every one of its ground pins is connected to ground.

The 80C188EB's IC technology is low-power CMOS. Logic levels at its input pins must be CMOS compatible. Like other CMOS devices, the power dissipated is a function of the system clock frequency. Several speed versions of the 80C188EB are available, including 13, 20, and 25 MHz. Early speed versions were 8 and 16 MHz. Numbers indicating a device's maximum speed are included as a suffix on the part number. For example, an 80C188EB20 is a 20-MHz part.

A particular speed version can be operated at any frequency up to and including its rated frequency. At a frequency of 0 MHz (DC), an 80C188EB requires less than 50 µA quiescent current. As the clock frequency is increased, power supply current increases at a rate of approximately 3 mA per MHz. The 80C188EB's supply current is denoted as I_{CC}. Thus, the power dissipated is $V_{CC} \times I_{CC}$.

10.3   System Clock, Reset, and Bus Cycles

A microprocessor is a clocked sequential machine. In the case of the 80C188EB, the modular core consists of two clocked sequential machines: the Execution Unit (EU) and the Bus Interface Unit (BIU). Most of the 80C188EB's integrated peripherals are also clocked sequential machines. Like all clocked sequential machines, the 80C188EB requires a system clock signal. The system clock signal establishes the time base for the BIU, EU, and integrated peripherals.

10.3.1   System Clock

The 80C188EB's system clock can be generated by using its on-chip clock generator, or the 80C188EB can be driven by an external clock oscillator.

The 80C188EB's on-chip clock generator requires the addition of a crystal. The 80C188EB's internal clock generator circuitry divides the output of its crystal oscillator by two to generate a two-phase internal clock. As a result, the **system clock frequency, f_s,** is one half of the **crystal frequency, f_c.**

$$fs = \frac{fc}{2}$$

For example, to run an 80C188EB20 at its maximum system clock frequency of 20 MHz, a 40-MHz crystal is required.

The oscillator circuit can use either a parallel resonant fundamental mode or a third-overtone mode crystal network. Figure 10.3-1 shows the crystal circuit and its connection to the 80C188EB's **CLKIN** and **OSCOUT** pins. When using a parallel resonant fundamental mode crystal, L1 and C1 are omitted. Capacitors are connected from pins CX1 and CX2 to ground. A typical capacitor value is 20 pF. When a third-overtone mode crystal is used, components L1 and C1 are required.

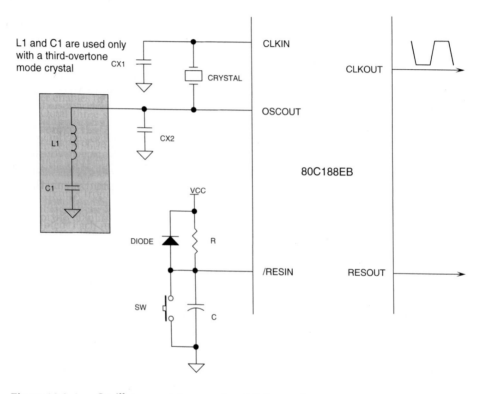

Figure 10.3-1   Oscillator crystal network and RC reset for an 80C188EB.

You must use care in the selection of the crystal, capacitor, and inductor. These components must be chosen to insure that the oscillator starts up and continues to oscillate over the system's entire operating temperature range. Many crystal manufacturers provide "microprocessor grade" crystals designed to be used with specific microprocessors. Using such a crystal simplifies the selection process.

Instead of using the internal crystal oscillator, an external oscillator can be connected directly to CLKIN. In this case, OSCOUT is left unconnected. Clock oscillators are available in 8- and 14-pin DIP packages. These clock oscillators are often called "canned oscillators."

One of the outputs of the two-phase internal clock is available at the **CLKOUT** pin. CLKOUT is a 50% duty cycle square wave that you can use as a clock signal for external peripheral devices. One period of CLKOUT, defined as being from one falling edge to the next, is defined as a *T state*. Changes in the address, data, and control signals are initiated only on transitions of CLKOUT. Therefore, all AC timing parameters are referenced to CLKOUT.

External peripheral devices often require a clock signal at a frequency lower than CLKOUT. One method for generating such a signal is to use one of the 80C188EB's on-chip timers. Two of these three timers have output pins. These two counter/timers can be programmed to provide at their output pins a signal whose frequency is a programmed fraction of CLKOUT's frequency.

10.3.2   Reset

A clocked sequential machine must be placed in a predefined starting state when power is first applied to the system. Resetting a system at power on is referred to as a **cold start** or **power-on reset**. Resetting a microprocessor is accomplished by asserting the microprocessor's reset input. The reset signal must continue to be asserted for a specified time after the microprocessor's power supply and oscillator outputs have stabilized. The amount of time required for a power supply's output to stabilize can vary considerably, depending on the power supply's characteristics. A crystal oscillator typically takes several milliseconds to stabilize.

An 80C188EB is reset by a logic 0 at its **/RESIN** input (Fig. 10.3-1). The 80C188EB provides a **RESOUT** signal that can be used to reset external devices. RESOUT remains asserted as long as /RESIN is asserted. Inclusion of a momentary contact switch allows the system to be manually reset after power on. Resetting a system after its power-on reset, is called a **warm start**.

/RESIN is a Schmitt trigger input. This allows a simple external RC circuit to generate the power-on reset signal. When the power supply is OFF, the voltage drop across capacitor C, V_C, is 0 V. This is the case because any voltage on the capacitor discharges through the low impedance path provided by the diode and the power supply's output impedance. The voltage at /RESIN is equal to V_C. When power is turned ON, /RESIN is initially 0, causing the 80C188EB to be reset.

The capacitor charges until the voltage across it equals the supply voltage V_{CC}. During the time that the voltage at /RESIN is in the logic 0 voltage range, the 80C188EB is held in its reset state. If, at power on, the power supply could reach its maximum output instantly, V_{CC} as a function of time would be given by the expression:

$$V_C(t) = V_{CC} \times \left(1 - e^{\frac{-t}{RC}}\right)$$

/RESIN must remain low for a minimum of 28 periods of CLKIN, after CLKIN and V_{CC} have stabilized, for the 80C188EB's pins to be placed in their reset state. /RESIN must remain low an additional 4 CLKIN periods after the pins have assumed their reset state. Thus, to guarantee reset at power on, /RESIN must be asserted for a total of 32 CLKIN periods.

A typical value for the RC time constant is 100 ms. However, the amount of time /RESIN is actually logic 0 after the supply reaches V_{CC} is a function not only of the capacitor and resistor values, but also of the rise time of the power supply's output. Therefore, V_{CC}'s rise time must also be taken into consideration. If the power supply's rise time is too long, /RESIN may not remain logic 0 long enough after V_{CC} reaches its minimum operating voltage.

If a proper /RESIN is not provided, the 80C188EB will start in an uninitialized state resulting in unspecified operation. Typically, the system crashes, or perhaps worse, writes random values into battery-backed or other forms of nonvolatile memory.

If appropriate values of R and C are not determined for the particular power supply being used, or if the power supply is later changed to one with a slower rise time, the reset signal's duration may be insufficient.

10.3.3   Microprocessor Supervisory Circuits

A more reliable method for providing a power-on reset signal, one that does not require a precise knowledge of the power supply's rise time, is desirable. In addition to its dependence on the power supply's rise time, an RC reset circuit does not handle brownout conditions. A **brownout** is a drop in the AC line voltage. This drop can cause the power supply's V_{CC} output voltage to drop below its required value. The 80C188EB, along with the other ICs in the system, requires that V_{CC} be within a specified range for proper operation. For example, an 80C188EB is not to be operated with V_{CC} above 5.5 V or below 4.5 V. When V_{CC} drops below 4.5 V, the 80C188EB can fail to operate properly.

Microprocessor supervisory circuits are ICs that provide a number of functions associated with monitoring the power supplied to a system. Functions provided typically include: generation of power-on reset signal, generation of a reset signal for low supply voltage or brownout conditions, power-fail warning, memory write protection, battery-backed memory switchover, and a watchdog timer. The reset features of a microprocessor supervisory circuit are the only ones of interest in this section. Other features are considered in later chapters when topics related to these features are discussed.

A variety of microprocessor supervisory circuits is available with different features and parameter values. A representative device, the Maxim **MAX807**, is shown in Fig. 10.3-2. The MAX807 contains several voltage comparators that monitor V_{CC}. Different versions of the MAX807 provide different reset comparator threshold voltages. The MAX807N's reset comparator causes it to assert both its active low and active high reset outputs whenever V_{CC} is below 4.575 V.

To reset an 80C188EB, the MAX807's /RESET output is connected to the 80C188EB's /RESIN pin (Fig. 10.3-3). The /RESET output holds the 80C188EB in its reset state during power on, power down, and brownout conditions. The MAX807 keeps its reset outputs asserted for a minimum of 140 ms after V_{CC} rises above 4.65 volts, no matter how long it takes V_{CC} to reach 4.65 V. This eliminates the power-on reset signal's dependency on the power supply's rise time.

A manual reset pin (/MR) allows a momentary contact switch to be connected from this pin to ground to provide a manual reset. No external pull-up resistor or debounce circuitry is required for the switch; the MAX807 provides this circuitry internally.

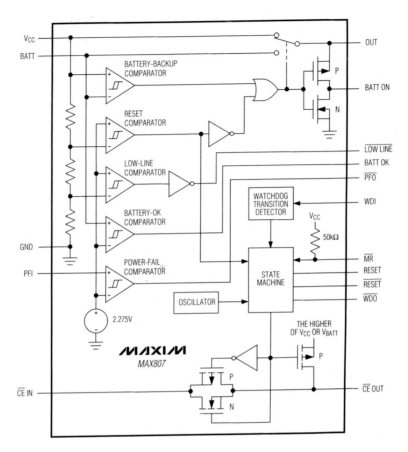

Figure 10.3-2   MAX807 microprocessor supervisory circuit block diagram. (Courtesy of
Maxim Integrated Products, Inc.)

10.3.4   T States and Bus Cycles

The bus cycle timing diagrams in Section 10.1 illustrate signal transitions at the system
bus. The paragraphs that follow describe bus cycles and signal transitions at the
80C188EB's pins.

The read bus cycle timing diagram for signals at an 80C188EB's pins is given in Fig.
10.3-4. The write bus cycle timing diagram is given in Fig. 10.3-5.

To I/O devices and memory, a bus cycle is an asynchronous event during which the
80C188EB first generates an address and /S2 to address a device, then asserts either a /RD
or a /WR strobe to cause a data transfer.

Recall from Chapter 3 that the 80C188EB's modular core consists of the Execution
Unit (EU) and Bus Interface Unit (BIU). The BIU generates the address, status, and control signals. The BIU executes a bus cycle only when instructions need to be fetched from
memory or when operands must be transferred from or to I/O or memory. When not executing a bus cycle, the BIU executes idle states. **Idle states (TI)** occur between bus cycles.

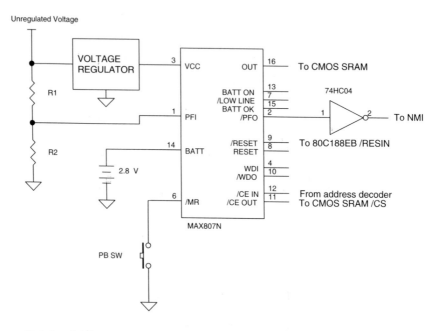

Figure 10.3-3   MAX807N microprocessor supervisory circuit and its connections to an
80C188EB system.

For example, one condition where idle states occur is when the instruction queue is full
and the EU is performing internal operations that do not require access to the bus.

A simplified representation of the BIU's state diagram (Fig. 10.3-6) shows the
sequence of state transitions in a bus cycle. A state transition occurs at the end of each
CLKOUT period. When /RESIN is asserted, the 80C188EB is reset and the BIU enters state
TI. When /RESIN is unasserted, the 80C188EB transitions to state T1 to start the first bus
cycle. (You will have to pay careful attention to the distinction between TI and T1, since
the I and 1 are very similar in the typeface used.) A bus cycle normally consists of four T
states, T1 through T4. Actions associated with each T state are summarized in Table 10.3-1.

As long as the current bus cycle is to be immediately followed by another bus cycle,
the transitions are from T1 through T2, T3, and T4, and back to T1. If another bus cycle
does not immediately follow the current one, state T3 is followed by state TI, instead of T4.
State transitions from TI back to TI continue until another bus cycle is initiated.

An integer number of WAIT states (TW) can be inserted between states T3 and T4.
Each WAIT state is actually a transition from T3 directly back to T3. WAIT states are
inserted in response to the 80C188EB's on-chip WAIT state generator or to external logic
that unasserts the 80C188EB's READY input.

During WAIT states, the bus signals maintain the same logic levels they had at the
end of T3. WAIT states are inserted to extend the duration of a bus cycle in order to accommodate a slow I/O or memory device. WAIT states and their generation are considered in
detail in Sections 11.7 and 13.3.

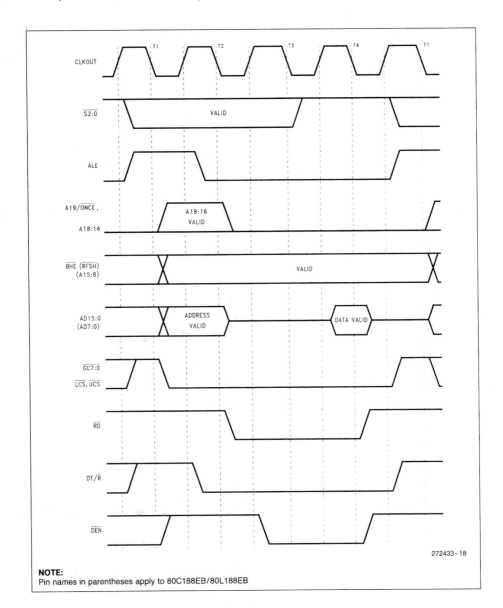

Figure 10.3-4   80C188EB read bus cycle timing diagram. (Courtesy of Intel Corp.)

Every bus cycle is preceded by a rising edge at the 80C188EB's ALE output and the generation of status signals /S2–/S0 (Figs. 10.3-4 and 10.3-5). /S2–/S0 indicate the impending bus cycle's purpose, or type. There are eight types of bus cycles (Table 10.3-2).

Two types of bus cycles, **Halt** and **Idle**, do not actually transfer data. The six bus cycles that do transfer data all share the basic timing relationships shown in Figs. 10.3-4 and 10.3-5.

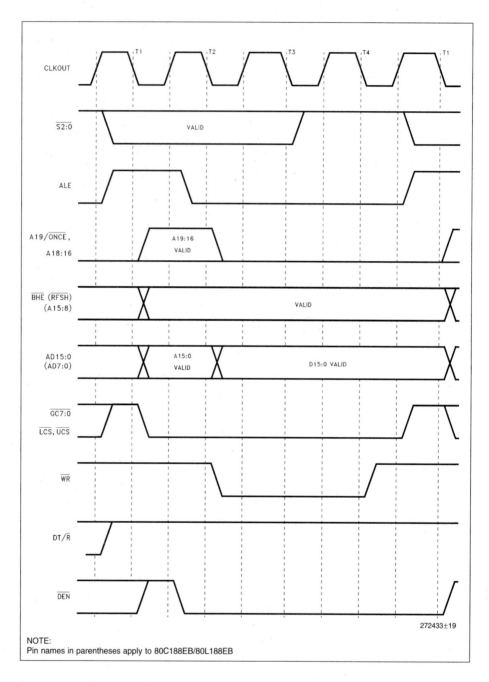

Figure 10.3-5   80C188EB write bus cycle timing diagram. (Courtesy of Intel Corp.)

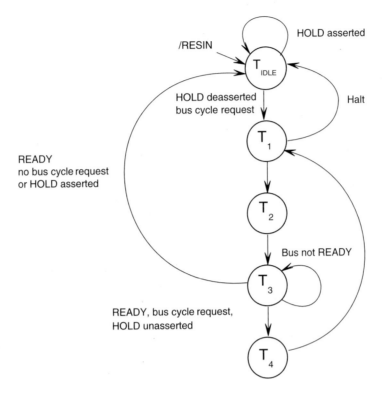

Figure 10.3-6   Simplified BIU bus cycle state diagram. TI has been written as T_{IDLE} in this diagram for clarity.

Table 10.3-1   Actions associated with each T state of a bus cycle.

T State	Actions
T1	Address, /S2–/S0, and DT/R generated. For write cycles, /DEN is asserted. ALE generated.
T2	A7–A0 is replaced by D7–D0 for a write and floated for a read. Either /RD or /WR is asserted. For a read cycle /DEN is asserted.
T3 and T4	Data transferred on AD7–AD0.
TW	WAIT state is inserted between T3 and T4 if READY negated.
TI	Idle states may be inserted for clock periods between bus cycles.

Table 10.3-2   80C188EB bus cycles.

/S2[a]	/S1[b]	/S0	Bus Cycle
0	0	0	Interrupt Acknowledge
0	0	1	Read I/O
0	1	0	Write I/O
0	1	1	Processor Halt
1	0	0	Instruction Prefetch
1	0	1	Read Memory
1	1	0	Write Memory
1	1	1	Idle (Passive)

a. /S2 = 0 for I/O access, /S2 = 1 for memory access.
b. /S1 = 0 for a read operation, /S1 = 1 for a write operation.

Distinctions between bus cycle types are based primarily on the direction of transfer and whether I/O or memory is involved. As can be seen from the table, status signal /S2 indicates whether the bus cycle accesses I/O (/S2 = 0) or memory (/S2 = 1). /S1 indicates the direction of transfer as a read (/S1 = 0) or a write (/S1 = 1). /S0 is needed to further distinguish between different types of bus cycles that involve the same address space and direction of transfer.

10.4   Address/Data Bus Demultiplexing

To reduce the number of pins required on the 80C188EB packages, address signals are time-multiplexed with data signals on the eight pins AD7–AD0, producing a time multiplexed address and data bus (Fig. 10.2-2).

A clock period, or T state, has two phases. The first half of a clock period, when CLKOUT is 0, is called **phase 1** (low phase) of the T state (Fig. 10.4-1(a)). The second half of a clock period, when CLKOUT is 1, is **phase 2** (high phase).

A simple bus cycle consists of the four states T1 through T4, as indicted in Fig. 10.4-1(b). Defining the start of a bus cycle at the beginning of T1 is consistent with the way external memory and I/O view a bus cycle. For a memory or I/O device, a bus cycle begins when a new address becomes valid.

A bus cycle is considered to have two phases, an **address/status phase** and a **data phase**. The address/status phase of a bus cycle starts during phase 2 of the T state preceding T1 and continues through T1. The data phase starts at T2 and continues through phase 1 of T4. Pins AD7–AD0 provide address bits A7–A0 during the address/status phase and transfer data bits D7–D0 during the data phase.

We have defined a bus cycle as starting at the beginning of T1 and ending at the end of T4. In this context, the address/status phase of the bus cycle starts 1/2 of a T state before the bus cycle starts. Correspondingly, the data phase ends 1/2 of a T state before the bus cycle ends.

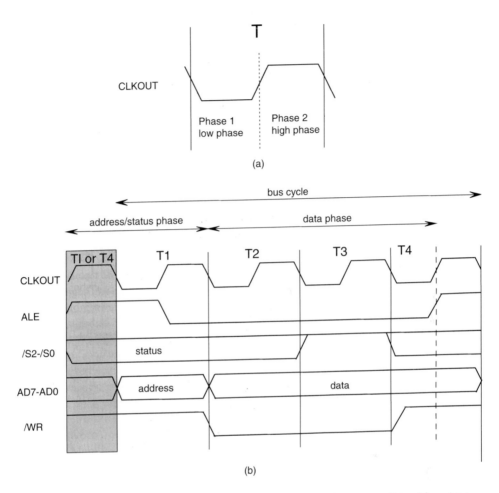

Figure 10.4-1   Clock and bus cycle phases: (a) phases of a T state; (b) address/status phase and data phase of a write bus cycle.

Some memory and I/O peripheral ICs are designed specifically for use with a microprocessor that has a multiplexed address/data bus. These ICs include on-chip address latches to demultiplex AD7–AD0. Demultiplexing accomplished outside of the CPU subsystem in the memory or I/O subsystems is called **remote demultiplexing**. An example of a system with remote demultiplexing is given in Section 10.7.

However, most memory and I/O peripheral ICs do not have on-chip address latches. These ICs require that an address remain stable at their address input pins throughout a bus cycle. Thus, the address signals on AD7–AD0 have to be demultiplexed, by latching them, to provide address bits A7–A0 that are stable on the system bus for the entire bus cycle. The most efficient way to accomplish this is with **local demultiplexing** in the CPU subsystem.

Local demultiplexing is accomplished using positive level triggered octal latches. In Fig. 10.4-2, one **74HC573 octal latch** is used to demultiplex address/data bus signals

AD7–AD0. Another latch is used to latch A19–A16 and /S2–/S0. Although A19–A16 and /S2–/S0 are not multiplexed with other signals, they are only valid during the address/status phase of the bus cycle (Figs. 10.3-4 and 10.3-5). The latched signals remain stable for the entire bus cycle. Latched signals are sometimes denoted with an L prefix to distinguish them from their unlatched counterparts. Accordingly, the outputs of the latches in Fig. 10.4-2 may be denoted LA19–LA16, /LS2–/LS0, and LA7–LA0.

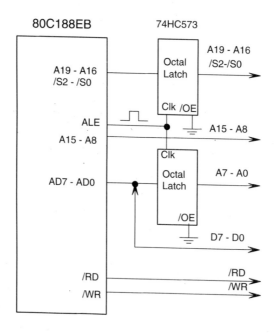

Figure 10.4-2   Demultiplexing the address and status for 80C188EB CPU subsystem.

In most systems, address bits A19–A16 and status bit /S2 are used as inputs to external address decoders that select memory and I/O ICs. If, instead, the 80C188EB's Chip Select Unit is used for all address decoding, these bits do not need to be latched.

The 80C188EB provides an **address latch enable** (**ALE**), strobe to clock external address latches for demultiplexing (Figs. 10.3-4 and 10.3-5). If a positive level triggered latch is used, it is transparent while ALE is asserted. Thus, the A7–A0, A19–A16 and /S2–/S0 values generated by the 80C188EB pass through the latches and are available on the system bus at the beginning of the bus cycle. These signals are then latched on the trailing edge of ALE (near the middle of T1) and held until the high phase of T4, when ALE is asserted in preparation for the next bus cycle.

During the beginning of T2, in a read bus cycle, the 80C188EB floats pins AD7–AD0. In response to /RD being asserted, the addressed input port or memory location must drive pins AD7–AD0 with the data, D7–D0, to be transferred.

During the beginning of T2 in a write bus cycle, the 80C188EB replaces address bits A7–A0 on pins AD7–AD0 with data, D7–D0, and asserts /WR. The addressed output port or memory location latches the data on the trailing edge of /WR (at the beginning of state T4).

10.5   A Fully Buffered 80C188EB CPU Subsystem

The CPU subsystem of Fig. 10.4-2 has limited **bus drive** capability. Its system data bus, D7–D0, system address bus bits A15–A8, and control signals /RD and /WR are driven directly from pins of the 80C188EB. The 80C188EB's address, data, and control pins can each source 2 mA at logic 1 and sink 3 mA at logic 0. If you connect loads to these pins that require more than this amount of current, the voltage levels of these signals may come within the logic's unallowed voltage range. As a result, the system may fail to operate properly.

As the number of ICs in the memory and I/O subsystems connected directly to the system bus increases, the CPU subsystem's bus drive capability can be exceeded. Figure 10.5-1 shows a **fully buffered** 80C188EB CPU subsystem. All address, data, and control lines are buffered. Buffering provides greater current drive capability. The 74HC573 (or **74HC372**) octal latches used to demultiplex AD7–AD0, A19–A16, and /S2–/S0 include output buffers, and therefore, inherently provide buffering. A 74HC573 can source 6 mA and sink 6 mA. Thus, the output pin of an octal latch can source three times more and sink two times more current than can an 80C188EB pin.

To provide greater drive capability for bits A15–A8, which do not need to be latched, a 74HC541 octal buffer is used. This buffer also sources 6 mA and sinks 6 mA. Two buffers from a second 74HC541 are used to buffer /RD and /WR. Buffered signals are sometimes denoted with a B prefix to distinguish them from their unbuffered counterparts, for example BA15–BA8.

For even greater drive capability, 74ACT latches and buffers can be used. 74ACT latches and buffers can source and sink 24 mA.

10.5.1   Data Bus Buffering

Buffering the data bus requires special consideration. Unlike address and control lines, data bus lines are bidirectional. The buffering scheme must drive data in the appropriate direction at the appropriate time. A buffer designed for this purpose is called a **transceiver**, a conjunction of the words transmitter and receiver.

The logical structure of a **74HC245 octal transceiver** is shown in Fig. 10.5-2. The transceiver's direction input, T/R, controls the direction of transfer. If T/R is 1, the top three-state buffer is selected to be enabled and data is transferred from "A" to "B," which corresponds to a transfer from the microprocessor to an external device. If T/R is 0, the bottom three-state buffer is selected to be enabled, and data is transferred from "B" to "A," which corresponds to a transfer from an external device to the 80C188EB. The selected buffer is enabled only while /OE is asserted. An **octal transceiver** provides eight pairs of these back-to-back buffers with shared control logic. The 74HC245 can source 6 mA and sink 6 mA.

The 80C188EB provides control signals **DT/R (Data Transmit/Receive)** and **/DEN (Data bus ENable)** to control a data bus transceiver. As shown in Figs. 10.3-4 and 10.3-5, DT/R indicates the direction of transfer for the bus cycle. For read bus cycles, DT/R is 0. For write bus cycles, DT/R is 1. /DEN is only asserted for that portion of a bus cycle during which data should actually be transferred. Only while /DEN is asserted is the selected

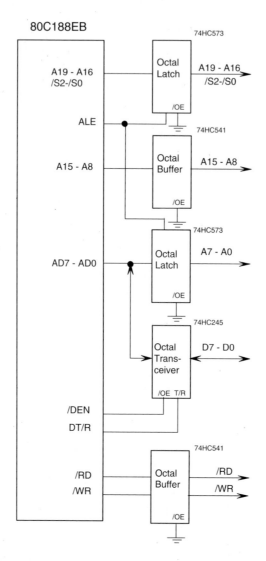

Figure 10.5-1   Fully buffered 80C188EB CPU subsystem.

buffer in every transceiver pair enabled. Note that /DEN is asserted for a much shorter time in a read bus cycle than in a write bus cycle.

A transceiver may be required on the data bus, even if there is no loading problem. Recall from Fig. 10.3-4 that during a read bus cycle, /RD is unasserted at the beginning of T4 to turn off the output data buffers in the device being read. The 80C188EB then drives pins AD7–AD0 with A7–A0 at the beginning of the next state, T1.

In Fig. 10.4-2, if after /RD is unasserted the device being read cannot float its data pins before the start of T1, bus contention occurs. This contention is the result of the device that was being read still driving data on AD7–AD0 while the 80C188EB has started to drive

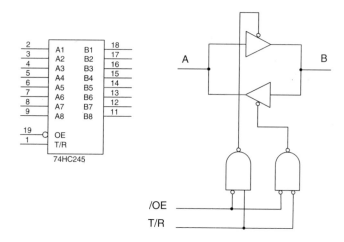

Figure 10.5-2   Transceiver logic structure.

address values A7–A0 onto these same bus lines. This problem frequently occurs with some older I/O peripheral ICs whose output buffers take a relatively long time to turn off.

In contrast, in Fig. 10.5-1 when /DEN is unasserted, the transceiver quickly isolates the device being read from the 80C188EB's AD7–AD0 pins. Thus, the addition of a transceiver eliminates the bus contention problem caused by a peripheral I/O device with slow output buffers.

An 80C188EB packaged in an 80-pin Quad Flat Package does not have a DT/R pin. However, the latched status signal /S1 provides similar information and can be used in place of DT/R.

The AD7–AD0 bus connection between the 80C188EB and the transceiver in Fig. 10.5-1 is referred to as the **local bus**. The bus connections between the transceiver and the memory and I/O subsystems are called the **buffered bus**. A fully buffered system has no memory or I/O devices directly connected to its local bus. If a system has memory or I/O devices connected to both its local bus and buffered bus, the system is called **partially buffered**. In a partially buffered system, the /DEN signal to the transceiver's /OE input must be qualified by another signal to prevent the transceiver from being enabled during a read of a device on the local bus. If this is not done, bus contention occurs between the device on the local bus and the transceiver when the local device is read.

A fully buffered 80C188EB CPU subsystem generates system bus signals that have timing waveforms like those of Figs. 10.1-2 and 10.1-3. That is, the address bits, A19–A0, are stable for almost the entire bus cycle. And the data bus, D7–D0, carries data only. When D7–D0 is not carrying data, it is in its high-impedance state.

Loading calculations, which consider the current required by all ICs interfaced to the system bus and the capacitive load presented by these ICs, must be carried out in order to determine whether buffering is needed.

10.6 Logic Family Compatibility, Loading, and Buffering

It is advantageous to implement an entire system using only a single logic family. However, some required IC functions may not be available in the preferred family. This situation leads to the need to mix logic families in a system. You must analyze both the logic voltage level and current drive requirements of the families being mixed to determine if the logic families are compatible.

The buffering required in a CPU subsystem depends on the load presented by other subsystems connected to the system bus. An address, data, or control line needs to be buffered if either its current or capacitive load is too large. Also, in the case of data lines, if a memory or I/O device cannot float its data outputs quickly enough to prevent bus contention, then buffering is required for isolation. This section outlines how to evaluate logic level compatibility and loading to determine when buffering is required.

10.6.1 Voltage Level Compatibility

Logic 0 and logic 1 voltage range definitions are illustrated in Fig. 10.6-1. Two sets of voltage ranges are defined, one for outputs (Fig. 10.6-1(a)) and another for inputs (Fig 10.6-1(b)).

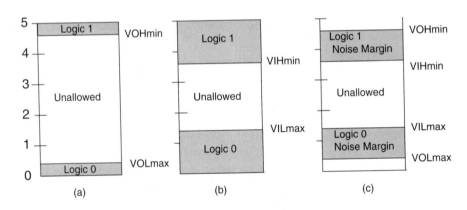

Figure 10.6-1   Logic level voltage ranges for a generic logic family: (a) output voltage levels; (b) input voltage levels; (c) DC noise margins.

The minimum high input voltage, V_{IHmin}, is the lowest voltage at an input pin that an IC is guaranteed to interpret as a logic 1. The minimum high output voltage, V_{OHmin}, produced by an output pin, must exceed V_{IHmin} for each of the inputs that it drives. The difference between these two voltages, $V_{OHmin} - V_{IHmin}$, is the logic 1 **noise margin** (Fig. 10.6-1(c)). This voltage margin provides some immunity to electrical noise.

For the logic 0 case, V_{ILmax} is the highest voltage at an input pin that an IC is guaranteed to interpret as a logic 0. The maximum voltage produced by an output pin for a logic

0 is guaranteed to be no more than V_{OLmax}. The difference, $V_{ILmax} - V_{OLmax}$, is the logic 0 noise margin.

When an output from a particular logic family drives only inputs from the same family, appropriate noise margins are maintained as long as the output's current driving specifications are not exceeded. If an output is connected to or drives too many inputs, its current specifications will be exceeded. When this is the case, either buffering is required or a device with greater current drive must be used.

Output and input voltage levels for an 80C188EB and for the 74HC, 74HCT, 74AC, 74ACT, 74LS, and 74ALS logic families are listed in Table 10.6-1.

Table 10.6-1 Representative values of primary voltage and current interfacing parameters.[a]

Parameter	80C188EB	74HC	74HCT	74AC	74ACT	74LS	74ALS
V_{OHmin}	$V_{CC} - 0.5V$	4.4 V[b] / 3.84 V	4.4 / 3.84 V	4.9 V / 3.76 V	4.9 V / 3,76	2.7 V	2.7 V
V_{IHmin}	$0.7 * V_{CC}$	$0.7 * V_{CC}$	2.0 V	$0.7 * V_{CC}$	2.0 V	2.0 V	2.0 V
V_{OLmax}	0.45 V	0.1 V / 0.33 V	0.1 V / 0.33 V	0.1 V / 0.37 V	0.1 V / 0.37 V	0.4 V	0.5 V
V_{ILmax}	$0.3 * V_{CC}$	$0.3 * V_{CC}$	0.8 V	$0.3 * V_{CC}$	0.8 V	0.8 V	0.8 V
I_{OHmax}	−2 mA	−0.02 mA / −4.0/6.0[c] mA	−0.02 mA / −4.0/6.0 mA	−0.05 mA / −24.0 mA	−0.05 mA / −24.0 mA	−0.4 mA	−0.4 mA
I_{IHmax}	+15 µA	+1 µA	+1 µA	+1 µA	+1 µA	20 µA	+20 µA
I_{OLmax}	+3 mA	+0.02 mA / +4.0/6.0 mA	+0.02 mA / +4.0/6.0 mA	+0.05 mA / +24.0 mA	+0.05 mA / +24.0 mA	+8.0 mA	+8.0 mA
I_{ILmax}	−15 µA	−1 µA	−1 µA	−1 µA	−1 µA	−0.4 mA	−0.2 mA
I_{OZH}[d]	+15 µA	+5 µA	+5 µA	+5 µA	+5 µA	+20 µA	+ 20 µA
I_{OZL}	−15 µA	−5 µA	−5 µA	−5 µA	−5 µA	−200 µA	−20 µA

a. All ratings are for device operation at 5.0 V supply ±10% and 25 degrees C. A specific component in any family may vary from this table's values. The manufacturer's data sheet should be consulted.
b. Upper value is for a CMOS load, lower value is for a TTL load
c. First value is for a standard output, second value is for a high-current output.
d. Ratings for three-state outputs in their high-impedance state.

The HC in **74HC** stands for High-speed CMOS. This CMOS logic family contains most of the logic functions available in earlier 74 series TTL families. 74HC logic operates at speeds comparable to 74LSTTL. 74HC logic is designed to be used with a supply voltage from 2.0 V to 6.0 V. The supply voltage for CMOS logic ICs is often designated by the symbol V_{DD} instead of V_{CC}. The more recent **74AC** logic family is a faster version of the 74HC family. 74AC logic has speeds comparable to 74ALS TTL and can source and sink more current than most TTL circuits.

The T in **74HCT** indicates that this CMOS logic family is TTL compatible. In order to provide this compatibility, 74HCT devices recognize TTL input voltage thresholds. 74HCT devices provide TTL logic level compatibility by using TTL-to-CMOS level translation input buffer stages. The output characteristics of 74HC and 74HCT are the same. 74HCT logic is designed to be operated at a supply voltage of 5.0 V. The **74ACT** family is a faster version of the 74HCT family.

    74ALS (Advanced Low-power Schottky) is a TTL family that requires less power and operates at higher speed than its TTL predecessors.

    When operated at 5.0 V, 74HC family logic is directly voltage level compatible with the 80C188EB, as can be seen from Table 10.6-1. To check voltage level compatibility, V_{OHmin} and V_{OLmax} of the driving logic must be compared, respectively, with V_{IHmin} and V_{ILmax} of the logic being driven. This comparison is to determine whether the voltage levels are compatible and if the noise margins are acceptable.

    Consider an 80C188EB driving a 74HC input, with both devices having a 5.0 V supply voltage. The 80C188EB's V_{OHmin} of 4.5 V and the 74HC's V_{IHmin} of 3.5 V provide a 1.0 V logic 1 noise margin. The 80C188EB's V_{OLmax} of 0.45 V and the 74HC's V_{ILmax} of 1.5 V provide a 1.05 V logic 0 noise margin. If the supply voltage is specified as 5.0 V ±10%, then the noise margins are reduced as the supply voltage approaches the low end of this range.

    For 74HC outputs driving 80C188EB inputs with $V_{CC} = 5.0$ V, a logic 1 noise margin of 0.9 V (4.4 V − 3.5 V) is provided. The table shows two values for 74HC outputs. The top entry is for a 74HC device driving CMOS inputs. The bottom value is for 74HC driving TTL inputs. For logic 0, the noise margin provided is 1.4 V (1.5 V − 0.1 V).

10.6.2   Current Drive Compatibility

In addition to input voltage level requirements, the input current requirements of a device must also be met. A logic device's inputs have a separate current requirement specification for each logic level. When an input is driven to logic 1, it may draw current as high as I_{IHmax} from the device driving it (Fig. 10.6-2(a)). When an input is driven to logic 0, it may provide current as high as I_{ILmax} to the device that drives it (Fig. 10.6-2(b)).

    When the driving device is generating a logic 1 output, it must be able to **source**, or provide, the total current required by all the inputs it drives, without its output voltage dropping below V_{OHmin} (Fig. 10.6-2(a)). The maximum current an output is guaranteed to be able to provide without its output voltage dropping below V_{OHmin} is denoted as I_{OHmax}. The maximum current an input will require at logic 1 is I_{IHmax}.

    When the driving device is generating a logic 0, it must be able to **sink**, or accept, the total input current from all the inputs it drives, without its output voltage rising above V_{OLmax}. The maximum current an output is guaranteed to be able to sink, without its output voltage rising above V_{OLmax}, is denoted as I_{OLmax}. The maximum current from an input at logic 0 is specified as I_{ILmax}.

    The input current requirements and output current drive capability for an 80C188EB and for the 74HC, 74HCT, 74AC, 74ACT, 74LS, and 74ALS logic families are included in Table 10.6-1. For the output currents, the upper current value is for a CMOS load and the lower value is for a TTL load. Values for CMOS driving TTL loads are specified for both CMOS standard outputs and high-current outputs (*standard/high-current*). High-current outputs are typical for buffer outputs.

    The sign associated with a current's value specifies the current's direction. The reference direction for currents is taken as *into* the pin. Therefore, a positive sign indicates that

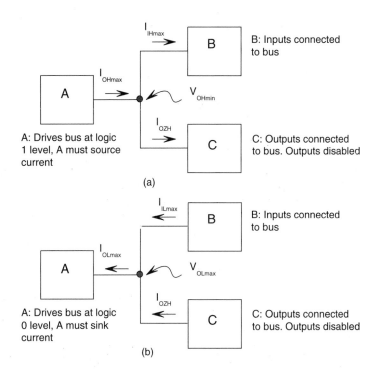

Figure 10.6-2   Input current requirements and output current drive capability: (a) logic
1 case; (b) logic 0 case. Current arrows correspond to actual (not reference) current directions.

the current is into the output. A negative sign indicates that the current is out of the output.

The number of inputs that an output can drive and still maintain its specified output voltage levels is called its **fanout**. Fanout is usually specified in terms of an output driving inputs from the same logic family. To determine fanout, the drive capability of an output must be compared with the current load from the inputs it drives for both the logic 1 and logic 0 states.

For example, for a 74HC output driving 74HC inputs to the logic 1 state, I_{OHmax} is -20 μA and I_{IHmax} is 1 μA. Therefore, a 74HC output can drive 20 74HC inputs. In the logic 0 state, I_{OLmax} for 74HC is 20 μA and I_{ILmax} is -1 μA. Therefore, one 74HC output can drive 20 inputs in the logic 0 state. The limits are the same for each case. Consequently, 20 74HC inputs can be driven by a single 74HC output. In other words, 74HC has a fanout of 20 (when driving 74HC).

The number of inputs an output can drive in each state is not the same for all logic families. For example, for an ALS output driving ALS inputs to the logic 1 state, I_{OHmax} is -400 μA and I_{IHmax} is 20 μA. Therefore, an ALS output can drive 20 ALS inputs. In the logic 0 state, I_{OLmax} for ALS is 8.0 mA and I_{ILmax} is -0.2 mA. Therefore, one ALS output can drive 40 ALS inputs to the logic 0 state. The limiting case is the logic 1 state. Consequently,

20 ALS inputs can be driven by a single ALS output. In other words, ALS has a fanout of 20 (when driving ALS).

A device that is driving the bus must meet the current requirements of all devices connected to the bus, not just the inputs. This includes the current requirements for other *outputs* connected to the bus! An output connected to a bus that is being driven by another device must be in its high-impedance state. An output in its high-impedance state can draw current when connected to a bus line that is at a logic 1 voltage level and can supply current when at a logic 0 voltage level! While the magnitudes of these currents are low, they still must be considered. These currents are specified as the off-state output current with a high voltage level applied, I_{OZH}, and the off-state output current with a low voltage level applied, I_{OZL} (Fig. 10.6-2). Worst-case values are given in Table 10.6-1.

If a device that drives the bus cannot meet the total current requirements of the devices to which it is connected, then its output must be buffered. The loading of the address, data, and control lines by subsystems connected to the bus must be calculated for both the logic 0 and logic 1 conditions to determine if the drive capability is exceeded.

10.6.3   Capacitive Loading

In addition to current loading, capacitive loading must also be considered. The timing specifications of an 80C188EB are guaranteed only if each 80C188EB pin's 50-pF maximum capacitive loading specification is not exceeded. If the load capacitance exceeds this value, the rise and fall times for signal transitions increase. As a consequence, timing specifications must be derated for loads of more than 50 pF per pin. Alternatively, and preferably, a buffer is used so that the 80C188EB's pin sees only the buffer's input capacitance.

The capacitive load for an 80C188EB pin includes the capacitances of all other pins (input and output) connected to the pin. Interconnect capacitance and parasitic capacitance must also be included in the capacitive load figure. Use of buffers significantly reduces the capacitance seen by the 80C188EB.

While this section focuses on the possible need for buffering in the CPU subsystem, similar computations must be done for each of the other subsystems as well. For example, during a bus cycle where the 80C188EB reads a memory location, it is the memory subsystem that drives the bus. Therefore, the memory subsystem must have adequate drive capability for the loading presented to it by the CPU subsystem as well as all the other subsystems connected to the bus.

Given all of the previous considerations, it may seem that it would always be preferable to design a fully-buffered CPU subsystem. After all, this results in the most conservative design, and maybe you wouldn't have to do all those loading calculations! In some situations, as when a system is being prototyped primarily to determine its feasibility, or the subsystems to be connected to the system's bus have not been completely determined, or when only a few systems are being built, this may be the case. However, in designs where production quantities are expected to be large, minimizing component cost, power dissipation, and printed circuit board area, and maximizing reliability are all important design criteria. Minimizing the number of ICs in a system helps you meet these criteria.

10.6.4   TTL to CMOS Compatibility

A comparison of output and input logic levels, similar to those done in Section 10.6.1, shows that a TTL device cannot directly drive a device that uses typical CMOS input levels. For example, a 74ALS TTL output cannot directly drive an 80C188EB input, because V_{OHmin} for 74ALS is 2.7 V and V_{IHmin} for the 80C188EB is 3.5 V.

Two approaches are commonly used to resolve this incompatibility to allow a TTL output to drive a CMOS input. One approach adds a pull-up resistor from the TTL output to V_{CC}. The pull-up resistor to V_{CC} pulls the TTL output voltage up to the V_{IHmin} value required by CMOS inputs.

To determine the pull-up resistor's value, upper and lower resistance limits are computed. A resistor value between these two limits is selected. The lower limit is determined by the current sinking capability of the TTL device. The TTL output must sink the current through the pull-up resistor plus the currents from the inputs, I_{IL} (Fig. 10.6-3(a)).

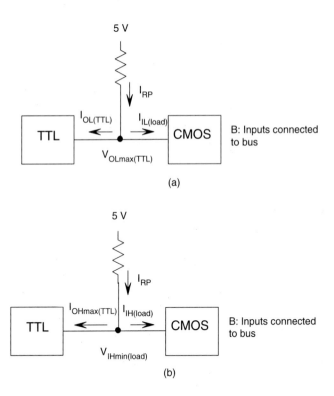

Figure 10.6-3   Circuits to compute the maximum and minimum limits for pull-up resistor based on current levels for a TTL output driving a CMOS input: (a) logic 0 case, TTL output sinks current from pull-up resistor and CMOS inputs; (b) logic 1 case, TTL output and pull-up resistor supply current to CMOS inputs. Current directions correspond to reference directions used to define logic family output and input currents.

The minimum value is given by the equation:

$$Rpmin = \frac{V_{CC} - V_{OLmin}(TTL)}{I_{OL}(TTL) + n \times I_{IL}(load)}$$

where n is the number of loads being driven. Note that the sign for the value of I_{IL} is negative. So, an increase in the number of inputs driven raises the minimum value for the pull-up resistor. However, since $I_{IL}(load)$ for CMOS is approximately 1 µA, its effect is negligible.

The upper limit is determined by two constraints: the total high-level input current that must be supplied to the loads and the rise time of the input signal. The equation for the maximum value of the pull-up resistor, based on the input load current constraint (Fig. 10.6-3(b)) is:

$$Rpmax = \frac{V_{CC} - V_{IHmin}(load)}{\left| n \times I_{IH}(load) - I_{OH}(driver) \right|}$$

For an **open collector TTL output,** $I_{OH}(driver)$ is zero. Therefore, all the current to the CMOS inputs must be supplied through the pull-up resistor. Since $I_{IH}(load)$ is approximately 1 µA for each CMOS input, $R_p max$ is a very high value.

This situation is also true for a **totem-pole output.** When the TTL output goes high, the pull-up resistor causes the top transistor of the TTL totem-pole output stage to be cut off, along with the bottom transistor. Therefore, I_{OH} is 0, and all the current to the CMOS input is supplied through the pull-up resistor.

The rise-time requirement, t, for the 74HC logic family is 500 ns. Generally, the rise time, rather than load current, is the limiting constraint for the maximum value of the pull-up resistor.

Consider an open collector TTL output. Since the current to the inputs is all being supplied by the pull-up resistor, a logic 0 to logic 1 transition will be exponential. The exponential rise time is governed by the time constant $R_p C_T$. The input voltage as a function of time is:

$$V_{IHmin} = V_{CC}(1 - e^{-t/R_p C_T})$$

where C_T is the total load capacitance. The time constant cannot exceed the rise-time requirement for the CMOS devices. Solving the above equation for Rp gives:

$$R_{pmax} = \frac{-t}{C_T \times \ln\left(1 - \frac{V_{IHmin}}{V_{CC}}\right)}$$

$$R_{pmax} = \frac{t}{1.2 C_T}$$

For a totem-pole TTL output, the output rises to 2.7 V (V_{OHmin}) in less than 10 ns (the rise time for a totem-pole TTL output). The output must then be pulled up to 3.5 V by the pull-up resistor. The time for this exponential rise is:

$$R_{pmax} = \frac{-t}{C_T \times \ln\left(1 - \dfrac{V_{IHminCMOS} - V_{OHminTTL}}{V_{CC} - V_{OHminTTL}}\right)}$$

$$R_{pmax} = \frac{t}{0.43\,C_T}$$

The value of t for this case is the 500 ns allowed for CMOS inputs minus the 10 ns it takes for the TTL output to reach 2.7 V.

The other approach to achieving compatibility is to use TTL-compatible CMOS logic families, such as 74HCT. The input logic levels of 74HCT are directly compatible with TTL output levels. Many CMOS peripheral ICs, such as ADCs and DACs, are designed so their inputs are TTL compatible.

One of CMOS logic's primary advantages is its low power dissipation. However, when a 74HCT input is driven by a TTL logic level, the CMOS device dissipates more power than if it were driven by a CMOS level. This is because the lower V_{OHmin} of the TTL signal does not completely turn OFF the "OFF" transistor in the CMOS output buffer. This results in a lower resistance path from V_{CC} to ground through the CMOS IC's output buffer transistors. This increases the power consumed by several orders of magnitude. For this same reason, unused CMOS inputs should be connected to either V_{CC} or ground.

10.7   A Minimum Component Complete System

To create a complete system, a CPU subsystem must be connected via the system bus to additional ICs that comprise the memory and I/O subsystems. The fully buffered CPU subsystem of Fig. 10.5-1 is appropriate for implementing systems of substantial complexity. In contrast, Fig. 10.7-1 shows a complete, though modest, 80C188EB system constructed from only two ICs.

One IC is the 80C188EB. The other IC is a **PSD311 Programmable Microperipheral with Memory**, from WaferScale Integration, Inc., WSI. The PSD311 contains $32K \times 8$ of EPROM and a $2K \times 8$ SRAM. The PSD311's architecture is shown in Fig. 10.7-2. Latches inside the PSD311 demultiplex AD7–AD0, providing remote demultiplexing. An internal programmable address decoder (PAD) allows you to map the PSD311's $32K \times 8$ of EPROM, in eight separate $4K \times 8$ blocks, to the locations in the memory address space you desire. As configured in Fig. 10.7-1, the PSD311 provides two eight bit I/O ports, pins PA7–PA0 and PB7–PB0. Each port bit is individually programmable as either an input or output. This system is particularly appropriate for small applications.

Figure 10.7-1 clearly illustrates the substantial differences that can exist between the conceptual organization of a system (Fig. 1.1-1) and the physical implementation of a particular system. Physically, the 80C188EB provides both CPU and I/O functions and the PSD311 provides both memory and I/O functions.

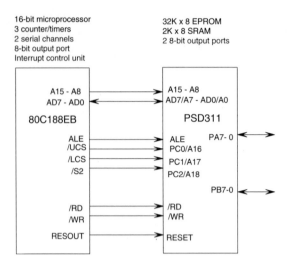

Figure 10.7-1   A minimum component two-chip 80C188EB system using a PSD311 integrated memory and peripheral IC.

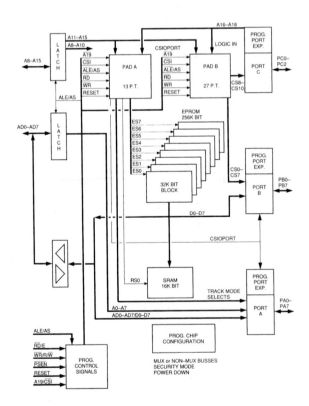

Figure 10.7-2   PSD311 family architecture block diagram. (Courtesy of WaferScale Integration Inc.)

The PSD311 is configurable for compatibility with a wide range of microprocessors and microcontrollers. A menu driven program from WaferScale, called MAPLE, makes it easy to produce the desired configuration data. The configuration data is programmed into the PSD311 along with the program's code.

Other devices in the PSD3xx product series provide as much as 128K × 8 of EPROM. WSI also provides a PSD4xx and PSD5xx product series. PSD4xx devices include, in addition to EPROM and SRAM, 40 programmable I/O pins and a general purpose high-density programmable logic device. PSD5xx devices include four 16-bit counter/timers and an eight-level priority interrupt controller, along with the EPROM and SRAM.

10.8   Single and Multi-Board Systems

There are several possible system configurations related to the partitioning of a system's ICs for placement onto printed circuit boards:

1. Custom single board system
2. Commercial off-the-shelf single board microcomputer
3. Custom multi-board system
4. Multi-board standard bus system

An application based on the two component system of Fig. 10.7-1 can easily place these components, as well as any other peripheral I/O device ICs, on a single, custom printed circuit board.

When an application is well defined and its level of complexity is limited, a custom single board approach can result in an optimal system. This approach is optimal if you design the printed circuit board to have only the hardware required for the application. This approach is particularly appropriate for systems that will be manufactured in large quantities. Its drawback is that there is no external access to the system bus, which precludes subsequent system expansion.

When the quantity of systems to be produced is not large, use of an existing off-the-shelf single board microcomputer may be appropriate. These single board microcomputers provide a microprocessor, memory, and I/O ports on a single printed circuit board. There are a large number of 80C188EB single board microcomputers available from a variety of manufacturers. Generally, any off-the-shelf single board microcomputer selected will be less than optimal, in the sense that it has some features or hardware that are not required for your application. However, using a single board computer has the advantage that the hardware is already available and pretested. You do not have to wait for printed circuit boards to be manufactured, nor carry out extensive board testing, as with a custom single board system.

Some single board systems allow for limited expansion in the form of **daughterboards**. Daughterboards are smaller boards that plug into a connector on the single board microcomputer (the motherboard). The connector and its signals are well defined and many manufacturers may make daughter boards that are compatible with a specific interconnection scheme. This means, for example, that several possible sources of ADC daughterboard subsystems are available from which to choose.

Custom multi-board systems can be created to handle applications where the complexity or flexibility required warrants this approach. Various subsystems are placed on separate printed circuit boards. These boards plug into a **backplane** printed circuit board that contains connectors for the subsystem boards. The system bus is carried in parallel to all the connectors by printed circuit traces on the backplane. Each subsystem board must include the bus interface logic required to allow it to properly connect to the backplane system bus.

For custom single and multi-board systems, the system bus is either the same as, or is an extension of, a specific microprocessor's bus. For multi-board **standard bus systems,** the system bus is typically defined to be independent of a particular microprocessor. Such bus standards allow some choice as to the CPU subsystem board and its microprocessor.

Bus standards define each signal's function and timing. Signals in a standard bus include address, data, control, power, and, for buses that allow multiple bus masters, bus arbitration signals. A bus standard also specifies the physical characteristics of the boards and connectors. Bus standards allow boards from various manufacturers that conform to the standard to be plugged into the system bus and operated successfully.

Most bus standards start out as a bus standard for a single manufacturer or a consortium of manufacturers. If the bus standard gains sufficient popularity, it may be proposed as a formal standard. In North America, the standards-making organization for backplane buses is the Institute of Electrical and Electronics Engineers (IEEE). Table 10.8-1 lists several industry bus standards.

Table 10.8-1   Some standard buses.

Characteristic	STD bus	Multibus	VME bus	IBM PC/AT	PC/104
IEEE Standard	P961	796	1014	P996	P996.1
Data bus	8	16	16 32 w P2	8 PC 16 AT	8 16 w P2
Address bus					
Bus control	semisync	async	async	semisync	semisync
Interrupt level	1	8	7	6	6
Multimaster arbitration	some versions	serial or parallel	4 levels w serial arb.	no, DMA only	no, DMA only
Connector type	card edge	card edge	pin and socket	card edge	pin and socket
Connector size	56 contact	86 and 60	96 pin P1 96 pin P2	62 PC plus 36 AT	64 P1 plus 40 P2
Board size	4.5 × 6.5	6.75 × 12	100 × 160 mm 233.4 × 270	4.2 × 13.2 PC 4.8 × 13.2 AT	3.55 × 3.78
Bus voltages	+5, −5 +12, −12	+5, −5 +12, −12	+5 +12, −12	+5, −5 +12, −12	+5, −5 +12, −12

By using a popular standard bus, it is often possible to create a complex system by selecting off-the-shelf boards appropriate for each specific application. In such situations, no other hardware design is required. In other situations, one or more custom boards designed to conform to the chosen bus standard are combined with off-the-shelf boards to create the system.

10.8.1   The PC/104 Bus

A bus standard that is particularly well-suited for uniprocessor systems with limited space is the **PC/104 bus**. This standard started out as a daughter board bus for Ampro's Little Board single board computer family. In 1992, a consortium of companies (the **PC/104 Consortium**) published a formal specification for this bus. PC/104 later evolved into an IEEE draft standard called the "P996.1 Standard for Compact Embedded-PC Modules."

PC/104 bus signals are functionally identical to those of the PC/AT bus (Table 10.8-2). The S prefix on address and data signals stands for "system." With this in mind, you can easily identify the address and data bus signals. The PC/104 bus provides hardware and software functional compatibility with the PC/AT architecture. For an 80C188EB or other 8-bit system, connector J2 is not used. The PC/104 bus standard's primary differences from the PC/AT bus standard are:

1. Small form factor
2. Stackthrough pin-and-socket bus connectors
3. Reduced bus drive capability

The motivation for the PC/104 bus was to provide PC/AT functionality in a small form factor. The 3.6 inch by 3.8 inch cards use 64-pin and 40-pin self stacking male/female headers. Eight bit data bus cards have only the 64-pin header. Sixteen-bit data bus cards add the 40-pin connector next to the 64-pin connector. Stacked cards are spaced 0.6 inches apart and held together by their stackthrough connectors and metal or plastic standoffs. PC/104 modules can be used in the form of a stand-alone module stack, or plugged into a custom carrier board, or used as daughter boards (expansion boards) on a motherboard.

The PC/104 standard's reduced bus drive specification of 6 mA per line lowers power consumption and allows the bus to be directly driven by HCT family logic devices. This reduces the cost and complexity of the boards by eliminating the need for bus driver ICs.

PC/104 microcomputer modules use microprocessors ranging from the 80C188EB to the 80486. A typical 80C188EB module contains the microprocessor, $128K \times 8$ RAM, $128K \times 8$ Flash memory, 24 TTL-compatible I/O lines, two RS232 serial channels, and a watchdog timer. More than 140 manufacturers make modules for the PC/104 bus. These modules include LCD and keypad interfaces, VGA drivers, floppy disk and IDE controllers, analog/digital converters, Ethernet adapters, and so on.

A further advantage of the PC/104 approach is that the relatively low cost development tools and software available for the PC can be used.

Table 10.8-2   PC/104 bus signal assignments.

Pin	J1/P1 Row A	J1/P1 Row B	J2/P2 Row C[a]	J2/P2 Row D
0	–	–	0V	0V
1	IOCHCK*	0V	SBHE*	MEMCS16*
2	SD7[b]	RESETDRV	LA23[c]	IOCS16*
3	SD6	+5v	LA22	IRQ10
4	SD5	IRQ9	LA21	IRQ11
5	SD4	–5V	LA20	IRQ12
6	SD3	DRQ2	LA19	IRQ15
7	SD2	–12V	LA18	IRQ14
8	SD1	ENDXFR*	LA17	DACK0*
9	SD0	+12V	MEMR*	DRQ0
10	IOCHRDY	(KEY)	MEMW*	DACK5*
11	AEN	SMEMW*	SD8[d]	DRQ5
12	SA19[e]	SMEMR*	SD9	DACK6*
13	SA18	IOW*	SD10	DRQ6
14	SA17	IOR*	SD11	DACK7*
15	SA16	DACK3*	SD12	DRQ7
16	SA15	DRQ3	SD13	+5V
17	SA14	DACK1*	SD14	MASTER*
18	SA13	DRQ1	SD15	0V
19	SA12	REFRESH*	(KEY)	0V
20	SA11	SYSCLK		
21	SA10	IRQ7		
22	SA9	IRQ6		
23	SA8	IRQ5		
24	SA7	IRQ4		
25	SA6	IRQ3		
26	SA5	DACK2*		
27	SA4	TC		
28	SA3	BALE[f]		
29	SA2	+5V		
30	SA1	OSC		
31	SA0	0V		
32	0V	0V		

a. Rows C and D are not required on 8-bit modules.
b. SD7–SD0 8-bit data bus D7–D0.
c. Address bits A23–A17, not latched.
d. SD15–SD8 high byte (D15–D8) of 16 bit data bus.
e. SA19–SA0 latched address bits A19–A0.
f. Buffered ALE.

10.9   Peripheral Control Block (PCB)

While, conceptually, a CPU subsystem does not contain any I/O, the fact that the 80C188EB has integrated peripherals means that any 80C188EB CPU subsystem also provides I/O (Figs. 10.1-1 and 10.2-1). The details of the integrated peripherals are covered in later chapters on memory and I/O subsystems. That part of the 80C188EB's register structure that allows its modular core CPU to communicate with its integrated peripherals is presented here. A complete register view of an 80C188EB must include these registers, as well as the modular core CPU registers introduced in Chapter 3.

To use any one of the 80C188EB's integrated peripherals requires that you first configure the peripheral for the mode of operation you desire. This is accomplished by your program writing to one or more of the peripheral's control registers. Most of the integrated peripherals also have status registers to monitor the peripheral's operation and data registers to store its data.

Control, status, and data registers for each integrated peripheral are physically located with the respective peripheral unit on the 80C188EB chip. However, the registers for all of the integrated peripherals are addressed as members of a single block of 128 contiguous word registers. This register block is called the **Peripheral Control Block** (**PCB**). Table 10.9-1 lists each PCB register's mnemonic and its offset from the PCB base address. All PCB registers are word registers that start at even addresses. Unassigned locations in the PCB must be treated as reserved and not written or read.

When an 80C188EB is reset, the default **PCB base address** is FF00H in the I/O space. Thus, initially, the PCB occupies the last 256 bytes of I/O space, FF00H to FFFFH. As a result, immediately after reset, the offsets in Table 10.9-1 are offsets from FF00H. For example, immediately after reset, the EOI register, which has an offset of 02H, is located at address FF02H in the I/O space.

In your program, you can equate the PCB register mnemonics to the sum of the PCB base address and the register's offset:

```
PCB_BASE        equ      0ff00h

EOI             equ      PCB_BASE + 02h
```

This technique allows the PCB registers to be referenced symbolically. It also makes it convenient to change the value of the base address, if the PCB is moved. Refer to section 10.9.1 for more information on moving (relocating) the PCB.

All transfers between the integrated peripherals and the 80C188EB's modular core are internal transfers that take place over a special 16-bit internal bus called the **F-Bus** (Fig. 10.2-1). However, for each access to a location in the PCB's address range, the 80C188EB still runs external bus cycles, even though there is no external data transfer. Any data on the external data bus during these bus cycles is ignored.

Writing a PCB register requires special consideration. Regardless of how they are coded, all transfers on the 80C188EB's internal F-Bus are 16-bit transfers. If DX points to a location in the PCB, execution of the instruction out dx,al causes the contents of AX (not AL) to be written to the PCB register. However, only one external bus cycle occurs because the instruction is a byte transfer instruction. If the instruction out dx,ax were used for the same purpose, the transfer would again take one internal bus cycle. But, because the

Table 10.9-1   80C188EB Peripheral Control Block, PCB, register mnemonics and offsets.

Offset	Register	Offset	Register	Offset	Register	Offset	Register
00H	Reserved	40H	T2CNT	80H	GCS0ST	C0H	Reserved
02H	EOI	42H	T2CMPA	82H	GCS0SP	C2H	Reserved
04H	POLL	44H	Reserved	84H	GCS1ST	C4H	Reserved
06H	POLLSTS	46H	T2CON	86H	GCS1SP	C6H	Reserved
08H	IMASK	48H	Reserved	88H	GCS2ST	C8H	Reserved
0AH	PRIMSK	4AH	Reserved	8AH	GCS2SP	CAH	Reserved
0CH	INSERV	4CH	Reserved	8CH	GCS3ST	CCH	Reserved
0EH	REQST	4EH	Reserved	8EH	GCS3SP	CEH	Reserved
10H	INTSTS	50H	P1DIR	90H	GCS4ST	D0H	Reserved
12H	TCUCON	52H	P1PIN	92H	GCS4SP	D2H	Reserved
14H	SCUCON	54H	P1CON	94H	GCS5ST	D4H	Reserved
16H	I4CON	56H	P1LTCH	96H	GCS5SP	D6H	Reserved
18H	I0CON	58H	P2DIR	98H	GCS6ST	D8H	Reserved
1AH	I1CON	5AH	P2PIN	9AH	GCS6SP	DAH	Reserved
1CH	I2CON	5CH	P2CON	9CH	GCS7ST	DCH	Reserved
1EH	I3CON	5EH	P2LTCH	9EH	GCS7SP	DEH	Reserved
20H	Reserved	60H	B0CMP	A0H	LCSST	E0H	Reserved
22H	Reserved	62H	B0CNT	A2H	LCSSP	E2H	Reserved
24H	Reserved	64H	S0CON	A4H	UCSST	E4H	Reserved
26H	Reserved	66H	S0STS	A6H	UCSSP	E6H	Reserved
28H	Reserved	68H	R0BUF	A8H	RELREG	E8H	Reserved
2AH	Reserved	6AH	T0BUF	AAH	Reserved	EAH	Reserved
2CH	Reserved	6CH	Reserved	ACH	Reserved	ECH	Reserved
2EH	Reserved	6EH	Reserved	AEH	Reserved	EEH	Reserved
30H	T0CNT	70H	B1CMP	B0H	RFBASE	F0H	Reserved
32H	T0CMPA	72H	B1CNT	B2H	RFTIME	F2H	Reserved
34H	T0CMPB	74H	S1CON	B4H	RFCON	F4H	Reserved
36H	T0CON	76H	S1STS	B6H	RFADDR	F6H	Reserved
38H	T1CNT	78H	R1BUF	B8H	PWRCON	F8H	Reserved
3AH	T1CMPA	7AH	T1BUF	BAH	Reserved	FAH	Reserved
3CH	T1CMPB	7CH	Reserved	BCH	STEPID	FCH	Reserved
3EH	T1CON	7EH	Reserved	BEH	Reserved	FEH	Reserved

instruction is a word transfer instruction, the 80C188EB would run two external bus cycles. Thus, the first coding approach saves the time of the additional bus cycle.

For example, either of the instruction sequences that follow writes the value in AX to the End-of-Interrupt register (EOI) in the PCB. The function of the EOI register is not important at this point.

```
mov     dx,EOI          ;DX <- address of EOI register
mov     ax,8000h        ;AX <- value to be written to 16 bit EOI
out     dx,al           ;write contents of AX, not AL, to EOI!
```

or

```
mov     dx,EOI          ;DX <- address of EOI register
mov     ax,8000h        ;AX <- value to be written to 16 bit EOI
out     dx,ax           ;write contents of AX to EOI
```

The first approach, which uses out dx,al is recommended for faster execution using an 80C188EB. However, its meaning may at first be less clear when reading the program. Examples in this text often use the slower, but clearer, approach. There is one case, discussed in the next subsection, where out dx,al must always be used.

Reads from registers in the PCB work similarly to external reads. If in al,dx is executed, while DX points to a PCB register, the low byte of the PCB register is placed in AL. To read an entire 16-bit PCB register, always requires a word read instruction, in ax,dx.

The functions of specific registers in the PCB are discussed throughout the remainder of the text. Determination of the bit pattern needed to program a specific PCB register can be made from the figures that define the function of the bits in each register, as is shown in the following subsection for the PCB's RELREG.

Another approach to determining the required bit patterns for programming PCB registers is to use an interactive application programming tool from Intel called **ApBUILDER**. This tool provides a software aid for determining the bit patterns. This program can also generate code in either ASM86 or C to implement the configuration decisions that you make interactively. The code generated can be cut and pasted into your program.

Figure 10.9-1 shows a window from ApBUILDER's Register Editor with bit values for programming the EOI register. The ASM86 code generated to implement the configuration decisions for the EOI register can be seen in the bottom right corner.

10.9.1   Relocating the PCB

The PCB is usually left at its default position. However, the entire PCB can be moved (relocated) so it starts at any 256 byte boundary in I/O space, or even in the memory address space. The need to move the PCB may arise in systems where the 80C188EB is being used to replace an earlier microprocessor, such as an 8088, and the previous design had external devices within the default I/O address range of the PCB. Examples in this text assume that the PCB is left in its default location, FF00H–FFFFH in the I/O space.

The relocation register (**RELREG**) is used to reposition the PCB (Fig. 10.9-2). RELREG has an offset of 00A8H from the PCB base address, giving it an address of FFA8H

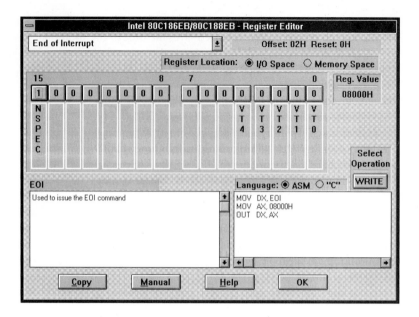

Figure 10.9-1   ApBUILDER Register Editor with the EOI register selected.

after reset. To relocate the PCB to any 256 byte boundary in either the I/O or the memory address space, RELREG is written to specify the new address space and base address.

If the PCB is to be moved to a new location in I/O space, eight of RELREG's bits, R15–R8, are used to specify bits A15–A8 of the new PCB base address. The lower 8 bits of the PCB base address are automatically zero. The MEM bit in RELREG specifies whether the PCB is to be moved to the memory or I/O space.

For example, the following sequence changes the PCB base address to 0C000H in the I/O space. Since the RELREG value specifies only bits A15–A8, and A7–A0 are always zero, loading RELREG with 00C0H changes the PCB base address to C000H. Of course, when the PCB is relocated, the relocation register also moves. RELREG will have an offset of 00A8H from whatever new PCB base address is specified.

```
mov     dx,RELREG        ;load the current RELREG address
mov     ax,00c0h         ;new RELREG value required
out     dx,al
```

If the PCB is to be moved to a location in the memory space, twelve bits of RELREG, R19–R8, are used to specify A19–A8 of the new PCB base address.

For the 80C188EB, a word write to RELREG creates a potential problem. Since RELREG is written internally by the first bus cycle, this cycle causes the PCB to be relocated. The second external bus cycle then attempts to write an address that is no longer in the PCB. This can create a problem if the system is designed as a "normally not ready" system, discussed in Section 13.3. It can also create a problem if an external output port with an address equal to RELREG+1 exists in the system. *Therefore, in an 80C188EB system, RELREG should only be written by a byte write and never by a word write.*

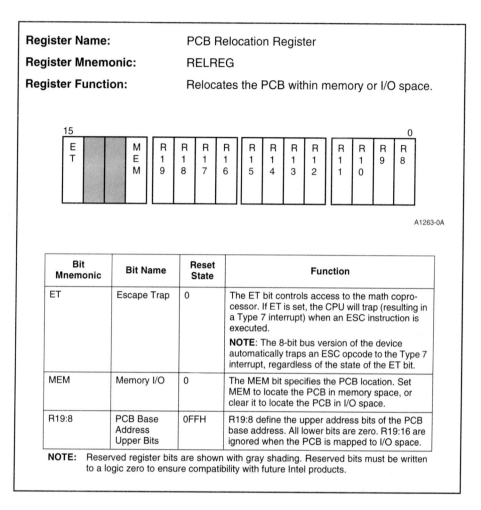

Register Name: PCB Relocation Register

Register Mnemonic: RELREG

Register Function: Relocates the PCB within memory or I/O space.

A1263-0A

Bit Mnemonic	Bit Name	Reset State	Function
ET	Escape Trap	0	The ET bit controls access to the math copro-cessor. If ET is set, the CPU will trap (resulting in a Type 7 interrupt) when an ESC instruction is executed. **NOTE:** The 8-bit bus version of the device automatically traps an ESC opcode to the Type 7 interrupt, regardless of the state of the ET bit.
MEM	Memory I/O	0	The MEM bit specifies the PCB location. Set MEM to locate the PCB in memory space, or clear it to locate the PCB in I/O space.
R19:8	PCB Base Address Upper Bits	0FFH	R19:8 define the upper address bits of the PCB base address. All lower bits are zero. R19:16 are ignored when the PCB is mapped to I/O space.

NOTE: Reserved register bits are shown with gray shading. Reserved bits must be written to a logic zero to ensure compatibility with future Intel products.

Figure 10.9-2   PCB relocation register. (Courtesy of Intel Corp.)

No word read or write operations should ever be performed to odd addresses in the PCB. This is because every register in the PCB is a word (16-bit) register that has an even address. If an odd address is read or written, two different registers are affected causing unknown results.

10.10   The 80C186EB Microprocessor

The 80C186EB and 80C188EB have identical EUs, and, therefore, can execute the same program. However, their BIUs differ in data bus width and instruction queue length. These bus width differences lead to differences in how fast the same program is executed on these two microprocessors when the microprocessors are running at the same clock speed.

In contrast to the 80C188EB's 8-bit data bus, the 80C186EB has a 16-bit data bus. The 80C186EB multiplexes 16 data bits, D15–D0, with address bits A15–A0 on its address/data bus pins, AD15–AD0. Demultiplexing is accomplished in the same manner as for an 80C188EB CPU subsystem. However, an additional octal latch is needed to demultiplex AD15–AD8. A second 8-bit transceiver is also needed to buffer the data bus.

The 80C186EB is capable of transferring a word (16 bits) of data in a single bus cycle. It can only do this when the word is appropriately aligned in memory. A word that has its low byte at an even memory address is said to be **word aligned** or simply **aligned**. An aligned word is transferred in a single bus cycle. Therefore, it is advantageous to align words in a data segment by preceding the directives that allocate storage for the words with the **EVEN** directive. The EVEN directive ensures that data (or code) following the directive starts at an even address. The assembler inserts a NOP if necessary to force the data to start at an even address.

A memory word with its low byte at an odd address is **unaligned**. The 80C186EB can access any two consecutive bytes in memory as a word, regardless of whether the word is aligned or not. However, an unaligned word requires two bus cycles to be transferred. The first cycle transfers the low byte of the unaligned word over the high byte of the data bus. The second bus cycle transfers the high byte of the unaligned word over the low byte of the data bus. When transferring an unaligned word, the BIU automatically redirects each byte from the high to the low side (or vice versa) on the 80C186EB's internal data bus.

The 80C186EB's BIU has a six byte instruction prefetch queue in contrast to the 80C188EB's four byte queue. The 80C188EB fetches an instruction byte whenever there is an empty byte in its queue. The 80C186EB fetches instruction bytes whenever two or more bytes in its queue are empty. The 80C186EB normally fetches two instruction bytes per bus cycle. However, if execution flow is transferred to an odd address, the BIU fetches a single instruction byte from the odd address and continues fetching words from subsequent even addresses.

Another 80C186EB difference is the signal /BHE. This signal does not exist on an 80C188EB. The **/BHE, Byte High Enable,** signal is asserted by the 80C186EB to enable data onto the high byte of the data bus. A0 is used to enable data onto the low byte of the data bus. The consequences of these differences on address decoder design for 80C186EB memory subsystems are covered in Section 11.8.

10.11   Summary

A CPU subsystem consists of a microprocessor and its support components. These support components are needed to make the microprocessor operable and to demultiplex and buffer the system's address, data, and control bus signals. The 80C188EB has a 20-bit system address bus, A19–A0, and an 8-bit system data bus, D7–D0. The system control bus consists of a number of signals. Only the three primary control signals required for data transfer, /RD, /WR, and /S2, were discussed in this chapter.

Since the 80C188EB includes integrated peripherals, its CPU subsystem also provides a second set of signals that provide direct connections to its integrated peripherals.

A microprocessor requires a system clock and a reset signal to place it in its initial state. A crystal, used in conjunction with the oscillator integrated onto the 80C188EB, generates the system clock. The microprocessor is reset by a signal from either an RC network or a microprocessor supervisory circuit. Use of a microprocessor supervisory circuit provides a more reliable reset signal, independent of the power supply's risetime.

Each byte of data transferred over the system data bus requires a bus cycle. Each bus cycle is normally four system clock periods. Some of the support components in a CPU subsystem are latches that demultiplex the 80C188EB's time multiplexed address/data and its status signals. These signals are latched so stable address and status signals are available on the system bus throughout an entire bus cycle. The 80C188EB provides a timing signal, Address Latch Enable (ALE) to clock the latches used for demultiplexing.

In addition to the components required to demultiplex the 80C188EB's address/data and latch its status signals, other components may be required to buffer some bus signals. Buffering provides additional current drive to handle the load presented to the system bus by memory and I/O subsystems. A special bidirectional buffer called a transceiver is used to buffer data bus signals. The 80C188EB provides the signal DT/R to control a data bus transceiver's direction and the signal /DEN to enable the transceiver's three state buffers.

The 80C188EB is a CMOS device. Other ICs used in the CPU subsystem are also typically CMOS. However, various CMOS logic families may be used, including TTL-compatible CMOS. In addition, TTL logic may need to be interfaced to the system bus. Careful analysis and design is required to insure that logic level compatibility exists between all interconnected ICs.

To determine the extent of buffering required, the current requirements and capacitance presented by memory and I/O subsystems must be analyzed. This requires a very careful analysis, particularly when different logic families are used in the various subsystems.

For applications that require only a small amount of memory and I/O, a minimum component system can be constructed using special ICs that provide memory and I/O in a single IC. The PSD311 includes demultiplexing latches, in addition to ROM, RAM, and I/O, thus allowing the creation of a complete, though modest, 80C188EB microcomputer system consisting of only two ICs.

The 80C188EB core module communicates with its integrated peripherals via a block of 128 word registers called the Peripheral Control Block (PCB). When the 80C188EB is reset, this block of registers is initially located in the highest 256 bytes of I/O space. It is possible to relocate the PCB to any 256 byte block in either memory or I/O space. Relocation of the PCB is usually not necessary.

An 80C186EB CPU subsystem is similar to an 80C188EB subsystem, except that the multiplexed address/data bus is 16 bits wide. So, additional latches are required to demultiplex address bits A15–A0, and, if the data bus is buffered, a second transceiver is required.

10.12   Problems

1. In an 80C188EB system, which bus signals control the reading and writing of memory and I/O? Of these signals, which provide both timing and direction of transfer information? Which signal specifies whether a transfer involves memory or an I/O port? Which two signals are never both asserted during the same bus cycle?

2. During a read bus cycle, what are the possible sources of data? What determines how long the data bus is driven with the data being read? During a write bus cycle, what is the source of data? What determines how long the data bus is driven with the data being written? When should a device being written to latch the data?

3. During the time a data byte is being written to the byte output port with address 4000H, what are the values of /S2, A19–A0, /RD, and /WR on the system bus?

4. During the time that a data byte is being read from memory location 01A2CH, what are the values of /S2, A19–A0, /RD, and /WR on the system bus?

5. What peripherals are integrated on an 80C188EB microprocessor chip?

6. In what package types is the 80C188EB available? How many pins does each of these package types have?

7. How many V_{CC} power connections are there to an 80C188EB in a PLCC package? How many of these must actually be connected to V_{CC}? How many ground connections are there? How many of these must actually be connected to system ground?

8. Approximately how much power supply current is drawn by an 80C188EB,

   a. at 13 MHz?

   b. at 20 MHz?

9. What are the frequencies, periods, and duty cycles of the CLKOUT signal when using:

   a. a 26 MHz crystal?

   b. a 40 MHz crystal?

10. Write an equation for the state time, T, as a function of the crystal frequency, f_c. Compute the state time for a system that uses a 20 MHz crystal.

11. For an 8 MHz 80C188EB, what is the minimum required /RESIN duration for a cold restart, in µs, after V_{CC} and CLKIN become stable? What is the duration for a 20 MHz 80C188EB?

12. If the power supply for an 80C188EB instantaneously reaches 4.5 V when switched on, what must the RC product be to produce a 50 µs reset pulse? If a 10 µF capacitor is chosen, what value should be used for R? Since a real power supply's output will not be a step function when turned on, how does this effect the choice of RC?

13. What would be the criteria for selection of a microprocessor supervisory circuit for use with an 80C188EB operated at 20 MHz in terms of the required V_{CC} reset threshold, duration of reset output, and polarity of reset?

14. What is the fundamental purpose of a bus cycle? What is the minimum duration of a bus cycle in periods of the system clock and what are these clock periods called?

15. Draw a timing diagram for a write bus cycle with no WAIT states showing the signals CLKOUT, ALE, AD7–AD0, and /WR at the 80C188EB's pins. Label the T states. Draw a second timing diagram with no WAIT states showing the signals CLKOUT, ALE, A7–A0, D7–D0, and /WR at the fully buffered system bus. Label the T states.

16. What are the eight types of 80C188EB bus cycles? For each type that involves a data transfer, what are the corresponding values of /S2 and DT/R? With what status signal does DT/R correlate?

17. How do the address and data bus signals generated at the 80C188EB's pins (Figs. 10.3-4 and 10.3-5) differ from the system address bus and data bus signals illustrated for the CPU subsystem in Figs. 10.1-2 and 10.1-3?

18. Why is it important that the address value remain stable on the system bus throughout a bus cycle? Which of the status signals can be used to determine whether the bus cycle's address references the memory or I/O space? Which status signal indicates the direction of transfer?

19. What support ICs are required to implement the simplest 80C188EB CPU subsystem with a locally demultiplexed system bus?

20. Describe any possible advantages or disadvantages in using positive edge triggered D-type flip-flops to demultiplex the address/data and status signals in an 80C188EB CPU subsystem.

21. What ICs are required to implement a fully buffered 80C188EB subsystem? List each IC's logic function and list specific ICs in the 74HC family that are suitable to provide the required functions.

22. In a system with a partially buffered bus, why can't the /OE input of the transceiver be directly driven by /DEN? How must /DEN be qualified before being used in controlling the /OE input of a transceiver in a partially buffered system?

23. What CMOS logic family would be most appropriate to demultiplex and fully buffer an 80C188EB's system bus if high-current drive capability is required? If some output devices generated TTL output levels, how could they be accommodated?

24. Assume that V_{CC} is 4.5 V and that a 74HC input port is being read by an 80C188EB. Also assume that neither I_{OH} nor I_{OL} max for the 74HC is exceeded. What are the values of the DC noise margins?

25. Discuss the feasibility of using a 74ALS245 bus transceiver to buffer the data bus for a fully buffered 80C188EB CPU subsystem implementation. Determine whether the voltage levels are compatible and whether current requirements are met. Assume that V_{CC} is 5.0 V.

	V_{OHmin}	V_{OLmax}	V_{IHmin}	V_{ILmax}	I_{OHmax}	I_{OLmax}	I_{IHmax}	I_{ILmax}
74ALS245	2.4 V	0.4 V	2.0 V	0.7 V	−12 mA	12 mA	20 μA	−0.1 mA
80C188EB	4.5 V	0.45 V	3.5 V	1.5 V	−2 mA	3 mA	15 μA	−15 μA

26. Write the directives and instructions to read the contents of the POLLSTS register in the PCB.

27. Write a sequence of instructions to:

   a. relocate the 80C188EB's PCB from base address FF00H in I/O space to base address 8000H in I/O space.

   b. relocate the PCB from base address FF00H in I/O space to base address 80000H in the memory space.

28. Two sequences of instructions are shown below, each of whose purpose is to relocate an 80C188EB's PCB.

    ```
    mov     ax,00a0h
    mov     dx,0ffa8h
    out     dx,ax

    mov     ax,00a0h
    mov     dx,0ffa8h
    out     dx,al
    ```

    Do both of these sequences successfully relocate the PCB? What, if any, is the difference in actions caused by these two sequences? For each case, to what base address and in what address space is the PCB relocated?

29. Draw a logic diagram showing the interconnection of buffers and latches to an 80C186EB to create a demultiplexed and fully buffered 20-bit address bus and 16-bit data bus. For the data bus transceivers draw the internal control logic and one representative set of buffers. During which T state is the address latched and what signal from the 80C186EB controls the latching? What is the preferred type of triggering for the latch?

11.1   Memory Subsystems

11.2   Logical Structure and Operation of Memory ICs

11.3   Static Random Access Memory (SRAM)

11.4   Erasable Programmable Read Only Memory (EPROM)

11.5   Flash Memory

11.6   Memory Subsystem Design

11.7   80C188EB Memory Subsystem Design

11.8   80C186EB Memory Subsystem Design

11.9   Memory Address Decoding

11.10   The 80C188EB's Chip-Select Unit

11.11   SSI and MSI External Address Decoders

11.12   PLD External Address Decoders

11.13   Summary

This chapter focuses on the logical design of a memory subsystem, including types of memory ICs, memory IC structure and operation, interconnection of ROM and RAM ICs to provide the required memory, and memory address decoding to select memory ICs in a subsystem.

Memory ICs first became available in the late 1960s. They have been of critical importance in making embedded systems practical and economical. An embedded system requires memory that is low cost, physically small, and reliable. Memory ICs provide these qualities.

Memory ICs are the technology driver for advanced MOS semiconductor technologies. Advanced semiconductor IC technologies are first applied to memories. After these process technologies are refined in the manufacture of memory, they are applied to the manufacture of microprocessors and other VLSI devices. Typically, microprocessors follow a generation behind memory in the use of a specific semiconductor technology.

The basic semiconductor bit storage element is the memory cell. Progress in the development of memory cells has lead to a variety of types of ROMs and RAMs. One very important memory innovation, the Intel 1702 Erasable Programmable Read Only Memory (EPROM) was introduced in 1971, the same year Intel introduced the first microprocessor, the 4004. The 1702 EPROM was a 256×8 (2 Kbit) device.

An EPROM is a nonvolatile ROM IC. EPROMs have the advantage that they can be erased with ultraviolet light and then electrically reprogrammed. As a result, EPROMs are an ideal type of ROM for storing your object code. If an error is found in the object code after an EPROM has been programmed, the EPROM can be removed from the system and erased. The EPROM can then be reprogrammed with the revised object code. Much of the success of early embedded systems design was due to the availability of EPROMs to speed up system development.

While a variety of memory cell types are available, each with specific advantages, the focus in this chapter is on Static Random Access Memory (SRAM) and EPROMs. These two types of memory ICs are typically used to provide the RAM and ROM in small to moderate size systems. They are also relatively easy to use. Also discussed is Flash memory, a type of ROM that can be reprogrammed in circuit. This more recent technology has become increasingly important, and may eventually replace EPROMs.

As memory IC technology has advanced, ICs with increasingly larger bit capacities have become available. These larger capacity memory ICs, along with Programmable Logic Devices (PLDs), have significantly reduced the effort required in the logical design of a memory subsystem.

11.1 Memory Subsystems

A ROM is nonvolatile; it retains its data when its power is turned off. Strictly speaking, a ROM cannot be written during normal system operation. The memory subsystem's ROM stores your program's instructions and constants. In contrast, RAM is volatile and loses its data if its power is turned off. RAM is read-write memory, meaning it can be written and read an unlimited number of times during system operation. The memory subsystem's RAM stores your variables and temporary data. Each specific application determines how many bytes of ROM and RAM are required.

Both ROM and RAM are random access. Any memory location (chosen at random) can be accessed in essentially the same amount of time as any other location. A serial memory's access time, by contrast, is a function of the location accessed.

The primary signals used to interface an 80C188EB memory subsystem to the system bus are A19–A0, D7–D0, and control signals /S2, /RD, and /WR (Fig. 11.1-1). With 20 address bits, an 80C188EB can directly address a maximum of $2^{20} = 1,048,576$ bytes of memory. The 80C188EB's memory address space was introduced in Section 3.2.

A memory subsystem's ROM and RAM are constructed from semiconductor memory ICs. The ideal memory IC is random access, low cost, low power, high speed, high density, nonvolatile, and in-circuit writable. Unfortunately, no single memory technology provides all these characteristics. As a result, there are a number of different types of ROM and RAM ICs. Each type excels with respect to one or more of the ideal device characteristics.

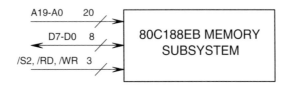

Figure 11.1-1   80C188EB memory subsystem and its primary connections to the system bus.

The ROM generic family includes masked ROM, programmable ROM (PROM), erasable programmable ROM (EPROM), electrically erasable PROM (EEPROM), and Flash. The RAM generic family includes static RAM (SRAM), dynamic RAM (DRAM), and pseudo-static RAM (PSRAM). Table 11.1-1 compares some important characteristics of each memory type.

Table 11.1-1   Types of ROM and RAM ICs and their characteristics.

	Type	Volatile	User Programmable	Erasable	In-circuit Programmable	Reprogram Times
ROM	Masked ROM	no	no	no	no	0
	PROM	no	yes	no	no	1
	EPROM	no	yes	yes	no	100
	EEPROM	no	yes	yes	yes	10,000
	Flash	no	yes	yes	yes	10,000
RAM	SRAM	yes	na[a]	na	na	na
	DRAM	yes	na	na	na	na
	Pseudo-static RAM	yes	na	na	na	na

a. na stands for not applicable

A masked ROM memory cell is a single transistor that is either present or absent. During the wafer fabrication process, the existence of a transistor at each cell position is programmed using a mask. Mask fabrication cost is high and the time it takes between ordering and receiving the devices, the turnaround time, is due to the long manufacturing process. As a result, masked ROM is only economical for large volume production of proven code. The code stored in a masked ROM cannot be modified. If an error is subsequently found, the large quantity of ROMs produced is worthless. A new mask must be created for the revised code, and another mask charge paid.

In contrast, a PROM is "user" programmable, or "field" programmable. The "user" is the designer of the embedded system, and "field" means outside of the semiconductor manufacturing facility. But, like a masked ROM, a PROM can only be programmed once. Bits were programmed into early bipolar PROMs by using a high current to melt fuses in the appropriate bit positions. This lead to the use of the expression "burning a PROM" to describe the programming of a PROM. If the code programmed into a PROM is later found to contain an error, the device is useless. However, PROMs can be programmed as needed, and any unprogrammed devices are still usable.

EPROMs, EEPROMs, and Flash are also user programmable. They have the added advantage that they can be erased and reprogrammed. So, if you have programmed one of these devices with code that contains an error, the device can be erased and reprogrammed with the corrected code. An EPROM package has a quartz window that allows light to reach the IC chip. An EPROM must be removed from the system and erased using ultraviolet light. EEPROMs and Flash have the advantage that they can be electrically erased in-circuit (without removing them from the system) and then reprogrammed. An EPROM and a Flash cell each contain a single transistor. An EEPROM cell requires two transistors and is, therefore, less economical than EPROM or Flash.

SRAM is the easiest type of RAM to design into a circuit. An SRAM memory cell is said to be **static** because it holds its data as long as its operating power is maintained, not because its contents are not changed during its operation. An SRAM cell is a bistable flip-flop circuit consisting of 6 transistors.

DRAM and PSRAM use a memory cell consisting of only a single transistor and a capacitor. This results in a much denser device, and a lower cost on a per bit basis. A DRAM or PSRAM memory cell is said to be **dynamic** because it cannot store a logic value indefinitely, even while its operating power is maintained. Charge on the capacitor represents the stored bit. Over a period of time (a few milliseconds), this charge decays. As a result, the capacitor's charge must be sensed and restored before it decays to too low a value. This process, which must be carried out periodically, is called **refreshing**. While the DRAM's memory array is being refreshed, it cannot be read or written. This reduces the memory's effective speed. Refresh requires additional logic to control the refresh operation. This logic overhead reduces the cost effectiveness of DRAMs in small and moderate size memory subsystems.

PSRAMs include refresh logic on the same IC as the memory. So, from the outside they look like SRAMs; hence their name pseudo-static RAM. Inclusion of this logic on-chip relieves you of the burden of designing refresh logic. However, inclusion of this logic results in a larger memory chip area, thus reducing PSRAM's density advantage.

Memory ICs must be interconnected, using address decoding logic, to create the desired memory subsystem. In addition to having the appropriate logical structure, the memory subsystem's timing must be compatible with that imposed by the 80C188EB. If the memory subsystem does not meet the 80C188EB's timing constraints, either the 80C188EB must be run at a slower clock speed or the duration of bus cycles that access the memory subsystem must be extended by inserting WAIT states. Timing details and WAIT states are discussed in Sections 13.4 and 13.5

11.2   Logical Structure and Operation of Memory ICs

While the differences in various ROM and RAM technologies and physical organizations are significant, there are similarities in their logical organization and in-circuit operation. These similarities are the focus of this section.

Memory ICs have an external or **logical organization** that differs from their internal or **physical organization**. A memory IC's external organization refers to the organization as seen at the IC's pins. The external organization is of concern when you design a memory subsystem. In contrast, the internal organization depends on the structure of the memory IC's memory array and internal decoding logic.

A memory IC is logically organized as a number of equal length registers, commonly referred to as memory locations (Fig. 11.2-1). The number of bits that can be stored in each register defines an IC's word length, or **width**. The total number of registers (locations) in a memory IC is referred to as its **depth**.

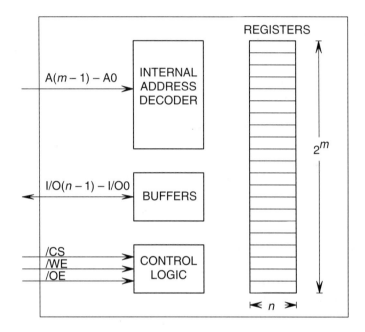

Figure 11.2-1   Logical organization of a $2m \times n$ memory IC with three control lines. Internal connections between the IC's logic and registers have been omitted for clarity.

A memory IC's interface includes pins for address, data, and control signals. One of the control inputs is **chip-select (/CS)**. As its name implies, the signal at this input selects the memory IC from among several memory ICs in the system. Unless it is selected, a memory IC cannot be written or read. The IC's address inputs further select the specific location to be written or read. The memory IC's internal address decoder decodes the address at its address inputs and accesses the corresponding memory cells. Data is written to, or read from, the IC on its data pins. Memory ICs used in embedded systems usually have bidirectional data pins, referred to as **common I/O**. Common I/O data pins are sometimes designated $I/O_{(n-1)} - I/O_0$, instead of D7–D0, to indicate their bidirectional nature.

11.2.1   RAM ICs with Three Control Inputs

RAM ICs typically have three control inputs. In addition to a chip select, the IC has a **write enable (/WE)**, input and an **output enable (/OE)** input (Fig. 11.2-1). Less common are RAMs with only two control inputs, /CS and /WE. The internal logic for each of these approaches is illustrated in Fig. 11.2-2.

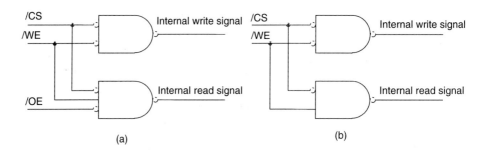

(a)   (b)

Figure 11.2-2   Control logic representation of the internal gating for a RAM with:
(a) three control inputs; (b) two control inputs.

The lower-order, or least significant, address bits from the system bus connect directly to the corresponding address pins of a memory IC (Fig. 11.2-3). The higher-order address bits (those not connected directly to the memory IC) must be externally decoded, along with /S2, to identify which of many possible memory ICs, is to be accessed. This decoding can be accomplished by either the 80C188EB's Chip-Select Unit or by a discrete external address decoder.

To write a RAM IC that has three control inputs involves the following steps (Fig. 11.2-4):

1. The address of the location to be written is placed on the address inputs.
2. /CS is asserted, to select the memory IC.
3. The data to be written is placed on the data inputs.
4. /WE is asserted.
5. /WE is unasserted, causing the data to be latched.
6. The data is removed from the data inputs.
7. /CS is unasserted, to deselect the memory IC.
8. The address is removed (changed).

Note that /OE remains unasserted throughout a write cycle.

The sequence of operations in Fig. 11.2-4 constitutes a RAM IC's **write cycle**. As shown, the signals to the RAM are unasserted in the opposite order of their assertion. The /WE input's function is analogous to that of the CLK input of a negative-level triggered latch. /WE is driven by /WR from the 80C188EB. To be reliably written, the RAM's timing requirements must be met. Timing requirements are considered in detail in Chapter 13.

To read a RAM that has three control inputs involves the following steps (Fig. 11.2-5):

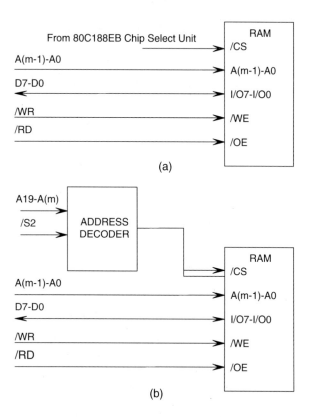

Figure 11.2-3   Selecting a RAM IC by decoding the high order address bits and /S2: (a) decoding accomplished by 80C188EB Chip-Select Unit (b) decoding accomplished by an external decoder.

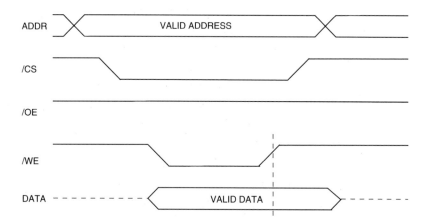

Figure 11.2-4   Relative timing relationship for the write cycle of a memory IC with three control inputs.

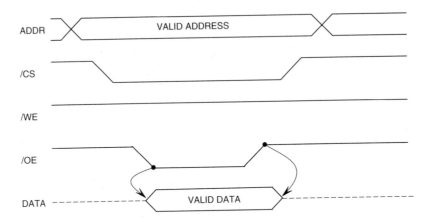

Figure 11.2-5   Relative timing relationship for the read cycle of a memory IC with three control inputs.

1. The address of the location to be read is placed on the address inputs.
2. /CS is asserted, to select the memory IC.
3. /OE is asserted, to enable the memory IC's output buffers.
4. The data driven on the data bus by the memory IC is latched by the 80C188EB.
5. /OE is unasserted, disabling the memory IC's output buffers.
6. /CS is unasserted, to deselect the memory IC.
7. The address is removed (changed).

Note that /WE remains unasserted throughout a read cycle.

The relative timing relationships in Fig. 11.2-5 constitute a **read cycle**. The 80C188EB must latch the data from the RAM before /OE is unasserted. The /OE input's function is analogous to that of the output control input (/OC) of an octal latch. Asserting /OE enables the RAM's output buffers, resulting in the data bus being driven by the data from the addressed RAM location. The /OE input is driven by /RD from the 80C188EB.

Read and write operations on a memory IC must be mutually exclusive, or bus contention results. Therefore, the memory IC's /WE and /OE inputs must never be asserted simultaneously.

11.2.2   RAM and ROM ICs with Two Control Inputs

RAM ICs with two control inputs have no /OE pin. When the IC is selected, it is either written or read, depending on whether /WE is asserted or unasserted.

If /WE is asserted when the RAM IC is selected, the RAM is written. When the RAM is written, the data is latched by the RAM on the rising edge of either /WE or /CS, whichever occurs first. However, when using conventional address decoding techniques in a system, the transition at /WE will always occur first.

If /WE is unasserted when the RAM IC is selected, the addressed location is read.

The advantage of using two control inputs, rather than three, is a reduction, by one, of the number of IC pins. This advantage has lost its importance as larger bit capacity ICs, with a larger number of pins, have become common. One drawback, of using a two control input IC, is that the external address decoding logic becomes slightly more complex.

Since it cannot be written, a ROM IC only needs two control inputs, /CE and /OE. The ROM's chip-select input is usually labeled **/CE** for **chip enable** instead of /CS. /CE of a ROM is logically equivalent to /CS of a RAM. The /OE input is used to enable the ROM's three-state output buffers.

11.3   Static Random Access Memory, SRAM

The easiest type of RAM to design into a memory subsystem is **static random access memory (SRAM)**. An SRAM's basic memory cell is similar to that of a D-latch. Like a D-latch, an SRAM is **volatile**. It retains data only while its operating power is maintained.

SRAM ICs typically have widths of 1, 4, 8, or 16 bits. A memory IC with an 8-bit width is called a **byte-wide memory**. A memory IC with a 16-bit width is called a **word-wide memory**. Specialty SRAMs exist with widths of 18 and 32 bits, but these are not of interest for 80C188EB systems. Table 11.3-1 lists some representative SRAMs and their logical organizations. In many applications, a single SRAM provides all the RAM required.

Table 11.3-1   SRAM Memory IC Logical Organizations.

Device	Organization	Pins	Control Lines	I/O Type
2114A	$1K \times 4$	18	2	common
2174H	$4K \times 1$	18	2	separate
6116	$2K \times 8$	28	3	common
5164	$8K \times 8$	28	3	common
62256	$32K \times 8$	28	3	common
52A512	$64K \times 8$	32	3	common
84100	$128K \times 8$	32	3	common

An SRAM has pins for address, data, control, power, and ground. The SRAMs in Table 11.3-1 all require +5 V power for operation.

To minimize the number of data pins, SRAMs with common I/O are used. SRAMs with common I/O are directly compatible with the 80C188EB's bidirectional data bus. If an SRAM with separate I/O is used with an 80C188EB, it must have its data outputs connected back to its corresponding data inputs through an external three-state buffer. The enable for this three-state buffer must only be asserted when the SRAM is selected and /RD is asserted.

11.3.1   SRAM Internal Organization

An examination of the internal organization, or architecture, of an SRAM provides a foundation for a better understanding of its operation and timing requirements. This examination also provides insight into the internal organization of EPROMs and Flash memory, whose internal organizations will not be considered here in detail. An SRAM IC contains:

1. An array of memory cells, each of which stores a single bit.
2. Internal address decoding logic to select any location.
3. Circuitry to allow writing and reading the selected location.
4. Input buffers, output buffers, and circuitry for address expansion.

All the circuitry in a memory IC, other than the memory array itself, is referred to as peripheral circuitry.

Memory manufacturers design the internal architecture of SRAMs to achieve high speed, large bit capacity, and low internal decoder and memory array costs. Manufacturing yield decreases with chip area. Therefore, minimizing an IC's chip area reduces its production cost. Chip area is reduced by organizing the IC's memory array and decoder logic for **two-level decoding**, or **coincident selection** (Fig. 11.3-1).

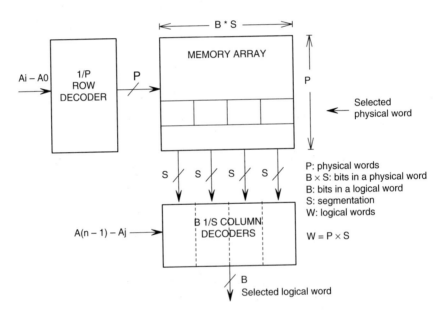

Figure 11.3-1   Representation of two level decoding in a memory IC.

With two-level decoding, the memory array is organized so that it is square or nearly square. A **physical word** consists of an entire row of the array. An internal **row decoder** selects a physical word in the array. Each physical word contains several logical words. The physical word selected is input to a column decoder. The column decoder selects one logical word from the physical word. Thus, a **logical word** consists of the bits, from a physical word, that are simultaneously selected and gated to the IC's output.

The **column decoder** actually consists of several identical multiplexer/demultiplexers, one for each output bit. The number of inputs to each multiplexer/demultiplexer is equal to the number of bits in a physical word divided by the number of bits in a logical word. This ratio is the memory IC's **segmentation**. While this specific use of the term segmentation differs from its use in describing memory address spaces, the central idea, that segmentation involves dividing something into smaller blocks, still applies.

A block diagram of the internal organization of an SRAM with 32,768 8-bit words ($32K \times 8$) organized with two-level decoding is shown in Fig. 11.3-2. This diagram is similar to one typically found on an SRAM's data sheet. The square memory array is 512×512 bits, thus it contains 512 physical words, each of which is 512 bits long. The 1-out-of-512 row decoder decodes nine address bits to select a physical word. Each 512 bit long physical word is divided (segmented) into 64 logical words. This division is in the form of eight blocks of 64 bits each ($8 \times 64 = 512$).

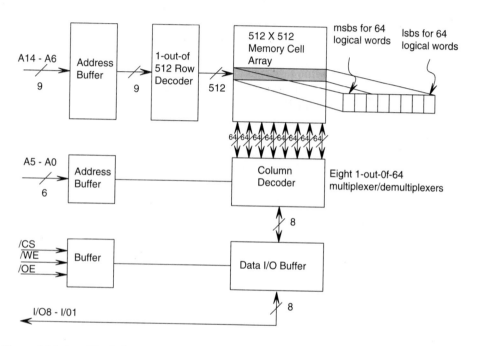

Figure 11.3-2   Block diagram of the internal structure of a 32 K × 8 SRAM with two-level decoding.

The leftmost block of a physical word contains the most significant bits of each of the 64 logical words contained in the physical word (compare with Fig. 11.3-1). The next block contains the next most significant bits of each of the 64 logical words, and so on. Column decoding requires eight 1-out-of-64 multiplexer/demultiplexers to provide the 8-bit logical word at the I/O pins. Six address bits connect to the column decoder.

When a memory is organized so the number of segments in a physical word equals the number of bits in the physical word, the memory is **bit organized.** Each logical word is one bit in length. A bit-organized memory has a single data output. For example, a 64K × 1 bit organized memory might consist of a 128 × 512 memory array, a 1-out-of-128 row decoder, and a 1-out-of-512 column decoder. In this example, the memory array is not square, but is nearly square.

The propagation delays associated with an SRAM's internal structure impose timing constraints on the sequencing of the address, data, and control signals to its pins. These constraints are specified on the manufacturer's data sheet in the form of AC characteristics and timing diagrams. Memory IC timing is considered in detail in Sections 13.4 and 13.5.

11.3.2   Battery Backed SRAM

An SRAM is volatile. When its V_{CC} power is removed or drops too low, the memory's contents are lost. Some applications require nonvolatile memory that can be written in-circuit and that has a very short write cycle time. Other applications require that some variables be protected from data loss in case of a power failure.

Low power CMOS SRAMs require so little standby power that their memory contents can be maintained from a battery. This standby voltage source can provide the power required to maintain a CMOS SRAM's memory contents during a power failure, or when the system's power is intentionally turned off. As a result, battery backed CMOS SRAM provides an ideal nonvolatile RAM for a finite period of time. However, over the long term, this approach must be considered volatile. Eventually, the battery will discharge.

While the standby voltage source is usually a lithium battery, a high energy density capacitor (over 3 Farads/cubic inch) can also serve as a standby voltage source and provide protection for short time periods. These capacitors provide a large capacitance, up to 2.2 F, in a small physical volume.

A battery (or capacitor) backed CMOS SRAM requires special external circuitry to handle two critical situations:

1. When V_{CC} drops too low, the SRAM's source of power must be switched from the system's V_{CC} source, derived from the AC power line, to the standby voltage source.
2. The SRAM must be protected from accidental writes during power on, power down, or brownouts. During these events, random signal transitions can occur on the system bus lines, including /CS and /WR. These signal transitions could cause one or more memory locations to be written with random data.

Microprocessor supervisory circuits include features that address these two problems. The MAX807 (Fig. 10.3-2) has two inputs for power sources. The system's +5 V, derived from the AC power line, is connected to the MAX807's V_{CC} input. The output from a backup voltage source is connected to the BATT input. OUT from the MAX807 is connected to the CMOS SRAM's V_{CC} input. Normally, the MAX807's OUT pin is internally connected to its V_{CC} input. However, when V_{CC} drops below the reset threshold and below the voltage at BATT, the MAX807 switches OUT's source to BATT.

To provide write protection, the chip select signal for the CMOS SRAM is routed to the MAX807's /CE IN input. The MAX807's /CE OUT drives the CMOS SRAM's /CS input. Normally the MAX807's /CE OUT is internally connected to its /CE IN. However, when V_{CC} drops below the reset threshold, /CE OUT becomes equal to OUT, providing a logical 1 to the SRAM's /CS input. This deselects the SRAM, preventing it from being written during power on, power down, or a brownout.

11.4   Erasable Programmable Read Only Memory (EPROM)

EPROMs provide user programmable and nonvolatile storage for software development and for low to moderate quantity production. EPROMs have read cycle times comparable to an SRAM. However, they cannot be written in circuit. They must be removed from the circuit and erased using ultraviolet light before being programmed. The internal organization of an EPROM is similar to that of an SRAM, with the EPROM's programming logic replacing the SRAM's write logic.

Each EPROM memory cell is a single transistor (Fig. 11.4-1). This transistor, developed by D. Frohman-Bentchkowsky in 1971, is called a floating polysilicon gate avalanche injection MOS (FAMOS) transistor. A FAMOS transistor resembles an ordinary MOS transistor, except for the addition of a floating gate. The floating gate is electrically isolated from the substrate on one side and the select gate on the other by layers of silicon dioxide, Thus, unlike the transistor's select gate, there is no connection to the floating gate.

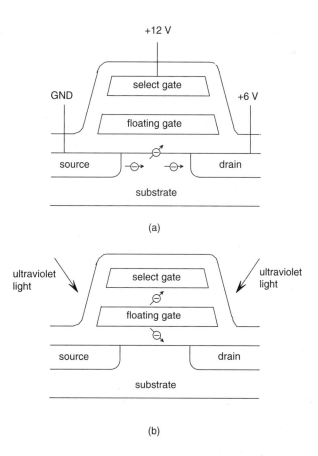

Figure 11.4-1   EPROM memory cell: (a) voltages applied to cell for programming; (b) ultraviolet light applied to cell for erasing.

An EPROM cell is programmed by charging its floating gate via the injection of electrons. This process is called avalanche injection, or hot electron injection. The voltages at the EPROM cell for programming are shown in Fig. 11.4-1(a). As electrons travel through the substrate from the source to the drain, under the influence of the positive drain voltage, some of them gain enough energy to jump the energy barrier at the interface between the silicon substrate and the silicon dioxide. The positive voltage on the select gate pulls these electrons through the silicon dioxide to the floating gate.

The charge on the floating gate alters the transistor's turn-on threshold voltage as seen by the select gate. In the unprogrammed state, there is no charge on the floating gate and the transistor has a low threshold. Under this condition, when the transistor is selected during read operations, by applying a positive voltage to its select gate, the transistor turns on. Sensing circuitry in the EPROM IC detects the transistor's drain current and interprets the cell's state as a 1. If the cell is in the programmed state, the charge on the floating gate causes the transistor to have a high turn-on threshold. Even with a positive voltage applied to the select gate, the transistor does not conduct. The sensing circuitry senses this condition as the 0 state.

EPROMs are programmed using a device programmer. An EPROM IC has a separate power supply pin, V_{PP}, for the programming voltage and a programming pin, /PGM, which places the EPROM in the programming mode. The device programmer uses these pins to apply the programming voltage and to place the EPROM in its programming mode.

EPROMs exhibit a wearout failure associated with the number of times a bit can be written. This characteristic is specified as the EPROM's **write endurance**. An EPROM's write endurance is typically less than 1,000 operations.

An EPROM cell is erased by photoemission of electrons from the floating gate to the select gate and substrate. Exposure to ultraviolet light increases the energy of the floating gate electrons to a level where they jump the energy barrier between the floating gate and silicon dioxide (Fig. 11.4-1(b)).

An EPROM IC is erased by exposing the entire IC chip to ultraviolet light through a quartz window on the IC package. Since the entire chip is exposed to ultraviolet light, all memory cells in the EPROM are erased simultaneously.

Erasure of an EPROM begins to occur upon exposure to light with wavelengths shorter than 4000 angstroms. Commercial EPROM erasers use mercury arc or mercury vapor lamps. These devices emit strong radiation with a wavelength of 2537 angstroms. A typical eraser completely erases an EPROM in 5 to 20 minutes. Sunlight, fluorescent light, and incandescent light are all capable of erasing an EPROM, if the length of exposure is sufficiently long. Therefore, after programming, the quartz window of an EPROM is covered with an opaque label to prevent inadvertent erasure.

One time programmable (OTP) versions of EPROMs, OTP-EPROMs, are also available. They have no quartz window and, therefore, once programmed, cannot be erased. Elimination of the quartz window reduces package cost, resulting in a lower cost device than a regular EPROM. Elimination of the quartz window also eliminates the possibility of accidental erasure by exposure to light.

Some low cost device programmers only program EPROMs, although they may be capable of programming all members of an entire family of such devices. In contrast, universal device programmers are capable of programming a wide range of programmable devices, including EPROMs, Flash memory, and programmable logic devices such as PALs.

Once programmed and placed in a system, an EPROM is only read. This is the mode of operation that is of concern to you when designing a memory subsystem.

An EPROM's external organization is also similar to that of an SRAM. However, once it is placed in a system, an EPROM can only be read, so it needs no /WE input. Two control inputs, /CE and /OE are provided. When their /CE inputs are unasserted, most EPROMs go into a low power mode of operation.

Although word-wide (16-bit) EPROMs are available, most EPROMs are byte-wide (Table 11.4-1). Byte-wide EPROMs and other byte-wide memory ICs are available that follow universal 28-pin or 32-pin DIP memory site standards adopted by the **Joint Electronic Devices Engineering Council**, or **JEDEC** (Fig. 11.4-2). Smaller 24-pin memory ICs conform to the 28-pin standard when positioned at the bottom of a 28-pin universal socket. On a printed circuit board, a 32-pin IC socket with a few jumpers allows any memory IC that conforms to either standard to be plugged into the socket. The jumpers on the printed circuit board are configured to accommodate the very few pins that have different functions for the different size ICs that conform to the two standards.

Table 11.4-1   Logical organization of some EPROM and Flash EPROM Memory ICs.

Device	Organization	Pins	Control Lines
27C128 EPROM	16K × 8	28	2
27C256	32K × 8	28	2
27C512 EPROM	64K × 8	28	2
27C4096	256K × 16	40	2
28F256A Flash	32K × 8	32	3
28F010 Flash	128K × 8	32	3
28F020 Flash	256K × 8	32	3

11.5   Flash Memory

Flash memory's primary advantage is that, unlike EPROM, it can be electrically erased and reprogrammed in-circuit. This allows its use when it is desirable to be able to load an updated version of your program's object code into memory through a serial interface. With this capability, you can update code without opening the system's case. You can even update code remotely over a telephone line. Flash memory is also useful for storing calibration and configuration data that must occasionally be changed by the system.

While EEPROMs are also in-circuit erasable and reprogrammable, they are less dense and typically more expensive than Flash.

Flash memory has some disadvantages in certain applications and systems:

1. Some Flash devices require 12 volts to program. However, 5 V only Flash memories are available.

2. The total number of erase/program cycles is limited. Typically, a Flash memory sustains 10,000 minimum to 100,000 typical erase/program cycles.

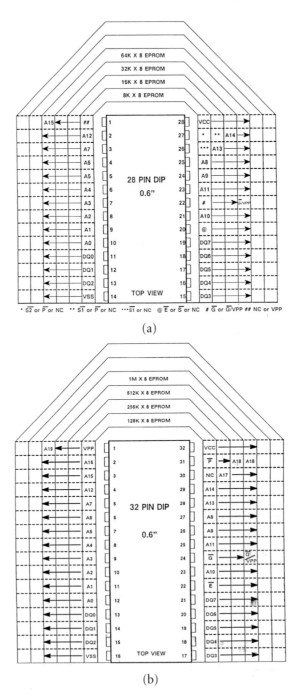

Figure 11.4-2   Byte-wide EPROM pinouts for dual in-line package (DIP): (a) 8 Kbytes to
64 Kbytes (b) 128 Kbytes to 1 Mbyte. (Courtesy of Electronic Industries
Association/JEDEC.)

3. Your system's microprocessor must execute erase and program algorithms for in-circuit reprogramming.

4. Large bit capacity Flash memories are most commonly available in surface mount packages only.

There are three predominate Flash memory technologies: NOR Flash, EEPROM Flash, and NAND Flash. Each provides the basic Flash attributes, but they differ in the details of the memory cell, peripheral circuits, and external organization. The NOR cell is derived from the EPROM cell and the EEPROM Flash cell is derived from the EEPROM cell. Structurally, the NAND cell looks like a NOR cell, but it programs and erases like an EEPROM cell. The NAND's peripheral logic is also significantly different. Data is read from the memory array serially.

Of these three technologies, only NOR Flash will be discussed further since it is the most prevalent.

11.5.1   NOR Flash Memory Cell

NOR Flash memory was introduced by Intel in 1988. The basic memory cell is a floating gate transistor similar to that of an EPROM. However, the oxide layer between the floating gate and substrate is much thinner in this transistor than in that of an EPROM. Intel calls this technology ETOX, for EPROM Thin Oxide.

When originally shipped, the default state of all cells in a NOR memory is a 1. This state corresponds to the erased condition. A cell can only be programmed to a 0. Once a 0 is programmed, the cell must be erased before it can be reprogrammed.

Programming can only change a cell's state from a 1 to a 0. Programming an ETOX cell is done through avalanche injection. This is the same process used to program an EPROM cell, as described in the previous section. The application of voltages to a cell for programming is shown in Fig. 11.5-1(a). If the floating gate is sufficiently charged, the transistor will not turn on when selected during a normal read operation. As a result, an output value of 0 is obtained.

The application of voltages to a cell for an erase operation is shown in Fig. 11.5-1(b). The select gate is grounded and +12 V is applied to the source. The electric field generated pulls electrons from the floating gate in a process called Fowler-Nordheim tunneling. Fowler-Nordheim tunneling is a quantum mechanical effect in which the electrons pass (tunnel) through the energy barrier of the very thin silicon dioxide layer. The physical mechanism for this process was developed in the 1960s by Fowler and Nordheim.

Like other memories, a Flash memory contains an array of memory cells. An individual byte can be read from or written to a Flash memory, but only the entire memory array, or blocks of the array, can be erased. In first generation NOR flash memories, the entire memory array is erased at one time. This process is called a **bulk erase.** The term "flash" refers to erasing the entire memory array at one time. Second generation NOR memory arrays are divided into blocks. Each block can be individually erased, independently of all other blocks. This approach is appropriately called **block erase.** Even though these second generation devices are erased in blocks, they are still called Flash memory.

First generation Flash memories require that all the details of erasure and programming be precisely controlled by your software. This includes the generation of several

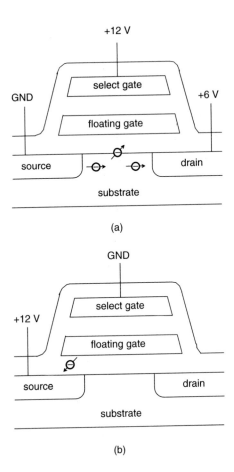

Figure 11.5-1   ETOX flash memory cell: (a) voltages applied to cell for programming; (b) voltages applied to cell for erasing.

accurate delays. Second generation Flash memories have algorithms for erasure and programming control that are automatically implemented by an on-chip state machine. Accordingly, second generation devices are much simpler to erase and program.

11.5.2   The 28F001BX-T CMOS Flash Memory

The Intel 28F001BX-T is an example of a second generation CMOS flash memory. The 28F001BX-T is organized as 128 K × 8 (1 M bit) and has a block architecture. In terms of its external organization, the 28F001BX-T is very similar to a 128 K × 8 SRAM (Fig. 11.5-2). It has 17 address inputs, 8 common I/O data pins, and /CE, /WE, and /OE inputs. During normal operation, it is read in the same manner as an SRAM or EPROM.

As expected, the 28F001BX-T has a V_{CC} input. An on-chip monitoring circuit disables the write circuitry, locking out writes, when V_{CC} falls below a value specified as V_{LKO}.

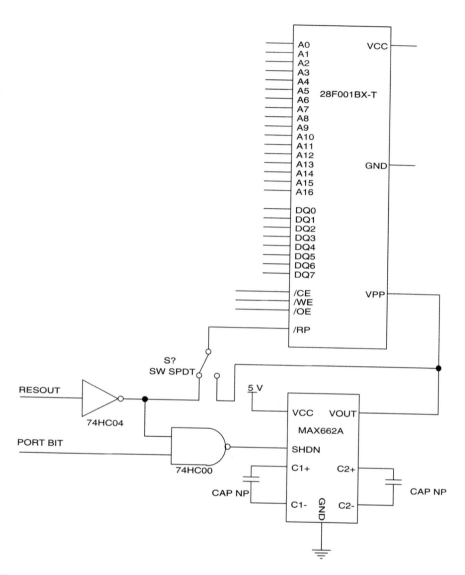

Figure 11.5-2   F001BX-T Flash memory with MAX662A memory programming supply.

V_{LKO} for the 28F001BX-T is 2.5 V. This provides one of the levels of protection to prevent spurious writes.

For purposes of erasing and programming, the 28F001BX-T is divided into four separate blocks: one 112 K $\times$ 8 main block, two 4 K $\times$ 8 parameter blocks, and one 8K $\times$ 8 boot block with hardware lockout (Fig. 11.5-3). Because its blocks are of different sizes, this architecture is called **asymmetrically blocked**. In any block structured architecture, erasing and reprogramming one block does not affect data stored in any other block.

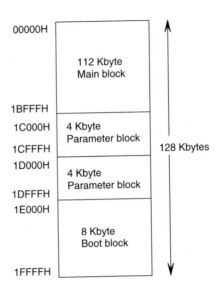

Figure 11.5-3   Block structure of asymmetrically blocked 28F001BX-T 128K × 8 Flash
memory.

In 5 V only systems, you can use a charge pump or other circuit to generate the 12 V
supply needed for programming from the 5 V supply. ICs, called **Flash memory programming supplies**, are specifically designed for this purpose. The +12 V in Fig. 11.5-2 is supplied from a **MAX662A** charge pump IC. Flash memory programming power supplies are
commonly specified in multiples of 30 mA. This value is the maximum I_{PP} current drawn
by a typical byte-wide Flash memory during erase and program cycles. The MAX662A
+12 V supply is specified for 30 mA. So, it can handle the current requirements of the
28F001BX-T.

The 28F001BX-T's external organization differs from an SRAM's in that it has two
additional inputs, V_{PP} and /RP. These inputs are used to control erasing and programming.
/RP is the powerdown input. When /RP is asserted, it puts the 28F001BX-T in a deep
powerdown mode. While /RP is asserted, all erase and program operations are locked out.
This provides write and erase protection for the device during power transitions. When
/RP is 5 V and the programming voltage, V_{PP}, is +12 V, any of the blocks in the device,
except the boot block, can be erased and programmed. To erase or program the boot
block, the /RP input must be +12 V.

In Fig. 11.5-2, a block protect jumper ties /RP to either the /RESET output from a
microprocessor supervisory circuit or to the output of the MAX662A. The /RESET output
is either 0 V or 5 V. When /RP is tied to /RESET, it is not possible to write the boot block.
This secures boot code. However, the other blocks can be erased and programmed, as long
as /RP is not asserted.

The output of the MAX662A is 5 V when it is shut down. When it is not shut down,
its output is 12 V. Strapping /RP to the output of the MAX662A allows erasure and programming of the boot block only when the MAX662A is not shut down.

Application or removal of 12 V from the MAX662A's output is controlled by its shutdown input (SHDN). In shutdown mode, V_{OUT} equals V_{CC}. With V_{CC} applied to V_{PP} and /RP unasserted, the 28F001BX-T can be read, but not erased or programmed. The signal driving SHDN is a function of an output port bit and the power fail, or reset output, of a microprocessor supervisory circuit. No block can be programmed unless the output port bit is 1. This allows software control of erase and programming. Furthermore, the /RESET output from the supervisory circuit must not be asserted. Thus, during power on or a brownout condition, the Flash cannot be inadvertently written.

As a second generation device, the 28F001BX-T has an automated erase and program algorithm implemented via an on-chip write state machine. /RP resets this internal state machine.

There is a command register and a status register on the 28F001BX-T. The command register does not occupy any memory locations, but instead is accessed during a write operation to the device. When using commands that are block specific, it is necessary to write the command to an address within the block. The 28F001BX-T's commands are listed in Table 11.5-1.

Table 11.5-1   28F001BX Command Definitions.

Command	Bus Cycles Required	Notes	First Bus Cycle			Second Bus Cycle		
			Operation	Address	Data	Operation	Address	Data
Read Array/Reset	1		Write	X	FFH			
Intelligent Identifier	3	1, 2, 3	Write	X	90H	Read	IA	IID
Read Status Register	2	2	Write	X	70H	Read	X	SRD
Clear Status Register	1		Write	X	50H			
Erase Setup/Erase Confirm	2	1	Write	BA	20H	Write	BA	D0H
Erase Suspend/Erase Resume	2		Write	X	B0H	Write	X	D0H
Program Setup/Program	2	1, 2	Write	PA	40H	Write	PA	PD

NOTES:
1.   IA = Identifier Address: 00H for manufacturer code, 01H for device code.
   BA = Address within the block being erased.
   PA = Address of memory location to be programmed.
2.   SRD = Data read from Status Register. See Fig. 11.5-4 for a description of the Status Register bits.
   PD = Data to be programmed at location PA. Data is latched on the rising edge of WE #.
   IID = Data read from Intelligent Identifiers.
3.   Following the Intelligent Identifier command, two read operations access manufacture and device codes.
4.   Commands other than those shown above are reserved by Intel for future device implementations and should not be used.

The definitions of the 28F001BX-T's status register bits are given in Fig. 11.5-4.

The erase algorithm is shown in Fig. 11.5-5. To erase a block, the command 20H is first written to an address in the block. Because the command register does not occupy an addressable memory location, the only requirement is that the address written be within

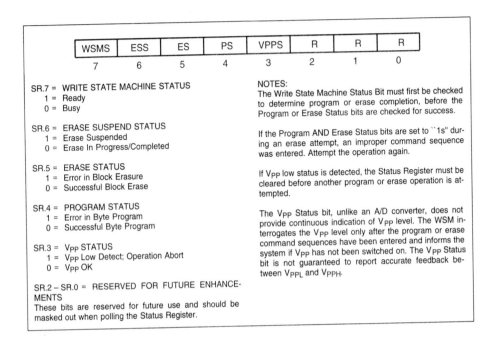

WSMS	ESS	ES	PS	VPPS	R	R	R
7	6	5	4	3	2	1	0

SR.7 = WRITE STATE MACHINE STATUS
   1 = Ready
   0 = Busy

SR.6 = ERASE SUSPEND STATUS
   1 = Erase Suspended
   0 = Erase In Progress/Completed

SR.5 = ERASE STATUS
   1 = Error in Block Erasure
   0 = Successful Block Erase

SR.4 = PROGRAM STATUS
   1 = Error in Byte Program
   0 = Successful Byte Program

SR.3 = V_{PP} STATUS
   1 = V_{PP} Low Detect; Operation Abort
   0 = V_{PP} OK

SR.2 – SR.0 = RESERVED FOR FUTURE ENHANCE-MENTS
These bits are reserved for future use and should be masked out when polling the Status Register.

NOTES:
The Write State Machine Status Bit must first be checked to determine program or erase completion, before the Program or Erase Status bits are checked for success.

If the Program AND Erase Status bits are set to ``1s'' during an erase attempt, an improper command sequence was entered. Attempt the operation again.

If V_{PP} low status is detected, the Status Register must be cleared before another program or erase operation is attempted.

The V_{PP} Status bit, unlike an A/D converter, does not provide continuous indication of V_{PP} level. The WSM interrogates the V_{PP} level only after the program or erase command sequences have been entered and informs the system if V_{PP} has not been switched on. The V_{PP} Status bit is not guaranteed to report accurate feedback between V_{PPL} and V_{PPH}.

Figure 11.5-4   28F001BX status register definitions. (Courtesy of Intel Corp.)

the block. Next, the erasure is confirmed by writing 0DH to the block. You must then wait until the Write State Machine status bit is ready. If this wait is too long, it may be necessary to suspend erasure and check the status. When the erasure is finished, the Erase, Program, and V_{PP} status bits need to be checked for errors. If no errors are detected, then the block was successfully erased.

The programming algorithm is shown in Fig. 11.5-6. When programming Flash memory, the location to be programmed must be erased first. To erase the location, the entire block must be erased. Programming starts with writing the Program Setup command (040H) to the address of the byte to be programmed. Next, the data is written to the same address. When done, the Program and V_{PP} status bits must be checked for errors. If no errors are detected, then the byte was successfully programmed.

Intel provides a software package, **SoftwareBuilder**, which is a hypertext version of Intel's Flash Memory Data Book. It includes erase and program algorithms in C and assembler that can be cut and pasted into your application.

11.5.3   Flash Memory Applications

The primary Flash memory applications are:

1. ROM replacement
2. In-circuit reprogrammable nonvolatile memory
3. Solid state disk

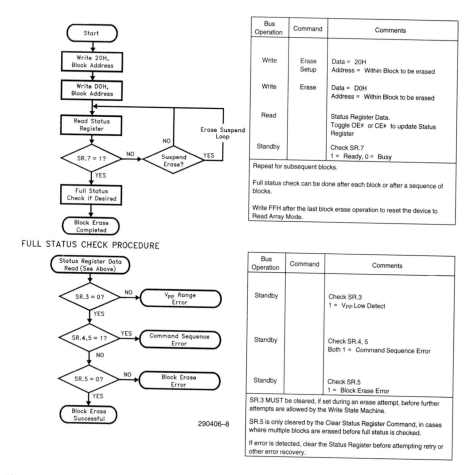

FULL STATUS CHECK PROCEDURE

Figure 11.5-5   28F001BX block erase algorithm flowchart.

As a ROM replacement, either first or second generation Flash can be used. When used for this purpose, a device can be initially programmed and reprogrammed by removing it from the system's printed circuit board and placing it in a device programmer. In this case, you do not need to concern yourself with erase/program algorithms; the device programmer provides them.

In applications that require in-circuit reprogrammability, you must provide the erase/program algorithms that the 80C188EB executes to erase and program a device.

One common use of in-circuit reprogrammability is to allow your program to be easily updated during development or in the field. A boot program, permanently stored in the Flash memory's boot block, can bring up the system, download code from a serial port, and program this code into other blocks of the Flash memory IC. The boot block must include the minimum code necessary to initialize the system and to reload code if your application code is inadvertently lost during an update, due to a power failure or other problem. Since a Flash memory cannot be read while it is being erased or programmed, the

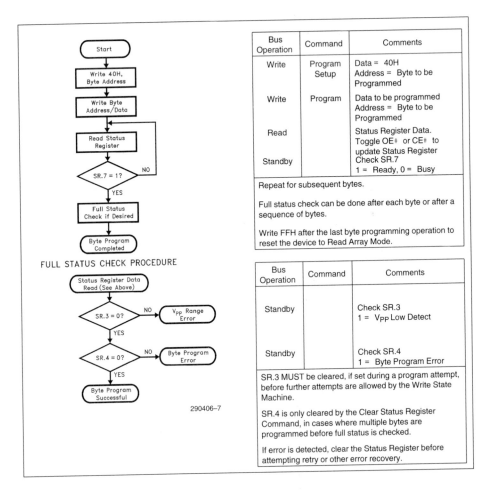

Figure 11.5-6   28F001BX byte programming algorithm flowchart. (Courtesy of Intel Corp.)

code for erase and reprogramming cannot be executed from the Flash memory being erased or programmed. This problem is solved by copying the erase and program algorithms to RAM and executing them from RAM.

Flash memories optimized for solid state disk replacement are available. These devices typically have blocks of equal size and are called **symmetrically blocked.** Using Flash memory as a solid state disk entails considerations that go beyond the scope of this text. However, one of these considerations, **wear leveling**, will be mentioned here.

Since Flash must be erased before it can be rewritten and the number of erase/program cycles is limited, the useful life of the Flash is extended by software that accomplishes wear leveling. Wear leveling replaces old data with new data by writing the new data into an erased portion of a block and leaving the old data intact, until all (or most) of the erased locations in a block have been used. Until this situation occurs, the block is not erased. This reduces the number of times the block is erased and extends the life of the Flash memory.

Because of their short erase times and ability to be programmed in-system, Flash memory is expected to largely displace EPROMs in the future.

11.6   Memory Subsystem Design

In its simplest form, an 80C188EB memory subsystem might consist of only one ROM IC and one RAM IC. In general, a single ROM IC with the necessary depth and width may not be available. The same is true for RAM. In such cases, several memory ICs are interconnected to provide the required depth and width. Another situation where multiple ROM or RAM ICs may be needed is when different types of ROM or RAM are required in a system. For example, both EPROM and Flash memory, or both SRAM and low-power CMOS SRAM might be needed.

To increase the depth, beyond that provided by a single memory IC, corresponding data lines of two or more memory ICs are interconnected and their chip selects are separately controlled. During a bus cycle, external address decoding logic decodes the higher order address bus bits to select the appropriate memory IC. The term external, when used to describe a memory address decoder, means the decoder is external to the memory IC. In Fig. 11.6-1, two 32K × 8 memory ICs are interconnected to provide a 64K × 8 memory appropriate for use in a system with an 8-bit data bus.

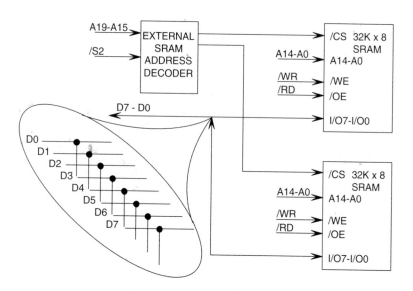

Figure 11.6-1   64K × 8 memory from two 32K × 8 memory ICs.

The external address decoder decodes the higher-order address bits to assert only one memory IC's chip select during a bus cycle. For a write operation, the /WR strobe appears at the /WE inputs of both memory ICs, but only the selected IC is written. For a read operation, the /RD strobe appears at the /OE inputs of both memory ICs, but only the selected memory IC's three-state output buffers are enabled. Three-state outputs on memory ICs allow data from multiple memory ICs to be multiplexed to one set of data lines.

Width is increased by placing the outputs of two or more memory ICs in cascade and connecting their chip-select inputs together. For example, two 32K × 8 ICs can be arranged to provide a 32K × 16 memory appropriate for a system with a 16-bit data bus. As shown in Fig. 11.6-2, the IC on the right provides bits D7–D0 and the IC on the left provides bits D15–D8. Connecting the chip-select inputs together allows sixteen bits of data to be simultaneously read from or written to the pair of memory ICs.

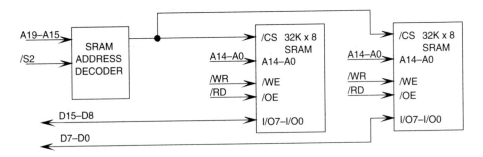

Figure 11.6-2   Word length expansion, combining two 32K × 8 memory ICs to create a 32K × 16 memory.

The steps in designing a memory subsystem are:

1. Estimate the total amount of ROM and RAM required.
2. Determine the address boundaries for the total ROM and RAM and draw an initial memory map.
3. Select the memory ICs to be used.
4. Determine the arrangement of the memory ICs that provide the required word length and number of words. Draw a detailed memory map showing all memory IC address boundaries.
5. Determine the programming of the 80C188EB's Chip-Select Unit or design external address decoding logic to generate the chip selects.
6. Include buffering if necessary.
7. Determine the required speed of the memory ICs.

Sections 11.7 and 11.8 focus on steps 2 and 4 for the 80C188EB and 80C186EB, respectively. Step 5 is covered in Sections 11.9 through 11.12. The results of steps 1 and 3, which are application dependent, are assumed as the starting point in these discussions. Step 6 was discussed in Chapter 10 and step 7 is discussed in Chapter 13.

Steps 4 and 5 differ for 80C188EB and 80C186EB memory subsystems. The logical representation of the memory address space for both subsystems is a single bank of 1,048,576 byte locations with addresses 00000H through FFFFFH (Fig. 11.6-3). For an 80C188EB system, with its 8 bit data bus, the physical implementation is structured the same as the logical representation. However, for an 80C186EB system, with its 16-bit data bus, the physical implementation consists of two **memory banks** each of 524,288 bytes. One bank, the even bank, is connected to the low byte of the data bus. The other bank, the odd bank, is connected to the high byte.

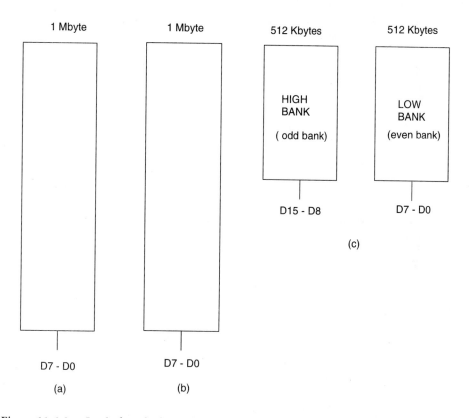

Figure 11.6-3   Logical and physical memory address spaces: (a) logical representation that applies to both the 80C188EB and 80C186EB; (b) 80C188EB physcial implementation; (c) 80C186EB physical implementation.

The data bus width differences between the 80C188EB and 80C186EB impact the arrangement of memory ICs and the design of the address decoding logic. These considerations are presented in the following two sections. 80C188EB memory subsystem design is more straightforward, and is examined first.

11.7   80C188EB Memory Subsystem Design

Consider the design of an 80C188EB system that requires 32K × 8 of SRAM and 16K × 8 of EPROM. The memory is to be constructed using a single 32K × 8 SRAM IC and a single 16K × 8 EPROM IC. Thus, no word-length expansion is required. The SRAM must begin at address 00000H and the EPROM must end at address FFFFFH. The remaining memory address space is unpopulated. The requirement of starting RAM at address 00000H and ending ROM at address FFFFFH holds for most 80C188EB embedded systems that have only one RAM IC and one ROM IC. The requirement on the placement of the ROM is because the reset address must be in ROM. The requirement on the placement of RAM has to do with the system's interrupt vector table, and will be covered later.

The **address bit map** in Fig. 11.7-1 is an expanded memory map. The address bit map shows which address bits are decoded by the memory ICs' internal decoders and which must be decoded by the 80C188EB's Chip-Select Unit or an external address decoder.

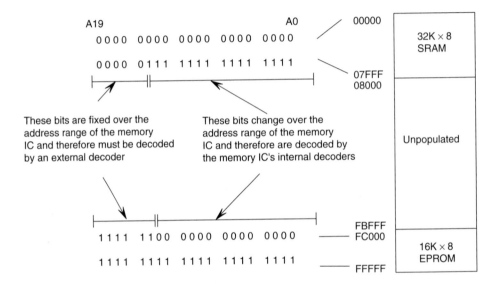

Figure 11.7-1   Address bit map and memory map.

A block diagram of the memory subsystem is shown in Fig. 11.7-2. For conceptual simplicity, two separate address decoders are shown. One selects the SRAM whenever the 80C188EB generates a memory address in the range 00000H through 07FFFH. It does this by asserting the SRAM's chip select only when bits A19–A15 equal 00000B and /S2 is 1. Recall that /S2 is 1 for all bus cycles that reference memory, as opposed to I/O. The inclusion of /S2 as a decoder input conditions the selection of the SRAM to bus cycles that reference the memory space.

The SRAM address decoder is a combinational circuit with six inputs and a single active low output. Methods for implementing external address decoders are presented in Sections 11.9 through 11.12. The SRAM's internal decoders decode the lower-order address bus bits, A14–A0, to select a single location within the SRAM.

In this example, the decoder that generates the chip enable for the EPROM must decode address bits A19–A14 and assert its active-low output when A19–A14 equals 111111B and /S2 is 1.

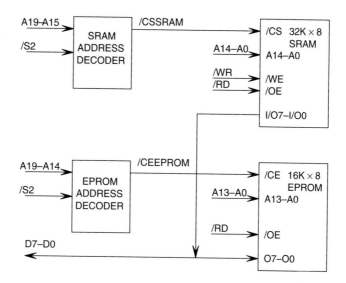

Figure 11.7-2   Memory subsystem using a 32K × 8 SRAM and a 16K × 8 EPROM.

Outputs from the SRAM and EPROM are multiplexed onto the data bus, D7–D0. Only while the SRAM is selected and its /OE input is asserted by a /RD strobe, does the SRAM drive the data bus. Conversely, only while the EPROM is selected and the /RD strobe is asserted, does the EPROM drive the data bus. To avoid bus contention, proper design of the external address decoding must preclude both the SRAM and EPROM from being selected simultaneously.

The propagation delay of the external address decoder adds to the delay of the memory IC to create the delay of the memory subsystem. Thus, it is desirable to design external address decoding logic so its delay is minimal.

11.8   80C186EB Memory Subsystem Design

An 80C186EB memory subsystem consists of an even and an odd memory bank (Fig. 11.6-3(c)). Address bus bit A0 along with /S2 are used by an external decoder to select the even memory bank (A0 = 0). As a result, all bytes in this bank have even addresses. **Byte high enable (/BHE = 0)** along with /S2 are used by the address decoder to select the odd bank. All bytes in this bank have odd addresses (A0 = 1). BHE is pin 7 of an 80C186EB in a PLCC package.

Since A0 from the address bus is used in the selection of the low bank, A1 from the address bus is connected to the A0 input pin of the memory ICs in both the low and high banks (Fig. 11.8-1). A2 of the address bus is connected to the A1 input pin of the memory ICs and so on. Any higher-order address bits not directly connected to the memory ICs are included as inputs to the external address decoders.

When an even byte is accessed, /BHE is 1 and A0 is 0 (Fig. 11.8-1(a)). Under these conditions, only the even bank is selected. The selected even byte is transferred on the low

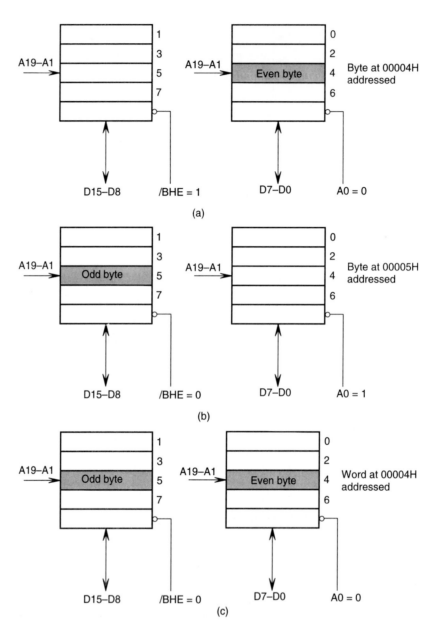

Figure 11.8-1   Data transfers to an 80C186EB memory: (a) byte transfer of an even byte;
(b) byte transfer of an odd byte. (c) transfer of an aligned word in a single
bus cycle. (d) transfer of the low byte of an unaligned word, first of two
bus cycles required; (e) byte transfer of the high byte of the unaligned
word.

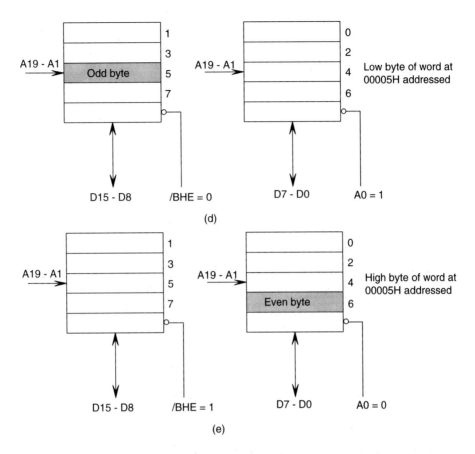

Figure 11.8-1   Data transfers to an 80C186EB memory: (a) byte transfer of an even byte; (b) byte transfer of an odd byte. (c) transfer of an aligned word in a single bus cycle. (d) transfer of the low byte of an unaligned word, first of two bus cycles required; (e) byte transfer of the high byte of the unaligned word. (Continued.)

byte of the system data bus, D7–D0. If the access were a read and the destination were the high byte of a register, the BIU would automatically redirect the byte internally from the low byte of the system data bus to the high byte of the 80C186EB's internal data bus. If the access were a write and the source were the high byte of a register, the BIU automatically redirects the byte to the low byte of the system data bus.

When an odd byte is accessed, /BHE is 0 and A0 is 1 (Fig. 11.8-1(b)). Only the odd bank is selected. The odd byte is transferred on the high byte of the system data bus, D15–D8. The BIU automatically redirects transfers from the high byte of the system bus to the low byte of the 80C186EB's internal bus, and vice versa, when necessary.

When a word that starts at an even address, an **aligned word**, is accessed, address bus bits A19–A1 select the byte within each bank (Fig. 11.8-1(c)). Both A0 and /BHE are 0, and both banks are simultaneously enabled. The aligned word is transferred in a single bus cycle.

Accessing a word that starts at an odd address, an **unaligned word**, (least significant byte at an odd address) requires two bus cycles. In the first bus cycle, the least significant byte is transferred on the high byte of the data bus (Fig. 11.8-1(d)). The second bus cycle transfers the most significant byte over the low byte of the data bus (Fig. 11.8-1(e)).

When object code is placed into the byte-wide ROMs for an 80C186EB memory subsystem, the even bytes of the object code must be programmed into ROMs that will be placed in the even bank and the odd bytes must be programmed into ROMs that will be placed in the odd bank. Usually, the object hex translator utility is used to separate the even and odd bytes of the object code into two separate hex files. Alternatively, the device programmer has the capability to program only the even or odd bytes of a hex file into an EPROM or Flash memory.

11.9   Memory Address Decoding

This section introduces several methods of address decoding. Specific techniques for implementing external memory address decoders are presented in the three sections that follow.

During a Read Memory or Write Memory bus cycle, the 80C188EB generates a 20-bit address to identify the specific memory location to be accessed. The memory subsystem must decode this address to select the memory location that is to respond to the bus cycle's /RD or /WR signal.

Lower-order address bits connect directly to a memory IC and are decoded by the memory IC's internal decoders. Higher-order address bits and /S2 are decoded by an external decoder. The external decoder's outputs provide the chip-select signals to each memory IC's /CS input. During a Read Memory or Write Memory bus cycle, only one of the decoder's outputs is asserted. Only the memory IC selected by the asserted decoder output can respond to /RD or /WR. To prevent bus contention, all other memory ICs are deselected during the bus cycle. In selecting a memory IC based on a particular higher-order address bit value, the external address decoder effectively determines the position of the IC in the memory address space.

11.9.1   Exhaustive Decoding

Address decoding can be exhaustive or nonexhaustive. With **exhaustive decoding**, all address bus bits that are not connected directly to a specific memory IC are decoded by the external address decoder that selects that memory IC. Exhaustive decoding creates a one-to-one mapping; each location in a memory IC has a single unique address. The term **fully-decoded** is also used to mean exhaustively decoded.

Exhaustive decoding for an 80C188EB memory subsystem requires that all 20 address bits and /S2 be decoded. For a memory IC with 2^m words, the m least significant bits of the address bus are decoded by the memory IC's internal decoders. The remaining j (where $j = 20 - m$) most significant address bits must be decoded by either the 80C188EB's

Chip Select Unit or by a discrete external address decoder. For this conceptual discussion, a discrete external address decoder is used.

The external address decoder's output provides the signal to the memory IC's chip-select, or chip-enable input. The external decoder decodes the j most significant address bits and /S2. The decoder's output is asserted over a range of 2^m addresses. The size of the address range over which a decoder's output is asserted is called its **granularity**.

As shown in Fig. 11.9-1, the most significant j address bits, decoded by the external address decoder, determine the starting position of the memory IC's block of 2^m locations in the memory address space. This is equivalent to specifying the range of addresses in the address space assigned to the memory IC. These j most significant address bits are referred to as the **block address**. Over the range of the 2^m addresses in the block, the j block address bits remain fixed and the least significant m address bits range from 0 to $2^m - 1$ (from m bits all 0s through m bits all 1s).

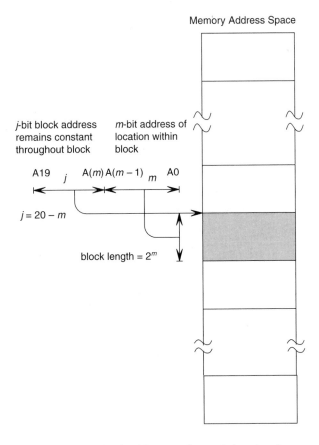

Figure 11.9-1   Effect of a j-bit block address in determining the placement of a block of 2^m locations, where $j + m = 20$.

The preceding discussion also applies to 80C186EB memory subsystems. However, to obtain 2^m bytes of memory in an 80C186EB memory subsystem, two 2^{m-1} byte memory ICs are used, one for the even bank and one for the odd bank. Address bit A0 is used as an input to the address decoder for even bank selection. /BHE is used as an input to the address decoder for odd bank selection. The least significant $m - 1$ address bits are connected directly to the two memory ICs' address inputs.

11.9.2   Non-exhaustive Decoding

With **nonexhaustive decoding** or **partial decoding**, some higher-order or block address bits are not decoded by the external address decoder. This simplifies the external address decoding logic. However, not decoding all the block address bits leads to a many-to-one mapping. Many different addresses are assigned to each location in a memory IC. If b block address bits are not decoded, each location in the memory IC will respond to 2^b different addresses. This may limit future expansion of a memory subsystem, since this partial decoding must be revised for any change in the memory map.

Two approaches to generating chip-select signals are discussed in the next three sections. The first section uses only the 80C188EB's integrated Chip-Select Unit. This approach is usually sufficient for small single board systems. The second section uses SSI and MSI devices, and the third section uses programmable logic devices. Discrete external address decoders, SSI, MSI, or PLD, are typically required in standard bus multiboard systems where the bus makes no provision to include chip-select signals and the CPU and memory subsystems are on separate boards.

11.10   The 80C188EB's Chip-Select Unit

The 80C188EB's Chip-Select Unit is the first of its integrated peripherals that we consider in detail. The 80C188EB's **Chip-Select Unit** (**CSU**) provides 10 programmable chip selects (Fig. 10.2-1). Two of these, the upper chip select, /UCS, and the lower chip select, /LCS, are dedicated pins. The other eight general chip selects, GCS7-GCS0, are multiplexed with the eight output bits of Port 1, on pins P1.7/GCS7-P1.0/GCS0. Each of these eight pins can be individually configured as either a chip select or an output port bit.

When an 80C188EB is reset, pins P1.7/GCS7-P1.0/GCS0 are automatically configured as general purpose chip selects. However, of the ten chip selects, only chip select /UCS is enabled. After reset /UCS is asserted for any address in the range from FFC00H to FFFFFH. This 1 Kbyte range allows a ROM that contains the bootstrap instruction to be selected immediately after power on. The bootstrap instruction is then fetched. The bootstrap instruction jumps to an initialization sequence, also in the active address range. You must write the initialization sequence to program all the chip selects needed by your application to their appropriate configurations and to enable them.

The ROM that contains the bootstrap instruction is normally larger than 1 Kbyte. Therefore, one of the steps in the initialization sequence is to program the starting address of the /UCS to a lower value to correspond to the larger ROM.

Each CSU chip select is independent and its operational characteristics are defined by its own **Chip-Select Start Register** and **Chip-Select Stop Register** (Figs. 11.10-1 and 11.10-2). These twenty registers are in the PCB at offsets 0080H through 00A6H (Fig. 10.9-1). For example, the Chip-Select Start Register for /UCS has offset 00A4H and its Stop Register has offset 00A6H.

Register Name:	Chip-Select Start Register
Register Mnemonic:	UCSST, LCSST, GCSxST (x=0-7)
Register Function:	Defines chip-select start address and number of bus wait states.

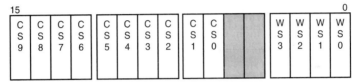

A1163-0A

Bit Mnemonic	Bit Name	Reset State	Function
CS9:0	Start Address	3FFH	Defines the starting (base) address for the chip-select. CS9:0 are compared with the A19:10 (memory bus cycles) or A15:6 (I/O bus cycles) address bits. An equal to or greater than result enables the chip-select.
WS3:0	Wait State Value	0FH	WS3:0 define the minimum number of wait states inserted into the bus cycle. A zero value means no wait states. Additional wait states can be inserted into the bus cycle using bus ready.

NOTE: Reserved register bits are shown with gray shading. Reserved bits must be written to a logic zero to ensure compatibility with future Intel products.

Figure 11.10-1   Chip-Select Start Register. (Courtesy of Intel Corp.)

A Chip-Select Start Register defines the starting address of the address range over which the chip select will be asserted. This register also specifies the number of WAIT states to be automatically inserted into bus cycles that access locations in the defined address range. The Chip-Select Stop Register defines the ending address for the chip select's address range. This register also specifies the chip selects's READY, ignore stop address, memory/IO, and enable options.

When an 80C188EB generates an address in the address range of an enabled chip select, the chip select output is asserted simultaneously with the appearance of the address on the 80C188EB's address bus. The 80C188EB's decision to assert the chip select is made just after the EU calculates the effective address, prior to the start of the bus cycle.

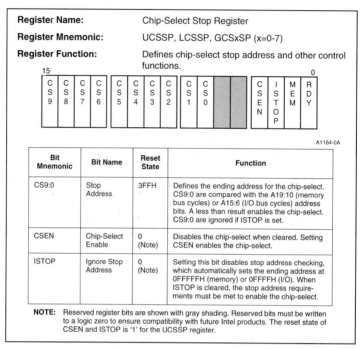

Register Name:	Chip-Select Stop Register
Register Mnemonic:	UCSSP, LCSSP, GCSxSP (x=0-7)
Register Function:	Defines chip-select stop address and other control functions.

A1164-0A

Bit Mnemonic	Bit Name	Reset State	Function
CS9:0	Stop Address	3FFH	Defines the ending address for the chip-select. CS9:0 are compared with the A19:10 (memory bus cycles) or A15:6 (I/O bus cycles) address bits. A less than result enables the chip-select. CS9:0 are ignored if ISTOP is set.
CSEN	Chip-Select Enable	0 (Note)	Disables the chip-select when cleared. Setting CSEN enables the chip-select.
ISTOP	Ignore Stop Address	0 (Note)	Setting this bit disables stop address checking, which automatically sets the ending address at 0FFFFFH (memory) or 0FFFFH (I/O). When ISTOP is cleared, the stop address requirements must be met to enable the chip-select.

NOTE: Reserved register bits are shown with gray shading. Reserved bits must be written to a logic zero to ensure compatibility with future Intel products. The reset state of CSEN and ISTOP is '1' for the UCSSP register.

Register Name:	Chip-Select Stop Register
Register Mnemonic:	UCSSP, LCSSP, GCSxSP (x=0-7)
Register Function:	Defines chip-select stop address and other control functions.

A1164-0A

Bit Mnemonic	Bit Name	Reset State	Function
MEM	Bus Cycle Selector	1	When MEM is set, the chip-select goes active for memory bus cycles. Clearing MEM activates the chip-select for I/O bus cycles. MEM defines which address bits are used by the start and stop address comparators. When MEM is cleared, address bits A15:6 are routed to the comparators. When MEM is set, address bits A19:10 are routed to the comparators.
RDY	Bus Ready Enable	1	Setting RDY requires that bus ready be active to complete a bus cycle. Bus ready is ignored when RDY is cleared. RDY must be set to extend wait states beyond the number determined by WS3:0.

NOTE: Reserved register bits are shown with gray shading. Reserved bits must be written to a logic zero to ensure compatibility with future Intel products. The reset state of CSEN and ISTOP is '1' for the UCSSP register.

Figure 11.10-2   Chip-Select Stop Register. (Courtesy of Intel Corp.)

11.10.1 Chip-Select Start Register

When a chip select is configured for the memory address space, ten bits, CS9–CS0, in the 16-bit Chip-Select Start Register specify the most significant 10 bits, A19–A10, of the starting physical address (Fig. 11.10-1). The remaining ten address bits are all 0s by default.

Since the Chip-Select Start and Stop Registers only allow the most significant 10 bits of an address to be specified, address ranges for memory chip selects can only be multiples of 1Kbyte. Correspondingly, the smallest possible address range is 1 Kbyte, in other words, a granularity of 1K. Since memory ICs come in multiples of 1 Kbyte, the active range for a chip select can be exactly matched to the number of bytes in the memory IC it selects.

Each chip select has WAIT state logic. Four bits in the Start Register indicate the number of WAIT states (0 to 15) to be inserted for all accesses in the chip select's address range.

11.10.2 Chip-Select Stop Register

The Chip-Select Stop Register has ten bits to specify the stop or ending address for the chip select's range. The actual value of the last address in the chip select's range is one less than the stop address value specified (Fig. 11.10-2). The address range defined by a chip select's Start Register and Stop Register is called the **active address range** for the chip select. The generation of any address in the active range of an enabled chip select causes the chip select to be active (asserted).

Four other bits in the Stop Register are used in configuring the chip select. The Chip-Select Enable bit (CSEN) when set, enables the chip select. If a chip select is not enabled, the logic level at the chip select pin is always 1.

When set, the Ignore Stop Address bit (ISTOP) causes the address specified in the Stop Register to be ignored. This makes the stop address for memory FFFFFH.

The Memory select bit (MEM) when set, causes the chip select to be asserted only for memory addresses in the specified address range. Otherwise, the chip select is asserted only for I/O addresses in the address range. Thus, MEM, in effect, specifies what /S2's value must be for the chip select to be asserted. When MEM is set, the chip select is referred to as a **memory-mapped chip select**. Recall that the bus cycles that reference memory are Instruction Prefetch, Read Memory, and Write Memory.

When MEM is 0, the chip select is an **I/O-mapped chip select**. The bus cycles that reference I/O are: Read I/O and Write I/O. The chip select outputs are never active for Interrupt Acknowledge or Halt bus cycles, or for accesses to the PCB.

When set, the external READY input bit (RDY) of the Chip-Select Stop Register causes the 80C188EB to respond to its external READY input, in addition to the programmed number of WAIT states. When an access is made within the chip select's address range, the programmed number of WAIT states is first inserted. After these WAIT states have elapsed, the READY input is checked. If READY is unasserted, additional WAIT states are inserted until READY is asserted.

When the 80C188EB is reset, /UCS is automatically programmed for 15 WAIT states. This results in 15 WAIT states being inserted into each bus cycle during the fetch of the bootstrap instruction and all other instructions and data within the /UCS address range.

This situation will persist until /UCS is reprogrammed. Using the CSU for WAIT state generation is discussed further in Section 13.3.

11.10.3 Programming the CSU

As an example, consider using the CSU to generate the chip selects for the memory subsystem of Fig. 11.7-1. Assume that /LCS selects the SRAM and /UCS selects the EPROM, and that the following equates have been defined:

```
LCSST          equ 0ffa0h          ;LCS start register address in PCB
LCSSP          equ 0ffa2h          ;LCS stop register address in PCB
UCSST          equ 0ffa4h          ;UCS start register address in PCB
UCSSP          equ 0ffa6h          ;UCS stop register address in PCB
```

The following instruction sequence configures the chip selects:

```
mov     dx,LCSST        ;DX <- Lower Chip-Select Start register
mov     ax,0000h        ;start address 00000h, 0 WAIT states
out     dx,al
mov     dx,LCSSP        ;DX <- Lower Chip-Select Stop register
mov     ax,080ah        ;stop address 07fffh (08000H-1)
out     dx,al           ;CSEN=1, ISTOP=0, MEM=1, RDY=0

mov     dx,UCSST        ;DX <- Upper Chip-Select Start register
mov     ax,0fc00h       ;start address fc000h, 0 WAIT states
out     dx,al
mov     dx,UCSSP        ;DX <- Upper Chip-Select Stop register
mov     ax,0ffCeh       ;stop address fffffh
out     dx,al
```

The placement of these instructions in memory requires careful consideration. Your program normally starts at the beginning of the ROM. Assume the first instruction in your program has the label start. The bootstrap instruction you would normally have automatically inserted by the locator jumps to start. However, if your ROM is greater than 1 Kbyte, then when the bootstrap instruction is executed, the system fails. This failure results from the 80C188EB trying to fetch the next instruction from an address outside the range for /UCS. /UCS is not asserted, so the ROM is not selected. When the 80C188EB generates /RD, no external device drives the data bus and the 80C188EB latches invalid data.

One technique for handling this problem is to place the instructions to reprogram /UCS's start address in memory, starting at the restart location, FFFF0H, and follow these instructions with the bootstrap instruction. The instruction sequence that you want at FFFF0H is:

```
mov     dx,UCSST        ;DX <- Upper Chip-Select Start Register
mov     ax,0fc02h       ;start address fc000h, 2 WAIT states
out     dx,al
jmp     far ptr start
```

This instruction sequence is only 12 bytes long, so it fits in the 16 memory locations from FFFF0H to FFFFFH. The only thing left is to get the locator to place these instructions starting at address FFFF0H.

There are two ways to resolve this problem. First, if the ROM is no larger than 64 Kbytes and you have a single module program, the instructions to reprogram /UCS can be placed starting at FFFF0H by placing these instructions at the end of your source file and preceding them with an ORG directive. The **ORG** directive allows you to control the assembler's location counter within the current segment. ORG has the form:

ORG expression

The expression associated with the ORG specifies the new value of the assembler's location counter. This value is the number of bytes from the beginning of the current segment to where the first instruction needs to be placed to end up at location FFFF0H. In this example, expression is equal to FFFF0H–FC000H or 03FF0H.

The second, and more common, approach will handle ROM of any size. Instead of using the ORG directive, a different code segment with a different class name is created. You use the locator's class directive to place this segment at FFFF0H. The example of this technique that follows involves multiple modules, which are not discussed in detail until Chapter 20. However, the following instructions give you an idea of how this is done. A separate file is created that defines a different code segment. In this example, the additional code segment's name is pwron. In this code segment, the Upper Chip-Select Start register is reprogrammed to the address that corresponds to the start of the EPROM. The instructions in the pwron segment are only 12 bytes long. They can fit from FFFF0H to the end of the memory space, FFFFFH. The last instruction is a FAR jump to the start of the program. At the start of the program, /LCS and any other chip selects are initialized.

```
name     pwron_reset


code     segment         public          'ROM'
EXTRN    start:far
code     ends


assume               cs:pwron
pwron                segment         public          'PWRON'
pwron_reset:
         mov     dx,UCSST         ;DX <- Upper Chip-Select Start Register
         mov     ax,0fc02h        ;start address fc000h, 2 WAIT states
         out     dx,al
         jmp     far ptr start
pwron    ends
         end     pwron_reset
```

The locator directive that causes the locator to automatically place a bootstrap instruction at FFFF0H must be removed from the locator configuration file. If not, the locator will attempt to write the bootstrap instruction over the instruction sequence you have placed at FFFF0H.

The correct sequence for programming a nonenabled chip select is Start Register first, followed by the Stop Register. This procedure was followed in the preceding example for /LCS. If a chip select that is already enabled is being reprogrammed to a new address range, generally the safest approach is to disable the chip select before reprogramming, to avoid problems that might occur from briefly having an unintended active address range. However, /UCS cannot be disabled for reprogramming because the instructions are being fetched from the ROM selected by /UCS. For this example, no problem occurs from reprogramming /UCS because only the start address is changed.

If additional SRAMs or EPROMs were required, general chip-select outputs could be programmed to select them. If the CSU's chip selects are used for selecting memory or I/O devices in a system, you must program the appropriate Chip-Select Start and Stop registers. This should be the first thing done after the execution of the bootstrap instruction.

11.11   SSI and MSI External Address Decoders

The most efficient way to generate memory chip-select signals is to use the CSU. The techniques discussed in this and the next section are appropriate when the number of chip-select signals needed in a system exceeds the number available from the CSU. These techniques are also appropriate in multi-board systems with standard buses where the bus does not include chip-select signals.

In its simplest form, an external address decoder is simply a combinational circuit with j address inputs and a single chip-select output. An external memory address decoder must also include /S2 as an input if the same addresses are used in both the memory and I/O address spaces. In practice, a single address decoder circuit is typically designed to generate chip selects for several memory ICs. Such implementations are simply multiple-input, multiple-output combinational circuits.

Each chip-select function, and its associated decoder output, can be defined by a Boolean sum-of-products expression consisting of a single product term. The expressions for the chip selects in the memory of Fig. 11.7-1 are:

$$CS = /A19 * /A18 * /A17 * /A16 * /A15 * /S2$$

$$CE = A19 * A18 * A17 * A16 * A15 * A14 * /S2$$

These equations are written for active-high signals, rather than the active-low signals required at the memory ICs' chip select inputs. Because most discrete ICs used for address decoding have active-low outputs, they inherently generate the complements of the functions they implement. Therefore, the equations are written for the complements of the signals desired.

Any method for implementing a combinational circuit with SSI gates can be used to design an external address decoder. However, for exhaustive decoding using SSI gates typically requires a number of ICs.

MSI 1-out-of-n decoders can generate multiple chip-select outputs from a single IC. These outputs select equal size contiguous blocks in the memory address space. In Fig. 11.11-1, two 74HC138 1-out-of-8 decoders are used to generate the chip selects /CS and /CE. The block sizes for these two chip selects differ. The 3-bit binary input code at the C,

B, and A inputs of each 74HC138 determines which of its active-low outputs is asserted, when the conditions at the decoder's enable inputs are met.

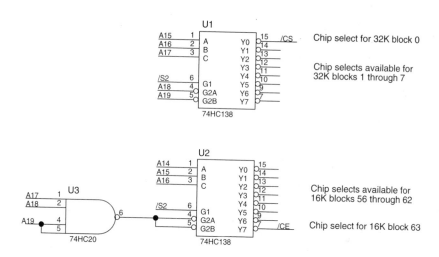

Figure 11.11-1   Address decoding using two 1-out-of-8 decoders.

If A19,A18,/S2 = 001B, decoder U1 is enabled, and if A17,A16,A15 = 000B, then output /Y0, which provides /CS, is asserted. Each output of decoder U1 corresponds to a block of 32K addresses. Output /Y0 is asserted for any address in the first 32K of the address space, 32K block 0. Output /Y1 is asserted for any address in the second 32K of the address space, 32K block 1, and so on.

Decoder U2 provides chip selects corresponding to eight 16K blocks. The last of these eight blocks is the last 16K block in the address space; therefore /CE is obtained from output /Y7. In an application where provisions for memory expansion are desired, use of 1-out-of-n decoders provides additional chip selects for expansion memory of the same block size.

11.11.1 Nonexhaustive Address Decoding

Using nonexhaustive decoding, chip selects for the 32K × 8 SRAM and 16K × 8 EPROM can be generated by decoding only one address bit, A19, and /S2, as shown in Fig. 11.11-2. This is possible because there are only two memory ICs in the system. By decoding A19, one IC is mapped to the lower 512K and the other to the upper 512K of the memory address space. A19 must be 0 and /S2 must be 1 in order to select the SRAM. The SRAM is selected for any address with A19 = 0, that is, any address in the lower 512K. A18–A15 (four address bits) are ignored in selecting the SRAM; therefore 16 addresses are mapped to each location in the SRAM. The 16 addresses mapped to a single location correspond to all the addresses that can be created when address bits A18–A15 are treated as "don't cares."

The multiple mapping of addresses that results from nonexhaustive decoding is called **foldback**. In Fig. 11.11-2, the single 32K × 8 SRAM IC acts like it is sixteen contigu-

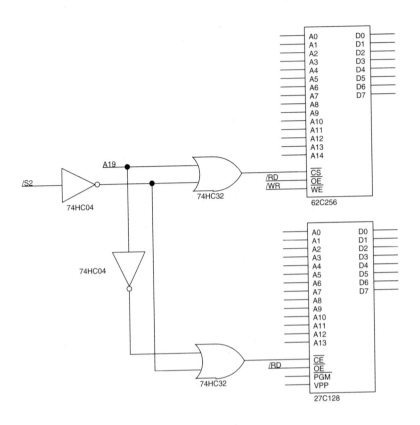

Figure 11.11-2   Nonexhaustive address decoding.

ous 32K × 8 memory ICs, filling the entire lower 512K. It appears this way because if any logical address in the lower 512K is written then read, the data that was written is read back. In this example, if no more than 32K × 8 of SRAM is required and the program uses only addresses in the same 32K block, there is no problem. However, if the program treats two logically different addresses that map to the same physical IC locations as distinct, errors will occur in the program's execution. This is the case because, in reality, the same memory location is being accessed.

11.12   PLD External Address Decoders

An efficient and flexible way to implement an external address decoder is to use a **programmable logic device** (**PLD**). A PLD is an IC that can be programmed by the user to perform logic functions. Advantages of using PLDs to replace discrete logic in systems include: reduction in the number of ICs required, increased reliability, and reduced cost. Also, since PLDs are user programmable, modification of their functions in completed designs can often be accomplished by reprogramming the PLD, without requiring printed circuit board modification.

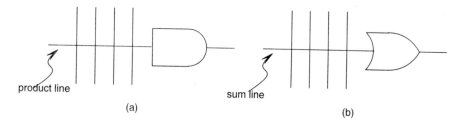

Figure 11.12-1   PLD gate input notation: (a) AND gate product line; (b) OR gate sum line.

A concise notation is used to represent inputs to the AND and OR gates available in PLDs (Fig. 11.12-1). Gates in PLDs have a large number of inputs. Their representation in logic diagrams by conventional symbols would be cumbersome. Instead, inputs to a gate are drawn as a single line. An AND gate's symbolic single input line is called its **product line**. Lines crossing the product line represent possible input connections to the gate. For an OR gate, the symbolic single line that represents its inputs is called its **sum line**.

The base architecture of simple PLDs consists of an AND gate array followed by an OR gate array (Fig. 11.12-2). External inputs are buffered, providing the normal and complement form of each. These input signals, the columns in the AND array, intersect the rows of AND gate product lines. The open circles at the intersections of the columns and rows indicate programmable connections.

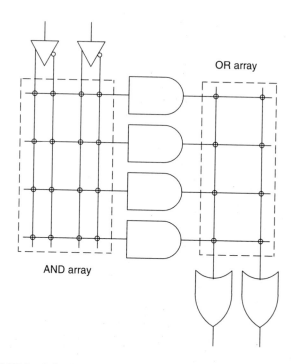

Figure 11.12-2   PLD basic logic structure, AND array followed by an OR array.

The outputs of the AND gates provide the rows of the OR array. The columns of the OR array are the OR gates' sum lines. Again, the open circles at the intersections of rows and columns indicate programmable connections. The outputs of the OR gates provide the PLD's outputs. This logic structure allows the direct implementation of combinational functions in a sum-of-products form. A PLD output can implement any Boolean function that "fits." The number of inputs to the AND gates limits the number of variables in any product term of the Boolean function. The number of AND gates limits the number of product terms that can be summed by the function.

A variety of types of PLDs exists and within each type there is a number of architectural variations. One basic difference in the types of PLDs is whether both the AND array and the OR array are programmable. For a **Programmable Logic Array** (**PLA**) both are programmable. For a **Programmable Array Logic** (**PAL**) the AND array is programmable and the OR array is fixed. For a Programmable Read Only Memory (PROM), a type of PLD, the AND array is fixed and the OR array is programmable.

11.12.1 Programmable Array Logic (PAL)

The simplest type of PLD is a PAL. PALs find wide application as address decoders in embedded systems.

At the detailed conceptual level, programming a PAL involves determining which intersections between the input lines and product lines need to be connected to implement the desired function.

In most PALs, all the connections in an unprogrammed device are made. The process of programming a device actually involves breaking unwanted connections. If connections for both the normal and complement forms of the same external input are left intact, the output of the associated AND gate is always 0. If all the connections to a product line are broken, the output of the AND gate is always 1. An X is used on a PLD logic diagram to indicate a programmed connection.

PALs differ in their number of inputs, number of AND gates, number of OR gates, and number of OR gate inputs. Early PALs have a simple fixed logic configuration following each OR gate output. In combinational PALs with asserted-high outputs, the OR gate outputs are connected directly to the PAL's output pins. In combinational asserted-low PALs, each OR gate's output is inverted and then connected to the output pin. A **registered PAL** uses the OR gate outputs as inputs to a register and the register's outputs are connected to the PAL's output pins. PALs with registered outputs include a clock input for the register.

One step in designing with PALs is selecting, from the many available devices, a PAL that efficiently provides the necessary logic capability for the functions to be implemented. This process is simplified by the use of PALs with programmable output structures called **macrocells**. The OR gate outputs in these PALs are input to a macrocell, and the macrocell's outputs provide the PAL's outputs. The macrocell is itself a programmable logic structure that allows configuration of an output as combinational or registered and as asserted high or asserted low. In addition, the macrocell's "output" pin can be configured as an input pin.

11.12.2 PALCE22V10

An example of a versatile PAL is the PALCE22V10. A block diagram of this device is shown in Fig. 11.12-3. The PALCE22V10 has 12 dedicated inputs, shown at the top of the diagram and 10 I/O connections shown at the bottom. The I/O connections can be configured as either inputs or outputs.

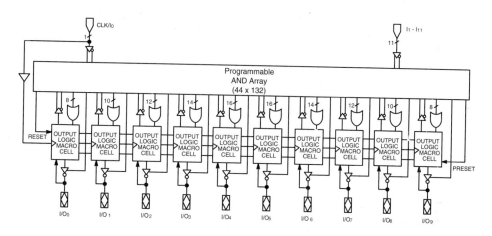

Figure 11.12-3 Block diagram of PALCE22V10. (Copyright © 1998, Vantis. Reprinted with permission of copyright owner. All other rights reserved.)

The PALCE22V10's logic diagram is shown in Fig. 11.12-4. Eleven of the 12 dedicated inputs are on the left side of this diagram. The twelfth input is on the bottom right. Each input is buffered and the buffered normal and complement forms of the input are connected to separate vertical lines, generating 24 vertical lines. For example, the buffered and normal forms of the input at pin 2 are available on columns 4 and 5, respectively.

The other 20 vertical lines are the normal and complement forms of signals from the 10 macrocells on the right side of the diagram. Together these 44 columns provide the normal and complement forms of the 22 possible inputs for the AND array. Practically speaking, only 21 inputs are available since in any useful application at least one macrocell needs to be configured as an output.

The rows of the AND array are the AND gate product lines. Each AND gate has 44 inputs. One of the AND gates associated with each output is used to control the output's inverting three-state buffer. The remaining AND gate outputs are inputs to the OR gate. The connections of AND gate outputs to OR gate inputs is fixed in a PAL. As a result, the fixed OR array is simply replaced by showing the outputs of each group of AND gates as inputs to an OR gate.

Not all of the PALCE22V10's OR gates have the same number of inputs (AND gate outputs). This can be seen more clearly in the block diagram. For example, the OR gate for output 0, I/O$_0$, has 8 inputs and the OR gate for output 4, I/O$_4$, has 16 inputs. As a result, output 0 can implement a sum-of-products expression that is the sum of 8 product terms,

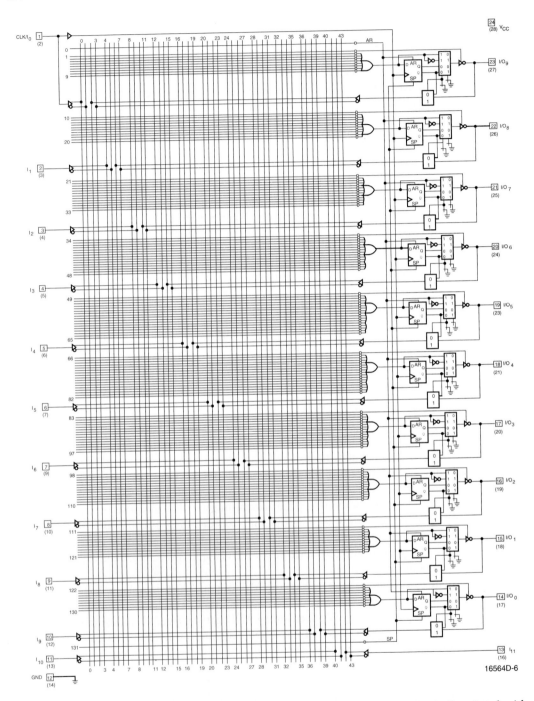

Figure 11.12-4 PALCE22V10 logic diagram. (Copyright © 1998, Vantis. Reprinted with permission of copyright owner. All other rights reserved.)

each of 22 variables, and output 4 can implement a sum-of-products expression that is the sum of 16 product terms, each of 22 variables.

The structure of the output macrocell is shown in detail in Fig. 11.12-5. The AND gate at the top of the diagram controls the three-state inverting output buffer. The product line for this AND gate can be programmed so the gate's output is fixed at 0, disabling the three-state buffer and making the I/O pin always an input. If this gate's output is fixed at 1, enabling the three-state buffer, the I/O pin is always an output. Alternatively, this gate's output can be a function of the PAL's inputs, allowing the I/O pin to be bidirectional (the direction being a function of one or more inputs).

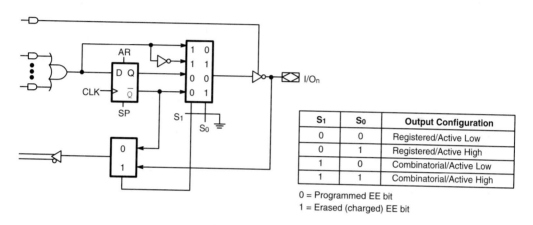

S_1	S_0	Output Configuration
0	0	Registered/Active Low
0	1	Registered/Active High
1	0	Combinatorial/Active Low
1	1	Combinatorial/Active High

0 = Programmed EE bit
1 = Erased (charged) EE bit

Figure 11.12-5   PALCE2V10 output logic macrocell diagram. (Copyright © 1998, Vantis. Reprinted with permission of copyright owner. All other rights reserved.)

When configured as an output, the output's type is controlled by the macrocell's four input multiplexer. The multiplexer's select inputs are programmable connections S_1 and S_0. For a combinational active high output, $S_1 S_0$ is 11. This selects the inverted output of the OR gate as the input to the inverting three-state buffer. For an active-low combinational output, $S_1 S_0$ is 10. Under this condition, the output of the OR gate is input to the inverting output buffer. In both cases S_1 is 1, so the two input multiplexer feeds the signal at the I/O pin back, in its normal and complement forms, as input to the AND array.

For a registered active high output, $S_1 S_0$ is 01 and the /Q output of the D flip-flop is input to the inverting output buffer. For a registered active low output, $S_1 S_0$ is 00 and the Q output of the D flip-flop is input to the inverting output buffer. For either registered output, S_1 is 0, and the /Q output of the flip-flop is fed back, in its normal and complement forms, to the AND array.

Each output macrocell is independently programmable, providing the PALCE22V10 with substantial flexibility. Programmable connections at the AND gate array and S_1 and S_0 are implemented in the PALCE22V10 by electrically erasable links. This allows a PALCE22V10 to be electrically erased and reprogrammed.

While this description has focused on the lower level implementation details of a PAL, design support tools used to program PALs make most of the lower level implementation details transparent. These tools consist of support software and a device programmer.

11.12.3 Programming PALs

A PAL is normally programmed by creating a source file that specifies the type of PAL to be used, the assignment of signals to the pins of the PAL, and the Boolean equation for each PAL output. The source file is input to a PAL assembler. The PAL assembler processes the source file and creates a fuse map output file. The **fuse map** specifies which "fuse" connections should be left intact by the device programmer. A fuse map is so named because the connections in early PALs were fusible links, which were burned by the device programmer to break connections. Fuse map output files normally conform to a JEDEC standard for fuse maps.

The sequence of operations in producing a programmed PAL is shown in Fig. 11.12-6 and is analogous to the operations performed to program an EPROM with the object code generated from an assembly language source file.

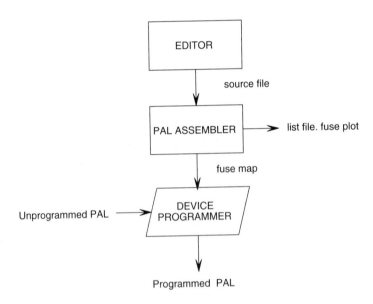

Figure 11.12-6   Steps to create a programmed PAL from a source file.

The address decoders represented as two blocks in Fig. 11.7-2 are implemented with a PALCE22V10 in Fig. 11.12-7. The unused PAL outputs could be programmed to provide additional memory or I/O chip selects.

A source file to program the PALCE22V10 is given in Fig. 11.12-8. This file follows the ABEL-HDL source file format. In addition to ABEL-HDL, other PLD compilers, such as PALASM and CUPL are available to produce a fuse map file from an appropriate source file.

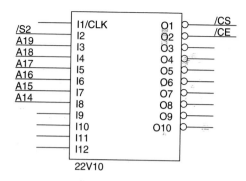

Figure 11.12-7   Implementation of an external memory address decoder for the memory of Fig. 11.7-2 using a PALCE22V10.

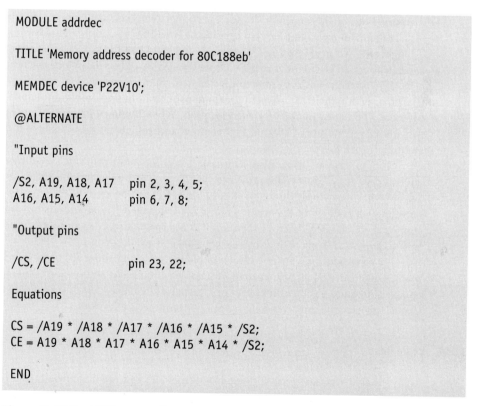

```
MODULE addrdec

TITLE 'Memory address decoder for 80C188eb'

MEMDEC device 'P22V10';

@ALTERNATE

"Input pins

/S2, A19, A18, A17     pin 2, 3, 4, 5;
A16, A15, A14          pin 6, 7, 8;

"Output pins

/CS, /CE               pin 23, 22;

Equations

CS = /A19 * /A18 * /A17 * /A16 * /A15 * /S2;
CE = A19 * A18 * A17 * A16 * A15 * A14 * /S2;

END
```

Figure 11.12-8   ABEL source file to program an external memory address decoder for the memory of Fig. 11.7-2.

11.13   Summary

The memory subsystem provides the ROM and RAM needed by a system. The amount of each required depends on your application. The required ROM and RAM are provided by one or more ROM and RAM ICs. These ICs are interconnected to provide the appropriate organization and total amount of each type of memory needed.

Each memory IC is itself a small memory subsystem. A memory IC's chip-select input and three-state data outputs, controlled by its output enable input, make the interconnection of multiple memory ICs to form a larger memory straightforward.

The simplest type of RAM memory IC to design into a system is an SRAM. SRAMs are volatile, but CMOS SRAMs can be used with a battery to provide nonvolatile battery backed memory. Microprocessor supervisory circuits provide functions that are useful in preventing battery backed memory from being inadvertently written when a system is powered on or powered down.

The two most commonly used types of ROM for development are EPROMs and Flash memory. Both of these memory types are nonvolatile. Their contents can be changed by erasing the memory IC and reprogramming it. For EPROMs, erasure is accomplished with UV light after removing the EPROM from the system. Flash memories are erased electrically and can be erased in-circuit or removed from the system and erased by a device programmer.

When memory ICs are interconnected to form memory locations with a longer word length, or width, their chip-select inputs are connected in common and each memory IC provides a subset of the bits for each location. When memory ICs are interconnected to provide a larger number of words, higher-order address bits must be decoded to appropriately select each memory IC.

The process of generating chip-select signals to memory ICs requires external address decoding. Address decoding can be accomplished by using the 80C188EB's Chip-Select Unit. Alternatively discrete SSI, MSI, or a PLD can be used. With exhaustive address decoding schemes, all of the address bus bits are decoded. Those address bits not directly connected to, and decoded by, a memory IC's internal address decoders are decoded either by the Chip Select Unit or by a discrete external address decoder.

External address decoding can be implemented using either SSI or MSI or Programmable Logic Devices. Nonexhaustive address decoding leaves some address bus bits undecoded. This simplifies the complexity of external address decoders, but results in hardware that allows each memory location to respond to multiple addresses.

11.14   Problems

1. What are the two generic catagories of memory in a memory subsystem? What kind of information is stored in each category of memory?

2. State the characteristics of an ideal memory IC.

3. What are the primary signals used to connect a memory subsystem to an 80C188EB system bus?

4. Draw a logic symbol for each of the following RAM ICs that reflects its external organization. Label all inputs and outputs.

    a. 32K × 8 with 3 control lines and common I/O

    b. 128K × 8 with 3 control lines and common I/O

    c. 1K × 4 with 2 control lines and common I/O

    d. 4K × 1 with 2 control lines and separate I/O

5. Draw a block diagram showing the external organization of a 256K × 8 SRAM with three control lines. Indicate what signal connects to each pin of the IC when it is used in an 80C188EB system. What is the bit capacity of this IC?

6. Draw a logic symbol for each of the following ROM memories that reflects its external organization. Label all inputs and outputs.

    a. 8K × 8

    b. 32K × 8

7. List the logic values for each of the control inputs in order to:

    a. write a RAM that has three control inputs

    b. read a RAM that has three control inputs

    c. write a RAM that has two control inputs

    d. read a RAM that has two control inputs

8. Sketch a timing diagram for a write cycle and for a read cycle of a RAM showing the relative timing relationships for the IC's signals.

9. Draw a block diagram of the internal structure of a 16K × 4 SRAM IC with three control inputs and common I/O. Indicate the size of the row and column decoders. Specify the number of logical words, the number of physical words, and the segmentation.

10. Draw a block diagram of the internal structure of a 128K × 8 SRAM IC with three control inputs and common I/O. Indicate the size of the row and column decoders. Specify the number of logical words, the number of physical words, and the segmentation.

11. Draw a block diagram of the internal structure of a 4K × 1 SRAM IC with three control inputs and common I/O.

12. Draw a block diagram of the internal structure of a 256K × 8 EPROM IC. Indicate the size of the row and column decoders. Specify the number of logical words, the number of physical words, and the segmentation

13. Draw a block diagram of the internal structure of a 64K × 16 EPROM IC. Indicate the size of the row and column decoders. Specify the number of logical words, the number of physical words, and the segmentation.

14. A Flash memory with a write endurance of 100,000 is used to develop software for an embedded system. If, on average, the software is revised and tested ten times a day, for how many weeks can the Flash memory be used? Assume a five day work week.

15. Design an 80C188EB memory subsystem that provides 64K of EPROM and 64K of SRAM. The SRAM starts at location 00000H. The EPROM is located so that it can contain the bootstrap instruction to the start of the application code. This instruction is executed when the microprocessor is reset. The SRAM is to be implemented using 32K × 8 ICs that have three control inputs and common I/O. The EPROM IC to be used is 64K × 8 and has two control inputs. Include a memory map of the subsystem that shows, in hexadecimal, the address range associated with each IC. Also

include an address bit map. Use an external address decoder and show it as a single block with all inputs and output labelled.

16. An 80C188EB memory subsystem requires 16K bytes of SRAM starting at address 0000H and 128K bytes of EPROM ending at address FFFFFH. The SRAM ICs to be used are $16K \times 4$ with three control inputs and common I/O. The EPROM IC is $128K \times 8$. Draw a memory map of the subsystem showing all memory IC address boundaries in hexadecimal. Draw an address bit map showing all memory IC address boundaries in binary. Write the Boolean equations for the address decoder chip-select and chip-enable outputs that implement exhaustive decoding. Draw the block diagram of the resulting memory subsystem.

17. An application requires $128K \times 8$ of SRAM and $128K \times 8$ of Flash. The IC components available are $64K \times 8$ SRAM memory ICs and $128K \times 8$ Flash memory ICs. The SRAM is to start at address 00000H and the Flash is to end at FFFFFH. Draw the memory map showing all device address boundaries.

18. An application requires $128K \times 8$ of SRAM and $256K \times 8$ of EPROM. The IC components available are $128K \times 8$ SRAM memory ICs with three control inputs and $128K \times 8$ EPROM ICs with two control inputs. The SRAM is to start at address 00000H and the EPROM is to end at FFFFFH. Draw the memory map showing all device address boundaries. Write the sum-of-products Boolean equations to select each IC. These equations are to be written for the complements of the select signals.

19. Using the least number of byte-wide memory ICs, design a memory subsystem for an 80C186EB microprocessor. The memory subsystem must provide 64K bytes of EPROM ending at address FFFFFH and 16K bytes of SRAM starting at address 00000H. The SRAM ICs have three control inputs and common I/O. Draw the logic diagram of the memory subsystem and its interface to the 80C186EB system bus. Indicate the external organization of each memory IC. Address decoding logic should be shown as a single block with all inputs and outputs labeled. Write the Boolean equation for each output. Use nonexhaustive decoding.

20. Why is the ISTOP bit necessary in the Chip-Select Stop Register? Support your answer with calculations.

21. Generate the chip select signals required in problem 13 using the 80C188EB's Chip-Select Unit. Assign appropriate CSU outputs to be the chip-select signals and write an instruction sequence that initializes the outputs. Assume that the SRAM requires 0 WAIT states and the EPROM requires 1 WAIT state.

22. Generate the chip select signals required in problem 14 using the 80C188EB's Chip-Select Unit. Assign appropriate CSU outputs to be the chip-select signals and write an instruction sequence that initializes the outputs. Assume that the SRAM requires 0 WAIT states and the EPROM requires 1 WAIT state.

23. Generate the external address decoding for the memory subsystem of problem 15 using only two 74AC138 1-out-of-8 decoders (recall that these decoders have three enable inputs, two active-low and one active-high). The 80C188EB's Chip-Select Unit is not to be used.

24. Design the address decoder of problem 15 using only NAND gates and inverters. Draw the logic diagram of the address decoder.

12.1   Basic I/O Ports

12.2   MSI I/O Ports

12.3   I/O Ports on Microprocessor Compatible ICs and Device Controllers

12.4   I/O Port Address Decoding

12.5   PLD External I/O Address Decoders

12.6   SSI and MSI External I/O address decoders

12.7   Conditional I/O

12.8   80C188EB Input/Output Unit

12.9   Interfacing I/O Ports to an 80C186EB

12.10   82C55A Programmable LSI I/O Port

12.11   Summary

More than anything else, I/O subsystems differentiate the hardware of one system from that of another. Accordingly, their I/O subsystems are what give each system its unique character.

In this chapter, the basic structure and design of I/O subsystems is examined in detail. The focus is on the logic required to interface an I/O device to the system bus. This interface includes ports and I/O address decoders. Various IC implementations of ports, from simple MSI circuits to programmable LSI circuits, are presented.

I/O address decoding logic is required for the selection of an individual port or an IC containing multiple ports. To efficiently accomplish I/O address decoding, a programmable logic device can be used alone, or in conjunction with the 80C188EB's Chip-Select Unit. However, in some cases for nonexhaustive decoding, SSI and MSI I/O address decoders might be preferred.

A port that supports conditional data transfer allows the microprocessor to determine, by polling a status flag, when an input device has new data, or when an output device can accept new data. The port must provide the handshaking logic required for conditional I/O.

Some simple I/O devices are also discussed in this chapter; more complex devices are introduced in later chapters.

12.1   Basic I/O Ports

Input/Output subsystems, or **I/O subsystems**, allow the CPU subsystem to transfer data to and from the outside world via the system bus (Fig. 12.1-1). While our conceptual block diagram of a system has shown only a single input subsystem and a single output subsystem, typical systems have several input and output subsystems. The application dictates the number and types of I/O subsystems required. Furthermore, many single I/O functions involve both input and output. As a result, block diagrams of systems show function-based I/O blocks, for example, a display block, an analog data acquisition block, and so on. Each block typically has both inputs and outputs.

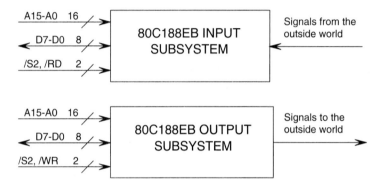

Figure 12.1-1   80C188EB input and output subsystems in isolated I/O space.

To simplify matters, we first consider subsystems that are either exclusively input or exclusively output.

12.1.1   Simple Input Subsystems

An input subsystem consists of an input device and hardware to interface the input device to the system bus. Input devices range from simple to complex. Simple input devices require only simple interface circuitry. The block diagram in Fig. 12.1-2 represents the simplest interface for an 8-bit input device. This interface consists of an octal three-state buffer and an I/O address decoder. The octal three-state buffer isolates the 8-bit input device's outputs from the system bus, except when the 80C188EB reads data from the device.

When enabled, the octal three-state buffer provides a pathway, or **port**, from the input device to the data bus. This pathway is called an **input port**. An input port can only be read by the 80C188EB. While the octal three-state buffer can be thought of as providing

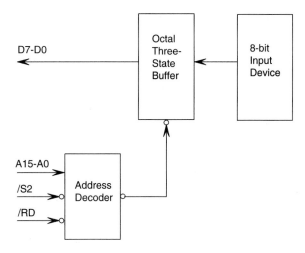

Figure 12.1-2   A simple input subsystem with an 8-bit input device.

a port or pathway from the input device to the data bus, it is equally important to think of it as isolating the input device's outputs from the data bus.

When its conditions are met, the I/O address decoder enables the octal three-state buffer. The octal three-state buffer then drives the input device's data onto the data bus. The conditions for the I/O address decoder to enable the three-state buffer are that the address on the bus is that of the input port and that the /RD strobe is asserted.

As an example, the eight switches of Fig. 4.2-2 constitute a simple input device. Figure 4.2-2's switch input subsystem is shown alone in Fig. 12.1-3. The circuitry needed to interface the switches to the system bus consists of pull-up resistors, a 74HC541 octal three-state buffer, and an I/O address decoder. The pull-up resistors are necessary to convert the switches' mechanical positions to logic levels. The switches' logic values are input to the system data bus through the octal three-state buffer.

The I/O address decoder decodes the bus address, /S2, and /RD, so the octal three-state buffer is enabled only when an instruction that reads the switches is executed. The I/O address decoder controls the three-state buffer to determine when the buffer should provide a pathway and when it should provide isolation.

In the program of Fig. 4.4-1, the input port's address, 8000H, was equated to the symbol SWITCHES:

    SWITCHES   equ   8000h

The instruction sequence that input the data was:

    mov   dx,SWITCHES
    in   al,dx

When the IN instruction is executed, the 80C188EB's BIU runs a Read I/O bus cycle with an address of 08000H. When the 80C188EB asserts /RD during this bus cycle, the decoder generates a 0 at its output. This 0 remains as long as /RD is asserted. During this period, the three-state buffer is enabled and the switch's data appears on the data bus. The

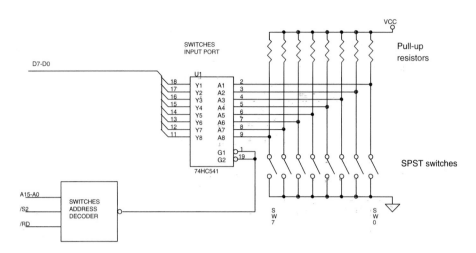

Figure 12.1-3   Switch input port from Fig. 4.2-2.

80C188EB latches this data into AL. When /RD is unasserted, the decoder's output returns to a 1, and the three-state buffer is disabled.

The port in the previous example is a byte input port. A word input port provides a 16-bit data value. Because of the 80C188EB's 8-bit data bus, this 16-bit value must be transferred as two bytes. A word input port is shown in Fig. 12.1-4. This port's address is 8010H. If this address is equated to the symbol SWITCHES_16,

        SWITCHES_16   equ   8010h

the data from this port is input by the instruction sequence:

        mov   dx,SWITCHES_16
        in   ax,dx

Execution of the IN instruction causes the 80C188EB's BIU to run two Read I/O bus cycles. During the first Read I/O bus cycle, the BIU generates the address 08010H. When the 80C188EB asserts /RD, the decoder generates a 0 at its output that is connected to the top three-state buffer. This 0 remains as long as /RD is asserted. During this period, only the top three-state buffer is enabled and the low byte of the 16-bit data appears on the data bus. The 80C188EB latches this byte into AL.

During the second Read I/O bus cycle, the BIU automatically generates the address 08011H. This address is one higher than the previous address. When the 80C188EB asserts /RD during the second bus cycle, the decoder generates a 0 at its output that is connected to the bottom three-state buffer. While /RD is asserted, the bottom three-state buffer is enabled, and the high byte of the 16-bit data appears on the data bus. The 80C188EB latches this byte into AH.

Input data must be held (stored) by the input device until the 80C188EB has the opportunity to read the data. In the previous example, each switch is a mechanical storage cell that holds the data. In general, a register is required to hold the input data until it is read (Fig. 12.1-5). This register may be part of the input device. This is the case when the

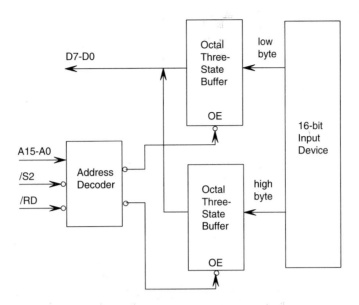

Figure 12.1-4   A simple 16-bit input subsystem, a word input port.

input device can store the data it generates until the data is read. When the input device does not have this storage capability, the input port must be an addressable register with three-state outputs. The register's data inputs and clock are driven by the input device. The register's three-state outputs are connected to the system data bus, and its output enable is driven by the I/O address decoder.

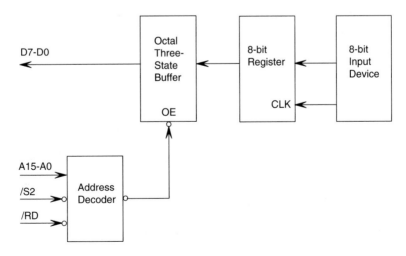

Figure 12.1-5   Using a register to store input data until it can be read by the micro-processor.

12.1.2   Simple Output Ports

The block diagram in Fig. 12.1-6 represents the simplest possible interface of an 8-bit output device to the system bus. The interface consists of an octal register and an I/O address decoder. The register holds the data that the 80C188EB outputs on the system data bus to the device. This register provides the pathway, or **output port**, from the system data bus to the output device. The 80C188EB can only write data to an output port.

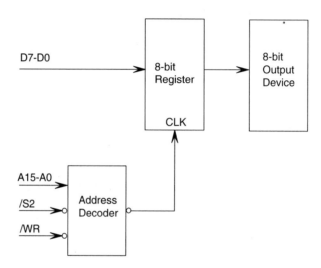

Figure 12.1-6   A simple output subsystem with an 8-bit output device.

When its conditions are met, the I/O address decoder clocks the register. The input conditions for the I/O address decoder to assert its output are that the address on the bus is that of the output port and that the /WR strobe is asserted. When /WR is unasserted, the rising edge of the I/O address decoder's output signal clocks the register. In general, an output port is an addressable register with its inputs connected to the system data bus and its outputs connected to an output device.

An LED is an example of a simple output device. When combined with a current limiting resistor and a buffer/driver, an LED can be turned ON or OFF by a logic level.

Figure 12.1-7 shows the LED output subsystem from Fig. 4.2-2. This output subsystem interfaces eight LEDs to the system bus. The 74HC574 octal D-type flip-flop provides the output port that connects the system data bus to the output device. The 74HC574 has three-state outputs. Because the enable input (/OC) is hardwired to ground, the three-state outputs in Fig. 12.1-7 are always enabled. The additional drive capability of its buffered outputs allows the 74HC574 to handle the LED's high current.

A 0 written to a port bit turns ON its associated LED, while a 1 turns the LED OFF. The octal D-type flip-flop stores the logic level, maintaining the LEDs in the desired ON or OFF states. Each LED remains ON or OFF until the 80C188EB writes a different value to the octal flip-flop.

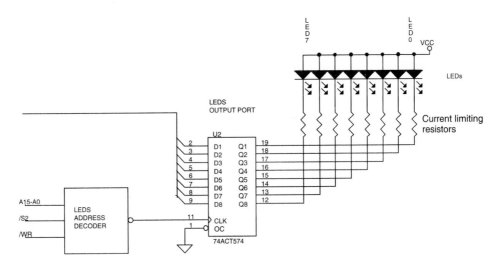

Figure 12.1-7   LEDs output subsystem from Fig. 4.2-2.

In the program of Fig. 4.4-1, the output port's address, 8000H, was equated to the symbol LEDS.

```
LEDS      equ      8000h
```

The instruction sequence that output the data was

```
mov       dx,LEDS
out       dx,al
```

When the OUT instruction is executed, the 80C188EB's BIU runs a Write I/O bus cycle with an address of 08000H. When the 80C188EB asserts /WR, the decoder generates a 0 at its output. This output is connected to the CLK input of the 74HC574 octal D-type flip-flop. When /WR is unasserted, the decoder's output is unasserted. The rising edge of the decoder's output signal latches the data in the D-type flip-flop.

A byte output port can be expanded to a word output port in a manner similar to the way the byte input port was previously expanded to a word input port.

The simple input and output ports presented in this section allow only unconditional I/O. Unconditional I/O requires that the input device always has new data ready whenever the microprocessor reads the port. For an output port, unconditional I/O requires that the output device is always ready to accept new data from the microprocessor.

Most I/O devices require that data transfers to or from them be conditioned on their having new data ready or their being ready to accept new data. Conditional I/O was introduced in Section 7.5.1 from a primarily software viewpoint. Hardware for conditional I/O is presented in Section 12.7.

Some IC implementations of simple I/O ports are presented next.

12.2   MSI I/O Ports

I/O ports can be implemented using MSI or LSI circuits that provide one or more input and/or output ports on a single IC. MSI circuits, considered in this section, usually provide a single byte port. Section 12.10 gives an example of an LSI circuit whose sole function is to provide multiple I/O ports.

12.2.1   MSI Input Ports

As previously stated, data generated by an input device must be stored until the 80C188EB has an opportunity to read the data. This stored data must be isolated from the system data bus until read. The simplest form of input port, a three-state buffer, is appropriate when the input device itself stores the input data, as was the case in the switch example. An input device select pulse from the 80C188EB's Chip-Select Unit or from an external I/O address decoder enables the three-state buffer.

Octal three-state buffer/drivers are available in noninverting and inverting forms. For example, the 74HC541 is a noninverting octal buffer/driver and the 74HC540 is an inverting octal buffer/driver (Fig. 12.2-1). These buffers have high current outputs that can

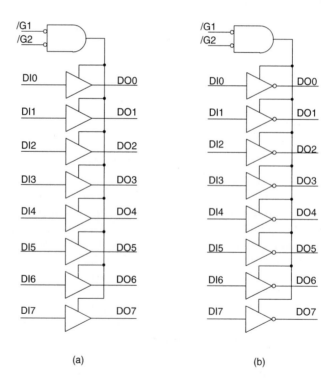

(a)   (b)

Figure 12.2-1   Octal buffers with three-state outputs: (a) 74HC541 noninverting octal buffer; (b) 74HC540 inverting octal buffer.

source or sink 6 mA. These buffers are enabled when their /G1 and /G2 inputs are both asserted. Both ICs have the same pinouts.

If an input device generates TTL output levels, a 74HCT541 or 74HCT540 with its TTL compatible input levels can be used. Alternatively, pull-up resistors can be used at the input device's outputs to provide logic levels compatible with CMOS inputs.

If an input device cannot store the data it generates, a register is required as part of the input port, in addition to a three-state buffer. ICs that contain both a register and a three-state buffer, such as the 74HC574 octal D-type flip-flop or the 74HC573 octal latch can be used (Fig. 12.2-2). The input device provides the data and the clock signal that writes the data into the register. An input device select pulse, generated in response to execution of an IN or INS instruction, controls the enabling of the register's three-state buffers (Figs. 12.2-3(a) and (b)).

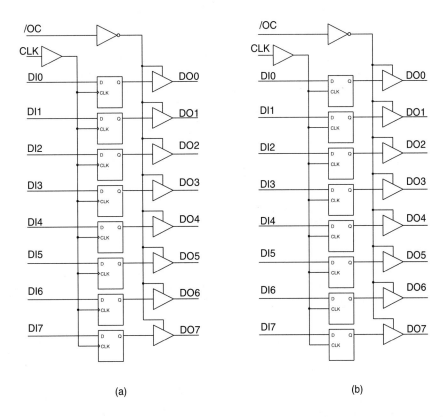

(a)   (b)

Figure 12.2-2   Registers with three-state outputs: (a) 74HC74 octal D-type flip-flop
                 (b) 74HC573 octal D-type latch.

12.2.2   MSI Output Ports

An output port must be able to store data output from the 80C188EB until the output device accepts the data. In its most basic form, an output port is a simple register. An 8-bit

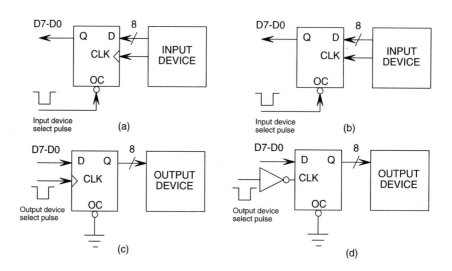

Figure 12.2-3   Octal flip-flops with three-state buffers as ports: (a) 74HC574 octal flip-
flop as an input port; (b) 74HC573 octal latch as an input port; (c)
74HC574 as an output port; (d) 74HC573 as an output port.

output port can be implemented with a single 8-bit register such as a 74HC574 or
74HC573. An output device select pulse from the 80C188EB's Chip-Select Unit or from an
external I/O address decoder is used to clock the register.

A 74HC574 used as an output port is shown in Fig. 12.2-3(c). Data from the
80C188EB's data bus is clocked into the 74HC574 on the rising (trailing) edge of the output device select pulse. Since the device select pulse is derived from /WR and the 74HC574
is positive edge triggered, the time at which the data is latched corresponds to the rising or
trailing edge of /WR. Data must be latched on the trailing edge of an output device select
pulse because the data is not valid at the leading edge.

If the output data must be continually available to the output device, the 74HC574's
three-state output buffers must be maintained in their enabled state. This is accomplished
by grounding the 74HC574's output control input (/OC).

The 74HC573 is an octal D-type positive level triggered latch. If the device select
logic creates an active low device select pulse, the pulse must be inverted so the data is
latched on the pulse's trailing edge. Connection of a 74HC573 as an output port is shown
in Fig. 12.2-3(d).

A variety of other MSI registers are also used as output ports. The two just discussed
have noninverting or **true outputs**; others are available with inverting outputs. Some, like
the 74HC574 and 74HC573, have **flow through** pin arrangements, with all input pins on
one side of the chip and all output pins on the other side. This arrangement simplifies
printed circuit board layout.

12.3   I/O Ports on Microprocessor Compatible ICs and Device Controllers

Complex I/O devices typically require complex interface logic. However, many complex I/O devices are realized as a VLSI circuit that includes most of the circuitry necessary to interface the IC to the system bus. These devices are referred to as **microprocessor compatible ICs** or as **peripheral ICs.** They are easy to interface to the system bus. The only thing missing from a microprocessor compatible IC is an I/O address decoder to decode the higher-order address bus bits.

An example of a microprocessor compatible IC input subsystem is the Maxim MAX166 analog-to-digital converter (ADC, Fig. 12.3-1). This 20-pin IC converts an analog voltage into an 8-bit binary number. It can be used, as in Fig. 4.3-1, to convert an analog signal from a transducer to binary for processing by a microprocessor. All the logic required to control the conversion and to interface the converter to the system bus is contained, along with the converter circuitry, on the IC.

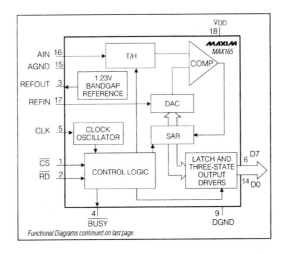

Figure 12.3-1   MAX166 microprocessor compatible 8-bit analog-to-digital converter. (Courtesy of Maxim Integrated Products, Inc.)

The MAX166's control logic allows it to be operated in any of three modes. In its simplest mode, Asynchronous Conversion, it continuously converts its analog input to binary. This mode of operation is selected by grounding the MAX166's MODE input pin. Using this mode, the ADC appears to a microprocessor as a single 8-bit input port. When the microprocessor wants the value at the MAX166's analog input, it simply reads the ADC's input port. The MAX166 is read by asserting its /CS and /RD inputs. This enables the MAX166 output data latch's three-state buffers. The data read is the result from the most recently completed conversion.

Some I/O devices require separate circuitry to both control their operation and to interface them to the system bus. **Device controller ICs** that provide this circuitry are available for many devices that are commonly interfaced to systems. Two examples are display controller ICs for multiplexed LED displays and floppy-disk controller ICs for floppy disk drives.

Device controller ICs, microprocessor compatible ICs, and peripheral interface ICs usually contain three types of registers distinguished by their use: control, status, and data (Fig. 12.3-2). **Control registers** are written by your program to control the mode of operation of the device controller IC or the I/O device it controls, and to initiate operations in the device. **Status registers** are read by your program to obtain information about the present state or mode of the device controller IC or the I/O device. **Data registers** hold data read from, or written to, an I/O device. The interface for a complex I/O device may contain multiple registers of each of these three types.

From a register viewpoint, an I/O subsystem is simply considered in terms of its control, status, and data registers.

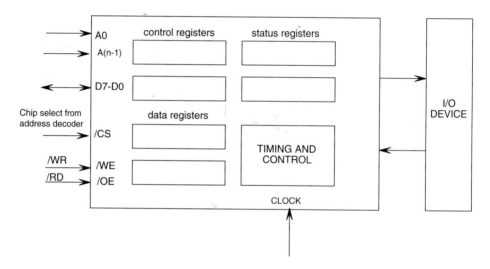

Figure 12.3-2   Generic IC device controller.

12.4   I/O Port Address Decoding

An 80C188EB allows I/O ports to be mapped to (located in) either its isolated I/O address space or its memory address space.

12.4.1   Isolated I/O

Only IN or INS and OUT or OUTS instructions transfer data from and to, respectively, registers in the isolated I/O space. When the 80C188EB initiates an I/O bus cycle to transfer the data, it makes /S2 a 0. During this bus cycle, the most significant four address bits, A19-A16, are 0H. Only the least significant 16 address bits, A15-A0, address the port. This allows any one of a maximum of 64K byte input ports and 64K byte output ports to be addressed.

The only 80C188EB registers that can be the source or destination for isolated I/O transfers are AL and AX. The I/O port address can be specified using either fixed port, variable port, or string port addressing as discussed in Section 6.2.

12.4.2   Memory Mapped I/O

By appropriate design of the external I/O address decoders or programming of the Chip-Select Unit, I/O ports can be placed in the memory address space. Ports in the memory address space are referred to as **memory mapped I/O**. Like ports in isolated I/O space, the same address can be used for two different I/O registers in the memory space, one a memory mapped input port and the other a memory mapped output port.

The design of the port hardware determines whether an input port and an output port with the same address are actually the same register. For example, assume that an octal D-type flip-flop is used as an output port and the outputs from the octal D-type flip-flop are connected only to an output device. Also assume that an octal three-state buffer is used as an input port. The inputs to the octal three-state buffer come only from an input device. The address decoders are designed so the input and output ports have the same address. However, in this case the input and output ports are physically independent. Therefore, what is written to the output port will not be what is read from the input port with the same address.

The input and output port structure just described could be modified so the outputs from the octal latch go to the output device and to the inputs of the three-state buffer. There is no separate input device. The result is an output port with readback capability. In effect, the input and output ports with the same address are the same register. What is written to the output port will be what is read back from the input port with the same address.

Any of the memory addressing modes in Section 6.6 can be used to read and write memory mapped I/O ports. During a Read Memory or Write Memory bus cycle that transfers data from or to a memory mapped I/O port, the 80C188EB makes /S2 a 1. Therefore, the I/O address decoder for a memory mapped I/O port must condition the device select pulse on /S2 being a 1.

Because of the memory addressing modes' greater power, more efficient software can be written to transfer data to and from memory mapped ports. However, since references to the memory address space use the full 20-bit address, memory mapped ports require that all 20 bits be decoded to implement exhaustive decoding. This results in more complex address decoding logic. However, this allows a system to have more than the 64K byte input ports and 64K byte output ports possible for isolated I/O.

Port I/O address decoder design techniques for ports in isolated I/O space are introduced in this section. The same principles apply to memory mapped I/O ports, with the exception that the condition on /S2 differs (/S2 is 1). Also, 20, not 16, address bits must be decoded for exhaustive decoding.

12.4.3   Read I/O and Write I/O Bus Cycles

For IN and INS, the bus cycle that transfers the data is a Read I/O bus cycle. For OUT and OUTS, data transfer is accomplished by a Write I/O bus cycle. During either bus cycle, /S2 is 0.

For a byte port, the transfer of data takes place during a single bus cycle. For word ports, two bus cycles are required. Bus cycles were described in detail in Section 10.3.4

Figure 10.3-4 shows the timing relationship between the availability of the address and the assertion of /RD during a Read I/O bus cycle. Figure 10.3-5 shows the timing relationship between the address and /WR during a Write I/O bus cycle. For a Read I/O bus cycle, the /RD strobe indicates to external hardware the exact time during which the input port's three-state buffer is to be enabled. For a Write I/O bus cycle, the /WR strobe indicates the exact time at which the output port should latch the data placed on the data bus by the 80C188EB.

12.4.4   I/O Chip Select and I/O Device Select Pulses

I/O ports and I/O peripheral ICs must be selected in order to be read or written. Peripheral ICs that can be both read and written typically have address inputs and three control inputs to select the register to be accessed (Fig. 12.3-2). These inputs are similar to those of the SRAMs of Chapter 11.

Generation of an exhaustively decoded chip-select signal for such a device requires decoding /S2 and all of the address bits A15–A0 that are not direct inputs to the device. This type of chip-select signal for an I/O port is referred to as an **I/O chip select**.

The peripheral's /WE input is driven by /WR, and its /OE input is driven by /RD.

A simple input port or a simple output port may have only one control input, such as an output enable for an input port or a CLK for an output port. In addition to the address and /S2, the selection of these devices must be further conditioned on either /RD or /WR being asserted. Such signals, which are conditioned on /RD or /WR, are referred to as **input device-select pulses** (**IDSP**), or **output device-select pulses** (**ODSP**).

For a word port, two device select pulses are required. A word port consists of two consecutive byte ports. If the address of the byte port that holds the low byte is *hhhh*H, then the address of the byte port that holds the high byte is (*hhhh* + 1)H.

I/O chip selects, and input and output device select pulses, can be generated either by the 80C188EB's Chip-Select Unit in combination with an external I/O address decoder or by an external I/O address decoder alone.

12.4.5   WAIT States for I/O Ports

Accessing simple I/O ports, or ports, in peripheral ICs and device controllers may require the introduction of WAIT states. This may be necessary to meet either the port's or the 80C188EB's timing requirements. Timing analysis and WAIT state generation logic for I/O ports is similar to that for memory, and is discussed in detail in Chapter 13.

Some peripheral ICs have modes of operation where the peripheral operates like it is a slow I/O device. For example, a second operating mode of the MAX166 ADC is its Slow Memory Interface mode. In this mode, a read operation of the MAX166's data register both starts the conversion and reads the result. Both the MAX166's /CS and /RD inputs must be continually asserted until the conversion has completed. When the conversion is complete, the data register contains the result. Since the ADC's conversion time is much longer than a normal bus cycle, WAIT states have to be introduced. The MAX166 includes logic that generates an output signal, /BUSY, indicating that it is busy carrying out a conversion. This signal can be used to directly request WAIT states.

12.4.6   CSU Generated I/O Chip-select and Device-select Signals

The 80C188EB's Chip-Select Start and Stop registers allow any of the CSU's chip-select outputs to be programmed as I/O chip selects (Figs. 11.10-1 and 11.10-2). Typically, one or more of the eight general chip select outputs, GCS7-GCS0, are used.

In determining whether to assert a chip select configured for I/O, the CSU compares 10 bits, CS9–CS0, of the chip select's start and stop addresses with bits A15–A6 of the bus cycle address. The 6 least significant bits of the start and stop addresses can't be programmed. This means the smallest granularity for a CSU generated I/O chip select is 64. The MEM bit in the Chip-Select Stop register must be cleared, so that the chip select is only asserted for I/O bus cycles. Thus, MEM = 0 takes care of the requirement that /S2 = 0.

To achieve exhaustive decoding or to generate input or output device select pulses, the chip-select signal from the CSU is used as an input to an external decoder. The external decoder decodes any of the least significant six address bits that are not decoded by the I/O device. For device select pulses, the external decoder must also include /RD or /WR.

For example, consider a peripheral IC with 3 address inputs (A2–A0) and control inputs /CS, /WE, and /OE. This peripheral IC is to be located in the isolated I/O space (Fig. 12.4-1). The address range for the peripheral IC's registers in the isolated I/O space is to be 0008H through 000FH. The I/O chip select signal is generated using /GCS0 and an external decoder. The sequence of instructions that programs /GCS0, assuming accesses to the peripheral IC require 2 WAIT states and the 80C188EB's external READY input is not to be used, is:

```
    mov     dx,GCS0ST        ;program /GCS0's start register
    mov     ax,0002h         ;start address 0000H, 2 WAIT states
    out     dx,al
    mov     dx,GCS0SP        ;program /GCS0's stop register
    mov     ax,0048h         ;stop address 003FH, CSEN = 1, ISTOP = 0
    out     dx,al            ;MEM = 0, RDY = 0
```

/GCS0 is asserted for all I/O addresses from 0000H to 003FH. This address range is 64 bytes, /GCS0's smallest granularity. To achieve exhaustive decoding, the external I/O address decoder has inputs /GCS0 and A5–A3. The external address decoder's decoding of /GCS0 and A5–A3 further reduces the address range to the desired 8-byte range. The output of the external decoder provides the peripheral IC's chip-select signal.

For input or output device select pulses, the external decoder must include /RD or /WR, respectively, as an input. A specific input device select pulse, /IDSP*hhhh*H, is generated only during the Read I/O bus cycle of an IN or INS. This pulse selects the port with address *hhhh*H. To generate an exhaustively decoded input device select pulse, the external address decoder must decode the least significant six address bits and /RD. The resulting input device select pulse enables the input port's three-state buffer.

A specific output device select pulse, /ODSP*hhhh*H, is generated only during the Write I/O bus cycle of an OUT or OUTS that addresses port *hhhh*H. To generate an

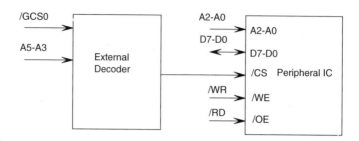

Figure 12.4-1   Generating a chip select for a peripheral IC using the CSU and external address decoder.

exhaustively decoded output device select pulse, the external address decoder has to decode the least significant six address bits and /WR. The resulting output device select pulse clocks the output port's register.

For small systems that require eight or fewer I/O chip selects, the granularity of /GCS7–/GCS0 is not a problem. Each chip select can handle an I/O device with as many as 64 input and output ports. If a peripheral device has fewer than 64-byte I/O registers and no external decoding is used, the resulting address decoding is nonexhaustive.

12.5   PLD External I/O Address Decoders

An efficient and flexible way to implement an external I/O port address decoder is to use a programmable logic device (PLD). The primary advantage of using a PLD is its flexibility in terms of generating outputs, each of which is a function of any, but not necessarily all, of its inputs. This allows the generation of both input and output device select pulses together with I/O chip-select outputs, which are not conditioned on /RD or /WR. In addition, the input and output device select pulses and chip selects do not have to be for adjacent addresses or blocks.

Consider the example in the previous section that required an external I/O address decoder be used in conjunction with /GCS0. The external decoder (Fig. 12.4-1) can be implemented using a PALCE22V10. An assignment of signals to the PALCE22V10 is shown in Fig. 12.5-1. The output of the PAL that drives the peripheral IC's /CS input is labeled /CSPIO. The I/O address decoder's output, /CSPIO, is to be asserted (/CSPIO = 0) when /GCS0 is asserted (/GCS0 = 0) and A5–A3 equals 001B. The equation for the complement of /CSPIO, CSPIO, is:

$$CSPIO = GCS0 * /A5 * /A4 * A3$$

This equation is written so CSPIO is 1 when the conditions for /CSPIO to be 0 are met. Note in particular that the product term uses GCS0 rather than /GCS0. When /GCS0 is asserted (/GCS0 = 0), then GCS0 is 1. If, at the same time, the address A5–A3 is 001B, then every literal in the product term is a 1 and CSPIO is 1.

An ABEL source file for PALCE22V10 design is given in Fig. 12.5-2.

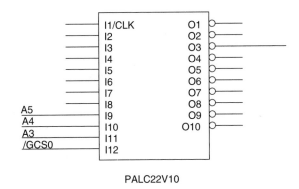

PALC22V10

Figure 12.5-1   Assignment of signals to a PALCE22V10 to implement the I/O address decoder of Fig. 12.4-1.

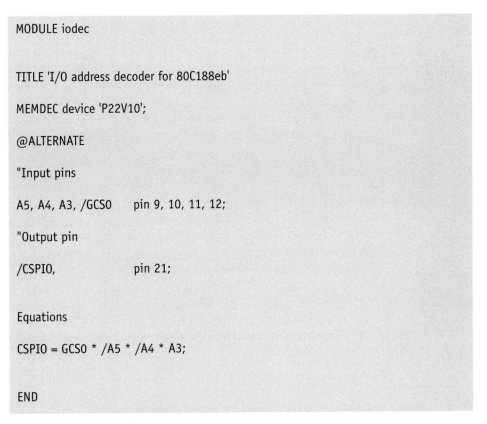

```
MODULE iodec

TITLE 'I/O address decoder for 80C188eb'

MEMDEC device 'P22V10';

@ALTERNATE

"Input pins

A5, A4, A3, /GCS0      pin 9, 10, 11, 12;

"Output pin

/CSPIO,               pin 21;


Equations

CSPIO = GCS0 * /A5 * /A4 * A3;


END
```

Figure 12.5-2   ABEL source file for I/O decoder of Fig. 12.5-1.

The assignment of signals to pins in Fig. 12.5-1 was chosen to illustrate that a single PAL can be used to generate different types of outputs. If the signal assignments in Fig. 11.12-7 and in Fig. 12.5-1 are combined, then a single PALCE22V10 can be used to implement the chip select signals for the system's ROM, RAM, and I/O. All that is required is that the information in source files of Figs. 11.12-8 and 12.5-2 be combined into a single source file.

A PAL can be used without using an output from the CSU as one of its inputs to generate input and output device select pulses and I/O chip-select signals. For exhaustive decoding, the PAL would have inputs /S2, A15–A0, /RD, and /WR. Since 19 inputs are required, a single PALCE22V10 could generate three device selects or I/O chip selects.

12.6   SSI and MSI External I/O Address Decoders

In general, the use of PLDs has largely replaced use of either SSI or MSI devices for I/O address decoding. However, there are still some occasions where SSI or MSI devices are used. Therefore, familiarity with these approaches is important.

The design of external I/O address decoding logic varies, depending on how many I/O devices are involved and what decoding logic is provided on the input and output port ICs themselves. If only a single input port and a single output port are required, address decoding is unnecessary. /S2 can simply be combined with /RD to generate a nonaddress specific input read strobe (/IOR) (Fig. 12.6-1). /IOR is to be asserted when /S2 is asserted *and* /RD is asserted. Since all these signals are asserted-low, the AND function is implemented with an OR gate. Remember, a positive logic OR gate is the same as a negative logic AND gate.

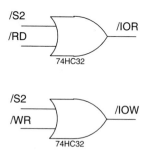

Figure 12.6-1   Generation of nonaddress specific input and output select pulses.

/S2 can be combined with /WR to generate a nonaddress specific output write strobe (/IOW). In a system with only one input port and one output port, these strobes can directly control the input buffer and the output latch, respectively. The port address of the I/O instruction is, in this case, a don't-care. But, of course, if fixed I/O port addressing is used, some port address must be specified in the IN and OUT instructions.

12.6.1   Linear Selection

In a typical application, more than one input port and one output port are required. The port address is decoded to generate a unique device select pulse for each input and each output port. The simplest form of nonexhaustive decoding is **linear selection**. With linear selection, one address bit is associated exclusively with each I/O port's selection. The address bit is logically combined with /S2 and either /RD or /WR to generate an input or output device select pulse, respectively (Fig. 12.6-2). Since there are only 16 bits in a port address, only 16 input and 16 output ports can be selected using linear selection. However, the resulting simplification of decoders may provide important savings in some very small systems.

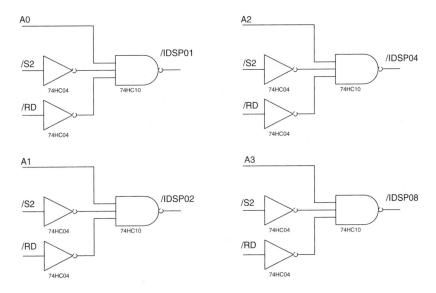

Figure 12.6-2   Linear selection I/O address decoding.

In Fig. 12.6-2, address bit A3 = 1 selects port 8. If the /RD strobe is inverted and then NANDed with A3 and /S2, an active-low input device select pulse, /IDSP08H, is generated. When connected to the active-low enable of a three-state buffer, /IDSP08H controls when the buffer drives the bus. If /RD is replaced with /WR in Fig. 12.6-2, the corresponding output device select pulses are generated. If an IC's three-state buffer has multiple enable inputs, the internal decoding logic of the three-state buffer reduces the number of external gates required for address decoding.

A disadvantage of linear selection is the possibility that a programming error can cause bus contention. If a port address that is not a power of two is accidentally used in the program, two or more input ports can be enabled and drive the data bus simultaneously. For example, suppose a design contains input ports 1H, 2H, 4H, 8H, and 10H, selected by address bits A0, A1, A2, A3, and A4. If IN AL,10 is written instead of IN AL,10H, instruction execution causes input ports 2 and 8 to be selected simultaneously, causing bus contention. Even if the port's three-state buffers are not damaged, excessive current drawn from the power supply as a result of the contention may cause the supply voltage to drop so low that data stored in volatile system memory or in ports may be lost. *When linear selection is used, extra care must be taken to ensure that two ports are not selected simultaneously!*

12.6.2   Conventional Decoding

All of the SSI and MSI implementation techniques used for memory address decoders in Chapter 11 can be used for I/O address decoders. The only differences are that for ports in isolated I/O space, only 16 address bits must be decoded for exhaustive decoding and /S2 must be 0.

Figure 12.6-3 shows two 74HC138 decoders used to generate eight input device select pulses and eight output device select pulses. Since only three address bits are decoded, the decoding is nonexhaustive and is only suitable for systems requiring eight or fewer input and eight or fewer output ports. Either /RD or /WR is connected to one of the asserted-low enables, and the other asserted-low enable is connected to /S2. The remaining asserted-high enable is connected to V_{CC}.

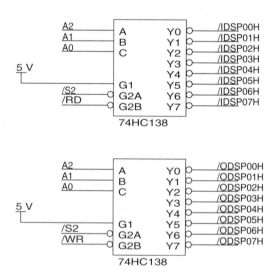

Figure 12.6-3   Generating device select pulses using 74HC138 decoders.

To provide device select pulses for larger numbers of input and output ports, 74HC138s can be cascaded. The first level 74HC138 is wired as in the previous case. Each of its outputs is connected to an asserted-low enable of a 74HC138 on the second level. The least significant three address bits go to each of the second level 74HC138s. The next more significant 3 address bits go to the first level 74HC138. Nine 74HC138s can generate 64 device select pulses in this manner.

12.7   Conditional I/O

An I/O data transfer can either be unconditional or conditional. Examples of unconditional transfers were given in Sections 4.2 and 4.3. Conditional transfers were introduced in section 7.5. Conditional I/O transfers are considered in greater detail in this section.

An **unconditional transfer** moves data to or from an I/O port without first determining whether the port has new data ready to be read (input port) or is ready to receive new data (output port). The assumption is that the port is always ready. The data transferred during an unconditional transfer may represent a command, status, or data to be processed. Commands are written to an output port to control the operation of an I/O device. Status is read from an input port and used to monitor the state of an I/O device. Data is transferred in either or both directions. Data is distinguished from commands or status by how it is used and its port address in a controller or peripheral IC.

For a **conditional data transfer**, execution of the I/O instruction that transfers the data is conditioned on the I/O device being ready. Readiness is determined by checking the status, obtained by an unconditional input of status from the I/O device. Status information, contained in the input bit pattern, indicates the present state of the I/O device. Typically, only a few bits in a register are required to indicate an I/O device's status. Unused bits are simply ignored by your software. If its status indicates that an I/O device is ready for a data transfer, a second I/O instruction is executed to transfer the data.

A single status bit can indicate when an input port has new data available (ready), or when an output port is ready to receive data. Instructions that test the status flag increase the total time associated with a conditional I/O operation. This additional time is called **I/O overhead.** The software process of testing the status bit is called **polling**.

Consider an input device that generates data at input port INDATA (Fig. 12.7-1). To indicate that new data is available, the input device sets a flag, bit 7 of input port STATUS. This type of flag is often called a **service request flag**. The input device is requesting service from the microprocessor. The service requested is for the microprocessor to read the new data generated by the input device. The use of flags in controlling conditional transfers is referred to as handshaking. This is the only way of knowing when data in a port should be processed as new data.

To determine the availability of new data, the program inputs the status byte from port STATUS and tests bit 7. If bit 7 is 1, new data is available and an instruction is then executed that inputs the data from port INDATA. The input device select pulse that enables the three-state buffers of port INDATA is also used to clear the data available flag of port STATUS.

The frequency with which a status flag is checked determines the minimum length of time it takes to detect that there is new data. An input procedure can execute a tight loop, sometimes called a **busy wait loop**, to check the status flag. The procedure, inbuff, in Fig. 12.7-2, for the system shown in Fig. 12.7-1, assumes that the number of bytes of data to be transferred is specified in CX and that BX points to the starting address of a data buffer in memory.

Use of a tight loop to check a status bit creates a problem in a system where no method is provided for exiting the loop. If the input device malfunctions and cannot set the status bit, the program hangs in an infinite loop. A solution to this problem is to write the test loop as a **controlled timeout.** This ensures that if the status flag is not set within a given time (number of loops), the loop is exited and appropriate action is taken for the no response condition.

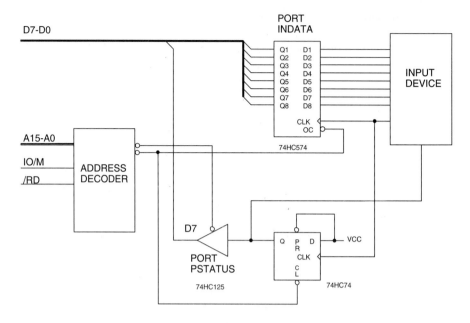

Figure 12.7-1   Conditional transfer of data from an input port.

```
;**********************************************************************
;NAME:        inbuf
;FUNCTION: performs conditional input of data from byte port to buffer
;ASSUMES: bx - pointer to buffer, cx - length of buffer
;RETURNS: input data in buffer
;**********************************************************************
inbuff        proc
chk_rdy:
              mov     dx,STATUS      ;input data valid status byte
              in      al,dx
              test    al,80h         ;if bit 7 = 0, no new data is available
              jz      chk_rdy        ;wait
              mov     dx,INDATA      ;input data
              in      al,dx
              mov     [bx],al        ;store in buffer
              inc     bx             ;increment buffer pointer
              loop    chk_rdy        ;loop if buffer is not full
              ret
inbuff        endp
```

Figure 12.7-2   Procedure to input data to a memory buffer from an input port using
                conditional I/O.

When several input devices are used, a polling procedure can check the service request flag of each device, in turn, to see which has data. Figure 12.7-3 shows four input devices with their flags combined into one status byte.

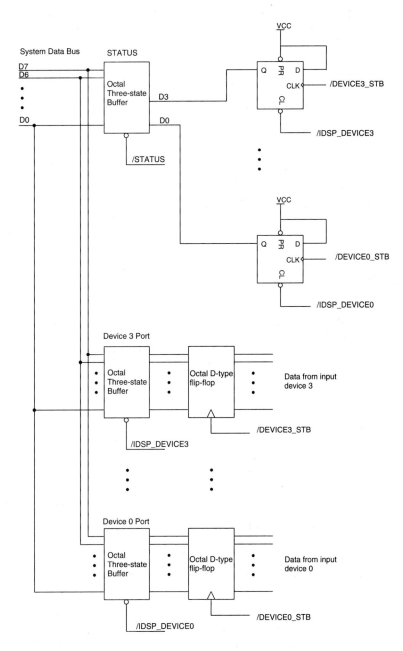

Figure 12.7-3   Combined status flags for four input devices.

The polling procedure in Fig. 12.7-4 checks each input device's status flag. If a device's service request flag is set, the device's service procedure is called. The order in which the polling procedure tests the service request bits defines the **priority** among the input devices. In this example, input device 3 has the highest priority. The service procedure for each device saves AL, then inputs and either stores in memory or processes the data. Inputting data from a particular device clears only that device's service request flip-flop. Before returning from the service procedure, AL is restored.

```
;****************************************************************;
;NAME: POLL
;FUNCTION: Polls service request flags from four devices.
;        If a device's flag is set, the device's service procedure
;        is called
;ASSUMES: Port STATUS bits 3-0 are service request flags for
;        devices 3-0
;RETURNS: appropriate service procedure executed
;CALLS: srv3, srv2, srv1, and srv0
;****************************************************************
;

poll    proc
        push    ax
        mov     dx,STATUS
        in      al,dx
d3?:    test    al,08h          ;Is flag for device 3 set?
        jz      d2?             ;no, check next device
        call    srv3            ;yes, service device 3
d2?:    test    al,04h          ;Is flag for device 2 set?
        jz      d1?             ;no, check next device
        call    srv2            ;yes, service device 2
d1?:    test    al,02h          ;Is flag for device 1 set?
        jz      d0?             ;no, check next device
        call    srv1            ;yes, service device 1
d0?:    test    al,01h          ;Is flag for device 0 set?
        jz      done            ;no, then done
        call    srv0            ;yes, service device 0
done:   pop     ax
        ret
poll    endp
```

Figure 12.7-4   Polling procedure for four devices.

For an output device, a service request flag can be used to indicate when the output device can accept the next data byte. This is necessary when an output device requires time to process data previously transferred to it, before it can accept new data. If a program writes new data without first checking whether the processing of the previous data has been completed, the previous data is overwritten. The error condition associated with overwriting data is referred to as an **overrun error**.

12.8   The 80C188EB Input/Output Unit

For applications that require a number of I/O port bits, external I/O ports are used. However, in some applications only a few I/O port bits are required. In other applications, a few more port bits are required beyond those supplied by a system's external I/O ports. In either of these cases, use of the 80C188EB's integrated Input/Output Unit can save you the expense of adding external I/O ports.

The 80C188EB has two general purpose 8-bit I/O ports, Port 1 and Port 2. Each port is multiplexed to pins shared with other integrated peripherals. **Port 1** is an output only port whose pins are multiplexed with the general purpose chip-select signals (Fig. 12.8-1). When the 80C188EB is reset, these pins are all configured as chip selects, but are not enabled. The initial logic level at each pin is a 1. Each pin can be individually configured, by the program, to be either an output port or a chip select.

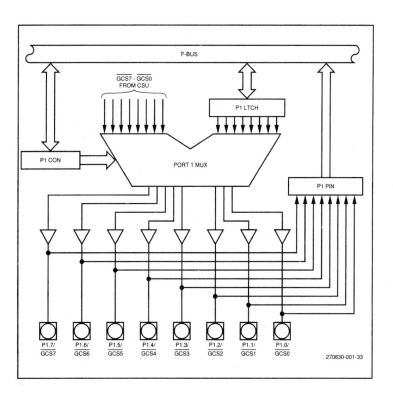

Figure 12.8-1   80C188EB Port 1 block diagram. (Courtesy of Intel Corp.)

Port 2 consists of one bidirectional, three input, two output, and two bidirectional open-drain pins (Fig. 12.8-2). The one bidirectional, three input, and two output pins are multiplexed with signals from the Serial Communications Unit. The two open-drain bidirectional pins are not multiplexed. When the 80C188EB is reset, those pins that are multiplexed with the Serial Communications Unit are initially configured for their serial communications functions. The two outputs used to transmit data (TXD0 and TXD1) are initially logic 1s. The output used as an interrupt request (SINT1) is initially logic 0.

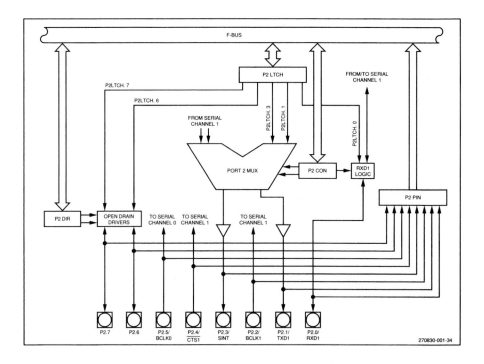

Figure 12.8-2   80C188EB Port 2 block diagram. (Courtesy of Intel Corp.)

12.8.1   Port Pin Logic Module

Each of the two I/O ports has its own set of four PCB registers: a Port Control register (P*x*CON), a Port Direction register (P*x*DIR), a Port Latch register (P*x*LTCH), and a Port Pin register (P*x*PIN). The eight registers' offsets from the PCB's base address range from 0050H to 005EH. Only the low byte of each word register is used. One bit in the low byte of each register is associated with each port pin.

P*x*CON selects the function, peripheral or port, for each pin. P*x*DIR controls the direction of bidirectional I/O pins. P*x*LTCH holds the value to be output for an output or bidirectional pin. And, P*x*PIN allows the current state of the port pins to be read. These PCB registers are shown in Fig. 12.8-3 through 12.8-6.

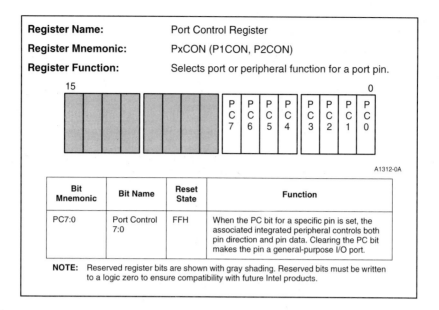

Figure 12.8-3   Port control register. (Courtesy of Intel Corp.)

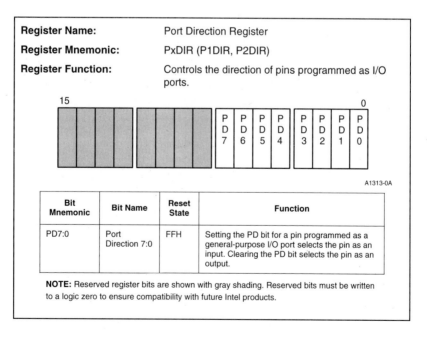

Figure 12.8-4   Port control register. (Courtesy of Intel Corp.)

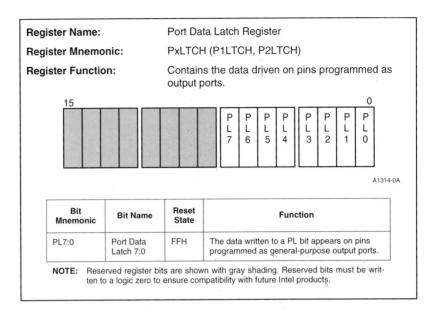

Figure 12.8-5   Port latch register. (Courtesy of Intel Corp.)

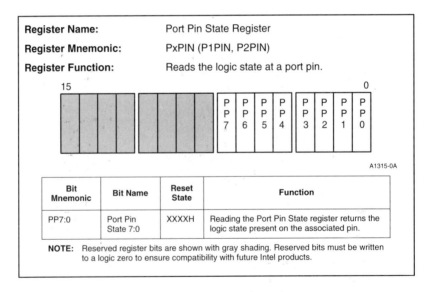

Figure 12.8-6   Port pin register. (Courtesy of Intel Corp.)

Each port pin is derived from the bidirectional logic module structure in Fig. 12.8-7. The three latches represent one bit from the registers PxCON, PxDIR, and PxLTCH. These bits are all associated with a single pin. These latches exist for all port pins, even those fixed as outputs or as inputs. No latch is shown corresponding to the PxPIN register. This read only "register" is actually a synchronizer and three-state buffer. This "register" provides the current value at the pin, synchronized with the system clock.

The overall operation of the bidirectional port pin in Fig. 12.8-7 can be easily understood by examining the function of each of the three latches in the module in turn. The bottom latch is the Port Control Latch. The Q output of this latch provides the select input to the bottom multiplexer. The /Q output provides the select input to the top multiplexer. The value written to the Port Control Latch exerts control through the two multiplexers.

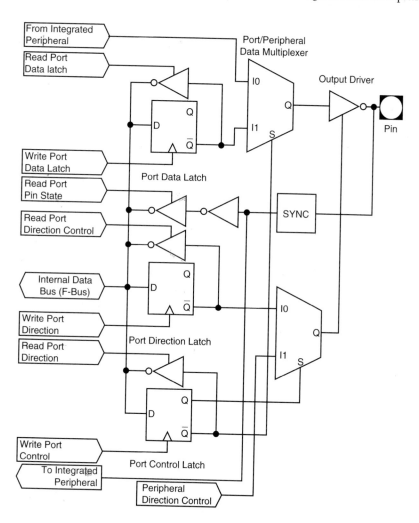

Figure 12.8-7   Simplified logic diagram of a bidirectional port pin. (Courtesy of Intel Corp.)

The bottom multiplexer selects whether an integrated peripheral function or the contents of the Port Direction Latch controls the enabling of the pin's output driver. The top multiplexer selects whether an integrated peripheral function or the Port Data Latch provides the data to the output driver. When a 1 is written to the Port Control Latch, the integrated peripheral determines the enabling of the output driver and the driver's input. When a 0 is written to the Port Control Latch, the Port Direction Latch controls the enabling of the output driver, and the Port Data Latch provides the input to the output driver.

Assuming that a 0 has been written to the Port Control Latch, so the pin is configured as a port pin, the Port Direction Latch, the middle latch, determines whether the port is an input or output port. A 1 written to the Port Direction Latch disables the output driver, making the pin an input. A 0 written to the Port Direction Latch enables the output driver, so the pin is an output.

If the Port Direction Latch contains a 0, making the port an output, the data written to the Port Data Latch becomes the input to the output driver, and therefore, the output at the port pin.

If the Port Direction Latch contains a 1, making the port an input port, the current logic level at the port pin can be read by reading the Port Pin "register."

The following two subsections describe each port in detail and specify how the port pins are variations of the bidirectional port pin of Fig. 12.8-7.

12.8.2   Port 1

The Port 1 Multiplexer Control register, P1CON (Fig. 12.8-3), determines whether each pin of Port 1 is driven by a general chip-select signal or by a bit from the Port 1 Data Latch. If a particular bit of P1CON is a 1, the associated pin is a general chip select. If it is a 0, the associated pin is an output from the Port Data Latch P1LTCH (Fig. 12.8-5).

Port 1 differs from the bidirectional logic module of Fig. 12.8-7 in that the connection from the bottom multiplexer to the output driver is omitted and the output driver is hardwired enabled. Since Port 1 is an output only port, the Port Direction register (P1DIR) has no effect in determining whether the port's bits are inputs or outputs. However, this "unused" register can be written and read as a simple storage register.

All the bits of P1CON become 1s when the 801C88EB is reset, so these eight pins are initially configured as general chip selects. The Port 1 multiplexing options are shown in Table 12.8-1.

The following instruction sequence configures bits 7–4 of Port 1 as general chip selects, /GCS7–/GCS4, and configures bits 3–0 as output port bits, P1.3–P1.0.

```
mov     dx,P1CON
mov     ax,00f0h
out     dx,al
```

Data written to Port 1's Data Latch (P1LTCH) appears at only those port pins configured as output ports. Data should be written to the Port Data Latch before configuring the pin as an output. If P1LTCH is read, it is the latch's content, not the state of the port's pins that is returned.

Table 12.8-1   Port 1 multiplexing option.

Pin Name	Peripheral	Port Function	Type
P1.7/GCS7#	GCS7	P1.7	output
P1.6/GCS6#	GCS6	P1.6	output
P1.5/GCS5#	GCS5	P1.5	output
P1.4/GCS4#	GCS4	P1.4	output
P1.3/GCS3#	GCS3	P1.3	output
P1.2/GCS2#	GCS2	P1.2	output
P1.1/GCS1#	GCS1	P1.1	output
P1.0/GCS0#	GCS0	P1.0	output

Even though Port 1 is an output port, the value at the port's pins can be read. The Port 1 Pin register (P1PIN) is a read only register. Reading this register returns the logic level at the port's pin. Signal changes at the port's pins are synchronized to the system clock. For pins configured as an output port, the level at the pins is the same as the value output to the port latch. For pins configured as chip selects, reading the pins returns all 1s, since the P1PIN register is in the PCB address space and all chip selects remain high during a PCB access.

12.8.3   Port 2

Pins P2.3 and P2.1 of Port 2 are outputs only (Fig. 12.8-2). Pins P2.5, P2.4, and P2.2 are inputs only. Pins P2.7 and P2.6 are open-drain bidirectional. Pin P2.0 is a special case. Pin 2.0 is bidirectional when used as a peripheral. It functions as an input for the asynchronous communications modes and as an output for the synchronous communications mode. However, when configured as a port, it functions only as an input, regardless of the value of its P2DIR bit. Port 2 multiplexing options are summarized in Table 12.8-2.

Table 12.8-2   Port 2 multiplexing options.

Pin Name	Peripheral	Port function	Port direction
P2.7	NONE	P2.7	open drain
P2.6	NONE	P2.6	open drain
P2.5/BCLK0	BCLK0 (input)	P2.5	input
P2.4/CTS1#	CTS1# (input)	P2.4	input
P2.3/SINT1	SINT1 (output	P2.3	output
P2.2/BCLK1	BCLK1 (input)	P2.2	input
P2.1/TXD1	TXD1 (output)	P2.1	output
P2.0/RXD1	RXD1 (I/O)	P2.0	input[a]

a. Serves as data output pin in mode 0 (synchronous) serial transfers.

The output pins, P2.3 and P2.1, are similar to the pins of Port 1. Clearing bits 3 and 1 in Port 2's Port Control register (P2CON) multiplexes Port 2 Data Latch's data to the pins. Setting bits 3 and 1 in P2CON multiplexes signals from the serial communications unit to the pins.

Bits P2.5, P2.4, and P2.2 are inputs only. For input only pins, the common logic structure is modified so that the output driver is hardwired disabled. These input pins are shared by the port and the Serial Communications Unit. The signals on these pins go to both P2PIN and the Serial Communications Unit. Since these pins are always shared, the associated bits in P2CON are not used. And, since their direction is fixed, the associated bits of P2DIR are also not used. Furthermore, with the output driver permanently disabled, the associated bits of P2LTCH are not used. All of these unused bits can be used for general storage. Data at the pins is read by reading register P2PIN.

Pin P2.0 is a special input pin shared with the RXD1 function of the serial communications unit. This pin functions as an input when configured as a port, but is not a dedicated input. This pin becomes an output during a synchronous transmission on channel 1, regardless of its P2DIR bit value. During a synchronous transmission, the data from the transmit buffer (TBUF) appears on this pin, if the associated P2CON bit is a 1. If the P2CON bit is 0, the corresponding bit from P2LTCH appears on the pin. When the synchronous transmission is completed, pin 2.0's driver enters its high-impedance state, and the pin becomes an input.

Reading P2PIN returns the values at Port 2's pins, regardless of whether particular pins are configured for port or peripheral functions.

12.8.4   Open-drain Bidirectional Pins

Pins P2.7 and P2.6 are open-drain bidirectional I/O pins that are not multiplexed with any integrated peripheral.

When the corresponding bit of P2DIR is 0, the pin is an output and its value is controlled by the content of P2LTCH. If the corresponding bit in P2LTCH is 0, the pin's N-channel open-drain output driver is turned ON and its output is 0. If the bit in P2LTCH is a 1, the driver is turned OFF and the output is in its high-impedance state.

If the associated bit in P2DIR is 1 or if P2CON is 1, the open-drain output is in its high-impedance state. An external pull-up resistor to V_{CC} is required for each open-drain output in order for it to produce a valid logic 1 value.

12.9   Interfacing I/O Ports to an 80C186EB

Byte ports interfaced to an 80C186EB can be connected to either the low or high byte of its 16-bit data bus. When a number of byte ports are involved, they can be split between the low and high bytes of the data bus to distribute bus loading. All ports connected to the low byte of the data bus have even addresses. Their port selection must be conditioned on A0 being 0. All ports connected to the high byte of the data bus have odd addresses. Their selection must be conditioned on /BHE being 0.

A microprocessor compatible peripheral IC with a byte-wide data bus and multiple registers must be connected to either the low byte or the high byte of the 80C186EB data bus. If it is connected to the low byte, all of its registers will have even addresses. In this case, A0 = 0 is a condition for selection of the peripheral IC and is an input to the external I/O address decoder. The peripheral IC's A0 address input pin connects to A1 of the address bus, its A1 input pin connects to A2 of the address bus, and so on.

A peripheral device with a 16-bit data bus should be interfaced to the system bus so its word registers are aligned (even addressed words). Data transfers to and from the peripheral device will then be accomplished in a single bus cycle.

12.10   82C55A Programmable LSI I/O Ports

The 80C188EB's port pins are limited in number and are not sufficient for most applications. In addition, if the integrated peripherals multiplexed with the port bits are used, which is likely, very few integrated port bits are available for use. Additional ports can be provided in the form of MSI ports, as already discussed. However, a more efficient approach is to use a programmable LSI I/O port.

Registers, three-state buffers, and flags interconnected to form multiple I/O ports are available as single LSI circuits. For versatility, these ports are software configurable. Each port's mode of operation is established by writing a control register in the IC. Once established, a port's mode is usually not changed during the execution of your program.

An example of a programmable LSI I/O port is the **82C55A Programmable Peripheral Interface.** This IC provides several programmable I/O ports in a 40-pin DIP or 44-pin PLCC package. The 82C55A can be used with many different microprocessors and is often included on single board microcomputers and PC/104 I/O modules. Unlike the 80C188EB's I/O ports, the 82C55A provides a mode of operation where input ports latch the input data under the control of an external clock signal.

The 82C55A contains a control register and three 8-bit I/O ports: A, B, and C (Fig. 12.10-1). Port C is actually two independently programmable ports, C-upper (C7–C4) and C-lower (C3–C0). In some modes of operation, Port C functions as a status register. The control register is shown functionally divided into a Group A Control (controls port A and port C upper) and a Group B Control (controls port B and port C lower).

The 82C55A's internal 8-bit bidirectional data bus buffer transfers data between the system data bus and either its control register or one of its I/O ports. The 82C55A is selected using its /CS input. When not selected, its data bus buffer is in its high-impedance state. When an 82C55A is selected, inputs A1 and A0 address either the control register or one of its ports (A, B, or C) for a data transfer (Table 12.10-1).

Table 12.10-1   82C55A Register Addresses.

A1	A0	Read Operation	Write Operation
0	0	Port A	Port A
0	1	Port B	Port B
1	0	Port C	Port C
1	1	none	Control

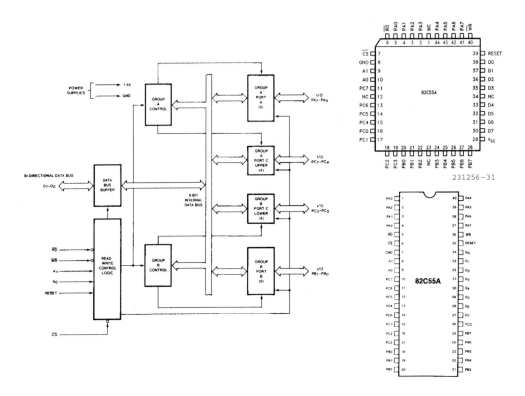

Figure 12.10-1   Block diagram and pinouts of 82C55A Programmable Peripheral Interface. (Courtesy of Intel Corp.)

At system power on, a reset signal applied to the 82C55A clears the control register and sets all ports to the input mode. The 82C55A stays in this mode until your program writes a byte to its control register. Writing the control register defines the 82C55A's subsequent mode of operation. The three basic modes of operation are:

1. mode 0, basic input-output.
2. mode 1, strobed input-output.
3. mode 2, bidirectional bus.

The control word's mode definition format is shown in Fig. 12.10-2.

12.10.1   82C55A Mode 0

Mode 0 provides two 8-bit ports (A and B) and two 4-bit ports (C-upper and C-lower). Any of these four ports can be input or output. Outputs are latched, but inputs are not. There are 16 possible input-output configurations in this mode. For example, the control word 8AH sets port A for output, port C-upper for input, port B for input, and port C-lower for output. For an 82C55A in the 80C188EB I/O space that is selected when A15

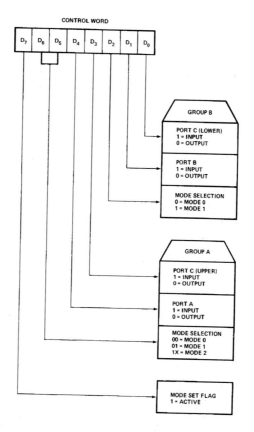

Figure 12.10-2   Mode definition format of control word for 82C55A. (Courtesy of Intel Corp.)

through A2 are all equal to zero, is initialized to the previous configuration by the instruction sequence:

```
mov    dx,CNTRL_REG
mov    al,8Ah           ;load A with control word
out    dx,al            ;write control word into control
                        ;register of 82C55A
```

where CNTRL_REG is equated to 0003H.

12.10.2   82C55A Mode 1

Mode 1 provides two strobed 8-bit ports, A and B. In this mode, both inputs and outputs are latched. Pins of the two 4-bit ports (C-upper and C-lower) are used to provide hand-shaking for ports A and B. Figure 12.10-3 shows the configuration definitions for an 82C55A for input and output in mode 1.

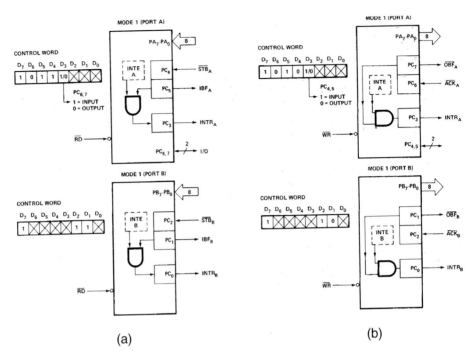

Figure 12.10-3   Mode 1 (a) and (b) output configuration for an 82C55A. (Courtesy of
                 Intel Corp.)

For port A as an input port in mode 1 (Fig. 12.10-3(a)) pins, PC3, PC4, and PC5 are
used for handshaking. For port B configured as an input port, PC0, PC1, and PC2 are used
for handshaking. Pins PC6 and PC7 can be programmed as input or output ports. An
input device places data at port pins PA7–PA0 (or PB7–PB0), then generates a strobe,
/STB$_A$ (or /STB$_B$), that loads the data into the input latch. This sets the input buffer full
(IBF) flag (Fig. 12.10-4(a)).

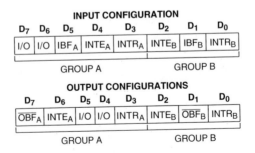

Figure 12.10-4   Mode 1 status word (port C) for 82C55A. (Courtesy of Intel Corp.)

In mode 1, port C provides status information as indicated in Fig. 12.10-4. The program can read port C to obtain the mode 1 status word and check the IBF bit to determine whether new data is available for input. The status word format differs depending on whether each port is configured as input or output. If both port A and port B are configured as input ports, then each has its own IBF flag (IBF_A and IBF_B) in the status word. If the associated IBF flag is asserted, the program can read new data from the port. Inputting data from a port clears its IBF flag.

For output in mode 1 (Fig. 12.10-3(b)) the 80C188EB writes data to port A (or B), causing the output buffer full flag, /OBF, to be asserted (Fig. 12.10-4(b)). The output device monitors /OBF to determine when output data is available. After it reads this data, the output device acknowledges reading by asserting the acknowledge input, /ACK. This action negates /OBF.

As an example of mode 1 operation, consider the configuration of the 82C55A in Fig. 12.10-5. Port A is input and port B is output. PC5-PC0 are used for handshaking and PC7 and PC6 are basic inputs. The command word to program the ports is 10111100B (0BCH). The following instruction sequence initializes the 82C55A:

```
mov    dx,CNTRL_REG
mov    al,0bch
out    dx,al
```

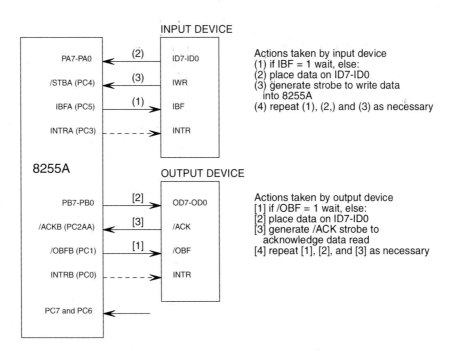

Figure 12.10-5   82C55A in mode 1 operation with Port A configured as an input port and Port B configured as an output port.

With port A in the input mode, the input device places data on inputs PA7–PA0, then strobes PC4. This loads the data into input port A and asserts the port A input buffer full flag (IBF_A), bit 5 of the status register. Your program can test the buffer full condition by reading the status register (port C) and checking bit 5. If the buffer is full, your program executes an IN instruction to transfer the data from input port A to register AL. The read strobe generated by this IN automatically negates IBF_A.

There can be a problem if an input device generates too long a strobe at pin PC4 of the 82C55A and the IBF_A flag of the status register is repeatedly tested in a program loop. The IBF_A flag is sensitive to the level of the signal at pin PC4. When a strobe from the input device occurs, IBF_A flag is asserted. Assume that your program tests IBF_A, finds it set, and executes an IN to input the data. The /RD strobe during the Read I/O bus cycle of the IN negates IBF_A. If a long strobe from the input device is still low, IBF_A is set again by the same strobe. Your program again inputs the same data from the port. Thus, if your program is in a tight loop waiting to read the next ten new bytes of data from the input port, it reads the same byte of data ten times!

This problem can be prevented by designing logic to limit the duration of the strobe from the input device. An easier solution is to test the INTR flag instead of IBF. INTR is only asserted when /STB returns to 1, the trailing edge of /STB. Thus, INTR is asserted only after the long strobe terminates. Reading the port clears INTR, and INTR remains cleared until the end of the next strobe.

Since IBF is also available at a pin of the 82C55A, the input device can test this signal to determine whether the 80C188EB has input the previous byte it strobed into port A. Thus, the input device can use the IBF pin's output to synchronize its operation with the 80C188EB to avoid overrun errors.

To use INTR from the 82C55A for this purpose, instead of using IBF, the initialization command to the 82C55A must enable the interrupt output ($INTE_A = 1$). This is accomplished by writing a *bit set* command for PC4 (09H) to the control register. The 82C55A's bit set/reset capability is explained at the end of this section. The internal $INTR_A$ flag in the status register is not affected by $INTE_A$.

Control signals also provide handshaking for an output port. In the previous example, port B is an output port, pins PC2–PC0 provide the handshaking control signals. In the output mode, the contents of the 80C188EB's AL register are transferred to output port B of the 82C55A by an OUT instruction that addresses port B. The /WR strobe resulting from the OUT asserts $/OBF_B$ (PC0). The output device monitors $/OBF_B$ to determine when there is valid output data. When the output device is ready to accept the data, it strobes PC2. The strobe signal at PC2 negates /OBF. The program reads the mode 1 status and tests bit 1 to see whether the output device has accepted the data.

12.10.3 82C55A Mode 2

Mode 2 configures port A as a single 8-bit bidirectional bus. Five bits of port C are read for status and written for control of port A. This handshaking capability is similar to that of mode 1. This mode allows an 82C55A to be used to pass bytes of data between two microprocessors. For more information on this mode of operation see the 82C55A's data sheet.

12.10.4   82C55A Bit Set/Reset

The 82C55A also has a bit set/reset capability for port C. When bit 7 of a control word is 0, the control word is interpreted by the 82C55A as a port C bit set/reset command. Any bit of port C can be set or cleared. The bit set/reset format is shown in Fig. 12.10-6. The ability to directly set or clear a single port bit is advantageous in applications where individual bits of port C control separate external functions. Bits of port C that are status or control bits in mode 1 or 2 can also be set or cleared using this capability, just as if they were data bits.

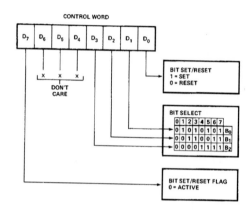

Figure 12.10-6   BitSet/ResetFormat. (Courtesy of Intel Corp.)

12.11   Summary

Useful systems require connections to the outside world. I/O subsystems allow the microprocessor to transfer data to and from the outside world via the system bus. An I/O subsystem consists of an I/O device and the device's interface to the system data bus. This interface includes a port that provides the actual pathway between the system bus and I/O device.

An input port can be as simple as a three-state buffer. An output port can be as simple as a register. Usually, the data to be transferred must be stored temporarily. In general, ports include some type of storage to hold the data to be transferred. As a result, input ports most often include a register in addition to a three-state buffer. The register is written by the input device and later read by the microprocessor. In contrast, an output port is written by the microprocessor and later read by the output device.

A port register can be a discrete register IC or may be integrated onto an IC peripheral device or device controller IC. Single discrete ports are provided by MSI registers and multiple ports are provided by general purpose programmable LSI I/O ports. Ports are also included in some multifunction LSI circuits like WSI's Programmable Microperipheral with Memory.

Single ports are selected by device select pulses. Multiport ICs are selected by I/O chip selects. Device-select pulses are similar to chip-select pulses, except that device-select pulses include conditioning on either /RD or /WR. Device-select pulses and chip selects can be generated using exhaustive or nonexhaustive address decoding.

The simplest way to accomplish address decoding for device select pulses and I/O chip selects is to use the 80C188EB's Chip-Select Unit in combination with an external decoder implemented with a PLD. This is especially true when WAIT states are required.

Data transfers between an I/O device and microprocessor usually need to be synchronized. This is necessary to avoid the data being overwritten by subsequent data before the first data is accepted. Synchronization can be accomplished using handshaking. Handshaking requires a service request flip-flop that is set when data is written into a port and cleared when the data is read from the port.

For an input port, the service request flip-flop is set by the input device when it loads data into the port. Before reading the data port, the microprocessor reads a status port to obtain the state of the service request flip-flop. If the flip-flop is not set, there is no new data and the microprocessor does not read the data port. If the flip-flop is set, there is new data, and the microprocessor reads the data port. When the microprocessor reads the data port, the service request flip-flop is automatically cleared. Programmable peripheral port ICs, like the 82C55A, include the flip-flops and other logic required for handshaking.

The 80C188EB provides two integrated 8-bit I/O ports, Port 1 and Port 2. However, all the bits of Port 1 are multiplexed with the Chip-Select Unit's general chip selects. Six of the bits of Port 2 are multiplexed with Serial Communications Unit signals. If the multiplexed pins are used as chip selects or for serial communications, they are not available for use as port bits. Nevertheless, in some applications the availability of just one or a few port bits on the 80C188EB can eliminate the need for an additional discrete port IC and its address decoding.

12.12   Problems

1. What signals are used to interface an input subsystem to an 80C188EB system bus? What signals are used to interface an output subsystem to an 80C188EB system bus?

2. What is the purpose of a register as part of a simple input port? What is the purpose of a register as part of a simple output port? Under what conditions would it not be necessary to include a register in an input port? Under what conditions would it not be necessary to include a register in an output port?

3. What are the three fundamental types of registers in peripheral and device controller ICs? What is the basic function of each of these register types?

4. Draw a block diagram of a 16-bit output port and its interface to an 80C188EB system bus. Label the inputs and outputs of all the blocks in your diagram.

5. Using a CMOS data book, (HC or HCT), list, by part number, function name, and features all the octal three-state buffers that are appropriate for implementing simple input ports. List all the octal D-type flip-flops and octal latches that are useful in implementing simple output ports.

6. Using Fig. 10.3-4, justify qualitatively the need for the inverter in Fig. 12.2-3(d).

7. Draw block diagrams similar to those in Fig. 12.1-1, representing an input subsystem and an output system in the memory address space. Show the appropriate signals to interface the I/O subsystem to the system bus.

8. What are the advantages and disadvantages of using isolated I/O instead of memory mapped I/O?

9. What does it mean for an IC to be microprocessor compatible?

10. Write a sequence of instructions to generate an I/O chip select using /GCS1. The chip select's active range should start at address F000H and be as short as possible. What is the actual active address range and what is the granularity for /GCS1? If the chip select is used to directly select a peripheral IC with address inputs A3–A0, is the address decoding exhaustive? If not, how could it be made so?

11. Using Fig. 12.5-2 as a starting point, modify the figure to represent a PROM as a type of PLD. What would be the external organization of the resulting PLD?

12. An 82C55A Programmable Peripheral Interface (Fig. 12.10-1) has the following bus interface signals, A1–A0, /CS, /RD, /WR, D7–D0. Use /GCS2 and a PALCE22V10 to provide exhaustive decoding and locate the 82C55A starting at address E000H. Draw a block diagram of the interface and write a sequence of instructions to configure /GCS2. Write and assemble a source file to program the PAL.

13. The only isolated I/O ports required in a particular system are two input ports (octal three-state buffers with active-low enables) with addresses 00H and 01H, and two output ports (octal positive edge triggered flip-flops) with addresses 00H and 01H. Draw a logic diagram of an implementation of the required I/O address decoder using only a single 74HCT139 dual 1-out-of-four decoder.

14. Write an instruction sequence to configure Port 1 to provide /GCS0 and /GCS1 and to use the remaining bits as port bits. Will these port bits be inputs or outputs?

15. What is the maximum number of input bits available using Port 1 and Port 2?

16. An 82C55A is to be programmed so port A is an input port that does not latch the data from its input device. Port B is also to be programmed as input port, but it must latch the data from its input device. Write the instruction sequence that initializes the 82C55A. The 82C55A is located in isolated I/O space. Refer to its registers symbolically; PORTA, PORTB, PORTC, and CNTRL. When programmed as specified, is Port A appropriate for conditional data transfers? Explain your answer.

17. Four 82C55As are to be located, one after the other, starting at address 0000H in the isolated I/O space. The four 82C55As are the only ports in the I/O space. Using a 74ASL138 and as few other gates or flip-flops as required, design address decoding logic that generates the chip-select signals for the four 82C55As. The address decoding is to be nonexhaustive. Draw the logic diagram for address decoding logic, and label all input and outputs. List the lowest address associated with the registers on each 82C55A.

13

TIMING

13.1   Time Constraints and System Architecture

13.2   Instruction Execution Times

13.3   WAIT States

13.4   Memory IC Timing Parameters

13.5   Memory Subsystem Timing Compatibility Calculations

13.6   I/O Timing Considerations

13.7   80C188EB Timer/Counter Unit

13.8   The 82C54 Programmable Interval Timer/Counter

13.9   Clock Calendar ICs

13.10   Watchdog Timers

13.11   Summary

Timing is a critical issue that must be considered from the very beginning of a design, and throughout a system's development. A successful design requires very careful attention to timing matters related to a number of very different aspects of the design. For example, a system must accomplish its overall function within an acceptable time constraint. In addition, some individual system tasks may have very strict timing requirements. Each task's time constraints determine whether it can be accomplished primarily in software or whether it must be done in hardware. These decisions define the system's architecture.

Estimating whether or not a software implementation of a task will be fast enough requires a knowledge of instruction execution times. Instruction execution time is in turn affected by whether or not WAIT states are inserted into bus cycles so slow memory and I/O devices can keep up with the microprocessor.

Determination of the number of WAIT states needed to reliably access a particular memory or I/O device requires that a timing compatibility analysis be performed. If the timing requirements of any single device in the system are not met, the entire system can fail to operate properly.

Some systems need to accurately measure time in order to perform time dependent tasks. Time intervals, from very short to very long, may need to be measured. Programmable timer/counters are used to measure relatively short time intervals. These same devices can be used to generate precisely timed output waveforms. Measurement of long time intervals and maintenance of time of day and date information are accomplished by a clock/calendar IC.

In mission critical applications, a watchdog timer can be used to monitor a system's operation by requiring that the microprocessor trigger the watchdog timer periodically. If this does not happen, the watchdog timer times out and either resets the system or interrupts the microprocessor, causing the execution of a procedure that shuts the system down.

A periodic signal from a timing circuit may be used to generate a time base signal to schedule and coordinate the overall sequencing of task execution in real-time systems.

13.1   Timing Constraints and System Architecture

The more critical time constraints are to the successful operation of a system, the more the system changes from a soft to a hard real-time system. Even in relatively nonreal-time and soft real-time systems, some individual tasks may still have very tight time constraints.

Timing constraints determine the overall system-level architecture, the selection of a microprocessor, and the microprocessor's clock speed. The overall system-level architecture must take into consideration the allocation of each task to either a primarily software or primarily hardware implementation. This allocation is based on each task's speed constraints and the cost of the hardware approach.

Any task can be executed most quickly by a dedicated hardware system designed and optimized to perform that specific task. This hardware may be available as a commercial IC, as in the case of a numeric coprocessor or a microprocessor compatible peripheral IC. Or, it may have to be specially designed as an application specific IC.

At one extreme, in terms of system-level architecture, is a system where all tasks can be implemented in software and still meet all timing constraints. When more restrictive timing constraints exist, some tasks may have to be accomplished in hardware, using either peripheral ICs or application specific integrated circuits (ASICs). Allocating some tasks to peripheral hardware can also allow multiple tasks to be executed concurrently.

The choice of a microprocessor's clock speed affects the overall system timing, and places timing constraints on the operation of all subsystems. The timing characteristics of subsystem components must be compatible with the timing constraints imposed by the microprocessor. Hardware timing compatibility is achieved through proper selection of speed-selected versions of components, introduction of WAIT states, or inclusion of additional subsystem hardware.

13.2   Instruction Execution Time

To estimate the execution time of a task, the execution time of its individual instructions must be known. You also need to know individual instruction execution times in order to write procedures that execute in the shortest possible time. Most tasks can be accomplished by several algorithms and each algorithm can, in turn, be performed by different instruction sequences. Knowledge of instruction execution times is needed to compare the speeds of various approaches. In applications where relatively low accuracy time delays are acceptable, they can be implemented in software, based on instruction execution times.

An instruction's execution time is the product of the number of system clocks (T states) required to execute the instruction and the system clock period. The system clock period is the reciprocal of the system clock frequency. For example, an 8-MHz system clock (16 MHz crystal) has a 125 ns clock period, and a 20-MHz system clock (40 MHz crystal) has a period of 50 ns.

The number of clocks required to execute individual instructions varies widely, from 2 clocks for instructions like CLC and CBW, to 51 (80C186EB) and 83 (80C188EB) for POPA. Because of their data bus width differences, the number of clocks required to execute the same instruction on an 80C186EB and an 80C188EB differ when the instruction's execution involves the transfer of words.

The number of clocks required to execute an instruction also varies depending on the particular form of the instruction: register-to-register, immediate-to-memory, etc. Instruction summaries in Intel data and reference books provide the information needed to determine the total number of clocks for each form of an instruction (Appendix D). These summaries give separate values for the 80C186EB and the 80C188EB. The values specified assume the instruction is in the prefetch queue at the time it is needed by the EU. It is also assumed that no WAIT states or bus holds occur during the instructions's execution. For the 80C186EB, it is further assumed that all word data is aligned.

In practice, a sufficient number of prefetched instruction bytes may not be in the queue. Thus, the actual execution time of a sequence of instructions is generally greater than the time determined by adding individual instruction execution times from the listings. This difference may be substantial for the 80C188EB, which, with its 8-bit data bus, has more difficulty keeping its instruction queue full.

For most instruction forms, the number of clocks is specified as a single integer, n. For example, the register-to-register form of ADD has $n = 3$. Thus, the total number of clocks for execution of a register-to-register ADD is 3, regardless of whether the registers involved are byte or word registers. With a 20 MHz system clock, this form of ADD takes 150 ns to execute (3 clocks $\times$ 50 ns/clock).

For instructions whose execution requires the transfer of data, the number of data bytes that can be transferred in a single bus cycle affects the execution time. Adding the contents of a memory byte and a register, with either as the destination, requires a minimum of 10 states or 500 ns at 20 MHz. On an 80C188EB, an additional 4 clocks must be added for each memory data transfer required to execute the instruction. If a register is the destination, only one memory transfer is needed and only 4 clocks must be added. But, if memory is the destination, two transfers are required, and 8 clocks must be added. An additional one or two clocks may also be required to initiate each transfer, due to the asynchronous handshake between the EU and BIU.

For conditional branch instructions, the execution time depends on whether the branch condition is met or not, so two values of n are given. The smaller value applies when the condition is not met, and the branch does not occur. The larger value applies when the condition is met, and the branch occurs. In the later case, n includes the clocks required to flush the instruction queue and fetch the next instruction's opcode. For example, the LOOP instruction requires 16 clocks if the branch occurs, and 6 if it does not. Figure 13.2-1 shows a software delay using LOOP and the calculation of the loop control value to achieve a desired delay.

```
       mov   cx,count      ;clocks = 4
delay: loop  delay         ;clocks = 16 if branch occurs
                           ;clocks = 6 if branch does not occur
```

for count > 0

      delay =   [mov clocks   4
                  + loop clocks, when branch occurs16 * (count - 1)
                  + loop clocks, no branch]6
                  * T

or

      delay =   [4 + 16 * (count -1) + 6} * T
               [16 * count - 6] * T

for T = 125 ns (8 MHz)

      delay = 2 us * count - 1.5 us

or to compute the value of count for a desired delay

      count =   (delay + 1.5 us)/2 us

Figure 13.2-1   Delay loop execution time computation.

Execution times for variable shift and rotate instructions depend on the number of bit positions the operand is shifted or rotated. The register form of SHL takes $5 + n$ states, where n is the number of bit positions shifted. If CL has been loaded with 3, then SHL AL,CL requires 8 clocks.

For instructions with a repeat prefix, such as MOVS, the number of states consists of two parts. A constant term gives the initial number of clocks required to start the instruction, and n is the number of clocks corresponding to the number of iterations. For MOVS, the number of clocks specified is $8 + 8n$. If words are being moved by an 80C188EB, 4 clocks must be added for each memory transfer and two such transfers occur for each repetition. So, the number of clocks is $8 + 16n$.

Though it is difficult to accurately compute, the execution time for a sequence of instructions is always repeatable, assuming the same operand values and external conditions (interrupts etc.). During development, execution times for instruction sequences or procedures can be measured precisely, using an in-circuit emulator or counter/timer instrument.

Because of the difficulty in accurately computing the execution time for a sequence of instructions, it is preferable to use one of the 80C188EB's internal counter/timers or an external counter/timer or clock calendar IC to generate or measure accurate time intervals. When one of the 80C188EB's integrated timer/counters is used, the tradeoff of hardware over software incurs no added cost.

13.3   Wait States

The 80C188EB's system clock and bus timing determine how long an address and data are valid on the system bus before and after /WR is asserted during a write bus cycle. This dictates how much time a memory or I/O device has to latch the data.

For a read bus cycle, the system clock and bus timing determine how long an address is valid before and after the 80C188EB asserts /RD. This dictates how quickly a memory or I/O device must drive data onto the data bus after /RD is asserted, and how quickly it must disable its three-state buffers after /RD is unasserted.

Memory and I/O subsystems must be fast enough to keep up with the 80C188EB. If they are not, they will not be written or read reliably. You must perform a timing analysis to determine whether your memory and I/O subsystems are fast enough. Timing analysis for memory and I/O subsystems is covered in Sections 13.4 through 13.6.

If a memory or I/O subsystem is too slow, various remedies are available. One is to use a lower frequency microprocessor crystal to make the duration of a T state longer. This approach results in slower overall system operation, and is generally not acceptable. Another possibility is to replace slow memory or peripheral ICs with higher speed versions, if they exist. This results in higher component costs.

Usually the best approach is to use the 80C188EB's WAIT state capability. WAIT states (TW) can be inserted into a bus cycle following state T3 (Fig. 10.3-6). Each WAIT state is essentially an additional T3 state and is one clock period in duration. During WAIT states, the address, data, and control signals remain in the same state they were in during T3. Since WAIT states are inserted after the control signal, /WR or /RD is asserted, they have the effect of stretching the duration of these pulses. This allows a memory IC or I/O port more time to respond (Fig. 13.3-1). The last WAIT state in a bus cycle is followed by T4.

If a memory IC's chip select is generated by the 80C188EB's Chip-Select Unit, the appropriate Chip-Select Start Register can be programmed to insert from 1 to 15 WAIT states into all bus cycles that access locations in the chip select's range. One to 15 WAIT states is more than sufficient to handle most memory ICs.

For cases where the chip select is generated by an external address decoder whose output is not conditioned on an output from the Chip-Select Unit, the 80C188EB's READY input can be used to insert WAIT states. The READY input pin must be asserted to terminate a bus cycle. The 80C188EB examines its READY input during state T3 of each bus cycle. If READY is asserted, the bus cycle continues normally. However, if READY is unasserted, the 80C188EB inserts WAIT states until READY is asserted.

There are two general approaches to using the READY feature, the normally not-ready approach and the normally ready approach. The **normally not-ready** approach assumes that memory and I/O devices in the system are too slow to meet the 80C188EB's

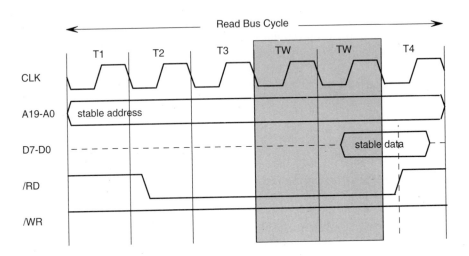

Figure 13.3-1   Read bus cycle timing diagram with two WAIT states. Signals as they
appear on the system bus, not at the 80C188EB's pins.

timing constraints without the insertion of WAIT states. The **normally ready** approach
assumes that the memory and I/O devices are fast enough to meet the 80C188EB's timing
constraints.

In a normally not-ready system, the READY input of the 80C188EB is normally
unasserted. When the addressed memory or I/O device is ready to complete the bus cycle,
external WAIT state control logic asserts READY. This approach requires that WAIT state
control logic be designed to assert READY for every access to each device in the system.
This results in more complex WAIT state control logic than the normally ready approach.
If no device responds during a bus cycle to assert READY, the system will hang executing
WAIT states indefinitely.

The normally ready approach is used in most simple systems. The READY input is
normally asserted. When a slow device is addressed, external WAIT state control logic
unasserts READY. This logic keeps READY unasserted long enough to extend the bus cycle
by a sufficient number of WAIT states. Since WAIT state control logic can be designed to
examine the address, /S2, /RD and /WR, WAIT states can be introduced for specific
address ranges, in either the memory or I/O space.

A selectable WAIT state generating circuit for a normally ready system is given in Fig.
13.3-2. When ALE is asserted, the 74HC164 shift register is cleared and its outputs are all
0s. If the chip select is also asserted, READY is unasserted and WAIT states are inserted.
When ALE is unasserted, a 1 is shifted into the shift register on each rising edge of
CLKOUT. Which output of the shift register is connected to the OR gate determines how
many CLKOUTs occur before READY is asserted and the bus cycle completes.

Some slow peripheral ICs contain internal logic that generates a busy output that is
asserted when an attempt is made to write or read the device. The busy output remains
asserted until the device is ready to complete the operation. Such an output can be used to
directly control the 80C188EB's READY input.

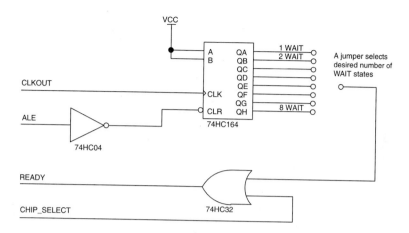

Figure 13.3-2   Shift register WAIT state generator.

For chip selects generated by the Chip-Select Unit, the programmed WAIT state feature and the READY input can be used in combination by setting the RDY bit in the Chip-Select Stop Register. If RDY is not set, the programmed number of WAIT states is inserted in a bus cycle and the READY input is ignored. If RDY is set, the programmed number of WAIT states is inserted. After the programmed number of WAIT states has elapsed, additional WAIT states are inserted until READY is asserted.

The 80C188EB internally generates a READY signal whenever an access is made to a location within the PCB. The external READY input is ignored for accesses in the PCB's address range.

There are timing compatibility problems other than a device being too slow. Some of these problems, as discussed in the Section 13.5, cannot be remedied by the insertion of WAIT states.

13.4   Memory IC Timing Parameters

Before a timing compatibility analysis can be started, the timing characteristics of the individual memory and I/O devices must be understood. Propagation delays through the internal architecture of a memory IC impose timing constraints on the sequencing of address, data, and control signals at the IC's pins. These constraints are listed as timing parameters in the manufacturer's data sheet, under the heading AC characteristics. These timing parameters are illustrated in timing diagrams. Most parameters specify the delay between two events, one of which is the cause and the other the effect. The names used to identify identical timing parameters can differ among IC manufacturers.

Typical timing parameters for the read cycle of a SRAM are illustrated in Fig. 13.4-1. These timing diagrams represent the signals at the IC's package pins. The 50 percent points of signal transitions are used here for reference. Other timing diagrams may use the 10 and 90 percent points.

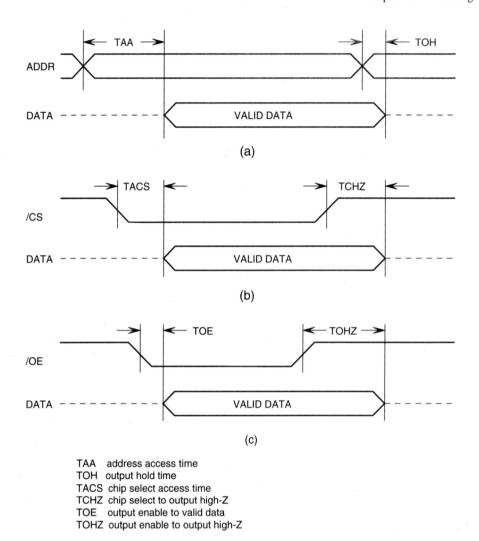

TAA   address access time
TOH   output hold time
TACS   chip select access time
TCHZ   chip select to output high-Z
TOE   output enable to valid data
TOHZ   output enable to output high-Z

Figure 13.4-1   Timing delays for a read operation on a memory IC: (a) parameters
                 related to address changes; (b) parameters related to changing /CS;
                 (c) parameters related to changing /OE.

13.4.1   Read Cycle Timing

For a read cycle, /WE remains unasserted, so its timing is not a concern. During a read
cycle, the address, /CS, and /OE change. Each signal change affects the desired output,
which is valid data. In Fig. 13.4-1, the effect of a change in each of these signals on the output data is illustrated separately.

In Fig. 13.4-1(a), /CS and /OE are assumed to be asserted throughout the operation
and, therefore, are not shown. The effect of changes at only the address inputs on valid
output data is illustrated in Fig. 13.4-1(a). The address signal (ADDR) represents all of the

IC's address inputs. The change in the address at the beginning of the cycle represents the time when the last address bit becomes stable for the new address. The change at the end of the cycle represents the time when the first address bit changes for the next address.

The delay from the application of a new address at the address pins to the appearance of the newly addressed data at the data pins, is the **address access time** (TAA). This time is simply the address valid to data valid delay of the memory IC.

With valid data at the output, if the address is changed, the output data remains valid for a short period of time. This delay is the **output hold time** (TOH).

In Fig. 13.4-1(b), the address and /OE are held fixed, with /OE asserted. The read operation is then controlled by /CS. With /CS unasserted at the beginning of the cycle, the memory IC's three-state buffers are disabled and its data pins are in their high-impedance state. When /CS is asserted, there is a delay before the output data becomes valid. This delay is the **chip select access time** parameter TACS. The delay from the negation of /CS until the three-state buffers turn OFF is the **chip select to output high Z** delay (TCHZ).

Finally, in Fig. 13.4-1(c) the address and /CS are fixed, with /CS asserted. The read operation is then controlled by /OE. The delay from the assertion of /OE until the data is valid is the **output enable to valid data** delay (TOE). The delay from unasserting /OE until the three-state buffers turn OFF is the **output enable to output high Z** delay (TOHZ).

Timing diagrams in manufacturers's data sheets are composites that show all these timing constraints on a single diagram. The composite timing diagram of Fig. 13.4-2 shows the application of address and assertion of /CS and /OE at the latest possible times in the read cycle for their effects on the output data to occur simultaneously. The primary reference points for a read cycle are the beginning (t_0) and end (t_1) of valid output data.

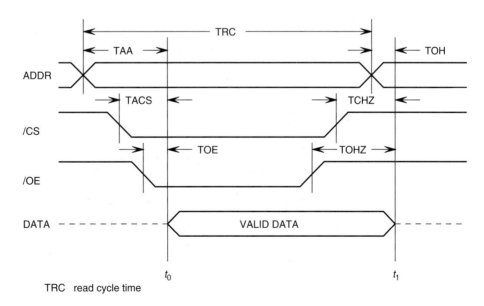

Figure 13.4-2   Timing diagram for a read cycle of a SRAM.

The timing relationships in Fig. 13.4-2 are the requirements at the IC's pins for a read operation. To have valid output data appear at the output pins at t_0:

1. The address must be valid at the address pins at least TAA ns (or more) prior to t_0.
2. /CS must be asserted at least TACS ns prior to t_0.
3. /OE must be asserted at least TOE ns prior to t_0.

As shown in the figure, TACS and TOE are usually smaller than TAA. This is due to the fact that /CS and /OE, together, directly control the output buffers. When the speed of a memory IC is expressed as a single number, for example "a 150 ns memory," the number usually represents TAA.

To insure the data remains valid until t_1, the address must remain valid until at least TOH ns before t_1.

Parameter TCHZ expresses both how long the data remains valid and how quickly the memory IC stops driving the data bus after /CS is unasserted. To use /CS to insure that the data bus is in its high impedance state after t_1, /CS must be unasserted TCHZ ns (or more) before t_1. Parameter TOHZ provides the same information with respect to unasserting /OE. To use /OE to insure that the data bus is in its high impedance state after t_1, /OE must be unasserted at least TOHZ ns before t_1.

The **read cycle time** (TRC) specifies the maximum rate at which different locations in the memory can be successively read.

13.4.2   Write Cycle Timing

For a write operation, the principal parameters are shown in Fig. 13.4-3. SRAM manufacturers usually specify two types of write cycles, **/WE controlled** and **/CS controlled**. The difference is in whether /WE or /CS is the last control signal to be asserted and the first to be unasserted during a write cycle. SRAMs used in microprocessor systems are usually /WE controlled. This is due to the fact that /CS is driven by the Chip-Select Unit or an external address decoder and is asserted before /WE and unasserted after /WE. /WE is directly driven by /WR. Figure 13.4-3 is the timing diagram for a /WE controlled write cycle.

The write pulse at the /WE input must have a minimum **write pulse width** (TW) to guarantee writing the slowest memory cells in the IC. The write pulse begins and ends the operation and is a convenient reference for specifying the parameters. For most memories, the levels on the data lines are not important until /WE is unasserted (makes its 0 to 1 transition) because most memories latch the input data at this transition. As a result, the primary reference point for most write cycle timing parameters is this transition, at t_0 in Fig. 13.4-3. This is similar to the situation that exists with a negative level triggered latch.

Data must be stable at the data input pins for a minimum period of time before t_0 to guarantee it will be accurately stored. This is the **data setup time** (TDW). Figure 13.4-3 shows TDW referenced to the 0 to 1 transition of /WE.

It is also necessary to hold the input data stable for a period of time (TDH) after t_0. This time period is the **data hold time**.

Whenever a memory IC's address inputs are changed, a finite amount of time elapses before the outputs of the memory IC's internal address decoders settle to their final value. During this settling time, transients occur at the decoder's outputs. These transients inad-

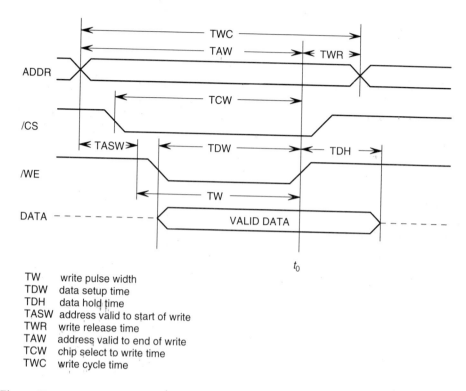

TW   write pulse width
TDW data setup time
TDH data hold time
TASW address valid to start of write
TWR write release time
TAW address valid to end of write
TCW chip select to write time
TWC write cycle time

Figure 13.4-3   Timing diagram for a /WE controlled write cycle of a SRAM IC.

vertently select other locations in the IC. If /WE is asserted *before* these transients end, the data may be erroneously written into other memory locations in addition to the one intended. To preclude this, the address lines must be stable for a period of time preceding and following the assertion of /WE. The **address valid to start of write** (TASW) indicates how long the address must be stable before /WE is asserted. The **write release time** (TWR) indicates how long the address must be held stable after /WE is unasserted.

The length of time the address must be stable before the end of the write pulse is expressed by the **address valid to end of write** parameter (TAW). Like the address inputs, /CS must be stable a period of time before the end of the write pulse. This period of time is the **chip select to end of write** (TCW).

The **write cycle time** (TWC) specifies the minimum time between successive write operations. On most static memory ICs, read and write cycle times are equal.

13.5   Memory Subsystem Timing Compatibility Calculations

The memory subsystem's timing must be compatible with that of the CPU subsystem. Memory ICs are available in different speed versions. Timing compatibility analysis is carried out to determine the slowest and least expensive version of each memory IC that is compatible with the desired microprocessor clock speed. In some applications, the fastest affordable memory ICs may still not be fast enough. In such cases, WAIT states must be introduced. Timing compatibility analysis then reveals how many WAIT states are needed.

The timing compatibility analysis in this section is based on the bus timing waveforms and AC characteristics given in the 80C188EB data sheets. These timing waveforms and AC characteristics specify the sequencing of address, data, and control signals at the 80C188EB's pins. The timing parameters are specified with respect to the transitions of CLKOUT.

Figure 13.5-1 defines the setup and hold parameters for input signals with respect to CLKOUT transitions. The required setup time for an input signal with respect to CLKOUT going high is TCHIS, and the hold time is TCHIH. Input signal setup and hold times with respect to the falling edge of CLKOUT are defined as TCLIS and TCLIH, respectively.

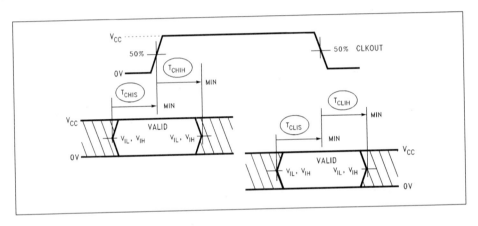

Figure 13.5-1   Input setup and hold. (Courtesy of Intel Corp.)

Values for these parameters are shown in Table 13.5-1, which gives the AC characteristics for 20 MHz and 13 MHz 80C186EBs (which also applies to the 20 MHz and 13 MHz 80C188EB).

With these parameters in mind, it can be determined from Fig. 10.3-4 that for a read bus cycle, data from the addressed device must be stable on the data bus TCLIS ns before the beginning of state t_4, and must remain stable for TCLIH ns after the beginning of t_4. These requirements are the setup and hold times the 80C188EB needs in order to latch the data. The 80C188EB assumes the appropriate external device will place data on the data bus at the correct time. Therefore, the 80C188EB interprets whatever is on the bus at the beginning of t_4 as valid data. If the device being read is too slow, it will not be able to drive the data bus soon enough after /RD is asserted to meet the 80C188EB's setup time requirement. As a result the data read will be invalid.

Consider the circuit in Fig. 13.5-2. In this circuit, /CS for the SRAM and /CE for the EPROM are generated by an external address decoder. Alternatively, they could have been directly driven by /LCS and /UCS, resulting in a simpler analysis. The timing compatibility analysis for this circuit must determine how fast the EPROM must be to be reliably read. For the SRAM, both read cycle and write cycle timing requirements must be analyzed.

Table 13.5-1   AC characteristics—80C186EB20/80C186EB13

Symbol	Parameter	20 MHz		13 MHz		Units	Notes
		Min	Max	Min	Max		
INPUT CLOCK							
T_F	CLKIN Frequency	0	40	0	26	MHz	1
T_C	CLKIN Period	25	∞	38.5	∞	ns	1
T_{CH}	CLKIN High Time	10	∞	12	∞	ns	1, 2
T_{CL}	CLKIN Low Time	10	∞	12	∞	ns	1, 2
T_{CR}	CLKIN Rise Time	1	8	1	8	ns	1, 3
T_{CF}	CLKIN Fall Time	1	8	1	8	ns	1, 3
OUTPUT CLOCK							
T_{CD}	CLKIN to CLKOUT Delay	0	17	0	23	ns	1, 4
T	CLKOUT Period		$2 \times T_C$		$2 \times T_C$	ns	1
T_{PH}	CLKOUT High Time	$(T/2) - 5$	$(T/2) + 5$	$(T/2) - 5$	$(T/2) + 5$	ns	1
T_{PL}	CLKOUT Low Time	$(T/2) - 5$	$(T/2) + 5$	$(T/2) - 5$	$(T/2) + 5$	ns	1
T_{PR}	CLKOUT Rise Time	1	6	1	6	ns	1, 5
T_{PF}	CLKOUT Fall Time	1	6	1	6	ns	1, 5
OUTPUT DELAYS							
T_{CHOV1}	ALE, $\overline{S2{:}0}$, $\overline{DEN}$, DT/$\overline{R}$, $\overline{BHE}$ ($\overline{RFSH}$), $\overline{LOCK}$, A19:16	3	22	3	25	ns	1, 4, 6
T_{CHOV2}	$\overline{GCS0{:}7}$, $\overline{LCS}$, $\overline{UCS}$, $\overline{NCS}$, $\overline{RD}$, $\overline{WR}$	3	27	3	30	ns	1, 4, 7
T_{CLOV1}	$\overline{BHE}$ ($\overline{RFSH}$), $\overline{DEN}$, $\overline{LOCK}$, RESOUT, HLDA, T0OUT, T1OUT, A19:16	3	22	3	25	ns	1, 4
T_{CLOV2}	$\overline{RD}$, $\overline{WR}$, $\overline{GCS7{:}0}$, $\overline{LCS}$, $\overline{UCS}$, AD15:0 (AD7:0, A15:8), $\overline{NCS}$, $\overline{INTA1{:}0}$, $\overline{S2{:}0}$	3	27	3	30	ns	1, 4
T_{CHOF}	$\overline{RD}$, $\overline{WR}$, $\overline{BHE}$ ($\overline{RFSH}$), DT/$\overline{R}$, $\overline{LOCK}$, $\overline{S2{:}0}$, A:19:16	0	25	0	25	ns	1
T_{CLOF}	$\overline{DEN}$, AD15:0 (AD7:0, A15:8)	0	25	0	25	ns	1
T_{CHIS}	$\overline{TEST}$, NMI, INT4:0, BCLK1:0, T1:0IN, READY, CTS1:0, P2.6, P2.7	10		10		ns	1, 8
T_{CHIH}	$\overline{TEST}$, NMI, INT4:0, BCLK1:0, T1:0IN, READY, $\overline{CTS1{:}0}$	3		3		ns	1, 8
T_{CLIS}	AD15:0 (AD7:0), READY	10		10		ns	1, 9
T_{CLIH}	READY, AD15:0 (AD7:0)	3		3		ns	1, 9

Table 13.5-1   AC characteristics—80C186EB20/80C186EB13 (Continued.)

Symbol	Parameter	20 MHz		13 MHz		Units	Notes
		Min	Max	Min	Max		
T_{CLIS}	HOLD, PEREQ, $\overline{\text{ERROR}}$	10		10		ns	1, 8
T_{CLIH}	HOLD, PEREQ, $\overline{\text{ERROR}}$	3		3		ns	1, 8

NOTES:
1. See Figs. 13.5-1, 13.5-3, and 13.5-7 for waveforms and definitions.
2. Measure at V_{IH} for high time, V_{IL} for low time.
3. Only required to guarantee I_{CC}. Maximum limits are bounded by T_C, T_{CH}, and T_{CL}.
4. Specified for a 50 pF load.
5. Specified for a 50 pF load.
6. T_{CHOV1} applies to $\overline{\text{BHE}}$ ($\overline{\text{RFSH}}$), $\overline{\text{LOCK}}$, and A19:16 only after a HOLD release.
7. T_{CHOV2} applies to $\overline{\text{RD}}$ and $\overline{\text{WR}}$ only after a HOLD release.
8. Setup and Hold are required to guaranee recognition.
9. Setup and Hold are required for proper operation.

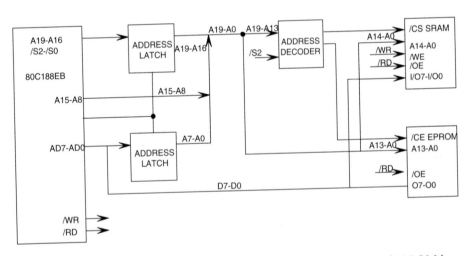

Figure 13.5-2   Memory subsystem with 32K × 8 of SRAM and 16K × 8 of EPROM interfaced to minimum mode unbuffered 80C188EB.

13.5.1   EPROM Timing Analysis

The EPROM's timing parameters are TACC, TCE, TOE, and TDF (Table 13.5-2). Each parameter must be individually considered and its requirements met.

Table 13.5-2   Timing Constraints for Read Cycle of EPROM and SRAM in Fig. 13.5-2.

EPROM Parameters	SRAM Parameters	System Constraints[a]
TACC	TAA	$< \text{TAVDV} - \text{address latch delay} + n_W T$[b]
TCE	TACS	$< \text{TAVDV} - (\text{address latch delay} + \text{address decoder delay})^c + n_W T$
TOE	TOE	$< \text{TRLDV} + n_W T$
TDF	TOHZ	$< \text{TRHAV}$

a. Where $\text{TAVDV} = 3T - \text{TCLOV2max} - \text{TCLISmin}$
  and $\text{TRLDV} = 2T - \text{TCLOV2max} - \text{TCLISmin}$
b. $n_W T$ is the product of the number of WAIT states and the state time
c. Address latch and address decoder delay are 0 if /CE is driven by a chip select from the Chip Select Unit.

TACC Analysis

TACC is the delay from a valid address applied at the EPROM's address inputs until valid data appears at its output. The system into which the EPROM is placed must allow the EPROM at least this much time to provide the data. If not, then the EPROM is too slow. The time allowed by the system is the time allowed by the 80C188EB reduced by the delays introduced by any other components in the signal paths between the 80C188EB and the EPROM.

Before carrying out this analysis, it is important to understand, from Fig. 13.5-3, that the delay from a CLKOUT transition until an output is valid is given by the parameters TCHOV with respect to high transitions and TCLOV with respect to low transitions. The minimum value for these two parameters specifies how long data remains valid after a clock transition. The maximum value specifies how long it takes for the data to become valid after a transition. Note that TCHOV and TCLOV parameters are used for both the assertion and unassertion of output signals. There are two different values for each of these parameters for different sets of output signals.

Examination of the 80C188EB read timing waveforms (Fig. 10.3-4) reveals that there is no single parameter that specifies the time from the 80C188EB's generation of a stable address to stable data being required at its AD7–AD0 pins. However, this time can be derived from the other timing parameters that are provided. If the desired parameter is defined as "address valid to data valid" (TAVDV), Fig. 13.5-4 shows how TAVDV is determined. The address is valid TCLOV2 ns after the beginning of t_1 and the data must be valid TCLIS ns before the beginning of t_4. Thus,

$$\text{TAVDV} = 3T - \text{TCLOV2max} - \text{TCLISmin},$$

where T is the time of one CLKOUT period. TCLIS is the setup time for valid data, referenced to the falling edge of t_4. By definition, only a minimum time requirement makes sense for a setup time. Therefore, TCLISmin is the only value defined for TCLIS, and is the value used.

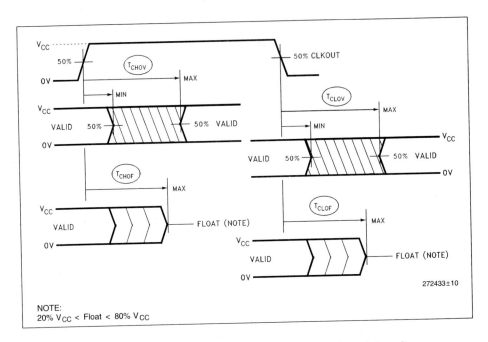

Figure 13.5-3   Output delay and float waveform. (Courtesy of Intel Corp.)

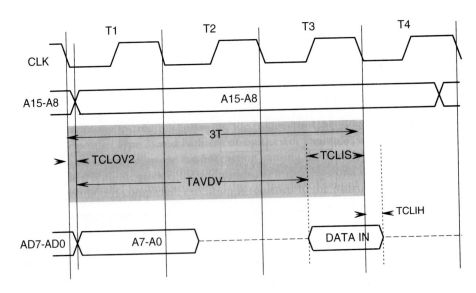

Figure 13.5-4   Derivation of TAVDV from timing diagram.

The fact that TAVDV is also clock period dependent (a function of T) means that if the 80C188EB is run at a slower clock speed, larger T, the amount of time available for TAVDV is increased.

As can be seen in Fig. 13.5-5 (a) and (b), there are two signal paths from the 80C188EB's address pins to the EPROM's address pins. Address lines A13–A8 of the 80C188EB are connected directly to the corresponding pins of the EPROM (Fig. 13.5-5(a)). For this path, the access time available for the EPROM corresponds to the time

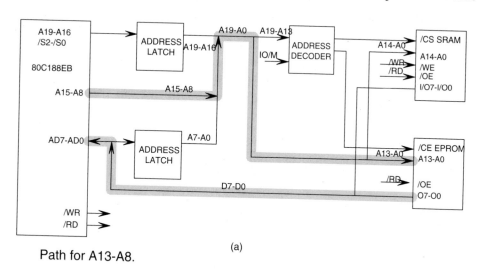

(a)

Path for A13-A8.

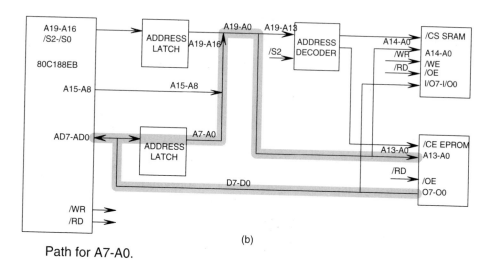

(b)

Path for A7-A0.

Figure 13.5-5   Signal path for timing analysis of the EPROM's TACC parameter: (a) path for address bits A13–A8; (b) path for address bits A7–A0.

from the 80C188EB generating a valid address to the time the 80C188EB requires valid data at its AD7–AD0 pins, or simply TAVDV. Thus, for this path the constraint is TACC < TAVDV.

The path for address bits A7–A0 from the 80C188EB is through an address latch (Fig. 13.5-5(b)). This path is the longest, in terms of delays, of the two paths and, therefore, is the worst-case path. This is because the access time available to the EPROM is reduced by the delay through the address latch. Thus, the timing constraint on TACC requires that the following inequality:

$$TACC < TAVDV - \text{address latch delay}$$

be satisfied.

The value on the right hand side of the previous expression is the upper limit for the address access time of the EPROM when used in the circuit of Fig. 13.5-2. If WAIT states were inserted, the value for TACC would be increased by T for each WAIT state. In this case, the relationship would be:

$$TACC < TAVDV - \text{address latch delay} + n_W T$$

Note that all the expressions involving inequalities specify constraints that must be meet, and are not statements indicating that the specified relationships actually exist.

TCE Analysis

Analysis of the time available for TCE, the "chip enable to valid data delay," involves two paths (Fig. 13.5-6 (a) and (b)). The EPROM's chip enable is derived from A19–A14. A15–A14 take one path to the decoder and A19–A16 take a second, longer, path. A19–A16 propagate through both an address latch and the address decoder (Fig. 13.5-6 (b)). This longer path yields:

$$TCE < TAVDV - (\text{address latch delay} + \text{address decoder delay}) + n_W T$$

TOE Analysis

TOE is the delay from asserting the EPROM's /OE input until valid data appears at its outputs. Since /OE is directly driven by /RD, a determination must be made of how long the 80C188EB allows from "read low until data valid," which is denoted as TRLDV. TRLDV is not specified directly, but is derived as:

$$TRLDV = 2T - TCLOV2max - TCLISmin.$$

With this parameter defined, the time allowed for TOE is:

$$TOE < TRLDV + n_W T.$$

TDF Analysis

The EPROM's TDF parameter indicates how quickly its three-state buffer floats after /OE is unasserted. TDF impacts two aspects of the timing, the hold time required by the 80C188EB, TCLIH, and whether data placed on the multiplexed address/data bus by the EPROM is removed soon enough so it does not conflict with the address placed on the address/data bus by the 80C188EB for the next cycle.

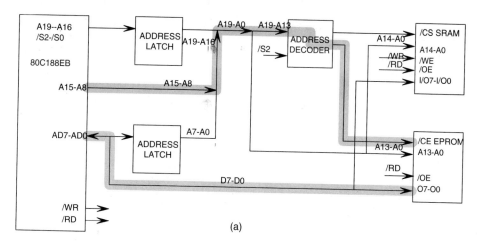

Path for A15–A14.

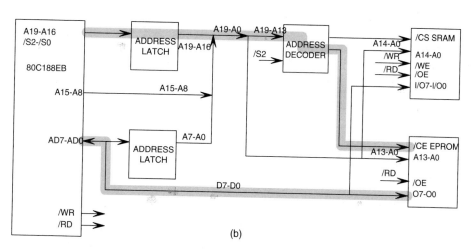

Path for A19–A16.

Figure 13.5-6   Signal path for timing analysis of the EPROM's TCE parameter: (a) path for address bits A15–A14; (b) path for address bits A19–A16.

The 80C188EB requires that data remains valid for TCLIH ns after the falling edge of the CLKOUT that starts t_4. The negation of /RD does not occur until TCLOV2 ns after the start of t_4. Therefore, even if the three-state buffer could turn off instantly, data would remain valid for at least TCLOV2 ns. Since TDF for the EPROM is not zero, TDF provides additional hold time for valid data. Thus,

$$TDF > TCLIHmin - TCLOV2min$$

The values for TCLIHmin and TCLOV2min are equal, making any nonzero value for TDF acceptable.

Examination of the 80C188EB relative signal timing diagram (Fig. 13.5-7) indicates that after /RD is unasserted, TRHAV ns elapse before the 80C188EB drives AD7–AD0 with address bits A7–A0 for the next bus cycle. The EPROM must stop driving the data bus before this happens or bus contention occurs. The resulting constraint is:

$$TDF < TRHAV$$

Note that insertion of WAIT states has no effect on this constraint.

Table 13.5-3 gives values for the relative timing parameters for 20 MHz and 13 MHz 80C188EBs.

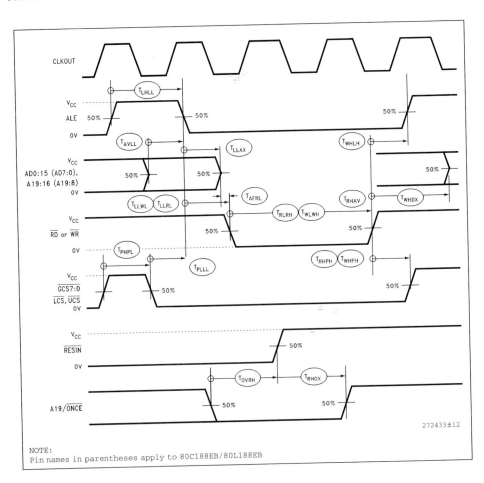

Figure 13.5-7   Relative signal waveform. (Courtesy of Intel Corp.)

Table 13.5-3   Relative Timings (80C186EB25, 20, 13/80L186EB16, 13, 8).

Symbol	Parameter	Min	Max	Units	Notes
T_{LHLL}	ALE Rising to ALE Falling	$T - 15$		ns	
T_{AVLL}	Address Valid to ALE Falling	$\frac{1}{2}T - 10$		ns	
T_{PLLL}	Chip Selects Valid to ALE Falling	$\frac{1}{2}T - 10$		ns	1
T_{LLAX}	Address Hold from ALE Falling	$\frac{1}{2}T - 10$		ns	
T_{LLWL}	ALE Falling to $\overline{WR}$ Falling	$\frac{1}{2}T - 15$		ns	1
T_{LLRL}	ALE Falling to $\overline{RD}$ Falling	$\frac{1}{2}T - 15$		ns	1
T_{WHLH}	$\overline{WR}$ Rising to ALE Rising	$\frac{1}{2}T - 10$		ns	1
T_{AFRL}	Address Float to $\overline{RD}$ Falling	0		ns	
T_{RLRH}	$\overline{RD}$ Falling to $\overline{RD}$ Rising	$(2 \times T) - 5$		ns	2
T_{WLWH}	$\overline{WR}$ Falling to $\overline{WR}$ Rising	$(2 \times T) - 5$		ns	2
T_{RHAV}	$\overline{RD}$ Rising to Address Active	$T - 15$		ns	
T_{WHDX}	Output Data Hold after $\overline{WR}$ Rising	$T - 15$		ns	
T_{WHPH}	$\overline{WR}$ Rising to Chip Select Rising	$\frac{1}{2}T - 10$		ns	1
T_{RHPH}	$\overline{RD}$ Rising to Chip Select Rising	$\frac{1}{2}T - 10$		ns	1
T_{PHPL}	$\overline{CS}$ Inactive to $\overline{CS}$ Active	$\frac{1}{2}T - 10$		ns	1
T_{OVRH}	$\overline{ONCE}$ Active to $\overline{RESIN}$ Rising	T		ns	3
T_{RHOX}	$\overline{ONCE}$ Hold from $\overline{RESIN}$ Rising	T		ns	3

NOTES:
1. Assumes equal loading on both pins.
2. Can be extended using wait states.
3. Not tested.

13.5.2   SRAM Timing Analysis

Timing analysis for the read cycle of the SRAM is similar to that for the EPROM. The equivalent timing parameters for the SRAM are also given in Table 13.5-2.

For the SRAM write cycle, the timing parameters are summarized in Table 13.5-4.

TW Analysis

The SRAM's /WE is directly driven by the 80C188EB's /WR (Fig. 13.5-2). The width of /WR is given as TWLWH (Fig. 13.5-7). As a result, the minimum duration write strobe required by the SRAM, TW, must be less than TWLWH:

$$TW < TWLWH + n_W T$$

TDW and TDH Analysis

Since the data pins of the SRAM are connected directly to AD7–AD0, no delays are introduced as far as data setup (TDW) and hold (TDH) are concerned. The setup time (TDVWH) provided by the 80C188EB is not given directly on the timing diagram. The

Table 13.5-4   Timing Constraints for Write Cycle of SRAM in Fig. 13.5-2.

SRAM Parameter	System Constraint
TW	$< \text{TWLWH} + n_W T$
TDW	$< \text{TDVWH}^{\text{a}} + n_W T$
TDH	$< \text{TWHDX}$
TASW	$< \text{TAVWL} - \text{address latch delay}^{\text{b}}$
TAW	$< 3T - \text{TCLOV2max} + \text{TCLOV2min} - \text{address latch delay} + n_W T$
TCW	$< \text{TAW} - \text{address decoder delay}$
TWR	$< \text{TWHLH} + \text{address latch delay}$
TWR	$< T - \text{TCLOV2max} + \text{TCLOV2min}$

a. $\text{TDVWH} = 2T - \text{TCLOV2max} + \text{TCLOV2min}$
b. $\text{TAVWL} = T - \text{TCLOV2max} + \text{TCLOV2min}$

data becomes valid TCLOV2max ns after the start of t_2 and /WR is unasserted TCLOV2min ns after the start of t_4. As a result:

$$\text{TDVWH} = 2T - \text{TCLOV2max} + \text{TCLOV2min}.$$

Therefore:

$$\text{TDW} < \text{TDVWH} + n_W T$$

The hold time is indicated directly as TWHDX. Thus:

$$\text{TDH} < \text{TWHDX}$$

and this constraint is not affected by WAIT states.

TASW, TAW, and TCW Analysis

The SRAM parameter TASW specifies the minimum time that the SRAM requires a valid address exist at its address pins before the start of the write pulse at its /WE input. The time from the 80C188EB generating a valid address until it asserts /WR, TAVWL, is not given directly but is derived as:

$$\text{TAVWL} = T - \text{TCLOV2max} + \text{TCLOV2min}.$$

Address pins A14–A8 of the 80C188EB are connected directly to the corresponding pins of the SRAM. Address bits A7–A0 are latched from pins AD7–AD0 of the 80C188EB. Of these two paths, the latter places the greatest constraint on the time available for TASW since the address latch reduces the time available for TASW via this path. Thus, the requirement is:

$$\text{TASW} < \text{TAVWL} - \text{address latch delay}$$

and is not affected by WAIT states.

The relationship for time available for the SRAM's "address valid to end of write" parameter (TAW) is determined in a similar fashion to be:

$$\text{TAW} < 3T - \text{TCLOV2max} + \text{TCLOV2min} - \text{address latch delay} + n_W T$$

The TCW, "chip select valid to end of write" time available to the SRAM, is the same as the time available for TAW minus the delay of the address decoder:

$$TCW < 3T - TCLOV2max + TCLOV2min - \text{address latch delay}$$
$$- \text{address decoder delay} + n_w T.$$

TWR Analysis

Write release time (TWR) the amount of time the address remains stable at the SRAM's address inputs after the end of /WR, must be derived. Two relationships can be obtained. The expression for the address bits that are latched is:

$$TWR < TWHLH + \text{address latch delay.}$$

And, the expression for the address bits that go directly to the SRAM is:

$$TWR < T - TCLOV2max + TCLOV2min.$$

These two expressions need to be evaluated numerically to determine which is the limiting case.

If a bidirectional buffer were included in the data bus path, the effect of its delay would have to be included in the calculations.

The results of the timing compatibility analysis allow the selection of the appropriate speed versions of the memory ICs and/or identifies the number of WAIT states that must be inserted. These types of calculations are vital to achieve a properly designed memory system.

13.5.3   Timing Margins and WAIT States

In conducting a timing analysis, all the constraints that have been discussed must be met. If all the delays in the circuit are considered in the timing analysis and their worst case values are used in the calculations, no additional timing margin is required. However, the above relationships don't include propagation delays of signals through wires and printed circuit board traces. Some additional margin, say 10 to 15 ns, should be included to compensate for these factors.

Using the results of the timing calculations, appropriate actions can be taken to insure compatibility. In many cases, inserting an appropriate number of WAIT states is the solution. In other cases, such as not meeting hold time requirements, WAIT states have no effect. In such a case, a memory IC with a less severe hold requirement might be substituted. Alternatively, a buffer can be added. The propagation delay of the buffer increases the hold time available to the memory IC.

13.6   I/O Timing Considerations

The same type of analysis used in Section 13.5 for memory subsystem timing applies to I/O subsystems. However, the options available to achieve compatibility are generally more limited. Many peripheral ICs are available in only one speed or with very few speed options. In addition, many peripheral ICs are significantly slower than typical memory ICs. This leaves the introduction of WAIT states as the primary approach to providing timing compatibility.

Generating exhaustively decoded chip selects for I/O peripherals generally requires the use of external decoders. The 64 byte granularity provided by the Chip-Select Unit when used to generate chip selects for the I/O address space is not sufficient by itself. However, as was shown in Sections 12.4 and 12.5, an external decoder may be used in combination with the CSU to generate an exhaustively decoded chip select.

One convenient way to generate WAIT states for I/O devices, while keeping external address decoders simple, is to use one or more of the 80C188EB's general chip select outputs as input to external decoders. For example, consider a system which has six peripheral devices. Two of these devices require 2 WAIT states, three require 5 WAIT states, and one requires 8 WAIT states. Three 80C188EB chip select outputs could be programmed to generate the desired WAIT states and to have nonoverlapping address ranges. The chip select outputs are then used as inputs to a PLD. Each I/O device would be assigned to an address in the range covered by the appropriate chip select. Each PLD output's Boolean equation would include the appropriate CSU chip select and lower order address bits.

In extreme cases of timing incompatibility, it may be necessary to interface a peripheral IC through a port rather than connect it directly to the system bus.

13.7   80C188EB Timer/Counter Unit

As has been shown, counting and timing functions can be implemented using procedures. However, in more complex applications, this software approach requires too much CPU time. A hardware approach is preferable. Also, when very accurate time intervals must be generated or measured, a hardware approach is required. A programmable timer/counter can be used to implement many kinds of counter-based functions in a system, such as an event counter, a real-time clock, a square-wave generator, a one-shot, or pulse width measurement. The 80C188EB's Timer/Counter Unit (TCU) provides three independent 16-bit binary timer/counters, Timer 0, Timer 1, and Timer 2.

13.7.1   Timers 0 and 1

Timers 0 and 1 are functionally identical. Timer 0 is conceptually represented in Fig. 13.7-1. Timer 1 would be represented similarly. The operation of Timers 0 and 1 will be described in terms of Timer 0.

Timer 0 has an input pin (T0IN) and an output pin (T0OUT). Four 16-bit PCB registers are associated with Timer 0. All four registers can be read or written at any time, even while the timer is operating. **Timer Control Register** (**T0CON**) controls Timer 0's mode of operation (Fig. 13.7-2). This register provides status bits in addition to control bits.

The other three registers associated with Timer 0 all hold 16-bit binary values. The **Timer Count Register** (**T0CNT**) holds the current count. The two **Timer Maxcount Compare Registers** (**T0CMPA** and **T0CMPB**) hold maximum count values that the TCU compares to the value in T0CNT. These two registers allow operation of the timer in either of two counting modes. In **single maximum count mode**, when idle, Timer 0's output (TOUT) is a 1. When Timer 0 is enabled to count, its output remains 1 until the count in T0CNT reaches T0CMPA. At the end of this time interval, T0CNT is cleared and an active-low output pulse is generated at T0OUT (Fig. 13.7-3). The active-low output pulse has a duration of one period of CLKOUT.

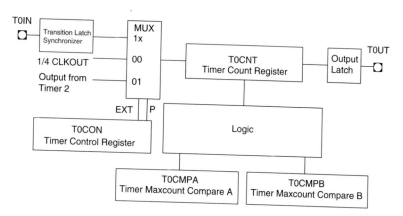

Figure 13.7-1   Functional representation of Timer 0 of the 80C188EB's Timer/Counter Unit. Timer 1 is functionally identical but independent of Timer 0.

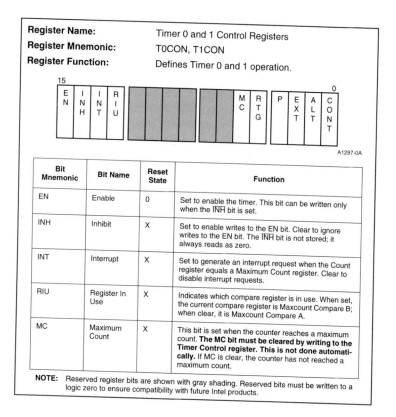

Figure 13.7-2   Timer 0 and Timer 1 control registers. (Courtesy of Intel Corp.)

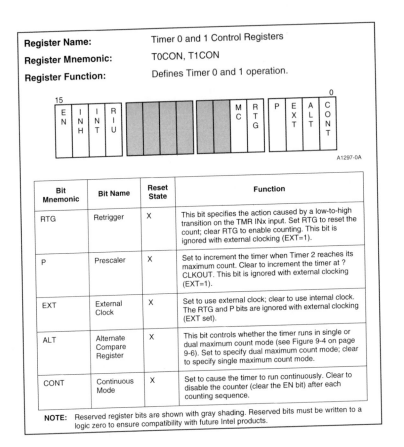

Figure 13.7-2   Timer 0 and Timer 1 control registers. (Courtesy of Intel Corp.)
(Continued.)

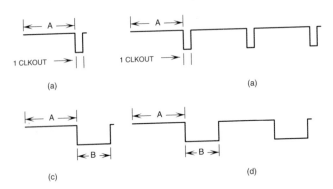

Figure 13.7-3   Timer 0 (and Timer 1) counting modes: (a) single maximum count mode
noncontinuous; (b) single maximum count mode continuous; (c) dual
maximum count mode noncontinuous; (d) dual maximum count mode
continuous.

In **dual maximum count mode**, Timer 0 holds its T0OUT high until T0CNT reaches T0CMPA. Then it resets T0CNT and holds T0OUT low until T0CNT reaches T0CMPB.

Incrementing T0CNT

T0CNT is incremented in response to each timer event. A **timer event** can be one of three possible occurrences depending on the timer event source selected. You use bits in T0CON (Fig. 13.7-2) to specify the source and the counting mode. There are three possible timer event sources, as shown in Fig. 13.7-1. Bits EXT and P in T0CON select the source (Table 13.7-1). Regardless of which source is selected, no counting occurs unless the enable bit (EN) is set. The enable bit is set by writing 1s to bit positions EN and /INH in T0CON. /INH is the inhibit bit. When /INH equals 0, it prevents a write to T0CON from changing the value of EN.

Table 13.7-1   Timer event sources for Timer 0.

EXT	P	Timer Event Source
0	0	1/4 CLKOUT
0	1	Output of Timer 2
1	0	0 to 1 transitions at T0IN
1	1	0 to 1 transitions at T0IN

Transitions from 0 to 1 at Timer 0's external input pin (T0IN) can be counted by setting the external bit (EXT). T0CNT is then incremented for each 0 to 1 transition at T0IN. Transitions at T0IN are synchronized to the 80C188EB's clock by the Transition Latch/Synchronizer at the T0IN input. Because of the way that Timer 0's counting element is implemented, the maximum rate at which 0 to 1 transitions can be counted is 1/4 of the 80C188EB's CLKOUT frequency. For example, for a 20-MHz 80C188EB the maximum count rate is 5 MHz. Since T0CNT is a 16-bit counter, the maximum count value that can be held in this register is 65,535.

When EXT is 0, either of two internal timer event sources can be selected based on the prescalar bit P. If P is 0, an internal signal with a frequency of 1/4 CLKOUT is counted. When P is 1, T0CNT is incremented each time Timer 2 reaches it maxcount. In the latter case, Timer 2 prescales (divides down) an internal signal that has a frequency of 1/4 CLKOUT.

When configured for internal clocking, an external enabling condition at T0IN must be met for T0CNT to count. The condition depends on the retrigger bit (RTG). If RTG is 0, the timer's input pin is level sensitive and the timer is enabled for counting when T0IN is 1.

If EXT is 0 and RTG is 1, the timer's input pin is edge sensitive. Counting is not enabled until a 0 to 1 transition occurs at T0IN. The first timer event after the 0 to 1 transition at T0IN clears T0CNT. Subsequent timer events increment T0CNT. The occurrence of a subsequent 0 to 1 transition at T0IN before maxcount is reached clears T0CNT, and counting continues from 0. This extends the timer cycle and is equivalent to retriggering a retriggerable one-shot (monostable multivibrator).

13.7.2   Counting Modes

As previously stated, Timer 0 can be operated in either of two counting modes, single maximum count mode and dual maximum count mode. The alternate (ALT) bit in T0CON selects the mode. For single maximum count mode, ALT is 0. Each time T0CON is incremented, its value is compared to the value in T0CMPA. If the values are equal, T0CNT is cleared, the maxcount bit (MC) is set, and a negative pulse of one CLKOUT duration is generated at T0OUT (Fig. 13.7-3(a)). The timer can also be programmed to generate an interrupt request when the maximum count is reached by setting the interrupt (INT) bit in T0CON. The actions of incrementing T0CNT, comparing it with T0CMPA, and resetting T0CNT (if justified) take place in one clock cycle. As a result, the maximum count value is never actually stored in T0CNT.

The time interval for the timer to count from 0 to its maximum count value is defined as a **timer cycle**. The single pulse at the T0OUT in Fig. 13.7-3(a) marks the end of the timer cycle. A maxcount value of 0 results in a timer cycle of 65,536 counts. If the continuous bit (CONT) in T0CON is 0, the timer executes a single timer cycle. When this single timer cycle is completed, the EN bit is automatically cleared and the counter stops counting. If CONT is 1, the timer executes timer cycles continuously and never clears EN. This results in periodic output pulses at T0OUT (Fig. 13.7-3(b)).

In the dual maximum count mode, the timer sets T0OUT and counts until it reaches the value in T0CMPA. This constitutes a timer cycle. The timer then clears T0OUT and T0CNT. Next the timer counts until its reaches the value in T0CMPB (Fig. 13.7-3(c)). This constitutes a second timer cycle, so T0CNT is again cleared. Whenever a maxcount is reached, maxcount bit (MC) is set. MC is set when maxcount A is reached and is set again when maxcount B is reached.

However, MC is not automatically cleared. The only way MC is cleared is by writing a 0 to the MC bit position in the T0CON register.

If the timer is programmed for continuous operation in the dual maximum count mode, the result at T0OUT is a variable duty cycle square wave, which is high for T0CMPA counts and low for T0CMPB counts (Fig. 13.7-3(d)).

Output pin T0OUT's value indicates which Maxcount Compare Register is in use. When T0OUT is 1, Maxcount Compare Register A is in use. When T0OUT is 0, Maxcount Compare Register B is in use. This information is also provided by the Register In Use bit (RIU) in T0CON. However, the sense of RIU is opposite that of T0OUT. RIU is 0 when maxcount register A is in use, and 1 when maxcount register B is in use.

In the dual maxcount mode, even if the timer is not programmed to run continuously, its output always goes high when the timer halts. If interrupts are enabled in the dual maxcount mode, an interrupt request occurs after maxcount A is reached and another interrupt is generated after maxcount B is reached.

The detailed operation of Timers 0 and 1 is illustrated in the flowchart of Fig. 13.7-4.

13.7.3   Timer 2

Timer 2 has no input or output pins and can only be clocked internally at a rate of 1/4 CLKOUT. Timer 2 has no Maxcount Compare Register B, and, therefore, only operates in

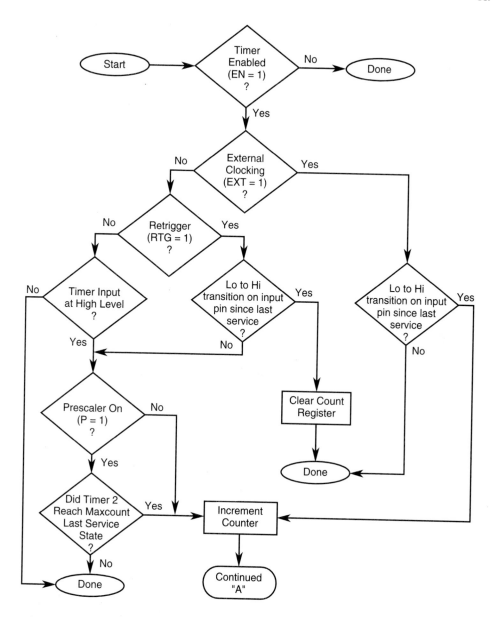

Figure 13.7-4   Timers 0 and 1 flow chart. (Courtesy of Intel Corp.)

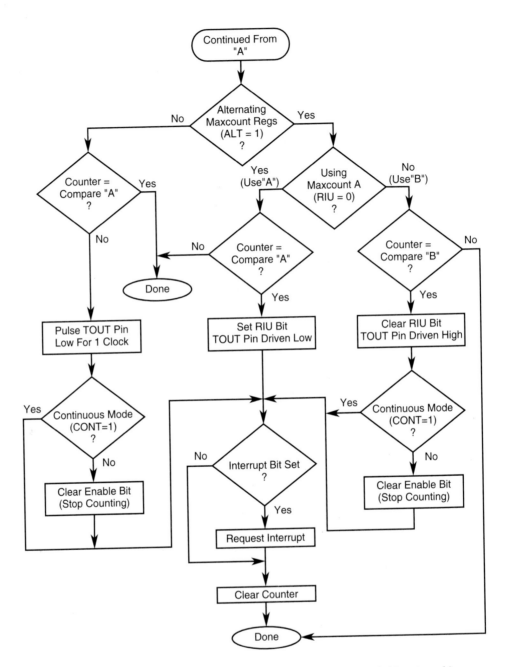

Figure 13.7-4   Timers 0 and 1 flow chart. (Courtesy of Intel Corp.) (Continued.)

single maximum count mode. Timer 2 is typically used to generate a free running real-time clock or as a prescalar for Timers 0 and 1. A **prescalar** simply divides down its input frequency to produce a lower output frequency. This lower (prescaled) frequency is input to a second timer. This technique allows the second timer to generate lower output frequencies than it could have by directly dividing down the original source frequency.

When used as a real-time clock, Timer 2 is used to generate a periodic interrupt. Each interrupt generated corresponds to a "clock tick." An example of this use of Timer 2 is given in Chapter 14.

The control register for Timer 2 is shown in Fig. 13.7-5.

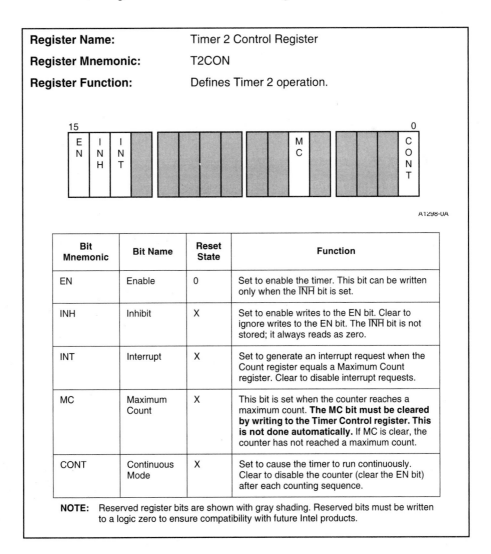

Figure 13.7-5   Timer 2 control register. (Courtesy of Intel Corp.)

13.7.4   Timer/Counter Application Example

As an example of the use of the 80C188EB's Timer/Counter Unit, consider an application that requires the measurement of an external square wave's frequency. Assume this frequency is no greater that 65 KHz. Also, assume the 80C188EB's clock frequency is 20 MHz.

The configuration of the Timer/Counter Unit to make this measurement uses all three timers (Fig. 13.7-6). Timer 0 counts 0 to 1 transitions of the unknown frequency for 1 second. Thus, after the 1 second interval, the value in Timer 0 is the measured frequency.

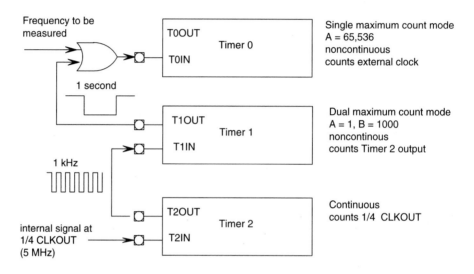

Figure 13.7-6   80C188EB Timer/Counter Unit configured to measure frequency.

A 1 second gate pulse is required to gate Timer 0 for the measurement. The asserted-low 1 second gate pulse is generated by Timer 1. Timer 1 uses the output of Timer 2 as the time base from which it generates the 1 second gate.

The sequence of instructions to initialize the Timer/Counter Unit prior to the first measurement is shown in Fig. 13.7-7. The timer/counter registers' values are indeterminate after reset and must be initialized to zero. The order of initialization of the timers is important. Timer 1 is initialized first, but is not enabled.

Timer 1 is initialized to operate in dual maximum count mode, with maxcount A = 1 and maxcount B = 1000. While Timer 1 is disabled, its T1OUT pin is 1. When it is enabled to make a measurement, T1OUT stays 1 for one count at T1IN. On the next count, T1OUT becomes 0 and remains 0 for 1000 counts at T1IN. After the 1000 counts, when maxcount B is reached, T1OUT returns to 1. Since Timer 1 is configured for noncontinuous operation, T1OUT remains 1.

```
;Initialize Timer 1 Count Register to zero
        mov     dx,T1CNT        ;zero counter
        mov     ax,0
        out     dx,ax

;Initialize Timer 1: dual maximimum count mode, A=1 and B=1000,
;noncontinuous operation, count output of Timer 2
        mov     dx,T1CMPA       ;maxcount A = 1
        mov     ax,1
        out     dx,ax
        mov     dx,T1CMPB       ;maxcount B = 1000
        mov     ax,1000
        out     dx,ax
        mov     dx,T1CON
        mov     dx,000ah        ;not enabled, external
        out     dx,ax           ;dual count mode, noncontinuous


;Initialize Timer 0 Count Register to zero
        mov     dx,T0CNT        ;zero counter
        mov     ax,0
        out     dx,ax

;Initialize Timer 0: single maximum count mode, A = 65,536
;non-continuous operation, counts gated external frequency
        mov     dx,T0CMPA       ;maxcount A = 0 (65,536)
        mov     ax,0
        out     dx,ax
        mov     dx,T0CON
        mov     ax,0c004h       ;enabled, external, continuous
        out     dx,ax

;Initialize Timer 2: continuous operation, counts 1/4 of CLKOUT
        mov     dx,T2CMPA       ;maxcount = 5000
        mov     ax,5000
        out     dx,ax
        mov     dx,T2CON
        mov     dx,0c001h       ;enable, no interrupt, continuous
        out     dx,ax
```

Figure 13.7-7   Initialization of Timer/Counter Unit for frequency measurement.

Timer 1 is configured for prescaling. Therefore, it counts pulses at its T1IN input from Timer 2. If the period of the input signal at T1IN is 1ms, a single asserted low pulse of 1 second duration appears at T1OUT, whenever Timer 1 is enabled by setting its EN bit.

Timer 0 is initialized and enabled next. It is initialized to count external events and to operate noncontinuously. It is initialized for single maximum count mode with a maximum count of 65,536 (0). It can never reach this count because it will only receive timer events for 1 second and the maximum frequency to be measured is 65 KHz. The maximum count possible is 65,000.

Lastly, Timer 2 is initialized and enabled. It generates the 1 KHz time base for Timer 1 by prescaling the internal 5 MHz input (1/4 of 20 MHz) and operating in the continuous mode.

After the initialization sequence (Fig. 13.7-7) is completed, the fact that Timer 1 is not enabled means the measurement is idle. To make a measurement, the procedure meas_freq in Fig. 13.7-8 is called. This procedure enables Timer 1 to start the measurement. The procedure then tests the Register In Use (RIU) bit first to determine if the 1 second gate has started, and then to determine when the gate has terminated.

```
meas_freq      proc
               mov     dx,T1CON
               mov     ax,0c00ah;enabled, external
               out     dx,ax            ;dual count, not continuous

gate_start?:
               mov     dx,T1CON;wait for gate to start
               in      ax,dx
               test    ax,1000h
               jz      gate_start?

gate_end?:
               mov     dx,T1CON;wait for 1 sec gate to end
               in      ax,dx
               test    ax,1000h
               jnz     gate_end?

               mov     dx,T0CNT;save measured frequency
               in      ax,dx
               mov     cx,ax
               xor     ax,ax            ;clear T0CNT
               out     dx,ax
               ret
meas_freq      endp
```

Figure 13.7-8   Frequency measurement procedure.

When maximum count B has been reached, the procedure reads the measured frequency from T0CNT. T0CNT is then cleared in preparation for the next measurement.

A drawback to the approach in meas_freq is polling to determine when the measurement is complete. This can be avoided by configuring Timer 1 to generate an interrupt at the end of its timing cycle. The meas_freq procedure would then be modified so all it does is enable Timer 1 to start the measurement and then return. The 80C188EB would then go on to other tasks until it is interrupted. A separate interrupt procedure, written to handle Timer 1's interrupt, would then read T0CNT to get the measured frequency and clear T0CNT in preparation for the next measurement.

13.8   82C54 Programmable Interval Timer/Counter

When additional timer/counter capability beyond that provided by the 80C188EB's Timer/Counter Unit is needed, a timer/counter peripheral IC can be used. A popular device for this purpose is the 82C54 Timer/Counter. The 82C54 is often used on single board microcomputers and on PC/104 Counter/Timer modules.

The 82C54 Programmable Interval Timer/Counter provides three independent 16-bit counters in a single 24-pin DIP or a 28-pin PLCC (Fig. 13.8-1). Each counter can be programmed to operate in any one of six modes. The counters can count in either binary or BCD. Unlike the timer/counters in the 80C188EB, the 82C54's counters are down counters. They are initialized with a nonzero count, and then counted down to zero. Each counter has its own clock input, gate input, and counter output. The 82C54-2 can handle clock inputs from DC to 10 MHz. In some modes of operation, the counter's output consists of a change in level after a programmed initial count is counted down to zero. In other modes, the output consists of a repetitive pulse train that is related to the input pulse train by the programmed count.

The 82C54 has four 8-bit ports. Three of these can be written or read and correspond to counter 0, counter 1, and counter 2. The fourth is a control register and can only be written. The 82C54's three 16-bit counters are programmed, initialized, and read through these four 8-bit ports. Each counter must be programmed before it is used. Programming a counter consists of writing its control word (a byte), followed by the initial count (a word). The 82C54's data sheet can be consulted for a detailed description of the programming procedure.

The 82C54 has six modes of operation, each of which is briefly explained in this section. This is an overview of the modes of operation. For a more detailed description of each mode, refer to the 82C54's data sheets.

Each counter is fully independent and can operate in a different mode than the other counters. For an 82C54 counter, a clock pulse is defined as a rising edge followed by a falling edge at its CLK input, and a trigger is defined as a rising edge at the GATE input. The gate must be 1 for counting to be enabled. A simplified representation of each mode is illustrated in Fig. 13.8-2. These waveforms illustrate the simple case where GATE = 1, or where a single trigger (GATE making a 0 to 1 transition) occurs.

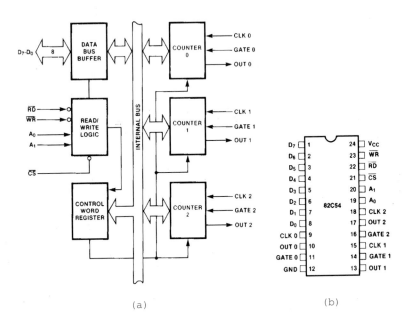

Figure 13.8-1   82C54 Programmable interval Timer: (a) block diagram; (b) pin configuration. (Courtesy of Intel Corp.)

13.8.1   Mode 0: interrupt on terminal count

After the control word is written, OUT is low. After the initial count is written, it is loaded into the counting element, CE, on the first CLK pulse. The first CLK pulse does not decrement the count. For an initial count of N, OUT goes high $N + 1$ CLK pulses later. If GATE is 0 when the initial count is written, the first clock pulse loads CE but following CLKs will not effect CE as long as GATE remains low. However, after GATE is asserted, the next CLK pulse decrements CE, and OUT goes high N clock pulses after GATE is asserted.

    With this mode, OUT can be used to generate a single interrupt after a specified number of events (CLKs) or a specified time interval has elapsed.

13.8.2   Mode 1: hardware retriggerable one-shot

After the control word and initial count are written, the counting element is armed. On the first CLK pulse following a trigger, the counter is loaded and OUT goes low. An initial count of N causes OUT to stay low for N CLKs following the trigger and then go high. The one-shot is retriggerable because if OUT is already low it will remain low for an additional N CLKs if an additional trigger occurs.

    This mode can be used to generate control pulses of a prescribed duration or to create a watchdog timer.

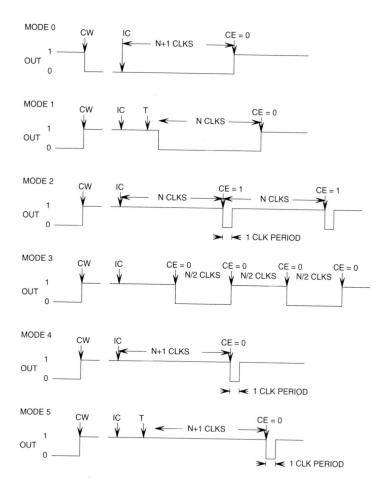

Figure 13.8-2   Simplified OUT waveform for modes of 82C54 counter timer.
CW = control word
IC = initial count
T = trigger
CE = counting element

13.8.3   Mode 2: rate generator

After the control word has been loaded, OUT is initially high. The next CLK pulse after the count is loaded, loads CE. When the count decrements to 1, OUT goes low for one CLK period then returns high. For an initial count of N, OUT goes low N CLK pulses after the initial count is loaded. The counter automatically reloads the initial count and the cycle repeats. Thus, OUT is periodic, going low for one CLK period, every N CLKs.

This mode can be used to generate an interrupt every N CLKs and is often used in the implementation of a real-time clock.

13.8.4   Mode 3: square wave mode

This mode is similar to mode 2, except that OUT is a square wave with a period of N. OUT is initially high and, when half the count has expired, goes low for half the count. OUT is a periodic waveform. For odd N, OUT is high for $(N + 1)/2$ counts and low for $(N - 1)/2$ counts.

Mode 3 can be used to create a square wave with a frequency that is equal to $1/N$ times the frequency of CLK. Clock sources for peripherals can be generated by using one of the 82C54's counters to divide down CLKOUT from the 80C188EB.

13.8.5   Mode 4: software triggered strobe

After writing the control word, OUT will initially be high. The first CLK after the initial count is written loads CE; this CLK does not decrement the count. When the initial count reaches 0, OUT will go low for one CLK period. For an initial count of N, OUT does not go low until $N + 1$ CLK pulses after the initial count is written. Writing the initial count triggers the counting. If an initial count is written before the strobe has occurred from a previous control word, the new count is loaded on the next CLK and the time interval before the strobes occurrence is extended by the new count. Thus, this mode is software retriggerable.

13.8.6   Mode 5: hardware triggered strobe

After writing the control word and initial count, CE is loaded on the first CLK pulse after a trigger. This CLK pulse does not decrement CE. For an initial count of N, OUT does not go low until $N + 1$ CLKs after the trigger. The counting sequence is retriggerable. OUT will not strobe low until $N + 1$ CLK pulses after any trigger.

13.9   Real-Time Clocks

Applications often require that time of day and date information be maintained. For example, this is necessary when measured data must be time stamped or when it is important to record the actual time when some event takes place. A simple programmable timer could be configured to generate a "clock tick" interrupt. The associated interrupt service routine would update memory locations containing the time of day and date for each clock tick. However, a more efficient hardware solution is readily available in IC form.

Real-time clocks or **clock calendar** ICs are microprocessor compatible CMOS circuits designed specifically to provide time of day and date information. A real-time clock consists of a time base oscillator whose output is prescaled then fed into a chain of counters. The first counter in the chain counts fractions of a second. The carry from this counter feeds a counter that counts seconds, followed by a counter that counts minutes, and so on. The last counter in the chain counts years. The counters are designed to automatically account for leap years, daylight savings time, and the number of days in each month. The counters typically count in BCD. The real-time clock IC is battery backed, so it maintains the correct time when power is turned off or lost.

The counters can be written to initially set or to change the time and date, and read to determine the time and date. Care must be taken when reading the time or date to deal with the possibility of reading the counters while they are in the process of being incremented. Most real-time clocks have hardware provisions or recommended techniques that can be used to avoid this problem.

The block diagram of National Semiconductor's **DP8572A Real-Time Clock** is shown in Fig. 13.9-1. The DP8572A requires a crystal and two capacitors to provide the

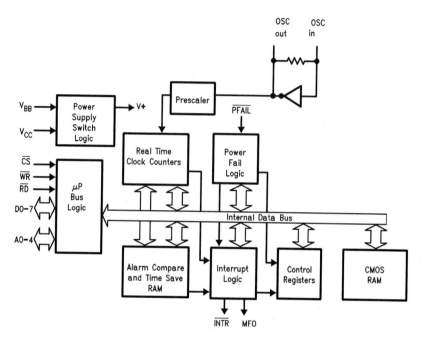

Figure 13.9-1   National DP8572A Real-Time Clock block diagram. (Courtesy of National Semiconductor Corporation.)

oscillator (OSC) signals. The oscillator's internal output is scaled to 100Hz before being input to the counter chain. The first counter in the chain counts every 0.01 seconds.

The counters in the chain are shown on the bottom left side of Fig. 13.9-2. The DP8752A looks like two software selectable 31-byte pages in I/O or memory space and a Main Status Register which is common to both pages. Page 0 contains the registers corresponding to the clock counters and control, data, and status registers. The control registers in page 0 are further split into two separate blocks selected by a register select bit. Page 1 consists of 31 bytes of CMOS RAM that can be used for general purposes. This small amount of nonvolatile RAM may be sufficient for many applications where nonvolatile RAM is required, obviating the need for a separate battery-backed CMOS RAM. The DP8572A has its own separate power input for a battery, V_{BB}. Circuitry on the DP8572A automatically switches from V_{CC} to the battery when V_{CC} drops too low.

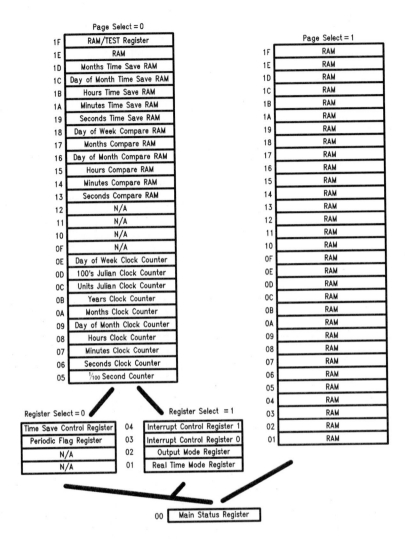

Figure 13.9-2   DP8572A Real-Time Clock memory map. (Courtesy of National Semi-
                 conductor Corporation.)

Registers in either of these two pages can be selected for reading or writing through
the DP8752 bus interface logic which provides a typical microprocessor interface.

Compare registers allow an interrupt to be generated when a preprogrammed date
and time of day are reached. This is similar to setting an alarm clock, except the alarm time
can be specified more precisely, from the month down to the second. The occurrence of an
alarm can be used to generate an interrupt. Thus, with a real-time clock it is possible to
cause a task to be executed at some specific time far into the future.

With a little ingenuity a system can be designed to go to sleep, then wake up at some
preprogrammed date and time and turn on its own AC power and perform its functions.

13.10   Watchdog Timers

A **watchdog timer** is a hardware circuit that, if its input is not pulsed at some minimum rate, generates an output signal indicating a fault. It is essentially similar to a retriggerable one-shot, which times out if it is not retriggered often enough.

Watchdog timers are used in embedded systems to detect certain types of system failures and to reset the system. These types of failures are often caused by electrical interference or programming errors that cause the system to fetch instructions from areas of memory that don't contain code. As a result, the system may end up in an infinite loop or hang up in some other way.

In a simple implementation, the application software periodically generates a device select pulse that retriggers the watchdog timer. If the application consists of a master loop that calls procedures to implement the system's function, an instruction that retriggers the watchdog timer could be placed in the master loop. If the system fails in such a manner that this instruction is not repeatedly executed, then the watchdog timer times out. The resulting time out signal can be used to either reset the microprocessor or generate a non-maskable interrupt.

If the choice is to reset the system, the assumption is that resetting the system will solve the problem. But this assumption may not be valid. Resetting is a rather brute force approach to error detection and recovery. Another approach is to have the time out signal generate a nonmaskable interrupt. This interrupt causes execution of a procedure that attempts a system recovery appropriate to the application. Nonmaskable interrupts are covered in the next chapter.

Some microcontrollers contain an integrated watchdog timer. Alternatively, a watchdog timer can be implemented using a retriggerable one-shot, a programmable counter, or a watchdog timer IC.

Many microprocessor supervisory circuits include a watchdog timer function. For example, the MAX807 microprocessor supervisory circuit (Fig. 10.3-2) includes a watchdog timer. Either a change of state or a pulse must occur at the MAX807's watchdog input (WDI) at least every 1.6 seconds or its watchdog output (/WDO) is asserted. /WDO can be used to either reset the system or generate a nonmaskable interrupt.

A provision to externally disable the watchdog timer should also be included. Disabling the watchdog timer is necessary during debugging because when a breakpoint is reached, the watchdog timer will not get retriggered and will reset the system. For the MAX807, the watchdog output is disabled if WDI is disconnected or allowed to float.

13.11   Summary

Timing requirements can dictate the system level architecture of a design. The speed of a software approach must be determined when trying to decide if a specific task should be implemented primarily in software or hardware. Computing a task's execution time based on the execution time of its instruction sequence can be difficult, due to the complex interaction between the 80C188EB's EU and BIU, and the fact that WAIT states may be used. Nevertheless, rough approximations can be made. And, for tasks that are ultimately done in software, knowledge of instruction execution times allows the code's speed to be optimized.

All components in a system must be compatible in terms of speed. The speed at which the microprocessor runs sets the overall timing constraints for the system. Each memory IC and peripheral IC has its own timing requirements. A timing compatibility analysis must be performed to determine whether each memory or peripheral IC is compatible with the microprocessor's timing. This analysis must consider the memory IC or peripheral in the context of the system's circuitry.

Introducing WAIT states into bus cycles is the primary way to handle timing compatibility problems resulting from a memory or peripheral IC being too slow. WAIT states can be introduced by the 80C188EB's Chip Select Unit or by an external WAIT state generator.

Measuring the time between external events and generating time based output signals are common tasks in embedded systems. Programmable counter/timer circuits are used for this purpose. The 80C188EB has three 16-bit counter/timers in its integrated Timer Counter Unit. Additional timer/counters can be provided by external programmable counter/timers such as the 82C54.

When date and time of day information are needed, a real-time clock or clock/calendar IC is used. These low power circuits are battery backed and can keep track of date and time information even when the AC power is removed.

13.12   Problems

1. An 80C188EB system uses a 40-MHz crystal. What is the least amount of time required to transfer a single byte of data between the 80C188EB and an external I/O port?

2. Compare the speeds of implementing the following operations:

   a. clearing a register using XOR rather than MOV r,0,

   b. incrementing a pointer by 2 using INC or SHL or ADD.

3. An 80C188EB uses a 40-MHz crystal. Determine the instruction execution time for each of the following instructions.

   ```
   (a) mov        cx,2732
   (b) mov        ax,wvar1        ;wvar1 is a word variable
   (c) mov        bx,wvar1
   (d) mov        bx,warray[si]   ;warray is an array
   (e) rol        ax,cl           ;assume CL is 5
   (f) rol        wvar1,cl        ;assume CL is 5
   ```

4. Compute the time required to move a block of 128 words from one buffer in memory to another, using MOV instructions in a loop. Compare this with the time required to accomplish the same task with a MOVSW in a loop, and, finally, with the MOVSW with a REP prefix. Assume the buffers do not overlap and the state time is 50 ns.

5. Write an expression that gives the delay time of the variable delay procedure of Fig. 8.5-1 as a function of the constant TENMSEC and the parameter passed to the procedure in CX. Is the value equated to TENMSEC correct for an 80C188EB operated at 20 MHz?

6. Analyze the operation of the shift register WAIT state generator circuit of Fig. 13.3-2. Draw a timing diagram for a read bus cycle showing CLK, /RD, QA, AB, and RDY for the case where the QA output of the shift register is used. Do the same for the case where the QB output is used. Are the setup and hold time requirements of the 82C84A RDY input met?

7. TWR is the write release (address hold from end of write) parameter for the write cycle of a SRAM. What is the consequence of not meeting the requirement indicated by this parameter?

8. Determine the time available for each of the EPROM parameters for the circuit in Fig. 13.5-2 for 80C188EB clock speeds of 13 MHz and 20 MHz. Assume the propagation delay through an address latch is 7 ns and through the address decoder is 25 ns.

9. The only EPROM available for use in the circuit of Fig. 13.5-2 has TACC = TCE = 450 ns. The circuit uses an 80C188EB operated at 13 MHz. Are WAIT states required? If so, how many?

10. Assume that a bidirectional buffer is added to the circuit of Fig. 13.5-2 to buffer the data bus. Draw a block diagram of the buffer onto Fig. 13.5-1 in the proper position. Label the control signals from the 80C188EB that control the buffer. Determine the time available for the EPROM parameters, TACC, TCE, TOE, and TDF in this modified circuit. And assume the 80C188EB is operated at 20 MHz.

11. Draw a timing diagram similar to Fig. 13.5-4 to show the derivation of TDW.

12. Draw a timing diagram similar to Fig. 13.5-4 to show the derivation of TWR.

13. An 80C188EB system's functions are written as tasks. The order and time of each task's execution is controlled by a simple scheduler procedure. The scheduler's software implementation of a real time clock requires an NMI interrupt every 100ms. How would you accomplish this using the 80C188EB's Timer/Counter Unit?

14. A motor has a shaft encoder that generates a single positive pulse for each revolution of the motor's shaft. If the motor's speed exceeds 6000 revolutions per minute for more than 1 second, the system will self-destruct. The system is controlled by an 80C188EB operated at 20 MHz. If the 80C188EB determines that the motor's speed is excessive, it can take corrective action. However, if the 80C188EB devotes its time to continually software monitoring the motor, it will not have time to implement other necessary system functions. Solve this dilemma by using the 80C188EB's TCU and as little other logic as possible. First describe the outline of your solution approach, then give as detailed a description of the solution implementation as possible.

14

INTERRUPTS AND EXCEPTIONS

14.1　　Fundamental Interrupt Concepts

14.2　　80C188EB Interrupts and Interrupt Processing Sequence

14.3　　Interrupt Vector Table

14.4　　80C188EB Hardware Interrupts

14.5　　80C188EB Interrupt Control Unit (ICU)

14.6　　Interrupt Service Routines (ISRs)

14.7　　Interrupt Driven Systems

14.8　　Software Interrupts and Exceptions

14.9　　Interrupt Priority and Latency

14.10　82C59A Priority Interrupt Controller

14.11　Debugging Systems That Use Interrupts

14.12　Summary

Polling to determine when an I/O device requires service has certain disadvantages. Consider an application where there are several I/O devices and the microprocessor must quickly respond to each one's request to preclude a loss of data. The need to frequently poll each device severely complicates the software's design. Constant polling also entails significant software overhead, reducing system throughput. As an alternative, interrupts can be used to allow each I/O device to directly signal the microprocessor when it requires service. Use of interrupts eliminates the need to poll.

A microprocessor's interrupt pin allows a signal from an external device to temporarily interrupt a program's execution flow and cause an interrupt procedure to be executed. The interrupt procedure executes the task required to service the external device. After the interrupt procedure completes execution, execution flow continues from the point of interruption. An interrupt capability makes it possible for a microprocessor to respond immediately to external events, such as an I/O device setting its service request flip-flop.

A typical microprocessor may have several interrupt pins, allowing signals from multiple external sources to interrupt the microprocessor. Each interrupt source has a separate interrupt procedure written to handle its specific needs. A priority is assigned to each interrupt pin, so if two interrupt requests occur simultaneously, the microprocessor knows which interrupt procedure to execute first.

Interrupts can be used as a basis upon which to structure a system's software architecture. Software can be designed so a program's execution flow is primarily determined by external events that generate interrupts. The microprocessor executes interrupt procedures according to the order of occurrence and priority of interrupt requests. The order and priority of interrupt requests then becomes the principal factor determining the sequence of task execution. Such a system is interrupt driven.

In addition to hardware interrupts, there are also software interrupts. Two kinds of sources of software interrupts exist, interrupt instructions and exceptions. An interrupt instruction causes an interrupt procedure to be immediately executed. An interrupt instruction is like a call instruction, except that an interrupt procedure is executed rather than a normal procedure. An exception causes an interrupt in response to an unusual condition that requires correction before normal program execution can continue.

Almost all embedded systems use interrupts to some degree; many use them extensively. Consequently, a clear understanding of interrupts is very important.

14.1   Fundamental Interrupt Concepts

Some fundamental interrupt concepts, applicable to most microprocessors, are presented in this section. The 80C188EB's interrupts are the focus of the remainder of this chapter.

An **event** is an action, occurrence, or happening to which a microprocessor must respond. Events are typically asynchronous. An **asynchronous event** is one that occurs at unpredictable points during a program's execution. Events include actions such as pressing a key on a keypad, an ADC's completion of a conversion, the closing of a limit switch, the receipt of a serial character by a UART, or detection of imminent power supply failure.

The microprocessor must respond to an event by executing an interrupt procedure that performs a task appropriate to the event. The microprocessor cannot always respond immediately. So, an **interrupt request flip-flop** is used to record the event until the microprocessor can respond.

The need to record an event until it can be responded to is not a new concept. This was also necessary with polling. With a polled interface, the flip-flop that records an event is called a service request flip-flop. What is different with interrupts is how the microprocessor detects and responds to an interrupt request flip-flop being set.

The output of an interrupt request flip-flop is connected directly to one of a microprocessor's interrupt pins (Fig. 14.1-1). When the interrupt request flip-flop is set by an event, such as an input device loading data into an input port, the microprocessor is interrupted and automatically transfers execution to the interrupt procedure. The interrupt procedure inputs and processes the data. After completion of this task, execution continues from the point of interruption.

In many applications, the system's overall effectiveness depends upon how quickly it can detect events and perform their associated tasks. Such requirements can make the use of

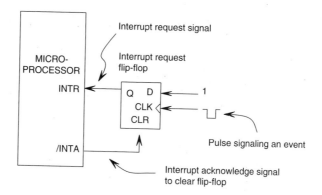

Figure 14.1-1   Direct connection of an interrupt service request flip-flop's output to a microprocessor's interrupt pin.

interrupts essential. In addition to reducing response time, use of interrupts has the potential to simplify software design by reducing software overhead and task scheduling decisions.

As shown in Fig. 14.1-1, a microprocessor's interrupt capability allows a device to directly signal the microprocessor concerning an event. The device is referred to as the **interrupt source**, and the signal it generates is an **interrupt request signal**. Usually an interrupt request flip-flop is set by the device and the flip-flop's output is connected directly to an interrupt pin to provide the interrupt request signal. For many peripheral ICs, the interrupt request flip-flop is contained in the IC. While the interrupt request signal is asserted, the interrupt is said to be **pending.** The interrupt request signal must remain asserted until the microprocessor acknowledges the request.

The microprocessor responds to an interrupt request by executing an **interrupt service procedure (ISP)** most often referred to as an **interrupt service routine (ISR)**, or **interrupt handler**. An ISR is simiiar, in most respects, to a normal procedure. When an ISR completes its execution, execution flow is returned to the point of interruption. Having I/O devices use interrupts to request service is referred to as **interrupt driven I/O**.

After the microprocessor responds to an interrupt request by transferring execution flow to the ISR, the interrupt request flip-flop must be cleared. This may be done automatically if the microprocessor provides an **interrupt acknowledge signal** as shown in Fig. 14.1-1. Alternatively, instructions in the ISR can be used to generate a device select pulse to clear the flip-flop.

An interrupt input is either maskable or nonmaskable. You can disable a **maskable interrupt** input by using an instruction in your program. A microprocessor ignores requests at a disabled interrupt input. A maskable interrupt input must be disabled immediately before the microprocessor executes a **critical section** of code, one where the occurrence of an interrupt could create a problem. After execution of the critical section of code, the interrupt input is reenabled.

A **nonmaskable interrupt** input cannot be disabled. Such an input is often used to handle a catastrophic event, one which must, under any circumstances, be responded to immediately. An example is the detection, by a microprocessor supervisory circuit, of the imminent failure of a system's power supply. In this case, the ISR might attempt to save, in nonvolatile memory, information about the system's state. When power is restored, the system can use the saved information to continue processing from the point where power was lost. In addition, or alternatively, the ISR might shut the system down in a fail-safe manner.

Interrupt inputs are either edge or level sensitive. An **interrupt request** exists, or is pending, at a **level sensitive interrupt input** while the signal at that input is asserted. The signal must remain asserted until the microprocessor acknowledges the request. If it does not, the request is lost. Of equal importance is the necessity to clear the interrupt request flip-flop before the ISR is completed. If this is not done, a single event continually generates interrupts. This causes the system to hang in an infinite loop.

For an **edge triggered** or **edge sensitive interrupt input**, an interrupt request exists if the signal at the interrupt pin makes the required transition, either positive or negative. Some edge triggered inputs also require the signal remain asserted after the transition until the interrupt is acknowledged. Other types of edge sensitive inputs have an internal interrupt request flip-flop. When the edge occurs, the internal flip-flop is set. When the interrupt is responded to, the internal flip-flop is automatically cleared.

If the signal at an edge triggered interrupt input has been previously asserted, it must first be changed to the opposite logic level then reasserted before it can generate a second interrupt. This requirement constitutes a **lockout feature**. For example, with a positive edge triggered interrupt input, a rising edge requests an interrupt. But, if the signal remains at the positive level after the interrupt request is acknowledged, the continued existence of the positive level alone is not sufficient to be considered a valid interrupt request.

A typical system rarely has just a single interrupt source. To handle interrupt requests from multiple interrupt sources, a microprocessor may provide several interrupt pins. Another approach is to use a single interrupt pin and connect the multiple interrupt request signals to a priority interrupt controller IC. This IC synchronizes and prioritizes the requests to provide a single interrupt request signal to the microprocessor (Fig. 14.1-2).

A unique ISR is associated with each interrupt source. When an interrupt request is acknowledged, the microprocessor automatically identifies which source caused the interrupt, and transfers execution to the appropriate ISR.

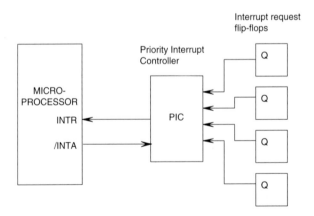

Figure 14.1-2   Using a priority interrupt controller to combine several interrupt requests into one.

In applications with more than one interrupt source, multiple events can occur simultaneously. Since the microprocessor can only execute a single ISR at a time, there must be a priority assigned to each interrupt source. The assigned **priority** determines to which interrupt request the microprocessor first responds. The microprocessor services each interrupt request in turn, according to its priority.

14.2   80C188EB Interrupts and Interrupt Processing Sequence

The 80C188EB has six external interrupt pins (Fig. 14.2-1). If this number is insufficient for your application, you can use an external Priority Interrupt Controller to expand the number of interrupt inputs (Section 14.10). In addition to these external hardware interrupts, the 80C188EB has two internal hardware interrupts associated with the Timer Unit and Serial Communications Unit on-chip peripherals.

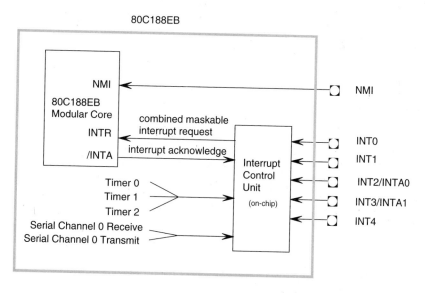

Figure 14.2-1   Hardware interrupt inputs to an 80C188EB modular core. NMI is directly from an external pin. The other external interrupts connect to the on-chip Interrupt Control Unit. Two internal interrupts combine the timer interrupt requests and serial channel 0 interrupt requests, respectively.

The 80C188EB also has software interrupts. Software interrupts can be directly generated by the execution of an interrupt instruction or indirectly generated by an exception. For clarity, it is important to make a distinction between an interrupt request, or pending interrupt, and the actual interruption of the 80C188EB's execution flow. An external source may generate an interrupt request, causing the associated interrupt to be pending. Or, the conditions for an exception may be valid, causing the interrupt associated with the exception to be pending. These situations are often casually referred to as interrupts.

However, under some conditions there may be a significant delay between an interrupt request and the 80C188EB's responding by transferring execution to the interrupt's ISR. This execution transfer constitutes the actual interrupt. In fact, under certain conditions it is possible that an external interrupt request never gets serviced. That is, the actual transfer of execution to the ISR, the interrupt, never occurs. Allowing a situation to occur where an interrupt request never gets serviced is unacceptable in most applications.

Situations that delay or prevent a pending interrupt from being serviced are discussed later. The focus will now be on how the 80C188EB processes an actual interrupt. The 80C188EB modular core handles an interrupt from any source in essentially the same manner. This common response is illustrated in Fig. 14.2-2, and comprises the **interrupt processing sequence**.

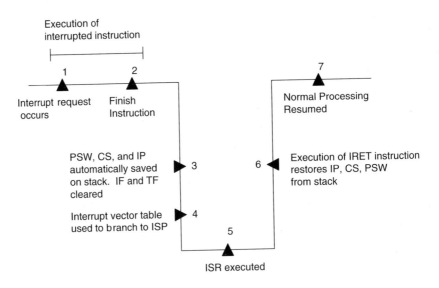

Figure 14.2-2   80C188EB Interrupt processing sequence.

Figure 14.2-2 shows an interrupt request occurring during an instruction's execution. For convenience, the instruction being executed when the interrupt request occurs is referred to as the **interrupted instruction**. This term is somewhat misleading since, except for a few special cases, the interrupted instruction's execution is actually completed before interrupt processing begins.

After the interrupted instruction's execution is complete, the 80C188EB acknowledges the interrupt request. In response to this acknowledgment, and depending on the kind of interrupt, the 80C188EB's modular core either receives a vector table offset directly or receives a type code from which it computes a vector table offset. The 80C188EB uses the vector table offset to transfer execution flow to the appropriate ISR. But, before this can happen the 880C188EB must save part of the current task's context. A task's **context** is the information needed to resume the task's execution if the task is stopped before its completion and some other task is executed. In the case of a task that is interrupted, the context includes the contents of the general purpose registers, segment registers, IP, and SP. To save part of the current task's context and transfer execution to the ISR, the interrupt processing sequence must:

1. Save the flags, by pushing PSW onto the stack.
2. Clear the IF and TF bits in PSW. Clearing these bits disables the maskable interrupts and the single step exception, respectively.
3. Save the return address by pushing CS and IP onto the stack.
4. Obtain the ISR's CS and IP values from the interrupt vector table and use them to transfer execution to the ISR.

These interrupt processing sequence steps are illustrated in Fig. 14.2-3 (a).

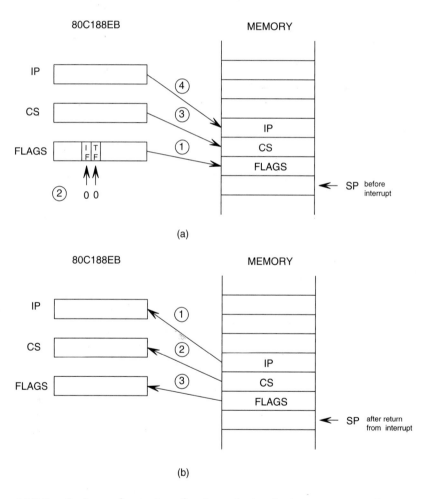

Figure 14.2-3   Saving and restoring of registers during the interrupt processing sequence: (a) registers saved on the stack at start of sequence; (b) registers restored at end of sequence.

The structure of the interrupt vector table and the table lookup process are explained in the next section. The new CS:IP value obtained from the interrupt vector table is the address of the first instruction in the ISR. In effect, step 4 is equivalent to an indirect far call. The indirection is through a double word in memory, the interrupt vector.

The ISR implements a task associated with the event that caused the interrupt. When the task is complete, the ISR is terminated by execution of an *interrupt return instruction*, **IRET** (Table 14.2-1). Execution of IRET:

1. Pops the saved IP and CS values from the stack.
2. Pops the saved PSW value from the stack.

These steps complete the interrupt processing sequence and are illustrated in Fig. 14.2-3(b). Instruction execution continues with the instruction following the interrupted instruction.

Table 14.2-1   Interrupt related instructions.

Mnemonic	Operands	Function	O	D	I	T	S	Z	A	P	C
IRET	none	Interrupt return	–	–	–	–	–	–	–	–	–
STI	none	Set interrupt enable flag	–	–	1	–	–	–	–	–	–
CLI	none	Clear interrupt enable flag	–	–	0	–	–	–	–	–	–
HLT	none	Halt	–	–	–	–	–	–	–	–	–
INT	type[a]	Interrupt	–	–	0	0	–	–	–	–	–
INTO	none	Interrupt on overflow	–	–	–	–	–	–	–	–	–
BOUND	reg,mem	Detect value out of range	–	–	–	–	–	–	–	–	–

a. Type is an 8-bit immediate value

14.3   Interrupt Vector Table

In order to transfer execution to the appropriate ISR, the 80C188EB must have a way to identify each interrupt source and to determine the starting address of the interrupt source's ISR. Each interrupt source is identified by a unique 8-bit **type code**. Thus, 256 different interrupts can be distinguished.

The 80C188EB gets the starting address of an ISR from the **interrupt vector table** in memory (Fig. 14.3-1). The interrupt vector table can contain 256 entries, one for each interrupt type code. Each table entry is a 32-bit address. These 32-bit addresses are called **interrupt vectors**. The position of an interrupt vector in the interrupt vector table is related to the type code of its associated interrupt.

Each interrupt vector is a double word pointer to an ISR. This pointer consists of the CS and IP values for the first instruction in the ISR. Each interrupt vector is stored with IP as the least significant word. Using CS and IP values from the interrupt vector table to transfer execution to an ISR is referred to as "vectoring to the ISR."

The interrupt vector table starts at physical address 00000H, and it is not relocatable. In most cases, the 80C188EB receives the interrupt vector table offset for the interrupt vec-

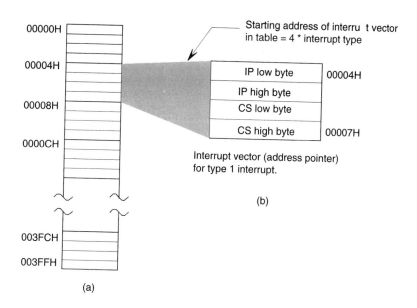

Figure 14.3-1   Interrupt vector table: (a) 1K byte vector table with space for 256 elements; (b) vector for type 1 interrupt (single step).

tor directly from internal logic. For interrupt requests from an external Priority Interrupt Controller, the 80C188EB receives from the external Priority Interrupt Controller the interrupt type code, not the offset. The 80C188EB multiplies the type code by 4 to obtain the interrupt vector's offset.

With a maximum of 256 type codes and four bytes per interrupt vector, a 1K byte table holds all possible interrupt vectors. The physical address range for the table is from 00000H through 003FFH. Interrupt vector 0, corresponding to interrupt type 0, starts at address 00000H and occupies the first four bytes. Interrupt vector 1, for interrupt type 1, starts at address 00004H and occupies the next four bytes, and so on.

The purposes of the first 32 interrupts, types 0 through 31, are either predefined or reserved by Intel. The predefined interrupts are assigned to the 80C188EB's interrupt pins, on-chip peripherals, and exceptions. Their names, vector table addresses, and type codes are given in Table 14.3-1. Note that type codes are often specified in decimal.

If compatibility with future Intel hardware and software products is desired, you should not use any of the reserved interrupts. Since 224 interrupts are still available, this restriction is not significant. Interrupt types 32 through 255 can be assigned as you like. Systems using DOS reserve interrupts 32 through 63 for use by the operating system. If all 256 interrupts are not used, the entire first 1K bytes of memory need not be allocated for the interrupt vector table.

For each interrupt used, its interrupt vector must be initialized by your software. Initialization entails placing the ISR's CS and IP values into the proper locations in the interrupt vector table. The details of the initialization process differ depending on whether the first 1K of the memory is ROM or RAM.

Table 14.3-1   Assignment of interrupt vectors to interrupt vector table.

Address in Vector Table (Hexadecimal)	Vector Type	Interrupt Name	Priority[a]
00H	0	Divide Error	1
04H	1	Single Step	1a
08H	2	Non-Maskable	1
0CH	3	Breakpoint	1
10H	4	Overflow	1
14H	5	Array Bounds	1
18H	6	Invalid Op-Code	1
1CH	7	ESC OP-Code	1
20H	8	Timer 0	2a
24H–2CH	9–11	Reserved	
30H	12	INT0	5
34H	13	INT1	6
38H	14	INT2	7
3CH	15	INT3	8
40H	16	Numerics (80C186EB)	
44H	17	INT4	4
48H	18	Timer 1	2b
4CH	19	Timer 2	2c
50H	20	Serial Channel 0 Receive	3a
54H	21	Serial Channel 0 Transmit	3b
58H–7CH	22–31	Reserved	
80H–FCH	32–255	Available	

a. Letter suffix indicates relative priority within level.

To initialize a vector when addresses 0H to 03FFH are in ROM, the vector must be part of your application's object code and be located to this address range. This is done by creating an absolutely located segment in the source file and using data allocation directives to generate the addresses as constants in the code.

Usually, the memory starting at address 00000H is RAM. In this case, instructions in your program must write the vector values to the vector table. For example, interrupt INT0 has type code 12. Assume the ISR for INT0 has the name INT0_ISR. The following instruction sequence initializes the interrupt vector for INT0:

```
push    ds              ;save DS
xor     ax,ax           ;set DS to 0000H
mov     ds,ax
```

```
mov    ax,offset int0_isr        ;get offset of ISR
mov    bx,12 * 4                 ;compute vector table offset
mov    [bx],ax                   ;put ISR offset into vector table
mov    ax,seg int0_isr           ;get segment of ISR
mov    [bx+2],ax                 ;put ISR segment into vector table
pop    ds                        ;restore original DS
```

Note that in the case of interrupt vectors located in ROM, initialization takes place at assembly time, or more precisely when the ROM is programmed. For the RAM case, initialization must take place at the beginning of your program, before interrupts are enabled. Since the response to an interrupt is the execution of a procedure, the stack must also be initialized before enabling interrupts.

14.4   80C188EB Hardware Interrupts

The 80C188EB's modular core has only two interrupt inputs. NMI (Non-Maskable Interrupt) and INTR (Interrupt Request) (Fig. 14.2-1). NMI is nonmaskable and INTR is maskable. The NMI signal comes directly from an 80C188EB pin and is directly handled by the modular core.

The INTR signal comes from the 80C188EB's integrated Interrupt Control Unit, (ICU), which synchronizes and prioritizes all hardware interrupt requests, except NMI. The ICU passes the combined interrupt request to the modular core. The ICU has five inputs from 80C188EB interrupt pins. The ICU also has an input from the Timer Control Unit (TCU) and an input from the Serial Control Unit (SCU). We will first consider the INTR interrupt input, then the NMI input.

14.4.1   Interrupt Request (INTR)

INTR is the maskable interrupt input to the 80C188EB's modular core CPU. It is masked by the interrupt enable flag (IF), which is part of the PSW. IF serves as the **global interrupt mask** for all maskable hardware interrupts. When IF is cleared, the INTR input is disabled, and the 80C188EB will not respond to any hardware interrupt request, except NMI. IF has no effect on NMI, the software interrupts, or the exceptions. When the 80C188EB is reset, IF is automatically cleared. Therefore, after reset, all maskable interrupts are initially disabled.

After the segment registers, stack, and appropriate interrupt vectors have been initialized, IF must be set in order to enable the maskable hardware interrupts. IF is set and cleared using the instructions *set interrupt enable flag* (**STI**) and *clear interrupt enable flag* (**CLI**) respectively (Table 14.2-1).

Each interrupt controlled by the ICU also has an individual mask. To use any one of these interrupts, you must also clear the interrupt's individual mask bit. This is done by writing the specific interrupt's control register in the ICU. Registers of the ICU and their functions are covered in the next section.

IF is automatically cleared during the interrupt processing sequence of *all* interrupts, not just the hardware interrupts (Fig. 14.2-2). Thus, INTR is disabled throughout the processing of an interrupt, unless the ISR sets IF, by executing a STI instruction. If an ISR executes STI to set IF, a subsequent request at INTR results in a new interrupt acknowledgment and a **nested interrupt** condition. When the second ISR has completed, execution is transferred back to the first ISR.

When an ISR has completed its task, it executes an IRET instruction. IRET pops the old PSW from the stack, restoring the previous state of IF (Fig. 14.2-3). This action reenables INTR, if IF was set prior to the interrupt. STI and IRET instructions do not actually enable IF until *after* the instruction following STI or IRET has been executed. These instructions are designed this way to reduce the likelihood of excessive build-up of return addresses on the stack.

The CLI instruction is used when you want your program to disable interrupts for a period of time. This is necessary before a critical section of code is executed, for example, a procedure that is also called by an ISR. Disabling INTR using CLI does not prevent an external interrupt request from occurring but does prevent its recognition by the 80C188EB. If an interrupt request is still pending when INTR is later enabled, then the request is recognized and acknowledged at that time. If an interrupt request is removed before INTR is enabled and the interrupt acknowledged is received, then the request is missed.

14.4.2   A Simple Interrupt Example

Quite a few details regarding 80C188EB interrupts have been presented. This section gives a simple example to put these details into context. Figure 14.4-1 shows a simple interface of a hardware debounced pushbutton switch to the 80C188EB's INT0 interrupt input. The pushbutton switch represents an I/O device that generates an event. Pressing and releasing the switch generates a positive pulse. This positive pulse is the event. We are interested in having the 80C188EB respond to this event by displaying the count of the total number of events since the system was reset.

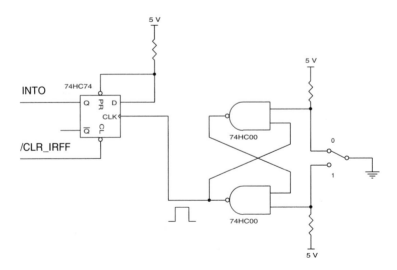

Figure 14.4-1   Using a momentary contact switch to generate an event.

On the leading edge (0 to 1 transition) of the positive pulse, the positive-edge trig-gered D-type interrupt request flip-flop is set. The output of this flip-flop is connected to the INT0 input of the 80C188EB. An output device select pulse from an address decoder is used to clear the interrupt request flip-flop.

At the beginning of the program IDEVNCT, in Fig. 14.4-2, symbolic addresses are equated to constants. The addresses I0CON and EOI are for INT0's Interrupt Control reg-ister and the End-of-Interrupt register, respectively. These addresses are based on the off-sets of these registers in the PCB. Memory for the variable count is allocated in the data segment, data. Since this program uses an interrupt, memory for a stack is also allocated in the segment stack.

Following the stack segment is the code segment, code. The initial code in this seg-ment is for the ISR, INT0_ISR, that increments and displays count in response to an inter-rupt. This code will be examined in detail in a moment.

The first executable instruction in the program follows the ISR. This instruction has the label start. When the program is executed, it first initializes the segment registers and stack. The interrupt vector for INT0 is then initialized. The variable count and the display are then cleared.

Next, the interrupt request flip-flop must be cleared. Since this flip-flop is not auto-matically cleared when the 80C188EB is powered on, by using /RESOUT, it might ran-domly power up in the set state. If this happens, once IF is set and INT0's individual mask bit is cleared, an interrupt will occur, even though the pushbutton has never been pressed. As a result of this interrupt, a count of 1 is displayed. The interrupt request flip-flop is cleared using an output device select pulse. This pulse asserts the flip-flop's asynchronous clear input.

After clearing the interrupt request flip-flop, the INT0 interrupt mask bit is cleared. Writing the word 0017H to I0CON, INT0's interrupt control register, unmasks the INT0 interrupt and configures it as level sensitive. Maskable interrupts are then globally enabled by setting the interrupt enable flag (IF) using STI.

The program then enters an infinite loop. In a practical application, this infinite loop would be replaced by a sequence of background tasks that are executed repeatedly.

When the pushbutton is pressed and released, the interrupt request flip-flop is set. At this point the interrupt is pending. After the 80C188EB completes executing its current instruction, it starts the interrupt processing sequence. The ICU provides the 80C188EB with the address 0048H, which is the memory address where the interrupt vector is stored. The 80C188EB obtains the interrupt vector and makes CS and IP equal to the interrupt vector. Thus, execution is transferred to the ISR int0_isr.

Looking at int0_isr, we see that first it saves all the 80C188EB registers on the stack. The purpose of this ISR is to increment and display count, which it does next. Having com-pleted its task, the ISR must prepare to return to the instruction following the interrupted instruction.

The interrupt request flip-flop is cleared by generating an output device select pulse to address CLR_IRFF. If this step were not carried out, once int0_isr is returned from, another interrupt would occur. This is because interrupt input INT0 was configured as level sensi-tive. The result would be that the display would be continuously incremented at a very rapid rate. If INT0 had been configured as edge sensitive, not clearing the interrupt request

```
        name    idevcnt
;*******************************************************************
;
;NAME:        IDEVCNT
;
;DESCRIPTION: This program counts the number of occurrences of an
;external event that generates an interrupt.
;*******************************************************************
;
.186

LEDS        equ     8000h
IOCON       equ     0ff18h
CLR_IRFF    equ     8007h
EOI         equ     0ff02h

data    segment 'RAM'
count   db (?)
data    ends

stack   segment 'STKRAM'
        dw      64 dup (?)
tos     label   word
stack   ends

assume cs:code, ds:data, ss:stack

code    segment public 'ROM'

;*******************************************************************
;
;NAME:        INT0_ISR
;
;function:    Increment and display the variable COUNT
;created:     02/16/97
;modifies:    COUNT
;called by:   INT0
;*******************************************************************
;
int0_isr proc   far
        pusha                   ;save all registers
        inc     count           ;increment count of events
        mov     al,count        ;output count to LEDS
        not     al
        mov     dx,LEDS
        out     dx,al
        mov     dx,CLR_IRFF     ;generate OPDSP to clear interrupt request
        out     dx,al           ;flip-flop, contents of AL unimportant
```

Figure 14.4-2   Interrupt driven program to count pushbutton switch events.

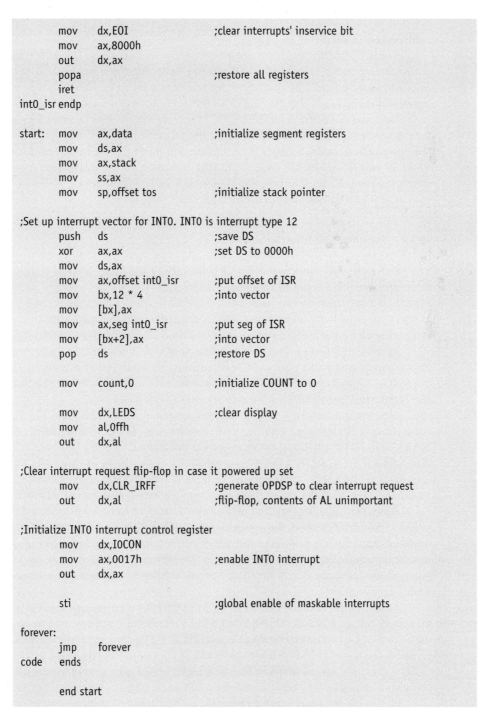

```
             mov     dx,EOI                    ;clear interrupts' inservice bit
             mov     ax,8000h
             out     dx,ax
             popa                              ;restore all registers
             iret
int0_isr endp

start:       mov     ax,data                   ;initialize segment registers
             mov     ds,ax
             mov     ax,stack
             mov     ss,ax
             mov     sp,offset tos             ;initialize stack pointer

;Set up interrupt vector for INT0. INT0 is interrupt type 12
             push    ds                        ;save DS
             xor     ax,ax                     ;set DS to 0000h
             mov     ds,ax
             mov     ax,offset int0_isr        ;put offset of ISR
             mov     bx,12 * 4                 ;into vector
             mov     [bx],ax
             mov     ax,seg int0_isr           ;put seg of ISR
             mov     [bx+2],ax                 ;into vector
             pop     ds                        ;restore DS

             mov     count,0                   ;initialize COUNT to 0

             mov     dx,LEDS                   ;clear display
             mov     al,0ffh
             out     dx,al

;Clear interrupt request flip-flop in case it powered up set
             mov     dx,CLR_IRFF               ;generate OPDSP to clear interrupt request
             out     dx,al                     ;flip-flop, contents of AL unimportant

;Initialize INT0 interrupt control register
             mov     dx,IOCON
             mov     ax,0017h                  ;enable INT0 interrupt
             out     dx,ax

             sti                               ;global enable of maskable interrupts

forever:
             jmp     forever
code         ends

             end start
```

Figure 14.4-2   Interrupt driven program to count pushbutton switch events.
                 (Continued.)

flip-flop in the ISR would prevent all subsequent presses of the pushbutton from incrementing the count.

The ICU contains an In-Service bit for each of its interrupts. The In-Service bit for a particular interrupt is set when the ICU asserts INTR. If this bit is not cleared, no additional interrupt requests from this interrupt input will be responded to. This bit is cleared by writing 8000H to register EOI in the PCB. This process is discussed further in the next section.

Next, the ISR restores all of the 80C188EB registers' values to what they were after the interrupted instruction completed execution. Finally, the IRET instruction is executed. IRET pops the IP and CS values of the instruction following the interrupted instruction. These IP and CS values are used to transfer execution to the instruction following the interrupted instruction. The program is now back in the forever loop.

The ICU is considered further in the Section 14.5.

14.4.3   Nonmaskable Interrupt (NMI)

The NMI interrupt input operates independently of the ICU. **NMI** is a **nonmaskable interrupt**, one that cannot be disabled by software. If you are not going to use this interrupt in your system, then you must ground the NMI pin. An NMI interrupt is predefined as type 2. Because it is nonmaskable, NMI is primarily used to handle catastrophic events, such as the imminent loss of system power or a timeout signal from a watchdog timer.

An NMI ISR for a power failure application typically saves the registers and other critical variables in battery backed CMOS memory so when power is restored, the system can resume normal operation from the point where it was interrupted. It also places all the external devices that the microprocessor controls in safe states.

A power-fail interrupt request can be generated by a MAX807N Microprocessor Supervisory Circuit (Fig. 10.3-2). This request can be generated using either the MAX807N's /LOW LINE output or its power fail output (/PFO). The MAX807N's reset threshold is 4.575 V. /LOW LINE is asserted 30 mV above this reset threshold. The elapsed time from /LOW LINE being asserted to the 80C188EB being reset is illustrated in Fig. 14.4-3 as t_1. The NMI ISR has only the brief time interval t_1 to complete its task.

Time interval t_1 is a function of the rate of decay of the power supply's output. The rate of exponential decay of the power supply's output is, in turn, a function of the size of its output filter capacitors and the amount of current drawn. Switching power supplies use smaller capacitors than older linear supplies. Therefore, their output decay rates are much faster. Values for t_1 can vary from a few milliseconds for switching supplies to seconds for some linear supplies.

An alternative approach is to use the MAX807N's power fail input (PFI) to monitor the supply voltage. PFI has a threshold of 2.275 V. A resistor divider is used to divide down the voltage being monitored so /PFO is asserted at the desired voltage level. If the resistor divider is connected to V_{CC}, resistor values can be chosen so PFI equals the 2.275 V threshold as soon as V_{CC} drops to 4.8 V. This provides a longer time period for the NMI ISR to complete its work.

Ideally, PFI is connected to monitor the unregulated DC voltage from which the regulated V_{CC} is derived. The resistor divider values are then chosen so that /PFI is asserted as soon as the unregulated voltage starts to drop. This method can provide a longer time, t_2,

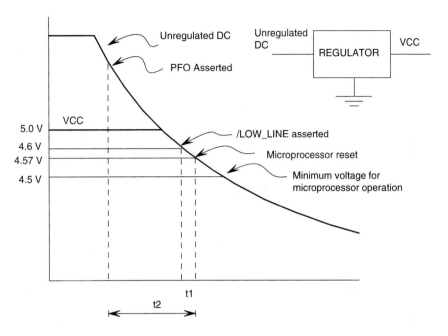

Figure 14.4-3   Use of a microprocessor supervisory circuit to generate a power fail interrupt.

between assertion of the NMI interrupt request and the microprocessor's reset. Unfortunately, in some applications the unregulated DC voltage may not be readily accessible.

The NMI input is rising edge triggered and level-latched. This input is synchronized with the 80C188EB's clock and must be held high for one clock cycle to guarantee recognition. The interrupt request signal may be removed before the NMI ISR is entered, as long as the one clock cycle requirement is met.

A rather infrequent use of NMI is based on the fact that if NMI is asserted within 10 clock cycles after RESET is negated, execution is vectored to the NMI ISR. This allows program execution to begin at an address other than the default start address, FFFF0H. However, this also requires that the interrupt vector table be in ROM, not RAM.

14.4.4   The Halt Instruction and Interrupts

Execution of a *halt* (**HLT**), instruction causes the 80C188EB to enter the halt state. This instruction is a processor control instruction that is used infrequently in embedded systems because usually you want your program to continue its execution indefinitely.

Once the processor halts, there are only two ways to cause it to exit the halt state. One way is to reset the 80C188EB. In this case, program execution begins again from the start. The other way is an interrupt request on NMI or INT0-INT4. In the case of a hardware interrupt, after the ISR is completed, execution continues with the instruction following the HLT. Thus, it is possible to use a HLT to stop the 80C188EB's execution until the occurrence of a specific hardware interrupt.

14.5   80C188EB Interrupt Control Unit

The function of the 80C188EB's on-chip **Interrupt Control Unit** (ICU), is to synchronize and prioritize interrupt requests from its seven interrupt inputs and provide a single combined interrupt request signal (INTR) to the modular core CPU (Fig. 14.2-1). In response to an /INTA signal from the modular core CPU, the ICU provides the offset address of the memory location in the vector table where the interrupt's vector is stored. The ICU's interrupt inputs are the five pins INT0–INT4 and two internal interrupt request signals. One of the later two signals is the combined interrupt requests from Timers 0, 1, and 2. The other signal is the combined receive and transmit interrupt requests from serial channel 0.

The ICU has 15 control and status registers. These registers are accessible through the PCB. Each ICU interrupt input has its own control register; this accounts for 7 of the 15 registers. The other 8 registers provide control and status for the ICU's operation.

The functions of the least significant four bits of the 7 interrupt control registers (I0CON, I1CON, I2CON, I3CON, I4CON, TCUCON, and SCUCON) are similar. One of these four bits is the individual interrupt's mask bit and the other three set the priority level for that interrupt. Other bit assignments for these registers are discussed later.

14.5.1   Interrupt Masking

All interrupts from the ICU can be masked both globally and individually. The interrupt enable flag (IF) provides the global enable and must be 1 for any interrupt from the ICU to be enabled. Each individual interrupt's mask bit must be 0 for the ICU to respond to that interrupt's request. A mask bit value of 1 disables the corresponding interrupt. The individual mask bits allow a specific interrupt to be temporarily disabled, while other maskable interrupts are still enabled. After reset, IF is 0 and the individual mask bits are all 1s, so initially all interrupts are both globally and individually masked. Before an interrupt request can actually cause an interrupt, IF must be set and the individual interrupt's mask bit must be cleared.

An individual interrupt's mask bit can be accessed from either of two registers. Bit 3 of each specific interrupt's control register is its mask bit (MSK). For example, bit 3 of I0CON, the control register for INT0, is the mask bit for INT0.

All the mask bits are also accessible from a single **Interrupt Mask register** (IMASK) (Fig. 14.5-1). For example, bit 4 of IMASK is the mask bit for INT0. Bit 3 of I0CON and bit 4 of IMASK are actually the same bit, which can be written to and read from either register. Modifying a mask bit in one register also modifies its image bit in the other register.

For example, either of the following sequences enables INT0:

```
        mov     dx,IMASK        ;enable INT0 by clearing bit 4 of IMASK
        in      ax,dx
        and     ax,00edh        ;clear bit 4 and reserved bits
        out     dx,ax
```

or

```
        mov     dx,I0CON        ;enable INT0 by clearing bit 3 of I0CON
        in      ax,dx
```

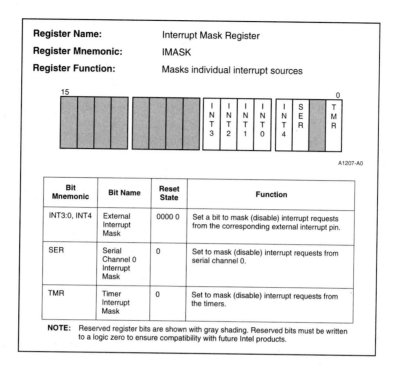

Figure 14.5-1   Interrupt Mask Register, IMSK. (Courtesy of Intel Corp.)

```
and     ax,0077h       ;clear bit 3 and reserved bits
out     dx,ax
```

The second instruction sequence clears only the interrupt mask bit, while leaving the other bits of I0CON, which are used to configure the interrupt, undisturbed.

14.5.2   ICU Interrupt Priority

One of the ICU's functions is to a prioritize interrupt requests. Prioritization is needed to handle two situations. The first situation occurs when the 80C188EB is not currently servicing an interrupt, and two or more interrupt requests occur simultaneously at unmasked ICU inputs. The ICU must determine which request has the highest priority. In response to simultaneous interrupt requests, the ICU asserts INTR. When the 80C188EB's modular core acknowledges this interrupt request, the ICU provides the vector table offset address for the highest priority interrupt request. The modular core CPU then transfers execution to the ISR for that interrupt source.

When this ISR completes execution, the ICU again asserts INTR. When the 80C188EB modular core acknowledges this interrupt request, the ICU provides the vector table offset address of the lower priority pending interrupt.

The second situation that requires prioritization is when an ICU interrupt is being serviced and an interrupt request occurs at another interrupt input. If the second interrupt request is of higher priority than the first, the ICU asserts INTR. If the ISR currently being serviced has set IF, then the current ISR is interrupted and execution is transferred to the second, higher priority, ISR. When an ISR **preempts** another in this fashion, the second ISR is said to be nested. An interrupt request cannot preempt a higher priority interrupt that is being serviced, nor can it preempt itself.

Each ICU interrupt has a priority level. The least significant three bits of each interrupt control register specifies the priority level. These bits, PM2–PM1, are called **priority mask bits**. Priority levels range from 0, the highest, to 7, the lowest. When the 80C188EB is reset, the three priority mask bits in every control register are set. Therefore, initially every hardware interrupt is at priority level 7, the lowest level.

Within the same priority level, the ICU applies a relative priority as shown in Table 14.5-1. After reset, with every ICU interrupt at level 7, the priority among the ICU interrupts is completely determined by Table 14.5-1.

Table 14.5-1   Default interrupt priorities.

Interrupt name	Relative priority[a]
Timer 0	0a
Timer 1	0b
Timer 2	0c
Serial Channel 0 Receive	1a
Serial Channel 1 Transmit	1b
INT4	2
INT0	3
INT1	4
INT2	5
INT3	6

a. Letter suffix indicates relative priority within level.

The priority of any ICU interrupt can be changed by writing a new value to its priority level bits. If two interrupts are assigned to the same priority level, their priorities within that level are determined by the priority assignment in Table 14.5-1.

Priority levels provide another way to mask interrupts. The **Priority Mask register**, (**PRIMSK**), has a three bit priority mask field (Fig. 14.5-2). This priority mask prevents any interrupts of lower priority (higher numerical value) from occurring. When the 80C188EB is reset, this value is initialized to 7 and does not mask any interrupts.

The priority assignment for ICU interrupts in Table 14.5-1 does not take into account the other 80C188EB interrupts. The 80C188EB's overall priority scheme includes NMI, interrupt instructions, and exceptions. The complete interrupt priority scheme is given in Table 14.3-1.

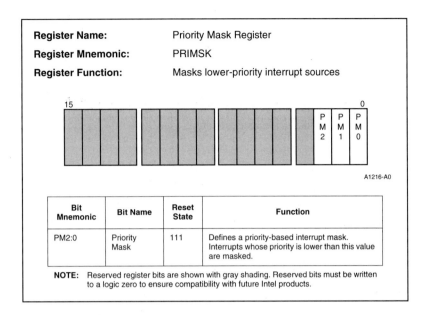

Register Name:	Priority Mask Register
Register Mnemonic:	PRIMSK
Register Function:	Masks lower-priority interrupt sources

Bit Mnemonic	Bit Name	Reset State	Function
PM2:0	Priority Mask	111	Defines a priority-based interrupt mask. Interrupts whose priority is lower than this value are masked.

NOTE: Reserved register bits are shown with gray shading. Reserved bits must be written to a logic zero to ensure compatibility with future Intel products.

Figure 14.5-2   Priority Mask Register, PRIMSK. (Courtesy of Intel Corp.)

14.5.3   ICU Interrupt Synchronization and Prioritization

The actions taken by the ICU to synchronize and prioritize interrupts is flowcharted in Fig. 14.5-3. Two ICU registers are involved in this process. These registers have a bit associated with each interrupt. When the ICU detects an interrupt request at one of its inputs, it sets this interrupt's Interrupt Request bit in the **Interrupt Request register** (**REQST**) (Fig. 14.5-4). This bit is set regardless of whether the interrupt is masked or not. A set Interrupt Request bit indicates that its corresponding interrupt is **pending**. For external interrupts the interrupt request signal must remain a 1 at the pin until the request is acknowledged. If the interrupt request signal goes low before the interrupt is acknowledged, the interrupt request bit is cleared and the interrupt request is missed.

The ICU checks all pending interrupts. If the highest priority unmasked pending interrupt is of higher priority than any interrupt currently being serviced, the ICU asserts INTR. When the 80C188EB's modular core CPU acknowledges the interrupt request, the ICU provides the vector table offset address, so the 80C188EB can obtain the interrupt vector and transfer execution to the ISR. The ICU then clears the interrupt's request bit in REQST and sets the interrupt's In-Service bit in the **In-Service register** (**INSERV**) (Fig. 14.5-5). A bit set in INSERV indicates that the corresponding interrupt is currently being serviced.

An instruction at the end of the ISR issues an **End-of-Interrupt command** (EOI) to clear the interrupt's In-Service bit. If the In-Service bit is not cleared, subsequent interrupts from this source will not be recognized. The EOI command is discussed in detail in the next section.

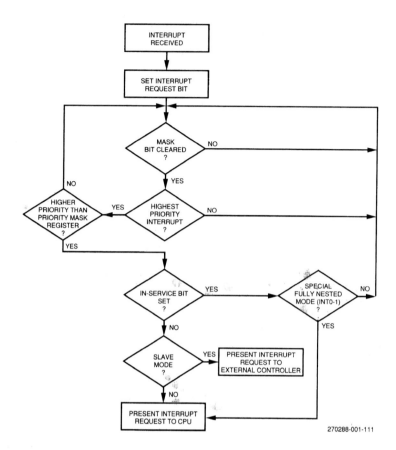

270288-001-111

Figure 14.5-3   Interrupt request sequencing. (Courtesy of Intel Corp.)

14.5.4   External Interrupts (INT0–INT4)

The **interrupt control registers** (**I2CON**, **I3CON**, and **I4CON**) for interrupts INT2, INT3, and INT4 are similar and shown in Fig. 14.5-6. The mask bit and priority level bits have been previously discussed. All interrupt control registers for external pins have a level bit (LVL) that selects level or edge triggering for the input.

Interrupt requests on pins INT0-INT4 are not latched, even if edge triggering has been selected! If one of these signals is asserted while the interrupt is disabled or a higher priority interrupt is in service, and is not held until accepted by the 80C188EB, the interrupt request is missed. This is true even though the interrupt's request bit in REQST may have been temporarily set. In general, this means that an external interrupt request flip-flop must be used to latch an event and provide the interrupt request signal to the 80C188EB's interrupt pin. In some cases, the interrupt request signal from a peripheral IC associated with the event may be latched in the peripheral IC, obviating the need for a discrete interrupt request flip-flop.

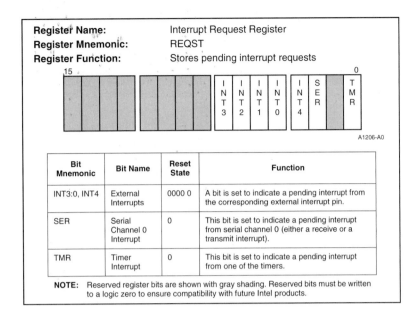

Register Name: Interrupt Request Register
Register Mnemonic: REQST
Register Function: Stores pending interrupt requests

A1206-A0

Bit Mnemonic	Bit Name	Reset State	Function
INT3:0, INT4	External Interrupts	0000 0	A bit is set to indicate a pending interrupt from the corresponding external interrupt pin.
SER	Serial Channel 0 Interrupt	0	This bit is set to indicate a pending interrupt from serial channel 0 (either a receive or a transmit interrupt).
TMR	Timer Interrupt	0	This bit is set to indicate a pending interrupt from one of the timers.

NOTE: Reserved register bits are shown with gray shading. Reserved bits must be written to a logic zero to ensure compatibility with future Intel products.

Figure 14.5-4   Interrupt Request Register, REQST. (Courtesy of Intel Corp.)

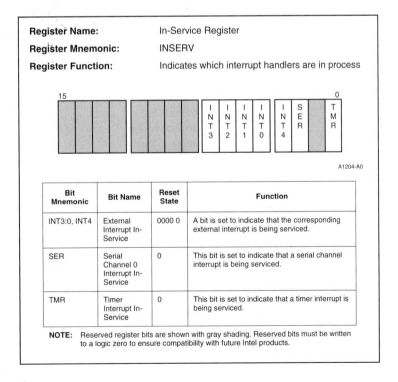

Register Name: In-Service Register
Register Mnemonic: INSERV
Register Function: Indicates which interrupt handlers are in process

A1204-A0

Bit Mnemonic	Bit Name	Reset State	Function
INT3:0, INT4	External Interrupt In-Service	0000 0	A bit is set to indicate that the corresponding external interrupt is being serviced.
SER	Serial Channel 0 Interrupt In-Service	0	This bit is set to indicate that a serial channel interrupt is being serviced.
TMR	Timer Interrupt In-Service	0	This bit is set to indicate that a timer interrupt is being serviced.

NOTE: Reserved register bits are shown with gray shading. Reserved bits must be written to a logic zero to ensure compatibility with future Intel products.

Figure 14.5-5   In-Service Register, INSERV. (Courtesy of Intel Corp.)

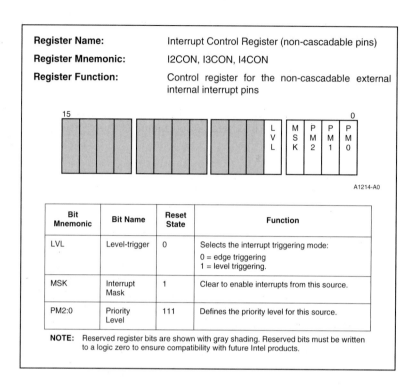

Register Name:	Interrupt Control Register (non-cascadable pins)
Register Mnemonic:	I2CON, I3CON, I4CON
Register Function:	Control register for the non-cascadable external internal interrupt pins

15   0

| | | | | | | | | | | | | L V L | M S K | P M 2 | P M 1 | P M 0 |

A1214-A0

Bit Mnemonic	Bit Name	Reset State	Function
LVL	Level-trigger	0	Selects the interrupt triggering mode: 0 = edge triggering 1 = level triggering.
MSK	Interrupt Mask	1	Clear to enable interrupts from this source.
PM2:0	Priority Level	111	Defines the priority level for this source.

NOTE: Reserved register bits are shown with gray shading. Reserved bits must be written to a logic zero to ensure compatibility with future Intel products.

Figure 14.5-6   Interrupt Control Register for noncascadable external pins. (Courtesy of Intel Corp.)

The control registers for **INT0** and **INT1** contain two additional bits (Fig. 14.5-7). The SFNM bit enables the **Specially Fully Nested mode**. This mode allows an interrupt request at INT0 or INT1 to be serviced even if its In-Service bit is set (Fig. 14.5-3). This mode is normally used in conjunction with the cascade mode which is enabled by setting the CAS bit. Cascade mode allows an external interrupt controller, such as the 82C59A, to be used to expand the number of interrupt sources that can be supported by either interrupt input INT0 or INT1. This mode of operation and the 82C59A priority interrupt controller, are discussed in Section 14.10

14.5.5   Timer and Serial Channel 0 Interrupts

All interrupt requests from the integrated peripherals are latched by the ICU. The interrupt control register for the timers (**TCUCON**) and serial channel 0 (**SCUCON**) are similar and contain only a mask bit and priority level bits (Fig. 14.5-8).

Each of the three timers in the Timer Control Unit (TCU) can generate its own interrupt request. The mask bit in TCUCON enables or disables interrupt requests from all three timers. In addition to clearing the mask bit in TCUCON, the INT bit in each specific timer's control register (**T0CON, T1CON, or T2CON**) must be set for that timer to generate an interrupt request (Figs. 13.7-2 and 13.7-4).

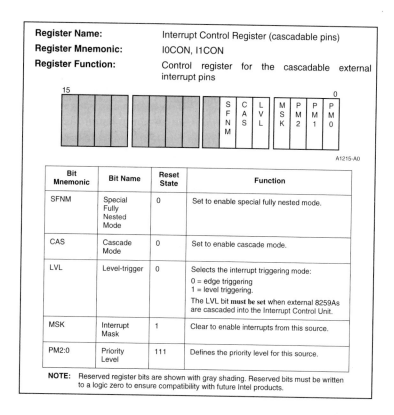

Bit Mnemonic	Bit Name	Reset State	Function
SFNM	Special Fully Nested Mode	0	Set to enable special fully nested mode.
CAS	Cascade Mode	0	Set to enable cascade mode.
LVL	Level-trigger	0	Selects the interrupt triggering mode: 0 = edge triggering 1 = level triggering. The LVL bit **must be set** when external 8259As are cascaded into the Interrupt Control Unit.
MSK	Interrupt Mask	1	Clear to enable interrupts from this source.
PM2:0	Priority Level	111	Defines the priority level for this source.

NOTE: Reserved register bits are shown with gray shading. Reserved bits must be written to a logic zero to ensure compatibility with future Intel products.

Figure 14.5-7   Interrupt Control Register for cascadable interrupt pins. (Courtesy of Intel Corp.)

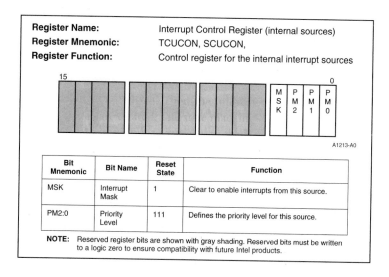

Bit Mnemonic	Bit Name	Reset State	Function
MSK	Interrupt Mask	1	Clear to enable interrupts from this source.
PM2:0	Priority Level	111	Defines the priority level for this source.

NOTE: Reserved register bits are shown with gray shading. Reserved bits must be written to a logic zero to ensure compatibility with future Intel products.

Figure 14.5-8   Interrupt Control Register for internal sources. (Courtesy of Intel Corp.)

For example, Timer 2 can be used to generate an interrupt request at fixed time intervals to cause a task to be executed periodically. Using this approach to time the task's execution eliminates the need for a software delay. This allows other tasks to be executed in the time interval between the interrupts. Assuming that Timer 2's interrupt vector has been initialized, the following sequence of instructions causes Timer 2 to generate an interrupt request every 20 ms, for an 80C188EB with an 8-MHz system clock.

```
;Initialize Timer 2: continuous operation, 20 ms interrupt
        mov     dx,T2CNT        ;clear timer count register
        mov     ax,0
        out     dx,ax
        mov     dx,T2CMPA       ;maxcount = 40000
        mov     ax,40000
        out     dx,ax
        mov     dx,T2CON        ;enable interrupt, continuous mode
        mov     ax,0e001h
        out     dx,ax
        mov     dx,TCUCON       ;unmask timer interrupts
        mov     ax,0007h
        out     dx,ax
        sti                     ;global enable of maskable interrupts
```

The interrupt requests from the three timers are combined to form a single interrupt request to the ICU. However, each timer interrupt has its own interrupt vector to point to its ISR. The interrupt request register (REQST) and the In-Service register (INSERV) also have only a single bit to represent the combined status of the three timers. However, the **Interrupt Status register (INTSTS)** has three separate bits (TMR2–TMR0) to indicate a pending interrupt from each timer (Fig. 14.5-9). Among the timers, Timer 0 has the highest priority and Timer 2 the lowest.

INTSTS acts as a second-level request register to process timer interrupts. When a timer interrupt request occurs, both the combined TMR bit in REQST and the individual timer bit TMRn in INTSTS are set.

When the shared timer interrupt request is acknowledged, the timer interrupt request with the highest priority is serviced and that timer's bit in INTSTS is cleared. If no other timers have interrupts pending, the shared timer interrupt request bit in REQST is also cleared. If other timers have interrupts pending, this bit remains set.

The shared In-Service bit in INSERV is set when the shared timer interrupt request is acknowledged. Since the shared timer In-Service bit is set, no other interrupt request from a timer, even if it has a higher priority, is responded to until this bit is cleared. Other timer interrupts simply remain pending. When the ISR for the timer being serviced executes an EOI command, the shared timer In-Service bit will be cleared and the other timer interrupts can be serviced.

The **Serial Communication Unit (SCU)** has two independent serial channels. Only serial channel 0 has a connection to the ICU. This connection is the combined interrupt request for the serial channel 0 receive and serial channel 0 transmit interrupts. The SRX and STX bits in INTSTS indicate whether channel 0's receiver or transmitter has an inter-

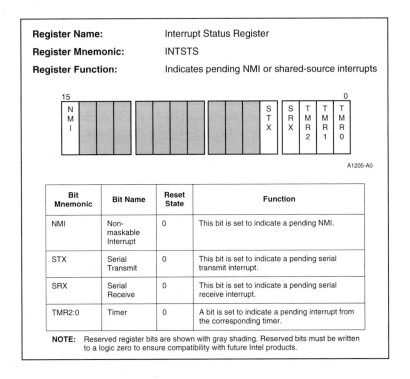

Register Name: Interrupt Status Register

Register Mnemonic: INTSTS

Register Function: Indicates pending NMI or shared-source interrupts

Bit Mnemonic	Bit Name	Reset State	Function
NMI	Non-maskable Interrupt	0	This bit is set to indicate a pending NMI.
STX	Serial Transmit	0	This bit is set to indicate a pending serial transmit interrupt.
SRX	Serial Receive	0	This bit is set to indicate a pending serial receive interrupt.
TMR2:0	Timer	0	A bit is set to indicate a pending interrupt from the corresponding timer.

NOTE: Reserved register bits are shown with gray shading. Reserved bits must be written to a logic zero to ensure compatibility with future Intel products.

Figure 14.5-9   Interrupt Status Register, INSTS. (Courtesy of Intel Corp.)

rupt pending. The serial channel receive interrupt has higher priority than the serial channel transmit interrupt.

The 80C188EB's second serial channel, channel 1, has no internal connections to the ICU. However, this serial channel's interrupt request signal, SINT1, can be externally connected to one of the interrupt input pins.

14.5.6   Polling Interrupt Requests

The individual mask bits for interrupt sources provide the flexibility to mask some interrupts and service them using polling while leaving other interrupt sources unmasked and servicing them using interrupts. Support for polling is provided by the Poll Status and Poll registers. These registers contain identical information (Fig. 14.5-10 and 11). The IREQ bit indicates whether there is a pending interrupt, and bits VT4–VT0 give the least significant five bits of the type code of the highest priority pending interrupt. The most significant five bits are 0s.

These registers differ in the effects caused by reading the register. Reading the **Poll Status register** (**POLLSTS**) simply gives the status information but does not acknowledge the pending interrupt or update any registers.

Reading the **Poll register** (**POLL**) acknowledges the interrupt by updating the REQST, INSERV, POLL and POLLSTS registers. The 80C188EB does not automatically

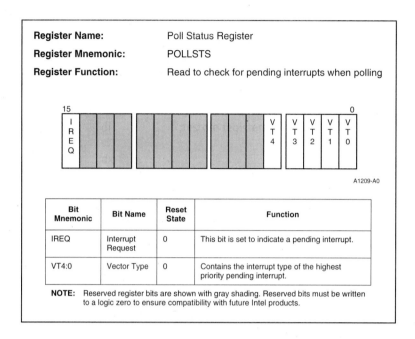

Figure 14.5-10   Poll Status Register, POLLSTS. (Courtesy of Intel Corp.)

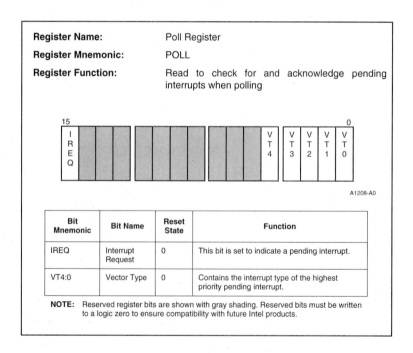

Figure 14.5-11   Poll Register, POLL. (Courtesy of Intel Corp.)

vector to the ISR. Your software must use the vector type code VT4–VT0 and compute the address in memory where the interrupt vector is stored. The interrupt vector is then used to transfer execution to the ISR. Before transferring execution to the ISR, you must push the PSW, so that after the transfer, the stack looks just the way it does after the 80C188EB transfers execution to an ISR at the start of the interrupt processing sequence.

```
        mov     dx,POLL              ;get the interrupt status and
        in      ax,dx                ;type code
        test    ax,8000h             ;is there a pending interrupt?
        jz      no_interrupt         ;no, skip interrupt servicing
        and     ax,001fh             ;mask to get type code
        shl     ax,2                 ; * 4 for vector table offset
        mov     bx,ax                ;save
        xor     ax,ax                ;clear AX
        push    ds                   ;save current DS
        mov     ds,ax                ;point DS to vector table
        mov     cx,[bx]              ;get IP value of vector
        mov     dx,[bx+2]            ;get CS value of vector
        pop     ds                   ;restore DS to data segment
        mov     isr_vector,cx        ;put vector IP in memory
        mov     isr_vector+2,dx      ;put vector CS in memory
        pushf                        ;put the PSW on the stack
        call    isr_vector           ;put the return CS and IP on stack
                                     ;and transfer execution to ISR
no_interrupt:
```

The variable isr_vector is a double word memory location allocated in the data segment. The interrupt's vector was copied from the vector table to isr_vector. The call instruction is an indirect call through a double word memory location. This causes the CS and IP values for the instruction following the call to be saved on the stack. The low word of isr_vector becomes the new IP and the high word becomes the new CS.

14.6 Interrupt Service Routines

Many examples of ISRs are presented in subsequent chapters. For most examples, the full program is not provided. For each of these examples, you must keep in mind that the following operations must be accomplished before an interrupt can be used.

1. A stack of sufficient size must be allocated.
2. The interrupt vector must be initialized.
3. The interrupt must be configured and individually enabled by writing the proper value to its control register.
4. Maskable interrupts must be enabled by using STI to set IF.

An ISR implements a task to handle the event that causes an interrupt. This task differs considerably depending on the nature of the event. In most respects, ISRs are similar to regular procedures. An ISR returns execution to the instruction following the interrupted instruction, just as a regular procedure returns execution to the instruction following its CALL.

However, it is critically important that the execution of an ISR have no unexpected effect on the interrupted process. Since, in general, an interrupt may occur at any point in a program, all registers used by the ISR must be saved on the stack at the beginning of the ISR, and restored at the end. This process is called saving and restoring the **system context** or **system state**.

As shown in Fig. 14.2-2, before execution is transferred to an ISR, the 80C188EB automatically pushes PSW, CS, and IP onto the stack. This is similar to an intersegment CALL, except that PSW is also saved. These operations save the minimal context of the task executing at the time of the interrupt. This information is popped from the stack when the ISR returns. After returning from an ISR, the program resumes exactly where it left off when interrupted, with no changes to its registers.

Figure 14.6-1 is a template for an interrupt service routine. This template shows the typical operations in an ISR.

```
isrn    proc
        push    ax                      ;save all registers used by
        push    bx                      ;interrupt procedure
        push    cx
        push    dx

        mov     dx,DSP_IREQ_F           ;generate device select pulse
        out     dx,ax                   ;to clear int req. flip-flop for external interrupt

        sti                             ;enable interrupts, if nesting is desired
        .
        .                               ;instructions to execute ISR's task
        .
        mov     dx,EOI                  ;send non-specific EOI command
        mov     ax,8000h                ;to clear In-Service register bit
        out     dx,ax
        pop     dx                      ;pop all saved registers in reverse order
        pop     cx
        pop     bx
        pop     ax
        iret                            ;pop IP, CS, and PSW
isrn    endp
```

Figure 14.6-1   Interrupt service routine template.

These operations are:

1. Save the interrupted task's context.
2. In an INT0–INT4 ISR, the external interrupt request flip-flop must be cleared.
3. Set IF, if you wish to allow other INTR interrupts during the execution of the current ISR.
4. Execute the instructions to accomplish the ISR's task.
5. Clear the interrupt source's In-Service bit in the INSERV register.
6. Restore the interrupted task's context.

Any 80C188EB registers modified by the ISR are pushed onto the stack at the beginning of the ISR to save the interrupted task's context. Instead of using individual PUSH's, the PUSHA instruction can be used. ISRs don't return results in registers like some procedures. Therefore, no return values get overwritten by using a POPA at the end of the ISR to restore the registers. The disadvantage in using PUSHA and POPA is the additional time taken if only a few registers need to be saved. Thus, in time critical applications, using PUSHA and POPA may not be preferable.

One advantage of using PUSHA and POPA is that later, when you modify the ISR, you do not have to worry about using a previously unsaved register and forgetting to save and restore it.

In an INT0–INT4 ISR, the external interrupt request flip-flop must be cleared. If this is not done before executing IRET, an interrupt input configured as level sensitive will continually generate interrupts. Clearing the interrupt request flip-flop can be accomplished using a separate device select pulse, if it is not accomplished as a side effect of the task carried out by the ISR. The internal interrupt request flip-flops for the timers and serial channels are automatically cleared when their interrupts are acknowledged.

Since IF is automatically cleared when any interrupt is recognized, a STI instruction must be executed to set IF, if other INTR interrupts are to be allowed during the execution of the current ISR. If IF is not set, then all maskable interrupts are ignored for the duration of the ISR. In some systems, this could result in a higher priority interrupt being missed.

Before returning, the ISR must clear the interrupt source's In-Service bit in the INSERV register. This is done by writing the ICU's End-of-Interrupt register (EOI, Fig. 14.6-2). If a STI was previously executed, it is critical that the interrupt request flip-flop be cleared before the EOI command is issued, otherwise the ISR may be reentered before its completion.

There are two methods for issuing the EOI command that is required in step 5. These methods correspond to the two forms of the EOI command. The simplest way is to issue a nonspecific EOI command by setting the NSPEC bit in the EOI register. This is done by writing 8000H to EOI. A nonspecific EOI simply clears the In-Service bit of the highest priority interrupt currently in service. NMI ISRs do not require an EOI command. There is no In-Service bit in INSERV for the NMI. Sending a nonspecific EOI during a NMI ISR clears the In-Service bit of the highest priority interrupt preempted by the NMI.

Alternatively, a specific EOI command can be used to clear a specific In-Service bit. To issue a specific EOI, bit NSPEC in the EOI register is cleared and bits VT4–VT0 are written with the least significant five bits of the type code for the particular interrupt. For

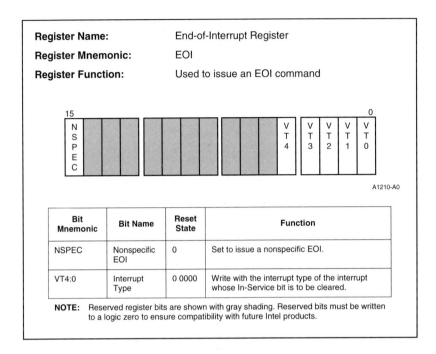

Figure 14.6-2   End-of-Interrupt Register, EOI. (Courtesy of Intel Corp.)

example, to clear the In-Service bit for INT1, 000DH is written to EOI to specify that interrupt type 13's In-Service bit is to be cleared.

For each group of shared interrupts a single type code is used. To issue a specific EOI for any timer, interrupt 0008H is written to EOI. To issue a specific EOI for channel 0's receive or transmit interrupt, 0014H must be written to EOI.

The ISR must pop, in reverse order, the registers it saved, then execute an interrupt return instruction (IRET) to restore the interrupted task's context. IRET pops IP, CS, and PSW, returning program execution to the instruction following the interrupted instruction. At this point, the previous context has been restored. ISRs must be terminated by IRET, not by RET, because RET does not pop the PSW.

It is very important, particularly in time critical applications, to keep your ISRs as short as possible.

14.6.1   Shared Procedures

The use of interrupts is highly advantageous because it allows concurrent processing. However, interrupts must be used with considerable care. One area of concern is shared procedures. The sharing of a procedure arises when a procedure called by the main program is also called by an ISR or when the same procedure is called by two nested ISRs.

As an example of the first case, assume that procedure procx is being executed as a result of a call by the main program. Then an interrupt occurs, and the ISR also calls procx.

The process of calling a procedure that has not completed execution is referred to as **reentering** the procedure. The result of reentering a procedure that was not written to allow reentrance can mean the loss of data and subsequent failure of the system.

Several approaches can be used to solve the **shared procedure** problem. A rather crude approach is to simply not share procedures. The procedure in question is simply duplicated rather than shared. Each copy of the procedure is given a unique name. Duplicated procedures must be totally independent of each other. Not only must they have different names, they must have different instruction labels if they are in the same module, and they cannot share memory variables. One cost of duplication is the additional memory required. Another is an increase in program complexity because it may not be obvious that several different procedures actually do exactly the same thing.

A better approach is to write a reentrant procedure. A reentrant procedure is one that can be invoked while it is currently executing, reentered, without the loss of intermediate results. Reentrant procedures are written as **pure procedures**, using a separate, dynamically allocated, temporary storage or work area for each entry into the procedure. Pure procedures also do not modify themselves in any way. All but the simplest procedures require temporary storage for parameters, data, and intermediate results. This storage, or work area, must be unique for each entry into a reentrant procedure.

There are two ways to provide unique temporary storage:

1. If the microprocessor's registers are sufficient to provide the temporary storage needed, these registers are saved on the stack at the beginning of the procedure and restored at the end of the procedure. As a result, the temporary work area is unique for each entry.

2. If a procedure requires a larger temporary work area, it is provided by using local variables in a stack frame, as discussed in Chapter 8.

You must insure that a reentrant ISR is, on average, returned from more often than it is invoked. Otherwise, the stack grows each time the procedure is entered, until it overwrites the data segment, causing the system to crash.

The shared procedure problem cannot always be handled by using duplicated or reentrant procedures. I/O driver procedures, for instance, cannot be duplicated. An I/O device and its associated I/O driver procedure are a single resource. It can only be serially shared. One task must complete its use of the I/O driver before another task can start to use the procedure. In such cases, reentry can be prevented by disabling the interrupts before the serially shared procedure is called. After returning from the procedure, interrupts are reenabled. This approach increases the system's interrupt response time to a value greater than the execution time of the shared procedure.

In a system where response times are critical, leaving the interrupts disabled while a serially shared procedure executes may not be acceptable. Preventing two or more tasks from using the same resource is called **mutual exclusion.** A semaphore can be used to reserve a shared resource and thereby provide mutual exclusion. A **semaphore** is a variable, used as a flag, with two operations defined on it. One operation, the P operation, requests the use of the shared resource. The other operation, the V operation, releases the resource for use by other tasks.

The P operation must be indivisible, an operation that while testing the semaphore does not allow any other task to gain use of the resource. Assume the variable semaphore has been allocated. When semaphore is a 0, the procedure is in use. When it is a 1, the procedure is free. The following instruction sequence is *not* indivisible.

```
p_op:           test        semaphore,1      ;check semaphore
                jz p_op                      ;wait if 0, resource busy
                mov         semaphore,0      ;clear semaphore to block others
                call        serially_shared
```

Assume that semaphore is initially 1, and the resource is free. The MOV instruction clears the semaphore, so no other task calls the serially shared procedure. This task then calls the procedure. However, if an interrupt occurs between the TEST instruction and the MOV instruction, the ISR also finds that semaphore is 1 and it calls the serially shared procedure. The procedure has now been reentered. The desired indivisible test and clear operation can be accomplished using an XCHG instruction as follows:

```
p_op:           mov         al,0
check:          xchg        semaphore,al     ;get and clear semaphore
                test        al,1
                jz          check
                call        serially_shared
```

The XCHG instruction accomplishes an indivisible test and clear operation. The 0 that was in AL is placed in the semaphore; this stops any other task from gaining access to the procedure. If the original value of the semaphore (now in AL) is 1, the tasks calls the serially shared procedure.

After returning from the serially shared procedure, the task does an indivisible V operation to release this resource.

```
v_op:           mov         semaphore,1
```

By using a semaphore, interrupts do not have to be disabled before calling the serially shared procedure. ISR's of interrupts that don't need to use the shared resource can execute to completion without regard to the status of the serially shared procedure. If an ISR is entered that needs to use the serially shared resource, it must check the semaphore. If the resource is in use, the ISR must wait. However, the ISR can reenable the interrupts so higher priority interrupt requests can still be responded to. To take this process to a higher level of sophistication requires that the ISR communicate with a background task that can schedule the ISR's task to be run at a later time when the resource is free. This allows the ISR to be returned from. This capability is, in effect, one of the functions of a real-time operating system and is beyond the scope of this text.

14.7   Interrupt Driven Systems

Interrupt driven I/O has been discussed in terms of achieving fast response to an I/O device's request for service. An unstated assumption was that the overall sequencing of tasks in the system was still essentially under program control.

Some applications are appropriate for implementation as interrupt driven systems. In an **interrupt driven system**, the order in which tasks are executed is primarily determined in response to interrupts from I/O devices and other peripherals. As shown in Fig. 14.7-1, software initializes the system and then transfers execution to a background task. In the extreme case, the background task can be as simple as a self loop implemented by a single instruction. When meaningful background tasks also exist, the resultant system is a **foreground/background** system. Any task that is not time critical can usually be placed in the background. This includes tasks like updating displays, outputting data to printers, and monitoring noncritical aspects of the system's operation.

The foreground tasks are executed as ISRs. These ISRs implement essentially independent tasks with minimal communication between them. The sequencing of tasks is dependent on the order of events (interrupts) and is not entirely deterministic. The result is interrupt driven task sequencing, instead of program driven sequencing.

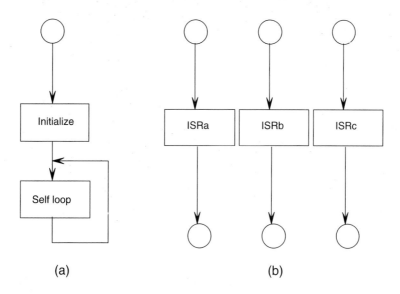

Figure 14.7-1   Interrupt driven system; (a) Initialize and wait for interrupts; (b) interrupt service routines to carry out system tasks.

Structuring a system as interrupt driven spares the designer from having to determine a precise order of execution for the system's tasks. An interrupt driven architecture may be appropriate when events associated with tasks are asynchronous and therefore the time and order of their occurrence cannot be predetermined.

14.8   Software Interrupts and Exceptions

In addition to having an interrupt occur in response to a request from a hardware device, your program can generate an interrupt directly by executing an interrupt instruction (INT). Such an interrupt is referred to as a software interrupt. Interrupts can also be generated indirectly by an instruction when its execution causes an exception. An **exception** is an unusual condition that requires attention before your program continues its normal instruction processing.

The 80C188EB handles software interrupts and exceptions similarly. Software interrupts and exceptions cannot be disabled by IF. However, like all other interrupts, their acknowledgment clears IF and TF, so their occurrence disables maskable interrupts and the single-step interrupt. In the case of software interrupts, the interrupt type is specified by the instruction. For exceptions, the interrupt type is predefined.

14.8.1   Software Interrupt Instruction (INT)

An *interrupt instruction* (**INT**) allows your program to generate an interrupt. INT generates an interrupt immediately upon the completion of its execution. This instruction has a single operand, *n*, which specifies the type code for the interrupt (Table 14.2-1). The value of *n* is assembled as the second byte of the two-byte instruction; the first byte is the opcode. The INT instruction's effect is similar to that of a hardware interrupt. The main differences are that the interrupt is caused by the execution of an instruction instead of a hardware event, and the type code is provided by the instruction.

If *n* is the type code of the NMI or one of the interrupts handled by the ICU, the associated ISR will be executed, but the corresponding bit in INTSTS is not altered. Since *n* can have any value from 0 (00H) to 255 (FFH), INT can also be used to test ISRs written to service hardware interrupts.

INT instructions are also frequently used as calls to an operating system (supervisor calls). For example, in 80C188EB systems using DOS, interrupt types 20H through 3FH are reserved by DOS.

14.8.2   Exceptions

Exceptions can be classified as either traps or faults. **Traps** are detected and serviced immediately after the instruction that causes the trap. The return address pushed onto the stack is the address of the instruction following the trapped instruction. All exceptions except the Escape Opcode (Type 7) and Numerics Coprocessor Fault (Type 16) are traps. **Faults** are detected and serviced before the instruction causing the fault is executed. The return address pushed onto the stack is the address of the instruction that caused the fault. After the ISR's execution is completed, execution is returned to the instruction that caused the fault and the instruction is restarted. A brief description of each of the 80C188EB's exceptions follows.

Divide Error, Type 0

A divide error, or Type 0 interrupt, occurs automatically following a DIV or IDIV instruction if the quotient is too large to fit in the destination. The ISR written to handle this situation is application dependent.

The divide error is sometimes loosely referred to as a "divide by zero" error. It is important to keep in mind that division by zero is only one example of a divisor value that produces this error. Depending on the value of the quotient, nonzero divisors can also cause this error.

In many embedded systems applications, it is possible to write the application program so conditions for a divide error can never occur. Whenever you use DIV or IDIV in a program, you must either know that divide errors are precluded by the design of the program, or you must provide an ISR to handle these errors.

Single Step, Type 1

This interrupt allows a software debugger to single step through a sequence of instructions. The single step interrupt is used by debuggers to allow the monitoring of registers and memory after each instruction in a sequence of interest is executed. The occurrence of a single step interrupt is conditioned on the trap flag (TF). If TF is set, a single step interrupt occurs immediately after an instruction is executed.

As shown in Fig. 14.2-2, whenever any interrupt occurs, the current value of TF is saved on the stack (as one of the bits in PSW), then TF is cleared. Clearing TF allows instructions in the debugger's single-step ISR to be executed without single stepping. When the ISR terminates, IRET restores the old value of TF when it pops PSW from the stack. The next instruction in the sequence being single stepped is then executed and, after its execution, another single step interrupt occurs.

When an 80C188EB is reset, TF is automatically cleared. The 80C188EB has no instructions to directly set or clear TF. To initiate single stepping, an instruction sequence can push PSW onto the stack using PUSHF, then set TF by ORing the top of the stack with 0100H. A POPF is then used to transfer the new flag settings to PSW.

```
push      bp                      ;save BP on the stack
pushf                             ;save flags image on stack
mov       bp,sp                   ;use BP to point to the top of the stack
or        word ptr [bp], 0100H              ;set TF in flags image
popf                              ;copy modified flags image to flags
pop       bp                      ;restore BP
```

To terminate single stepping, TF can be cleared by ANDing the PSW image saved on the stack with 0FEFFH.

Breakpoint Interrupt, INT3, Type 3

INT3 is a special one byte form of the INT instruction, and it has the opcode CCH. INT3 is often used as a **breakpoint instruction** by debuggers and monitors. A debugger uses this one-byte instruction to implement a breakpoint by saving the first byte of the instruction at the location where the breakpoint is to occur, and then replacing it with the object code CCH. When execution of the program reaches the "breakpointed" instruction, the interrupt occurs. The ISR allows any desired debugging, such as displaying the registers and memory, to be carried out. To remove the breakpoint, the debugger replaces the CCH byte with the byte saved from the original instruction. Since the object code for INT3 is only one byte long, it can be substituted for any instruction.

Interrupt on Overflow, INTO, Type 4

Interrupt on overflow (**INTO**) is a conditional interrupt instruction (Table 14.2-1). An interrupt on overflow occurs if the overflow flag (OF) is set and an interrupt on overflow instruction (INTO) is executed. When placed following arithmetic instructions that operate on signed operands, INTO causes an overflow error ISR to be executed if an overflow occurred.

Array Bounds Check, Type 5

An array bounds interrupt occurs when the array index is outside the array bounds during execution of a *bound* (BOUND) instruction (Table 14.2-1). The array's bounds are in memory at a location specified by one of the BOUND instruction's operands. The instruction's other operand indicates the value of the index to be checked.

Invalid Opcode, Type 6

An invalid opcode interrupt is caused by the 80C188EB's attempt to execute an undefined opcode.

Escape Opcode, Type 7

The escape opcode fault is used for floating point emulation. An 80C187 coprocessor can be used with the 80C186EB. When floating point instructions must be emulated because an 80C187 is not present in a system, the Escape Trap (ET) bit in the Relocation register is set when the system is initialized. When a floating point instruction is executed with the escape trap bit set, the escape opcode fault occurs and the ISR emulates the floating point instruction.

The 80C188EB does not support operation with an 80C187, so it always generates an escape opcode fault when a floating point instruction is encountered.

Numeric Coprocessor Fault, Type 16

A numeric coprocessor fault is caused by an 80C187 coprocessor when it encounters a problem in executing an instruction. This fault is only applicable in an 80C186EB system with a coprocessor.

14.9   Interrupt Priority and Latency

The relative priorities of the ICU's interrupts have already been discussed. This section explains the overall priority of all of the interrupts. Also discussed is the amount of time required for the 80C188EB to respond to an interrupt request.

14.9.1   Interrupt Priority

The 80C188EB's interrupt priorities are listed in Table 14.3-1. The priority of any non-maskable interrupt (NMI, software interrupt, or exception) is higher than that of any maskable interrupt. The nonmaskable interrupts are all listed as having a priority of 1 or 1a. The maskable interrupts have default priorities from 2 through 8.

The priority indicated specifies which interrupt is vectored to first, when multiple interrupts are recognized within a single instruction boundary. For simultaneous maskable interrupts, this priority also indicates which ISR is executed first. This is the case because, during the interrupt acknowledgment, all other maskable interrupts are automatically disabled and the ISR can execute to completion.

When simultaneous interrupts involve two or more nonmaskable interrupts or a maskable interrupt and a nonmaskable interrupt, the situation becomes more complicated. This complication results from the fact that the ISR vectored to first is not necessarily the ISR executed first.

For example, consider a situation where a NMI and a maskable interrupt are pending during the same instruction's execution. At the completion of the instruction's execution, IF will be cleared and the NMI's ISR will be vectored to. As you would expect, the NMI's ISR executes and, when done, pops the PSW, setting IF. The maskable interrupt's ISR is then vectored to and executed.

However, if an exception and an NMI are both pending during the same instruction's execution, the exception has priority, in terms of vectoring, over the NMI. The exception's vector is taken first and execution is transferred to the exception's ISR. But, since NMI is nonmaskable, the exception's ISR is interrupted and the NMI is vectored to. Therefore, the exception's ISR is preempted, and the NMI's ISR is executed. Thus, even though the exception has the highest priority in terms of vectoring, it is the NMI's ISR that is actually executed first.

Normally only one type of exception can occur at an instruction boundary. However, single step interrupts are a special case. The only time more than one exception can occur is if the second exception is the single step exception. If a single step occurs with any other interrupt, the other interrupt's ISR is vectored to first, followed by an immediate vector to the single step ISR. Therefore, the single step's ISR is executed before the other interrupt's ISR.

There is an exception to this priority ranking when a software interrupt, a NMI interrupt, and a single step interrupt request occur simultaneously. In this case, transfer of execution to the software interrupt's ISR followed by the NMI causes both the NMI's and software interrupt's ISRs to be executed, respectively, without single stepping. Single stepping resumes with the instruction following the one that caused the software interrupt—the next instruction in the routine being single stepped.

14.9.2   Interrupt Latency and Response Time

The quickness with which a microprocessor responds to an interrupt request is an important consideration in real-time systems. The delay in response can be expressed as the sum of two components, interrupt latency and interrupt response time. **Interrupt latency** is the maximum time from the occurrence of an interrupt request until the 80C188EB starts to acknowledge the request. **Interrupt response time** is the time from when the 80C188EB starts to acknowledge the request until the first instruction in the ISR is fetched.

A slightly different definition of interrupt response defines it as the time from when the 80C188EB starts to acknowledge the request until the execution of the first "useful" instruction in the ISR. This second definition includes, as part of the interrupt response, the time required to execute push instructions to save the registers that are not automatically saved.

Note that for hardware interrupts, the execution time of the interrupted instruction must be included in the determination of interrupt latency. This additional time can be considerable. The longest latencies occur when a division, multiplication, or variable-bit shift or rotate instruction has just begun execution and the interrupt request occurs.

There are a few special cases where a hardware interrupt occurs at a time other than immediately after the execution of the interrupted instruction is completed. This leads to the concept of an instruction's boundary. An **instruction's boundary** is the point during or after an instruction's execution when an interrupt is allowed to occur.

In some cases, an interrupt cannot occur until the completion of execution of the instruction following the interrupted instruction, for example, when a repeat or segment override prefixes an instruction. Since a prefix is actually considered part of the instruction it prefixes, an interrupt is not recognized between a prefix and its associated instruction.

For string instructions with a repeat prefix, interrupt latency would be extremely long had these instructions not been designed to accommodate interrupts. As shown in Fig. 7.8-1, interrupts are allowed on each repetition of the string primitive.

An interrupt cannot occur until after the instruction following an instruction that MOVs to a segment register or POPs to a segment register. These constraints protect a program that is changing to a new stack by updating SS and SP. If an interrupt were acknowledged after SS is changed but before SP is changed, the 80C188EB would push PSW, CS, and IP into the wrong memory locations. Accordingly, whenever a segment register and another register are to be changed together, the segment register should be changed first, followed immediately by the instruction that changes the other register.

In a system with multiple interrupts, the worst case latency must be determined by taking into consideration the execution time of higher priority ISRs and lower priority ISRs that don't reenable the interrupts. Therefore, a minimum latency, based on no higher priority interrupts occurring, and a maximum latency, which takes into account higher priority interrupts, exists. Accurately determining the maximum latency is usually very difficult.

After an interrupt is recognized by the 80C188EB's modular core CPU, the interrupt response time varies depending on the particular interrupt. Interrupts that supply their own type vectors take 62 states (42 for the 80C186EB). The maskable interrupts require 67 states (47 for the 80C186EB). The additional 5 states are required for the ICU to provide the vector table entry address.

When INT0 or INT1 are used in the cascade mode, the interrupt response time is 75 states (55 for the 80C186EB). In this case, an external interrupt controller (82C59A) provides the interrupt type code from which the 80C188EB calculates the vector table offset address.

WAIT states, DMA, and refresh operations all extend response time. Direct Memory Access (DMA) is discussed in Chapter 19.

In a real-time system with multiple interrupts sources, interrupt requests occur in an asynchronous fashion. The system must insure that each interrupt request is serviced within its real-time constraint. If an interrupt request from a source is in-service and another request from the same source is pending, and the same source generates a third event, causing a third request, the third request will be missed since there is no place to store it.

14.10   82C59A Priority Interrupt Controller

For applications that require more than its five external interrupt inputs, the 80C188EB provides support for expansion of the number of interrupt inputs through the use of external 82C59A priority interrupt controller ICs. One 82C59A can be connected to input INT0 and a second can be connected to INT1, if these inputs are programmed in the cascade mode. When INT0 is programmed for cascade mode, pin INT2 becomes an output and functions as the interrupt acknowledge signal (/INTA0) to the external controller (Fig. 14.10-1). When INT1 is programmed in the cascade mode, INT3 functions as its interrupt acknowledge, /INTA1.

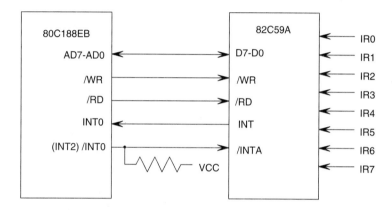

Figure 14.10-1   Connection of 82C59A Programmable interrupt controller to an 80C188EB.

An 82C59A **Priority Interrupt Controller** (**PIC**) combines interrupt requests from up to eight independent sources into a single interrupt request signal. The PIC accepts interrupt requests from devices and, when simultaneous requests occur, determines which has the highest priority. If the highest priority new request has a priority higher than the interrupt currently being serviced, the 82C59A asserts its INT output.

If an 82C59A is used, the Special Fully Nested mode must be selected for INT0 or INT1 when the ICU is initialized. This is necessary so the ICU will allow a second interrupt request at one of these inputs to preempt a previous interrupt that is still in service. This must be done to allow the 82C59A to maintain its own preemptive priority allowing its higher priority interrupt requests to preempt lower priority interrupts.

For simplicity, the discussion that follows refers to a single 82C59A connected to pins INT0 and /INTA0 (INT2). The discussion applies in a similar fashion to a second 82C59A connected on INT1 and /INTA1 (INT3).

When INT0 is programmed for cascade mode, the interrupt's type is not fixed and must be specified by an 8-bit interrupt type code provided to the 80C188EB's data bus during a special bus cycle. When INT0 is programmed for cascade mode, the 80C188EB acknowledges an interrupt request at INT0 by executing two consecutive **Interrupt Acknowledge bus cycles** (Fig. 14.10-2). Interrupt Acknowledge bus cycles are similar to

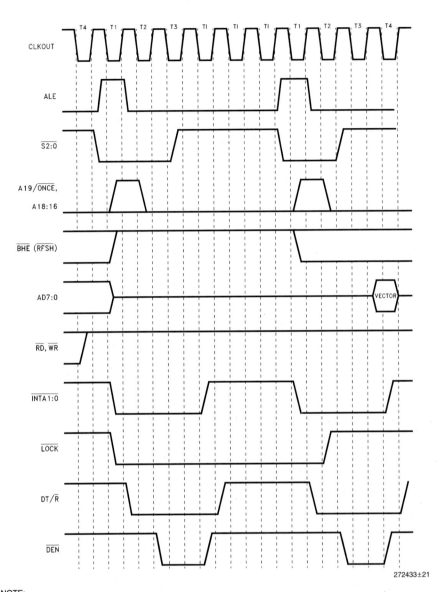

Figure 14.10-2   Interrupt acknowledge bus cycles. (Courtesy of Intel.)

Read I/O Port bus cycles, except, instead of asserting /RD, the 80C188EB asserts its /INTA0 output. The first Interrupt Acknowledge bus cycle signals that an interrupt acknowledge sequence is in progress. This allows the 82C59A time to prepare to generate the type code to identify the interrupt. When /INTA0 is asserted during the second Interrupt Acknowledge bus cycle, the 82C59A drives the data bus with the interrupt type code assigned to the interrupting source.

The 80C188EB multiplies the type code by 4 to get the offset into the interrupt vector table of the interrupt's vector. The 80C188EB transfers execution to the ISR pointed to by this vector.

The block diagram and pin configuration of an 82C59A are shown in Fig. 14.10-3. The 82C59A's eight interrupt request inputs are IR7–IR0. Input IR0 has the highest priority. The 82C59A's INT output is connected to the 80C188EB's INT0 input pin. The 82C59A's /INTA input receives interrupt acknowledge pulses from the 80C188EB's /INTA0 output. The interrupt's type code is sent by the 82C59A over the data bus in response to the second /INTA0 pulse of the Interrupt Acknowledge bus cycle.

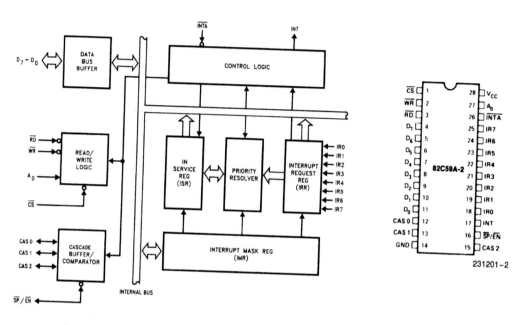

Figure 14.10-3   Block diagram and pinouts of 82C59A Programmable Interrupt Controller. (Courtesy of Intel Corp.)

The 82C59A is programmable and must be initialized by several command words sent from the 80C188EB after power-on. One of these command words specifies the most significant five bits that will be common to all of the eight different 8-bit interrupt type codes that can be generated by the 82C59A. The least significant three bits of each interrupt type code corresponds to the interrupt request being serviced. For example, if the most significant five bits have been specified as 01000B and an interrupt at IR3 is being responded to, the type code generated is 01000011B.

The priority resolving logic in the 82C59A is similar to that of the 80C188EB's ICU. Three 8-bit registers in the 82C59A have bits associated with each one of the eight interrupt request inputs. The bits in these registers have functions similar to their counterparts in registers in the 80C188EB's ICU. The Interrupt Request register (IRR) has bits indicating each of the current interrupt requests. The In Service register (ISR) indicates which interrupts are currently being serviced. And, the Interrupt Mask register (IMR) holds the individual interrupt mask bits. Each of these three registers can be read as a status register.

In the 82C59A's **nonspecific end of interrupt mode**, the ISR must send a nonspecific EOI command byte to the 82C59A. When the 82C59A receives the nonspecific EOI command, it clears the highest priority bit set in its In-Service register.

14.11   Debugging Hardware Interrupts

Debugging systems that use interrupts can become perplexing as the number of interrupt sources and the frequency of interrupt requests increases. In addition, some remote debuggers use one of the 80C188EB's interrupts for communication between the prototype and host computer. As a consequence, the debugger's operation can be affected when debugging an interrupt or can affect the debugging of an interrupt. These interactions can be particularly troublesome when using a breakpoint in an ISR or when single stepping an ISR.

The first step in debugging a system that uses interrupts is to make sure that everything is properly initialized before STI is executed. You must have an adequate size stack, interrupt vectors must be properly initialized, external devices that generate interrupts must be properly configured, and the individual interrupt mask bit for each interrupt used must be cleared. These preliminaries should be checked by reviewing a hardcopy of your code before you start a debugging session.

During debugging, initialization is checked by placing a breakpoint before STI in the background task. At this breakpoint, you can check the stack size by viewing the 80C188EB's SS and SP registers. Memory can be viewed to see that the interrupt vectors are in place. Some debuggers allow you to examine the PCB's registers symbolically. For example, Paradigm DEBUG's view menu has a target selection that symbolically displays the registers in the ICU. You can then examine the values in the control registers to see if they have been properly initialized.

In some aspects, an ISR is like a procedure and the debugging considerations raised in Section 8.8 are applicable. Both a procedure and an ISR, when returned from, should leave the stack in the state it was in prior to their execution. In addition, an ISR should return with all the 80C188EB's general purpose registers in their previous state.

For a procedure, it is easy to check SS and SP before and after the procedure's execution. For an asynchronous hardware interrupt, this is more difficult. You don't know where in the execution of your program the interrupt will occur. Therefore, you can't place breakpoints in the interrupted code prior to and following an interrupt.

There is also the practical matter of causing an interrupt to occur. For some interrupt sources, like the previous pushbutton interrupt example, causing an interrupt to occur just when you want it to while debugging is easy. For other interrupt sources, you may have little control over when an interrupt request occurs.

One way to cause a hardware interrupt's ISR to be executed is to simulate the hardware interrupt using an INT instruction. An INT that has the same interrupt type code as the hardware interrupt. This approach works because the interrupt sequence is the same for hardware and software interrupts. An INT instruction can be temporarily inserted in the background task and a breakpoint placed before and after this instruction. Values for SS and SP at the two breakpoints can then be compared.

To determine whether an interrupt actually occurs in the operation of a system, or to examine the operation of an ISR in detail, requires that a breakpoint be placed in the ISR. What happens when the breakpoint occurs depends on the design of the debugger. If a breakpoint is set in the ISR before the ISR reenables the interrupts, all maskable interrupts are disabled when the breakpoint occurs. Remote debuggers typically use one of the 80C188EB's interrupts for serial communication. If the debugger uses a maskable interrupt for communications, the host will no longer be able to communicate with target prototype and the debugger will be inoperable.

If the debugger is designed to enable the interrupts or if a breakpoint is placed after the ISR enables the interrupts, higher priority interrupts will be serviced while you single step the ISR. Depending on the application, this may produce confusing results.

Most debuggers will not halt when the HLT instruction is executed.

One debugging issue related to exceptions and unused interrupts warrants consideration. Exceptions cannot be masked, so if an exception occurs, the 80C188EB will vector to its ISR, regardless of whether you have initialized the exception's interrupt vector and written its ISR. If the vector has not been initialized, the 80C188EB will simply use whatever values are in the vector table as the new CS and IP. Execution will be transferred to some random location in memory with undesired consequences. For example, if you use a DIV or IDIV instruction anywhere in you program, you must initialize the Divide Error interrupt vector and write an appropriate ISR.

One way to deal with unexpected exceptions or interrupts is to include a loop in your program that initializes all interrupt vectors to point to a single unexpected interrupt ISR. Then you would initialize the interrupts you intend to use. Placing a breakpoint in this unexpected interrupt ISR causes execution to stop if an unexpected interrupt occurs. You must then track down the source of the interrupt.

14.12   Summary

Using interrupts allows a system to respond quickly to I/O devices and other external events. In many applications the use of interrupts is the only way you can provide the speed of response and total throughput required. Interrupt use can also simplify your software's architecture with regard to scheduling tasks in the proper sequence.

Use of interrupts requires careful attention to details. The stack must be of sufficient length. Interrupt vectors and the control registers for individual interrupts must be initialized. When all initializations are complete, the maskable interrupts can be globally enabled.

Each ISR must save the context of the interrupted task, so when the ISR completes execution, the interrupted task can be resumed with none of its data corrupted. An ISR for an external device must clear its interrupt request flip-flop and its In-Service bit before returning.

Each ISR must be as short as possible to reduce the latency for other interrupts. Very short ISRs can be allowed to execute to completion without their reenabling the interrupts. To reduce latency further, an ISR can reenable interrupts during its execution by using an STI instruction. If there is any chance that an ISR can be invoked during its execution, then the ISR must be written to be reentrant. Any procedures called by an ISR that are used by other tasks must also be written to be reentrant.

Interrupt driven systems can simplify a system's software architecture. However, if a system is interrupt driven, a careful analysis is required to insure that each interrupt request is serviced within its time constraint.

One other issue that requires that systems using interrupts be carefully designed is the difficulty in debugging such systems.

Though they must be used with great care, interrupts are used in almost all embedded systems.

14.13   Problems

1. Define an event.
2. What are the advantages of using an interrupt to conditionally input data from a port as opposed to using polling?
3. How is an interrupt similar to a procedure call and how is it different?
4. Explain the difference between a maskable and a nonmaskable interrupt input. In what situations is each type appropriate?
5. Explain the difference between a level sensitive and an edge sensitive interrupt input.
6. Why is it so important to clear an interrupt request flip-flop before the execution of its ISR completes?
7. What is the significance of the priority assigned to interrupt inputs?
8. Compare and contrast the specific actions involved in the transfer of execution to, and the return from, an ISR to the actions involved in an intersegment call to and return from a regular procedure.
9. While an ISR is executing, no other maskable interrupts will be responded to unless the ISR itself makes this response possible. But, when the ISR has completed its execution, the microprocessor will again respond to maskable interrupts. Explain the mechanism that makes this possible and how the ISR itself can make it possible for maskable interrupts to be responded to during its execution.
10. What is the difference between a near return, a far return, and an interrupt return. What instruction(s) would be used to achieve each?
11. At what address in memory would the starting address for the ISR for each of the following interrupts be found?

    a. An INT0 interrupt
    b. int 8 instruction
    c. A type 21 interrupt
    d. An NMI interrupt

12. For your assembler, write an instruction sequence that initializes the vector for Timer 2 assuming that its ISR's name is RTC_TICK and the first 1K bytes of memory are ROM.

13. Since the stack and interrupt vectors must be initialized before an interrupt is allowed, what, if anything, prevents an NMI interrupt from occurring before these initializations are carried out?

14. A system has two interrupt sources, event A and event B. Each generates a 100 ns negative pulse. Event A should cause a type 40H interrupt and event B should cause a type 41H interrupt. Event A has the highest priority. Using small and medium scale ICs, draw a diagram of logic that generates the signal at the 80C188EB's INTR input in response to an event, and the logic to generate the type code. Interrupt requests are to be cleared by device select pulses generated by the ISRs. Show the logic to generate the device select pulses as a single block.

15. Port B of an 8255 is to be used for interrupt driven I/O. Draw a logic diagram showing the interface of the 8255 and its input device to an 80C188EB. The 8255 is located in isolated I/O space. Show address decoding logic as a single block. Also show a simple logic structure to generate a type 60H interrupt. Assume the type 60H interrupt is the only one in the system. Write an instruction sequence to initialize the 8255 and an instruction sequence to enable interrupts from port B. Port A should be initialized as an input port that does not latch its data and the unused bits from Port C as output bits. Refer to the 8255's registers symbolically: PORTA, PORTB, PORTC, and CNTRL.

16. An 82050 UART is to interrupt an 80C188EB when a character is received from a terminal and send (echo) the character back to the terminal. To echo the character, the 80C188EB polls the 82050's line status register (LSR) to determine when its transmit buffer is empty. The 82050 UART is to be placed in the I/O address space starting at address 0000H. Partial address decoding is to be used. Use a MAX 233 to buffer the UART's serial input and output for RS232 compatibility. The clock input to the 82050 is provided by OSC from the 8284. The interrupt generated when the UART receives a character is to be a type 40H interrupt. This interrupt will be the only external interrupt in the system. Draw a logic diagram of the interface of the 82050 to the system bus. Write the entire program. Communications between the 82050 and the terminal take place at 9600 baud, with 7 data bits, one stop bit, and even parity. After initializations, the program remains in a self loop until an interrupt. The ISR is not returned from until the character is echoed.

17. The contents of a 20-byte memory buffer (DBUFF) is to be transferred to an output device (ODATA) in the isolated I/O space. After a byte is written to the output device, it generates a type 42H interrupt once it has emptied its data register. Write a procedure (STRANS) that initiates the transfer of data from the memory buffer to the output device. Write an ISR (NXBYTE) that responds to an interrupt from the output device and transfers the next byte from the buffer, if all 20 bytes have not been transferred.

18. A stepper motor is controlled by Darlington drivers connected to the least significant four bits of output port STEP. For clockwise rotation, the step sequence is 0AH, 09H, 05H, 06H, and repeat. Stepping through the sequence in reverse order creates counter-clockwise rotation. Write an interrupt procedure that reads bit 0 of port DIR, and if it is 1, steps the motor one step clockwise and returns. If bit 0 of DIR is 0, the procedure steps the motor one step counter-clockwise and returns.

19. Using two 82C59A priority interrupt controllers with an 80C188EB, how many external interrupt inputs can be provided?.

20. A minimum mode 80C188EB system uses a single 82C59A Priority Interrupt Controller. Each interrupt source generates a 200ns pulse when it needs service from the microprocessor. The ISR, written for each interrupt source, issues a nonspecific end of interrupt command before its completion. The interrupt vectors for the 82C59A are located starting at address 200H in memory. The 82C59A is located in isolated I/O space starting at symbolic port address B82C59A. Write a sequence of instructions to initialize the 82C59A. What type code will be generated by the 82C59A for an interrupt from the interrupt source connected to interrupt request input IR5 of the 82C59A?

15

DATA ENTRY
AND DISPLAY

15.1   User Data Entry

15.2   Mechanical Switches

15.3   Keypads and Keyboards

15.4   Optical Shaft Encoders

15.5   Displays

15.6   Light Emitting Diodes, LEDs

15.7   Multiplexed Eight Digit LED Display Driver

15.8   Liquid Crystal Display (LCD) Modules

15.9   Vacuum Fluorescent Display (VFD) Modules

15.10   Summary

Signals from the outside world to input devices, or from output devices to the outside world, can be either digital or analog. On the system bus side of an I/O device the signals must always be digital and compatible with the logic levels of the bus. I/O devices that convert digital signals to analog and analog signals to digital are presented in Chapters 17 and 18, respectively. I/O devices that handle digital data in serial form are covered in Chapter 16. This chapter presents some important I/O devices that are used specifically for a system's user interface. A user interface allows a user to enter commands and data to a system and to receive status and results from a system.

Switches, keypads, keyboards, and shaft encoders are common user input devices. Individual LEDs, seven-segment LED displays, liquid crystal displays, and vacuum fluorescent displays are common user output devices. The input and output devices presented in this chapter are useful for providing a user interface for a wide variety of systems. The concepts presented also apply to more complex user interface devices and to a variety of I/O devices that do not involve user interaction.

15.1   User Data Entry

User data entry is the direct input of data by a human operator. In contrast, electronic data entry involves the direct input of data by another electronic system. With either method, provision of appropriate digital input data may require one or more of the following operations:

1. Conversion: distinguishing between the two logic states of an input device and generating an electrical signal with the appropriate voltage for each state.
2. Sensing: detecting a change in state of an input signal corresponding to the occurrence of new data.
3. Debouncing: providing a single transition for each change of state of a mechanical switch
4. Encoding: converting a multivalued input state to a binary code.

Techniques for carrying out these operations vary considerably depending on the physical nature of each input device. Usually, there is considerable opportunity for hardware/software tradeoffs in implementing these types of input subsystems. Hardware/software tradeoffs are emphasized in the next three sections as mechanical switches, keypads, keyboards, and optical shaft encoders are considered as user input devices.

15.2   Mechanical Switches

Two-position switches are commonly used to input data. There are a variety of methods for creating a binary signal from the physical states of a two-position switch. Switches may be classified in terms of these methods, such as: electromechanical, capacitive, magnetic, and optical.

Electromechanical, or simply mechanical switches, are used for data entry in many systems. The amount of data input to a system through mechanical switches varies from a small amount, at system initialization, to large amounts throughout a system's operation. The latter situation is the case with interactive systems. Accordingly, selection of devices for manual data entry is based on the type and quantity of data to be entered, and the time and the frequency at which data is entered.

A variety of mechanical switches are available, including **Single-pole/single-throw** (SPST) and **single-pole/double-throw** (SPDT) switches. These switches exist as either toggle (maintained contact) or pushbutton (momentary contact) switches (Fig. 15.2-1).

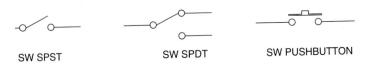

SW SPST   SW SPDT   SW PUSHBUTTON

Figure 15.2-1   Symbols for simple mechanical switches: single-pole/single-throw, SPST, maintained; single-pole/double-throw, SPDT, maintained; SPST momentary contact.

A mechanical switch's position must be converted to an electrical signal compatible with the system's logic family. In Fig. 15.2-2 a switch and a pull-up resistor connected to +5 V provide a signal compatible with CMOS or TTL circuits. When the switch is closed, it provides an output voltage of 0 V. When open, the switch provides a voltage of $V_{out} = 5\text{ V} - I \times R$, where I is the total I_{IHmax} current required by the load connected to the switch.

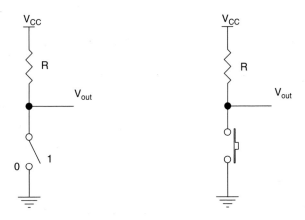

Figure 15.2-2   Conversion of a switch's position to logic levels using a pull-up resistor.

The pull-up resistor's value is chosen to limit the power dissipated when the switch is closed, but still provide a current above I_{IHmax} at a voltage above V_{IHmin} when the switch is open. If a switch's output is to be input to the system data bus, its load is the input current of the three-state buffer that isolates the switch's output from the data bus (Fig. 15.2-3).

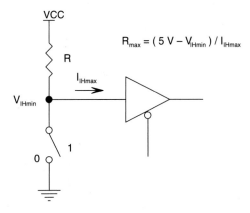

$$R_{max} = (5\text{ V} - V_{IHmin}) / I_{IHmax}$$

Figure 15.2-3   Computation of the maximum value for a pull-up resistor.

15.2.1   Mechanical Switch Bounce

When a mechanical switch is operated, closed or opened, its contacts **bounce**. The contacts actually open and close many times before coming to rest. A typical switch's contacts may bounce for from 1 to 20 ms. Higher quality switches have shorter bounce periods. As a result of this bouncing, multiple logic transitions appear at the switch's output, instead of a single transition (Fig. 15.2-4). Note that the switch bounces when it is closed and bounces again when it is opened.

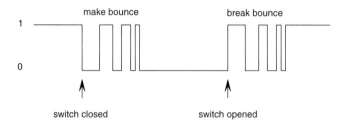

Figure 15.2-4   Multiple signal transitions caused by the contact bounce of a mechanical switch.

    If a microprocessor repeatedly inputs a switch's output during the bounce period, it can detect multiple logic state transitions. Thus, it appears to the microprocessor that the switch has been operated several times, instead of just once. To preclude this possibility, the switch must be debounced.

    A switch can be debounced using hardware or software. **Hardware debouncing** produces a signal with a single transition from the multiple transitions that appear at the switch's output when the switch's contacts bounce. **Software debouncing** insures that the multiple transitions at the switch's output are treated by the software as a single transition.

    Use of an RS latch to debounce a single-pole/double-throw switch is shown in Fig. 15.2-5. The latch's output changes state only once when the switch's position is changed. RS latches can be constructed from cross-coupled NAND gates or from cross-coupled NOR gates. If NOR gates are used, the resistors must be pull-down resistors, connected to ground rather than to 5 V. Use of an RS latch requires that the switch be single-pole/double-throw.

    In contrast, any type of switch can be debounced using software. A software debouncing approach is illustrated in Fig. 15.2-6. This code counts the number of times a pushbutton switch is operated. Each time the pushbutton is operated, the count is updated and displayed on the LEDs. The count shown on the LED display is incremented by 1 each time the pushbutton is pressed, but does not change when the pushbutton is released.

    When the pushbutton is not pressed, its output is 1. The pushbutton's output is connected to bit 0 of input port PBSW. After initialization, the program loops, at wait_for_0, inputting the pushbutton's value. To exit this loop, the pushbutton must be 0. Thus, exiting this loop corresponds to detecting a pushbutton press, a 1 to 0 transition of the pushbutton. A 20 ms delay procedure is then called. The delay period is chosen to be slightly longer that the pushbutton's bounce. After the delay, the pushbutton is again tested. If the push-

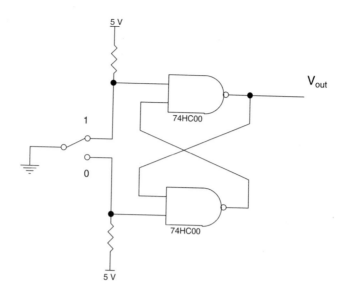

Figure 15.2-5   Use of an RS latch to debounce a single-pole/double-throw switch.

button is still 0, the press is accepted as valid and the count of presses is incremented and displayed.

The code then loops, at wait_for_1, waiting for the pushbutton to be released. When a 1 is detected, the code jumps back to the beginning to wait for the next pushbutton press.

If the call to the delay procedure is commented out, and the program containing this code is reassembled and run, pressing the pushbutton results in the count being incremented by a random value. This value corresponds to the number of 1 to 0 transitions that the code detected when the pushbutton bounced on being pressed. When the pushbutton is subsequently released, the count is again incremented by a random value. This value corresponds to the number of 1 to 0 transitions detected when the pushbutton was released.

The drawback of the code in Fig. 15.2-6 is that during the 20 ms software delay, the 80C188EB cannot do any other useful work. Furthermore, if an application has several pushbuttons to debounce and a number of other tasks to execute, each with its own time constraint, the amount of time spent in the software delay could pose a problem.

One possible solution involves replacing the 20 ms delay with a number of tasks whose total execution time is 20 ms. However, most tasks of any complexity have numerous execution paths, based on current status or data values and external events. So, it is difficult to guarantee that the execution time of a collection of tasks will not vary substantially.

15.2.2   Debouncing a Switch Using a Software State Machine

A more efficient switch debouncing approach uses a hardware timer to provide the 20 ms debounce delay. Timer 2 can be programmed to generate an interrupt every 20 ms. The task of its ISR is to debounce the pushbutton. While the timer is counting down the delay, the 80C188EB can be executing other tasks.

```
        name    debouncr

;***********************************************************************
;
;NAME:        DEBOUNCE
;
;DESCRIPTION: This program reads a switch PBSW connected to bit 0 of
;port PBSW and counts the number of 1 to 0 transitions of PBSW.
;Debouncing is used. The purpose is to illustrate the effects of
;debouncing
;
;***********************************************************************
;

        .186

PBSW        equ     8001h
LEDS        equ     8000h

stack   segment 'STKRAM'
        dw      32 dup (?)
tos     label   word
stack   ends



        assume cs:code, ss:stack

code    segment public'ROM'

;***********************************************************************
;
;NAME: VDELAY
;
;FUNCTION: Variable software delay
;
;CREATED:
;REVISED:
;
;ASSUMES: AX = delay time as a multiple of 10ms
;RETURNS: nothing
;MODIFIES: CX, AX, and F
;
;CALLS: nothing
;CALLED BY:
;
```

Figure 15.2-6   Program to debounce a pushbutton.

```
;DESCRIPTION: Variable software delay. Delay varies in 0.1 ms steps
; from 0.1 ms to 0.109 minutes. Delay as a multiple of 0.1 ms is passed
; in AX. AX = 1 provides approximately 0.1 ms delay for 80C188EB operated
; at 8 MHz. AX = 2 produces 0.2 ms delay etc. AX = 0 provides maximum
; delay. For 80C188EB clock speeds other than 8 MHz TENMSEC must be
; recomputed.
;
;
;*********************************************************************

tenthmsecequ 50

vdelay  proc

vdly0:  mov     cx,tenthmsec
vdly1:  loop    vdly1
        dec     ax
        jnz     vdly0
        ret

vdelay  endp


start:  mov     ax,stack
        mov     ss,ax
        mov     sp,offset tos

        xor     bl,bl           ;clear BL to hold presses count
        mov     al,bl           ;clear display
        not     al
        mov     dx,LEDS
        out     dx,al


        mov     dx,PBSW         ;input PBSW, and wait for a 0

wait_for_0:

        in      al,dx
        and     al,01h
        jnz     wait_for_0      ;if switch is not 0, wait
```

Figure 15.2-6   Program to debounce a pushbutton. (Continued.)

```
        mov     ax,200          ;1 to 0 transition detected
        call    vdelay          ;delay longer than bounce

        mov     dx,PBSW         ;input PBSW, must still be a 0
        in      al,dx
        and     al,01h
        jnz     wait_for_0      ;input not 0, false 1 to 0


        inc     bl              ;1 to 0 transition detected
        mov     al,bl           ;increment and display count
        not     al
        mov     dx,LEDS
        out     dx,al

        mov     dx,PBSW         ;input PBSW and wait for a 1
wait_for_1:
        in      al,dx
        and     al,01h
        jz      wait_for_1

        jmp     wait_for_0      ;1 has been detected, go back and
                                ;wait for a 0


code    ends

        end star
```

Figure 15.2-6   Program to debounce a pushbutton. (Continued.)

The debounce code in Fig. 15.2-6 cannot be modified to create the desired ISR. In the code of Fig. 15.2-6, information about the state of the process of debouncing the pushbutton is represented by the point of execution in the program. For example, when the program is in a loop waiting to detect a 0 (wait_for_0), the pushbutton remains released.

An ISR cannot store the state of a process in terms of its point of execution, because each time it is invoked, the ISR must execute to completion, without delay. Thus, the process state must be stored somewhere else. An obvious approach is to use a software finite state machine (FSM). A state diagram for debouncing a pushbutton is given in Fig. 15.2-7. Every 20 ms, when the Timer 2 interrupt occurs, the ISR looks at the present state and input and determines the next state and output. The input to the state machine is the value read from the pushbutton. TASK0 of the state machine does nothing. TASK1 increments the count of pushbutton presses.

At reset, the state machine is placed in State 0. This state corresponds to the pushbutton not being pressed. In State 0, if the value read from the pushbutton is 0, the pushbutton has just been pressed. For this input value a transition to State 1 takes place. State 1

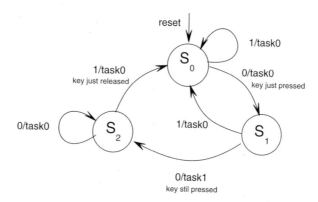

Figure 15.2-7   State diagram for debouncing a switch.

corresponds to the pushbutton having just been pressed. At this point, although the pushbutton has been pressed, it has not yet been checked after the 20 ms debounce period to see if the press is to be accepted as valid.

In State 1, the first time that the pushbutton is read as a 0 corresponds to the pushbutton still being pressed 20 ms after it was first pressed. This situation causes a transition to State 2 and the execution of TASK1. State 2 represents that a valid pushbutton press has occurred. The transition to State 2 is the only situation that causes the execution of TASK1, which increments and displays COUNT. On subsequent Timer 2 interrupts in State 2, if the pushbutton's value is 0, we do not wish to execute TASK1. This situation corresponds to the pushbutton remaining pressed.

In State 2, if an input of 1 is read, the pushbutton has just been released and a transition to State 0 occurs.

The state machine of Fig. 15.2-7 can be implemented by the FSM procedure of Fig. 8.7-2 if the FSM's inputs and state table are appropriately modified. Figure 15.2-8 shows the complete program with the state machine's input symbols and state table modified as required to implement the state diagram in Fig. 15.2-7. The modified FSM procedure is named dbnc_sw.

The program starts executing at the instruction labeled start. First the segment registers and stack pointer are initialized. Then the interrupt vector for Timer 2 is initialized and count and the display are cleared. The state machine's present state, pstate, is initialized to the offset of s0. This corresponds to initializing the state machine to State 0.

Timer 2 is then initialized to generate an interrupt every 20 ms. Finally, the timer interrupts are unmasked, and maskable interrupts are globally enabled. The program then enters an infinite loop. In a practical application, instead of being in an infinite loop doing nothing, the program would be in an infinite loop executing other tasks of the application.

When a Timer 2 interrupt occurs, the ISR pbisr is executed. pbisr inputs the pushbutton's value and masks it to create an input to the state machine. The dbnc_sw procedure is then called. dbnc_sw uses the input and present state to determine the next state and task to be executed. If task1 is executed, it will increment and display count.

As you can see, the seemingly trivial operation of directly inputting the closure of a momentary switch turns out to require careful consideration. What is logically a single

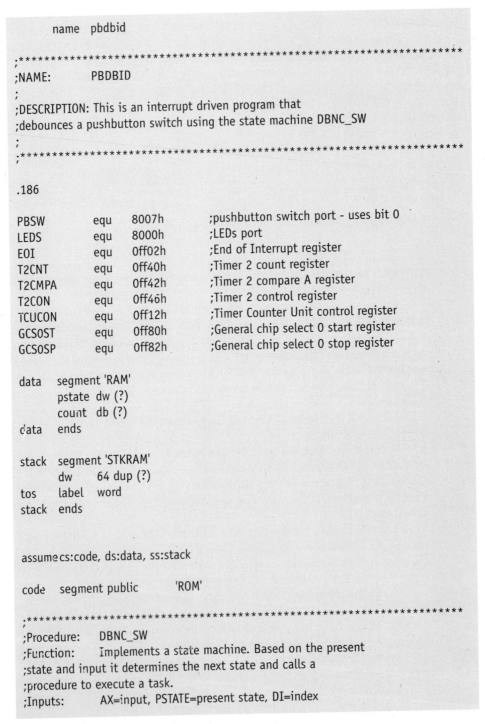

```
        name    pbdbid

;**********************************************************
;NAME:       PBDBID
;
;DESCRIPTION: This is an interrupt driven program that
;debounces a pushbutton switch using the state machine DBNC_SW
;
;**********************************************************

        .186

PBSW       equ    8007h       ;pushbutton switch port - uses bit 0
LEDS       equ    8000h       ;LEDs port
EOI        equ    0ff02h      ;End of Interrupt register
T2CNT      equ    0ff40h      ;Timer 2 count register
T2CMPA     equ    0ff42h      ;Timer 2 compare A register
T2CON      equ    0ff46h      ;Timer 2 control register
TCUCON     equ    0ff12h      ;Timer Counter Unit control register
GCS0ST     equ    0ff80h      ;General chip select 0 start register
GCS0SP     equ    0ff82h      ;General chip select 0 stop register


data    segment 'RAM'
        pstate dw (?)
        count  db (?)
data    ends

stack   segment 'STKRAM'
        dw      64 dup (?)
tos     label   word
stack   ends


assume cs:code, ds:data, ss:stack


code    segment public       'ROM'

;**********************************************************
;Procedure:   DBNC_SW
;Function:    Implements a state machine. Based on the present
;state and input it determines the next state and calls a
;procedure to execute a task.
;Inputs:      AX=input, PSTATE=present state, DI=index
```

Figure 15.2-8   Program to debounce a pushbutton using a software finite state machine.

```
;Ouputs:        PSTATE and task execution
;Modifies:      FLAGS
;Calls:         tasks
;************************************************************************
;equate input symbols to input codes
i0      equ     0
i1      equ     1
eol     equ     0ffh    ;end of list of specific inputs

;state table

;pstate state   input           next state      task

s0              dw i0,          s1,             task0
                dw i1,          s0,             task0
                dw eol,         s0,             task0

s1              dw i0,          s2,             task1
                dw i1,          s0,             task0
                dw eol,         s0,             task0

s2              dw i0,          s2,             task0
                dw i1,          s0,             task0
                dw eol,         s2,             task0

dbnc_sw         proc    near
                push    ax              ;save registers
                push    bx
                push    cx
                push    dx
                push    si
                push    di

                mov     si,0            ;zero index into  subtable
                mov     bx,pstate       ;get present state (address)
search:         cmp     ax,cs:[bx][si]  ;does subtable entry match input
                jz      match           ;yes

                                        ;is this the last entry in subtable?
                cmp     word ptr cs:[bx][si],eol
                jz      match           ;if so, it is considered a match
                add     si,6            ;no, add 6 to go to next input entry
                jmp     search          ;continue search
```

Figure 15.2-8   Program to debounce a pushbutton using a software finite state machine. (Continued.)

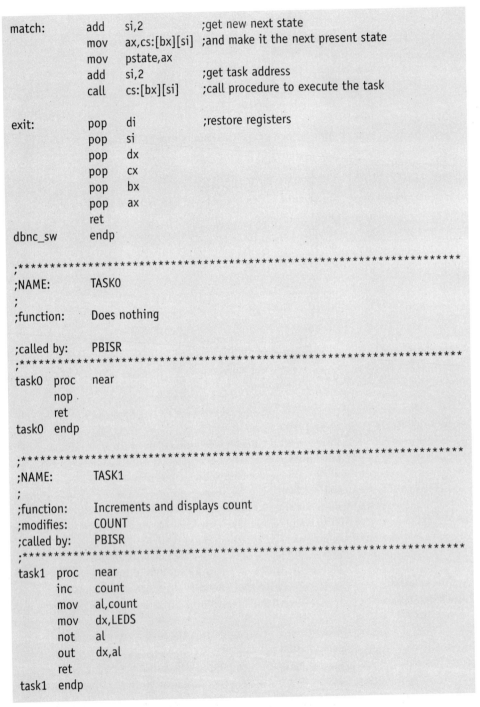

```
match:      add   si,2             ;get new next state
            mov   ax,cs:[bx][si]   ;and make it the next present state
            mov   pstate,ax
            add   si,2             ;get task address
            call  cs:[bx][si]      ;call procedure to execute the task


exit:       pop   di               ;restore registers
            pop   si
            pop   dx
            pop   cx
            pop   bx
            pop   ax
            ret
dbnc_sw     endp

;*******************************************************************
;NAME:      TASK0
;
;function:  Does nothing

;called by: PBISR
;*******************************************************************
task0  proc  near
       nop
       ret
task0  endp


;*******************************************************************
;NAME:      TASK1
;
;function:  Increments and displays count
;modifies:  COUNT
;called by: PBISR
;*******************************************************************
task1  proc  near
       inc   count
       mov   al,count
       mov   dx,LEDS
       not   al
       out   dx,al
       ret
task1  endp
```

Figure 15.2-8   Program to debounce a pushbutton using a software finite state machine. (Continued.)

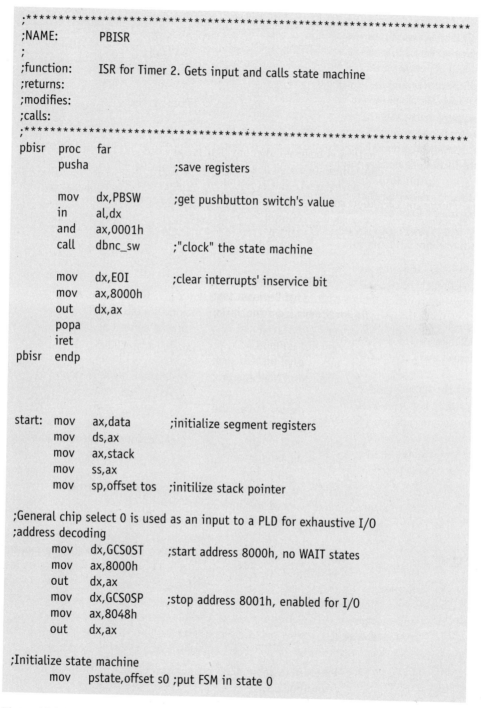

```
;********************************************************************
;NAME:        PBISR
;
;function:    ISR for Timer 2. Gets input and calls state machine
;returns:
;modifies:
;calls:
;********************************************************************
pbisr   proc   far
        pusha                   ;save registers

        mov    dx,PBSW          ;get pushbutton switch's value
        in     al,dx
        and    ax,0001h
        call   dbnc_sw          ;"clock" the state machine

        mov    dx,EOI           ;clear interrupts' inservice bit
        mov    ax,8000h
        out    dx,ax
        popa
        iret
pbisr   endp




start:  mov    ax,data          ;initialize segment registers
        mov    ds,ax
        mov    ax,stack
        mov    ss,ax
        mov    sp,offset tos    ;initilize stack pointer

;General chip select 0 is used as an input to a PLD for exhaustive I/O
;address decoding
        mov    dx,GCS0ST        ;start address 8000h, no WAIT states
        mov    ax,8000h
        out    dx,ax
        mov    dx,GCS0SP        ;stop address 8001h, enabled for I/O
        mov    ax,8048h
        out    dx,ax

;Initialize state machine
        mov    pstate,offset s0 ;put FSM in state 0
```

Figure 15.2-8   Program to debounce a pushbutton using a software finite state machine. (Continued.)

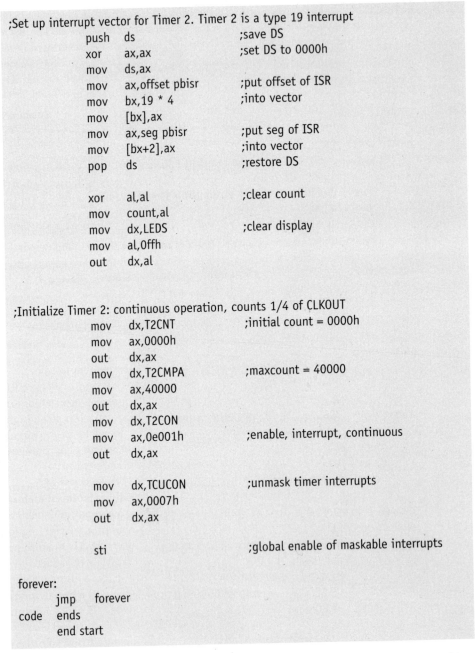

```
;Set up interrupt vector for Timer 2. Timer 2 is a type 19 interrupt
            push    ds                      ;save DS
            xor     ax,ax                   ;set DS to 0000h
            mov     ds,ax
            mov     ax,offset pbisr         ;put offset of ISR
            mov     bx,19 * 4               ;into vector
            mov     [bx],ax
            mov     ax,seg pbisr            ;put seg of ISR
            mov     [bx+2],ax               ;into vector
            pop     ds                      ;restore DS

            xor     al,al                   ;clear count
            mov     count,al
            mov     dx,LEDS                 ;clear display
            mov     al,0ffh
            out     dx,al


;Initialize Timer 2: continuous operation, counts 1/4 of CLKOUT
            mov     dx,T2CNT                ;initial count = 0000h
            mov     ax,0000h
            out     dx,ax
            mov     dx,T2CMPA               ;maxcount = 40000
            mov     ax,40000
            out     dx,ax
            mov     dx,T2CON
            mov     ax,0e001h               ;enable, interrupt, continuous
            out     dx,ax

            mov     dx,TCUCON               ;unmask timer interrupts
            mov     ax,0007h
            out     dx,ax

            sti                             ;global enable of maskable interrupts

forever:
            jmp     forever
code    ends
        end start
```

Figure 15.2-8   Program to debounce a pushbutton using a software finite state machine. (Continued.)

switch closure must be correctly interpreted as such. In addition, the microprocessor must read a switch's output often enough so that the switch's operation is not missed. Achievement of these objectives becomes more difficult when many switches are involved and numerous other tasks must be executed.

15.3   Keypads and Keyboards

When user entry of a large number of different data symbols is necessary, keyboards with 100 or more momentary contact switches, or **keys**, are commonly used. The term **keypad** is typically applied to keyboards consisting of a small number (typically 10 to 20) of keys. When dealing with keypads and keyboards, the terms switch, key, and keyswitch are used interchangeably. Each key of a keypad or keyboard has associated with it a particular code or binary value that identifies the key. When a key is pressed, its corresponding code must be generated by an encoding operation.

When the number of keys is less than or equal to 16, keys are efficiently encoded into parallel data using combinational circuitry. For example, the **74HC148 Priority Encoder** encodes eight contact closures into a 3-bit code (Fig. 15.3-1). The encoder's /EO output is asserted if any one of its inputs is asserted. This output is used by hardware or software that debounces the encoder's output, or is latched and used to generate an interrupt. Two 74HC148s and a few gates can encode 16 keys.

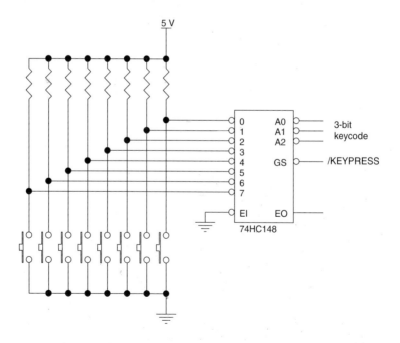

Figure 15.3-1   Use of a 74HC138 priority decoder to encode an eight-key keypad.

The keys in Fig. 15.3-1 all have one of their contacts connected in common. This is a linear key arrangement. Instead of a linear arrangement, keys can be arranged at the intersection of wires to form a **key matrix** (Fig. 15.3-2(a)). A matrix arrangement is advantageous for a large numbers of keys, because it reduces the amount of hardware required for scanning and encoding.

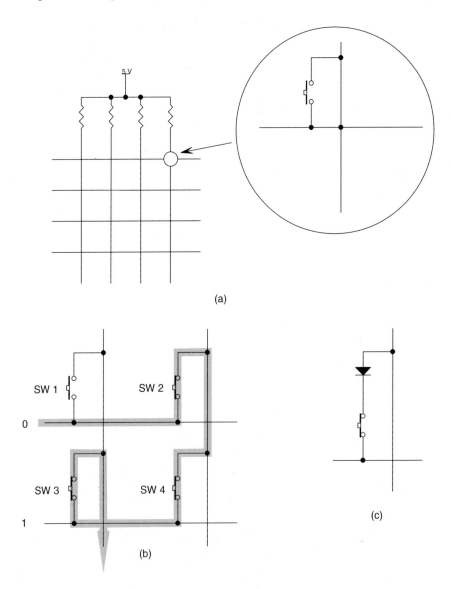

Figure 15.3-2   Keyboard: (a) keyboard switch matrix; (b) sneak path in a switch matrix—key 1 appears pressed when keys 2,3, and 4 are actually pressed; (c) diode orientation to prevent sneak paths.

15.3.1   Software Keymatrix Scanning

A keymatrix is **scanned** to determine if a key has been pressed, and, if so, to identify the key. Scanning is accomplished using either software or hardware. Here the hardware/software trade-off decision is usually based on whether the system can afford the software overhead required for scanning.

Hardware to support software keymatrix scanning is shown in Fig. 15.3-3. The key matrix rows are controlled by an output port and the columns are sensed through an input port.

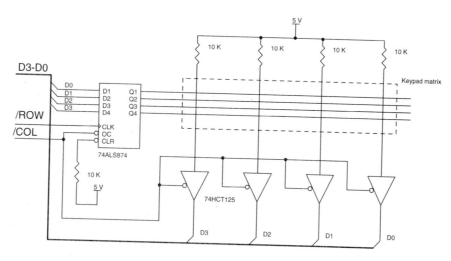

Figure 15.3-3   Hardware for software scan of 4 × 4 key matrix.

The keymatrix of Fig. 15.3-3 can be scanned to determine the state of each key by checking the keys on each row in turn. To check the keys on row 0, a bit pattern is output to the port that makes row 0 a 0 and all other rows 1s. The input port is then read. The value read is the state of the keys in row 0. If a bit read is 0, the corresponding key is pressed. If a bit read is 1, the corresponding key is released.

This process is repeated for each row in turn. In other words, the 0 is walked down the rows and the columns are read each time a row is made 0.

Half of a **74ALS874 Dual 4-Bit D-type Edge-Triggered Flip-Flop** is used as an output port in Fig. 15.3-3. The 74ALS874 has three-state outputs. Instead of being hardwired to ground, the 74ALS874's output enable input is connected to the output enable inputs of the 74LS125 three-state buffers. As a result, the output port only drives the rows of the matrix while the input port is being read. This approach is used to minimize the amount of time that a row output that is 1 can be connected to the row output that is 0, a situation that occurs when two keys in the same column are pressed simultaneously. This approach limits the amount of time these outputs can be subjected to a high current.

The state machine method of debouncing a switch is easily extended to handle the keypad of Fig. 15.3-3. Instead of having a single FSM, sixteen FSMs are used, one for each key. The expansion is fairly simple. Instead of using a single variable pstate, a 16 word pstate array is allocated to hold the present state of each of the 16 FSMs. Although there are 16 FSMs, only one copy of the procedure dbnc_sw is needed. This one copy is called 16 times for each Timer 2 interrupt.

The Timer 2 ISR, kpadisr, is given in Fig. 15.3-4. kpadisr first scans the keypad. The value read for each of the switches is placed in BX. The scan is from top row to bottom row. The key values are right shifted into BX. As a result, bit 0 of BX is the value of key 0, the rightmost key in the top row. Bit 1 of BX is the value of key 1, the key to the immediate left of key 0, and so on.

A loop is then executed 16 times. In each loop iteration, the least significant bit of BX is used as the input for the FSM dbnc_sw. When dbnc_sw is called, it determines the next state and the task to be executed. If TASK1 is executed, the loop index is used to form the keycode, and the keycode is output to the display. When dbnc_sw is returned from, BX is right-shifted in preparation for the next iteration.

When this program is run, pressing a key causes the key's code to be displayed.

Problems arise when two or more keys are pressed almost simultaneously. This situation is called **rollover**. In the previous case, if rollover occurs, the key code returned depends on the order of detection by the scan procedure, and not on the order in which the keys were actually pressed.

Either of two techniques is commonly used to handle rollover. Two-key and N-key rollover refer to the manner in which a keyboard is scanned and key closures are accepted. Two-key rollover successfully handles cases where no more that two keys are pressed simultaneously. With **two-key rollover,** a key closure is accepted, provided all other keys are released. When a key is pressed, that closure is processed, and the keyboard is ignored until the key is released. If a second key is pressed before the first is released, the second key will be recognized only after the first key is released.

N-key rollover processes each key closure in the order in which it is detected during the scan, regardless of the status of all other keys. This mode of operation is used when data entry is rapid, for example, when the operator may press a second and possibly a third key before releasing the first.

Implementation of N-key rollover requires additional considerations. As shown in Fig. 15.3-2(a), each row–column intersection in the matrix simply contains a switch, which connects the two when closed. Consider the situation in Fig. 15.3-2(b), where row 1 has been selected in the scan, and switches 2, 3, and 4 are pressed. There is an electrical path, called a **sneak path,** through switches 2–4–3 that makes column 1's output 0. Since row 1 is selected and column 1 is 0, it appears that switch 1 has been pressed when, in reality, it has not. The key that appears to be pressed is called a **phantom key**. A diode connected in series with each switch (Fig. 15.3-2(c)) prevents sneak paths in a matrix.

15.3.2   Hardware Keymatrix Scanning—Encoder ICs

For hardware key matrix scanning, **keyboard encoder** ICs are available that scan small and large keyswitch arrays and produce an encoded output corresponding to the key pressed. The **MM74C923 20-Key Encoder** IC can handle 20 keys (Fig. 15.3-5).

Examination of the MM74C923's logic diagram reveals that it implements, in hardware, an algorithm similar to the software scan algorithm previously described. A 2-bit

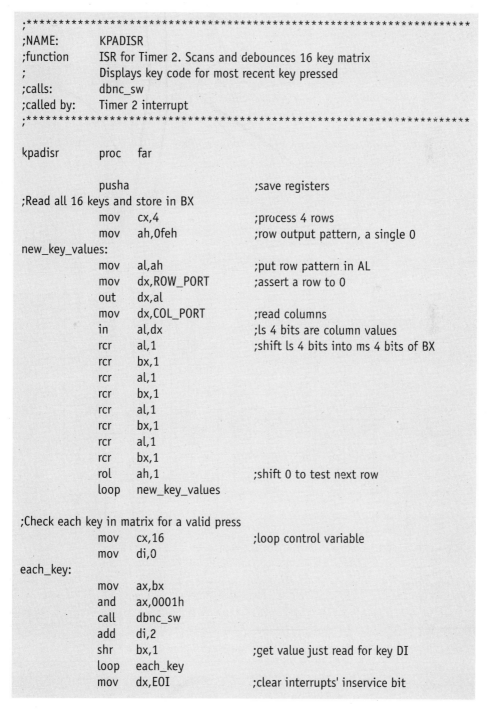

```
;****************************************************************
;
;NAME:        KPADISR
;function     ISR for Timer 2. Scans and debounces 16 key matrix
;             Displays key code for most recent key pressed
;calls:       dbnc_sw
;called by:   Timer 2 interrupt
;****************************************************************
;

kpadisr       proc    far

              pusha                        ;save registers
;Read all 16 keys and store in BX
              mov     cx,4                 ;process 4 rows
              mov     ah,0feh              ;row output pattern, a single 0
new_key_values:
              mov     al,ah                ;put row pattern in AL
              mov     dx,ROW_PORT          ;assert a row to 0
              out     dx,al
              mov     dx,COL_PORT          ;read columns
              in      al,dx                ;ls 4 bits are column values
              rcr     al,1                 ;shift ls 4 bits into ms 4 bits of BX
              rcr     bx,1
              rcr     al,1
              rcr     bx,1
              rcr     al,1
              rcr     bx,1
              rcr     al,1
              rcr     bx,1
              rol     ah,1                 ;shift 0 to test next row
              loop    new_key_values

;Check each key in matrix for a valid press
              mov     cx,16                ;loop control variable
              mov     di,0
each_key:
              mov     ax,bx
              and     ax,0001h
              call    dbnc_sw
              add     di,2
              shr     bx,1                 ;get value just read for key DI
              loop    each_key
              mov     dx,EOI               ;clear interrupts' inservice bit
```

Figure 15.3-4   ISR to scan and debounce a 16 key matrix.

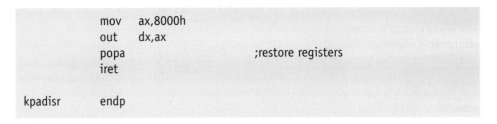

```
            mov     ax,8000h
            out     dx,ax
            popa                            ;restore registers
            iret

kpadisr     endp
```

Figure 15.3-4   ISR to scan and debounce a 16 key matrix. (Continued.)

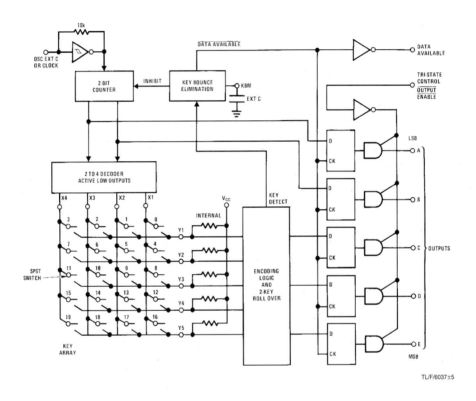

TL/F/6037±5

Switch Position	0	1	2	3	4	5	6	7	8	9	10	11	12	13	14	15	16	17	18	19
	Y1,X1	Y1,X2	Y1,X3	Y1,X4	Y2,X1	Y2,X2	Y2,X3	Y2,X4	Y3,X1	Y3,X2	Y3,X3	Y3,X4	Y4,X1	Y4,X2	Y4,X3	Y4,X4	Y5*,X1	Y5*,X2	Y5*,X3	Y5*,X4
A	0	1	0	1	0	1	0	1	0	1	0	1	0	1	0	1	0	1	0	1
B	0	0	1	1	0	0	1	1	0	0	1	1	0	0	1	1	0	0	1	1
C	0	0	0	0	1	1	1	1	0	0	0	0	1	1	1	1	0	0	0	0
D	0	0	0	0	0	0	0	0	1	1	1	1	1	1	1	1	0	0	0	0
E*	0	0	0	0	0	0	0	0	0	0	0	0	0	0	0	0	1	1	1	1

(Row label at left: DATA OUTPUT)

*Omit for MM54C922/MM74C922

Figure 15.3-5   74C923 20-Key encoder IC block diagram and truth table. (Courtesy of
National Semiconductor Corporation.)

counter and a two-to-four (1-out-of-4) decoder scan the columns of the switch matrix. Scan frequency is set by an external oscillator, or by a capacitor when using the MM74C923's internal oscillator. Encoding logic senses the rows and detects a key closure. Additional circuitry provides contact bounce elimination and two-key rollover. The debounce period can be set by an external capacitor.

When a key closure is accepted, three bits from the encoding logic and two bits from the counter are latched into a 5-bit register by the /DATA_AVAILABLE signal. This signal is asserted as long as the accepted key remains pressed. When this key is released, /DATA_AVAILABLE is unasserted, even if another key is pressed. If a second key is pressed before the first key is released, /DATA_AVAILABLE is automatically asserted again, after the debounce period elapses. Thus, /DATA_AVAILABLE, indicates the availability of new data corresponding to the second key pressed.

Use of a MM74C923 removes from the software the burden of frequently scanning a keypad. The DATA_AVAILABLE output signal can be used to interrupt the 80C188EB, allowing keyboard scanning to take place concurrently with other 80C188EB operations.

There are a variety of keyboard encoders that handle 88 or more keys. However, most of these provide a serial output compatible with the keyboard interface for IBM PC or PS/2 computers. Keyboard encoders with parallel outputs aren't as common, but are usually preferable for embedded systems.

USAR System's **P25C8 Keyboard Encoder** provides a parallel output and can scan and debounce an 8×11 switch matrix (Fig. 15.3-6). The debounce period is fixed at 20 ms and the scan algorithm provides 2-key rollover. The P25C8 provides an ASCII output at pins B8-B1 and a parity bit at its PARITY pin. Parity can be configured as even or odd by hardwiring the COL9/PRINV pin to either V_{CC} or ground through a 100K ohm resistor. The COL9/PRINV pin has a dual function: it serves as a column select output during normal operation and is read at power on to determine whether parity should be odd or even.

The STROBE signal is asserted after a key press has been debounced and is unasserted when the key is released. The output data and parity are valid 200 µs before STROBE is asserted. The output data bits and STROBE can be configured to be asserted low or high by wiring the COL10/INV to V_{CC} (asserted low) or ground (asserted high) through a 100K ohm resistor. This pin is checked by the P25C8 at power on to determine whether the output and STROBE should be inverted. Thereafter, this pin serves as a column select output. USAR also provides one-time programmable (OTP) as well as masked ROM versions of the P25C8 that allow you to specify the keycode assignments.

A single-chip microcomputer can be programmed to function as a dedicated keyboard scanner. Single-chip microcomputers, such as the 8048 and its derivatives, are often used in keyboards for personal computers and for monitors. In such situations, the row and columns of the key matrix are driven and sensed through the single-chip microcomputer's on-chip I/O ports. The microcomputer scans the key matrix and detects and debounces key closures and releases. The scan algorithm is written to detect and reject phantom key closures. A unique 8-bit scan code is generated for a key's closure and another unique scan code for the key's release.

The single-chip microcomputer places the scan codes in a FIFO buffer implemented in software in its RAM. Each scan code is in turn taken from the FIFO, converted from parallel to serial, and transmitted to the system to which the keyboard is connected. When a key is pressed and held longer than a given time (e.g., 0.5 seconds) the microcomputer can

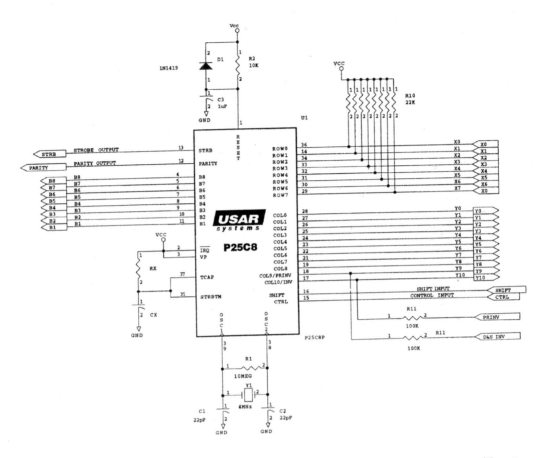

Figure 15.3-6   Pinouts of P25C8 88 key encoder with parallel outputs. (Courtesy USAR0)

implement a **typematic** or automatic repeat function by repeatedly sending the key's scan code (at for example, ten characters per second) until the key is released. The microcomputer handles the formatting of the serial data, adding the start-bit, stop-bit, and parity-bit before transmission. The single-chip microcomputer also handles commands sent to the keyboard from the system and the protocol to allow bidirectional serial communication between the system and keyboard over a single serial line.

15.4   Optical Shaft Encoders

An **optical shaft encoder,** or simply **optical encoder,** can be used where a rotary input device is desired. Such a need often arises on instrument front panels to allow a user to enter or adjust settings. An optical encoder designed for panel mounting is often called a **digital potentiometer** (Fig. 15.4-1). However, this term is also used to describe a completely different device, a digitally controlled resistor, as discussed in Section 17.5. Optical encoders are used in many other user and machine input devices. For example, a track ball can use two optical encoders to provide X and Y position information. Optical encoders are also used in a variety of mechanical motion and position sensing devices.

Figure 15.4-1   Panel mounted optical shaft encoder, digital potentiometer. (Courtesy of Hewlett-Pcakard Co.)

An optical encoder translates the rotation of a shaft into interruptions of a light beam that are then converted to electrical pulses. In effect, an optical shaft encoder converts rotary mechanical motion into a serial digital output. An optical encoder with quadrature outputs produces two digital output waveforms, designated channel A and channel B. These waveforms are in quadrature (have a phase difference of 90 degrees). For clockwise (CW) shaft rotation, B leads A. This means that the rising edge of B occurs before the rising edge of A (Fig. 15.4-2). For counterclockwise (CCW) rotation, A leads B. Optical encoders that provide from 16 to 512 pulses per revolution are common.

When used with appropriate software, a panel mounted optical encoder allows a user to increment or decrement a displayed parameter. For example, CW rotation of the shaft might cause the parameter to be incremented and CCW rotation cause the parameter to be decremented.

Each channel of an optical encoder has a light emitting diode (LED) and two phototransistors or two photodiodes, Fig. 15.4-2. LEDs are discussed further in Section 15.6. When light from an LED strikes a phototransistor it conducts, i.e. is turned ON. When light is blocked from the phototransistor it turns OFF. The phototransistors are separated from the LEDs by a code wheel that is connected to the shaft of the optical encoder. The **code wheel** is a disk with N equally spaced apertures around its circumference.

The physical positioning of each LED and phototransistor pair is such that as the disk is rotated, one transistor in the pair and then the other is exposed to light from an LED. When one transistor is fully exposed, the other is fully blocked. An analog comparator compares the output from a phototransistor pair with a reference voltage level. The comparator's output is a digital signal. Each LED and phototransistor pair creates a square

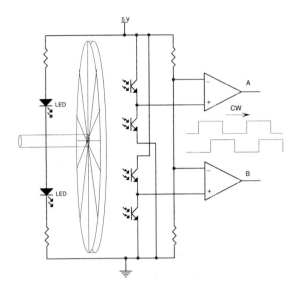

Figure 15.4-2   Optical shaft encoder with quadrature outputs.

wave as the shaft is rotated. The relative positioning of the two transistor pairs provides the phase shift required to place the two signals in quadrature.

An interface of an optical encoder to a system bus, designed for polled operation, is shown in Fig. 15.4-3. If the optical encoder's output is TTL compatible, but not CMOS compatible, HCT (or ACT) three-state buffers are used. The 80C188EB must continually poll the port DPOT and test A and B to detect a change in the shaft's position. Once a change is detected, a determination is made as to whether it was caused by CW or CCW rotation. Comparing the new values of B and A with the old values indicates the direction of rotation as shown in Table 15.4-1.

Table 15.4-1   Determinations of rotation direction
from new and old values of B and A.

New BA	Old BA	Composite	Rotation
10	00	08H	CW
11	10	0EH	CW
01	11	07H	CW
00	01	01H	CW
01	00	04H	CCW
11	01	0DH	CCW
10	11	08H	CCW
00	10	02H	CCW

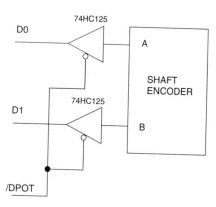

Figure 15.4-3   Determination of rotation direction from new and old values of B and A from shaft encoder.

The procedure digpot in Fig. 15.4-4 polls the optical encoder. Before this procedure is called, the main program must initialize memory location oldba with the initial values of B and A obtained from the optical encoder at power on. Procedure digpot inputs the current values of B and A and compares them with the previous values. If they are the same, the shaft has not been rotated and the procedure is exited.

If the new values of B and A differ from the previous values, then it must be determined whether the shaft rotation was CW or CCW. This is done by creating a composite positional status byte with the new values of B and A as bits 3 and 2, and the previous values of B and A as bits 1 and 0 (Table 15.4-1). This composite value is compared with the four composite codes that correspond to CW rotation. If the composite positional status corresponds to one of these codes, memory location param is incremented. If not, param is decremented.

In the procedure digpot, param is incremented by a constant value in response to each pulse from A. For fine tuning a parameter, this is very efficient. However, when a parameter must be changed by a large value, many turns of the shaft are required. An alternate approach is to make the amount that the parameter is incremented in response to each A pulse a function of the angular velocity of the shaft. Angular velocity is determined by measuring the time between successive A pulses. When the time between the A pulses is short, the angular velocity is high, and the parameter is changed by a large value. If the time between pulses is long, the angular velocity is low, and the parameter is changed by a small value. The time between pulses can be measured using one of the 80C188EB's Counter/Timers.

An interrupt driven interface of the optical encoder to a system bus is shown in Fig. 15.4-5. The rising edge of A sets the interrupt request flip-flop. In addition, this edge is used to clock a second flip-flop that stores the value of B. The ISR, dpotisr (Fig. 15.4-6) simply reads the direction flip-flop, bit 7 of port DIR, to determine whether the shaft was rotated CW or CCW. If the shaft was rotated clockwise, B (the contents of the DIR flip-flop) is 1. Reading port DIR clears the service request flip-flop as a side effect. This obviates the need to use an output instruction in the ISR specifically for this purpose.

```
name    digpot

;equates
DPOT    equ 8000h;input port for digital pot

data    segment 'RAM'
        oldba  db ?              ;old values of B and A
        param  db ?              ;parameter to be incremented or decremented
data    ends

stack   segment 'STKRAM'
        dw 14 dup(?)
tos     label word
stack   ends

assume          cs:code, ds:data, ss:stack

code            segment 'ROM'

;****************************************************************
;
;
;NAME: digpot
;
;FUNCTION: detects rotation of digital potentiometer
;
;ASSUMES: oldba initialized
;RETURNS: new value for oldba, param
;MODIFIES: oldba, param
;
;DESCRIPTION: reads the output of the digital potentiometer and
;determines if the pot has been rotated since the procedure was last
;called. The value of param is incremented if rotation is CW and
;decremented if the rotation is CCW. Digpot must be called often
;enough so that the pot has not been rotated more than
;360 degrees/(16 * 2) = 11.25 degrees
;****************************************************************
;

digpot          proc
                mov    dx,DPOT      ;get digital pot output
                in     al,dx
                and    al,03h       ;mask all bits except 1(B),0(A)
```

Figure 15.4-4   Program to increment and decrement a parameter using a digital
               potentiometer.

```
                cmp     al,oldba        ;compare with old B,A
                jz      done            ;if equal, no rotation occurred
                mov     ah,al           ;save new B,A
                mov     al,oldba        ;get old B,A
                mov     oldba,ah        ;replace old with new
                shl     ah,1            ;create composite position byte
                shl     ah,1            ;new B,A bits 3 and 2
                or      al,ah           ;old B,A bits 1 and 0
                cmp     al,08h          ;compare composite with the four
                jz      cw              ;codes corresponding to CW rotation
                cmp     al,0eh
                jz      cw
                cmp     al,07h
                jz      cw
                cmp     al,01h
                jz      cw
                dec     param           ;rotation was not CW
                ret
cw:             inc     param           ;rotation was CW
done:           ret
digpot          endp

;initialize segment registers and stack pointer
start:          mov     ax,data
                mov     ds,ax
                mov     ax,stack
                mov     ss,ax
                mov     sp,offset tos

;execute program
                mov     dx,DPOT         ;initialize B and A
                in      al,dx
                and     al,03h
                mov     oldba,al
                mov     param,0         ;initialize PARAM
again:          call    digpot
                jmp     again
code            ends
                end     start
```

Figure 15.4-4   Program to increment and decrement a parameter using a digital potentiometer. (Continued.)

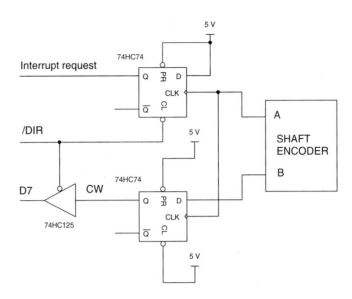

Figure 15.4-5   Interrupt interface of shaft encoder to microprocessor.

The previous two interfacing approaches require little hardware or software. However, both approaches involve significant software overhead.

For the polled interface, the polling procedure must be called often enough to prevent missing a pulse from the optical encoder. If a spinner knob is used, it is possible for the optical encoder's shaft to be rotated at a relatively high angular velocity. In this case, the software's architecture must be designed to call the polling procedure over and over. During the system's operation, the vast majority of times the polling procedure is called, the optical encoder's position will not have changed.

The interrupt approach eliminates the need for polling, reducing the software overhead. However, an interrupt occurs for each pulse from the shaft encoder. So, when the shaft is rotated at a high angular velocity, the interrupt service routine is continuously called, resulting in significant overhead.

A hardware approach to interfacing an optical encoder uses an IC specifically designed for this purpose. Hewlett Packard makes three quadrature decoder/counter interface ICs, the **HCTL-2000, HCTL-2016,** and **HCTL-2020.** Each of these ICs performs quadrature decoding and counting, and provides an 8-bit bus interface. The HCTL-2000 has a 12-bit counter. The HCTL-2016 and HCTL-2020 have 16-bit counters. The HCTL-2000 and HCTL-2016 are available in 16-pin DIP packages. The HCTL-2020 is available in a 20-pin DIP.

These ICs have inputs for the quadrature signals A and B (Fig. 15.4-7). The quadrature input signals are digitally filtered. The filter output waveforms can change only after an input level has the same value for three consecutive rising edges at the CLK input. The maximum clock frequency is 14 MHz. The filtered waveforms are decoded to increment or decrement the binary up/down counter. The HCTL-2020 has outputs that indicate when the inputs have changed state, CNTD_{CDR}, the direction of rotation, $U/\overline{D}$, and counter over-

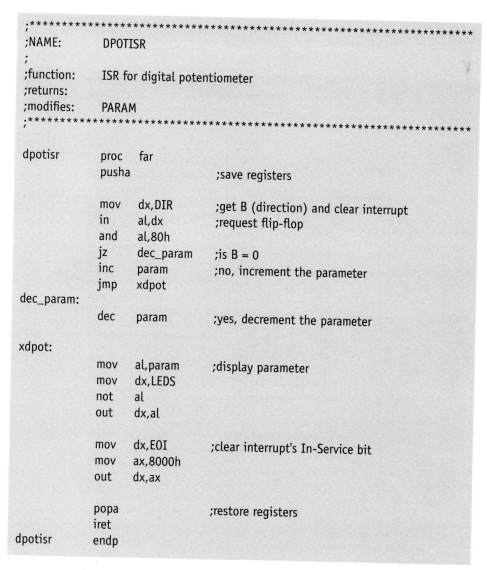

```
;*******************************************************************
;NAME:        DPOTISR
;
;function:    ISR for digital potentiometer
;returns:
;modifies:    PARAM
;*******************************************************************

dpotisr        proc   far
               pusha                  ;save registers

               mov    dx,DIR          ;get B (direction) and clear interrupt
               in     al,dx           ;request flip-flop
               and    al,80h
               jz     dec_param       ;is B = 0
               inc    param           ;no, increment the parameter
               jmp    xdpot
dec_param:
               dec    param           ;yes, decrement the parameter

xdpot:
               mov    al,param        ;display parameter
               mov    dx,LEDS
               not    al
               out    dx,al

               mov    dx,EOI          ;clear interrupt's In-Service bit
               mov    ax,8000h
               out    dx,ax

               popa                   ;restore registers
               iret
dpotisr        endp
```

Figure 15.4-6   ISR for digital potentiometer. Increments or decrements PARAM depending on direction of rotation.

flow and underflow, CNT_{CAS}. $U/\overline{D}$ and CNT_{CAS} allow you to cascade an external counter with the HCTL-2020 to extend the maximum count.

An 80C188EB can read the count as two bytes. Logic within the HCTL device prevents the count value being read from changing during the reading. When SEL input is 0 and /OE is asserted, the device provides the high byte. When SEL is 1 and /OE is asserted, the device provides the low byte. A clock input (CLK) accepts the required external clock signal. This input can be driven by CLKOUT from the 80C188EB.

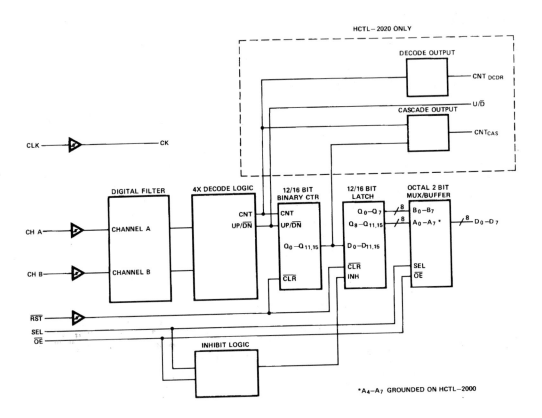

Figure 15.4-7   Block diagram of HCTL-20XX family quadrature decoder/counter interface ICs. (Courtesy of Hewlett-Packard.)

15.5 Displays

Electronic displays range in complexity from simple annunciators (ON-OFF lights) to
graphic displays utilizing cathode ray tubes (CRTs). A wide range of technologies are used
to implement and control display devices. Each technology has advantages and disadvantages with respect to the density of information displayed, power consumption, reliability,
and ease of use.

The visible portion of a display is comprised of an arrangement of light emitting or
light modulating elements. The physical arrangement of display elements is called a display
font. The font determines what characters can be displayed. Some common fonts are
shown in Fig. 15.5-1. Fonts with seven elements are capable of displaying decimal and
hexadecimal numeric characters. Dot matrix fonts, such as a 5×7 matrix, can display
numeric, alphabetic, and some symbolic information. Graphic displays have a large number of elements (called picture elements or **pixels**) and can display pictorial information
with high resolution. They can be thought of as very large dot matrix displays.

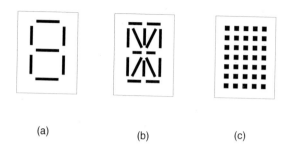

(a)   (b)   (c)

Figure 15.5-1   Display fonts: (a) 8 segment; (b) 16 segment; (c) 5 × 7 dot matrix.

As the number of elements in a display increases, so does the complexity of the electronics necessary to control the display. Three popular low density displays are: LED displays; Liquid Crystal Displays (LCDs); and Vacuum Fluorescent Displays (VFDs). These types of displays are considered in the remaining sections of this chapter.

15.6   LED Displays

One of the simplest display technologies is the **light-emitting diode** (LED). LEDs are solid state devices, p-n junctions, that emit light when stimulated by a low voltage direct current. LEDs can be designed to emit light with wavelengths from ultraviolet, through the visible spectrum, to infrared. The most efficient LED is in the visible spectrum and emits red light. While red is the most commonly used color for LED displays, yellow, green, and blue LEDs are also available.

LEDs are popular display devices because they can be operated from low voltages, are compatible with systems that use ICs, are small, lightweight, and mechanically rugged. As solid state devices, they are highly reliable and have a typical operating life of more than 100,000 hours. LEDs are available as single devices or packaged together in various fonts for displaying binary, numeric, and alphanumeric information.

A symbol for an LED is shown in Fig. 15.6-1(a). An LED emits light when forward biased. The intensity of the light is a function of the current through the LED. The voltage drop of a forward biased LED is essentially fixed, typically 1.6 or 2.4 V. When driven as shown in Fig. 15.6-1(b), a resistor limits the LED's current to the desired value. For DC operation, the nominal operating current is typically 20 mA for standard red LEDs and 10 mA for high efficiency red LEDs. Some low current LEDs can operate at a current of 1 mA.

In general, most logic ICs cannot directly drive a high-current LED, because they can't sink 20 mA. For example, standard 74HCxxx series ICs can only sink 4 mA. However, ICs with high-current outputs, like the 74HC534, can sink 6 mA (Fig. 15.6-2). 74ALSxxx series ICs can sink 8 mA and those with high-current outputs, like the 74ALS534, can sink 24 mA.

Logic circuits with open collector outputs can be used to drive LEDs as shown in Fig. 15.6-3. For example, a 74ALS1005 open collector inverter can sink 24 mA.

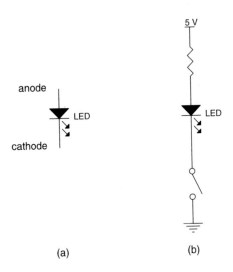

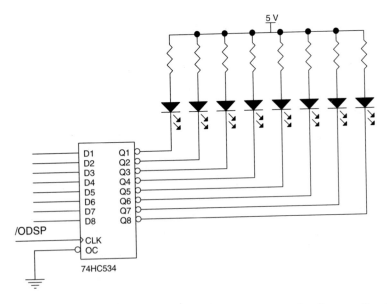

Figure 15.6-1   Light-emitting diode, LED: (a) circuit symbol; (b) circuit using a mechanical switch and current limiting resistor.

Figure 15.6-2   Using a 74HC534 noninverting octal D-type flip-flop to directly drive LEDs.

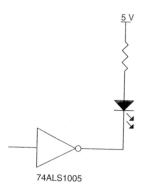

Figure 15.6-3   Driving an LED with an open collector inverter.

15.6.1   Seven Segment Displays

Decimal digits and some letters of the alphabet can be displayed using a seven segment (element) font (Fig. 15.5-1). Seven segment LED displays have an LED (or sometimes two in series) for each segment. There are two variations of seven segment display connections, Fig. 15.6-4. In one, **common anode**, all of the LEDs' anodes are connected in common. In the other, **common cathode**, all of the LEDs' cathodes are connected in common. The common connection is brought out to a package pin. These two variations require differ- ent drive arrangements. Each segment can be driven by 1 bit of an output port (Fig. 15.6-2) or decoder-driver ICs can be used.

BCD-to-seven segment and hex-to-seven segment decoder driver ICs are available for driving seven-segment displays. Figure 15.6-4 shows the connection of a common anode and a common cathode seven-segment display to appropriate BCD-to-seven seg- ment drivers. In one case, the anode is connected to the 5 V supply, and a low decoder- driver output voltage turns a segment ON. In the other, the cathodes are connected to ground. In this case, a high decoder-driver output voltage turns a segment ON.

15.6.2   Multiplexed Displays

To display a small number of digits, each LED segment can be **directly driven** by an output port, or by a decoder driver connected to an output port, as previously discussed. Since each digit requires its own port and/or decoder driver, the number of ports and drivers increases in direct proportion to the number of digits in the display.

Multiplexing techniques allow one set of decoding and driving circuitry to be shared by all the digits in a display. Figure 15.6-5 shows the hardware for an 8-digit software- driven multiplexed LED display. In a multiplexed display, each digit is turned ON and then OFF in sequence. This is done at a rate that makes it appear that all of the digits are con- stantly ON.

To display a digit, the display ISR first writes to the digit select output port, DSEL, a pattern that turns OFF all digits (Fig. 16.5-6). The ISR then writes the segment pattern to be displayed to the segment output port, LED_SEGS. Next a digit pattern is written to DSEL to

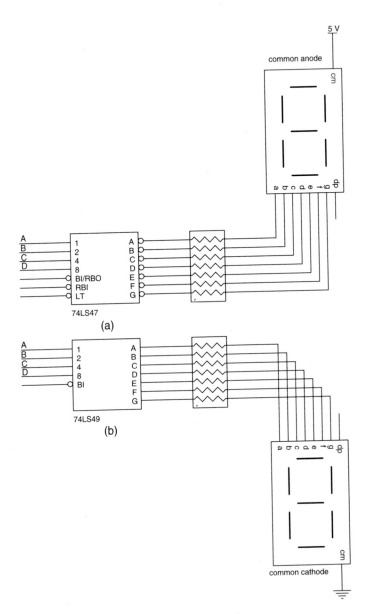

Figure 15.6-4   Driving seven-segment LEDs from BCD inputs using decoder drivers: (a) common anode circuit; (b) common cathode circuit.

turn ON only the digit driver for the selected seven-segment display. Within a specified period, the ISR must be invoked again to repeat this process for the next digit in the sequence. Whenever port DSEL is written, the retriggerable one-shot is triggered. When the one-shot times out, it generates an interrupt request.

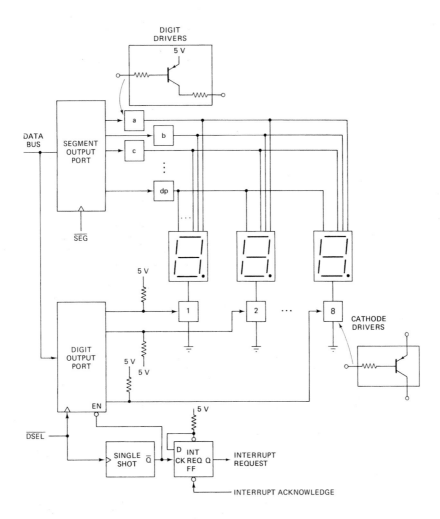

Figure 15.6-5   Eight-digit multiplexed LED display.

Each digit is turned ON, or **refreshed**, at a frequency called the **refresh rate**. If a digit is refreshed often enough, it appears to the human eye to be constantly ON. The minimum practical refresh rate is usually 100 Hz. Typically, multiplexed displays are refreshed at 1 kHz, or higher. For N digits refreshed at f Hz, the maximum ON time t_p, for each digit is:

$$t_p = \frac{1}{f \times N}$$

The **duty factor** for a single digit is the ratio of the time that the digit is ON to the refresh period, and is $1/N$.

Multiplexing is not only efficient in terms of shared decoding and driving circuitry, it is also the most efficient way of operating an LED. For a given average power dissipation,

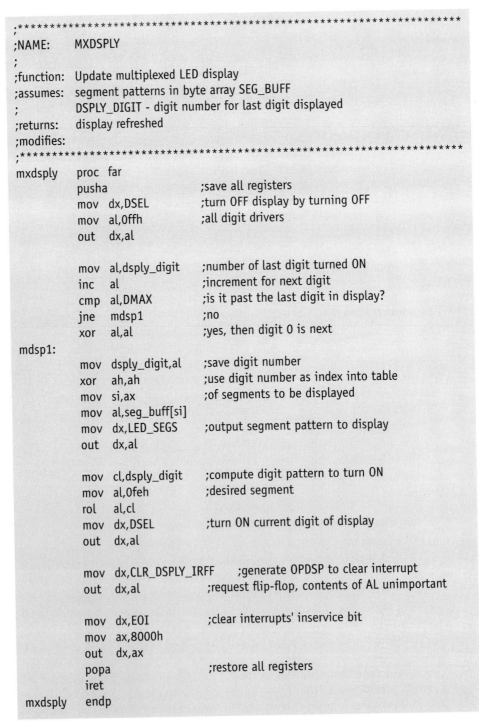

```
;*****************************************************************
;NAME:      MXDSPLY
;
;function:  Update multiplexed LED display
;assumes:   segment patterns in byte array SEG_BUFF
;           DSPLY_DIGIT - digit number for last digit displayed
;returns:   display refreshed
;modifies:
;*****************************************************************
mxdsply    proc far
           pusha                    ;save all registers
           mov   dx,DSEL            ;turn OFF display by turning OFF
           mov   al,0ffh            ;all digit drivers
           out   dx,al

           mov   al,dsply_digit     ;number of last digit turned ON
           inc   al                 ;increment for next digit
           cmp   al,DMAX            ;is it past the last digit in display?
           jne   mdsp1              ;no
           xor   al,al             ;yes, then digit 0 is next
mdsp1:
           mov   dsply_digit,al     ;save digit number
           xor   ah,ah             ;use digit number as index into table
           mov   si,ax             ;of segments to be displayed
           mov   al,seg_buff[si]
           mov   dx,LED_SEGS        ;output segment pattern to display
           out   dx,al

           mov   cl,dsply_digit     ;compute digit pattern to turn ON
           mov   al,0feh            ;desired segment
           rol   al,cl
           mov   dx,DSEL            ;turn ON current digit of display
           out   dx,al

           mov   dx,CLR_DSPLY_IRFF    ;generate OPDSP to clear interrupt
           out   dx,al               ;request flip-flop, contents of AL unimportant

           mov   dx,EOI             ;clear interrupts' inservice bit
           mov   ax,8000h
           out   dx,ax
           popa                    ;restore all registers
           iret
mxdsply    endp
```

Figure 15.6-6   ISR to update 8-digit multiplexed LED display of Fig. 15.6-5.

strobing an LED at a high peak current and low duty factor provides greater light output than does direct drive.

The peak segment currents allowable when a display is multiplexed exceed the allowable average segment currents. Thus, if a digit in a multiplexed display is accidently left ON for an extended period of time, it can be damaged. In Fig. 15.6-5, the one-shot times out the digit ON time. The outputs of port DSEL are enabled only during the one-shot's pulse. This insures that no seven-segment display is left on too long.

15.7   Multiplexed Eight-Digit LED Display Driver

Operation of a multiplexed display is significantly simplified by the use of a display driver IC. The ICM7218 series of CMOS eight-digit display drivers includes devices to handle common anode (A, C, and E versions) and common cathode (B and D versions) seven-segment LEDs. Each device in the series contains the necessary digit drivers, segment drivers, and multiplex scan circuitry. The outputs of an ICM7218 consist of eight segment strobes and eight digit strobes. Each segment strobe is connected to the corresponding segment of all eight seven-segment displays. Each digit strobe is connected to the common segment connection of only one seven-segment display.

The ICM7218 contains an 8×8 SRAM. The 80C188EB simply writes the information to be displayed to the ICM7218's SRAM. Internal scan circuitry in the ICM7218 automatically multiplexes the information from the SRAM to the LED digits. Display data is written to the A and B versions of the ICM7218 in byte serial form. These versions have no address inputs to select specific locations in the 8×8 SRAM. Thus, to change a single displayed digit, you must write all eight digits. The C, D, and E versions have address inputs and are random access. The data displayed by a single digit is changed by simply writing the associated SRAM location.

The ICM7218B and its interface to a system bus are shown in Fig. 15.7-1(a). Inputs ID0–ID7 are driven from the data bus. A control input, MODE, selects either the ICM7218B's control register or the SRAM locations to be written in response to a write pulse at /WRITE. This input is controlled by the output of a flip-flop. To change the data displayed, a 1 is written to the mode flip-flop. Then a control byte is written to the control register. A 0 is then written to the mode flip-flop and then eight data bytes are written to the SRAM, Fig. 15.7-1(b). The first data byte written to the SRAM corresponds to digit 1 of the display and the last corresponds to digit 8.

The control word (a byte) uses bit 7 to indicate that data will be written immediately following the control word (Fig. 15.7-2(a)). Bits 6 and 5 specify how the ICM7218B is to use the data in the SRAM to control the segments in each digit. There are two decode formats, Hexa Code and Code B, and a no decode format available. The decode formats use the least significant 4 bits of each data byte to encode the information to be displayed. Hexa Code is the common hexadecimal code. Code B encodes the ten decimal digits plus six special characters. If bit 5 is 0, the decode format is selected by bit 6. If bit 5 is 1, no decode is selected.

With no decode, each bit in a byte directly controls a segment of a seven segment display. The association of bits with segments in the display is also shown in Fig. 15.7-2(b). Note that the decimal point is turned ON by a 0, while all other segments are turned ON

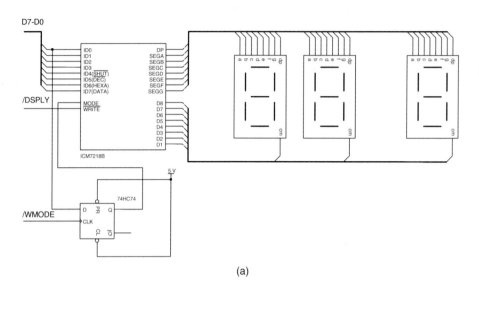

Figure 15.7-1   IMC7218B 8-digit display driver: (a) interface to system bus; (b) control
                  and data byte sequencing.

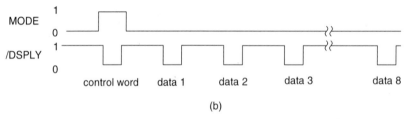

Figure 15.7-2   IMC7218B bit assignments: (a) control word; (b) no decode data byte.

by 1s. Since the no decode option allows segments to be directly controlled, it is possible for the display driver to control a mix of seven-segment displays and annunciators. The annunciators are simply assigned as segments of a digit and controlled independently. When bit 4 is 0, the display is shut down to save power. However, even when shut down, the data in the ICM7218's SRAM is maintained.

One approach to software control of the display is to maintain an eight-byte display image buffer in the system's RAM. For the no decode format, each bit that is a 1 in the buffer should cause its associated segment to be turned ON. With the exception of the DP segment, this is the same convention for a no decode data pattern written to the ICM 7218B. Thus, the DP bit in the buffer must be complemented before being written to the ICM7218B. The contents of the image buffer are manipulated by your program to create the bit patterns desired for the ICM7218B's SRAM. After the contents of the display image buffer have been changed, the procedure update, shown in Fig. 15.7-3, is called to update the display.

update sets the mode and then writes the necessary control word to the ICM7218B's control register. update then clears the mode and transfers the eight data bytes from the display image buffer, dsplyi, to the ICM7218B's SRAM. A LABEL directive is used prior to allocating the bytes for the image buffer. This allows the symbol dsplyi to be used as the base address for the array. Each digit in the array is also addressable by name to allow digits in the buffer to be easily manipulated individually.

When digits in a multiplexed display are controlled by hardware, the possibility of ghosting must be considered. **Ghosting** occurs when segments in a digit are dimly lit, when they should be OFF. These segments are those that are to be lit in the next digit to be turned ON in the multiplexing sequence. This problem is the result of the digit driver transistor of one digit being turned OFF while the digit driver transistor of the next digit is simultaneously being turned ON. Since transistors are able to turn ON faster than they can turn OFF, the digit turning OFF momentarily displays the new segment information of the digit turning ON.

Ghosting is prevented by having the multiplexing hardware provide a short period of time between digits being turned ON where all digits are OFF. This time is called the **interdigit blanking time**, t_b. The ICM7218B provides an interdigit blanking time of 10 μs. The digit on time, t_p, is 500 μs. Thus, the refresh period is 8×510 μs = 4.08 ms, and the refresh frequency is 245 Hz.

15.8   Liquid Crystal Display (LCD) Modules

Liquid Crystal Displays (LCDs) use the ability of a liquid crystal material to rotate the polarization of light passing through the material, or when an electric field is applied, to not rotate the light's polarization. Using this characteristic, a display can be constructed where each display element causes light to either be absorbed or reflected, depending on the element's state. When an element absorbs light, the area it encompasses on the surface of the liquid crystal display appears black. Since an LCD does not produce light, it is a **passive display** and cannot be seen in the dark.

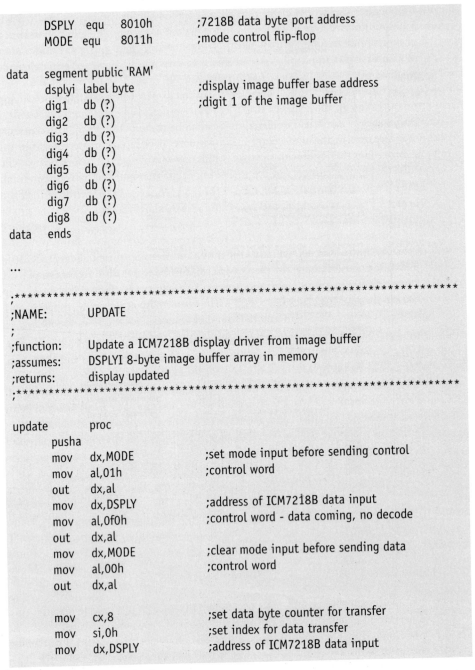

```
        DSPLY  equ    8010h        ;7218B data byte port address
        MODE   equ    8011h        ;mode control flip-flop

data    segment public 'RAM'
        dsplyi label byte          ;display image buffer base address
        dig1   db  (?)             ;digit 1 of the image buffer
        dig2   db  (?)
        dig3   db  (?)
        dig4   db  (?)
        dig5   db  (?)
        dig6   db  (?)
        dig7   db  (?)
        dig8   db  (?)
data    ends

...

;***************************************************************
;
;NAME:       UPDATE
;
;function:   Update a ICM7218B display driver from image buffer
;assumes:    DSPLYI 8-byte image buffer array in memory
;returns:    display updated
;***************************************************************
;

update         proc
        pusha
        mov    dx,MODE             ;set mode input before sending control
        mov    al,01h              ;control word
        out    dx,al
        mov    dx,DSPLY            ;address of ICM7218B data input
        mov    al,0f0h             ;control word - data coming, no decode
        out    dx,al
        mov    dx,MODE             ;clear mode input before sending data
        mov    al,00h              ;control word
        out    dx,al

        mov    cx,8                ;set data byte counter for transfer
        mov    si,0h               ;set index for data transfer
        mov    dx,DSPLY            ;address of ICM7218B data input
```

Figure 15.7-3   Allocation of memory for image buffer and procedure to update ICM7218B display from image buffer.

```
xfer:   mov     al,dsplyi[si]        ;get byte from image buffer
        xor     al,80h               ;complement DP bit
        out     dx,al                ;output to display driver
        inc     si                   ;increment index to next digit
        loop    xfer                 ;loop until done
        popa
        ret
update endp
```

Figure 15.7-3   Allocation of memory for image buffer and procedure to update ICM7218B display from image buffer. (Continued.)

LCDs have the advantage of very low power consumption. In addition, their elements can be arranged to create numerous font styles including: seven-segment, sixteen-segment, and dot matrix fonts.

LCDs are multiplexed. The specific multiplexing techniques used are considerably more complex than those for LEDs. Because of this complexity, LCDs are often provided as modules that have the LCD display mounted on one side of a printed circuit board and one or two ICs that implement the multiplexing, driving, control, and microprocessor interface mounted on the back.

15.8.1   LCD Character Module

LCD dot matrix character displays consisting of from 1 to 4 rows with 16 or 20 characters per row are common. For example, a widely used LCD dot matrix character display module has two 16-character rows. Versions of such a module are available from several manufacturers including: AND, EPSON, Hantronix, IEE, Rohm, and Shelly Associates. The LCD panel and its driver and controller IC are mounted on a single printed circuit board (Fig. 15.8-1). The only power required is +5 V. Each character is formed as a 5×7 dot matrix.

Figure 15.8-1   A 1×16 and a 2×16 Liquid crystal display (LCD) module. (Courtesy of Industrial Electronic Engineers (IEE), Inc.)

The controller IC includes a character generator ROM that allows the display of any of 160 different alphanumeric characters, symbols, and other signs. Each character is specified by an 8-bit character code. Characters in the ASCII character set are represented by their ASCII codes (Table 15.8-1). In addition to the character generator ROM, a character generator RAM allows you to create eight of your own programmed 5×7 dot matrix patterns.

Table 15.8-1   Character patterns for LCD module input codes.

The controller's functional block diagram is shown in Fig. 15.8-2. Two 8-bit registers, an Instruction Register (IR) and a Data Register (DR) are written to control the module's operation. IR receives the instruction codes (Table 15.8-2) that control the display's operation.

Table 15.8-2   Table of instructions for LCD module.

			Instruction Code[a]							
RS	R/W	Instruction	D7	D6	D5	D4	D3	D2	D1	D0
0	0	Display Clear	0	0	0	0	0	0	0	1
0	0	Cursor Home	0	0	0	0	0	0	1	X
0	0	Entry Mode Set	0	0	0	0	0	1	I/D	S
0	0	Display ON/OFF Control	0	0	0	0	1	D	C	B
0	0	Cursor Display Shift	0	0	0	1	S/C	R/L	X	X
0	0	Function Set	0	0	1	DL	1	0	X	X
0	0	CG RAM Address Set	0	1	Address for CG RAM					
0	0	DD RAM Address Set	1	Address for DD RAM						
0	1	Busy Flag/Address **Read**	BF	Address in AC register						
1	0	Write Data	Data for CG or DD RAM							
1	1	Read Data	Data from CG or DD RAM							

a.   I/D = 1: increment   I/D = 0: decrement
S = 1: shift display   S = 0: freeze display
D = 1: display ON   D = 0: display OFF
B = 1: blink character at cursor B = 0: do not blink
S/C = 1: display shift   S/C = 0: cursor shift
R/L = 1: right shift   R/L = 0: left shift
DL = 1: eight bit interface   DL = 0: four bit interface
BF = 1: doing internal operation BF = 0: internal operation complete

To display a character, the 80C188EB must first write a *DD RAM Address Set* instruction byte to IR. This instruction specifies the position at which the character is to be displayed. The display address, A_{DD}, contained in this instruction byte is then automatically transferred to the Address Counter (AC) to address the Display Data RAM (DD RAM). Next, the 80C188EB writes the character's code to the Data Register (DR). Data written to DR is automatically transferred into the DD RAM location whose address is in the AC.

The same controller IC used in this 2-row × 16 characters/row LCD module can be used with LCDs having several different row and character per row organizations. The 80-byte DD RAM can hold 80 characters. For this LCD module, only 32 of those characters can be displayed. Unused DD RAM locations can be used as general purpose RAM. The leftmost character position on the top display line has DD RAM address 00H. The rightmost position on the top line is at address 0FH. On the bottom line, the leftmost position has address 40H, and the rightmost has address 4FH.

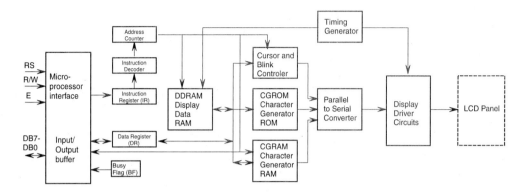

Figure 15.8-2   Dot matrix liquid crystal display controller/driver block diagram.

The LCD module's circuitry transforms each character code into that character's 5×7 dot-matrix pattern and displays this character pattern at the appropriate position on the LCD screen.

The Address Counter is either incremented or decremented automatically after each character entry. Thus, successive character codes can be entered after specifying only the position of the initial character.

Other LCD module instructions turn the display ON and OFF, clear the display, blink the cursor and/or a character, and shift displayed data. The LCD module's busy flag must be tested before instructions or data are written.

15.8.2   LCD Module/80C188EB Interface

The signals used to control transfers to and from the LCD module are shown at the bottom of Fig. 15.8-2. The timing relationships for these signals are shown in Fig. 15.8-3. The LCD module has two control inputs, R/W and E, instead of the more familiar /RD and /WR control inputs. Control signals /RD and /WR each provide both direction and timing information. In contrast, with R/W and E, direction is established by one signal and timing by the other. The direction of a transfer is controlled by R/W, which is 1 for a read and 0 for a write. Timing is controlled by the enable signal E. Read and write operations occur on the falling (trailing) edge of E.

The signals R/W and E are referred to as "**Motorola-style control signals**," since they are representative of the signals typically generated by Motorola family microprocessors to control bus transfers. In contrast, /RD and /WR are referred to as "**Intel-style control signals**."

LCD module input RS is an address input. RS = 0 selects register IR, and RS = 1 selects register DR. One method of interfacing the LCD module to an 80C188EB system bus is to connect A0 to RS. The LCD module's R/W input must be stable at the beginning of the bus cycle. Therefore, either the complement of DT/R, S0, or an address bit can be connected to R/W.

Use of an address bit is appropriate if the other signals are not available in a particular application. For example, assume that A1 is connected to R/W. E is then driven by an

INTERFACE TIMING CHARACTERISTICS

WRITE OPERATION

ITEM	SYMBOL	MIN	MAX	UNIT
Enable Cycle Time	t_{cycle}	1000	—	ns
Enable Pulse Width—"High Level"	PW_{EH}	450	—	ns
Enable Rise/Fall Time	t_{Er}, t_{Ef}	—	25	ns
Address Set-up Time—RS, R/W	t_{AS}	140	—	ns
Address Hold Time	t_{AH}	10	—	ns
Data Set-up Time	t_{DSW}	195	—	ns
Data Hold Time	t_H	10	—	ns

READ OPERATION

ITEM	SYMBOL	MIN	MAX	UNIT
Enable Cycle Time	t_{cycle}	1000	—	ns
Enable Pulse Width—"High Level"	PW_{EH}	450	—	ns
Enable Rise/Fall Time	t_{Er}, t_{Ef}	—	25	ns
Address Set-up Time—RS, R/W	t_{AS}	140	—	ns
Address Hold Time	t_{AH}	10	—	ns
Data Delay Time	t_{DDR}	—	320	ns
Data Hold Time	t_{DHR}	20	—	ns

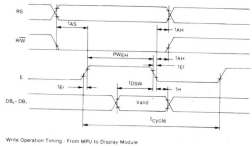

Write Operation Timing - From MPU to Display Module

Read Operation Timing - From Display Module to MPU

Figure 15.8-3   Write timing diagram for LCD module.

address decoder output that is asserted whenever address bits A15–A2 are the LCD module's address and either /RD or /WR is asserted. With this assignment of signals, a write to IR requires A1,A0 = 00B. A read with A1,A0 = 10B returns the busy flag and the contents of the Address Counter. DR is written with A1,A0 = 01B and read with A1,A0 = 11B.

Since the minimum pulse width for E is 450 ns, the LCD module requires WAIT states in most applications. Also, a minimum of 1000 ns is required between successive assertions of E. This requirement can be met by placing other instructions between successive reads or writes to the LCD module.

The LCD module has an internal reset circuit for implementing an automatic reset at power on. However, this reset circuit will operate properly only if V_{CC} to the module has a rise time to 4.5 V of between 0.1 and 10 ms. If these conditions are not met, the module must be initialized by the microprocessor. The initialization sequence required for most displays of this type is shown in Fig. 15.8-4. The LCD module is assumed to be assigned to the isolated I/O space and interfaced as described in the previous paragraph. A procedure to accomplish this initialization is given in Fig. 15.8-5.

A procedure to write an ASCII message to the display is given in Fig. 15.8-6. This procedure updates both lines of the display from two 16-byte buffers, in the data segment. Line 1 of the display is filled with the contents of dsp_buff_1 and line 2 is filled with the contents of dsp_buff_2. In this approach the characters to be displayed are manipulated in the display buffers and then all characters on the display are updated at once. Alternatively, the characters on the display can be manipulated directly in the DD RAM using the LCD module's instructions.

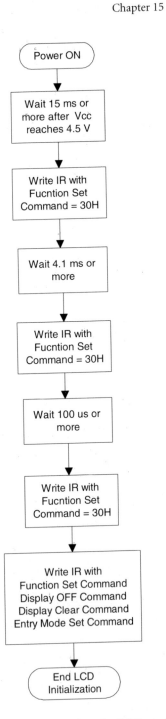

Figure 15.8-4   Software initialization procedure for LCD module.

```
;*******************************************************************
;NAME: INIT_DSP

;FUNCTION: Initializes a 16 character x 2 line LCD display module.
;MODIFIES:   no registers are altered.
;CALLS:    delay
;
;DESCRIPTION:  This procedure performs a complete reset and initialization
;of the display module using instructions.  The display is configured
;with the following settings: no cursor, auto increment (of address
;counter), no shifting (of displayed characters).
;
;DSP_CMD_WR    Address to write IR DSP_CMD_RD    Address to read IR
;DSP_DAT_WR    Address to write DR DSP_DAT_RD    Address to read DR
;
;*******************************************************************

init_dsp       proc    near

start_init:
     pushf                            ;Save registers not be be altered.
     push   ax
     push   cx

dly_30ms:
     mov    cx,15000                  ;Load counter and delay for ~30 ms.
     call   delay                     ;(2uS per count in cx).

func_set1:
     mov    al,30h                    ;Load 'function set' value and
     mov    dx,DSP_CMD_WR             ;Output to the display cmd reg.
     out    dx,al

dly_4p1ms:
     mov    cx,2050                   ;Load counter and delay for ~4.1 ms.
     call   delay                     ;(2uS per count in cx).

func_set2:
     mov    al,30h                    ;Load 'function set' value and
     mov    dx,DSP_CMD_WR             ;Output to the display cmd reg.
     out    dx,al
```

Figure 15.8-5   Procedure to initialize LCD display module.

```
dly_100us:
        mov     cx,50              ;Load counter and delay for ~30 ms.
        call    delay              ;(2uS per count in cx).


func_set3:
        mov     al,30h             ;Load 'function set' value and
        mov     dx,DSP_CMD_WR      ;Output to the display cmd reg.
        out     dx,al


ck_bsy_1:
        mov     dx,DSP_CMD_RD      ;Read command reg and test
        in      al,dx
        test    al, 80h            ;busy flag (1 = busy).
        jnz     ck_bsy_1           ;Cont to chk until busy = 0.


func_set:
        mov     al,00111000b       ;Send func set, 8-bit mode.
        mov     dx,DSP_CMD_WR
        out     dx,al


ck_bsy_2:
        mov     dx,DSP_CMD_RD      ;Read command reg and test
        in      al,dx
        test    al, 80h            ;busy flag (1 = busy).
        jnz     ck_bsy_2           ;Cont to chk until = 0.


set_dsp_off1:
        mov     al,08h             ;Send dsp off, no curser/blink cmd.
        mov     dx,DSP_CMD_WR
        out     dx,al


ck_bsy_3:
        mov     dx,DSP_CMD_RD      ;Read command reg and test
        in      al,dx
        test    al, 80h            ;busy flag (1 = busy).
        jnz     ck_bsy_3           ;Cont to chk until = 0.


clr_dsp1:
        mov     al,01h             ;Send clear display command.
        mov     dx,DSP_CMD_WR
        out     dx,al
```

Figure 15.8-5   Procedure to initialize LCD display module. (Continued.)

```
ck_bsy_4:
        mov     dx,DSP_CMD_RD           ;Read command reg and test
        in      al,dx
        test    al, 80h                 ;busy flag (1 = busy).
        jnz     ck_bsy_4                ;Cont to chk until = 0.

mode_set1:
        mov     al,00000110b            ;Send mode (incr/no shift) cmd.
        mov     dx,DSP_CMD_WR
        out     dx,al

ck_bsy_5:
        mov     dx, DSP_CMD_RD          ;Read command reg and test
        in      al,dx
        test    al, 80h                 ;busy flag (1 = busy).
        jnz     ck_bsy_5                ;Cont to chk until = 0.

;initialization complete, turn on display.
dsp_on:
        mov     al,0ch                  ;Send 'display on' cmd.
        mov     dx,DSP_CMD_WR           ;Output to the display.
        out     dx,al

ck_bsy_6:
        mov     dx,DSP_CMD_RD           ;Read command reg and test
        in      al,dx
        test    al, 80h                 ;busy flag (1 = busy).
        jnz     ck_bsy_6                ;Cont to chk until = 0.

end_init:
        pop     cx                      ;Restore regs.
        pop     ax
        popf
        ret
init_dspendp
```

Figure 15.8-5   Procedure to initialize LCD display module. (Continued.)

```
;*********************************************************************
;
;NAME:        update
;FUNCTION:    Updates the information being displayed by a 16 character x 2 line
;             LCD display.
;ASSUMES:     two (2) 16 byte memory buffers; dsp_buff_1, dsp_buff_2
;RETURNS:     nothing.
;MODIFIES:    ax,cx,si,fr
;CALLS:       nothing
;CALLED BY:
;
;DESCRIPTION: This procedure updates the display using the two 16 byte
;             buffers, defined in the data segment, dsp_buff_1 and
;             dsp_buff_2. Line 1 of the display is filled with the contents
;             of dsp_buff_1 and Line 2 is filled with dsp_buff_2 contents.
;*********************************************************************
;

update proc    near

        mov    cx, length dsp_buff_1        ;Load cx with length of buffer.
        push   cx                           ;Save a copy for later.


wr_line_1:
        mov    si, offset dsp_buff_1        ;Load si as a pointer to 1st
                                            ;byte of buffer for line 1.
;set DDRAM address to 1st position of first line.
test_busy0:
        mov    dx,DSP_CMD_RD                ;read busy flag (= d7).
        in     al,dx
        test   al,80h                       ;if '1', then busy.
        jnz    test_busy0                   ;if busy keep checking.
        mov    al, 80h                      ;Set addr to 00h (with d7=1) and
        mov    dx,DSP_CMD_WR                ;output to the display cmd reg.
        out    dx,al


test_busy1:
        mov    dx,DSP_CMD_RD                ;Read busy flag (= d7).
        in     al,dx
        test   al,80h                       ;If '1', then busy.
        jnz    test_busy1                   ;If busy keep checking.
```

Figure 15.8-6   Procedure to update LCD module from memory buffers.

```
get_byte:
        mov    al, [si]                 ;Read byte from buffer and
        mov    dx,DSP_DAT_WR            ;output to the display.
        out    dx,al
        inc    si                       ;Adjust ptr to nxt buff location.
        loop   test_busy1               ;Loop til cx=0, all bytes written.
        pop    cx                       ;Reload cx with buffer length.

wr_line_2:
        mov    si, offset dsp_buff_2     ;Load si as a pointer to 1st
                                         ;byte of buffer for line 2.

;set DDRAM address to 1st position of second line.
test_busy:
        mov    dx,DSP_CMD_RD            ;read busy flag (= d7).
        in     al,dx
        test   al,80h                   ;if '1', then busy.
        jnz    test_busy                ;if busy keep checking.
        mov    al, 0c0h                 ;Set addr to 40h (with d7=1) and
        mov    dx,DSP_CMD_WR            ;output to the display cmd reg.
        out    dx,al

test_busy2:
        mov    dx,DSP_CMD_RD            ;Read busy flag (= d7).
        in     al,dx
        test   al,80h                   ;If '1', then busy.
        jnz    test_busy2               ;If busy keep checking.

get_byte2:
        mov    al, [si]                 ;Read byte from buffer and
        mov    dx,DSP_DAT_WR            ;output to the display.
        out    dx,al
        inc    si                       ;Adjust ptr to nxt buff location.
        loop   test_busy2               ;Loop til cx = 0.
        ret

update  endp
```

Figure 15.8-6   Procedure to update LCD module from memory buffers. (Continued.)

15.9   Vacuum Fluorescent Display (VFD) Modules

Vacuum fluorescent displays (VFDs) are active displays. Their high brightness makes them good for applications with high ambient lighting. Most VFDs emit blue-green light. Like LCD modules, VFD modules provide all the multiplexing and drive logic required. They also come in a variety of configurations in terms of fonts, characters per line, and number of lines.

Noritake's **CU20025ECPB-U1J**, VFD module is a drop in replacement for 2 x 20 LCD displays similar to the 2 x16 LCD module of the previous section. The controller architecture for the CU20025ECPB-U1J is similar to the LCD module's, so the same driver software can be used.

The CU20025ECPB-U1J has a jumper that can be used to configure its interface signals to be compatible with either Motorola or Intel style control signals. When Motorola style is selected, two pins on the interface connector are configured as R/W and E. With this selection, the CU20025ECPB-U1J's timing waveforms are similar to those of Fig. 15.8-3. When Intel style is selected, the same two control pins are configured as /WR and /RD.

IEE's FLIP 2 x 16 VFD module (Fig. 15.9-1) has large 0.44 inch 5 x 7 dot matrix characters. This module can be interfaced to a microprocessor by using either its parallel data bus or serial data input. A jumper allows selection of either the parallel or serial interface.

Figure 15.9-1   2 × 16 vacuum fluorescent display (VFD) module. (Courtesy of Industrial Electronic Engineers (IEE) Inc.)

The parallel interface is bidirectional and uses Intel style control signals. To obtain the maximum parallel loading rate, the status of the device's input buffer can be read to determine when the buffer is empty. Alternatively, for more efficient operation an interrupt output is provided so that the microprocessor can be interrupted when the input buffer is empty.

The software operation of this display module is somewhat similar to the LCD of the previous section, although it uses a different command set.

You can simplify the interface hardware by using the serial interface. The serial interface is unidirectional. The serial signal can be jumper selected to accept TTL or RS232 level input. The transfer rate of the serial data is 1200 baud. Serial I/O interfaces are discussed in detail in the next chapter.

15.10   Summary

As the material in this chapter demonstrates, even the design of an apparently simple user input or output subsystem can present you with substantial implementation choices and subtle design complexities. The first major choice you must make is what kind of input or output device is most appropriate for the type and quantity of data that will be input or displayed in your application.

Once you have chosen a particular kind of input or output device, you must select a specific device from that category. Most IC I/O peripheral devices include interface and control logic as part of the device. In contrast, many electromechanical I/O devices include little or no interface and control logic.

Implementation of interface and control logic allows a substantial tradeoff between software and hardware. A critical factor affecting this decision is the real-time aspects of even simple I/O devices when controlled directly. For example, if a 16-key keypad is selected as an input device, there is substantial tradeoff in how the keypad is scanned.

If the scanning is done in software, then your software must deal with debounce time and scan rate. You must insure that the scan procedure is called often enough so that no keypress is missed. Whether you can accomplish this in software depends on the time constraints of the other tasks the microprocessor must execute in the specific application.

If scanning is accomplished in hardware using a 16-key encoder IC, such as the MM74C922, no software is required for scanning the keypad. The only interface decision you must make is whether to design the interface to poll the keypad or to be interrupt driven.

Similar decisions must be made when designing a display subsystem. First you have to choose the appropriate display device and then decide how it will be driven and interfaced. For example, if you need to display eight digits on an instrument panel and you need an active display with relatively large digits, you might chose to use seven-segment LEDs. Choosing a display driver IC to drive the LEDs drastically simplifies the hardware and software design.

The user input and output devices presented in this chapter are appropriate for low data rate and low data density applications. A large variety of these devices and associated driver ICs are available. A similarly large number of devices and driver ICs are available to handle higher data rate and data density applications.

15.11   Problems

1. What are the four operations commonly associated with generating digital input data from user input devices?

2. Using the information in Table 10.7-1, for each logic family in the table, compute the maximum value of pull-up resistor that can be used with a mechanical switch whose output drives a three-state buffer from that logic family (Fig. 15.2-3). In each case, how much power does the pull-up resistor dissipate when the switch is closed?

3. Draw the logic diagram for the input and output subsystems and write a program that measures the contact bounce (in milliseconds) of SPST switches. Both the oper-

ate and release contact bounce times should be measured. The measured operate and release bounce times are to be displayed on two-digit seven-segment displays.

4. Analyze the operation of the RS latch of Fig. 15.2-5 for an input waveform like that of Fig. 15.2-4. Verify that the RS latch debounces the SPDT switch.

5. Instead of the cross-coupled NAND gates of Fig. 15.2-5, draw a circuit that uses cross-coupled NOR gates to debounce a SPDT switch. Label the 0 and 1 positions of the switch. Analyze the circuit's operation and verify that this latch debounces the SPDT switch.

6. A momentary contact switch is used to count events that cause its operation. The switch's output must increment an 8-bit binary counter each time the switch is pressed. The counter is a 74HC590 8-Bit Binary Counter with 3-State Output Register. This counter counts positive edges. The counter's output is read by an 80C188EB through its octal three-state buffer. Draw a logic diagram for the interface using isolated I/O. Indicate any required component values and show their computation. Use 74HC devices for any additional logic required. The address decoder can be shown as a single block with its inputs and outputs labeled. Should the momentary contact switch be a SPST or a SPDT switch?

7. Explain how the program of Fig. 15.2-6 can successfully debounce both the press and release of the switch, if the delay is only called after the switch is pressed.

8. Four BCD thumbwheel switches are used to enter a single 4-digit control parameter into an 80C188EB system while the system is running. Write a procedure that checks the BCD switches' outputs and updates, if necessary, the value of the control parameter in memory. Assume that the procedure is called approximately once every 10 seconds. Consider the time required for an operator to alter the value of all four thumbwheel switches before designing your solution.

9. Two 74LS148 priority encoders and a quad two-input NAND gate can be used to encode the 16 keys of a keypad that has one terminal of each key connected in common. Draw the logic diagram to accomplish this.

10. Eight momentary contact switches are required in an application for a function keypad. The switches are arranged in a linear fashion and their outputs are input through a single byte port, KEYS. Write a procedure that returns a key's code only if no other keys are pressed and the key that is pressed has been held longer than the debounce period. The keycode assigned to a key corresponds to its bit position in the input port. The procedure returns a valid key code in AL with CF set. When the procedure is not returning a valid keycode, it returns with CF clear. The procedure calls a second procedure, bdelay, to delay for debouncing. This delay procedure should be called only when necessary. Do not write the procedure bdelay. Draw a logic diagram for the circuit. Show the address decoding as a single block. The port address for KEYS is 8000H.

11. The MM74C923 keyboard scanner of Fig. 15.3-4 has a DATA_AVAILABLE output that makes a 0 to 1 transition when a key is pressed and remains 1 until the key is released. Draw the logic diagram for an interrupt driven interface of the MM74C923 to an 80C188EB system. Assume that this is the only interrupt in the system and include logic to generate the interrupt vector. The output of the MM74C923 is input

through port KEYSW. Write a service procedure that calls another procedure, prskysw, to process the keyswitch.

12. Modify the procedure digpot so that the parameter, param, can never be incremented above 255 nor decremented below 0.

13. Write an interrupt procedure, dpin, for the optical encoder with interrupt interface of Fig. 15.4-5. The procedure increments or decrements param by 1 for each interrupt. However, param is never to be incremented above 255 or decremented below 0.

14. Draw the logic diagram of a circuit, based on Fig. 15.4-5, that includes an 8254 counter/timer to allow the period of either A or B to be determined. This allows the computation of a velocity dependent value by which param is incremented or decremented. Assume a 10Hz square wave signal is available to be used in the determination. The circuit must allow the interrupt service procedure to determine the period by reading the 8254 as soon as the interrupt occurs. Use SSI logic as required. In what mode is the 8254 operated? Describe the operation of your circuit and how the velocity would be determined.

15. In an application, HLMP-0300 annunciator LEDs are directly driven by a 74ALS564A octal flip-flop. The 74ALS564A can sink 24 mA, I_{OL} = 24 mA. Assume $V_{OL\ TYP}$ = 0.35 V @ 24 mA and V_{CC} = 5.0 V. The LED is to be driven at 20 mA. The forward voltage drop across the HLMP-0300 diode is approximately 2.1 V @ 20 mA. Calculate the value of the current limiting resistors to properly limit the current through the LEDs.

16. A common anode seven-segment display is to be directly driven by a 74ALS574 and used to display hexadecimal digits. Draw a logic diagram the interconnection of the seven-segment display to the 74ALS574. Segments a through g should be driven by bits D6 through D0, latched from the data bus. Determine the bit pattern required to display each of the hexadecimal digits.

17. An eight-digit, multiplexed display, similar to the display in Fig. 15.6-5, is to be refreshed at a refresh rate of 100 Hz. The display interrupts an 80C188EB when it requires service. If the interrupt service procedure requires 60 μs to execute, what is the ON time for each digit? What percentage of time is the 80C188EB devoted to servicing the display? At what rate must the display interrupt the 80C188EB? What is the duty factor for a digit being ON?

18. An eight-digit, multiplexed, seven-segment display is to be refreshed at a refresh rate of 250 Hz. The display is software driven with the segments controlled by output port SEG and the digits controlled by output port DEG. Draw the logic diagram and write the initialization sequence required to use an 8254A to interrupt the 80C188EB each time a new digit must be turned on. How can the 8254A be used to protect the display from damage in a situation where the 80C188EB is delayed from responding to the display interrupt because of a higher priority task?

19. A procedure, bcdseg, is to be written for use with the ICM7218B multiplexed eight-digit display driver. This procedure has an unpacked BCD digit passed to it in AL. The procedure must convert the BCD digit to the seven-segment pattern (Fig. 15.7-2) required to display the digit when the pattern is written to the ICM7218B. The pattern is returned in AL.

20. A procedure, segon, is to be written for the ICM7218B multiplexed eight-digit display driver. This procedure allows the segments of a digit to be used as separate annunciators, rather than as a seven-segment display. The procedure receives two parameters in AH and AL. AL contains a bit pattern with a single 1 in the position which corresponds to the segment to be turned ON. AH specifies which digit of the display this segment is associated with. The procedure writes the necessary segment pattern into the specified digit position of the display buffer dsplyi (Fig. 15.7-3). This pattern must not affect any other segments in the digit. Note that the calling sequence can load AL symbolically, assuming that constants have been associated with the symbols using equate statements, for example, SEGA equ 01000000B. Also note that the decimal point segment must be handled differently from the others.

21. Repeat problem 20 for a procedure segoff that turns off the specified segment in the specified digit. Try to create a single procedure to handle both cases, segon and segoff.

22. Using SSI gates draw a logic diagram of a circuit that generates Intel-style control signals, /RD and /WR, from Motorola-style control signals R/W and E. Can a circuit be designed that generates Motorola-style control signals from /RD and /WR? If so, design the circuit. If not, is there any set of 80C188EB signals that allows R/W and E to be easily generated? If so, draw the logic diagram of the circuit.

16

SERIAL I/O SUBSYSTEMS

16.1   Serial Data Transfer

16.2   Universal Asynchronous Receiver/Transmitters (UARTs)

16.3   The 80C188EB's Serial Control Unit (SCU)

16.4   SCU Asynchronous Serial Transfers

16.5   Circular Memory Buffers

16.6   RS-232 and Other Serial Communication Interfaces

16.7   Flow Control for Serial Data Transfer

16.8   "PC Type" UARTs

16.9   SCU Asynchronous Serial Transfer for Multiprocessor Systems

16.10   Clocked Synchronous Serial I/O Devices

16.11   Clocked Synchronous Serial Transfers Using the SCU

16.12   Summary

Data transfers between an 80C188EB CPU subsystem and I/O subsystems on the system bus are normally parallel transfers of eight bits at a time. However, there are many situations where serial data transfer is preferred or required. Serial data is transferred as a stream of bits, one bit at a time, on a single data line. Data can be transferred serially using one bit of the data bus, while ignoring the other seven bits. But, usually a separate dedicated serial data line is used.

Three common situations where a microprocessor needs to transfer data serially are when:

1. An I/O device is inherently serial in operation.
2. An I/O device is a great distance from the microprocessor.
3. A peripheral IC has a serial interface.

I/O devices, such as CRT terminals, magnetic tape storage systems, and serial printers, are inherently serial in operation. Consequently, they are constrained by their design to receive and transmit data serially. The only data connection available to such devices is a serial interface connector.

If a great distance separates the microprocessor and I/O device, serial transfer is usually required even when the I/O device is inherently parallel in operation. The cost of running a cable with as many conductors as there are data bus bits is high. Not only is the multiple conductor cable costly, but multiple line drivers and receivers are also necessary. Beyond a certain distance, serial data transfer is more economical in spite of the additional hardware or software required to convert parallel data to serial for transmission, and serial data to parallel upon reception.

In contrast to the second situation, the third situation involves an extremely short distance between a microprocessor and a peripheral IC on the same printed circuit board. Many peripheral IC functions, including DACs, ADCs, and ROM are available in serial versions. These serial ICs are primarily intended for applications where small package size and low cost are critical.

No matter what reasons dictate serial transfer, several operations are required to interface a serial device to a microprocessor:

1. Conversion between parallel and serial data formats.
2. Translation of logic signals to signals appropriate for transmission over a particular type of serial channel.
3. Buffering received or transmitted data.
4. Controlling the flow of data, so that data is not lost.

After introducing fundamental serial data transfer concepts, this chapter presents software and hardware approaches for implementing serial data transfer. Hardware approaches presented include use of the 80C188EB's integrated Serial Control Unit and use of discrete IC Universal Asynchronous Receiver Transmitters.

Serial data is usually transmitted and received at logic levels that differ significantly from those of either CMOS or TTL. Driver and receiver ICs used to translate between these levels and CMOS or TTL are discussed.

For most applications, having the hardware and software in place to receive and transmit a byte of data is just the beginning. Data is usually received and transmitted in groups, with one data byte following immediately after the next. Often, the microprocessor cannot process the data received on a byte-by-byte basis because of time constraints placed on the microprocessor by other tasks. The data bytes received (or transmitted) must usually be placed in a memory buffer until the microprocessor has a chance to process the data. Implementing circular memory buffers for this purpose is discussed in this chapter.

If a large amount of serial data is being received faster than it can be processed, then eventually the memory buffer will overflow. Methods of flow control that coordinate the flow of data between a transmitter and a receiver to prevent buffer overflow are presented.

16.1   Serial Data Transfer

Electronic transmission of encoded information from one point to another over relatively large distances is referred to as **data communications**. This field of study substantially predates that of embedded systems design. Data communications terminology is applied to serial data transfer in embedded systems, even when the distances involved are not large. Some data communications terminology important to embedded systems design is introduced in this section.

16.1.1   Serial Communications Channels

Serial data transfer involves a transmitter (source) and a receiver (destination). The electrical transmission path between the two is called a **communications channel**. This channel can be as simple as a single wire or coax cable, or more complex such as fiber optic cables, telephone lines, or a portion of the radio frequency spectrum.

    Serial channels are classified in terms of their direction of transfer as simplex, half duplex, or full duplex (Fig. 16.1-1). A **simplex** channel can transfer data in only one direction. A **half-duplex** channel can transfer data in either direction, but in only one direction at a time. A **full-duplex** channel can transfer data in both directions simultaneously.

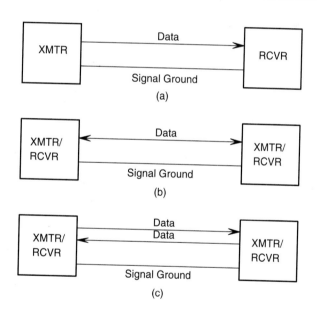

Figure 16.1-1   Serial data connections classified by direction of transfer: (a) simplex; (b) half-duplex; (c) full-duplex.

    When the communications channel consists of wires or lines, the minimum number required for a simplex channel is two: the data, or signal line, and a signal ground. A half-duplex channel also requires only two lines, signal and ground. However, there must be some method to "turn the line around" when the direction of transfer is to change. This involves a protocol and logic to establish one device as the transmitter and the other as the receiver. After transfer in one direction is complete, the roles of transmitter and receiver are reversed and transfer takes place in the opposite direction, on the same signal line. Full-duplex channels require two signal lines and a signal ground. Each signal line is dedicated to data transfer in a single direction, allowing simultaneous transfer in opposite directions.

The number of signal changes per second on a communications channel is its **baud rate**. Since binary signals can only change between one of two possible values, their baud rate is equivalent to the number of **bits per second** (**bps**) transferred. A communication channel's **capacity** is the maximum baud rate the channel can support. If data is transmitted at a rate beyond a channel's capacity, the number of transmission errors increases significantly.

16.1.2   Information Codes

Serial data may be textual or pure binary. Textual data is often encoded in the **American Standard Code for Information Interchange** (**ASCII**). Each ASCII character requires seven bits for encoding. Characters in the ASCII code represent letters, digits, punctuation, symbols, and control codes (Appendix A). Control codes, 00H through 1FH, are used by devices like terminals to control their operation and are not printed or displayed.

Sometimes even pure binary data is transmitted as ASCII characters. This allows the received data to be viewed on a terminal or printed. An example is the Hex-ASCII code, used in Chapter 4 for transmitting binary object code to a device programmer. In Hex-ASCII, each binary byte is split into two hexadecimal values, each of which is encoded as an ASCII character. So, transmitting pure binary data in Hex-ASCII is only half as efficient as transmitting it in binary.

Another reason for sending binary data as Hex-ASCII characters is that some commercial software and hardware are designed to handle only ASCII. These products can't handle arbitrary 8-bit data. For example, an 8-bit pure binary value that happens to be the same bit pattern as an ASCII form feed control character, 0CH, if sent to a printer, might affect the printer's operation in an unintended fashion.

16.1.3   Synchronization Techniques

A clock signal is needed to synchronize the receiver's timing to the incoming serial data so that the receiver can latch each data bit. Serial data transfers can be classified as either asynchronous or synchronous, based on the nature of the clock signal.

In **asynchronous transfer**, the transmitter and receiver do not share a common clock signal. Each provides its own independent clock. Both clocks run at the same nominal frequency. Asynchronous serial data is transmitted as a group of sequential bits called a **frame** (Fig. 16.1-2). Synchronization is established on a frame-by-frame basis, and only for the duration of each frame. The advantage of asynchronous transfer is its low cost. It is used primarily where transmission of frames is irregular, or where large blocks of data do not need to be transmitted at high speed.

In **synchronous transfer,** either a common clock signal exists between the transmitter and receiver, or the receiver is capable of deriving a clock signal from the transitions of the received data signal. Synchronous transfers are described in sections 16.10 and 16.11 and are encountered in later chapters with respect to some serial peripheral ICs. The other sections of this chapter focus on asynchronous transfer.

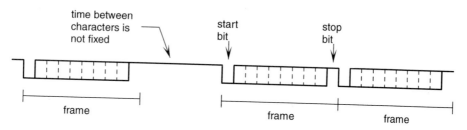

Figure 16.1-2   Asynchronous serial transfer.

16.1.4   Asynchronous Serial Data Transfer

The time that a single data bit is valid during a serial transfer is referred to as the **bit time**. The bit time is the reciprocal of the baud rate. In asynchronous data transfer, once the transmitter starts to send a frame, the receiver must synchronize itself with the frame's bit time. To do this, the baud rate of the transmitter and receiver must be equal.

A frame is sent by the transmitter whenever it becomes available for transfer. Thus, the time interval between the arrival of any two frames at the receiver is unknown. But, the time interval between bits in a single frame is always fixed (Fig. 16.1-3).

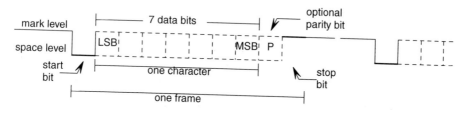

Figure 16.1-3   Seven bit asynchronous character and its framing.

When a frame is not being sent, the transmitter holds its output at 1. In this condition, the data line is said to be **idle** or **marking**. To signal the start of a frame, the transmitter causes the serial data line to transition from 1 to 0 by sending a **start bit.** A start bit is a 0 bit that marks the start of the frame. The receiver detects the 1 to 0 transition and uses its own clock to synchronize its operation with that of the transmitter. After detecting the 1 to 0 transition, the receiver implements **false start bit detection** by waiting one-half of a bit time and sampling its input to make sure it is still 0. If the data line is still 0, the previously detected 1 to 0 transition is assumed to have been the beginning of a start bit, rather than a noise spike.

After detecting the start bit and sampling the data line one-half of a bit time later, the receiver continues to sample the data line at intervals of one bit time. This **center sampling** insures that the data line is sampled near the middle of each data bit. Since the leading and trailing edges of transitions on the data line are distorted by line capacitance, inductance, and leakage, center sampling eliminates errors that might result if sampling occurred near the distorted beginning or end of a bit time. Center sampling also eliminates errors due to a slight mismatch in the transmitter's and receiver's clock frequencies.

After the start bit, data bits are transmitted, least significant bit first. The data bits may be followed by an optional parity bit. When parity is used, the parity bit is set or cleared by the transmitter to produce either even or odd parity. For **even parity**, the parity bit is set or cleared so that the total number of 1s in the data bits and the parity bit is even. For odd parity, this total is made odd by the choice of the parity bit's value.

Finally, a **stop bit** is transmitted. The start bit and stop bit are said to frame the data (Fig. 16.1-3). A stop bit in combination with the next start bit guarantees that there will always be a 1 to 0 transition to signal the start of each frame.

For transfers of ASCII characters, the 7-bit ASCII character is preceded by a start bit and usually followed by a parity bit and one stop bit. The resulting frame transmitted is ten bits long. In asynchronous transfer there is always overhead, in terms of bits, that comprises a significant percentage of the frame. For example, in a 10-bit frame there are 7 data bits and three overhead bits, or 30% overhead.

Asynchronous serial data transfers typically occur at rates of 1200, 2400, 4800, 9600, 14.4 k, 19.2 k, 38.4 k and 115 kbps. These baud rates are commonly used by manufacturers of commercial communications equipment. For example, asynchronous transfer of information between a CRT terminal and an 80C188EB system might take place at 9.6 kbps, or 9600 bits per second. At this rate, one bit time, is 104 μs. If each frame is ten bits, each character takes 1.04 ms. Thus, 960 characters can be transmitted per second, assuming there is no idle time between frames.

16.1.5   Hardware/Software Trade-offs for Serial Data Transfer

The logical formatting of data for serial transfer and the generation of the one-half and full-bit time delays can be done in software. A low-cost software serial receiver can input data through one bit of an input port. A receive procedure polls to detect the start bit and then center samples each of the incoming bits. This procedure also converts the serial data to parallel and, if necessary, checks the parity bit. The 80C188EB's JPE and JPO conditional branch instructions are designed for checking parity. In this software approach, hardware is needed only for the 1-bit input port and the electrical interface to the communications channel.

A low-cost software serial transmitter consists of one bit of an output port and a transmit procedure that outputs the start bit, data bits, parity bit, and stop bit with the appropriate timing.

The disadvantage of software formatting and timing of serial transfers is that the microprocessor is completely dedicated to the transfer for the duration of each frame. It takes 8.33 ms to transfer a single frame at 1200 bps. In this period of time, assuming an average instruction execution time of 2 μs, approximately 4,162 instructions could be executed, enough instructions to do many other useful tasks.

The software approach can be improved by using a hardware timer to time the bit times and generate an interrupt when either the next bit should be sampled or output. Even this approach starts to become a problem if full-duplex transfers must be accommodated. Implementation of this approach becomes even more difficult as the number of other tasks that need to be carried out simultaneously with the serial transfers increases.

The most efficient approach and one that simplifies a system's software architecture is to use dedicated hardware. For asynchronous serial transfer this dedicated hardware is called a UART.

16.2   Universal Asynchronous Receiver/Transmitters (UARTs)

A **Universal Asynchronous Receiver/Transmitter (UART)** provides all the logic needed for full-duplex asynchronous serial transfers. A UART handles the detailed timing, serialization, and deserialization aspects of asynchronous data transfer. UARTs are available as discrete ICs or integrated onto a microprocessor or multifunction IC. UARTs are used so often in embedded systems that the 80C188EB provides two UARTs in its Serial Communications Unit (SCU).

Whether implemented as a discrete IC or integrated onto a microprocessor IC, all UARTs share some common architectural features and functions that are the focus of this section. A block diagram of a generic UART is shown in Fig. 16.2-1. This UART interfaces to a microprocessor's parallel data bus in a manner similar to other parallel peripheral ICs. The UART contains a number of control, status, and data registers, which appear to the microprocessor as I/O ports.

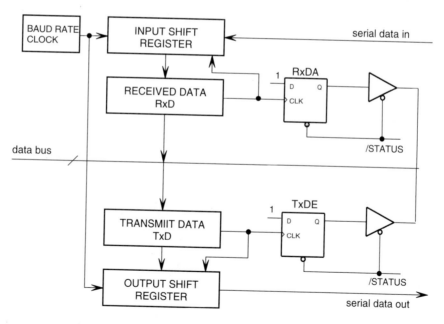

Figure 16.2-1   Hardware implementation of a serial receiver and transmitter, both using double buffering.

16.2.1   Baud Rate Generator

A clock source, referred to as a **baud rate clock,** is required for a UART's operation. Some UARTs include an oscillator to provide the baud rate clock. In this case, all that is required is the addition of an external crystal. Other UARTs require that the baud rate clock be generated externally. Integrated UARTs usually provide a programmable divider circuit that divides down the system clock to create the baud rate clock.

For a specific baud rate, the baud rate clock must oscillate at a multiple, called the **clocking factor,** of the baud rate. Clocking factors of 8, 16, or 64 times the baud rate are common. The clocking factor allows the UART's receiver to count baud rate clock pulses equal to one-half a bit time after the start bit's transition to begin center sampling. The UART then counts baud rate clock pulses equal to one bit time to center sample each of the subsequent bits. UARTs include a divider to divide down a fixed baud rate clock so that the UART is programmable for different baud rates.

When the baud rate clock is generated from the system clock, a small error exists for standard baud rates. This error exists because an integer system clock frequency is not divisible by another integer to produce exactly the required clocking factor needed for standard baud rates. For example, an 8 times baud rate clock for 9600 bps must be 76.8 kHz. The required divisor to divide down an 8 MHz system clock to 76.8 kHz is 104.1667. The closest integer divisor is 104, which results in an error of 0.16%. Errors in the baud rate clock of less than approximately 3% are usually not a problem.

16.2.2   UART Control and Status Registers

A UART's frame format and operational modes are programmable. Control register(s) are written to specify the format of the transmitted and received frames. Format parameters include: the number of data bits, number of stop bits, whether a parity bit should be sent or checked, and whether the parity should be odd or even. A UART is able to generate interrupt requests when the transmission of a frame is completed and after a frame is received. Bits in a UART's control register are written to enable or disable these interrupts.

For polled operation, a UART's status register provides bits that indicate when a data byte can be sent and when a data byte has been received. The status register also indicates whether any of several possible errors have occurred during the reception of a frame.

16.2.3   UART Transmitter

To transmit data after a UART has been initialized, the data is written, in parallel, to the UART's Transmit Data register (TxD). Logic associated with TxD automatically transfers the data to the output shift register. This parallel-input serial-output shift register performs the formatting and parallel-to-serial conversion (serialization) necessary to transmit the frame. After the frame has been shifted out of the output shift register, a Transmit Data register Empty status flag (TxDE) is set to indicate that TxD and the shift register are both empty.

Another byte can be written to TxD while a previously written byte is being shifted out. This two-register structure is called a **double buffer** or **dual rank.** The program can poll the TxDE flag to determine when the TxD register can be written with the next byte. Alternatively, the setting of TxDE can be enabled to generate an interrupt request, invoking an ISR that writes the next byte to TxD.

16.2.4   Data, Byte, Character, or Frame?

The terms data, byte, character, and frame are often used interchangeably when discussing asynchronous serial data transfer. However, it is helpful at this point to emphasize some distinctions between them. The data format of the frame transmitted by a UART is usually programmable to have from 5 to 8 data bits. What is written to the TxD register and read from the Receive Data register (RxD) by the microprocessor is always a byte. The 5 to 8 data bits are right justified in the byte. In general, the data byte written or read can represent binary data or a character code.

The UART automatically adds framing bits (start and stop) and possibly a parity bit to the data loaded into the transmit shift register before transmitting a frame. The UART strips off the framing bits and parity bit from a frame in the receiver shift register before transferring the data byte to RxD. In summary, what is serially transmitted or received by the UART is a frame. The frame contains data, which in many applications represents a character code. In such cases, it is accurate to say that a character is serially transmitted or received.

16.2.5   UART Receiver

To receive serial data, an input shift register inputs the data bit stream, removes the framing and parity bit information, and loads the data, in parallel, into the RxD register (Fig. 16.2-1). Double buffering allows the microprocessor a full frames's time in which to read data from RxD, before that data is possibly overwritten by the next byte received. Without double buffering, the microprocessor would have only one stop bit's time in which to read the data before it is possibly overwritten.

When data is transferred to RxD, the Received Data Available status flag (RxDA) is set to indicate that new data is available. A program can poll this flag, and if it is set, read the RxD register. Alternatively, setting RxDA can be enabled to generate an interrupt. This latter approach relieves the microprocessor from polling and results in increased efficiency.

As increasingly faster transmission rates have come into use, the time that a microprocessor has to carry out other tasks between servicing a UART's active serial channel has been substantially reduced. In an interrupt driven interface, with frames being received at 1200 bps, an interrupt is received every 8.3 ms. At 19.2 kbps, a frame is received and an interrupt occurs every 520 µs.

To handle the higher baud rates, some UARTs replace the single Receive Data register and the single Transmit Data register with on-chip **first-in first-out (FIFO)** memory buffers. For example, the 16C552 UART, described in Section 16.8, has a 16-byte receive FIFO and a 16-byte transmit FIFO. This means that microprocessor has roughly 16 times as long to respond to a receive interrupt without characters being lost. For transmissions, it means that the microprocessor can output as many as 16 bytes to the UART at once.

16.2.6   UART Modem Control Signals

UARTs also provide several logic inputs and outputs. Most of these are simply programmable port bits. However, they often have names that correspond to some of the signals used to control modems, and can be used for that or for another purpose. Modem control signals are discussed in Section 16.7.

16.3   The 80C188EB's Serial Communications Unit, SCU

The 80C188EB's integrated **Serial Communications Unit** (**SCU**) provides two independent serial communications channels, channel 0 and channel 1 (Fig. 16.3-1). Either channel can be programmed to operate in one of four asynchronous modes or a single synchronous mode. When operated in one of its asynchronous modes, a serial channel acts like a UART. Each channel has its own baud rate clock, receive shift register, receive buffer, transmit buffer, transmit shift register, and interrupt capability.

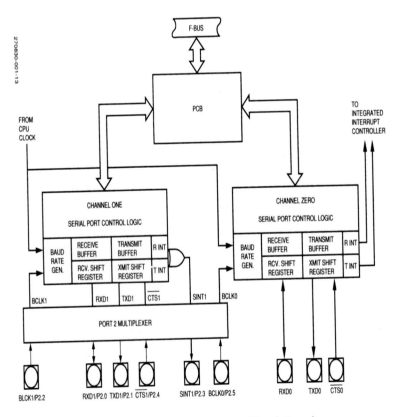

Figure 16.3-1   SCU block diagram. (Courtesy of Intel Corp.)

Each serial channel has its own six registers in the PCB for control, status, and data. These registers' PCB offsets range from 60H through 6AH for channel 0 and 70H through 7AH for channel 1. The two channels are identical in operation, except for how their interrupts are supported by the ICU.

The four different asynchronous modes, modes 1 through 4, all provide frames with seven, eight, or nine data bits. Transmission and reception is full duplex. Both transmission and reception for a channel occur at the single baud rate programmed for that channel.

Asynchronous mode 1 has either 8 data bits or 7 data bits and a parity bit. Mode 1 is used in the next section to illustrate the basic operation of the SCU. Mode 4 has 7 data bits and no parity and is provided to accommodate older serial devices that use a seven-bit data frame.

Asynchronous modes 2 and 3 are primarily used together to support a master/slave multi-microprocessor communications protocol. This protocol allows easy communications, using a shared serial channel, between multiple 80C188EBs, or other microprocessors (e.g. 8051, 80196) that also support this protocol. Multiprocessor asynchronous transfers are discussed in Section 16.9.

Mode 0, a clocked synchronous mode, transmits and receives data on one line (half-duplex) and generates a synchronization clock for the data transfer on a second line. This mode is useful for transferring data to and from serial peripheral devices such as ADCs and DACs and is discussed in Sections 16.10 and 16.11.

16.4 SCU Asynchronous Serial Transfers

In modes 1 through 4, frames consists of a start bit, followed by 7 to 9 data bits, and a stop bit. For frames with 8 or 9 data bits, the last data bit can be replaced by a parity bit. **Mode 1** is the common 8 data bit asynchronous communications mode. Each mode 1 frame has a start bit, eight data bits, and a stop bit. Enabling the parity feature replaces the eighth data bit with a parity bit.

Before a channel can be used, it must first be initialized. The procedure SC0INIT (Fig. 16.4-1) initializes channel 0 in mode 1 for interrupt driven communications at 9600 bps with an 8 MHz system clock. The steps are:

1. Load the serial receive and transmit interrupt vectors.
2. Set the baud rate.
3. Set the mode and frame format.
4. Clear any spurious serial interrupts, then enable the interrupts.
5. Enable the serial receiver

16.4.1   Initializing a Serial Channel

SC0INT first sets up interrupt vectors to point to the receive and transmit interrupt routines. The offset and segment addresses of the receive interrupt routine, RX0ISR, and then the offset and segment addresses of the transmit interrupt routine, TX0ISR, are loaded into the

```
;*****************************************************************
;
;NAME:        sc0init
;
;function:    Initialize serial channel 0
;assumes:     rx0isr and tx0isr ISRs, 8 MHz system
;returns:     nothing
;modifies:    AX,BX,PSW
;
;DESCRIPTION:Loads interrupt vectors types 20 and 21. Sets baud
;            rate for 9600, mode 1, even parity. Clears pending
;            channel 0 interrupts, then enables channel 0 interrupt
;            and globally enables maskable interrupts
;
;*****************************************************************
;
sc0init proc
        push    ds                      ;set up serial 0 interrupt vectors
        xor     ax,ax                   ;set DS to 0000h to address table
        mov     ds,ax
        mov     bx,4*20                 ;load type 20 and 21 interrupt vectors
        mov     word ptr [bx],offset rx0isr
        mov     word ptr [bx+2], seg rx0isr
        mov     bx,4*21
        mov     word ptr [bx],offset tx0isr
        mov     word ptr [bx+2], seg tx0isr
        pop     ds                      ;resore DS

        mov     dx,B0CMP                ;load baud rate control reg
        mov     ax,8067h                ;and init with 1843200/(8X baud).
        out     dx,ax

        mov     dx,S0CON                ;load control reg
        mov     ax,0019h                ;and init for 10-bit async even parity
        out     dx,ax

        mov     dx,S0STS                ;clear any old RI and TI
        in      ax,dx                   ;by reading S0STS

        mov     dx,SCUCON               ;enable serial channel 0 interrupts
        mov     ax,0007h                ;by clearing bit 3
        out     dx,ax
```

Figure 16.4-1   Procedure to initialize channel 0 for interrupt driven operation.

```
        mov    dx,SOCON                ;enable channel 0's receiver
        in     ax,dx
        or     al,00100000b           ;set receive enable bit, REN
        and    ah,00000001b
        out    dx,ax


        sti                           ;globally enable maskable interrupts
        ret
scOinit endp
```

Figure 16.4-1   Procedure to initialize channel 0 for interrupt driven operation.
                  (Continued.)

interrupt vector table. Serial channel 0's receive interrupt is predefined as type 20 and serial channel 0's transmit interrupt is predefined as type 21.

Two registers in the PCB, Baud Rate Counter and Baud Rate Compare, must be loaded to initialize the baud rate. The most significant bit of the **Baud Rate Compare** (**B0CMP**) register (Fig. 16.4-2) selects the source for the baud rate clock. The source can be either the CPU clock or an external clock signal applied to pin BCLK0, Fig. 16.3-1. The **Baud Rate Counter** (**B0CNT**) is a 15-bit free running counter that divides down the baud rate clock. The least significant 15 bits of B0CNT (Fig. 16.4-3) are compared to B0CMP after each pulse from the baud rate clock. If these values are equal, the baud rate generator outputs a pulse and resets B0CNT. This output from the baud rate generator is the sample clock with a clocking factor of 8 times the desired baud rate.

The Baud Rate Counter register is automatically reset to 0H when the 80C188EB is reset. Therefore, there is no need to clear it during initialization.

The equation for the required baud rate compare value is:

$$CMPVAL = \frac{FCPU}{8 \times BAUDRATE} - 1$$

The baud rate compare value for 9600 baud using the internal 8 MHz CPU system clock is 103 or 67H. Thus, the Baud Rate Compare register is loaded with 8067H to select the internal clock as the baud rate clock and to use a compare value of 103.

After setting up the baud rate, the desired asynchronous mode and frame format are selected by writing the **Serial Control** register (**S0CON**). Bit assignments for this register are given in Fig. 16.4-4.

When the 80C188EB's Clear To Send input (/CTS) is enabled by setting CEN, the /CTS input must be asserted externally before the transmitter can send a frame. This allows the external receiver to control when a byte in the transmitter shift register is actually sent. In this example, the channel is configured to disable /CTS. The receiver is not yet enabled. Even parity is selected and enabled and mode 1 is selected. The value that must be loaded into S0CON to achieve all of this is 0019H. S0CON is a read/write register. Reading this register does not effect its contents.

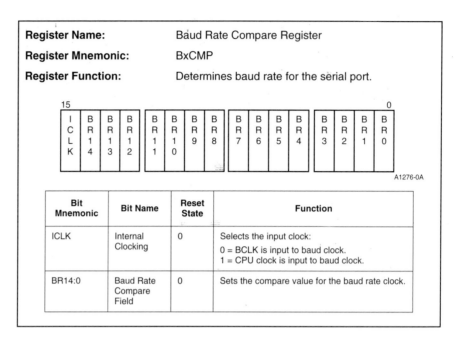

Figure 16.4-2   Baud Rate Compare register. (Courtesy of Intel Corp.)

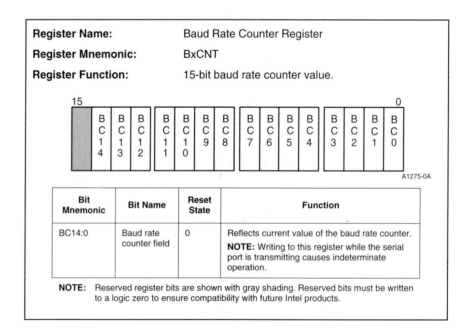

Figure 16.4-3   Baud Rate Counter register. (Courtesy of Intel Corp.)

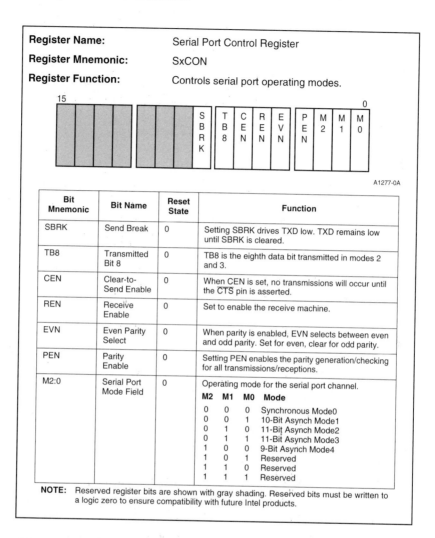

Figure 16.4-4   Serial Control Registers. (Courtesy of Intel Corp.)

The **Serial Status** register (**S0STS**) is used to monitor the current state of the channel and provides a number of status bits, Fig. 16.4-5.

Two of these bits, RI and TI, are request bits for interrupts and are cleared to clear any old pending interrupts. Reading S0STS clears all bits in this register, except CTS. CTS is always the complement of the value on the /CTS pin. Next, the interrupt mask bit in SCUCON (Fig. 16.4-4) is cleared to allow interrupts from the SCU.

The receiver must still be enabled before reception can occur. The receiver is enabled by setting the REN bit in S0CON. Once enabled, the receiver begins sampling the RXD line. The initialization procedure for channel 0 is now complete, and the procedure returns.

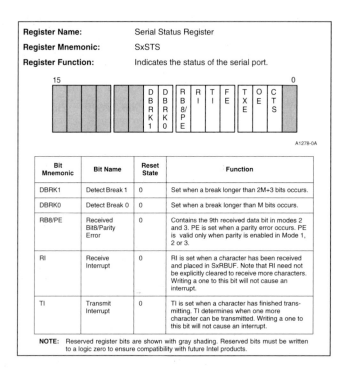

Bit Mnemonic	Bit Name	Reset State	Function
DBRK1	Detect Break 1	0	Set when a break longer than 2M+3 bits occurs.
DBRK0	Detect Break 0	0	Set when a break longer than M bits occurs.
RB8/PE	Received Bit8/Parity Error	0	Contains the 9th received data bit in modes 2 and 3. PE is set when a parity error occurs. PE is valid only when parity is enabled in Mode 1, 2 or 3.
RI	Receive Interrupt	0	RI is set when a character has been received and placed in SxRBUF. Note that RI need not be explicitly cleared to receive more characters. Writing a one to this bit will not cause an interrupt.
TI	Transmit Interrupt	0	TI is set when a character has finished transmitting. TI determines when one more character can be transmitted. Writing a one to this bit will not cause an interrupt.

NOTE: Reserved register bits are shown with gray shading. Reserved bits must be written to a logic zero to ensure compatibility with future Intel products.

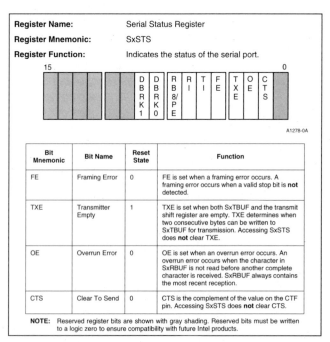

Bit Mnemonic	Bit Name	Reset State	Function
FE	Framing Error	0	FE is set when a framing error occurs. A framing error occurs when a valid stop bit is **not** detected.
TXE	Transmitter Empty	1	TXE is set when both SxTBUF and the transmit shift register are empty. TXE determines when two consecutive bytes can be written to SxTBUF for transmission. Accessing SxSTS does **not** clear TXE.
OE	Overrun Error	0	OE is set when an overrun error occurs. An overrun error occurs when the character in SxRBUF is not read before another complete character is received. SxRBUF always contains the most recent reception.
CTS	Clear To Send	0	CTS is the complement of the value on the CTF pin. Accessing SxSTS does **not** clear CTS.

NOTE: Reserved register bits are shown with gray shading. Reserved bits must be written to a logic zero to ensure compatibility with future Intel products.

Figure 16.4-5   Serial Status Register. (Courtesy of Intel Corp.)

16.4.2   Transmitting a Character

With the initialization accomplished, a frame can be transmitted by simply writing data to the **Serial Transmit Buffer** register (**S0TBUF**) in the PCB (Fig.16.4-6). If parity is enabled, the parity bit's value is automatically determined. Data written to S0TBUF is transferred to the transmit shift register and output on the TXD pin. Start and stop bits are automatically appended to the transmitted frame. As the frame's stop bit is shifted out, a transmit interrupt request is generated and the transmit interrupt bit TI is set.

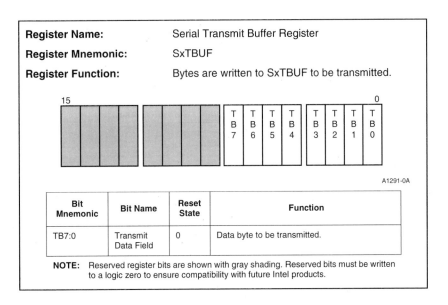

Figure 16.4-6   Serial Transmit Buffer Register. (Courtesy of Intel Corp.)

In response to the transmit interrupt, the transmit ISR can write the next character to be transmitted to S0TBUF. Serial channel 0's transmit ISR must also handle the interrupt generated after the last character in a sequence of characters is transmitted. When the ISR in invoked in this case, it must return without writing a new character to S0TBUF.

16.4.3   Receiving a Character

Once enabled, the receiver begins sampling the RXD pin, at eight times the baud rate, looking for the 1 to 0 transition that indicates the beginning of a start bit. To improve noise immunity, each data bit is sampled three times near the center of its bit time. A two-out-of-three majority logic circuit determines the value assigned to the data bit. At the middle of the stop bit, the received data is copied to S0RBUF, Fig. 16.4-7.

As a frame's reception is completed, a receive interrupt is generated and the receive interrupt flag RI is set. The receiver detects parity errors, framing errors, and overrun errors and sets the appropriate bits, PE, FE, and OE, respectively, in S0STS. Reading

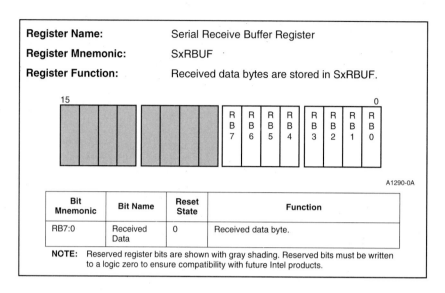

Figure 16.4-7   Serial Receive Buffer Register. (Courtesy of Intel Corp.)

S0RBUF returns the data in the low byte, and the value of the high byte is undefined. Serial channel 0's receive ISR can read the received byte from S0RBUF and store it in memory, or process it immediately. A serial channel receive ISR that reads S0RBUF and places the data byte in a circular memory buffer is discussed in Section 16.5.

16.4.4   Polled Operation

Serial channels are typically operated as interrupt driven. However, in some simple applications, and for initial testing purposes, polled operation may be used. The instruction sequence that follows echoes a character sent to the serial channel. The channel would be initialized as in Fig. 16.4-1, except there would be no need to load the interrupt vectors and the serial channel interrupt in SCUCON would not be unmasked.

```
nxt_char:
        mov     dx,S0STS        ;check RI for next character
        in      ax,dx
        test    ax,40h
        jz      nxt_char        ;wait
        mov     dx,S0RBUF       ;input character from S0RBUF
        in      ax,dx
        add     dx,2            ;output character to S0TBUF
        and     ax,007fh        ;mask all but ASCII character
        out     dx,ax
        jmp     nxt_char
```

In the above sequence, bit TXE of S0STS was not tested. When the Transmit Empty (TXE) status bit is a 1, it indicates that both the transmit buffer and the transmit shift register are empty. Under this condition, it is acceptable to write two data bytes to S0TBUF.

In general, TXE should be tested before writing data to S0TBUF, especially if the clear-to-send feature is enabled. When clear-to-send is enabled, transmission of a frame will not begin until /CTS is asserted. If /CTS has been negated and TXE is not tested before writing to S0TBUF, data in S0TBUF can be overwritten.

16.4.5   Serial Channels 0 and 1 Differences

Serial channels 0 and 1 are identical in operation, except for their interrupt circuitry and the fact that the pins for channel 1 are multiplexed with output port 2. Serial channel 0 is directly supported by the integrated Interrupt Control Unit (ICU) as has been previously described. In contrast, serial channel 1 has no direct connections to the ICU. Instead, output pin SINT1 provides an interrupt request signal that can be connected to one of the interrupt inputs, INT0–INT4, if desired. SINT1 is the logical OR of the bits RI and TI in S1STS. Therefore, when either RI or TI is set, SINT1 is asserted.

If SINT1 is used to generate an interrupt, the ISR can read S1STS to determine if the interrupt is the result of the reception or transmission of a frame and proceed accordingly. Reading S1STS clears RI and TI and is the only way SINT1 can be negated.

Since SINT1 is the OR of RI and TI, an interrupt request can be generated by the application program setting either of these bits, without either the receipt or transmission of a frame. This is not true for channel 0, because the internally generated interrupt request for channel 0 is derived from the signals that are used to set RI and TI, not from RI and TI. For channel 0, setting RI or TI does not generate an interrupt request. Also, failing to clear RI or TI does not prevent subsequent requests from occurring.

16.5   Circular Memory Buffers

A **memory buffer** is a temporary storage area in memory used to pass data from one task to another. The task that generates the data is often called the **producer** and the task that uses the data is called the **consumer**. Often, it is preferable for a receive ISR (the producer) to place each data byte into a buffer for some other task (the consumer) to process at a later time. Putting data into a buffer for later processing also allows the ISR to be written to execute in the least possible time.

A particularly appropriate type of buffer for this purpose is a first-in first-out (FIFO) structure called a **circular memory buffer, circular queue,** or **ring buffer** (Fig. 16.5-1). To implement this structure, an *n*-byte memory array is allocated. The FIFO property of the buffer is effected by controlling two pointers to the buffer. Data is placed in the buffer at the location pointed to by the **tail pointer** or **write pointer** and is removed from the buffer location pointed to by the **head pointer** or **read pointer**. These pointers are incremented modulo *n*, so that when a pointer points to the last location in the array, it will next point to the first location in the array.

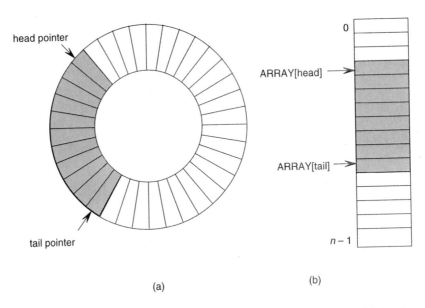

Figure 16.5-1   Circular memory buffer: (a) conceptual representation; (b) implementation using pointers.

The receive ISR, rx0isr, in Fig. 16.5-2, uses indexed addressing and index variable tail to maintain the tail pointer to the buffer CIRC_BUFF. The task that processes the data in the buffer uses a second index variable, HEAD, to maintain the head pointer. Variable nchars indicates the number of bytes in the buffer and is used to determine whether the buffer is empty or full. head, tail, and nchars are all initialized to 0 outside of RX0ISR.

rx0isr checks nchars to determine whether the buffer is full before it attempts to write a byte. If the buffer is not full, rx0isr writes the new byte into the buffer at index position tail. After rx0isr writes a byte to the buffer, it increments tail, modulo n, and increments nchars. Incrementing tail modulo n, when tail equals $n-1$, causes tail to be incremented from $n-1$ to 0. Thus, after a byte has been written to circ_buff[n-1], the next byte will be written to circ_buff[0], giving the buffer its circular characteristic.

The task that processes the data, disables the serial receiver interrupt, then checks whether nchars is nonzero to determine if data is available to be read. If there is no data to be read, the task reads a byte from the buffer at index head. After the task removes a byte from the buffer, it must increment head, modulo n, and decrement nchars. When the task has finished reading data from the buffer, it re-enables the serial receive interrupts.

16.6   RS-232 and Other Serial Communications Interfaces

Several physical-level serial communications standards and conventions find widespread use in embedded systems. **Physical-level standards** cover data and control signals, pin assignments, electrical characteristics, timing, and mechanical connectors. Many of the conventions in use are variants of the RS-232 standard.

```
;*************************************************************
;NAME:        rx0isr
;
;function:    ISR for channel 0 receive interrupt
;assumes:
;returns:     Received character in circ_buff
;modifies:    circ_buff, tail, chars
;
;DESCRIPTION: If CIRC_BUFF is not full, the byte received is written
;             to the buffer and index TAIL and byte counter NCHARS
;             are incremented. If the buffer is full, the received
;             byte is discarded and TAIL and NCHARS are not modified.
;
;*************************************************************

rx0isr  proc
        pusha                   ;save context
        mov     dx,S0RBUF       ;get received byte
        in      al,dx           ;mask out most significant bit
        and     al,07fh
        cmp     nchars,n        ;is n byte buffer full?
        je      er_bf           ;yes, discard byte
        mov     si,tail         ;no, put byte in buffer
        mov     circ_buff[si],al
        inc     si              ;increment index
        cmp     si,n            ;is index equal n?
        jne     new_tail;no
        xor     si,si           ;yes, set index to 0
new_tail:
        mov     tail,si         ;save index
        inc     nchars          ;increment bytes in buffer counter
er_bf:  mov     dx,EOI          ;clear interrupt's in-service bit
        mov     ax,8000h
        out     dx,ax
        popa                    ;restore context
        iret
rx0isr  endp
```

Figure 16.5-2   Receive ISR that places data in circular memory buffer.

16.6.1   RS-232 Standard

The formal name for the RS-232 standard is "Interface between Data Terminal Equipment and Data Circuit-Terminating Equipment Employing Serial Binary Data Interchange." The RS-232 standard concerns serial data transfer at relatively low speeds (up to 20 kbps) over relatively short distances (up to 50 feet). The standard includes definitions of the voltage levels to be used for data and control signals, the signal names, signal functions, and the assignment of signals to connector pins. Some of the parameters associated with this and other serial interface standards are listed in Table 16.6-1.

Table 16.6-1   Popular serial interface standards.

Parameter	RS-232	RS-423	RS-422	RS-485
Operation	single-ended	single-ended	differential	differential
Number of drivers allowed	1	1	1	32
Number of receivers allowed	1	10	10	32
Maximum cable length	50[a]	4000	4000	4000
Maximum data rate	20 kbits	100 kbits	10 Mbits	10 Mbits
Maximum common mode voltage	±25 V	±6 V	6 V	
Driver output	±5 V min ±15 V max	±3.6 V min ±6.0 V max	±2 V min	±1.5 V min
Driver load	3 to 7 kohm	450 min	100 ohm min	60 ohm min

a. Later versions of the standard eliminate the length limit and instead specify a maximum capacitance of 2,500 pF at the receiver.

The situation envisioned by the original version of the RS-232 standard, published in 1979, is the connection of a terminal to a modem in order to communicate with a remote computer over telephone lines (Fig. 16.6-1(a)). A **modem** is a circuit that consists of a modulator and a demodulator. A **modulator** uses serial logic levels to modulate either the frequency or phase of an analog signal that it transmits over telephone lines. On the receiver side, a **demodulator** converts the frequency or phase changes of the analog signal, back to serial logic levels. Modems are also referred to as **data sets**.

The terminal and computer, one at each far end of the connection, are both classified as **data terminal equipment** (**DTE**). The terminal is connected to the telephone line by a modem. On the other end of the phone line, the computer is also connected to the telephone line by a modem. The modems are both classified as **data circuit-terminating equipment** (**DCE**).

In practice, The RS-232 standard is often applied to serial data transfer applications other than those for which it was originally intended. For example, a peripheral device is connected to a PC's serial RS-232 port (Fig. 16.6-1(b)). Embedded systems are also often connected to a PC via one of the PC's RS-232 ports (Fig. 16.6-1(c)). Finally, two embedded systems may communicate with each other via an RS-232 interface (Fig. 16.6-1(d)).

The RS-232 standard includes the specification of a 25-pin connector and the assignment of signals and their functions to 22 of the 25 pins. The full set of signals are defined to support serial communications between data terminal equipment, and data circuit-terminating equipment. The standard includes recommended subsets of signals for specific data communications applications.

Although a PC may use a 25-pin D shell connector (DB-25), at most only 13 of the signals are used. PCs often use a 9-pin D shell connector (DB-9) and an assignment of sig-

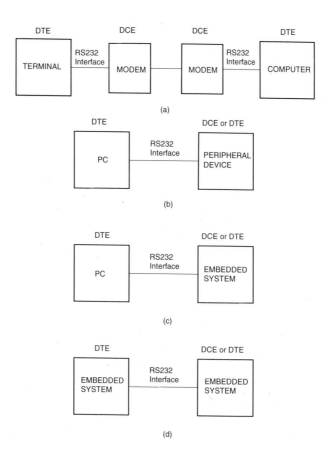

Figure 16.6-1   Common connections using the RS232 standard: (a) originally envisioned connection of a terminal to a printer over telephone lines; (b) connection of a peripheral device to a PC; (c) connection of an embedded system to a PC; (d) connection of two embedded systems.

nals to pin numbers that differ from the RS-232 standard. The signals often used by PCs and their assignments to the 25- and 9-pin connectors is shown in Table 16.6-2. These signals are named with respect to the DTE. For example, transmitted data (TD) is an output from the DTE, and received data (RD) is an input to the DTE.

In most respects, serial ports on PCs follow the RS-232 standard. The PC usually functions as the DTE and has a male connector. The peripheral device functions as a DCE and uses a female connector. This assignment of a male connector for the DTE and a female connector for the DCE is specified in revision E of the RS-232 standard.

In embedded systems, either of the previous sets of signals and assignments may be used, sometimes an even smaller subset may suffice. As few as three signals are sometimes used: transmitted data, received data, and signal ground.

Table 16.6-2   The nine RS-232 signals used by personal computers.

DB-9 pin number	DB-25 pin number	Input or output[a]	Description
1	8	Input	DCD Data Carrier Detect
2	3	Input	RX Receive Data
3	2	Output	TX Transmit Data
4	20	Output	DTR Data Terminal Ready
5	7		GND Signal Ground
6	6	Input	DSR Data Set Ready
7	4	Output	RTS Request to Send
8	5	Input	CTS Clear to Send
9	22	Input	RI Ring Indicator

a. Direction is with respect to DTE (personal computer)

16.6.2   RS-232 Modem Control Signals

RS-232 signals are either data, control, status, or ground signals. The control and status signals are usually referred to as modem control signals. Terms used to describe these signals relate to their intended use to control the interaction between a terminal and modem, as in Table 16.6-2. Most UARTs provide a few programmable input and output bits labeled with the names of the modem control signals. These bits can be used to control a modem. If they are not needed for that purpose, they can be used for general purpose I/O. These signals are also used to control the flow of serial data in applications where no modem is involved. Their use for flow control is described in Section 16.7.

16.6.3   RS-232 Voltage Levels

In some applications, it is primarily the voltage level requirements of the RS-232 standard that are followed. These voltage ranges are bipolar, involving both magnitude and polarity to represent logic levels. The valid output voltage ranges are −5 V to −15 V and +5 V to +15 V (Fig. 16.6-2). Data signals follow a negative logic convention. Logic 1 corresponds to the more negative voltage range. Therefore, a logic 1 data value is output as a −5 V to −15 V signal, and a logic 0 is output as a +5 V to +15 V signal. For control signals, positive logic is used.

RS-232 receiver inputs must accept voltages in the ranges −3 V to −25 V and +3 V to +25 V. The differences in the minimum output voltage and maximum input voltages provide a 2 V DC noise margin.

IC **line drivers** and **line receivers** are available that translate CMOS or TTL voltages to voltages compatible with the RS-232 standard. Usually, IC line drivers and receivers are inverters. For example, the MAXIM MAX233A provides two RS-232 transmitters and two receivers in a single 20-pin IC (Fig. 16.6-3). This CMOS IC requires only a +5 V supply and

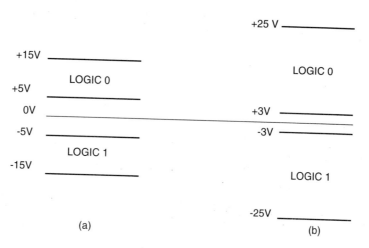

(a)

(b)

Figure 16.6-2   RS-232 negative logic levels defined for data: (a) driver output levels; (b) receiver input levels. In contrast, RS-232 control logic levels follow the postive logic convention, the logic 0 and 1 levels are interchanged.

contains an on-chip charge pump that generates +10 V and –10 V supplies from its single +5 V supply input. The drivers convert a TTL logic 1 input to a –9 V output and a TTL logic 0 input to +9 V output. The receivers convert a –3 V to –15 V input to a TTL logic 1 output, and a +3 V to +15 V input to TTL logic 0 output.

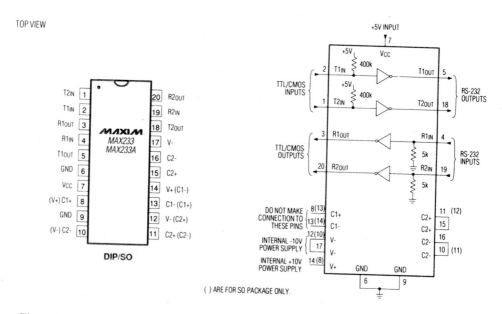

Figure 16.6-3   Maxim MAX233A RS-232 driver/receiver. (Courtesy Maxim Integrated Products, Inc.)

Because of the inversion provided by line drivers and receivers, control signals at a UART's modem control pins are the complement of what they are on an RS-232 line. For example, a UART would have an output pin labelled /RTS, which after inversion by a line driver produces the RS-232 control signal, RTS.

16.6.4   Other Serial Communications Interface Standards

Although RS-232 is most common, there are several other physical-level serial interface standards. Specifications for three other standards are included in Table 16.6-1. RS-423, like RS-232, is single ended (Fig. 16.6-4). **Single-end** or **unbalanced** means that each signal is a voltage on a single wire measured with respect to ground. The primary differences between RS-232 and RS-423 is that the RS-423 driver can drive 10 receivers, rather that just one. RS-423 can also transfer data faster and over a longer distance using smaller voltage levels.

Differential or **balanced** means that each signal is the difference between voltages on two different serial lines measured with respect to ground. RS-422 uses a differential connection and can drive 10 receivers (Fig. 16.6-4(b)).

RS-485 is also differential but allows multiple drivers, up to 32, and up to 32 receivers on a common pair of differential lines (Fig. 16.6-4(c)). RS-485 is used for applications where multiple microprocessors communicate over a single serial channel and is discussed in Section 16.9.

16.7   Flow Control

In many applications, the transmitter is capable of sending data faster than it can be accepted and processed by the receiver. Both transmitter and receiver are operating at the same baud rate, but either the processing required for each byte received or the existence of other higher priority tasks does not allow the receiver time to keep up. When the receiver cannot process the incoming data fast enough, an overrun error occurs and some of the incoming data is lost. Some mechanism must be provided to prevent overruns.

This section discusses software and hardware **flow control** protocols that implement handshaking to allow the receiver and the transmitter to cooperatively control the flow of data to prevent overruns.

16.7.1   Software Flow Control

The most common software flow control protocol is the **XON/XOFF protocol**. In this technique, the receiver sends the transmitter either of two ASCII control characters to start or stop the transfer of data. The character sent by the receiver to start a transfer is the **XON** character, ASCII character DC1 (11H). This character is also referred to as the **release character**. The character sent by the receiver to stop the transmitter from sending data is the **XOFF** character, control character DC3 (13H). This character is sometimes called the **holdoff** character.

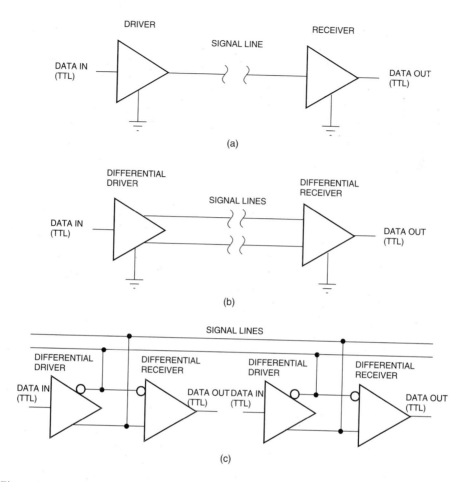

Figure 16.6-4   Line driver and receiver connections: (a) single-ended; (b) balanced differential (c) multidrop differential.

Transmitter software simply monitors the characters it receives. If XOFF is received, the transmitter stops sending characters until it receives a subsequent XON. If the receiver places the received characters into a memory buffer, it can check after each character is placed in the buffer whether or not the buffer is near full. If the buffer is near full, the receiver sends the transmitter the XOFF character. After some task has processed all, or an appropriate portion, of the data in the memory buffer, the task sends XON to continue the transmission of data.

16.7.2   Hardware Flow Control

A typical hardware flow control technique uses the Request To Send (RTS) and Clear To Send (CTS) RS-232 control lines in a nonstandard way. As envisioned by the standard, a DTE would assert RTS when it wishes to transmit data over the telephone lines. The DCE, a modem, would assert CTS when it was ready to receive data from the DTE. In half-duplex communication systems, the DCE interprets the assertion of RTS as a request to "turn the line around" from receive to transmit. Once it has turned the line around, the DCE asserts CTS, so the DTE can transmit the data. The DTR and DSR signals are often used as a pair in a similar fashion to implement handshaking.

For example, in an application where a PC is connected to a serial printer, the PC is the DTE and asserts RTS when it wishes to send data to the printer. When the printer asserts CTS, the PC starts sending data. If the printer's buffer is about to overflow, it will negate CTS. The PC will then suspend sending data until the printer again asserts CTS. An embedded system connected to a PC or another embedded system, can use this same technique for hardware flow control.

16.8 "PC Type" UARTs

Some applications require more than the two serial channels provided by the 80C188EB. In these situations, discrete UART ICs may be included in the system. Many UART ICs use, or are backward compatible with, a common register set used on the UART in the original IBM PC. This compatibility also extends to the UART function in highly integrated PC chip-sets used in later PCs. Consideration of "PC Type" UARTs is also important because embedded systems are often interfaced to a PC via its serial port.

The UART in the original IBM PC is National Semiconductor's **INS8250**. The popularity of the PC, coupled with the amount of software written to interact with the 8250, have caused many subsequent UART designs to utilize the 8250's register set or a superset thereof. National Semiconductor's series of register compatible UARTs includes the NS16450, NS16550AF and NS16C552. The 16450, a CMOS version, is faster than the 8250 and adds a scratchpad register. The 16550AF adds a 16-byte receive FIFO, a 16-byte transmit FIFO, and a DMA interface. The 16552 contains two independent UARTs, essentially two 16550AFs.

While these UARTs are register set compatible, there are differences among them, such as in technologies and packaging. 8250 compatible UARTs are also available from manufacturers other than National Semiconductor. For example, Intel's 82510 provides 8250 backward compatibility and has FIFOs.

16.8.1 "PC Type" UART Common Register Set

This subsection discusses, in a generic fashion, the common register set and operation of the types of UARTs used in PCs. For simplicity, "PC type" UARTs will simply be referred to as UARTs. Data sheets for the specific devices should be consulted for details. The UART's bus interface circuitry includes the usual address, data, and control signals for interfacing to a system bus. Serial data is output at the SOUT pin and input at the SIN pin (Fig. 16.8-1). Modem control inputs and outputs are also provided.

An external clock signal is required for operation. This signal can be provided by an external clock driving the XIN input, or the on-chip clock oscillator. The on-chip oscillator requires a crystal connected between pins XIN and XOUT.

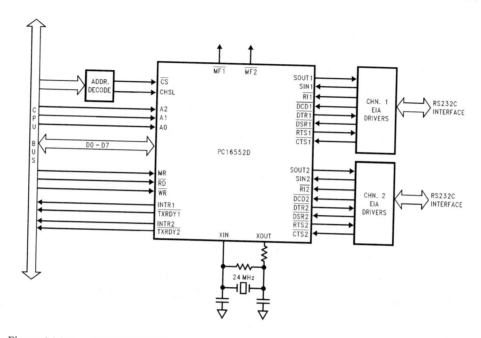

Figure 16.8-1   16C552 UART and its interface to the system bus and serial channels. (Courtesy of National Semiconductor Corporation.)

Once reset, the UART is configured for operation through its register set. There are eleven basic registers. These registers and their bit definitions are included in Table 16.8-1. This table provides the register definitions for a 16C552 UART, which is a superset of that of most PC type UARTs. All the registers are accessed using only 3 address bits and the state of the Divisor Latch Access Bit (DLAB), which is the most significant bit of the Line Control Register (LCR). A register is selected based on DLAB and the address at pins A2–A0.

An instruction sequence that initializes the UART must load the two divisor count registers, DLL and DLM, used by the internal baud rate generator to divide down the crystal frequency to produce a baud rate clock 16 times the desired baud rate.

$$\text{baud rate divisor} = \text{crystal frequency}/(16 \times \text{baud rate})$$

This clock is used internally to establish bit times and to accomplish center sampling for the receiver. To write DLL and DLM, the most significant bit of LCR, DLAB, must be set. As indicated in the rightmost columns of Table 16.8-1, when DLAB is set, writing to addresses 0 and 1 loads DLL and DLM, respectively. Setting or reading the baud rate divisor byte is the only time DLAB needs to be a 1.

LCR is then written with a byte with bit 7 equal to 0 to clear DLAB. The other bits of this byte establish the format of the frame to be transmitted and received. This determines the number of data bits (5 to 8), number of stop bits, and type of parity.

With DLAB cleared, writing addresses 0 and 1 writes the Transmit Holding Register (THR) and Interrupt Enable Register (IER) respectively.

Table 16.8-1 Register Summary for an Individual Channel.

Bit No.	0 DLAB=0 Receiver Buffer Register (Read Only) RBR	0 DLAB=0 Transmitter Holding Register (Write Only) THR	1 DLAB=0 Interrupt Enable Register IER	2 Interrupt Ident. Register (Read Only) IIR	2 FIFO Control Register (Write Only) FCR	3 Line Control Register LCR	4 MODEM Control Register MCR	5 Line Status Register LSR	6 MODEM Status Register MSR	7 Scratch Register SCR	0 DLAB=1 Divisor Latch (LS) DLL	1 DLAB=1 Divisor Latch (MS) DLM	2 DLAB1 Alternate Function Register AFR
0	Data Bit 0 (Note 1)	Data Bit 0	Enable Received Data Available Interrupt (ERDAI)	"0" if Interrupt Pending	FIFO Enable	Word Length Select Bit 0 (WLS0)	Data Terminal Ready (DTR)	Data Ready (DR)	Delta Clear to Send (DCTS)	Bit 0	Bit 0	Bit 8	Concurrent Write
1	Data Bit 1	Data Bit 1	Enable Transmitter Holding Register Empty Interrupt (ETHREI)	Interrupt ID Bit	RCVR FIFO Reset	Word Length Select Bit 1 (WLS1)	Request to Send (RTS)	Overrun Error (OE)	Delta Data Set Ready (DDSR)	Bit 1	Bit 1	Bit 9	$\overline{BAUDOUT}$ Select
2	Data Bit 2	Data Bit 2	Enable Receiver Line Status Interrupt (ELSI)	Interrupt ID Bit	XMIT FIFO Reset	Number of Stop Bits (STB)	Out 1 (Note 3)	Parity Error (PE)	Trailing Edge Ring Indicator (TERI)	Bit 2	Bit 2	Bit 10	$\overline{RXRDY}$ Select
3	Data Bit 3	Data Bit 3	Enable MODEM Status Interrupt (EMSI)	Interrupt ID Bit (Note 2)	DMA Mode Select	Parity Enable (PEN)	Out 2	Framing Error (FE)	Delta Data Carrier Detect (DDCD)	Bit 3	Bit 3	Bit 11	0
4	Data Bit 4	Data Bit 4	0	0	Reserved	Even Parity Select (EPS)	Loop	Break Interrupt (BI)	Clear to Send (CTS)	Bit 4	Bit 4	Bit 12	0
5	Data Bit 5	Data Bit 5	0	0	Reserved	Stick Parity	0	Transmitter Holding Register (THRE)	Data Set Ready (DSR)	Bit 5	Bit 5	Bit 13	0
6	Data Bit 6	Data Bit 6	0	FIFOs Enabled (Note 2)	RCVR Trigger (LSB)	Set Break	0	Transmitter Empty (TEMT)	Ring Indicator (RI)	Bit 6	Bit 6	Bit 14	0
7	Data Bit 7	Data Bit 7	0	FIFOs Enabled (Note 2)	RCVR Trigger (MSB)	Divisor Latch Access Bit (DLAB)	0	Error in RCVR FIFO (Note 2)	Data Carrier Detect (DCD)	Bit 7	Bit 7	Bit 15	0

Note 1: Bit 0 is the least significant bit. It is the first bit serially transmitted or received.
Note 2: These bits are always 0 in the 16450 Mode.
Note 3: This bit no longer has a pin associated with it.

Recall that after the baud rate divisor has been written, the DLAB bit in register LCR is cleared so that subsequently writing register 0 writes register THR, and writing register 1 writes IER.

The Line Status Register (LSR) holds the status of the serial communications link. When LSR is read, all of its bits are cleared. For serial transmission of data using polling, LSR is read and the TxD Empty bit, bit 5, is tested. If this bit is 1, the program can write the next byte to be transmitted to the Transmit Data register, TxD. Once a byte has been written to TxD, the UART can do other useful work. When several bytes are to be transmitted, the program must poll the UART to determine if it is ready to accept the next byte for transmission.

To receive data using polling, the LSR register is read and the Data Ready bit (DR) is tested. If this bit is 1, new data is available in the Receiver Buffer Register, RBR. When this bit is 1, other status bits in LSR indicate whether an overrun, parity, or framing error occurred when the frame was received.

A UART can be programmed so that its interrupt output (INT) is asserted whenever a new frame is received or when the UART can accept another byte for transmission. This signal can be used to interrupt an 80C188EB.

16.8.2   The 16C552 UART and Its FIFOs

The 16C552 contains two independent UARTs. This IC is often used on serial I/O expansion modules, such as PC/104 modules. The two UARTs share their system bus interface and external frequency source. Each UART has its own register set. The device's CHSL input pin is used to select which UART is referenced by the microprocessor.

For low baud rates, an 80C188EB can poll a UART to determine if a byte has been received or whether the UART can accept the next byte for transmission. To efficiently handle moderate baud rates, you need to make the interaction between the 80C188EB and UART interrupt driven. For high baud rates, even interrupt driven transfers between an 80C188EB and a UART with double buffering may not be adequate.

The problem is most critical on the receiver side. When a frame is received, the UART generates an interrupt. The 80C188EB must respond to the interrupt and read and store the received byte in one frame time, or the next byte received may cause an overrun error. At 19.2 kbaud one frame time amounts to only 520 µs. In some applications, the 80C188EB may not be able to immediately respond to the interrupt, perhaps because a higher priority interrupt is being processed.

The 16C552 provides a solution to this problem. The concept of double buffering is extended by replacing the single receive register with a receive FIFO buffer, RCVR FIFO, and replacing the transmit register with a transmit FIFO buffer, XMIT FIFO. The receive shift register transfers each byte received into the 16-byte RCVR FIFO. The FIFOs can be configured for polled or interrupt operation. The 16C552 can be programmed so that it generates an interrupt only after either 1, 4, 8, or 14 bytes have been received. This programmable **FIFO interrupt trigger level** means that the 80C188EB has to respond to fewer UART interrupts to handle the same number of bytes. In the best case, the 80C188EB would only have to execute an interrupt procedure 1/16th as often. Once an interrupt has occurred, the UART can still receive bytes without an overrun error until the FIFO is filled.

To keep the interrupt rate low, a high trigger level is programmed. A low trigger level is used when the microprocessor cannot quickly respond to an interrupt. The microprocessor may not be able to quickly respond to an interrupt due to higher priority interrupts or to a slow system clock speed.

The RCVR FIFO is designed to handle the case where the number of bytes received is less than the trigger level. This situation is handled by a time-out interrupt. The interrupt is activated when there is at least one byte in the RCVR FIFO and neither the microprocessor nor the receiver shift register has accessed the RCVR FIFO within four frame times of the last frame received.

In addition to holding 16 bytes of received data, the RCVR FIFO also holds 3 bits of error data per byte.

The XMIT FIFO buffer allows an 80C188EB to transfer as many as 16 bytes to the UART in response to a single interrupt. After a byte has been loaded into the empty XMIT FIFO, the UART waits one frame time before issuing a Tx FIF0 empty interrupt request. If two or more bytes were loaded into the XMIT FIFO at once, an interrupt request is generated immediately upon the XMIT FIFO becoming empty.

Programming the 16C552 to enable the FIFOs and set the receive FIFO trigger level is done by writing a control byte to the FIFO control register (FCR) Bits 7 and 6 select the trigger level, and bit 0 enables the FIFO buffers.

16.9   SCU Asynchronous Serial Transfer for Multiprocessor Systems

One method of coping with the complexity and speed requirements of a complex system is to allocate or distribute the system's tasks to multiple microprocessors. This task allocation can be done in various ways. The simplest scheme is to have each microprocessor responsible for executing a fixed set of tasks, with one microprocessor, the **master**, responsible for the overall coordination of the system. The other microprocessors, the **slaves**, carry out their tasks in response to commands from the master and report results back to the master.

Communications between the master and slave microprocessors can be in serial over a single serial bus. SCU **modes 2** and **3** can be used together to implement serial communications for a master/slave multi-microprocessor system (Fig. 16.9-1). Several microcontroller families have integral UARTs that can function in modes equivalent to the 80C188EB SCU's modes 2 and 3. Intel's 8051 family (including many of its derivatives) and 80196 family are examples. Therefore, a serial multiprocessor system may have a mix of microprocessor types.

In Fig. 16.9-1, the single master transmit line is driven by the master microprocessor's TXD pin and is used by the master to transmit to the slaves. Each slave's RXD input is connected to this line. Each slave's TXD line is connected through a three-state buffer to the master's receive line, RXD. Each slave controls the three-state buffer between its TXD pin and the master receive line using one of its port pins.

Modes 2 and 3 both have nine data bits resulting in an 11-bit frame. For transmission, the ninth bit is bit TB8 in the SxCON register. In multiprocessor applications, this bit must be set or cleared to specify the ninth data bit for each frame to be transmitted. In other applications, this bit can be left at 0, which is its value after the 80C188EB is reset, or it can be selected to be replaced by the parity bit. Transmission in modes 2 and 3 is identical.

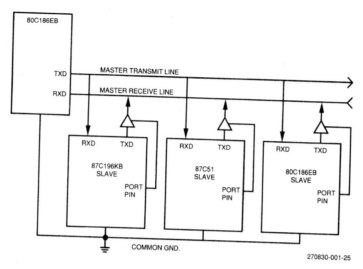

Figure 16.9-1   Serially interconnected multimicroprocessor system. (Courtesy of Intel Corp.)

Reception in modes 2 and 3 differs. In mode 2, reception will not complete unless bit 9 of the data frame is a 1. Any data received with bit 9 cleared is completely ignored. No flags are set, no interrupts generated, and no data is transmitted to the receive buffer. In contrast, reception in mode 3 completes regardless of the value of bit 9.

The master always operates in mode 3. The slaves are all initialized to receive in mode 2. Two types of data transfer occur:

1. A global command transfer from the master to all the slaves.
2. A bidirectional data transfer between the master and a selected slave.

When the master wants to broadcast a command byte to all of the slaves, the master transmits a frame with the ninth data bit a 1. All the slaves, operating in mode 2, receive and respond to the command. The lower 8 bits of this frame are the command. Commands can be used to cause all the slaves to carry out some operation or to enter a particular operational mode.

In order to transfer data to or from a single slave, the master sends an address command to all the slaves. This address command has the ninth data bit set so that all of the slaves receive and respond to the command. As its response, each slave compares the address field in the command to an address permanently assigned to the slave. If the addresses are equal, the slave knows it has been selected and writes its SxCON register to change its mode of operation to mode 3. The selected slave also enables the three-state buffer that connects it to the master's receive line.

The master and selected slave then communicate normally, both operating in mode 3. Each frame transmitted by the master during this communication is sent with the ninth bit a 0 so that the none of the other slaves are interrupted. Because the other slaves are not interrupted for each byte transferred from the master to the selected slave, processing of their other tasks is not negatively impacted.

When the transfer of data between the master and the selected slave is complete, the slave turns off its three-state buffer and places itself back in mode 2.

The buffering scheme in Fig. 16.9-1 is adequate as long as the microprocessors are in very close physical proximity. When the microprocessors are separated by some distance, buffering of the communication lines is necessary, similar to the case of a single microprocessor and I/O device using RS-232 drivers and receivers. The connection in Fig. 16.9-1 is referred to as a **multidrop** connection. RS-232 buffers cannot be used for multidrop connections because they don't have three-state output capability.

An RS-485 transceiver that can be used for this purpose is shown in Fig. 16.9-2. This transceiver's control inputs, Drive Enable (DE) and /Receive Enable (/RE) as well as its Data Input (DI) and Receive Data Output (RO) are CMOS and TTL compatible. On the RS-485 side the connection is differential. The information is carried in the voltage between lines B and A.

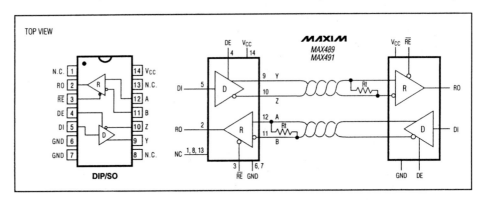

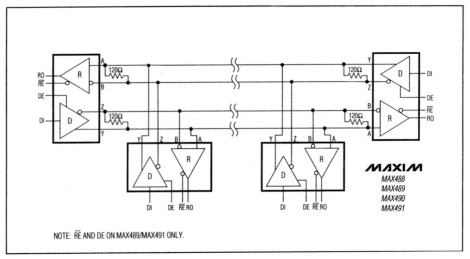

Figure 16.9-2   RS485 transceiver. (Courtesy of Maxim Integrated Products, Inc.)

16.10   Synchronous Serial Data Transfer

There are two common kinds of synchronous serial data transfer, one related to data communications and the other to serial peripheral ICs. In data communications, synchronous serial transfers are self clocking, and have no shared clock signal. In **self-clocking synchronous transmission**, one frame is sent immediately after the other, Fig. 16.10-1. Frames do not have start and stop bits for synchronization. Whenever another data character is not immediately ready for transmission, the transmitter repeatedly sends a special SYNC character until it can transmit the next data character.

The transmitter and receiver have independent clocks, but the receiver's clock is synchronized to the received signal's transitions. Since start and stop bits are not required, this approach has low overhead and is typically used for transferring large blocks of data at high speeds. Since this form of synchronous serial transfer is not prevalent in embedded systems, it is not considered further in this text.

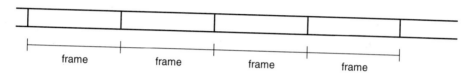

frame   frame   frame   frame

Figure 16.10-1   Self-clocking synchronous serial transfer. Frames sent without start or stop bits.

The second kind of synchronous serial transfer is commonly used with serial peripheral ICs. A separate line is used to carry a common clock signal used by the transmitter and receiver for synchronization (Fig. 16.10-2). This form of synchronous serial transfer is important in embedded systems. In some versions of this scheme, the clock signal is generated by the transmitter, and in others it is generated by the receiver.

16.10.1   Clocked Synchronous Serial Peripheral ICs

Clocked synchronous serial transfer is often used for transfers between a microprocessor and ICs with serial interfaces. The distances over which the data is transferred is usually very short. Typically, the serial peripheral ICs are on the same printed circuit board as the microprocessor.

There are several different protocols available for clocked synchronous serial transfer. These interfaces typically involve two or three wires and may be simplex or half-duplex channels. In a **two-wire scheme** (Fig. 16.10-2(a)), one wire is the serial clock, which defines the bit times, and the other is the serial data. The third wire for signal ground is not included in the count. Nor is any possible chip-select signal counted. If the serial peripheral is the receiver and provides the clock, it is said to be **self-clocked** or **internally clocked**. If the clock is provided by the transmitter, the receiver is said to be **externally clocked**. Two-wire schemes can also provide bidirectional data transfer. In such cases, the single data line is half-duplex.

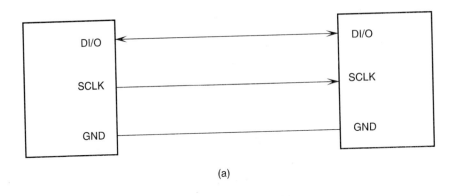

(a)

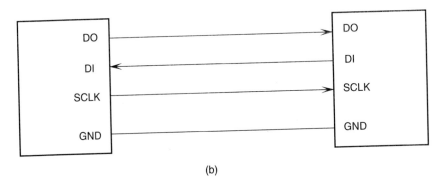

(b)

Figure 16.10-2 Synchronous serial transfer with a common clock: (a) 2-wire scheme; (b) 3-wire scheme.

A **three-wire** scheme has two data lines and the serial clock (Fig. 16.10-2(b)). However, data transfer usually occurs in only one direction at a time.

Examples of clocked synchronous serial transfers are given in Chapters 17 and 18 for DACs and ADCs.

16.11   Clocked Synchronous Transfers Using the SCU

The SCU's synchronous **mode 0** is used to interface two-wire externally clocked serial peripherals. In mode 0, the TXD pin provides the synchronizing serial clock for both transmission and reception (Fig. 16.11-1). The RXD pin is used in a half-duplex fashion for both transmitting and receiving data. Data is transmitted and received in eight-bit frames, there is no start, parity, or stop bit in a frame.

A byte is transmitted in mode 0 by writing it to SxTBUF. This data is shifted out, least significant bit first, on the RXD pin. The receiving circuit must sample the data on the rising edge of the synchronizing clock provided on the TXD pin. When the transmission is

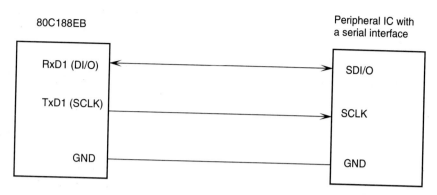

Figure 16.11-1   Synchronous serial 2-wire transfer using mode 0 of serial channel 1 of an 80C188EB.

complete, the TI request bit in SxSTS is set. The RXD (data) pin then goes to its high-impedance state. The TXD (clock) pin remains in the 1 state between transmissions.

To receive a byte, the receiver enable bit (REN) must be set and the receiver interrupt request bit (RI) must be cleared. These actions "turn the line around." When these conditions are met, eight clock pulses are automatically generated at the TXD (clock) pin. Each time the signal at TXD goes low, the circuit that is providing the data must drive RXD with the input data bit, least significant bit first. The received data is sampled by the SCU just prior to the rising edge of TXD. The device driving the RXD pin must adhere to the 80C188EB's setup and hold times for TXD. When the eighth bit is received, the receive interrupt request (RI) bit is set and the input byte is transferred to the low byte of SxRBUF.

16.12   Summary

Serial data transfer is common in embedded systems and may be either asynchronous or synchronous. The serialization and deserialization of data can be done in either software or hardware. A software approach is only appropriate in systems without significant time constraints.

For most practical systems, serialization and deserialization are handled by hardware. For asynchronous transfers, the hardware used for this purpose is called a UART. UARTs are available as discrete ICs and integrated onto microprocessors or multifunction support ICs.

The 80C188EB provides two independent serial channels in its integrated Serial Communications Unit (SCU). These channels can be configured for any of four asynchronous modes of operation or a single synchronous mode. When configured for asynchronous operation in mode 1, an SCU channel provides the functions of a typical UART.

Asynchronous modes 2 and 3 when used together provide a structure for serial data transfer between a master microprocessor and multiple slave microprocessors over a single pair of signal lines.

When asynchronous applications require more than the two serial channels provided by the 80C188EB, discrete UARTs can be added to the system. Most discrete UARTs have register sets compatible with the 8250 UART used in early PCs. Some of the more advanced UARTs provide FIFO receive and transmit buffers to minimize the rate at which the microprocessor must respond to the UART.

The 80C188EB's serial channels and PC-type UARTs can be operated in either a polled or interrupt driven mode. When data rates are high, interrupt driven operation is often essential.

For many low and medium complexity embedded systems, serial synchronous transfer is used for interfacing to synchronous serial IC peripheral devices.

In addition to the serialization and deserialization required for serial data transfer, the communications channel's electrical requirements must also be considered. For standards like RS-232, the voltage levels are neither TTL nor CMOS compatible. Driver and receiver ICs that translate between TTL or CMOS levels and the levels required for the standard are readily available.

Finally, some method of flow control may need to be provided to keep the transmitter from sending bytes faster than they can be processed by the receiver. One common software flow control protocol has the receiver send the transmitter the ASCII character XOFF to stop the transmitter from sending data and to send the character XON to have the transmitter resume sending data. One common hardware flow control approach uses the modem control signals RTS and CTS to provide handshaking for flow control.

16.13   Problems

1. What are the hexadecimal values of the ASCII control codes for:

    a. carriage return, CR

    b. line feed, LF

    c. horizontal tab, HT

    d. escape, ESC

2. What are the bit times for data transferred at the following rates:

    a. 4800 baud

    b. 14.4 kbaud

    c. 38.4 kbaud

    d. 115 kbaud

3. Draw the 10-bit frame for the asynchronous transfer of the following ASCII characters with even parity.

    a. a

    b. A

    c. 7

    d. CR (carriage return)

4. Write a serial transmit procedure, serial_out, that transmits a 10-bit frame containing an ASCII character at 9600 baud with even parity. The hardware consists of a 1-bit output port connected to D0 with I/O address XMIT. When the procedure is called, the ASCII character is in AL. Assume that a delay procedure, one_bit_time, is available to delay one bit time.

5. Repeat the previous problem but use bit P1.7 of the 80C188EB instead of a separate output port.

6. Write a serial receive procedure, serial_in, that receives a 10-bit frame with even parity. The procedure returns the ASCII character in AL, with CF set if there is a parity error. Assume that two delay procedures are available, half_bit_time and one_bit_time.

7. Repeat the previous problem but use P1.6

8. Modify the previous procedure to set CF if there is a parity error (PE), framing error (FE), or overrun error (OE). Use AH to return bits indicating the specific errors, bit 2—PE, bit 1—FE, and bit 0—OE.

9. Define double buffering and explain its advantage with regard to a UART's transmitter and receiver.

10. What is the purpose of a UART generating an interrupt after the completion of the transmission of a frame?

11. How many different modes of operation are available for the 80C188EB's serial channels? Of these, how many are asynchronous modes and how many are synchronous?

12. Determine the value for B0CMP for a baud rate of 19.2 kbaud using a 20 MHz 80C188EB. What, if any, is the error in the resultant baud rate clock?

13. Draw the connections required to have channel 1 cause an INT4 interrupt upon the receipt or transmission of a frame. Modify Fig. 16.4-1 to be the initialization procedure for channel 1 using INT4. Assume that the 80C188EB operates at 16 MHz and that the desired baud rate is 4800 baud.

17

ANALOG DATA AND
ANALOG OUTPUT SUBSYSTEMS

17.1   Analog Data and Analog I/O Subsystems

17.2   Digital-to-Analog Converters (DACs)

17.3   DAC to System Bus Interface

17.4   Basic DAC Circuits

17.5   Loading and Impedance Considerations

17.6   Operational Amplifiers

17.7   Analog Demultiplexers

17.8   Track-Holds

17.9   Digital Potentiometers

17.10   Summary

Input and output subsystems presented in previous chapters processed digital, or discrete, signals. Many applications require monitoring or control of physical quantities such as temperature, position, or pressure.

For instrumentation applications, monitoring, or measuring, such signals is the primary goal. The quantity being measured is referred to as the **measurand**. Signals associated with physical measurands are analog, or continuous, signals. For each physical measurand a transducer is required that generates an electrical signal that varies in proportion to the measurand. Such a signal is called an analog signal.

For an analog signal to be input to an embedded system, an analog input subsystem is required. An analog input subsystem converts an analog signal to a digital number. This number can then be input by the microprocessor and processed.

Control applications can be broadly characterized as either open loop or closed loop. In an open loop control application, a setpoint value, entered by a user or computed by the system, must be converted to an analog signal to control a process. This requires an analog output subsystem. The analog output signal is transformed by an output transducer to some other form of energy.

In a closed loop control application, the value of the physical measurand to be controlled must first be measured before it can be controlled. A closed loop control system requires both an analog input subsystem and an analog output subsystem. A signal from the measurand's transducer is fed back and compared to the setpoint value to control the process.

An understanding of analog input and analog output subsystems and the circuits commonly used to construct them is crucial for many embedded system designs. Analog-to-digital converters and digital-to-analog converters provide the fundamental interface between analog and digital signals. Other circuits used in analog input and output subsystems include operational amplifiers (op-amps), filters, track-holds, analog multiplexers, and analog demultiplexers.

After providing a brief overview of analog data and analog input and output subsystems, this chapter focuses on the design of analog output subsystems. Chapter 18 focuses on analog input subsystems and their associated circuits. Analog output subsystems are treated first, because the key component in an analog output subsystem, a digital-to-analog converter, is sometimes used to build the key component in an analog input subsystem, the analog-to-digital converter.

17.1   Analog Data and Analog I/O Subsystems

Analog data is data that can have any one of an infinite number of values within some range. In electronic systems, analog data is represented by analog signals. At any time, an **analog signal** has one of a continuous set of values in a restricted range. Except for limitations imposed by electrical noise, the resolution of an analog signal is infinite.

Like all electrical signals, an analog signal is characterized by a pair of variables, voltage and current. The information in an analog signal is associated with one or the other of these two variables. Most commonly, but certainly not exclusively, the voltage carries the information. For simplicity, we will usually assume that the information is represented by a signal's voltage. In Section 17.6, a circuit that converts an information-carrying current to a voltage is presented.

The exact voltage at a given time is important because this value represents the information embodied in the signal. For example, Motorola's **MPX4115 Altimeter/Barometer Absolute Pressure Sensor** generates an output voltage that ranges from 0.2 V to 4.8 V. This voltage is directly proportional to pressures that range from 15 to 115 kPa. Reading a voltage of 2.0 V from this sensor corresponds to a pressure of 54 kPa. One kiloPascal (kPa) equals 0.145 pounds per square inch (PSI).

17.1.1   Analog Input and Analog Output Subsystems

Figure 17.1-1(a) shows a block diagram of an **analog input subsystem.** The input to the analog input subsystem comes from an analog input device. The analog input device is usually an input transducer, or sensor, that converts some form of energy, such as heat, pressure, position, or light, into an analog voltage or current.

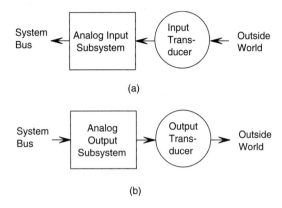

Figure 17.1-1   Analog I/O subsystems: (a) analog input device or input transducer provides analog input signal to analog input subsystem; (b) analog output subsystem provides analog signal to output device or output transducer.

For almost every type of physical measurand, numerous input transducers exist. A few transducers directly generate a digital output, like the optical shaft encoder of Chapter 15, which transforms angular position to digital output pulses. However, we are now interested in input transducers that generate an analog output. An analog input subsystem must convert the transducer's analog output voltage into a digital number or code so that it can be read by the microprocessor.

The task of an **analog output subsystem** is just the opposite of that of an analog input subsystem (Fig. 17.1-1(b)). A digital number or code is converted to an analog voltage or current. A system may need to generate output data in analog form to provide analog control signals, drive analog output transducers, or to synthesize analog waveforms. An analog output device is often called an **output transducer** or **actuator**. The output transducer changes the analog voltage to some other form of energy, for example mechanical position, rotation, pressure, or light.

17.1.2   Components of an Analog Output Subsystem

An analog output subsystem is typically comprised of the components shown in Fig. 17.1-2.

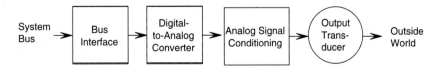

Figure 17.1-2   Single channel analog output subsystem.

The bus interface allows the microprocessor to write a digital value to the digital-to-analog converter. The **digital-to-analog converter** (**DAC**) converts digital data from the system bus to a piecewise continuous analog output. At the DAC's output, analog signal conditioning is often necessary to amplify, filter, buffer, or scale the analog voltage to the output transducer. Since a single analog output is generated in Fig. 17.1-2, this subsystem is referred to as a **single channel** analog output subsystem.

A **multichannel** analog output subsystem, sometimes called a **data distribution system,** provides several independent analog outputs. A separate DAC can be used to produce each output, creating a **DAC per channel** multichannel subsystem. However, an alternative approach using a demultiplexer can generate multiple analog outputs by time multiplexing a single DAC. The single DAC is followed by an analog demultiplexer with a separate track-hold for each output (Fig. 17.1-3). The **analog demultiplexer** is a digitally controlled analog switch that routes the DAC's output to the selected track-hold.

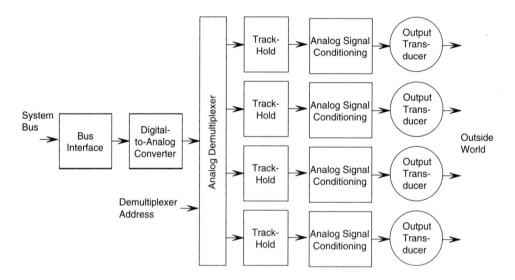

Figure 17.1-3   Multichannel multiplexed analog output subsystem.

When in its **track mode**, a **track-hold** (or **sample-hold**) circuit's output tracks (follows) its analog input. This mode is used to acquire a new output value. When switched to hold mode, the track-hold holds (latches) its analog input's value at the instant the track-hold was switched to hold mode.

In the following sections, each of the components in Fig. 17.1-2 and 17.1-3 is examined in detail, starting with the DAC.

17.2   Digital-to-Analog Converters (DACs)

A DAC, or D/A, accepts n-bits as input and provides an analog current or voltage as output (Fig. 17.2-1). A DAC's output is usually a linear function of its digital input. DAC's exist that have an intentionally nonlinear output function. These types of DACs are less common and are not of interest in this text. The DAC in Fig. 17.2-1 accepts parallel input data. Serial DACs require that their input data be serially shifted into the DAC.

Figure 17.2-1   Digital-to-analog converter (DAC).

A simple DAC consisting of a register, a DAC circuit, a voltage reference, and an op-amp current-to-voltage converter is shown in Fig. 17.2-2. Op-amps are discussed further in Section 17.6. The register holds the digital input to the DAC circuit, allowing the DAC to be interfaced to the system bus. The term DAC is generally used to refer to both the DAC circuit that accomplishes digital to analog conversion and to the larger conversion subsystem that includes this circuit. In this text, the expression DAC circuit is used to distinguish it from the larger subsystem, when this distinction is important.

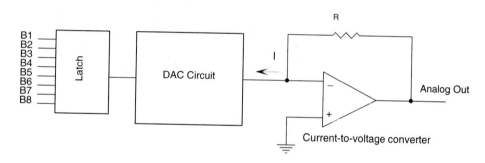

Figure 17.2-2   Digital to analog converter (DAC).

The **DAC circuit** consists of electronic analog switches and a network of either precision resistors or capacitors. Each bit of the digital input controls one or more switches. The switches in turn control currents or voltages derived from the reference voltage. The result is an output current or voltage that is proportional to the input code.

The voltage reference and current-to-voltage converter may or may not be included on a DAC IC. If not, an external voltage reference and an external op-amp are used.

The output of an ideal (error free) DAC that accepts an n-bit straight binary code is:

$$V_O = V_{REF} \times (B_1 2^{-1} + B_2 2^{-2} + \ldots + B_n 2^{-n})$$

where B_1 is the most significant bit, and B_n the least significant bit of the binary input. The DAC's output voltage is the product of the reference voltage and the binary fraction

$0.B_1B_2...B_n$. Some DACs require V_{REF} to be a constant value for the equation to be valid. Some DACs have a negative output voltage. The sign of the output voltage is a function of the type of DAC circuit and the polarity of the voltage reference.

Multiplying DACs are DACs for which the previous equation is valid even if V_{REF} varies from 0 to full scale. The output of a multiplying DAC is the product of two variables, the digital input and the analog voltage reference.

17.2.1   Ideal DACs

An error-free DAC is referred to as being ideal. The transfer function of an ideal 3-bit DAC with a straight binary input code is shown in Fig. 17.2-3. The **transfer function** plots the circuit's output versus its input. The analog output is not continuous, but has one of eight possible values corresponding to the eight possible 3-bit input codes. In general, an *n*-bit DAC with a fixed reference voltage can have only 2^n possible output values. Thus, using a DAC you can only approximate a desired analog value by using the DAC's closest discrete output value.

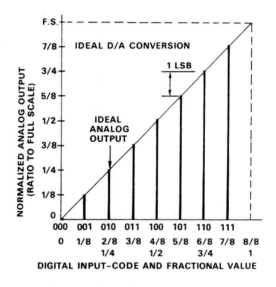

Figure 17.2-3   Conversion relationship for an ideal 3-bit straight binary D/A converter. (Courtesy of Analog Devices, Inc.)

The DAC's binary inputs are written as numbers that range from 000 through 111. Although a binary point is not written, these numbers actually represent eight fractions from 0.000 through 0.111 (from 0 through the maximum).

An ideal DAC's maximum output voltage is

$$V_{OMAX} = V_{REF} \times (1 - 2^{-n})$$

For $n = 3$, the maximum output is 7/8 of the **nominal full scale (FS)**, or **full scale range (FSR)** output. If a 3-bit DAC has a FS value of 10 V, the actual maximum output is 8.75 V. Table 17.2-1 gives some output voltages for an 8-bit, 10 V FS DAC as a function of its binary input.

Table 17.2-1   Output vs. binary coding for a +10 V FS 8-bit unipolar DAC.

Binary	Scale	V_{OUT}
00000000	0	0.00
00000001	+1 lsb	+0.04
00100000	+1/8 FS	+1.25
01000000	+1/4 FS	+2.50
10000000	+1/2 FS	+5.0
11000000	+3/4 FS	+7.50
11111111	+FS − 1 lsb	+9.96

The size of the change at a DAC's output for a one least significant bit (1 lsb) change in its input code is called a **step** and equals $FS/2^n$. For a 3-bit, 0 to 10 V DAC, the step size is $10/2^3$, or 1.25 V.

IC DACs with 8- to 16-bit inputs are common. The determination of the required size (number of bits) for a DAC is a function of the application. DACs with a larger number of bits have a correspondingly reduced step size. A DAC with an 8-bit straight binary input code has 256 distinct output values, one for each possible input code. The step size for an 8-bit 10 V FS DAC is 39.06 mV.

Table 17.2-2 shows the resolution of a DAC with a straight binary input as a function of the number of input bits. **Resolution** is the measure of the output step size relative to FS and equals $1/2^n$. Resolution is also a measure of a DAC's precision and is expressed in bits or as a percentage. An 8-bit binary DAC has a resolution of 1 part in 256 or 0.3906 percent or 3906 ppm (parts per million).

Consider an application where a system must generate an analog control voltage that ranges from 0 to +5 V. This control voltage is used to set a high-voltage power supply's output voltage within the range of 0 to 10,000 V. If it is necessary to cause changes as small as 1 V in the high-voltage power supply's output, a DAC with 14 or more bits is required. A 14-bit DAC provides a resolution of 1 part in 2^{14}, or 1 part in 16,384. With this resolution you can cause the high-voltage power supply's output to change 0.6 V (10,000/16,384) for a 1 lsb change at the DAC's input. A 13-bit DAC has a resolution of only 1 part in 8,192. A 1 lsb input change for a 13-bit DAC would change the output of the high-voltage power supply by 1.2 V.

Table 17.2-2   Number of output values and resolution as a function of the number of bits for a binary DAC.

Bits	Output values	Resolution			
		Percentage	PPM	dB	millivolts (for 10 V FS
1	2	50	500,000	−6	5000 mV
6	64	1.6	15,625	−36	156 mV
8	256	0.4	3,906	−48	39.1 mV
10	1,024	0.1	977	−60	9.77 mV
12	4,906	0.024	244	−72	2.44 mV
16	65,536	0.0015	15	−96	0.153 mV
20	1,048,576	0.0001	1	−120	0.00954 mV
24	16,777,216	0.000006	0.06	−144	0.000596 mV

17.2.2   Practical DACs

Accuracy is a measure of the error in a DAC's analog output. A specification of absolute accuracy must be traceable to an international standard. For this reason, relative accuracy is used instead. **Relative accuracy** is the deviation of a DAC's output from a straight line drawn through the endpoints of the DAC's transfer function. This error is specified relative to FS in fractions of a lsb, as a percent, or in ppm.

The value normally referred to as *accuracy* is actually an *inaccuracy*, or error. For example, a device referred to as "having an accuracy of 1 percent" is, in fact, 99 percent accurate. "Accurate to within 1 percent," is a clearer statement.

Many DAC data sheets do not give an overall accuracy specification. Instead, values are given for the constituent errors that contribute to the DAC's inaccuracy. These constituent errors are specified as static or dynamic parameters. The static or DC parameters are offset error, gain error, integral nonlinearity error, and differential nonlinearity error. These errors are most important in applications where the data rates are low and the exact timing of conversions is unimportant. This is the case in most measurement and control applications.

The DAC's output equation written to include offset and gain error is:

$$V_O = G \times V_{REF} \times (B_1 2^{-1} + B_2 2^{-2} + \ldots + B_n 2^{-n}) + V_{OS}$$

where G is the gain error and V_{OS} is the offset error. For an ideal DAC, $G = 1$ and $V_{OS} = 0$.

Offset error corresponds to an offset, or vertical shift, of the DAC's transfer characteristic from its ideal position (Fig. 17.2-4(a)). An offset error affects each output voltage by the same fixed amount. It is often measured as the actual output of the DAC when the code for zero output is applied.

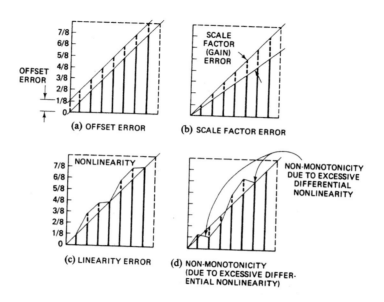

Figure 17.2-4   Typical sources of error for a 3-bit DAC. (Courtesy of Analog Devices, Inc.)

Gain error, or **scale error**, is the error in the slope of the DAC's transfer characteristic (Fig. 17.2-4(b)). Gain error is often measured as the departure of the actual output from the ideal output for the code that produces the maximum output.

Some DACs can be calibrated by adjusting external trim resistors so that their offset error and gain error are zero at room temperature. A DAC is calibrated for offset by applying the zero input code and adjusting an external offset trim resistor to produce an analog output of 0 V.

To eliminate gain error, the offset error is first zeroed, then the full-scale digital input is applied and an external gain trim resistor is adjusted to give an output voltage of FS − 1 lsb. Many DACs are laser trimmed during manufacture and do not require or provide connections for external trim.

A calibration operation to eliminate offset and gain errors is only valid for the temperature at which the calibration is performed. Changes in temperature cause offset and gain errors referred to as **offset drift** and **gain drift**, respectively. Offset drift and gain drift specified in parts per million per degree centigrade (ppm/ degree C) indicate the sensitivity of a DAC to changes in temperature.

The other sources of error in a DAC cannot be trimmed to zero. **Endpoint linearity**, or **integral nonlinearity** (**INL**), specifies the maximum deviation of the DAC's output from a straight line drawn through the end points of its transfer function. This specification is a major indicator of a DAC's performance (Fig. 17.2-4(c)). Endpoint linearity, integral linearity, **integral nonlinearity**, and **relative accuracy** are different terms that mean the same thing.

Differential nonlinearity (**DNL**) is the difference between the actual voltage step size for any two adjacent DAC input codes and the ideal 1 lsb step size (Fig. 17.2-4(d)). Differential nonlinearity is a measure of the smoothness of the DAC's output curve. A curve is monotonic if there is no change in the sign of its slope. For a DAC to be **monotonic**, each step must be greater than or equal to zero. A differential nonlinearity specification of less than or equal to ±1 lsb guarantees monotonicity.

A DNL of −1 means that the step size in going from at least one input code to its adjacent input code is 0. If the DNL is more negative than −1 lsb, then there is at least one case where the output in going from one input code to the next higher code decreases. When this is the case, the DAC is nonmonotonic. Monotonicity is especially important if a DAC's output is used as a control signal in a closed loop (feedback) control system. Non-monotonicity can change negative feedback to positive feedback.

The output of an "actual" 2-bit DAC is shown in Fig. 17.2-5. The dashed line represents a straight line through the outputs for the ideal (error free) DAC. The solid line represents a line connecting the measured outputs of an "actual" 2-bit DAC.

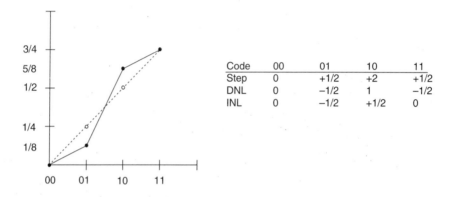

Code	00	01	10	11
Step	0	+1/2	+2	+1/2
DNL	0	−1/2	1	−1/2
INL	0	−1/2	+1/2	0

Figure 17.2-5   Comparison of transfer characteristics for an ideal 2-bit DAC and an "actual" 2-bit DAC.

The first row of the table in Fig. 17.2-5 gives the size in lsbs of the output step in going from one input code to the next adjacent code. The second row gives the DNL at each input code. The DNL value for a given input code is simply the step size (to that input code) −1 lsb. The third row gives the INL. The INL value for each input code is the sum (integral) of the DNLs up to and including the DNL for that code.

The previous specifications all concern static performance. Other DAC specifications relate to dynamic, or AC, performance. Dynamic specifications are critical in applications where a signal is constructed or reconstructed from digital data. **Latency** is the time required, after an input code change, for the output to settle to within a specified band of the final value (Fig. 17.2-6). This band is usually ±1/2 lsb. Latency is primarily a function of the type of switches, resistors, and output amplifier used in the DAC circuit.

Settling time is the time that elapses from the point at which the output *begins to change* to the point when the output settles to within a specified band of its final value. Settling time excludes the delay from the time the input code changes to the time the output starts to change. This time is included in the latency specification.

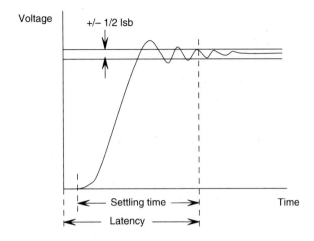

Figure 17.2-6   Settling time and latency for a DAC.

A major contributor to the settling time of a DAC circuit is the presence of glitches. During a glitch, the output is driven toward a value beyond the initial or final values. A **glitch** is an output transient associated with an input code change. A glitch may result when one or more intermediate input states occur during the input code transition. Intermediate input states occur because one or more switches in the DAC circuit change faster than the others. Consider the input of an 8-bit DAC being changed from 10000000 to 01111111 (Fig. 17.2-7). If the most significant bit (msb) switches faster than the other bits, an intermediate state of 00000000 occurs. This intermediate state momentarily drives the output toward 0 V.

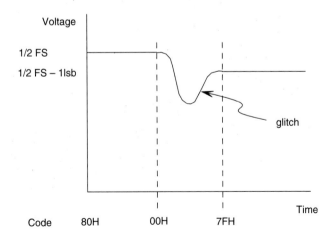

Figure 17.2-7   Glitch at a DAC's output due to an input change.

The severity of a glitch is defined by the glitch impulse specification. A **glitch impulse** is the product of the glitch's amplitude and its duration. Glitch impulse is often specified in units of nanovolt-seconds (nV-s). It is referred to as glitch energy even though its units are not actually energy.

17.2.3   DAC Input Codes

The previously discussed DACs are unipolar; they provide a single polarity output. **Bipolar DACs** can provide both positive and negative output voltages. Correspondingly, input codes for bipolar DACs must be able to represent positive and negative values. Several different signed input codes are used, including sign-plus-magnitude, two's complement, and one's complement. Also used is a code called **offset binary**, which is nearly identical to two's complement, except that the msb is complemented. Table 17.2-3 lists some output values for bipolar converters, with nominal −5 V to +5 V ranges, as a function of offset binary and two's complement input codes.

Table 17.2-3   Binary coding for a ±5 V FS 8-bit bipolar DAC.

Offset Binary	2's Complement	Scale	V_{OUT}
00000000	10000000	-FS	−5.00
00000001	10000001	-FS + 1 lsb	−4.96
00100000	10100000	−3/4 FS	−3.75
01000000	11000000	−1/2 FS	−2.50
10000000	00000000	0	0.00
11000000	01000000	+1/2 FS	+2.50
11100000	01100000	+3/4 FS	+3.75
11111111	01111111	+FS − 1 lsb	+4.96

17.3   DAC to System Bus Interface

In principle, any DAC can be interfaced to a system's bus. However, **microprocessor compatible DACs** include, on the DAC IC, the necessary registers and control logic to make interfacing easy. The digital input to a DAC may be serial or parallel. In either case, part of the interface logic is the register that holds the code that is the input to the DAC circuit.

17.3.1   Parallel Input DACs

The interface logic on a microprocessor compatible, parallel input DAC with 8, or fewer, bits is simply a single register. This register's inputs are connected to the data bus, and its outputs are the inputs to the DAC circuit. The register appears to the microprocessor as a byte output port. All that is required is an output device select pulse to write the register.

Interfacing a DAC with 9 or more bits to an 8-bit data bus requires at least two registers. For example, for a 12-bit DAC designed to be interfaced to an 8-bit data bus, one register holds the least significant 8 bits and the other the most significant 4 bits. However, these two registers alone still don't provide an adequate interface.

In many applications, it is important that the analog output change monotonically from one output value to the next. The DAC's two registers are loaded by two Write I/O bus cycles. These Write I/O bus cycles result from the execution of either two separate instructions that write byte ports or a single instruction that writes a word port. After the first register is written, and until the second register is written, the data in one of the registers is from the new 12-bit word and the data in the other register is from the old 12-bit word. This intermediate input to the DAC circuit may produce a significant glitch.

Double buffering is used to solve this problem (Fig. 17.3-1). The eight lsbs of a 12-bit word are first output to latch 1. The 4 msbs are then output to latch 3. The output device select pulse that clocks the 4 bits from the data bus into latch 3, simultaneously clocks the output of latch 1 into latch 2. Thus, all 12 bits, $B_0...B_{11}$, appear at the input to the DAC circuit nearly simultaneously.

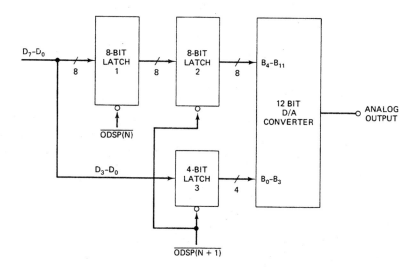

Figure 17.3-1   Double buffering the inputs to a DAC.

A single word port OUT instruction can transfer all 12 bits. The instruction's first Write I/O bus cycle transfers AL to latch 1. Its second Write I/O bus cycle transfers the least significant 4 bits of AH to latch 3 and simultaneously clocks the contents of latch 1 to latch 2.

Even with double buffering, glitches from data loading can exist. These glitches result from the timing relationship between /WR and valid data during a write or output bus cycle and the fact that most DACs use level-triggered latches. The 80C188EB asserts /WR at the same time that it starts to drive valid data onto the data bus. If the DAC's registers are level-triggered, they will be transparent as soon as /WR goes low. The DAC will initially respond to invalid data. During this time a glitch can be generated.

A simple way to avoid this problem would be for DAC manufacturers to use edge-triggered flip-flops instead of level triggered latches. However, DAC registers are usually level-triggered so that the DAC can also be used in nonmicroprocessor applications, by simply hardwiring the latches' clock inputs to the appropriate level, leaving the latches transparent. If the elimination of glitches is critical, a track-hold can be used at the output of the DAC to further suppress glitches.

17.3.2   AD7248A Parallel 12-bit (8 + 4 Loading) DAC

Analog Devices' **AD7248A Parallel 12-bit DAC** is an example of an 8-bit data bus compatible 12-bit multiplying DAC IC with voltage output. The AD7248A contains an on-chip output amplifier and voltage reference. It can be configured to produce any one of three output voltage ranges; 0 to +5 V, 0 to +10 V, or −5 V to +5 V. For bipolar operation, offset binary code is used. The input control structure of the AD7248A (Fig. 17.3-2) makes interfacing easy. There are two input registers, a least significant byte register (an 8-bit latch) and a most significant byte register (a 4-bit latch). Each register has its own select input.

AD7248A FUNCTIONAL BLOCK DIAGRAM

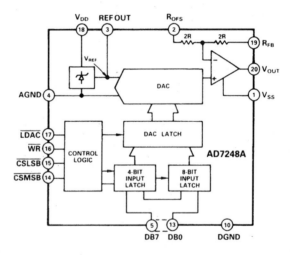

Figure 17.3-2   AD7248A 12-bit DAC block diagram. (Courtesy of Analog Devices, Inc.)

When both the /CSLSB and /WR inputs are asserted, the DAC's least significant byte register is written. When both /CSMSB and /WR are asserted, the most significant byte (actually 4-bit) register is written. Loading the two input registers does not change the inputs to the DAC circuit. The DAC circuit has its own 12-bit register, the DAC latch. The DAC latch is loaded from the input registers when both /LDAC and /WR are asserted.

The AD7248A's double buffered control structure has several advantages. Loading the two input registers separately from the DAC register eliminates the problem of glitches due to invalid data on the bus when /WR is asserted. With this approach, it takes three bus cycles to update the output. Another advantage of this structure occurs in applications where several DACs must have their outputs change simultaneously. To accomplish this, the DACs have their /LDAC inputs connected together. After the input registers of all the DACs have been loaded, a single /LDAC strobe updates all the DACs simultaneously.

If glitches caused by invalid bus data when /WR is asserted are not a problem in a particular application, then the 12-bit output can be updated in two Write I/O bus cycles. In this approach, /LDAC is connected to either /CSLSB or /CSMSB. If /LDAC is connected to /CSMSB, the 12-bit data value can be transferred by a single word port OUT instruction. For this case, the addresses assigned to /CSLSB and /CSMSB must be consecutive, with /CSLSB having the lower address.

In Fig. 17.3-3 an AD7248A is configured to produce a 0 to +5 V output.

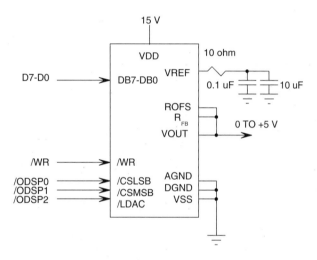

Figure 17.3-3   AD7248A 12-bit DAC interface to an 80C188EB system bus.

17.3.3   AD7243 12-bit Serial Input DAC

A serial input DAC requires fewer pins and can be placed in a smaller package. Thus, it requires less printed circuit board space. The primary disadvantage of a serial input DAC is that it takes longer to transfer input data to the DAC. This precludes the use of a serial DAC in applications where an analog output must be updated at a fast rate, such as in waveform generation.

Analog Devices' **AD7243** is an example of a 12-bit serial DAC. It includes an output amplifier and voltage reference. The AD7243's block diagram is given in Fig. 17.3-4. A serial to parallel shift register provides the input to the DAC latch (Fig. 17.3-5). The clear input (/CLR) allows the AD7243's DAC register to be quickly initialized to zero.

In one of its modes of operation (DCEN = 0), asserting the AD7243's /SYNC input provides frame synchronization for the serial data value. To load a serial word of data, /SYNC is first asserted, then the serial data is input, msb first, at the SDIN input (Fig.

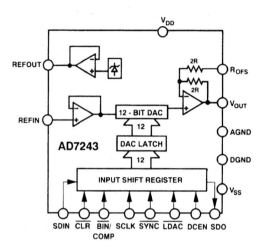

Figure 17.3-4   AD7243 serial input 12-bit DAC. (Courtesy of Analog Devices, Inc.)

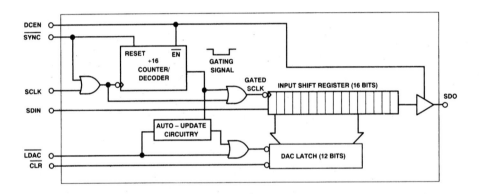

Figure 17.3-5   Simplified loading structure of AD7243. (Courtesy of Analog Devices, Inc.)

17.3-6). Each data bit is clocked into the shift register by a falling edge at SCLK. Sixteen bits of data must be clocked into the shift register. The first four bits are don't cares and only the last 12-bits are transferred to the DAC latch.

For unipolar operation, 0 to +5 V or 0 to +10 V output, the data format is straight binary. For bipolar operation, −5 V to +5 V output, the choice of format is controlled by the AD7243's /BIN pin. If this pin is 1, the data format is 2's complement; if it is 0, the data format is offset binary.

To update the analog output, the DAC latch can be loaded from the shift register in either of two ways. If /LDAC is 0 when /SYNC is asserted, the DAC latch is automatically updated when the last of the 16 data bits is clocked into the shift register. If /LDAC is 1 when /SYNC is asserted, the DAC latch is updated by asserting /LDAC anytime after the

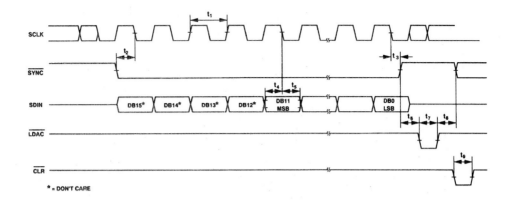

* = DON'T CARE

Figure 17.3-6   AD7243 timing diagram for stand-alone mode. (Courtesy of Analog
Devices, Inc.)

16-bit data transfer is complete. In this approach, /LDAC must be unasserted before the
next data transfer is initiated.

In Fig. 17.3-7, an AD7243 is configured for a 0 to +5 V output. One method of interfacing the AD7243 to an 80C188EB is to connect SDIN to one bit of the data bus and to
control /SYNC from an output port bit. /LDAC is hardwired to ground. PLD address
decoding logic that conditions its output on /WR and produces a positive device select
pulse is used to generate the clock input to SCLK. To transfer data to the DAC, a 0 is output
to the port bit that drives /SYNC. Then, a loop is executed that outputs each bit of the 16-
bit word, from most to least significant bit. To complete the transfer, a 1 is output to the
port bit driving /SYNC.

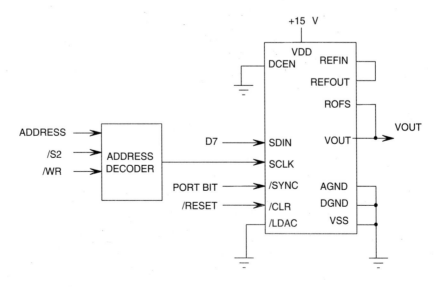

Figure 17.3-7   AD7243 serial 12-bit DAC configured for 0 to +5 V operation.

17.4   Basic DAC Circuits

Typically, basic DAC circuits are either networks of electronic switches and resistors or networks of electronic switches and capacitors. A very simple 2-bit **resistor divider DAC circuit** is shown in Fig. 17.4-1. This circuit uses a resistor divider to divide down a reference voltage into all of the possible discrete analog outputs needed for a 2-bit DAC. The equal value resistors in the divider produce the desired voltages at the divider taps as long as no current is drawn from the divider.

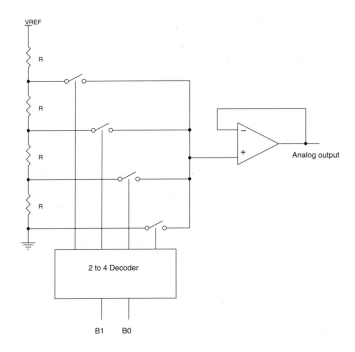

Figure 17.4-1   Resistor divider 2-bit DAC.

The 2-bit input is decoded into four mutually exclusive outputs by a two-to-four decoder. The switch corresponding to the asserted output is closed, and the analog voltage from the selected divider tap is buffered and then output. The unity gain op-amp buffer prevents a load connected to the DAC from drawing current from the resistor divider.

The main drawback with this circuit is that the number of components needed increases exponentially with the number of bits. A n-bit resistor divider circuit requires 2^n resistors, 2^n switches, and an n-to-2^n decoder. Thus, this circuit is impractical for values of n above 8.

Two versions of resistor DAC circuits where the number of components required increases linearly with n are presented in the following two subsections. These circuits are both R-$2R$ ladder implementations.

17.4.1   R-2R Ladder DACs

An **R-2R ladder** DAC circuit is shown in Fig. 17.4-2. This circuit has the advantage of only requiring resistors with the precise ratios of R and $2R$. The circuit in Fig. 17.4-2 is a **current steering mode R-2R circuit**. This circuit creates a current, I_S, at the summing junction of the op-amp that is proportional to its input code. The op-amp converts this current to an output voltage with:

$$V_{OUT} = -I_S R$$

where I_S is the sum of the currents through those switches that are in their logic 1 positions.

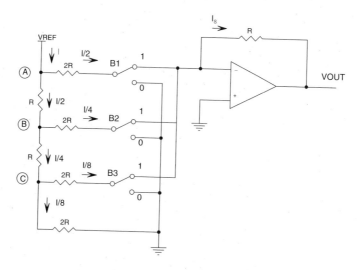

Figure 17.4-2   Current steering R-2R ladder network voltage output DAC.

The input to the circuit is a 3-bit word, $B_1 B_2 B_3$, which represents a straight binary fraction. B_1, the msb, has a weight of 2^{-1}, B_2 has a weight of 2^{-2}, and B_3, the lsb, has a weight of 2^{-3}. Each bit controls an analog switch. When B_i is 1, its analog switch passes a current through the associated horizontal $2R$ resistor and into the op-amp's summing junction. The op-amp's summing junction is held at ground potential by negative feedback through feedback resistor R. The current into the summing junction due to B_i being a 1 is:

$$I_i = \left(\frac{V_{REF}}{R}\right) 2^{-i}$$

When B_i is 0, the analog switch directs the current through its associated horizontal resistor to circuit ground, instead of into the op-amp's summing junction.

Due to the virtual ground effect of the op-amp in this negative feedback configuration, the inverting (–) terminal of the op-amp is effectively at ground potential. Thus, the right side of each $2R$ resistor is connected to ground through its associated switch, regardless of whether the switch is in its 0 or 1 position.

The Thevenin equivalent of the resistor ladder looking into the terminal connected to V_{REF}, is simply R. Thus, the current into the circuit from the reference supply is always:

$$I = \frac{V_{REF}}{R}$$

The equivalent resistance of the ladder network below node A is $2R$. Thus, the current I into node A splits in half, resulting in a current $I/2$, through the horizontal $2R$ resistor associated with B_1. The other half of the current is through the vertical resistor R and into node B. The equivalent resistance below node B is also $2R$. Thus, the current $I/2$ into node B splits, causing a current $I/4$ in the horizontal resistor associated with bit B_2. A continuation of this analysis shows that the current splits at each subsequent node, resulting in currents through the horizontal resistors that are weighted by powers of two. For each switch in its 1 position, the current through its associated horizontal resistor is into the op-amp's summing junction. Thus, I_S is the sum of these weighted currents.

$$I_S = I(B_1 2^{-1} + B_2 2^{-2} + B_3 2^{-3})$$

The op-amp current-to-voltage converter converts I_S to an output voltage:

$$V_{OUT} = -I_S R$$
$$= -I(B_1 2^{-1} + B_2 2^{-2} + B_3 2^{-3})R$$
$$= -V_{REF}(B_1 2^{-1} + B_2 2^{-2} + B_3 2^{-3})$$

This output voltage is directly proportional to the input code. The factor of proportionality is equal to V_{REF}. If V_{REF} is -10 V, the DAC's output ranges from 0 V to $+8.75$ V (seven-eighths of full scale), corresponding to input codes ranging from 000 to 111, respectively.

A **voltage switching mode R-2R circuit** can also be constructed (Fig. 17.4-3). Here, the reference terminal and the output terminal are interchanged compared to the current-steering mode. The effective resistance to ground of all resistors below a given node is $2R$. If B_1 alone is 1, the voltage at node A is $1/2$ V_{REF}. If B_2 alone is 1, the voltage at node A is $1/4$ V_{REF}. The contribution of each bit is a voltage at node A that is $1/2$ the voltage contributed by the preceding bit. By superposition, the voltage at node A, and correspondingly at the output of the unity gain op-amp, is:

$$V_{OUT} = V_{REF}(B_1 2^{-1} + B_2 2^{-2} + B_3 2^{-3})$$

The output of a voltage switching mode DAC has the same polarity as its reference voltage. In contrast, the polarity of a current steering DAC's output is the negative of its reference voltage.

17.4.2   Reference Voltages

For nonmultiplying DACs, a stable and accurate reference voltage is essential. Many DACs have an internal reference voltage derived from the supply voltage by a circuit that uses a temperature compensated Zener diode. Alternatively, some DACs allow the optional use of an external voltage reference for greater accuracy. Other DACs have no internal voltage reference and require an external reference.

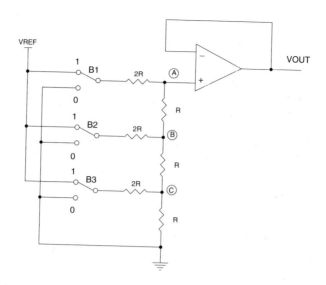

Figure 17.4-3   Voltage switching R-2R ladder network voltage output DAC.

Discrete voltage references using temperature compensated Zener diodes are available in IC form. In these devices, the Zener diode is driven by a current regulator and buffer amplifier. Output voltage accuracies are as high as ±0.01 percent.

17.4.3   Multiplying DACs

If the external reference voltage to a DAC changes, the DAC's output voltage changes. Some DACs are designed so that the change in the output current, I_S, is linear with respect to changes in V_{REF} over the entire range from 0 to the maximum allowable V_{REF}. These DACs' outputs are the product of their digital input and the analog voltage at their reference input. DACs designed for this type of operation are called multiplying DACs.

A multiplying DAC designed to accept a unipolar digital code and a positive reference voltage operates in a single quadrant. A multiplying DAC designed to accept a bipolar digital code operates in two quadrants. Two-quadrant multiplication also results when a multiplying DAC accepts only a unipolar digital code but can operate with a reference voltage of either polarity. Four-quadrant multiplication results when a multiplying DAC can operate with bipolar digital codes and a bipolar reference.

17.5   Loading and Impedance Considerations

A DAC's output may require signal conditioning before being applied to an output transducer (Fig. 17.1-2). The same is true for a track-hold's output in a multichannel analog output subsystem (Fig. 17.1-3). The required signal conditioning may include any combination of buffering, amplification, filtering, level shifting, current-to-voltage conversion, or some other operational modification.

The next section provides an overview of some common op-amp circuits for signal conditioning. Before considering those op-amp circuits, this section provides a brief review of some fundamental input and output impedance concepts. This review will emphasize the importance of input and output impedance in information and power transfer. As a result, the impact of the input and output impedance of op-amp circuits will be better appreciated.

When several signal conditioning operations need to be carried out on a signal, individual signal conditioning circuits are cascaded. The output of one circuit provides the input to the next circuit in the cascade. Consider the two analog circuits S and D where the output of the first circuit is connected to the input of the second (Fig. 17.5-1(a)). The top wire carries the analog signal between the two circuits. The bottom wire is the common or ground signal. As stated previously, all analog signals involve both a voltage and a current. The signal's voltage is the voltage from the signal wire to ground. The signal's current is the current though the signal wire. The signal's information is vested in either its voltage or its current. The product of the signal's voltage and current is its power.

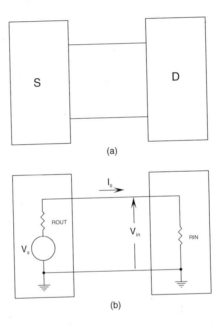

(a)

(b)

Figure 17.5-1   Loading effect of cascading two circuits: (a) input of circuit D connected to output of circuit S; (b) Thevenin equivalent circuits for the output of S and the input of D.

An analog signal can provide both information and power. Normally, the purpose of a specific signal is to provide either one or the other. When information transfer is the objective, it is the information in the signal that is valued. This information must be preserved in going from one intermediate stage of signal conditioning to the next. From the final stage to the output transducer, it may be either the signal's information content or its power that is important.

17.5.1   Maximum Information Transfer

Assume that we are interested in information transfer and that the information is embodied in the signal's voltage. The information is being transferred from S to D in Fig. 17.5-1(a). Figure 17.5-1(b) shows the Thevenin equivalent of the output of circuit S and the Thevenin equivalent of the input of circuit D. The Thevenin equivalent output of S consists of a voltage source, V_S and series resistance, R_{OUT}. The voltage source is a dependent source, its output voltage being a function of the analog signal of interest.

   Ideally, the voltage at the input of D should be identical to the voltage of the dependent source, V_S. When this is the case, information is transferred between the two circuits without any loss. However, R_{OUT} and R_{IN} form a voltage divider. The voltage at D, $V_{IN,}$ is:

$$V_{IN} = V_S \frac{R_{IN}}{R_{IN} + R_{OUT}}$$

   For V_{IN} to be exactly equal to V_S, either R_{OUT} has to be zero, or R_{IN} has to be infinite. In a practical circuit, neither of these conditions is met. However, you create a condition closest to the ideal for information transfer if you make R_{OUT} as small as possible and R_{IN} as large as possible.

   Circuit D's input impedance is said to load circuit S. The loading effect on S is increased as the value of R_{IN} is decreased.

   If the information in the signal between S and D is embodied in the signal's current, a similar analysis can be performed. In this case, D's output is modeled by a dependent current source and parallel output resistance, R_{OUT}. This is the Norton equivalent of S's output. D's input is modeled as before. In contrast, analysis of such a circuit reveals that the current into D is closest to that of the dependent current source when R_{OUT} is as large as possible and R_{IN} is as small as possible.

17.5.2   Maximum Power Transfer

In the previous cases, it is the information content of the signal that is important. In going from the last stage of the signal conditioning to an output transducer, sometimes it is the power in the signal that is important. Therefore, R_{IN} and R_{OUT} are chosen to maximize the power transferred. The power received by R_{IN} is:

$$P_{IN} = \frac{V_{IN}^2}{R_{IN}}$$

$$= \left(\frac{V_S R_{IN}}{R_{IN} + R_{OUT}}\right)^2 \frac{1}{R_{IN}}$$

$$= \frac{V_S^2 R_{IN}}{(R_{IN} + R_{OUT})^2}$$

Taking the derivative of P_{IN} with respect to R_{IN} and setting it to zero yields:

$$\frac{dP_{IN}}{dR_{IN}} = \frac{V_S^2(R_{OUT} - R_{IN})}{(R_{OUT} + R_{IN})^3} = 0$$

Thus, to maximize power transfer, R_{OUT} and R_{IN} must be equal. *The requirement for maximum power is quite different from the requirement for maximum information transfer.*

17.6   Operational Amplifiers

Op-amp ICs are used for signal conditioning because of their low cost, high reliability, and ease of application. Op-amps are the building blocks for current-to-voltage converters, voltage amplifiers, buffers, active filters, track-holds, and a variety of other linear and non-linear analog circuits. They are available as discrete linear ICs and are used as components in larger ICs.

An op-amp is a very high gain amplifier with two analog signal inputs, and one or two analog signal outputs. In addition to the signal inputs and outputs, DC supply voltage(s), usually two of opposite polarity, are required for the op-amp's operation. The basic op-amp circuit symbol is shown in Fig. 17.6-1(a). All voltages applied to an op-amp are specified with respect to the circuit's ground terminal. The two signal inputs are the **inverting input** (–) and the **noninverting input** (+). The voltages at these inputs are labeled v_- and v_+, respectively. For op-amps operating with opposite polarity supply voltages, input voltages can be positive or negative.

17.6.1   The Ideal Op-Amp

For purposes of this analysis, the op-amp is assumed to be ideal. The output voltage of an ideal op-amp is a function of the difference between its two input voltages, $v_+ - v_-$. This voltage difference is referred to as the **differential input voltage**.

An op-amp has three regions of operation (Fig. 17.6-1(b)). In the linear region, the output voltage, v_o, is the product of the op-amp's open loop gain, A_{OL}, and its differential input voltage, $v_+ - v_-$. In the two saturation regions, the output is at either the positive or negative saturation voltage, and is no longer a linear function of $v_+ - v_-$.

A simple equivalent circuit for an ideal op-amp in its linear region of operation is given in Fig. 17.6-2. The input resistance at the inverting and noninverting terminals is assumed infinite for the ideal op-amp. Therefore, the currents into these terminals are zero: $i_- = i_+ = 0$. The output resistance of the ideal op-amp is assumed zero. The dependent voltage generator, $A_{OL}(v_+ - v_-)$ models the output as a function of the differential input.

Open loop gains, A_{OL}, for practical op-amps range from 10^4 to 10^6. DC supply voltages are usually no greater in magnitude than 15 V. The values of saturation voltages are usually 1 or 2 volts below the supply voltages. Thus, a limit must be placed on the differential input voltage $(v_+ - v_-)$ that can be applied to the op-amp and still maintain linear operation. For example, with a gain of 10^6 and a saturation voltage of ± 14 V, the differential input voltage must be less than 14 microvolts (μV).

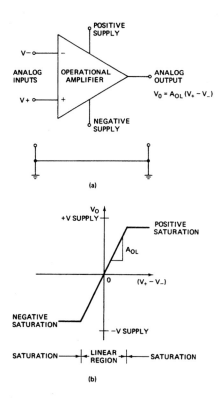

Figure 17.6-1   Operational amplifier: (a) basic circuit symbol; (b) voltage transfer characteristic.

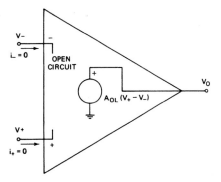

Figure 17.6-2   Equivalent circuit for an ideal op-amp.

Most applications involve input voltages of a much larger magnitude. Even if the input voltages were of a very low magnitude, the magnitude of the electrical noise signals present in most environments would cause the output of an open-loop op-amp to saturate or to oscillate. For these reasons, op-amps are not operated open loop in linear applications.

For closed loop operation, a portion of the output signal is fed back to one of the input terminals via an external connection. **Negative feedback**, used in implementing linear op-amp circuits, results when the feedback connection is made to the inverting terminal. **Positive feedback** results if the feedback connection is to the noninverting terminal. Positive feedback is intentionally used to produce some linear and nonlinear circuits.

17.6.2   Common Op-Amp Circuits

When an op-amp with a high open loop gain is used with negative feedback to implement a linear circuit, the circuit's closed loop gain, or transfer characteristic, and its input and output impedance are, to a first approximation, determined entirely by external feedback components. As a result, analysis and design of linear signal processing circuits using op-amps is relatively straightforward.

Some commonly used op-amp circuits employing negative feedback are summarized in Fig. 17.6-3. The circuit characteristics listed are approximations determined from the circuit's feedback configuration, and the assumption that the op-amp is ideal. However, for many applications, these approximations predict, with sufficient accuracy, the operation of the circuit when it contains a nonideal op-amp. The derivation of these equations is not provided here, but can be found in any introductory text on op-amps.

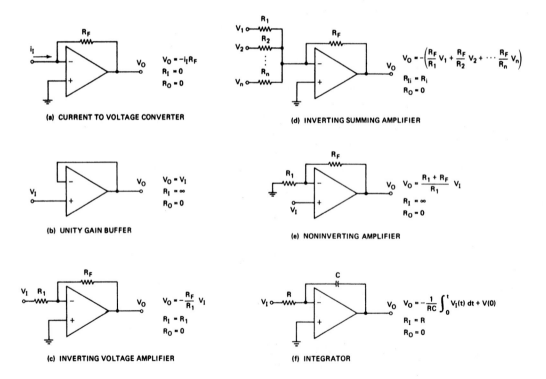

Figure 17.6-3   Common operational amplifier circuits.

We have already encountered some uses of op-amp circuits. The **unity gain buffer** (Fig. 17.6-3(b)) provides an "infinite" input impedance and a "zero" output impedance, while producing an output voltage equal to its input voltage. This buffer is used between two signal conditioning circuits to keep one from loading the other. A unity gain op-amp was used in Fig. 17.4-1 to keep a load connected to the resistor divider DAC's output from loading the resistor divider.

The **current-to-voltage converter** circuit (Fig. 17.6-3(a)) has an input impedance of zero ohms. However, the input impedance at the op-amp's input is infinite. Therefore, any current into the circuit flows through the feedback resistor. This produces an output voltage of $V_O = i_I R_F$. A current-to-voltage converter was used in the current steering R-$2R$ DAC of Fig. 17.4-2 to produce a voltage output.

17.6.3   Power Op-Amps

Power op-amps are operational amplifiers that are capable of providing significant power to a load. A power op-amp IC may have been designed to provide high currents at moderate voltages or to provide high voltages at moderate currents. The maximum operating voltages and currents for these devices are substantially higher than those of common op-amps.

Among their many applications, power op-amps are used to drive DC motors, loudspeakers, and piezo transducers. Figure 17.6-4 shows a circuit that uses a DAC to control a power op-amp to create a programmable high-voltage power supply. Programmable high voltage power supplies find widespread use in automatic test equipment (ATE), scientific, and medical applications.

17.7   Analog Demultiplexers

An **analog demultiplexer** is a digitally controlled connection of analog switches with a common input and several outputs. This arrangement allows an analog input signal to be routed to a selected output (Fig. 17.7-1). Except that its data input and data outputs are analog signals, an analog demultiplexer is functionally similar to a digital demultiplexer.

The analog demultiplexer's channel address inputs select the output to which the input data is routed. IC analog demultiplexers include the necessary decoding logic for channel selection, level translators for the digital control inputs, switch drivers, and the analog switches. Eight channel (one-of-eight) and sixteen channel (one-of-sixteen) demultiplexers are common. Some demultiplexers include a latch for the channel address. Latchable demultiplexers are particularly appropriate for use with microprocessors.

You may not find analog demultiplexers listed in your linear data books. However, you will find analog multiplexers. Most multiplexers are usable as demultiplexers. The pinout of the industry standard **DG528 8-Channel Single-ended Latchable Multiplexer** is given in Fig. 17.7-2. When used as a demultiplexer, the common D pin is the input and pins S1-S8 are outputs.

When the enable input EN is 0, all the multiplexer's switches are open, or OFF. The EN input allows multiple DG528s to be combined to build larger multiplexers. When EN is 1, the switch selected by the three address inputs A2-A1 is closed, or ON.

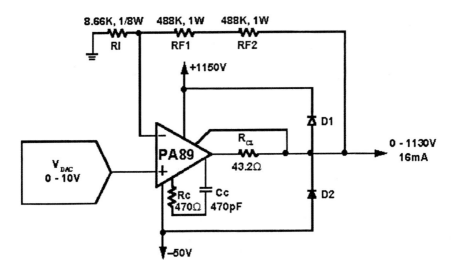

Figure 17.6-4   High voltage programmable power supply using a DAC and power op-amp. (Courtesy of Apex Microtechnology Corp., Tucson, AZ.)

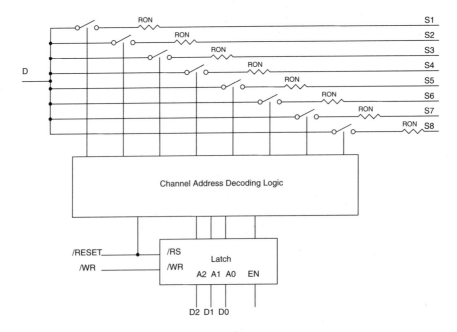

Figure 17.7-1   Functional diagram of an 8-channel demultiplexer (multiplexer) with an onboard address and control latch.

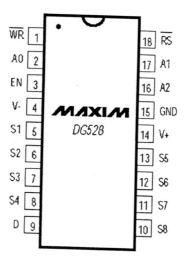

Figure 17.7-2   DG528 8-channel single-ended latchable multiplexer. (Courtesy of Maxim Integrated Products.)

The DG528 contains a negative level triggered address and control latch. When /WR is 0, the latch is transparent and the DG528 operates like a DG508 multiplexer, which has no latch. A change in the address inputs changes the selected channel. Each channel's switches are **break-before-make** to prevent momentary shorting of the outputs. The address inputs are latched along with EN on the rising edge of /WR. The addressed channel remains selected until there is a new address and /WR is asserted.

When asserted, the reset input (/RS) clears the latch and the enable bit. This leaves all of the switches OFF.

Many manufactures have pin compatible versions of the DG528, making it an industry standard. These versions may differ in their ON and OFF channel resistance values, the variation in ON resistance between channels, switching speeds, and other parameters.

The ON resistance of a channel should ideally be zero, and the OFF resistance should be infinite. For typical demultiplexers, ON resistances range from 25 to 3500 ohms, depending on the specific demultiplexer. OFF resistances are typically greater than 10 Mohms.

A demultiplexer is used in Fig. 17.1-3 to route the output signal from a single DAC to one of several track-holds. The DAC is loaded with the code to generate the output voltage for a specific channel. The demultiplexer is loaded with that channel's address. The voltage appears at the addressed channel only as long as the DAC remains loaded with the desired code and the channel remains selected by the demultiplexer.

In a multichannel analog output subsystem, it is usually necessary to provide voltages from all the channels simultaneously. Therefore, the output voltage from each multiplexer channel must be latched. A track-hold is used at each demultiplexer output to latch the analog voltage.

17.8   Track-Holds

A **track-hold** or **sample-hold** does for an analog signal what a D latch does for a digital signal (Fig. 17.8-1). When tracking, the track-hold's analog output follows its analog input (the track-hold is "transparent"). In response to a digital control signal ("the clock"), a track-hold stores ("latches") the instantaneous value of its analog input. The stored analog value is available at the track-hold's output until the track-hold is subsequently commanded to again track its input. One of the reasons analog information is most often represented as a voltage rather than a current is that track-holds can be easily designed to store a voltage. In contrast, it is not practical to design a track-hold for current.

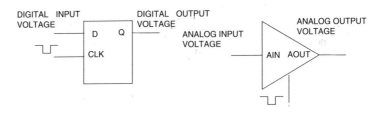

Figure 17.8-1   Analogy between a D-latch and a track-hold: (a) digital D latch; (b) analog track-hold.

An ideal track-hold can be represented by a switch and a capacitor (Fig. 17.8-2). The capacitor is the analog voltage storage element. When the switch is closed, the circuit is in the track mode. In the track mode, the output signal, v_o, follows the input signal, v_i. Since the circuit in this figure is ideal, the output voltage is exactly equal to the input voltage. When the switch is open, the circuit is in the hold mode. In the hold mode, the capacitor holds the voltage that existed at the instant the switch was opened.

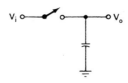

Figure 17.8-2   Idealized circuit representation of a track-hold as a switch and capacitor.

The distinction between a track-hold and a sample-hold is only in how the device is operated. A track-hold spends most of its time tracking the input and is switched into the hold mode for only brief intervals. A sample-hold samples (tracks) the input for a short time while spending most of its time in the hold mode. Most track-hold and sample-hold circuits are identical.

A practical track-hold circuit must buffer the switch and capacitor from being loaded by the finite output impedance of its source and the finite input impedance of its load. For the simple open-loop track-hold architecture of Fig. 17.8-3, this is accomplished using two unity gain op-amp buffers. Input buffer A_1 presents a high input impedance to the analog input voltage source, v_i, and a low output impedance to the switch and capacitor. The high input impedance of A_1 prevents the switch and capacitor from loading the source that produces voltage v_i.

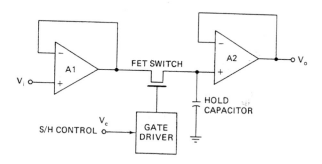

Figure 17.8-3   Implementation of a practical sample and hold circuit.

The low output impedance of A_1 allows the capacitor to be quickly charged when the switch is closed. Assume that the track-hold is holding a value of 0 V and its input is changed to its full scale voltage. The elapsed time from the assertion of the track command to the point at which the track-hold's output has transitioned from 0 V and settled to within a specified error band of its full scale output is known as the **acquisition time**. Once the output is within this specified error band, the output tracks the input (Fig. 17.8-4).

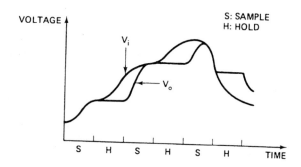

Figure 17.8-4   A plot of output voltage versus time for a track-hold.

A MOS transistor is typically used as the analog switch. The MOS transistor's gate voltage controls the resistance between its source and drain. When the control signal is switched to the hold state, the MOS switch opens (very high channel resistance), and the track-hold is in its hold mode. The time elapsed between the transition of the control signal to the hold state and the actual opening of the switch is the **aperture time**. The sampling, or storing, of the input signal is delayed by this time interval. The hold command would have to be advanced by this amount of time to have the sample actually occur at the desired time.

The time required for all output transients to settle to within a specified error band after switching from the track to hold mode is the **hold setting time.** An offset may exist between the track-holds's output voltage in the track mode and its output voltage when switched to the hold mode. This error is called the **hold step** or **pedestal error.** The hold step offset results from charge injected by the switch onto the hold capacitor.

While in the hold mode, the hold capacitor is not perfectly isolated from the input. A change in the input can cause a small change in the output. The fraction of the input signal variation that appears at the output in the hold mode is specified as **feedthrough.** Feedthrough is caused by the existence of parasitic source-gate and gate-drain capacitance.

The purpose of unity gain buffer A_2 is to provide isolation between the hold capacitor and the output. The high input impedance of A_2 buffers the capacitor's voltage from the load that is connected to the track-hold. Without A_2, the capacitor would discharge quickly through a low resistance load. Even with A_2 and the switch open in the hold mode, the charge on the hold capacitor still decays. However, the decay is over a much longer period of time. The decay occurs because the OFF resistance of the open MOS switch and the resistance of the noninverting input terminal of A_2, although very large, are not infinite.

Thus, a practical track-hold circuit cannot indefinitely hold its output voltage. The rate at which the output voltage decays in the hold mode is the track-hold's **decay** or **droop rate.** Using a larger capacitor reduces a track-hold's decay rate but increases its acquisition time, leading to a design trade-off.

Table 17.8-1 gives some specifications for a representative selection of track-holds.

Table 17.8-1   Some typical characteristics of track-holds.

Model	Specified accuracy %	Acquisition time ns	Aperture time ns	Hold settling time ns	Droop rate V/s
AD1154	0.00076	5.0	80	0.4	0.1
SMP10	0.01	3.5	50	7	0.02
SMP18	0.01	3.5	45	1	0.04
AD9101	0.1	0.007	0.5	0.004	18

IC track-holds contain the buffer amplifiers, analog switch, and switch driver in a single package. Because of their included op-amps, they are often called **Track-hold Amplifiers (THA)** or **Sample Hold Amplifiers (SHA).** An external hold capacitor completes the circuit. The symbol shown in Fig. 17.8-1 represents an entire track-hold.

Multichannel track-holds provide multiple THAs on a single IC, significantly reducing the parts count in multiplexed applications. For example, the **SMP18 Octal Sample-and-hold with Multiplexed Input** provides eight THAs with internal hold capacitors and an input demultiplexer with eight outputs in a 16-pin IC (Fig. 17.8-5). A 3-bit channel address selects the track-hold that will acquire the input data. The SMP18 allows a very cost effective implementation of the multichannel analog output subsystem of Fig. 17.1-3.

Returning to Fig. 17.1-3, assume the objective is to maintain the voltage at each track-hold's output at a constant value. For each channel, the following four steps are required:

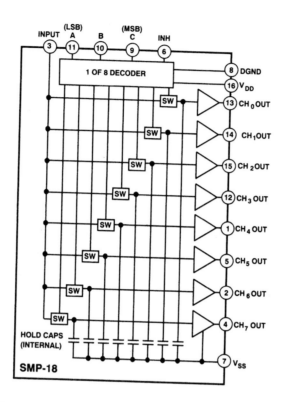

Figure 17.8-5   SMP18 Octal sample and hold block diagram. (Courtesy of Devices, Inc.)

1. Load the DAC to produce the voltage for the channel.
2. Write the channel's address to the multiplexer.
3. Put the channel's track-hold in its track mode to acquire the voltage.
4. Put the channel's track-hold in its hold mode to hold the voltage.

Each of these steps must be carried out for each channel in turn. After each channel is loaded, the output of the channel's track-hold starts to decay. Therefore, the entire process must be repeated often enough to refresh each track-hold to prevent any channel's output from decaying unacceptably. The minimum required refresh rate to keep an output within 1/2 lsb is:

$$\text{Minimum refresh time} = \frac{V_{FS}}{2^{n+1} \times \text{Decay rate}}$$

The SMP-18's droop rate of 40 mV/s requires a refresh within 250 ms to maintain the output within 1/2 least significant bit for an 8-bit accuracy with a full scale voltage of 5 V. For 10-bit accuracy, the refresh must be within 60 ms. For 12-bit accuracy it must be within 15 ms.

The worst case minimum refresh period achievable, assuming all eight channels are used, is eight times the sum of the DAC's settling time, the multiplexer's settling time, the track-hold's acquisition time, and the track-hold's aperture time.

In addition to its software burden, refreshing several track-holds produces a ripple in each track-hold's output. In an application where the analog output voltages must be extremely stable, this ripple may be unacceptable. If so, demultiplexing cannot be used, and a separate DAC must be provided for each output. There are numerous ICs that provide multiple DACs in a single package, reducing the cost of the DAC per channel approach.

Other advantages provided by multi-DAC ICs include: fast update rates, synchronized outputs, power on reset, and readback of the DAC registers. Synchronized outputs are particularly important in some ATE applications. Power on reset clears the DAC's registers at power on. This feature is particularly helpful in an application where the DAC's output is used to control a motor's speed or the output of a programmable high-voltage power supply.

17.9   Digital Potentiometers

Traditional potentiometers are electromechanical variable resistors with three terminals (Fig. 17.9-1(a)). Two terminals are the ends of the resistive element. The third terminal is the connection to a wiper that can be mechanically moved along the resistive element.

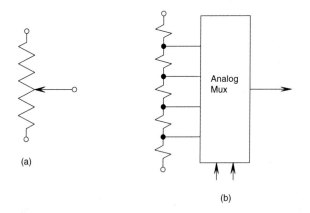

Figure 17.9-1   Potentiometers: (a) electromechanical; (b) digitally controlled.

A potentiometer can be used as a variable resistor or as an adjustable voltage divider. If connections are made to one of the end terminals and the wiper, the potentiometer functions as a variable resistor. Potentiometers are used in this manner as trim resistors. If a voltage is applied across its end terminals and the output taken from the wiper terminal, the potentiometer functions as an adjustable resistive voltage divider. Potentiometers are used in this manner to provide mechanically adjustable analog setpoint voltages to analog circuits.

As more and more electronic systems became controlled by microprocessors, a solid state equivalent of a potentiometer, one that could be adjusted by a microprocessor, was needed. A multiplying DAC can be used as a digitally programmed resistor. And, as is clear from Fig. 17.4-1, a DAC is a digitally programmed voltage divider. However, ICs called digital potentiometers have been specifically designed as digitally programmed potentiometers. They can be used to allow a microprocessor to tune or adjust analog circuits. As a result, systems can be designed with automatic tuning and automatic self calibration. Note that these digital potentiometers are not to be confused with optical shaft encoders of Section 15.4, which are also called digital potentiometers.

A digital potentiometer IC has a number of resistors connected in series (Fig. 17.9-1(b)). A connection (tap) is made from one side of each resistor to the input of an analog multiplexer. The output of the analog multiplexer is the potentiometer's wiper output. The potentiometer's address input is stored in a register and determines which of the multiplexer's analog inputs is selected. Changing the value in this register changes the wiper's position.

Digital potentiometers are available with nonvolatile registers. When these ICs are powered up, the wiper is in the same position it was left in the last time the system was used. This is analogous to the electromechanical counterpart, whose wiper does not change position when power is applied or removed.

Xicor's **X9Cxxx** family of **Digitally Controlled Potentiometers** has 99 resistors and 100 wiper tap points (Fig. 17.9-2). These devices are packaged in an eight-pin DIP. Family members differ in their total resistance from end to end. For example, the X9C102 has a 1 kohm total resistance and the X9C104 has a 100 kohm total resistance. The voltages applied to the end terminals can be from –5 V to +5 V.

A 7-bit up-down counter provides the address inputs to the decoder, which selects the tap to connect to the wiper. The value in this counter is automatically loaded from the 7-bit nonvolatile register when power is applied.

The wiper tap position is changed by counting the counter up or down. Control inputs consist of a chip select, /CS, an up/down control input, $U/\overline{D}$, and a clock input, /INC. A negative edge at the /INC input increments or decrements the counter, moving the wiper up (toward V_H) or down (toward V_L), depending on the value at $U/\overline{D}$. The counter cannot be incremented above the top tap position or decremented below the bottom tap position.

Storage of the current counter value in the nonvolatile register is initiated when /CS is returned to a 1, while /INC is also a 1. The X9Cxxx takes approximately 20 ms to complete the storage operation. The /CS and /INC pins are normally pulled up to V_{CC} through a resistor to prevent inadvertent incrementing or decrementing of the counter during power up.

Another example of a digital potentiometer with a very different mode of operation is Dallas Semiconductor's **DS1867 Dual Digital Potentiometer.** This IC provides two 256-position potentiometers in a 14-pin DIP. DS1867s are available with total resistance values of either 10, 50, or 100 kohms. Each wiper's position is set by an 8-bit value. The two 8-bit values and a Stack Select bit are serially entered into a 17-bit register. This 17-bit register has an EEPROM shadow register in which its contents are automatically stored upon power down and from which its contents are restored upon power up.

The two internal potentiometers can be externally connected in series to create a larger total resistance. When this is done, the Stack Select bit controls an internal multiplexer to select one wiper's output to appear at a third pin as the combined potentiometer's wiper output.

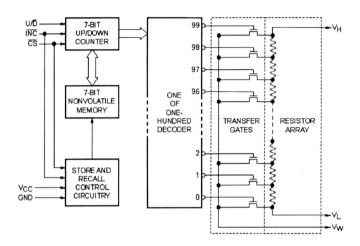

Figure 17.9-2   X9C10x Nonvolatile digital potentiometer. (Courtesy of Xicor, Inc.)

17.10   Summary

Acquiring, processing, and generating analog signals are important operations in many embedded systems. A DAC is the fundamental component for generating an analog voltage whose value is determined by a digital code. Since this digital code can be provided by a microprocessor, the microprocessor can produce and control an analog output voltage.

Microprocessor compatible DACs include registers to accommodate either the parallel or serial input of a digital code to the DAC. For parallel input DACs of more than 8 bits, double buffering is used to minimize glitches on the output due to input code changes. For serial input DACs, the serial input register and the DAC register also form a double buffer.

A DAC's output voltage may require additional analog signal conditioning to produce an analog signal appropriate for the analog output device. Such signal conditioning is normally accomplished with op-amps. The signal conditioning operation performed by an op-amp, and the op-amp's input and output impedance, are determined by the interconnection of external components, resistors and capacitors, to the op-amp. Current-to-voltage conversion, buffering, amplification, integration, and filtering are some of the analog operations easily accomplished using op-amps.

When multiple analog outputs are to be created using a single DAC, demultiplexers and track-holds are required. An analog demultiplexer routes an analog signal to one of several destinations in a fashion similar to the way a digital multiplexer routes a digital signal. A track-hold stores its analog input signal in response to a digital command. A track-hold is the analog equivalent of a digital level-triggered latch. The output of the track-hold is the "latched" analog input value.

Finally, there exists a class of ICs called digital potentiometers that are also used to generate a voltage that is proportional to a digital code. These devices are designed to allow a microprocessor to control the type of trim operations in a system that were done manually in the past. Digital potentiometers are usually nonvolatile, so their last setting is available at power on.

17.11   Problems

1. How does a voltage that is an analog signal with a range from 0 to +5 V differ from a voltage that is a digital signal that also has a range of 0 to +5 V?

2. The Motorola MPX4115 Altimeter/Barometer Absolute Pressure Sensor described in Section 17.1 has an input pressure range from 15 to 115 kPa and an output voltage range from 0.2 V to 4.8 V. Draw a graph of the transfer characteristic (output voltage vs. pressure) for this transducer. Derive the equation for input pressure as a function of output voltage. What are the input pressures for the following voltages: 1.46 V, 3.3 V, and 4.75 V? If the output voltage changes by 0.8 V, what was the change in pressure?

3. Give the output voltage for an 8-bit 5 V FS DAC with straight binary input for each of the following input codes:

    a. 00000000B

    b. 10000000B

    c. 11010100B

    d. 11111111B

4. For each DAC listed below, give the output voltage for the specified digital input. Assume that each DAC is ideal and its inputs are coded in straight binary.

    a. 8-bit 5 V FS DAC with input 01011110B

    b. 10-bit 5 V FS DAC with input 1001110110B

    c. 12-bit 10 V FS DAC with input 110010110011B

    d. 16-bit 2.5 V FS DAC with input 91A2H

5. Specify the step size for each of the following DACs:

    a. 8-bit 5 V FS DAC

    b. 10-bit 5 V FS DAC

    c. 12-bit 10 V FS DAC

    d. 16-bit 2.5 V FS DAC

6. For a 5 V 12-bit binary DAC, specify the following:

    a. resolution as a percent

    b. step size in volts

    c. maximum output voltage

7. A voltage to frequency (V/F) converter IC has been configured to provide an output of 0 to 100 kHz for an input voltage range of 0 to +5 V. If the input to the V/F converter is from a 0 to 5 V FS 12-bit DAC, what is the smallest change in output frequency that can be programmed?

8. An 8-bit multiplying DAC accepts binary input codes and a reference that can range from 0 to +5 V. For each of the input combinations that follows, what is the output voltage?

    a. 00010010B and 3.25 V

    b. 00000001B and 5.00 V

c. 11001010B and 1.25 V

d. 00100011B and 4.40 V

9. An 8-bit 0 to +5 V FS DAC has a gain error specification of ±2 lsbs maximum. If the DAC has no other errors, what will be the voltage range for the maximum output?

10. The outputs from a 3-bit DAC are measured for each input code giving the following values expressed in lsbs:

Code	000	001	010	011	100	101	110	111
Output	0	3/16	4/16	5/16	6/16	9/16	11/16	14/16

Determine the step size, differential nonlinearity (DNL), and integral nonlinearity (INL) at each input code. Specify all values in lsbs. What are the DNL and INL specifications for the DAC? Is the DAC monotonic?

11. What is the output of an 8-bit DAC that takes offset binary inputs and has a −5 V to +5 V FS output range for each of the following input codes:

a. 00000000

b. 10000000

c. 11010100

d. 11111111

12. If a microprocessor asserts /WR before it places valid data on the data bus, it momentarily provides invalid data to a DAC that it is writing. Depending on the DAC's input buffering scheme, this may cause a glitch at the DAC's output. Using the 80C188EB's data sheet determine the worst case time from /WR being asserted until valid data.

13. Draw a block diagram of the interface of an AD7284A Parallel DAC (Figs. 17.3-2 and 17.3-3) to an 80C188EB. A 22V10 PLD is to be used for address decoding. Use a separate device select pulse to transfer the data from the input latches to the DAC latch. Label the PLD's inputs and outputs. Write the Boolean equations for the PLD outputs. Write a procedure that loads the DAC from a memory word DAC_LOAD_VAL. The 12-bit data value to be loaded is right justified in the memory word.

14. A 12-bit AD7248A DAC has internal double buffer latches as shown in Fig. 17.3-2. Two of these DACs are to be used in an application where the outputs of the DACs, when updated, must change simultaneously. Address decoding is to be exhaustive. Use /GCS1 and a 22V10 PLD to implement the necessary address decoding. The addresses assigned to DAC0 are 8000H and 8001H. The addresses for DAC1 are 8002H and 8003H. The address that causes the DAC outputs to be updated is 8004H. The DACs are located in I/O space. Write the instructions required to configure /GCS1. Write the Boolean equations for each output in the form required for an ABEL source file.

15. Write a single procedure, LOADDAC, that can load either of the DACs in the previous problem. The procedure loads a 12-bit value into the DAC's input latches. It does not load the 12-bit DAC latch. Parameters are passed to the procedure in the

80C188EB's registers. Register DX contains the address corresponding to the 8-bit input latch (/CSLSB) and register AX contains the right justified 12-bit load value. Also write a sequence of instructions that use LOADDAC to load DAC2 with the value 8F4H and then cause the output voltage of the DAC to be updated to this value.

16. A 16-bit DAC, designed for interface to 16-bit microprocessors, has data inputs D15–D0 and a single control input /LDAC. The control input is connected to the DAC's internal negative level triggered 16-bit DAC latch. Draw a block diagram of the interface of this DAC to an 80C188EB. The interface should be designed to minimize glitch impulses on the DAC's output.

17. The AD7243 has three output configurations, 0 to +5 V, 0 to +10 V, and –5 to +5 V. For each of these configurations write the binary code that must be loaded to produce a +2.5 V output.

18. Draw a block diagram of the interface of an AD7243 Serial DAC (Figs. 17.3-4 to 17.3-6) to an 80C188EB. A 22V10 PLD is to be used for address decoding. Use the approach shown in Fig. 17.3-7 and described in Subsection 17.3-3. Label the PLD's inputs and outputs. Write the Boolean equations for the PLD outputs. Write a procedure that loads the DAC from a memory word DAC_LOAD_VAL. The 12-bit data value to be loaded is right justified in the memory word.

19. Assume the R-$2R$ current steering DAC of Fig. 17.4-1 uses a –10 V reference and has $R = 10$ Kohm. For each of the following input codes, B_1-B_3 give the value of the current I_S and the output voltage.

   a. 001B
   b. 011B
   c. 100B
   d. 111B

20. Assume the R-$2R$ voltage switching DAC of Fig. 17.4-2 has a 5 V reference and $R = 10$ kohm. For each of the following input codes, B_1–B_3, give the value of the voltage at node A and the output voltage.

21. For the circuit of Fig. 17.5-1(b), assume $V_S = 10.0$ V, $R_{OUT} = 1$K, and $R_{IN} = 10$K. What is the value of v_{in}? What should this value be ideally? If R_{IN} is increased to 1 Mohm what is the value of v_{in}?

22. An 8-bit parallel binary input DAC with a 0 to +5 V output must be used in an application requiring the generation of a 0 to +10 V output. Design an op-amp circuit that conditions the DAC's output to provide the required voltage range.

23. Using a single chip 8-bit parallel input binary DAC with a 10 V output and op-amp(s), design an 8-bit two's complement DAC with a –5 V to +5 V output.

24. The summing amplifier of Fig. 17.6-3(d) can be used to create a two-digit weighted resistor DAC. The DAC is to accept a two digit BCD code. This requires that the circuit of Fig. 17.6-3(d) have eight inputs and that the input resistor's ratios correspond to the BCD code's weighting. Draw the circuit diagram and indicate the values of all resistors. The smallest input resistor to be used is 1 kohm. The output of the DAC is to be 0 to 10 V, nominal. What is the resolution and step size of this converter?

25. As shown below, an 8-bit multiplying DAC is used in the feedback loop of an op-amp circuit. Assume that the polarity of the DAC's reference input and its output voltage are the same. Derive a relationship for the gain of the circuit, V_O/V_p, as a function of B_1-B_8. What are the maximum and minimum values of gain for the circuit and to what values of B_1-B_8 do they correspond? How does the gain change for a one-bit change in the binary input to the DAC?

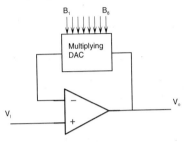

26. Design the logic to connect two DG528 8-channel latchable multiplexers to form a 16-channel demultiplexer with an interface to the 80C188EB's system bus. Draw a logic diagram for the implementation of this logic using standard SS and MSI components. Create a source file (in ABEL or some other HDL) for an alternate implementation of this logic using a PLD such as a 22V10.

27. The output of a 12-bit 0 to +5 V FS DAC is demultiplexed to eight track-holds. If the output impedance of the DAC is __ ohms and the input impedance of the track-holds used is __, what is the maximum RON for any channel of the demultiplexer if the demultiplexer is not to add any more than 1/4 lsb bit of error to the circuit.

28. A track-hold has a droop rate of 50 mV/s. How often must this track-hold be refreshed to allow it to hold the output from a 16-bit 10 V DAC to within 1/2 lsb?

29. A Xicor X9Cxxx digital potentiometer has 99 resistors. What is its resolution? If a DAC were to be used in place of this potentiometer how many bits would it need?

30. A straightforward way to interface a Xicor X9Cxxx digital potentiometer to an 80C188EB system might be to drive U/D from a port bit, drive /INC from /WR, and generate /CS from an address decoder or the CSU. The X9Cxxx has a setup time requirement from /CS to /INC of 100 ns and a low duration requirement for /INC of 1 μs. Analyze the impact of these requirements on the feasibility of the interface described for an 80C188EB operated at 20 MHz.

31. Timing requirements aside, the interface described in the previous problem would have /CS returning to 1 while /INC is a 1. This condition results in the initiation of storage of the counter's value in the nonvolatile register. Once this occurs, the X9Cxxx cannot be selected again for 20 ms. In contrast, if /CS is asserted and held low, /INC can be pulsed every 4 μs to adjust the output voltage. Describe how the interface for this type of operation could be implemented.

32. Consider the circuit shown in Fig. 17.6-3(e) with R1 and RF replaced by a 10 kohm Xicor X9Cxxx digital potentiometer. One terminal of the potentiometer is connected to ground, and the other is connected to the op-amp's output. The digital potentiometer's wiper is connected to the negative input of the op-amp. Determine the function and range of gains over the range of possible wiper positions.

CHAPTER

18

ANALOG INPUT
SUBSYSTEMS

18.1   Analog Data Acquisition

18.2   Input Transducers

18.3   Analog Input Signal Conditioning

18.4   Track-holds in Analog to Digital Conversion

18.5   Analog-to-Digital Converters (ADCs)

18.6   ADC Direct Conversion Techniques

18.7   ADC Indirect Conversion Techniques

18.8   Analog Multiplexers

18.9   Multichannel Data Acquisition Systems

18.10   Summary

As discussed in Chapter 17, many embedded applications involve monitoring or controlling physical measurands. For an instrumentation application, monitoring one or more measurands is the primary objective. In a closed loop control application, control of a measurand is the primary objective. However, monitoring a measurand is a necessary prerequisite for its control. A measurand's value must be determined before decisions required for its control can be made.

For each physical measurand, an input transducer, or sensor, is required that generates an electrical signal proportional to the measurand. This analog signal must be converted to a digital number before it can be input by a system and processed. This chapter introduces analog components used to generate and manipulate an analog signal before it reaches an analog-to-digital converter. The architecture and operation of analog-to-digital converters are also described.

18.1 Analog Data Acquisition

Analog data conversion typically requires several analog functions. Together these functions comprise a **data acquisition system** (**DAS**) (Fig. 18.1-1). The analog input signal to a data acquisition system is often the output of an input transducer, or sensor. The input transducer converts energy from the quantity being measured to an analog voltage or current.

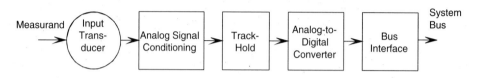

Figure 18.1-1   Single channel analog data acquisition subsystem.

When a transducer's output voltage range and an analog-to-digital converter's input voltage range do not match, analog signal conditioning in the form of amplification or scaling is required. Many transducers output **low level analog signals** of less than 1 V in amplitude. Frequently, as is the case with a thermocouple, such signals are in the millivolt or even microvolt range. Amplification is then required to convert a low level analog signal to a **high level analog signal** (1 to 10 V) compatible with the ADC's input range.

Filtering, another form of signal conditioning, may be required to eliminate noise or undesired frequency components in an analog signal. Other analog signal conditioning circuits implement operations such as buffering, clamping, and linearization. All these operations are used to transform a transducer's output into a signal suitable for conversion.

Because of their architecture, some types of ADCs require that their analog input remain constant during a conversion. In addition, some applications require that the analog input's value at a precise instant be determined. Use of a track-hold circuit allows both these requirements to be met. When used at the input of an ADC, a track-hold latches the analog input signal at the precise time dictated by its control signal. The ADC then converts the track-hold's output voltage.

The appropriately conditioned analog signal is converted to digital data by an **analog-to-digital converter** (**ADC** or **A/D**). The output of the ADC is a binary number or code that is proportional to the ADC's analog input.

A simple data acquisition subsystem was presented earlier in Chapter 4, Fig. 4.3-1. Let's analyze the constituent parts of this subsystem to begin our study of analog data acquisition subsystems. In that subsystem, only three of the components in Fig. 18.1-1 were required: a transducer, an ADC, and the bus interface. The LM34 temperature transducer's output voltage range is compatible with the input voltage range of the MAX166 ADC. So, the transducer's output was connected directly to the ADC's input. No analog signal conditioning was required. Also, since ambient temperature changes slowly, no track-hold was required. However, the MAX166 contains a built-in track-hold. The MAX166 is microprocessor compatible, so it also provides the basic bus interface. All that was needed to complete the interface to the system bus was an address decoder.

While a data acquisition system can consist of a single channel, the term data acquisition system usually implies a multichannel system. In the multichannel data acquisition system of Fig. 18.1-2, an analog multiplexer is used to select an analog input for conversion. Analog multiplexers were introduced in the previous chapter. A digital code at the analog multiplexer's channel address inputs selects which input channel's voltage appears at the multiplexer's output.

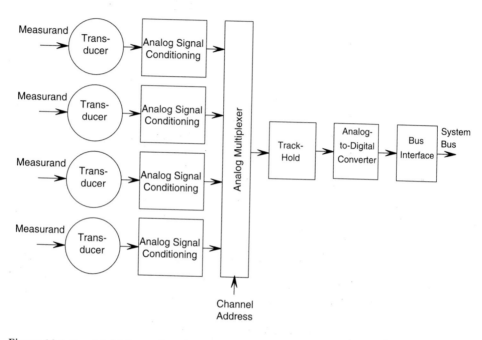

Figure 18.1-2   Multichannel analog data acquisition subsystem.

In the multichannel data acquisition system of Fig. 18.1-2, a single ADC converts several analog inputs in a time multiplexed fashion. The microprocessor selects the channel to be input to the ADC by supplying the appropriate channel address to the multiplexer (Fig. 18.1-2). The microprocessor then causes the track-hold to latch the multiplexer's output. Finally, the microprocessor initiates the conversion. After the conversion is complete, the microprocessor can select another channel and initiate the next conversion.

Multichannel systems can also be implemented using a dedicated converter for each channel. This approach is called, appropriately, **converter per channel.** Using a converter per channel eliminates the need for multiplexing but is more costly. Each approach has its advantages and disadvantages.

18.2   Input Transducers

A distinction is sometimes made between a sensor and a transducer. The definitions that follow correspond to the most commonly made distinction. An element that senses one form of energy, or a change in that form of energy, and transforms it into another form of energy, or change in another form of energy, is a **sensor**. An **electrical sensor** converts a measurand, or a change in a measurand, to an electrical signal. In contrast, a transducer is a device composed of a sensor and other elements that convert the sensor's output to a signal that is more appropriate to the application. For the purposes of this text, this distinction is not important. The term transducer will be used for both sensors and transducers.

For a specific physical measurand, there are usually many different types of transducers from which to choose. We will focus on transducers that convert other forms of energy to an electrical signal. Transducers are classified according to their transduction principle or according to the class of physical measurands they transduce.

The **transduction principle** is the physical principle upon which the operation of a transducer is based. Some examples are: resistive, capacitive, inductive, piezoelectric, photoconductive, photovoltaic, and electromagnetic transduction. These principles are involved in the transduction of various **classes of physical measurands** such as: acceleration, displacement, flow, force, humidity, light intensity, liquid level, pressure, sound, strain, temperature, and velocity.

To illustrate the variety of transducers available for a single measurand, a few common temperature transducers are listed in Table 18.2-1. These transducers differ in transduction principle, temperature range, linearity, sensitivity, stability, and cost.

Table 18.2-1   Some common temperature transducers.

Transducer	Transduction Principle	Self-generating	Linear	Output Level	Features
Thermocouple	thermoelectric	yes	no	low	self-generating
Thermistor	resistive	no	no	high	most sensitive
IC Sensor	band gap	no	yes	high	most linear

Some transducers are **self-generating**, directly producing an electrical signal. For example, a **thermocouple**, produced by joining the ends of two dissimilar metal wires, directly generates a voltage proportional to its junction temperature. However, a thermocouple's output is a low level signal that changes only tens of microvolts for a 1 degree Fahrenheit change in temperature. A thermocouple's output is also nonlinear.

Non-self-generating transducers do not directly generate an electrical signal. Instead, they are used to control a signal. A **thermistor** is a nonlinear temperature sensitive resistor composed of semiconductor materials. It is non-self-generating. When used as one of the components in a resistive voltage divider, it controls a voltage that varies with temperature. Most thermistors have a negative temperature coefficient (their resistance decreases with an increase in temperature).

The National Semiconductor **LM34 Fahrenheit Temperature Sensor** used in Fig. 4.3-1 is an **IC temperature transducer** that produces an output voltage proportional to temperature. It is non-self-generating and requires a supply voltage between 5 and 20 V. The LM34's output is linear, changing 10.0 mV/degree Fahrenheit.

In recent years there has been a substantial growth in the availability of microelectronic transducers, such as the National Semiconductor LM34 Fahrenheit Temperature

Sensor and the Motorola MPX4115 Altimeter/Barometer Absolute Pressure Sensor. Micro-electronic transducers are small in size and are mass produced using many of the techniques used to produce semiconductors and integrated circuits. Some of the technologies used in microelectronic transducers are silicon technology, thin-film technology, thick-film technology, and hybrid technology.

The production of transducers using microelectronic techniques results in smaller, less costly, and easier to use devices. Microelectronic transducers are easier to use because they often include signal conditioning integrated onto the device. This results in devices with high-level linear outputs. These outputs can often be connected directly to an ADC's input. The lower cost of microelectronic transducers increases the number of applications that are economically feasible for embedded systems.

Microelectronic transducers have made possible novel approaches to sensing traditional physical measurands and have made practical the sensing of measurands not easily detected in the past. For example, a wide range of biosensors are now available for sensing gases, ions, chemicals, and biological activity.

18.3   Analog Input Signal Conditioning

The analog signal from a transducer or other analog input device is often not in the form needed for direct input to an ADC. The signal is either too small, too noisy, has too high an output impedance, is not referenced to ground, or has some other deficiency. Thus, signal conditioning is required.

In an analog input subsystem, the purpose of signal conditioning is to provide the ADC with a noise free signal compatible with its input range. Amplification and filtering are the most commonly required signal conditioning operations.

Several op-amp circuits useful for signal conditioning were presented in Section 17.6. They are useful for conditioning high level signals in both analog output and analog input subsystems. Other circuits that are particularly important for analog input subsystems are presented in the subsections that follow.

18.3.1   Differential and Instrumentation Amplifiers

Many transducers produce low level voltages or currents. Amplification of low level signals, particularly in the presence of electrical noise, requires careful consideration.

Analog signals can be divided into two categories: single-ended and differential. A **single-ended signal** appears on a single wire and is measured with respect to the circuit ground (Fig. 18.3-1(a)). Single-ended signals are usually high level signals. For short distances, the signal is transmitted over a single wire and referenced to circuit ground. For longer distances, a pair of twisted wires is used to minimize noise pickup. One of the wires is grounded, and the other carries the signal. Alternatively, a shielded cable may be used to reduce the effects of electrical noise on the circuit. The circuits in Fig. 17.6-3 are all designed for single-ended inputs and generate single-ended outputs.

A low level signal is best handled as a **differential signal.** This approach requires two signal wires. The information is represented by the difference between the voltages on the

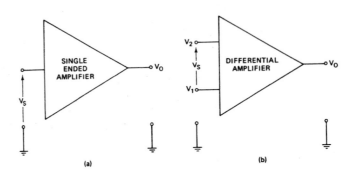

Figure 18.3-1   Generalized amplifier signal connections: (a) single-ended input single-ended output; (b) differential input single-ended output.

two signal wires, each measured with respect to ground (Fig. 18.3-1(b)). Many low level transducers, like bridge circuits, directly generate differential signals.

A transducer's environment may induce electrical noise onto its output signal. For our purposes, any signal other than the desired signal is considered noise. For low level signals, the magnitude of this noise may be comparable to the magnitude of the signal itself.

A differential amplifier is designed to handle differential input signals. Its output is usually a high level, single-ended signal that can then be processed by single-ended circuits, such as those of Fig. 17.6-3.

Figure 18.3-2 represents the type of situation where a differential or instrumentation amplifier is required. A transducer generates a low level signal represented by the voltage source, v_d. This signal is proportional to the measurand. In addition to v_d, the model of the transducer contains a voltage source v_{CM}, a **common mode voltage**.

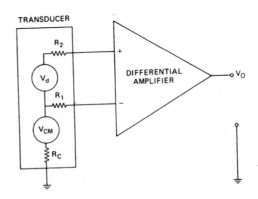

Figure 18.3-2   Simplified transducer model with differential outputs.

A portion of v_{CM} may result from the design of the transducer, as is the case with a bridge circuit. Also included in v_{CM} is noise induced in the conductors between the transducer and amplifier input and any difference in the ground potential at the transducer and the amplifier. If the two conductors carrying the signals follow the same physical path, they will be exposed to the same noise environment. This is the justification for using the single signal generator v_{CM} to model the noise.

If a single-ended connection is used between the transducer and the amplifier (v_2 is used as the signal input and v_1 is grounded), the signal amplified is $v_d + v_{CM}$. If v_d is a very low level signal, v_{CM} can be of comparable or greater magnitude. This results in a low **signal to noise ratio (SNR)**, at the input of the amplifier. The noise is amplified along with the signal. At the amplifier's output, it is impossible to determine what portion of the output is noise and what portion is signal.

However, if a differential signal is obtained from the transducer, an amplifier designed to amplify the differential signal and reject the common mode signal can be used. Such an amplifier is called a differential amplifier. The output of a **differential amplifier** is the product of the amplifier's gain and the voltage difference between its two input signals:

$$v_o = G(v_2 - v_1)$$

Figure 18.3-3 shows the circuit diagram of a differential amplifier constructed from a single op-amp. The circuit's output is:

$$v_o = \frac{R_2}{R_1}(v_2 - v_1)$$

Thus, the output is the input voltage difference ($v_2 - v_1$) multiplied by the gain ($G, = R_2/R_1$). A basic drawback of this circuit is that the differential input impedance (i.e. the impedance from input to input) is only $2R_1$. This impedance loads, and possibly attenuates, the signal source.

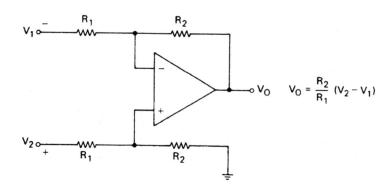

Figure 18.3-3   Differential amplifier constructed from a single op-amp.

The amplifier of Fig. 18.3-3 has additional limitations. If high input impedance and high gain are required, the input resistance has to be very large, and the feedback resistance even larger. This entails the difficult matching of two very high valued resistors. If matching is not achieved, the common mode signal is also amplified. Furthermore, changing the gain requires changing two matched resistors in the circuit.

An **instrumentation amplifier** that uses three operational amplifiers to solve these problems is shown in Fig. 18.3-4. This circuit's transfer function is:

$$v_o = \left(1 + \frac{2R_2}{R_1}\right)(v_2 - v_1)$$

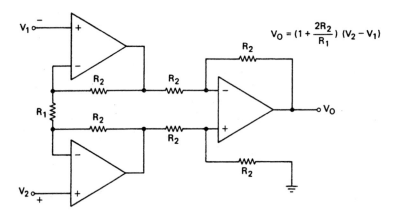

Figure 18.3-4   Instrumentation amplifier constructed from three op-amps.

The two input op-amps provide a very high input impedance. The gain of the circuit can be adjusted by changing the single resistor R_1. For high gain, the R_2 resistors that must be matched need not be excessively large. This type of instrumentation amplifier is available as a single IC with R_1 as an external resistor. For example, Analog Device's **AD620 Instrumentation Amplifier** can have its gain programmed to any value from 1 to 1000 using an external resistor.

For practical differential and instrumentation amplifiers, the ideal characteristics predicated on perfectly matched resistors and ideal op-amps are unattainable. The quality of a practical circuit is measured by its common mode rejection ratio (**CMRR or CMR**). This is the ratio of the circuit's gain for differential signals, A_d, divided by its gain for common mode signals, A_{CM}.

$$\text{CMMR} = \frac{A_d}{A_{CM}}$$

In an ideal circuit, $A_{CM} = 0$, resulting in an infinite CMRR. In practical IC circuits, **CMRRs** between 10^3 and 10^6 are typical.

The common mode rejection ratio is often specified in decibels as:

$$\text{CMMR(dB)} = 20\log_{10}\frac{A_d}{A_{CM}}$$

The CMRR of an AD620 programmed for a gain of 100 is 110 dB minimum. The value 110 dB is 20×5.5, so 110 dB equals $10^{5.5}$ or 316,227.77. The differential input signal we want to amplify is multiplied by 100 by the amplifier. The common mode signal, which we don't want in the output, is multiplied (scaled) by A_d/CMRR or $10^{-3.5}$ or 0.000316.

While some instrumentation amplifiers are programmable by a single external resistor, others can be programmed by either pin strapping or digital inputs. Those with digitally programmable gains are called **Programmable Gain Amplifiers** (**PGAs**). Digitally programmable gains are usually either powers of 10 (1, 10, 100, and 1000) or powers of two (1, 2, 4, and 8).

18.3.2   Filtering

Analog input signals are filtered to minimize unwanted frequency components, including electrical noise. Depending on the application, either a low-pass, high-pass, or band-pass filter may be needed. For many input transducers, the information in the signal is contained in the signal's low frequency components. In such cases, a filter that blocks higher frequency signal components reduces the noise in the signal without affecting the information. Low-pass filters are used for this purpose.

A **passive low-pass filter** is shown in Fig. 18.3-5(a). The gain of this filter in the frequency domain is:

$$G = \frac{V_{out}}{V_{in}} = \frac{1}{1 + j\omega RC}$$

where $\omega = 2\pi f$. The DC component of the signal ($f = 0$ or equivalently $\omega = 0$) sees a gain of 1 and is passed through the filter unattenuated. Higher frequency components of the signal see a gain of less than 1, with the gain decreasing as the frequency increases. For a signal at the filter's cutoff frequency, the low-pass filter's output voltage is half of its input voltage. The cutoff frequency, f_c, is given by:

$$f_c = \frac{1}{2\pi RC}$$

An **active filter**, one that combines amplification with filtering, can be created by placing a capacitor in parallel with the feedback resistor of Fig. 17.6-3(e), producing the circuit of Fig. 18.3-5(b). The gain for this circuit is:

$$G = -\frac{R_F}{R_1}\left(\frac{1}{1 + j\omega R_F C_F}\right)$$

For the DC component of the signal ($\omega = 0$), the gain is $-R_F/R_1$.

This is a **first-order filter**. A filter's **order** determines the rate of gain attenuation beyond its cutoff frequency. Increased order appears on the filter's transfer characteristic, gain versus frequency, as steeper rolloff. Low-pass filter circuits with order higher than one can be constructed. Higher order filter circuits require additional components.

Active high-pass and band-pass filter circuits can be constructed using op-amps, resistors, and capacitors. For example, a simple high-pass filter can be constructed from Fig. 17.6-3(e) by adding a capacitor in series with R_1.

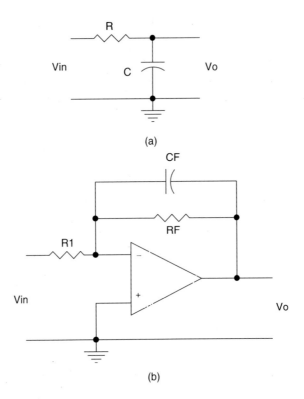

(a)

(b)

Figure 18.3-5   Low-pass filters: (a) passive filter with a maximum gain of 1; (b) active filter with a maximum gain of $-R_F/R_1$.

There are numerous books devoted exclusively to filter design. A few of these are listed in this chapter's bibliography. Also listed in the bibliography are some CAD programs for filter design. These programs compute the component values needed to achieve a desired gain and cutoff frequency for a given filter circuit.

Integrated circuit active filters allow high performance filters to be constructed using a single IC and a few external resistors. For example, Burr-Brown's **UAF42 Universal Active Filter** is a 16-pin IC that can be configured for a wide range of low-pass, high-pass, band-pass, and band-reject filters. You can use this IC to create filter types such as Butterworth, Bessel, and Chebyshev. The UAF42 contains four operational amplifiers, one configured as an inverting amplifier, two configured as integrators, and one uncommitted. The capacitors required are also integrated onto the IC. Burr-Brown provides a CAD program that guides you through the filter design process for the UAF2 and automatically calculates the component values.

18.3.3   Clamping Analog Signals

Most ADCs must have their analog input protected from being overdriven. Often the ADC cannot tolerate its analog input exceeding its positive supply voltage by more than 0.3 V, or exceeding its negative supply or ground by less than –0.3 V. Overdriving an ADC's input can be the result of an input signal exceeding the ADC's power supply voltage, applying an input signal to an unpowered ADC, or power supply sequencing at power on that drives the ADC prior to applying power to the ADC. Overdriving can cause permanent damage to an ADC.

Operational amplifiers are designed to operate with either dual power supplies or a single power supply. Dual power supply voltages of ±5 V, ±12 V, or ±15 V are common in systems. A typical circuit might use an op-amp to amplify a transducer's output. Such an op-amp operating from ±12 V supplies can generate outputs up to its saturation voltages, approximately ±11 V. The op-amp's output provides the ADC's input. If the ADC uses a single +5 V supply, or dual ±5 V supplies, it can easily be damaged by the op-amp's output. Thus, some way of limiting or clamping the value of the ADC's input is necessary.

A simple clamping circuit is shown in Fig. 18.3-6. The Schottky diodes prevent the ADC's input signal from exceeding the ADC's power supply voltages by more than 0.3 V.

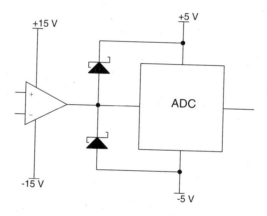

Figure 18.3-6   Simple clamping circuit using Schottky diodes to protect an ADC's input from an input signal that exceeds the ADC's power supply voltage.

Another approach to limiting the input signal to an ADC is to use an IC specifically designed for this purpose. Analog Devices' AD8036 **Clamp Amp** can be operated with ±5 V supplies and can clamp its output to voltages within this range. The clamp levels are determined by voltages at additional inputs, VH and VL, of the clamp amp. The only restrictions on VIN, VH, and VL are that the maximum voltage difference between VIN and VH or VL should not exceed 6.3 V, and all three of these voltages must be within the clamp amp's supply voltage range.

18.4   Track-holds for Analog to Digital Conversion

In Sections 18.6 and 18.7 we will consider different types of ADC architectures. Some ADCs require their inputs to be held constant, usually within 1/2 lsb, during the conversion process. If the signal to be converted can change more than this amount within a conversion period, a track-hold must be used to sample the signal and provide a constant input to the ADC.

For example, if the input signal is a sine wave, the allowed change in the signal determines the maximum sine wave frequency that can be converted without using a track-hold. This maximum frequency is often a surprisingly low value.

Assume that the maximum change in an ADC's input must be limited to within 1/2 lsb within the conversion time t_{conv}, or

$$\left. \frac{dv}{dt} \right|_{max} \leq \frac{1/2 \text{ lsb}}{t_{conv}}$$

An n-bit ADC's full input voltage range expressed in bits is 2^n bits. If the input to the ADC is a sine wave with a peak to peak value that is equal to the ADC's full input range, then in terms of bits, the sine wave's amplitude is 2^{n-1} bits. The maximum rate of change of the sine wave is:

$$\left. \frac{d}{dt} 2^{n-1} \sin \omega t \right|_{max} = \pi f 2^n$$

Setting the two expressions equal and solving for f gives:

$$f_{max} \leq \frac{1}{\pi 2^{n+1} t_{conv}}$$

For an ADC with a conversion time of 20 μs and a resolution of 12 bits, the maximum input frequency is 2 Hz! If you wish to convert sine waves with frequencies above 2 Hz and meet the constraint that the signal being converted not change more that 1/2 lsb during the conversion, then you must use a track-hold. The sine wave is input to the track-hold. The output of the track-hold provides the input to the ADC. The track-hold provides a constant input to the ADC during the ADC's conversion time. The structure and operation of track-holds was discussed in Section 17.8.

18.5   Analog-to-Digital Converters (ADCs)

Before considering specific ADC architectures and their operation, some fundamental analog-to-digital conversion concepts must be introduced. To convert an analog signal to a digital code, ADCs perform two basic operations, quantization and coding. **Quantization** is the mapping of the analog signal into one of several possible discrete ranges, or **quanta**. **Coding** is the assignment of a digital code to each quantum. The same codes used for inputs to DACs are also used in coding outputs from ADCs.

Figure 18.5-1 is the transfer characteristic of an ideal 3-bit binary unipolar ADC. An n-bit binary ADC has 2^n distinct output codes. Thus, the 3-bit converter has eight output codes represented on the vertical axis.

On the horizontal axis, the analog input range is divided into quanta by **transition points** or **decision levels**. **Quantization size** is $Q = FS/2^n$, where FS is the nominal full

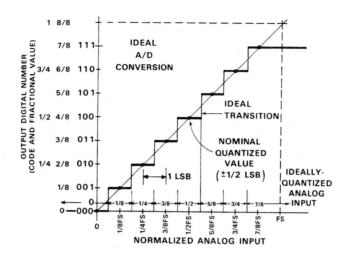

Figure 18.5-1   Conversion relationship for an ideal 3-bit ADC. (Courtesy of Analog Devices, Inc.)

scale input voltage. The quantization size represents the maximum input voltage change required to cause a change in the output of one least significant bit. Equivalently, a quantum change is the smallest change in the input signal that the ADC is guaranteed to detect.

In an ideal ADC, the first transition point occurs at $Q/2$, and each of the remaining transition points is spaced Q volts apart. The midpoint of each quantum is the voltage that is exactly (without error) represented by the output code.

For example, transition points at 1/16 FS and 3/16 FS bracket the 1/8 FS point. Any analog input in the quantum from 1/16 FS to 3/16 FS is assigned the output code representing 1/8 FS (001B). Thus, quantization produces an inherent **quantization error** of $\pm Q/2$. Accordingly an output, M, from an ADC indicates that the analog input has a value of $M \pm Q/2$ ($M \pm \mathrm{FS}/2^{n+1}$).

Since quantization error is inherent in the conversion process, the only way quantization error can be reduced is by selecting an ADC with a larger number of bits. In a practical converter, the transition points are not perfectly placed and nonlinearity, offset, and gain errors result. These errors are in addition to the inherent quantization error.

Errors in ADCs are defined and measured in terms of the location of the actual transition points in relation to their ideal locations (Fig. 18.5-2). If the first transition does not occur at exactly +1/2 lsb (+1/2 Q), there is an **offset error**. If the difference between the points at which the last transition and first transition occur is not equal to FS – 2 lsb, there is a **gain error**. **Linearity error** exists if the differences between transition points are not all equal, in which case the midpoints of some decision quanta do not lie on a straight line between 0 and FS. The midpoints between transition points should be 1 lsb apart. **Differential nonlinearity** is the deviation between the actual difference between midpoints and 1 lsb, for adjacent pairs of codes. If the differential nonlinearity is equal to or more negative than −1 lsb, then one or more codes will be missing.

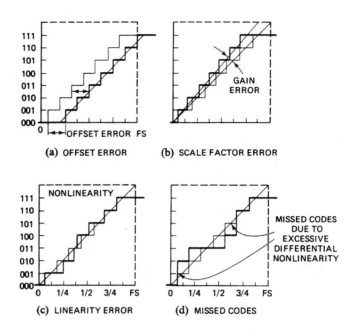

Figure 18.5-2   Typical sources of error for a 3-bit A/D converter. (Courtesy of Analog Devices, Inc.)

ADCs differ in how the operations of quantization and coding are accomplished. Several types of ADCs and their associated conversion techniques are presented in the next two sections.

18.5.1   Analog Comparators

One component associated with all ADC architectures is an analog comparator. An analog comparator is, itself, a 1-bit ADC. Even with its large quantization error, it is useful for determining whether an analog signal is above or below some threshold value (transition point). An analog comparator is also a key component in the construction of multi-bit ADCs.

An analog comparator is essentially an open loop op-amp. The open loop op-amp's output saturates at its highest positive level if its noninverting (+) input terminal is more positive than its inverting (−) input terminal (Fig. 18.5-3(a)). If, on the other hand, the inverting terminal is more positive than the noninverting terminal, the output saturates at its most negative value. The op-amp's output is clamped at the appropriate logic levels to provide a digital output.

The transfer characteristic of a comparator with 5 V CMOS logic level outputs is shown in Fig. 18.5-3(b). When the comparator is used as a threshold detector, the inverting input is connected to a reference voltage equal to the threshold, and the analog signal is connected to the noninverting input. When the analog signal exceeds the threshold, the comparator outputs a logic 1. When it is below threshold, the output is logic 0.

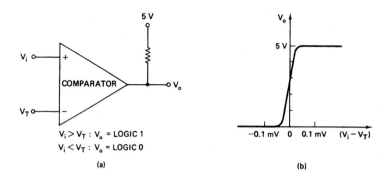

Figure 18.5-3   Comparator: (a) circuit; (b) voltage transfer characteristics.

The conversion relationship for a comparator implementing a 1-bit ADC with a nominal range of 0 to 10 V is shown in Fig. 18.5-4. The single transition point is placed at +1/2 lsb, where 1 lsb is equal to 5 V. A reference voltage of 2.5 V provides the single transition level at +1/2 lsb, dividing the 0 to 10 V FS range into two quanta. The endpoints of the transfer characteristic are 0 V and 5 V (FS – 1 lsb). The effect of actual full scale being nominal full scale minus 1 lsb is very clear in this figure and worth noting.

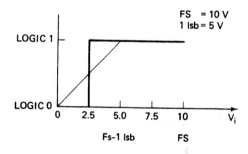

Figure 18.5-4   Conversion relationship of a comparator connected to provide a 1-bit A/D converter with a nominal 0 to 10 V input range.

18.5.2   Conversion Techniques

To construct ADCs of n bits, two broad categories of techniques are used, direct conversion and indirect conversion. With **direct conversion**, the analog voltage to be converted is compared to the output of a reference DAC. The reference DAC's output is changed as a result of each comparison, until it is eventually equal to the analog input voltage. The DAC's input is then equal to the desired output code. The various direct conversion techniques differ in the way the inputs to the DAC are sequenced to obtain a value equal to the unknown analog voltage. For ADCs with binary outputs, the desired binary code has been obtained when

$$\left| V_I - V_{FS} \sum_i B_i 2^{-i} \right| < (1/2) lsb$$

where V_I is the analog voltage to be converted.

With **indirect conversion**, the analog input voltage is transformed to the time or the frequency domain. Digital logic converts the time interval or the frequency into a digital output code. Indirect conversion techniques are slower than direct conversion techniques.

18.6   Direct Conversion Techniques

Four direct conversion techniques are presented in this section: flash, half-flash, counting, and successive approximation.

18.6.1   Flash Converters

The fastest and conceptually simplest ADC is a **flash** (parallel or simultaneous) **converter**. This converter directly implements the quantization operation using a voltage divider consisting of 2^n resistors and 2^n-1 comparators. The coding operation is implemented by a digital encoder that translates the digital outputs of the 2^n-1 comparators into an n-bit code (Fig. 18.6-1).

The resistors in the voltage divider divide the reference voltage into 2^n-1 voltages corresponding to the 2^n-1 transition points needed for quantizing an analog input. The inverting input of each comparator is connected to one of the transition point reference voltages. The resistor voltage divider provides a threshold for each comparator that is one lsb higher that the threshold for the comparator immediately below. The unknown analog voltage is connected to the noninverting input of each comparator. All comparators with transition point threshold voltages below that of the unknown voltage have outputs of 1. All comparators with transition point threshold voltages above the unknown voltage have outputs of 0.

The output from the comparators is a thermometer code. A **thermometer code** is a code consisting of a column with j consecutive 1s at the bottom and k consecutive 0s at the top, where $j + k$ is a constant.

The comparator's thermometer code outputs are latched. The latched outputs provide the input to a digital encoder. The digital encoder has 2^n-1 inputs, but only 2^n possible output codes. This combinational circuit can be designed to produce any output code format desired.

Flash ADCs are the fastest converters available. Conversion time is the sum of the delay through the comparator stage and the encoders. Because of the flash converter's conversion speed, a track-hold is usually not needed.

The flash ADC's drawback is the number of comparators required. An 8-bit converter requires 255 comparators! Practical IC flash converters range in size from 4 to 10 bits.

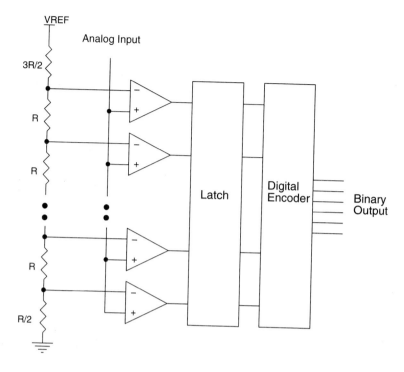

Figure 18.6-1   Parallel (flash) ADC.

The number of analog comparators required can be reduced by using the **half-flash** technique (Fig. 18.6-2). With this technique, the conversion is done in two steps and a track-hold is usually required. In the first step, an $n/2$ bit flash conversion produces the most significant $n/2$ bits of the result. These $n/2$ bits are input to a DAC to generate a voltage corresponding to the value they represent. This value is subtracted from the unknown analog input. The difference is then converted by a second $n/2$ bit flash converter to produce the least significant $n/2$ bits of the result. An 8-bit half-flash converter requires only 30 comparators, as opposed to the 255 required by an 8-bit flash converter.

18.6.2   Counting (Ramp) Converters

A simple direct conversion technique is that of the **counting** or **ramp converter**. Hardware for a counting converter that has its conversion algorithm implemented in software is shown in Fig. 18.6-3. To produce the ideal transfer characteristic of Fig. 18.5-1, the output of the DAC must be offset so that when the DAC is loaded with all zeros, its output voltage corresponds to +1/2 a least significant bit.

The conversion process consists of repeatedly outputting incrementally higher binary values to the DAC until the comparator changes state. Starting from a value of 0, each subsequent value output is 1 lsb greater than the previous value. The resulting output

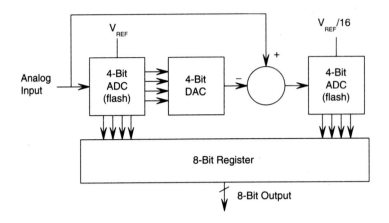

Figure 18.6-2   Analog-to-digital conversion in two stages, half-flash.

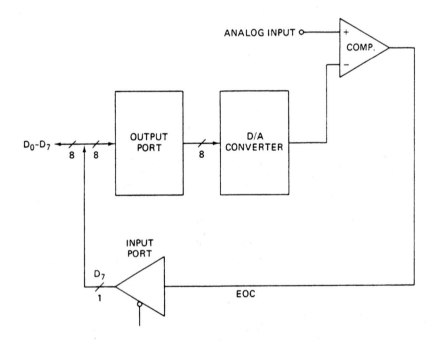

Figure 18.6-3   Basic hardware structure for software ADC conversion routines.

from the DAC is a piecewise continuous ramp. The following code implements an 8-bit ramp conversion using the hardware of Fig. 18.6-3.

```
ramp_ad           proc
          mov     cx,256          ;maximum steps in ramp, 2**n
          mov     al,0ffh         ;initial DAC load value - 1 (0 - 1)
ramp:
          inc     al              ;increment DAC load value
          mov     dx,DAC          ;step DAC output
          out     dx,al
          nop                     ;DAC and comparator settling time
          mov     dx,COMP         ;check comparator output, bit 7
          in      al,dx
          test    al,80h
          loopnz  ramp            ;loop if comparator output is 0
          ret
ramp_ad           endp
```

CX is initialized to 256 (2^8) to control a loop that allows a maximum of 256 steps to be generated. AL acts as the "counter" and holds the value output to the DAC. Since the value in AL is incremented in the loop, before being output to the DAC, AL is initially loaded with 0FFH. After AL is incremented, the first value output to the DAC is 0.

After allowing the DAC's and comparator's outputs to settle, the comparator's output is read. If the comparator's output is a 1, the analog input is greater than the DAC output. Therefore, the binary value output to the DAC is too small. AL is again incremented and output to the DAC. This process continues until either the comparator's output is 0 or the loop has been executed 256 times. The LOOPNZ instruction terminates the loop as soon as either of these conditions occurs. Since AL must be counted up to the value corresponding to the analog input, the conversion time is proportional to the analog input voltage. The maximum conversion time is approximately 2^n times the time for one loop iteration.

18.6.3   Successive Approximation Converters

The most popular direct conversion method is **successive approximation**. This method has the advantage of a fixed conversion time proportional to the number of bits, n, in the code and independent of the analog input value. The successive approximation algorithm consists of successive comparisons of the unknown voltage to a voltage generated by a DAC (the approximation).

Starting with the most significant bit, each comparison determines one bit of the final result and the approximation to be used for the next comparison. The successive approximation algorithm is, in effect, a **binary search**.

A successive approximation converter uses a DAC to generate the voltage that is compared to the unknown voltage. A software implementation of a successive approximation converter uses the same hardware used for the counting converter (Fig. 18.6-3). However, for a successive approximation converter, the offset required when the DAC is loaded with all 0s must be $-1/2$ lsb, rather than $+1/2$ lsb.

The steps in the successive approximation algorithm are as follows:

1. An initial approximation code is used to determine the most significant bit of the result. This code has a 1 as its most significant bit, and all its other bits are 0s.

2. The approximation code is output to the DAC

3. The comparator output is read. If it is 0, the bit being determined in the approximation is changed to a 0. If not, it is left as a 1.

4. If all bits have not been determined, the next most significant bit is tested. To test the next most significant bit, the next bit in the approximation code that resulted from step 3 is made a 1, and then step 2 is repeated. When all bits have been determined, the conversion process is complete.

The effect of this algorithm is to first test whether the analog input voltage is greater or less than 1/2 FS. If the analog input is greater than 1/2 FS, having a 1 as the most significant bit of the approximation code output to the DAC for the first comparison makes the comparator output a 1. When this is the case, the most significant bit is left as a 1. The next most significant bit in the approximation code is then set to 1, and the analog input is again tested (second comparison) to see whether it is greater than 3/4 FS.

In contrast, if during the first comparison the analog input is less than 1/2 FS, the comparator's output is a 0, and the most significant bit is changed to a 0. The next most significant bit is then set to 1, and a test is made to determine whether the unknown voltage is greater than 1/4 FS. This process is repeated in succession for each bit until the last bit is tested.

A procedure to implement a software-driven 8-bit successive approximation conversion is given in Fig. 18.6-4.

This procedure uses register BL to keep track of the position of the bit being tested. BL is initialized to 80H. The approximation is constructed in AH. Each approximation is created by ORing AH and BL. This value is then moved to AL and output to the DAC. If the comparator's output is a 0, BL is XORed with AH to clear the bit being tested, otherwise this bit is left as a 1. BL is then right shifted one position in preparation for creating the next approximation during the next pass through the loop. After eight iterations of the loop, the conversion is complete.

In IC implementations of successive approximation ADCs, the binary search algorithm is implemented by a **Successive Approximation Register** (**SAR**) state machine that takes as its inputs the output of the comparator and a clock signal and produces the correct successive approximation values for loading into the DAC.

If the input changes more than 1/2 lsb during the conversion, a track-hold is required to hold the input constant while the conversion is carried out. Successive approximation converter ICs with an on-chip track-hold are called **sampling ADCs**. An example was given is section 18.4 for determining the maximum sine wave frequency that can be converted without a track-hold.

```
;**********************************************************************
;NAME:        SA_ADC
;
;function: b-bit successive approximation analog-to-digital conversion
;returns: AL = result
;modifies: AX,BL,CX,DX and PSW
;DESCRIPTION:
;
;**********************************************************************

sa_adc proc
        mov     bl,80h          ;set position of 1st bit tested
        mov     ah,00h
        mov     cx,8            ;number of bits in result
next_bit:
        or      ah,bl           ;create approximation in AH
        mov     dx,dacsa        ;output approximation to DAC
        mov     al,ah
        out     dx,al
        nop                     ;wait for DAC and comparator to settle
        mov     dx,cmpsts       ;read comparator output
        in      al,dx
        or      al,al           ;set flags
        js      skip            ;if comparator out is 1 leave bit tested 1
        xor     ah,bl           ;comparator out = 0, clear bit
skip:   shr     bl,1            ;position for next bit
        loop    next_bit
        mov     al,ah
        ret
sa_adc endp
```

Figure 18.6-4   Procedure for an 8-bit software-driven analog-to-digital conversion successive approximation.

18.6.4   AD7875 12-bit Successive Approximation ADC

An example of a microprocessor compatible successive approximation ADC IC is the AD7875 (Fig. 18.6-5). On this 12-bit ADC's block diagram can be seen the 12-bit DAC, a comparator, and a SAR. These elements together comprise the successive approximation ADC. Also included on the IC are a voltage reference, track-hold, control logic, and bus interface.

Conversion results can be read from the AD7875 in serial or in either of two parallel formats. Only the parallel formats are discussed here. One parallel format transfers the result as a single 12-bit word, the other transfers the result as two bytes.

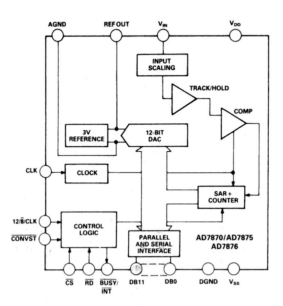

Figure 18.6-5   AD7875 12-bit sampling ADC. (Courtesy of Analog Devices, Inc.)

The AD7875 can be operated in either of two modes. Mode 1 is used for an interrupt driven interface. Using this mode, the microprocessor generates a device select pulse at the /CONVST input to initiate a conversion. The microprocessor then goes on to other tasks. When the conversion is complete, the ADC interrupts the microprocessor. The microprocessor executes an ISR to read the conversion result.

The rising edge of the negative pulse at the /CONVST input, which initiates the conversion, puts the track-hold in its hold mode. The /BUSY or /INT output functions as /INT in this mode. /INT is normally high and goes low at the end of the conversion. This signal can be polled or inverted and used to interrupt the microprocessor. The falling edge of /CS and /RD during a read of the ADC returns the /INT line high. If the three-function input 12/8/CLK is +5 V, the conversion result is read as a 12-bit word. If this input is 0 V, the result is read as two 8-bit words. Either the low byte or high byte of the result can be read first, depending on the HBEN input's value. Whichever byte is read first returns /INT high.

Mode 2 is used for an extended bus cycle interface. A read operation starts the conversion and the ADC requests WAIT states until the conversion is complete. The /BUSY or /INT line is used as a /BUSY line to request WAIT states. For this mode of operation, /CONVST is hardwired low and a conversion is started by taking /CS low while HBEN is low. /BUSY goes low at the start of the conversion and returns high when the conversion is complete. /BUSY is used to generate the signal to the 80C188EB's READY input.

18.7 Indirect Conversion Techniques

Two popular indirect conversion techniques are dual slope integration and delta-sigma conversion. Both techniques are presented in this section.

18.7.1   Dual-Slope Integrating Converters

Integrating ADCs use an indirect method of conversion where the analog input voltage is converted to a time interval. The output of an integrating ADC represents the average value of its analog input. Integrating ADCs are useful for precisely measuring slowly varying signals. There are several variations of the integrating ADC: single-slope, dual-slope, and multi-slope. The dual-slope or dual-ramp operation is employed in many ADC ICs. Multi-slope ADCs also include the dual-slope process.

For a dual-slope ADC, two time intervals are involved. During the first time interval, the analog input voltage is integrated for a fixed length of time. The output of the integrator at the end of the first time interval is a voltage that represents the average value of the analog input over the first time interval. A reference voltage of opposite polarity to the input is then integrated until the output of the integrator is zero. The time required to integrate to zero (deintegrate) creates a second time interval. The length of the second time interval is measured by a counter. The counter's output holds the result of the conversion.

A dual-slope ADC circuit is shown in Fig. 18.7-1. Logic controls an electronic switch that can select either the analog input voltage or a reference voltage as the integrator's input. The polarity of the reference voltage is opposite to that of the analog input. At the start of the conversion, the counter is cleared, and the analog input voltage is selected as the integrator's input. When the output ramp of the integrator crosses the comparator's threshold, $v_0 = 0$ V, the counter is enabled to count clock pulses.

The counter counts for a fixed time interval, T, until it overflows. For a constant value analog input, the slope of the integrator's output ramp is proportional to the unknown input. Thus, the integrator's output voltage at the end of the fixed time interval, T, is proportional to the analog input. If the analog input varies during the fixed time interval, the integrator's output at the end of this interval is proportional to the average value (integral) of the input, v_I, over the fixed time interval.

$$v_o(T) \; = \; - \frac{1}{RC}\int_0^T v_I dt$$

At the end of the time interval T, the input of the integrator is switched from the analog input to the reference voltage, making the integrator output a ramp with a fixed positive slope. The counter counts the time required for the integrator's output to reach the comparator's threshold. When the threshold is reached, the counter is stopped. The value in the counter is the code for the analog voltage. This can be verified by examining the relationship for $v_o(T + \tau)$:

$$v_o(T+\tau) \; = \; - \frac{1}{RC} \int_T^{(T+\tau)} (-V_{REF}) dt + v_o(T)$$

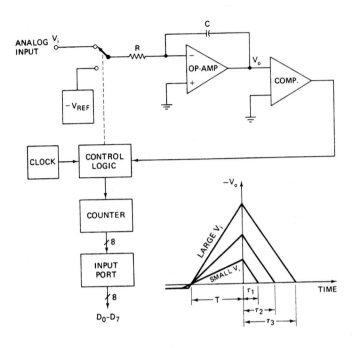

Figure 18.7-1   Dual-slope integrating A/D converter.

$v_o(T)$ is the initial condition at time T; thus:

$$v_o(T+\tau) = -\frac{1}{RC}\int_{T}^{(T+\tau)}(-V_{REF})\,dt - \frac{1}{RC}\int_{0}^{T}v_I\,dt$$

since $v_o(T+\tau) = 0$

$$\frac{1}{RC}\int_{T}^{(T+\tau)}V_{REF}\,dt = \frac{1}{RC}\int_{0}^{T}v_I\,dt$$

$$V_{REF}\tau = \hat{v}_I T$$

$$\hat{v}_I = \frac{\tau}{T}V_{REF}$$

Note that the time interval T is determined by incrementing an n bit counter until the counter overflows. When the counter overflows, there is a carry of 1 and the n bits in the counter are all 0s. Thus, the time interval T can be considered as being equal to a 1 with n zeros, $1.0_{n-1}\ldots0_0$. The value left in the counter after the time interval τ can then be considered as a fraction, $0.B_{n-1}\ldots B_0$. As a result, the average value of v_I, $\hat{v}_I$, is equal to this count multiplied by V_{REF}.

Because the values of R, C, and the clock frequency remain the same for both the charge and discharge cycles, and the output is the ratio of discharge time to charge time, the result is independent of any long term drift in R, C, or the clock frequency. Furthermore, by making the input integration period a multiple of the line frequency period, excellent AC line noise rejection is achieved.

Hardware integrating ADCs are, typically, low-speed devices. However, they are capable of high accuracy at low cost. Commercial integrating ADCs are generally multiple phase, or multi-slope. They include an additional phase(s) that precedes the first phase in Fig. 18.7-1. During this additional phase, the device carries out a self-calibrating autozero operation to eliminate offset errors.

18.7.2   Delta-Sigma Converters

Delta-Sigma (or **oversampling**) converters use oversampling and digital filtering to achieve high performance conversion and noise filtering at low cost. Delta-sigma converters convert an analog voltage by balancing the average current produced by the analog input voltage over the conversion period with an equal amount of current generated internally by the converter. A simplified functional diagram of a delta-sigma converter is shown in Fig. 18.7-2.

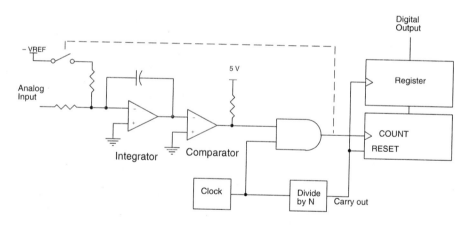

Figure 18.7-2   Simplified block diagram of a delta-sigma converter.

The analog input voltage produces a current into the integrator's summing junction charging the integrator's feedback capacitor and causing its output voltage to go negative. When the inverting input of the comparator goes negative, the comparator's output becomes 1. While the comparator's output is 1, -VREF is switched to the integrator's other input for the duration of one clock period. The current from the integrator's summing junction caused by switching -VREF into the circuit removes a fixed amount of charge from the capacitor during the one clock period. As long as the integrator's output is negative, an equal amount of charge is removed during the next clock period. In effect, the converter switches -VREF into the circuit often enough to maintain a zero average current into the integrator's summing junction. The name delta-sigma refers to the fact that the differences (delta) of the integrator's current inputs are summed (sigma) over time.

The comparator's output is a bit stream of 0s and 1s. A digital filter generates an *n*-bit binary output based on this bit stream. A simple implementation of the digital filter is a counter that counts the number of times the comparator's output is 1 for a fixed number of clock periods. The contents of the counter after the fixed number of clock periods is proportional to the average value of the input over the counting period and is the converter's result. Practical delta-sigma converters use higher order modulators and more sophisticated digital filters.

Delta-sigma converters are particularly useful for high-resolution conversion of low-frequency signals. IC delta-sigma converters typically range from 16 to 21 bits.

18.8   Analog Multiplexers

Because they are the same devices used in different ways, you have already been introduced to analog multiplexers during the discussion of analog demultiplexers in Section 17.7. When used as a multiplexer, the independent switch terminals are the inputs and the common terminal is the output (Fig. 18.8-1). Any unused inputs should be grounded.

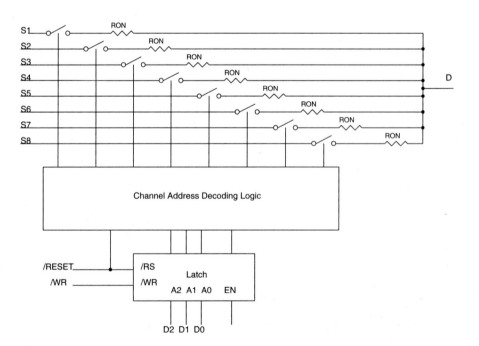

Figure 18.8-1   Functional diagram of an 8-channel multiplexer (demultiplexer) with an onboard address and control latch.

The DG528 multiplexer introduced in Section 17.7 is a single ended 1-of-8 multiplexer with an on-chip address latch. Multiplexers with differential inputs and outputs are also available for routing differential signals. The DG529 is a 2-of-8 differential multiplexer. It consists of two banks of four switches each. Each bank of switches has its own common output connection (Fig. 18.8-2). The channel address closes the corresponding switch in each bank.

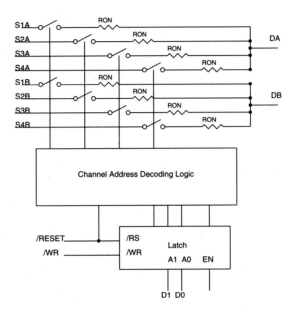

Figure 18.8-2   Functional diagram of a 4-channel differential input multiplexer (demultiplexer) with an onboard address and control latch.

The ON resistance, R_{ON}, of a multiplexer channel can significantly attenuate the input signal if the multiplexer drives a load directly. In Fig. 18.8-3(a), V_S and R_S represent the voltage and output resistance of a transducer. R_{ON} is the ON resistance of a multiplexer channel, and R_L is a load connected directly to the multiplexer's output. Ideally, we want the voltage across the load, V_L, to be equal to V_S. However, in this case V_L is:

$$V_L = \frac{R_L}{R_S + R_{ON} + R_L} V_S$$

The situation where the transducer is followed by a unity-gain buffer is represented in Fig. 18.8-3(b). In this case, the buffer supplies an output resistance that is so low it can be treated as zero. As a result,

$$V_L = \frac{R_L}{R_{ON} + R_L} V_S$$

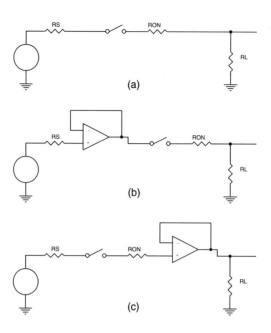

Figure 18.8-3   Connection of a load to a transducer through a multiplexer: (a) trans-
                 ducer connected directly to multiplexer input and load connected directly
                 to multiplexer output; (b) unity gain buffer used at input to multiplexer;
                 (c) unity gain buffer connected to output of multiplexer.

In Fig. 18.8-3(c) the output of the multiplexer is isolated from the load by a separate buffer amplifier or the input of the load is internally buffered, as in the case of a load which is a track-hold amplifier, programmable gain amplifier, or ADC with a high input imped-ance. This corresponds to the ideal situation and

$$V_L = V_S$$

R_{ON} is usually slightly dependent on the input signal level, referred to as $\boldsymbol{R_{ON}}$ **modu-lation**. Therefore, in addition to its attenuation effect, R_{ON} can cause distortion in the out-put signal if the multiplexer's output is not buffered from the load.

The high value of R_{OFF} resistance should isolate an OFF channel signal from affecting the output. The amount of coupling from one analog input channel to another one is spec-ified in dB as **cross-coupling.** High frequency input signals at OFF channels can have addi-tional coupling to the output through an equivalent capacitance that shunts an open switch from S input to D output. The proportionate amount of input signal coupled to the output is specified in dB as **OFF isolation.**

A multiplexer has several timing specifications. The output ON switching time, t_{ON}, is the time required to connect an analog input to the analog output. This time is measured from a change in the channel address. The output OFF switching time, t_{OFF}, is the time required to disconnect an analog input from the analog output. This time is measured from the change in the channel address. Because of the break-before-make operation of most multiplexers, the OFF switching time is faster that the ON switching time.

The output settling time, t_s, is the time required for an output to reach its final value, within a specified error band, after the channel address is changed. Because a multiplexer can be switched from a channel with a most negative input to a channel with a most positive input, or vice versa, this time specification is for a full range swing in the input voltage.

18.9   Multichannel Data Acquisition System

A **multichannel data acquisition system** (**DAS**), can acquire and convert a number of channels of analog data (Fig. 18.1-2). If there is no analog signal conditioning in each channel prior to the multiplexer, to create a signal whose full scale range corresponds to that of the ADC, then a single PGA can be placed at the multiplexer's output. The gain of the PGA is changed when the channel address is changed to provide the amplification needed for the channel selected.

The **sampling rate** for a DAS is the rate at which channels can be successively read. This rate is dependent upon the delay times associated with the components in the input signal's path. For the DAS in Fig. 18.1-2, after a new channel is selected, the output of the multiplexer must settle, the track-hold must acquire the new channel's signal, and the ADC must convert the signal.

When channels are being successively read and the components can be individually controlled, the multiplexer's channel address can be changed as soon as the track-hold is placed in the hold mode. This results in the multiplexer's settling time for the new channel occurring in parallel with the conversion time, Fig. 18.9-1. During the conversion, the track-hold must remain in the hold mode. As a result, the track-hold cannot be changed to the track mode to acquire the next channel's signal until the conversion is complete. Under these conditions the total time required is:

$$t_s = t_{acq} + t_{conv}$$

The sample rate is then:

$$f_s = \frac{1}{t_s}$$

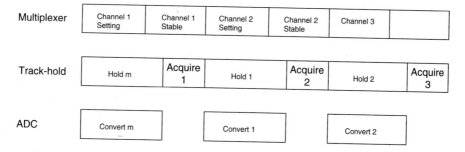

Figure 18.9-1   Overlap of multiplexer settling time and conversion time in conversions of successive channels.

For a DAS with m inputs the maximum sample rate per channel is:

$$f_s = \frac{1}{mt_s}$$

If a PGA follows the multiplexer, its gain can be changed when the multiplexer's channel address is changed. In this case, the settling time for the PGA overlaps with the later part of the conversion period.

18.9.1   A Single IC DAS

Microprocessor compatible data acquisition systems are available as single ICs. An example is the **MAX182 4 Channel 12-bit ADC**. The MAX182 contains a calibrated 4-channel 12-bit successive approximation ADC with track-hold and internal reference. Each conversion is preceded by an auto-zero cycle that reduces zero error to typically less than 100 μV. As can be seen in the block diagram of Fig. 18.9-2, one of the four analog inputs, AIN0-AIN3, is selected for conversion by the analog multiplexer. While the selected signal is held by the track-hold, the successive approximation register (SAR) carries out the conversion. Once the conversion is complete, the 12-bit result is read out as two bytes via on-board three-state buffers.

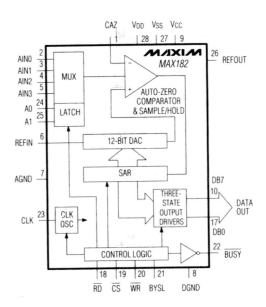

Figure 18.9-2   Maxim MAX182 calibrated 4-channel 12-bit ADC with track-hold and reference. (Courtesy of Maxim Integrated Products, Inc.)

Starting a conversion is simple. A write to the MAX182 selects the channel to be converted and starts the conversion. The value of address bits A1–A0 during this write is the channel address.

There are three ways to determine when the conversion is complete: software delay, poll, or interrupt.

After starting a conversion, the 80C188EB can simply delay for a period of time in excess of the conversion time. When the on-chip clock is used, the typical conversion time is 120 μs. However, due to manufacturing variations, the actual frequency of the on-chip oscillator can differ from chip to chip resulting in conversion times that range from 90 to 140 μs. A software delay would have to accommodate the worst case conversion time.

Completion of a conversion can be determined by polling. A read of the MAX182 with the byte select (BYSL) input high returns the high byte of the 12-bit result. The high byte contains the most significant four bits of the result in bit positions 3–0, and uses bit 7 as a BUSY flag. If bit 7 is 1, the conversion is still in progress. So, polling involves reading the high byte and testing bit 7. If bit 7 is 0, the conversion is complete. The least significant 4 bits of this byte are the most significant four bits of the result. The low byte is then read to obtain the least significant eight bits of the result. If BYSL is connected to A0, a read to an even address in the address range assigned to the MAX182 provides the low byte and a read to an odd address provides the high byte.

An interrupt driven approach uses the output from the /BUSY pin to interrupt the 80C188EB at the end of a conversion. The /BUSY output goes low during the conversion. The rising edge of /BUSY is used to set an interrupt request flop-flop. The ISR reads the result and clears the interrupt request flip-flop.

18.10   Summary

To measure a physical quantity, an analog input subsystem uses an input transducer to convert the energy from the physical measurand into an analog electrical signal. This analog signal, usually a voltage, is then converted to a code or number so it can be processed by the microprocessor.

The actual conversion of the signal from analog to digital is carried out by an ADC. But before the signal is input to the ADC, it may require conditioning so it is compatible with the ADC's input range.

Two common signal conditioning operations are amplification and filtering. Low-level signals are typically amplified using instrumentation amplifiers that have differential inputs. An instrumentation amplifier has the advantage that it amplifies the signal between its two inputs, but does not amplify electrical noise common to its two inputs.

The most commonly needed filter operation is to block high frequency components in a signal while passing the low frequency components. With most transducers for physical measurands, the high frequency signal components are associated with electrical noise. The operation just described is performed by a low-pass filter. Active low-pass filters provide a sharp rolloff at low cost. Active filters can also provide gain, in addition to filtering.

ADCs can be classified into two categories, direct conversion and indirect conversion, based on how they convert their input signals. Direct conversion compares the voltage to be converted to voltages generated from a reference voltage. These voltages are often generated by a DAC. Popular direct conversion techniques include flash converters, ramp converters, and successive approximation converters.

With indirect conversion techniques, the voltage to be converted is transformed to a time interval or a frequency. The time interval or frequency is measured and the measured value represents the input voltage. Popular indirect conversion techniques include dual-slope integrating converters and delta-sigma converters.

Advancements in analog integrated circuit design and fabrication techniques have resulted in high levels of integration for analog data conversion components. This has resulted in readily available high performance and reliable data acquisition components such as active filters, instrumentation amplifiers, multiplexers, track-holds and ADCs in IC form. The levels of integration are so high that complete data acquisition systems are available as single ICs. Use of these components significantly simplifies your work designing data acquisition input subsystems.

18.11 Problems

1. Four analog input signals must be converted to binary in a system. Compare and contrast the advantages of using a separate ADC for each signal with using a single multiplexed ADC. Assume that the converter per channel approach requires each of the functions of Fig. 18.1-1, and that the multiplexed approach requires each of the functions of Fig. 18.1-2.

2. Give a brief functional description of each of the blocks in Fig. 18.1-1, and briefly explain why it is needed.

3. For an ideal 4-bit ADC, what is the size of a quantum in terms of the nominal full scale input range (FS)? What are the locations of the first and last transition points in terms of FS?

4. Specify the quantum sizes and quantization errors for 8-, 12-, and 16-bit ADCs with a 0 to +5 V input range.

5. A pressure transducer generates an output that varies linearly from 0.2 V to 4.8 V for pressures that range from 15 kPa to 115 kPa. The output of the pressure transducer is to be converted to binary by an n-bit ADC with a 0 to +5 V input range. Assume that n-bit ADC are available for even values of n from 8 to 16. What value of n is necessary to make it possible to detect changes in pressure as small as 0.1 kPa? Show the calculations required to determine your answer. For the converter size chosen, what is the maximum upper bound, in kPa, on the accuracy of the measurements?

6. A particular ADC is designed to be interfaced to a microprocessor as a slow memory device that requests WAIT states until it completes a conversion. To a microprocessor, the ADC looks like a 1×8 ROM. It has a /CS and a /RD input, 8 data bits output, and a /BUSY output. When a conversion is desired, the ADC is simply read. In response to its being selected and its /RD input being asserted, the ADC asserts its /BUSY output until it completes the conversion. When the conversion is complete, the ADC negates its /BUSY output and drives its output data lines with the results of the conversion. The /BUSY line is used to request WAIT states from the microprocessor while the conversion is in process. Draw a block diagram representation of the interface of the ADC to an 80C188EB system. If the parameter TRLBL (read low to busy low) specifies the time the ADC takes to assert its /BUSY output after its /RD

input is asserted, derive an equation which specifies the TRLBL allowed by an 80C188EB. For an 80C188EB operated at 20 MHz, what is the value of TRLBL?

7. Use an 8-bit DAC and a comparator to implement a counting (ramp type) ADC. Assume the DAC output port address is DAC, and the comparator's output is input as bit 7 of input port STATUS. The comparator has an open collector output that is logic 0 when the DAC's output is greater than or equal to the unknown voltage being converted. Draw a block diagram of the circuit. Write a procedure, CONVERT, that implements the conversion and returns the result in register AL.

8. An 8-bit microprocessor compatible DAC contains an 8-bit latch. This DAC is to be combined with a comparator and a noninverting three-state buffer to implement a successive approximation A/D converter. The analog input is connected to the inverting terminal of the comparator. The buffered output of the comparator is connected to bit D7 of the data bus. The DAC has the symbolic name DACSA, and the three-state input port has the name CMPSTS. Both ports are in the I/O space and have the address 14H. Draw the logic diagram of the required hardware. Show the address decoding as a single block. Write the Boolean equations for each of the address decoder's outputs. Write a procedure, ADC, that implements the conversion and leaves the result in AL.

9. Draw the block diagram of a 10 V FS 4-bit successive approximation ADC that is driven by a microprocessor under software control. Draw the graph of the ideal conversion relationship for the converter showing only the first three quanta and first three binary outputs. Show clearly the transition points. Label the quanta and transition points as a fraction of full scale and in volts. To achieve the ideal conversion relationship, what must the output of the DAC be when its input is 0000B? For an input voltage of 6.65 V, determine the sequence of binary value output to the DAC during the conversion sequence.

10. An 8-bit analog-to-digital converter, ADC, has a start of conversion (SOC) input that must be pulsed high for at least 50 ns to start a conversion. The ADC has a /BUSY output that is asserted as soon as a conversion starts and remains asserted until the conversion completes. Data is read from the ADC by asserting its /OE input. Draw a logic diagram of the interface of the ADC to an 80C188EB so that the completion of a conversion can be detected by polling. Use a PAL and /GCS1 to accomplish exhaustive address decoding. Assume that /GCS1 is properly programmed. Use only addresses 8026H and 8027H in I/O space. Write the equations for all required PAL outputs. Write a procedure, ADC_POLL, that, when called, starts a conversion and then waits until the conversion is complete and reads the result. This procedure writes the result to the low byte of the memory word AD_RESULT and sets the most significant bit of the high byte of that word.

11. The task of the previous problem is to be accomplished using the same ADC, but the ADC is to interrupt the 80C188EB when it completes a conversion. Draw a logic diagram for the interface of the ADC to the 80C188EB. Use INT2 as the interrupt input. Write an interrupt service routine ADC_INT that, when called, reads the result and stores it in memory. The procedure then starts a new conversion before returning.

12. An 8-bit DAC and a comparator are used to implement a tracking ADC that displays its results on 8 LEDs. A tracking or servo ADC is similar to a ramp ADC, except that

once it steps up from 0 to the unknown input voltage value it is able to follow relatively slow changes in the input voltage. Draw the block diagram for the hardware required to implement the tracking ADC and the 8 LEDs that constantly display the result. Write a program whose sole purpose is to implement the tracking ADC.

13. A voltage to frequency ADC is to be designed using a voltage to frequency converter with a 0 to 10 V input range and a corresponding output range of 10 Hz to 10 kHz. The ADC is to provide a 10-bit binary output to an 8-bit microprocessor. The gate strobe is to be provided as 1 bit of an output port controlled by the microprocessor.

   a. Draw a block diagram of the ADC and the circuitry required to interface it to an 8-bit microprocessor. It is not necessary to show address decoding.

   b. What is the duration of the gate strobe for maximum resolution? For this value of gate strobe duration, what is the A/D output count for the following input voltages: 0 V, 2.5 V, and 5 V?

19.1   Programmed I/O and Interrupt Driven I/O Data Transfer Rates

19.2   Hardware FIFO Buffers

19.3   DMA Transfers

19.4   The 80C188EB's Support for DMA and Multiple Bus Masters

19.5   82C37A DMA Controller

19.6   80C18xEx Family Members with On-Chip DMA

19.7   Summary

Some I/O devices are designed to generate or receive data in blocks or bursts. Each block or burst consists of many data bytes transferred in a very short time. Such data needs to be temporarily stored in memory. For instance, temporary storage of input data may be necessary because the data is generated too rapidly to be processed on a byte-by-byte basis. While one byte is being processed, the next byte generated by the input device may be missed. In other cases, the nature of the processing may simply require that all the data be available before being processed.

Temporary storage in memory of output data is required for an output device that requires data to be transferred to it as a block, with no significant intervals between bytes.

The I/O techniques presented in previous chapters are inadequate to handle the block or burst data rates of many devices. Programmed I/O requires a significant amount of software overhead to transfer a small amount of data per unit time, resulting in a low data transfer rate. In addition to the software overhead required to poll an I/O device, every data byte transferred between an I/O device and memory has to pass through a register in the 80C188EB. This creates a bottleneck that has a substantial effect when trying to transfer a block of data quickly. Another drawback is that the 80C188EB cannot carry out other tasks during programmed I/O transfers.

Interrupt driven I/O eliminates polling, but does not increase the data transfer rate. However, interrupt driven I/O does allow concurrent processing. But if interrupts are generated on a byte-by-byte basis, the time spent entering and leaving the ISR can impact any concurrent processing to an unacceptable degree.

After first defining block and burst data, the speed limitations of programmed I/O and interrupt driven I/O are considered. Next, two approaches for handling block and burst I/O data are presented. The first approach uses a hardware FIFO memory to buffer the data. The second approach, direct memory access, involves the direct transfer of data between an I/O device and system memory, without the data passing through an 80C188EB register.

19.1   Programmed I/O and Interrupt Driven I/O Data Transfer Rates

For the purpose of later discussions it is helpful to characterize I/O data with respect to the temporal relationship between the data bytes generated or received. The programmed I/O and interrupt driven I/O transfers discussed in previous chapters assumed that data was generated asynchronously at a low data rate (Fig. 19.1-1(a)). For example, this is the case for data from a keypad. In some other cases, data was generated at a more uniform and slightly higher rate (Fig. 19.1-1(b)). This is the case for serial data from a UART.

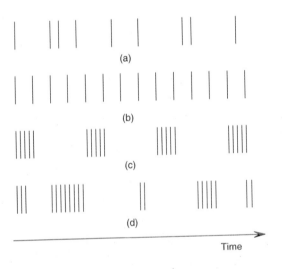

Figure 19.1-1   Temporal relationship between rates at which data is generated by an input device: (a) low data rate randomly generated data; (b) higher data rate uniformly generated data; (c) high data rate block data; (d) high data rate burst data.

Figures 19.1-1(c) and (d) represent the kind of data generation of primary interest in this chapter. Figure 19.1-1(c) represents data generated in blocks. **Block data** consists of a group of data bytes sent at a relatively high data rate. The number of bytes in a block is usually constant and known. Data received from reading a sector of a disk is an example of block data. Blocks are separated by intervals where no data bytes are generated.

Burst data generation is represented in Fig. 19.1-1(d). **Burst data** also consists of groups of data bytes generated at a relatively high data rate followed by relatively long intervals during which no or very little data is generated. In contrast to block data, the number of bytes in each group and the interval between groups varies substantially and is somewhat random. The rates at which the data are generated in Figs. 19.1-1 (c) and (d) are inherent to the device generating the data, but are assumed to be relatively high.

All the data transfers represented in Fig. 19.1-1 are asynchronous in that the generation of data is not synchronized to the 80C188EB's system clock. While most of the discussions in the following subsections use examples involving input devices, the same considerations apply to output devices as well.

19.1.1   Data Transfer Rates for Programmed I/O

Before presenting high data rate I/O techniques, we need to know what rates to consider as high for an 80C188EB. With programmed I/O, the highest data transfer rate you can achieve is by using string I/O with an appropriate I/O device. The following example demonstrates this concept.

The byte input device in Fig. 19.1-2 is assumed to always have the next data byte available. It is further assumed that the memory is always ready, no WAIT states are used, and interrupts are disabled. The fastest programmed I/O transfer rate from an input device to memory is achieved using an INSB instruction with a REP prefix:

```
mov      ax,seg mem_buff            ;segment address of buffer
mov      es,ax
mov      di,offset mem_buf          ;offset address of buffer
mov      dx,PORT_ADDR               ;input port address
mov      cx,NUM_BYTES               ;number of bytes to transfer
rep insb                           ;input bytes until CX = 0
```

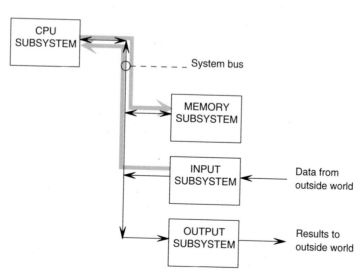

Figure 19.1-2   A programmed I/O input transfer using the INSB instruction. Each byte transferred passes through the 80C188EB.

The number of states required for an 80C188EB to execute an INSB instruction is 8 + 8n, where n is the number of bytes transferred. Thus, a byte is transferred every 8 states. For an 80C188EB operated at 25 MHz, each state is 40 ns, so a byte is transferred every 320 ns. The resulting transfer rate is 3.125 Mbytes/sec. This is a reasonably fast data transfer rate. For an 8 MHz system clock, the transfer rate is reduced to 1 Mbyte/second.

Each byte transferred by INSB is read from the input device to a temporary register in the 80C188EB and then written to memory. Thus, two bus cycles are required to transfer each byte, one to read and one to write. Each bus cycle requires 4 states, resulting in a total of 8 states per byte transferred. During the transfer, the 80C188EB is completely occupied performing the transfer and cannot do any concurrent processing.

To achieve the data rate described, the input device is not polled and must always have the next data byte available. Only a few input devices inherently meet this requirement. The addition of a FIFO buffer to an input device, as described in the next section, allows this requirement to be met.

The previous instruction sequence ignores another important practical issue. When should execution of the sequence be initiated? This is usually determined by polling a status byte or by an interrupt. Use of an interrupt allows the 80C188EB to execute other tasks until the data transfer is required. The ISR invoked can incorporate the previous instruction sequence to transfer the data.

19.1.2   Data Transfer Rates for Interrupt Driven I/O

The use of an interrupt to signal the start of a data block allows the 80C188EB to respond quickly. If the ISR contains the instruction sequence from the previous subsection, the data can be transferred at a relatively fast rate. In contrast, using a separate interrupt to transfer each individual data byte results in a relatively low data rate. The overhead penalty of the ISR is incurred for each byte. Figure 19.1-3 is an ISR that transfers one byte of a block each time it is invoked. This ISR illustrates the significant overhead involved. Prior to the interrupt being enabled, the memory buffer index, mb_ndx, is cleared. The ISR disables the interrupt after a block of length NUM_BYTES has been transferred to memory buffer mem_buff.

19.2   Hardware FIFO Buffers

In some applications, there is a significant difference in the rate at which an I/O device generates (or receives) data and the rate at which an 80C188EB can receive (or generate) the same data. One common situation involves an input device that generates high data rate blocks or bursts. The 80C188EB may not be able to directly handle the data transfer for the following reasons:

1. The 80C188EB is executing another task that it must complete without interruption.
2. The 80C188EB's maximum data transfer rate is slower than the peak data transfer rate of the I/O device.

```
;***********************************************************************
;NAME:     INBYTE_ISR
;
;function:  Transfer a byte from input port PORT_ADDR to memory buffer MEM_BUFF
;assumes:   MB_NDX (index) initialized
;returns:
;DESCRIPTION:
;
;***********************************************************************
inbyte_isr    proc
        push    ax                      ;save all registers used by
        push    di                      ;interrupt procedure
        push    dx
        mov     di,mb_ndx               ;get memory buffer index
        mov     dx,PORT_ADDR            ;load port address
        in      al,dx                   ;input byte
        mov     mem_buff(di),al         ;store in buffer
        inc     mb_ndx
        cmp     mb_ndx,NUM_BYTES        ;all bytes transferred?
        jne     clr_ireq
        mov     dx,IOCON                ;disable interrupt
        mov     ax,001Fh
        out     dx,ax
clr_ireq:
        mov     dx,DSP_IREQ_FF          ;generate device select pulse
        out     dx,al                   ;to clear int req. FF for external
        mov     dx,EOI                  ;send non-specific EOI command
        mov     ax,8000h                ;to clear In-Service register bit
        out     dx,ax
        pop     dx                      ;pop all saved registers in reverse order
        pop     di
        pop     ax
        iret                            ;pop IP, CS, and FLAGS
inbyte_isr    endp
```

Figure 19.1-3   ISR to input a byte and transfer it to a memory buffer.

19.2.1   Using a FIFO to Buffer Data from a Flash ADC

If the 80C188EB can handle an I/O device's data rate averaged over a relatively long period, then a FIFO can be used to buffer the I/O data and accommodate the rate differences. For example, a flash ADC and FIFO can be used to digitize an analog signal (Fig. 19.2-1). When started, the ADC generates a block of data at a data rate of 10 Mbytes/sec. The maximum programmed I/O data rate for a 25 MHz 80C188EB was found to be 3.125 Mbytes/sec in the previous section.

However, if the analog signal represents an event of limited duration or a periodic signal, a limited number of samples is sufficient to characterize the signal. In this example, the FIFO buffer stores 16 Kbytes sampled at the 10 Mbyte rate of the ADC. The 80C188EB subsequently reads this data at its lower 3.125 Mbytes/sec data rate.

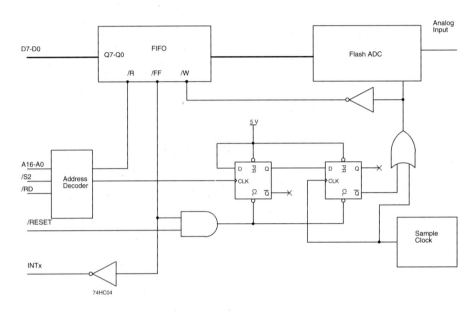

Figure 19.2-1   Use of a FIFO to buffer the output of an ADC.

First-in First-out (FIFO) memory buffers were introduced in Chapter 16. A purely software implementation, in the form of a circular memory buffer, was discussed in Section 16.5. A software FIFO would be far too slow for the application in Fig. 19.2-1. Hardware FIFOs were also introduced in Chapter 16 in terms of their inclusion in some UARTs.

Stand-alone hardware FIFO buffer ICs are available. These FIFOs can handle very fast data rates and buffer large quantities of data. A block diagram of **Integrated Device Technology's IDT7203/6 FIFO** series is shown in Fig. 19.2-2. FIFOs in this series range is size from 2K × 9 to 16K × 9. Data can be written to and read from these devices at rates up to 50 MHz. Like most recent high speed and high capacity FIFO ICs, they are a direct hardware implementation of the two-pointer circular buffer of Section 16.5. The major functional differences between the software and hardware implementations is that the hardware FIFO can be written and read simultaneously and at different rates.

When the IDT7206 FIFO of Fig. 19.2-2 is reset, both its write and read pointers are set to 0, thus, pointing to the first location in the RAM array. The circuit of Fig. 19.2-1 uses a start of sample (/SOS) device select pulse to set the sample gate flip-flop to start the collection of 16,384 samples. This flip-flop's output is synchronized by the second flip-flop, whose output gates the 10 MHz crystal oscillator output. The gated oscillator signal clocks the ADC and writes the FIFO.

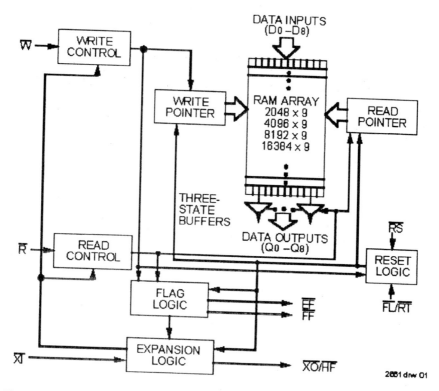

Figure 19.2-2   IDT Asynchronous FIFO. (Courtesy of Integrated Device Technology, Inc.)

The flash ADC samples its analog input on each falling edge at its clock input. The result from a specific sample is available on the rising edge of the clock 2.5 clock periods later. The inverter at the FIFO's write input causes this sample to be clocked into the FIFO 0.5 clock periods later. Thus, on each falling edge of the ADC's sample clock, a sample is taken and a result is clocked into the FIFO. Data at the FIFO's inputs is written into the FIFO by a rising edge at its /W control pin. On any specific falling edge of the sample clock, the result clocked into the FIFO corresponds to the sample taken 3 clock periods earlier. This operation is consistent with that of **Analog Devices AD775 8-bit 20 MSPS** (million samples per second) subranging **ADC**.

Three internal hardware flags available at pins of the FIFO indicate the amount of data in the FIFO. The /EF flag indicates that the FIFO is empty, the /HF flag indicates half full, and the /FF flag indicates full.

When the FIFO is full, it inhibits write attempts. Thus, write attempts on a full FIFO have no effect on either the FIFO's write pointer or RAM array contents. The device writing the FIFO should monitor the /FF flag and not attempt to write when the FIFO is full.

In Fig. 19.2-1, when the FIFO is full, its /FF output clears the sample gate flip-flop. This disables further writes to the FIFO. /FF is also inverted and used to interrupt the 80C188EB. The ISR is given in Fig. 19.2-3. The ISR uses REP INSB to read the FIFO. The FIFO's three-state outputs are enabled and data is read from the FIFO while its /R control input is asserted. The first read operation unasserts /FF, removing the interrupt request. The ISR sets a memory flag, new_buff_flg, that the 80C188EB later polls to process the data. Alternatively, the ISR could call a procedure to process the data immediately.

```
;**********************************************************************
;
;NAME:        FIFO_ISR
;
;function:    Transfer 16,384 bytes from input port PORT_ADDR to memory
;             buffer MEM_BUFF
;assumes:
;returns:
;DESCRIPTION:
;
;
;**********************************************************************
;
fifo_isr        proc
        pusha
        mov     ax,seg mem_buff      ;ES:DI pointer to destination
        mov     es,ax
        mov     di,offset mem_buff
        mov     cx,16384             ;number of bytes to transfer
        mov     dx,FIFO_ADDR         ;FIFO port address
        rep     insb                 ;input bytes
        mov     new_buff_flg,1
        popa
        ret
fifo_isr        endp
```

Figure 19.2-3   Interrupt service routine for flash ADC with FIFO buffer.

In this example, it is assumed that 16,384 samples are sufficient. If a larger FIFO were needed, the /XI and /XO control pins can be used to cascade multiple IDT7206 FIFOs.

19.2.2   Determining FIFO Buffer Length

In the previous example, the /SOS signal was asserted under program control to start filling the FIFO with samples. The 10 MHz sample clock causes a byte to be written into the FIFO every 0.1 μs. When the FIFO is completely filled, the FIFO full, /FF, flag disables further writes to the FIFO. As a result of this design, the arrival time of the first byte in a block, the rate of arrival of bytes, and the total number of bytes in a block is known. Furthermore, since a block is started under program control we are assured that we can empty the FIFO before another block starts to be received. Data is not read from the FIFO until it is full.

In some applications, the reading of data from the FIFO may begin just after the first byte is written into the FIFO. In this case, the FIFO may not need to be as large as the block to be received. Assume the block size is B. If the rate at which data is written to the FIFO

(WF) and the rate at which data is read from the FIFO (RF) are known and constant, then the required buffer length (BL) is:

$$BL = (WF - RF)\frac{B}{WF}$$

$$= \left(1 - \frac{RF}{WF}\right)B$$

In applications involving burst data, the start of a burst may not be precisely known, nor the interval between bytes in a burst, nor the burst duration. In these cases, the determination of the required length of the FIFO buffer is nontrivial and requires the use of queuing theory. The number of bytes in the FIFO is treated as a discrete random variable and requires that the process be modeled by a probability distribution function.

19.3   DMA Transfers

Programmed I/O and interrupt driven I/O both require that the microprocessor perform the data transfer. In contrast, **direct memory access (DMA)** transfers data between an I/O device and memory without the microprocessor's intervention. The microprocessor must have features that allow the use of DMA in the system. Additional hardware, in the form of a **DMA controller**, actually performs the data transfers.

When it transfers data, the DMA controller is the bus master. A **bus master** is a device that can generate address and control signals to transfer data on the bus. The DMA controller must request and be granted control of the system bus by the microprocessor before it can generate address and control signals to perform a data transfer.

Figure 19.3-1 illustrates the basic components of a conventional DMA controller and the controller's interface to the system bus and I/O device. The controller illustrated is capable of handling transfers between a single I/O device and memory. The DMA controller contains an address register, a word count register, and control logic for reading data from, or writing data to, memory. Also included in the DMA controller, but not shown on the figure, are a control register and status register. The steps required in a DMA transfer from an input device to a memory buffer are:

1. Initialize the DMA controller. Initialization requires writing the controller's address register with the starting address of the memory buffer and writing the word count register with the number of bytes to be transferred. The DMA controller is enabled to make the transfer by writing its control register.

2. Initialize the input device's controller. This initialization is dependent on the specific device controller, but generally involves writing commands to the device controller. Initializing the device controller results in the input device starting whatever process generates the data. After the device controller has been initialized, the microprocessor goes on to other tasks that are not part of the DMA transfer.

3. When the input device has data ready to be transferred, the input device controller issues a DMA request (DRQ) to the DMA controller to transfer the data.

4. The DMA controller uses its hold request (HRQ) output to request control of the system bus. When the microprocessor is ready to give up bus control, it suspends any of its processing that requires use of the bus. The microprocessor then puts its address, data, and control lines in their high-impedence states, effectively disconnecting itself from the system bus. The microprocessor uses its hold acknowledge (HOLDA) output to signal that the DMA controller can take control of the system bus.

5. The DMA controller is now the bus master. It drives the address bus with the memory address for the transfer causing the appropriate memory ICs to be selected. The DMA controller then asserts its request acknowledge (/DACK) output to select the input device controller for the transfer.

6. The DMA controller generates an /IOR strobe that the input device controller uses to enable its data bus buffers and drive the data bus with the byte to be transferred. While /IOR is active, the DMA controller generates a /MEMW strobe to write the data into memory.

7. After each data byte is transferred, the DMA controller increments its address register and decrements its word count register.

8. If after being decremented, the word count register is zero, all the bytes have been transferred. The DMA controller then unasserts /DACK and /HRQ, giving control of the system bus back to the microprocessor. If after the word count register is decremented it is not zero, then there are more bytes that must be transferred. In this case, steps 6, 7, and 8 are repeated until the word count reaches zero.

9. After the DMA transfer is complete, the microprocessor must be notified so that it can process the data in the memory buffer. The microprocessor can either poll a status bit in the DMA controller that indicates that the transfers are complete, or the DMA controller can be programmed to interrupt the microprocessor to indicate completion. The DMA controller in Fig. 19.3-1 uses its end of process signal (/EOP) to interrupt the microprocessor.

There are several key points in the previous description that warrant further emphasis.

1. The microprocessor sets up the DMA transfer by initializing the DMA controller and device controller. Then the microprocessor goes on to other, non-DMA, tasks.

2. To transfer a byte of data, the DMA controller must first request control of the system bus from the microprocessor. A DMA transfer cannot take place until the microprocessor relinquishes the bus.

3. During a transfer, the DMA controller generates the memory address and the /IOR and /MEMW timing signals, but it is the I/O device controller that generates the data and drives the data onto the system data bus.

4. The microprocessor must test for, or be notified, when the DMA transfer is complete so that it can process the data in the memory buffer.

In Fig. 19.3-1, data is transferred from an input device to memory. A transfer in this direction is referred to as a **DMA write**. When data is transferred from memory to an output device, the operation is called a **DMA read**.

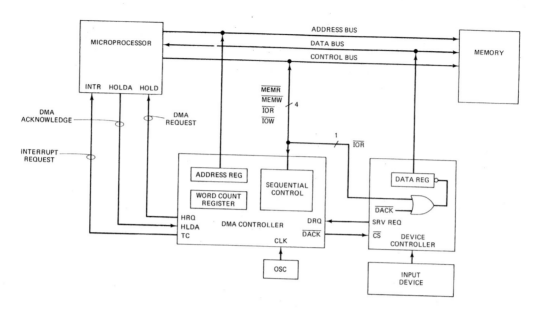

Figure 19.3-1   DMA controller controlling an input device.

DMA transfers can be classified as: block or burst, single transfer or cycle stealing, demand, or transparent. In **block** or **burst DMA**, once the DMA controller takes control of the system bus, it transfers the entire block of data before returning control of the bus to the microprocessor. The previous list of steps is for a block DMA transfer.

Block DMA transfers data at the highest possible rate. The maximum data rate of a block DMA transfer is limited only by the read or write cycle time of the memory and the speed of the DMA controller. The speed of the microprocessor is not relevant. Below this maximum, the transfer rate is limited by how fast the I/O device can supply or receive data. Block DMA transfers are commonly used in transferring data to or from a floppy disk or refreshing a CRT display.

In **single transfer** or **cycle stealing DMA**, control of the system bus alternates between the microprocessor and the DMA controller if the I/O device is fast enough. Each time the DMA controller releases its hold request after a byte is transferred, the microprocessor takes control of the system bus for the next bus cycle. The microprocessor executes a bus cycle to perform some task. Then, the DMA controller executes a bus cycle to transfer a byte. Thus, the DMA controller "steals" bus cycles from the microprocessor to transfer data bytes. In effect, the DMA transfers occur concurrently with other tasks performed by the microprocessor. The microprocessor's processing is slowed accordingly.

The steps in single transfer DMA are similar to those for block DMA except that after one byte of data is transferred, if the desired number of data bytes has not been transferred (word count register is not zero after step 7), then the DMA controller releases its hold request, returning control of the system bus to the microprocessor. Steps 4 through 8 are then repeated for each data byte, until all bytes have been transferred.

Demand transfer DMA allows the I/O device to briefly suspend the DMA transfer, giving control back to the microprocessor when the I/O device needs time to catch up in generating or receiving data.

For some microprocessors, a DMA controller can be used in a manner where single transfers occur only during internal processing when the system bus is not being used by the microprocessor. Such DMA transfers are called **transparent DMA.** They are transparent to the microprocessor in that they do not interfere with, or slow down, its normal rate of instruction execution. Transparent DMA requires, in addition to the usual DMA logic, logic to detect the occurrence of microprocessor states during which the microprocessor does not require use of the bus. This logic is usually contained in the microprocessor.

For all the types of DMA transfer, the only software required is that necessary to initialize the DMA controller and the I/O device controller.

19.4   The 80C188EB's Support for DMA and Multiple Bus Masters

The 80C188EB can transfer control of the system bus between itself and other bus masters. Its hold request input (**HOLD**) and hold acknowledge (**HLDA**) output provide a handshake capability between the 80C188EB and other bus masters to coordinate bus control transfers.

To gain control of the bus, a bus master, such as a DMA controller, must assert the 80C188EB's HOLD input and wait for a HLDA response (Fig. 19.3-1). When the 80C188EB can relinquish the bus, it three-states its address, data, and control pins (including /RD, /WR, /S2-/S0, /DEN and DT/R). ALE is not three-stated. The 80C188EB continues internal processing and then enters its hold state. By floating its address, data, and control buses, the 80C188EB effectively disconnects itself from the system bus. The DMA controller must keep the 80C188EB's HOLD input asserted until it no longer requires use of the system bus.

Hold requests and hold acknowledges are handled by the BIU. The elapsed time between a request and the corresponding acknowledge is called the **bus latency.** The shortest possible bus latency is two T states. Factors such as the bus being in a not-ready state, the need to complete the current bus cycle, and the bus being locked, produce longer latencies.

The bus can be locked by the execution of a *lock the bus*, **LOCK**, instruction (Table 19.4-1). This instruction prevents the 80C188EB from issuing a HLDA until all the bus cycles that comprise the execution of the instruction following the LOCK instruction are completed.

Table 19.4-1   Lock the bus instruction.

Mnemonic	Operands	Function	O	D	I	T	S	Z	A	P	C
LOCK	none	Locks the bus	–	–	–	–	–	–	–	–	–

When the BIU grants a hold acknowledge, the EU continues to execute instructions from the instruction queue until an operand transfer is required or there are no more instructions in the queue. As a result, there can be a significant overlap in the operation of the EU and the use of the bus by a DMA controller.

When the DMA controller unasserts HOLD, the 80C188EB responds by unasserting HLDA. The 80C188EB then exits its hold state and continues its previous operation from the point at which it was suspended. When the 80C188EB next requires the bus, it enables its address, data, and control lines. It is possible that for brief periods after the DMA controller has dropped its hold request, that neither the DMA controller nor the 80C188EB is driving the bus. As a result, pull-up resistors should be connected to control lines /RD, /WR, and /S2 to prevent inadvertent operations during transfers of bus control.

Unlike other members of the 80C18xEx family, the 80C188EB does not have an on-chip DMA controller. So, an external IC DMA controller, like the 82C37A, must be used.

19.5   82C37A DMA Controller

A separate IC DMA controller that can be used with the 80C188EB is the 82C37A. This section provides a brief overview of the 82C37A's architecture and operation. The 82C37A is packaged in a 40-pin DIP. One 82C37A can control four separate DMA channels, Fig. 19.5-1. Each channel operates in an identical fashion and has its own set of Current Address, Current Word Count, Base Address, Base Word Count, and Mode registers. Only one such set of registers is shown in Fig. 19.5-1. Other registers, such as Status and Command, are shared by the four channels. The 82C37A-5 when operated from a 5 MHz clock can transfer data at 1.6 Mbytes/sec.

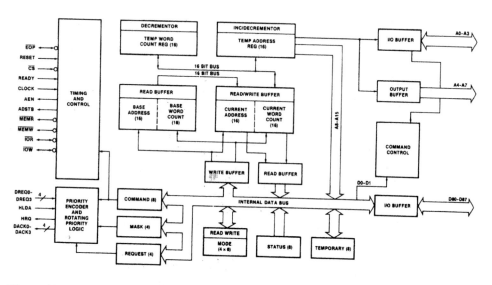

Figure 19.5-1   DMA controller block diagram. (Courtesy of Intel Corp.)

In addition to its registers, the 82C37A's three logic subsystems are also shown in Fig. 19.5-1. The Timing and Control block generates internal timing and external control signals using an externally provided clock. The Command Control block decodes commands written to the 82C37A by your program and also decodes the Mode Control word. The

Priority Encoder Logic resolves priority between DMA channels simultaneously requesting service. Only one channel can be active, perform a DMA transfer, at a time. There is a separate DMA request input, DREQ0–DREQ3, and a separate DMA acknowledge output, DACK0–DACK3, for each channel. Using fixed priority, DREQ0 has the highest priority and DREQ3 the lowest.

The 82C37A produces a 16-bit address. The least significant 8 bits of this address, A7–A0, are provided directly from 82C37A pins. Address bits A15-A8 are generated by the 82C37A and multiplexed on data pins DB7–DB0. These address bits must be latched externally. The 82C37A provides an address strobe (ADSTB) to clock an external latch. A second external latch is required to hold the most significant 4 bits of a 20-bit address.

Before it can function in a system, the 82C37A must be initialized. This is accomplished by your program writing several of its registers. When the 82C37A is addressed by the 80C188EB, address decoding logic asserts the 82C37A's chip-select input, /CS. This allows the 80C188EB to write the 82C37A's registers as output ports. During this process, the programming data is transferred to the addressed registers via the 82C37A's data bus, DB7–DB0.

Initialization must be carried out for each channel used. This process is described here for a single channel. The Current Address register holds the address for a DMA transfer. This register is initialized to the starting memory address for the transfer. The application program does this by writing the 16-bit starting address to the Current Address register as successive bytes.

The 82C37A's register addressing capability is expanded by an internal **First/Last Flip-Flop** that allows a single external address to be used to write both bytes of the 16-bit Current Address register. The First/Last Flip-Flop is cleared using the *Clear First/last* command. Then the low byte of the address is written to the Current Address register. Writing this byte causes the First/Last Flip-Flop to be toggled. The next write to the Current Address register writes the high byte of this register.

After a DMA transfer of a byte, the value in the Current Address register is automatically incremented or decremented. Whether this register is incremented or decremented depends on a bit in the mode register, which is set or cleared during initialization. This choice allows a block of data to be transferred from the lowest memory address to the highest, or vice versa.

The Current Word Count register is initialized to a value one less than the number of bytes to be transferred. To transfer n bytes, this 16-bit register is initialized to n-1. The value in this register is decremented each time a byte is transferred during a DMA operation. When this register is decremented from 0000H to FFFFH, the channel's terminal count (TC) bit in the status register is asserted, indicating that the DMA operation is complete.

Each channel's Base Address and Base Word Count registers are automatically written when their associated Current registers are written. When a channel's auto initialization feature is enabled, the Current registers are automatically reloaded with the values in the Base registers at the end of the DMA operation. This eliminates the need to reinitialize these registers when repeated DMA operations involving the same memory block and number of bytes are to be carried out.

Several other registers: Command, Mode, Request, Mask, and Status, are used to control and monitor the 82C37A's operation. The functions of these registers are not discussed here in detail.

The 82C37A can be initialized to transfer data in one of four modes. In the **block transfer mode**, DREQ only needs to be asserted until the DACK response is received. Once the 82C37A has control of the bus, it continues to make transfers until the entire block of data has been transferred.

In **single transfer mode**, the DREQ signal must be asserted by the I/O device controller until DACK is received in order to be recognized. In response to assertion of its DREQ input, the 82C37A generates a hold request (HRQ). When the hold acknowledge (HLDA) is received, the 82C37A transfers a single byte and then decrements the word count and increments or decrements the address. If DREQ is held active throughout this transfer, HRQ goes inactive and releases the bus to the 80C188EB. HRQ will then automatically be reasserted, and when the HLDA is received the 82C37A will transfer another single byte. The result is that the 80C188EB will have one full machine cycle between each DMA cycle. When the word count is decremented from 0 to FFFFH, the DMA transfer terminates.

In **demand transfer mode** the 82C37A continues to make transfers until a terminal count (TC) or external /EOP is encountered, or until DREQ becomes unasserted. This allows transfers of a block of data to continue until the I/O device has temporarily exhausted its data. When the I/O device can continue the transfer, it reasserts DREQ and the 82C37A again gains control of the bus and continues transferring the block of data. During the time DREQ is unasserted the 80C188EB has control of the bus. The DMA transfer is terminated when the word count register has been decremented to FFFFH or an external /EOP pulse is generated.

A cascade mode is available that allows multiple 82C37As to be cascaded so that more than four channels of DMA can be handled by a system.

There are two significant drawbacks to using the 82C37A. First, the maximum transfer rate of 1.6 Mbytes/sec is only about half of what can be accomplished using the REP INSB instruction. Second, two latches are required in addition to the 82C37A to provide the most significant 12 address bits, and a PLD is required to provide the necessary address decoding. There are some advantages in using the 82C37A. First, it can provide four DMA channels. Second, hardware DMA allows the I/O device to initiate the transfer once the DMA controller has been initialized. Finally, the 82C37A can provide modes of transfer other that just block transfer. Still, in many applications, it is preferable to consider using either an 80C188EA or 80C188EC microprocessor, both of which provide on-chip DMA controllers.

19.6   80C18xEx Family Members with On-Chip DMA

If your application requires DMA, the use of an 80C188EA or 80C188EC microprocessor may be preferable to using an 80C188EB. 80C186EA/80C188EA and 80C186EC/80C188EC microprocessors have on-chip DMA Units that provide multiple DMA channels (Table 1.5-2). This reduces the chip count for designs requiring DMA. However, there are some tradeoffs. The 80C188EA does not have the serial I/O channels and parallel I/O ports that the 80C188EB provides. The 80C188EC has all of the 80C188EB functions, plus DMA and a watchdog timer. It requires a 100-pin package and is more expensive.

The DMA Unit in the 80C186EA/80C188EA and 80C186EC/80C188EC uses the BIU to perform its data transfers. The DMA Unit working in conjunction with the BIU provides all the functions of a conventional DMA controller. The DMA Unit provides address and word count information. The BIU uses this information to actually perform the DMA transfer. The DMA Units provide greater capability and are simpler to use than an 82C37A.

The 80C186EA/80C188EA's DMA Unit has two independent DMA channels. Each channel can accept DMA requests from one of three sources:

1. an external request pin, DRQ0 or DRQ1
2. an internal request from Timer 2
3. an internal request from your program

The DMA Unit can transfer data between any combination of memory and I/O space. This includes memory to memory and I/O to I/O transfers. I/O to I/O transfers are not possible with the 82C37A.

The 80C186EC/80C188EC's DMA Unit is similar to that of the 80C186EA/80C188EA, except it has four independent DMA channels. Each channel can accept DMA requests from one of four sources. The additional source is the Serial Communications Unit. This allows the serial ports to make DMA requests and transfer data directly from a serial receiver to memory or from memory to a serial transmitter. This avoids the latency required in servicing serial interrupts.

Since the DMA Units for these microprocessors are similar, the 80C188EB will be used to illustrate their capabilities. A few differences between the 82C37A DMA controller and the 80C188EA on-chip controllers are also highlighted in this section. For a full description of these on-chip DMA units, see their respective Intel User's Manuals.

19.6.1   The DMA Unit's PCB Registers

Each DMA channel has six PCB registers. These are:

1. DMA Source Address Pointer High, DxSRCH
2. DMA Source Address Pointer Low, DxSRCL
3. DMA Destination Address Pointer High, DxDSTH
4. DMA Destination Address Pointer Low, DxDSTL
5. DMA Transfer Count Register, DxTC
6. DMA Control Register, DxCON

The registers for a channel must be programmed prior to a DMA transfer by that channel. The start bit (STRT) in a channel's Control register is set to enable or arm the channel. The channel can then perform a DMA transfer in response to a request. The DMA Control register bit assignments and functions are shown in Fig. 19.6-1.

Each on-chip DMA channel has a 20-bit source address pointer and a 20-bit destination address pointer. The most significant 4 bits of the source address pointer are contained in DxSRCH and the least significant 16 bits are contained in DxSRCL. The most significant 4 bits of the destination address pointer are contained in DxDSTH and the least

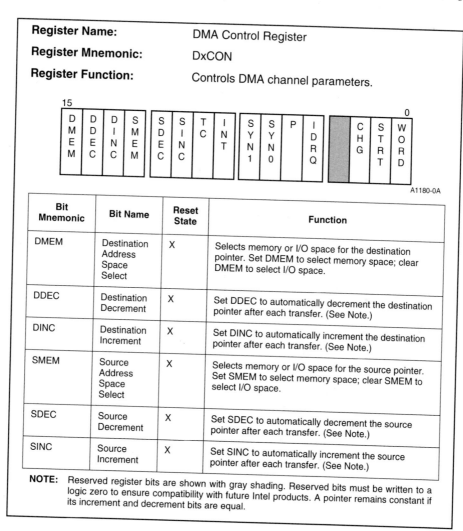

Bit Mnemonic	Bit Name	Reset State	Function
DMEM	Destination Address Space Select	X	Selects memory or I/O space for the destination pointer. Set DMEM to select memory space; clear DMEM to select I/O space.
DDEC	Destination Decrement	X	Set DDEC to automatically decrement the destination pointer after each transfer. (See Note.)
DINC	Destination Increment	X	Set DINC to automatically increment the destination pointer after each transfer. (See Note.)
SMEM	Source Address Space Select	X	Selects memory or I/O space for the source pointer. Set SMEM to select memory space; clear SMEM to select I/O space.
SDEC	Source Decrement	X	Set SDEC to automatically decrement the source pointer after each transfer. (See Note.)
SINC	Source Increment	X	Set SINC to automatically increment the source pointer after each transfer. (See Note.)

NOTE: Reserved register bits are shown with gray shading. Reserved bits must be written to a logic zero to ensure compatibility with future Intel products. A pointer remains constant if its increment and decrement bits are equal.

Figure 19.6-1   DMA Control Register for 80C188EA. (Courtesy of Intel Corp.)

Register Name: DMA Control Register

Register Mnemonic: DxCON

Register Function: Controls DMA channel parameters.

15														0
D M E M	D D E C	D I N C	S M E M	S D E C	S I N C	T C	I N T	S Y N 1	S Y N 0	P	I D R Q	C H G	S T R T	W O R D

A1180-0A

Bit Mnemonic	Bit Name	Reset State	Function
TC	Terminal Count	X	Set TC to terminate transfers on Terminal Count. This bit is ignored for unsynchronized transfers (that is, the DMA channel behaves as if TC is set, regardless of its condition).
INT	Interrupt	X	Set INT to generate an interrupt request on Terminal Count. The TC bit must be set to generate an interrupt.
SYN1:0	Synchroni- zation Type	XX	Selects channel synchronization: **SYN1 SYN0 Synchronization Type** 0 0 Unsynchronized 0 1 Source-synchronized 1 0 Destination-synchronized 1 1 Reserved (do **not** use)
P	Relative Priority	X	Set P to select high priority for the channel; clear P to select low priority for the channel.
IDRQ	Internal DMA Request Select	X	Set IDRQ to select internal DMA requests and ignore the external DRQ pin. Clear IDRQ to select the DRQ pin as the source of DMA requests. When IDRQ is set, the channel must be configured for source-synchronized transfers (SYN1:0 = 01).

NOTE: Reserved register bits are shown with gray shading. Reserved bits must be written to a logic zero to ensure compatibility with future Intel products.

Figure 19.6-1   DMA Control Register for 80C188EA. (Courtesy of Intel Corp.)
                 (Continued.)

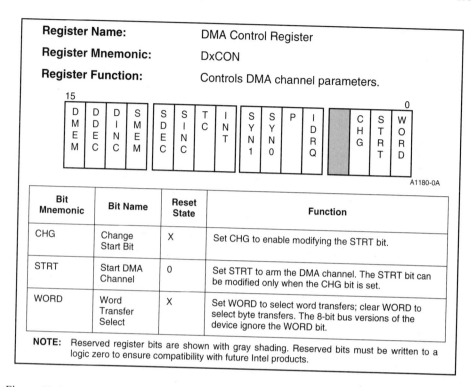

Figure 19.6-1   DMA Control Register for 80C188EA. (Courtesy of Intel Corp.) (Continued.)

significant 16 bits are contained in DxDSTL. These 20-bit pointers provide the physical addresses of the source and destination for a transfer.

Each pointer can be programmed to address either the memory space or I/O space using the SMEM and DMEM bits in the DMA register. By using the SDEC, SINC, DDEC, and DINC bits in the DMA Control register, these pointers can be programmed to automatically increment, decrement, or remain constant after each transfer. For use with a microprocessor with a 16-bit data bus, the pointers can be programmed to increment or decrement by two, for word transfers, using the WORD bit.

For example, for a conventional DMA write, the source address pointer would be programmed to address I/O space and to not increment or decrement. The destination address pointer would be programmed to address memory space and to increment.

When a DMA request is granted, the BIU performs each DMA transfer of a byte using two indivisible bus cycles, a fetch bus cycle followed by a deposit bus cycle. During the fetch bus cycle, the source address is used and /RD is asserted. A byte is read from the data source and placed in a temporary register in the microprocessor. During the deposit bus cycle, the destination address is used and /WR is asserted. The byte is written from the temporary register to the destination. Recall that the 82C37A normally uses only a single bus cycle and directly transfers a byte. The 82C37A does not use a temporary data register nor does it require two bus cycles for a transfer, unless it is performing memory to memory DMA .

By programming both address pointer registers for the I/O space, I/O to I/O transfers are possible. This type of transfer is not possible with an 82C37A.

The on-chip DMA controllers view the 1 Mbyte memory space as linear (unsegmented). In contrast, the 82C37A DMA controller uses a single 16-bit pointer. The high byte of this pointer, A15–A8, must be externally latched. An additional external latch is required to provide the most significant four address bits, A19–A16.

An address pointer programmed for the I/O space generates a complete 20-bit address. The most significant 4 bits of this address must be programmed to 0H, or addresses beyond the 64 Kbyte I/O space will be generated. The CSU will not assert a chip-select for addresses above 64 Kbytes. If external address decoding hardware ignores these bits, as is normally the case, it makes no difference whether they are 0H are not. On the other hand, these four bits could be decoded to allow bank switching of multiple 64 Kbyte I/O address spaces.

Each channel in a DMA Unit has its own 16-bit DMA Transfer Count register, DxTC. This register controls the total number of transfers the channel runs. This limits the maximum number of transfers for a single DMA operation to 65,536. To accomplish additional transfers, the channel must be reprogrammed. The transfer count register is decremented by 1 for each byte or word transferred. A DMA channel can be programmed to terminate its transfers when its Transfer Count register reaches zero. When programmed to terminate on terminal count, the DMA channel disarms itself when the transfer count value reaches zero. No further transfers take place until the channel is rearmed by your program.

19.6.2   External DMA Requests

An external I/O device requests a DMA transfer by asserting a DREQ input pin of the 80C188EA. The DMA Unit does not provide a discrete DMA acknowledge signal, as does a conventional DMA controller. When the BIU is ready to transfer a byte it will run the two bus cycles required. The BIU's accessing of the I/O device constitutes the acknowledgment of the request. If the DMA transfer is a DMA write, your address decoding logic will select the input device during the read bus cycle. In response to receiving its input device select pulse, the input device drives the data bus with the appropriate data. The channel will continue performing transfers as long as the request is active and programmed transfer count has not been exceeded.

External DMA requests are classified as source synchronized or destination synchronized. The type of synchronization a channel uses is programmed. In source synchronized transfers, the request originates from an input device. The maximum DMA transfer rate is the system clock frequency divided by 8 ($F_{CPU}/8$). Thus, a 20 MHz 80C188EA has a destination synchronized maximum transfer rate of 2.5 Mbytes/sec. This rate is twice as high for the 16-bit data bus versions of these microprocessors, since each transfer can be a word.

For destination synchronized transfers, the DMA request originates from an output device. Destination synchronized transfers have two idle states that follow the 8 states of the two bus cycles that transfer the data. The two idle states are inserted to allow the output device to unassert the DRQ input to prevent another DMA cycle from following the current one. This results in a total of 10 states per transfer. As a result, the maximum transfer rate for a destination synchronized transfer is the system clock frequency divided by 10 ($F_{CPU}/10$). Destination synchronized transfers give up the bus during the idle states allowing any other bus master to take control.

19.6.3   Internal DMA Requests

Internal DMA requests can originate from Timer 2 or your program. A DMA transfer can be initiated by Timer 2. Each time Timer 2 reaches a maximum count one transfer is performed by the DMA channel. For example, a memory buffer can be filled with the binary values needed to generate a waveform. Each value in the buffer corresponds to the waveform's value at a particular time increment. A DMA transfer from this buffer to a DAC will generate the waveform at the DAC's output.

Direct programming transfers are unsynchronized. After the appropriate PCB registers are initialized, the transfer is started by setting the Start bit in the control register. Once started the transfers continue until the Transfer Count register reaches zero. At this point, the DMA transfer is terminated. Direct programming transfers can be used to perform memory to memory DMA.

Each DMA channel can be programmed to generate an interrupt request when its transfer count reaches zero.

When the DMA Unit has a pending request it signals the BIU. If the BIU has no other higher priority requests, it runs the DMA cycle. If a DMA channel accesses memory or I/O within the programmed range of a chip select, the chip select will be asserted. A chip select will not be asserted for an I/O DMA cycle that accesses I/O space above 64K.

The DMA Unit has arbitration logic to handle simultaneous DMA requests from its two channels. Each channel has a priority bit in the control word to set its priority. If one channel is programmed for high priority and the other for low priority then the priorities will be fixed as programmed. If both channels are programmed for high priority, or both channels are programmed for low priority, then the priority will rotate.

19.6.4   A DMA ADC Example

In Fig. 19.2-1, an ADC was used with a FIFO buffer to sample an input signal at a 10 MHz rate. The FIFO generated an interrupt when it was full. The ISR then transferred the contents of the FIFO to a memory buffer, using a REP INSB instruction. For the AD775 Flash converter a simpler interface that transfers data directly from the ADC to a memory buffer using software initiated DMA can be created. The falling edge of an input device select pulse generated from /RD during the read cycle of the DMA transfer is used to clock the ADC and simultaneously read the result from the conversion of the sample taken three clocks earlier.

Because no FIFO is used and the ADC is clocked from a device select pulse, the sample rate is limited to the data transfer rate of the DMA.

A procedure to initialize the DMA channel and start the transfer is given in Fig. 19.7-2. Since the 20-bit destination address used by the DMA channel is a linear address, it must be computed from the segmented address of the memory buffer. The least significant 16 bits of the linear address are the sum of the least significant 12 bits of the memory

```
;*****************************************************************
;NAME:          DMA_ADC
;
;function:      Transfers 16,384 bytes from input port PORT_ADDR to
;               memory buffer MEM_BUFF
;returns:
;DESCRIPTION:
;
;*****************************************************************
;

dma_adc proc
;Calculate values for destination pointer registers and initialize.
        mov     ax,seg mem_buff     ;get segment addr. of destination
        rol     ax,4                ;put ms 4-bits of seg addr in BX
        mov     bx,ax
        and     ax,0fff0h           ;left shifted ls 12-bits of seg addr
        add     ax,offset mem_buff  ;add offset of destination
        adc     bx,0                ;add carry to ms 4-bits of seg addr
        and     bx,000fh            ;mask all but ms 4-bits of pointer

;AX contains ls 16-bits of pointer, BX contains ms 4-bits of pointer
        mov     dx,D0DSTL           ;ls 16-bits to DMA Unit
        out     dx,ax
        mov     dx,D0DSTH           ;ms 4-bits to DMA Unit
        mov     ax,bx
        out     dx,ax

;Initialize source pointer
        mov     ax,ADC_PORT         ;port address of ADC
        mov     dx,D0SRCL           ;ls 16-bits to DMA Unit
        out     dx,ax
        mov     dx,D0SRCH           ;ms 4-bits to DMA Unit
        xor     ax,ax
        out     dx,ax

;Initialize transfer count
        mov     ax,16384            ;number of bytes to transfer
        mov     dx,D0TC             ;output to Transfer Count register
        out     dx,ax
```

Figure 19.6-2   Procedure for a software initiated DMA transfer from a flash ADC to a
memory buffer.

```
;Initialize control register -
        ;Destination memory, post increment pointer
        ;source I/O, no ptr change
        ;terminate on terminal count, no interrupt, unsynchronized
        ;high priority, start channel, byte transfer
        mov    ax,1010001000100110b
        mov    dx,D0CON
        out    dx,ax
        ret
dma_adc endp
```

Figure 19.6-2   Procedure for a software initiated DMA transfer from a flash ADC to a
                 memory buffer. (Continued.)

buffer's segment address left shifted four bits and the memory buffer's offset address. The most significant 4 bits of the linear address are the sum of the most significant 4 bits of the memory buffer's segment address and the carry from the previous addition.

The Control register is initialized to have memory as the destination of the transfer and to post increment the destination pointer. The source of the transfer is I/O and the source pointer is not altered after a transfer. The transfer is programmed to be unsynchronized and to terminate when the Transfer Counter register reaches zero. The STRT bit is set to arm the channel for the transfer. Once the Control register is written, the transfer starts immediately.

19.7   Summary

Some I/O devices are capable of generating blocks or bursts of data where the data transfer rate during the block or burst is very high. Programmed I/O or interrupt driven I/O that transfers data on a byte-by-byte basis is typically too slow to handle such devices. The data generated must usually be placed in some form of memory buffer until it can be processed at a later time.

The 80C188EB provides two instructions, INSB and OUTSB, that were not available in previous microprocessors in this family. These are string I/O instructions that, when used with a REP prefix, can transfer data between the system memory and I/O at relatively high speeds. Each byte transferred between I/O and memory requires two bus cycles. The BIU controls the transfer of data and stores the data in one of its temporary registers between the two bus cycles. For an 80C188EB operating at 25 MHz, the transfer rate is 3.125 MHz. For an 80C186EB operated at this same frequency, the transfer rate is doubled.

A hardware approach to handling very high data rates is to use a FIFO memory buffer. Data can be simultaneously written to and read from the FIFO buffer at different rates. A high speed input device writes data into the FIFO buffer at its high data rate, and the microprocessor reads the data from the FIFO at its slower data rate. The FIFO must be large enough so that no data is lost. FIFO buffers that can be read and written at speeds of up to 50MHz are readily available.

Another traditional hardware approach to handling high speed data transfers is to use a hardware DMA controller. Typically, this is an IC device that can request control of the system bus in order to transfer data directly between an I/O device and memory. When the microprocessor grants the DMA controller control of the system bus, the DMA controller generates the memory address and control signals, and the I/O device generates or accepts the data. Each byte of data is transferred in a single bus cycle. The rate of transfer is not affected by the speed of the microprocessor but is determined only by the speed of the I/O device, DMA controller, and memory.

The 80C188EB provides the bus control arbitration signals HOLD and HLDA that allow it to share the system bus with a DMA controller. Unfortunately, the speed of the 82C37A DMA controller that would typically be used has not kept up with that of the 80C188EB. The fastest 82C37A can only transfer data at 1.6 Mbytes/sec. This data transfer rate is slower than that achievable with programmed I/O using string instructions. However, the DMA controller can handle four separate I/O devices and allows the I/O device to initiate the transfer, once the controller has been initialized. The DMA controller also has several modes of operation and can interleave its use of the bus with that of the 80C188EB to allow concurrent operation.

The 80C188EA and 80C188EC have on-chip multichannel DMA controllers. Using one of these microprocessors may be preferable to using an 80C188EB and 82C37A when DMA is required. These DMA controllers use the BIU to drive the address and control buses. While the data transfer rate is no faster than using string I/O, transfers can be initiated by the I/O devices and several modes of operation are possible.

19.8 Problems

1. Estimate the execution time for the INBYTE_ISR ISR of Fig. 19.2-3. From your estimate, determine the approximate data rate. How could you determine the actual data rate for a system that uses this ISR?

2. Give an example of an output device that requires that data be transferred to it as blocks with a high data rate.

20

MULTI-MODULE AND
MULTI-LANGUAGE PROGRAMS

20.1   Multi-Module Programs

20.2   Linking Modules

20.3   Makefiles

20.4   Segment Groups

20.5   Mixed Language Programs

20.6   Memory Models

20.7   Interfacing C and Assembly Language Modules

20.8   Simplified Segment Directives

20.9   Startup Code

Modular programs are comprised of self-contained portions of code that can be independently written, understood, tested, and debugged. The two primary ways of achieving modularity are through the use of procedures and multiple source modules. Procedures were introduced in Chapter 8 and extensively used in subsequent chapters. In this chapter, procedures are also considered, but in the context of their use in multiple source module programs.

Programs in previous chapters were all single source module (single source file) programs. A single source module is appropriate for small programs and for instructional purposes. However, because of their size and complexity, most practical programs are constructed as multiple source module (multi-module) programs.

Structuring a large program as a multi-module program has several advantages over using a single module:

1. Dividing a program into separate modules makes it easier and faster to manage software development and maintenance.

2. Since any one module is only a small portion of the entire program, it is easier to separately conceive and code each source module.

3. A single source module assembles faster than an entire program.

4. When the code in a particular module needs to be modified, only that module is edited and reassembled.

5. Some modules can be written in a high-level language such as C, FORTRAN, or Pascal.

6. Code from one or more libraries of modules containing previously developed procedures can be linked into a program as needed.

As with procedures, if your division of a program into modules is not done judiciously, the use of multiple modules loses many of its benefits. Modules should be functionally meaningful and coherent within the context of your application. You should divide your program into modules that are as independent as possible and that have the least possible interaction, or linkage, with other modules. All procedures that deal with a specific subsystem or subfunction should be placed in the same module.

Usually programs are divided such that a main module controls the program's overall execution flow by calling procedures in other modules. For complex applications or applications with large code size, it is often advantageous to write the main module in a high-level language, such as C. Some of the other modules can also be written in C, and some can be written in assembly language. The result is a multi-module mixed language program.

20.1   Multi-Module Programs

Multi-module programs consist of multiple source files. Each file is a module that is separately assembled or compiled. The object code modules (files) that result from assembling the individual source modules are linked together to build the complete program.

For ASM86 programs, four assembler directives define modules and specify the linkage between them. Two of these, NAME and END, introduced in Chapter 4, give a module its name and define its extent. The other two, PUBLIC and EXTRN, communicate symbol information among modules.

Each source module must begin with a NAME directive. The name directive follows the syntax:

    name   *modname*

Each module must end with an END directive. The END directive has the syntax:

    end   [*label name*]

One, and only one, of the modules that comprises a program has a *label name* with its END directive. This module is the program's **main module**. The *label name* is the label of the first instruction to be executed in the program. Since all of the previous programs were single module programs, each module was a main module and had a label name.

For separate modules to work together as a single program, interconnections must be established between them. One kind of interconnection allows a module to read and write a **shared variable** in another module. A second kind of interconnection allows a module to transfer execution to a location in another module. These inter-module references join modules into a single program.

PUBLIC and EXTRN directives define the interconnection between modules. The **PUBLIC** directive lists those symbols defined in a module that can be accessed by other modules. It has the syntax:

public   *name*, [,...]

The list of names can include variables, labels, or constants. Unless declared PUBLIC, the symbol for a variable, label, or constant is only known in the module in which it is defined and is unknown to other modules. If not declared as PUBLIC, the same variable name can be used to allocate storage in two different modules and the name will correspond to two distinct memory locations. In effect, every variable name is qualified by its module name.

The external directive (**EXTRN**) specifies those symbols that are referenced in the current module, but are defined and declared PUBLIC in some other module. EXTRN has the syntax:

extrn   *name:type*, [,...]

Each symbol listed in an EXTRN directive must have its type specified along with its name. The assembler must be told the symbol's type in order to assemble instructions that reference the symbol. Since modules are separately assembled, the assembler cannot ascertain on its own the type of any symbol not defined in the current module.

If a *name* in an EXTRN directive is that of a constant, its type is **ABS**, for absolute. If a name is a variable, its type is BYTE, WORD, or DWORD. If a *name* is a structure name, its type is the number of bytes allocated in the structure definition. If a *name* is a record name, its type is either byte or word, as appropriate. If name is a label, its type is NEAR or FAR.

A simple example of a multi-module program is a program for an instrumentation system that, among its other functions, measures some analog values. The program consists of many modules, including the main module and modules for analog-to-digital conversion, display, operator input, serial I/O, etc. In this example, portions of two modules are presented, the main module, main.asm, and the analog-to-digital conversion module, ad.asm.

To perform an analog-to-digital conversion, the module main needs to call two procedures in module ad.asm. One procedure, adinit, initializes the analog-to-digital converter. The other procedure, adconv, causes a conversion to take place. The ADC subsystem is multi-channel. Byte variable, adchnl, specifies the channel to be converted. Word variable adresult is used to return the result. Module main.asm is given in Fig. 20.1-1.

The term PUBLIC, in the SEGMENT directive for the data segment, is not to be confused with the PUBLIC directive. PUBLIC is used in the SEGMENT directive to specify the segment's *combine-type*. Combine-types are explained in the next section.

The EXTRN directive inside the data segment tells the assembler that there are two variables (adchnl, adresult) referenced in this module, but defined in the segment data of some other unspecified module. Since these two variables are not defined in this module, the EXTRN directive also tells the assembler the variables' types. adchnl is a byte variable and adresult is a word variable.

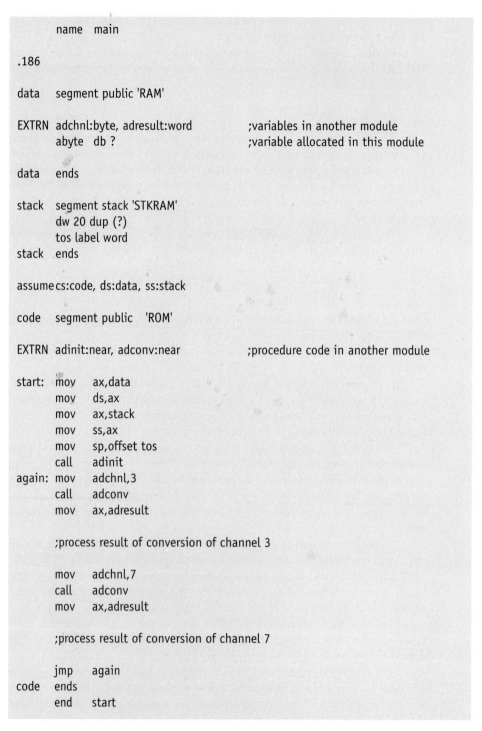

```
            name    main

.186

data    segment public 'RAM'

EXTRN   adchnl:byte, adresult:word          ;variables in another module
        abyte   db ?                        ;variable allocated in this module

data    ends

stack   segment stack 'STKRAM'
        dw 20 dup (?)
        tos label word
stack   ends

assume cs:code, ds:data, ss:stack

code    segment public  'ROM'

EXTRN   adinit:near, adconv:near            ;procedure code in another module

start:  mov     ax,data
        mov     ds,ax
        mov     ax,stack
        mov     ss,ax
        mov     sp,offset tos
        call    adinit
again:  mov     adchnl,3
        call    adconv
        mov     ax,adresult

        ;process result of conversion of channel 3

        mov     adchnl,7
        call    adconv
        mov     ax,adresult

        ;process result of conversion of channel 7

        jmp     again
code    ends
        end     start
```

Figure 20.1-1   Main module (MAIN) for a multi-module program.

The EXTRN in the segment code tells the assembler that procedures adinit and adconv are defined in the segment code of some other module and that both are NEAR procedures.

EXTRN directives should be placed within a SEGMENT/ENDS pair. It is important to place EXTRNs for symbols belonging to a segment that exists in the current module inside that SEGMENT/ENDS pair in the current module. List other external symbols (belonging to none of the logical segments in the current module) outside of all SEGMENT/ENDS pairs.

The label name on the END directive in Fig. 20.1.1 indicates that this is a main module and specifies the first instruction to be executed in the program.

Variables, procedures, and constants defined by EXTRNs in a module can be used just as if they were defined in the module. The call to adinit transfers execution to this procedure in the segment code of another module. When adinit's RET is executed, execution is transferred back to the instruction following the call in the module main. The ADC is initialized only once, at the beginning of the program.

To carry out a conversion, the ADC's channel must first be selected by loading the channel number into byte variable, adchnl. Then the procedure adconv is called. After returning from adconv, the result of the conversion, adresult, is moved into AX for further processing.

The module ad.asm, which contains procedures adinit and adconv, is given in Fig. 20.1-2.

The PUBLIC directive inside segment data in module ad tells the assembler that variables adchnl and adresult are public. As a result, these variables can be referenced by instructions in other modules. It is not necessary for this directive to tell the assembler the types of these variables, since their types are defined in this module. The PUBLIC directive in the segment code tells the assembler that the two procedures, adinit and adconv, are public and can be called from other modules.

All the procedures that control the ADC subsystem are contained in the single module ad. Thus, software changes to the ADC subsystem are confined to this module. If procedures related to the ADC subsystem need to be modified, or if there is a problem with the ADC subsystem, the code involved is confined to this one module. Putting all the procedures related to a particular subsystem or function into the same module is an objective of multi-module program design.

If the ADC hardware is changed, only the software in module ad needs to be revised. If adresult is to be treated as a 12-bit unsigned right justified number, then it is up to adconv to place such a value in adresult before returning. The ADC hardware may generate its result low byte first, high byte first, as a word, or serially. The 12-bit value may be generated right justified or left justified. The value might not even originate as an unsigned value or even as a 12-bit value. It is procedure adconv's responsibility to control the hardware conversion, format the data as necessary, and place the properly formatted data in adresult.

20.2   Linking Multiple Modules

Each source module in a multi-module program is separately assembled and produces its own object file. When a particular module is assembled, the assembler does not know the addresses of external symbols nor the values of external constants. Therefore, the assembler

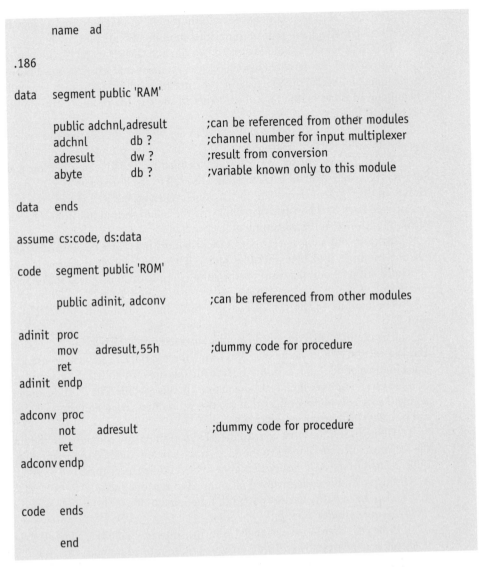

```
        name   ad

.186

data    segment public 'RAM'

        public adchnl,adresult      ;can be referenced from other modules
        adchnl      db ?            ;channel number for input multiplexer
        adresult    dw ?            ;result from conversion
        abyte       db ?            ;variable known only to this module

data    ends

assume cs:code, ds:data

code    segment public 'ROM'

        public adinit, adconv       ;can be referenced from other modules

adinit  proc
        mov    adresult,55h         ;dummy code for procedure
        ret
adinit  endp

adconv  proc
        not    adresult             ;dummy code for procedure
        ret
adconv  endp


code    ends

        end
```

Figure 20.1-2   Analog to digital conversion module (AD) for multi-module program.

cannot generate all the object code for those instructions that reference external symbols. The assembler allocates the appropriate number of bytes for each of these values, but it cannot fill in the actual values. If a source module references symbols defined in other modules, its object file includes information about these incomplete inter-module references.

After all source modules have been separately assembled, the linker is used to combine the separate object modules into a single program. In order to do this, the linker must resolve all inter-module references. References to external constants, variables, and labels are called **external references.** A module that contains external references is called an

unsatisfied module. What is missing (unsatisfied) are the values of externally defined constants and the addresses of externally defined variables and labels.

The linker must satisfy each external reference by finding the module in which the external symbol is declared public. The linker uses the address or value information provided in the object module where the symbol is defined and declared public to provide the missing information in the unsatisfied module. Obtaining the value of a constant is straightforward. However, determining the address of a variable or label is more complicated.

An external variable or label's type is already known from its EXTRN directive. If the EXTRN appears within a SEGMENT/ENDS pair, the segment address is also known. The offset of the variable or label is the only missing information. The offset given in the module where the variable or label is defined is the offset from the start of the logical segment in that module. If, during linking, this logical segment is combined with similarly named logical segments from other modules, the linker must determine the variable's or label's offset from the beginning of the composite logical segment.

Segments in different modules that have the same segment name can be combined into a single logical segment. When combined into a single segment, they are referenced using the same segment register value. To combine such segments, the linker adjusts the relative addresses of all the variables or labels in the combined segments. If logical segments with the same name are not combined, each segment address is different (has a different value), even though they use the same logical name. Not combining logical segments with the same name complicates addressing, since values in the segment registers have to be changed during the program's execution.

The SEGMENT/ENDS directive tells the linker how a logical segment can be combined with segments in other modules. A simplified form of the SEGMENT/ENDS directive was used in the previous chapters. That simplified form usually left a segment as non-combinable with any segments in other modules.

The full form of SEGMENT/ENDS is:

name   SEGMENT *[align-type][combine-type]* *['classname']*

name   ENDS

The **combine-type** tells the linker how a segment can be combined with other segments with the same segment name in other modules. The three choices of interest here are: none specified, PUBLIC, and STACK. In the programs of previous chapters, no combine-type was usually specified. As a result, the logical segments were not combinable with segments of the same name in other modules. However, if two logical segments with the same name appear in the same module, they are always combined at assembly time.

The linker combines a segment having the **PUBLIC combine-type** with other segments having the same segment name and a PUBLIC combine-type. When segments with the PUBLIC combine-type are combined, they are concatenated (placed adjacently, one after the other) to form one logical segment. The offsets in all the segments combined, after the first, are automatically adjusted to account for the total number of bytes in the preceding combined segments.

The **STACK combine-type** is used for stack segments. This combine-type causes the linker to combine segments so that the length of the combined segment is the sum of the lengths of its component segments. Offsets within each stack segment are combined so that the highest addressed byte in each stack segment coincides with the last byte in the combined segment. This is done so that the top of the empty stack may be referenced by the symbol for the first location past the end of the stack. This symbol is created using the LABEL directive.

In the previous example, the module main contained a stack segment, but the module ad did not. In this example, only one of the modules to be combined contains a stack segment, so the STACK combine-type is not used.

The **align-type** specifies on what boundary in memory a segment can be located. If no align-type is specified, the alignment defaults to paragraph. With paragraph alignment, a segment begins on an address divisible by 16, or equivalently, an address that has its least significant four bits equal to 0H. Other align-type choices are:

BYTE   segment may start at any address

WORD   segment must start at an even address

PAGE   segment must start at an address with the least significant equal 00H

INPAGE entire segment must fit into 256 bytes and when located cannot overlap a page boundary

When using an 80C186EB, word data should be placed in a data segment that is WORD aligned. Or, the WORD directive should be used immediately preceding the allocation of the data words. Either approach allows the 80C186EB to access each word in a single bus cycle.

The following command links two modules using Turbo Assembler's linker, TLINK:

```
tlink            main.obj ad.obj
```

The locator places segments with the same **classname** near each other in memory. This does not cause the segments to be combined, only to be near each other in physical memory. Usually the classname is used to place segments that should be in ROM near each other and into that portion of the memory space that is populated by ROM. Segments that should be in RAM are handled in a similar manner.

20.2.1   Object Modules from Libraries

A **librarian utility** is used to put a number of object modules into a single library file. The modules in the library file remain independent. The collection of object modules can then be referenced by the library's name. A librarian utility has commands to create a library and to add, list, and delete modules from the library.

Libraries provided with assemblers or compilers or through third parties provide modules for many common operations such as floating point arithmetic and string processing.

Object modules in a library can be linked into a program by including the library's filename as the last item in the list of files to be linked together. As the linker links the object modules, it maintains a list of unsatisfied external references. When it reaches the library file, it examines each object module in the file to see if that object module can satisfy one or more of the unsatisfied external references. If an object module satisfies an unresolved external reference, that module is automatically linked into the program and included in the object code produced.

Any object modules in the library that are not needed to satisfy unresolved external references are not linked into the final object code. An object module is indivisible. If an object module contains ten procedures and only one of these is required to satisfy an unresolved external reference, all ten procedures still end up in the final object code. For this reason, it is advantageous to only group procedures that are likely to be used together into the same module in a library.

20.3   Managing Multi-module Programs with a Make Utility

One advantage of creating a large program from multiple modules is that making a change to the program usually requires that only one source module be edited and reassembled. The reassembled module's object code is then linked to the program's other object code modules and the result located to create an updated executable version of the program. When several changes are made in a program, several modules may be modified. In this situation, care must be taken to ensure that the executable version of the program is the result of linking object files corresponding to the most recent version of each source module.

As the number of modules in a program increases, managing them during program development can become tedious and error prone. Failing to reassemble a source module you have changed or that depends on some other file, such as an include file you have changed, leaves you with an executable file that is not up-to-date. If a change is made in one source or include file, some, but not all, of the other source files may need to be reassembled.

One approach to insuring that all the object files linked together correspond to the most recent versions of the source modules is to put the commands to assemble, link, and locate all source files into a **batch file.** The batch file causes all the source modules to be reassembled each time it is executed. This approach becomes very time consuming when debugging large programs because the advantage of separate assembly of modules is lost.

A better approach is to use a make utility. A **make utility** is a program that automates the process of building an up-to-date version of your program. It creates the new version in the simplest possible way and without error. Use of a make utility provides you with two advantages:

1. Only those source modules that need reassembly are reassembled.
2. A record of every detail needed to assemble, link, and locate your program's source modules is provided.

A make utility examines the date and time stamps in the directory entry of each of the files that comprise your program. The make utility can automatically invoke the necessary assembler, compiler, or other tools to update only those object modules that require updating to keep the executable file current.

To accomplish its task, a make utility requires a makefile. A **makefile** is a text file that contains a description of how your program's source and object files should be processed and what dependencies exist among these files. A makefile consists of a set of interdependent instructions or rules. These rules tell the make utility how your program's source and object files must be processed to build the program.

Figure 20.3-1 is a simple makefile executable by Borland's make utility, MAKE. This makefile is written to produce an AXE version of a program, myprog, that is to be run using Paradigm's debugger.

```
myprog.axe: myprog.exe
        c:\locate -cmyprog.cfg myprog.exe

myprog.exe: main.obj module2.obj module3.obj
        tlink /s /v main.obj module2.obj module3.obj, myprog.exe

main.obj: main.asm
        tasm /c /l /zi module2.asm

module2.obj: module2.asm
        tasm /c /l /zi module2.asm

module3.obj: module3.asm
        tasm /c /l /zi module3.asm
```

Figure 20.3-1   A makefile using explicit rules.

Rules are used to tell MAKE what files depend on each other and what commands MAKE should execute to create the rule's target file. An **explicit rule** specifies complete file names and has the form:

Target: Dependency list
            Command list

The **target file** is the name and extension of the file to be updated. Each explicit rule tells how one specific target file depends on other files. The rule's dependency line (*Target: Dependency list*) must start in the first column. Each rule has associated with it one or more commands to create the updated target file. Commands must start with a space or tab. Commands typically invoke the assembler, compiler, linker, or locator. However, any command the operating system recognizes can be used in a makefile.

The makefile in Fig. 20.3-1 consists of five explicit rules. For example, the last rule in Fig. 20.3-1:

```
module3.obj: module3.asm
        tasm     /c /l /zi module3.asm
```

has a dependency line that indicates module3.obj depends on module3.asm. This rule lists the command for MAKE to execute to create the latest version of module3.obj. The command is to invoke TASM on module3.asm with the specified assembler switches.

The syntax to invoke MAKE at the DOS prompt is:

make *[options...] [target...]*

The name of the makefile that MAKE is to use can be specified as an option on the command line. If no makefile is specified, MAKE uses the file with the name makefile in the current directory. MAKE builds the targets you specify on its command line. If you type MAKE without a target specified, MAKE uses the first target specified in an explicit rule in the makefile as the ultimate target.

When MAKE is invoked, it reads the makefile to determine the dependencies. MAKE understands that it must update the files upon which a target file depends before it updates the target file itself. This requirement is called **linked dependency** and can cause the processing of a number of files.

In Fig. 20.3-1, the target of the first explicit rule is myprog.axe, so this is the ultimate target for the make operation. The rule for myprog.axe says that myprog.axe depends on myprog.exe. So, MAKE looks at the rule for creating myprog.exe. The rule for myprog.exe states that it depends on three object modules, main.obj, module2.obj, and module3.obj. MAKE compares the date and time stamp for main.obj against the date and time stamp for main.asm. If main.asm's date and time stamp is more recent, then it has been modified since is was last assembled. If this is the case, or if main.obj does not exist, then MAKE executes the command associated with the rule for updating main.obj. As a result, TASM is invoked and an updated version of main.obj is created.

Once MAKE has checked each of the OBJ dependencies, it checks the myprog.exe file's date and time against those of the OBJs upon which it depends. If any OBJ file is more recent than the EXE file, or if the EXE file does not exist, TLINK is executed to produce an up-to-date version of myprog.exe. Finally, the AXE file is checked against the EXE file. If the EXE file is more recent, or if the AXE file does not exist, MAKE invokes the locator.

If after being invoked once, MAKE is invoked again without any changes to the source files having been made, none of the files is reassembled and neither the linker nor locator is invoked.

Figure 20.3-2 shows a second makefile, functionally equivalent to the first. This makefile contains macros and an implicit rule. A **MAKE macro** is a variable that gets expanded into a string whenever the macro is invoked in a makefile. One macro definition, at the beginning of the file, specifies that AFLAGS = /c /l /zi. When this macro is invoked using $(AFLAGS), the text $(AFLAGS) is replaced by /c /l /zi. Macros simplify the appearance of a makefile and make it easier to maintain.

Implicit rules state how to make one type of file from another, based only on the file's extensions. The dependency line in an implicit rule is different from that of an explicit rule, but the commands are the same. The form for an implicit rule is:

    .Source_ext.Target_ext
    Command list

MAKE uses implicit rules if it can't find explicit rules for a given target. For example, the implicit rule in Fig. 20.3-2,

.ASM.OBJ

    tasm $(AFLAGS) S*.ASM

says that when an OBJ file is needed, it is made from an ASM file with the same filename by invoking the assembler TASM with the specified switches. The assembler options are spec-

```
AFLAGS = /c /l /zi
LFLAGS = /s /v

CFG = cfg

OBJS = main.obj module2.obj module3.obj

.ASM.OBJ:
        tasm $(AFLAGS) $*.ASM

myprog.axe:myprog.exe
        c:\locate -ccds.$(CFG) myprog.EXE

myprog.exe: $(OBJS)
        tlink $(LFLAGS) $(OBJS)
```

Figure 20.3-2   A makefile equivalent to the one in Fig. 20.3-1, but which uses macros and
                  an implicit rule.

ified by the $(AFLAGS) macro. The $* macro is one of several built-in macros provided by
MAKE. MAKE replaces $* by the name of the file being built, without the file's extension.

The makefile in Fig. 20.3-2 can serve as a template makefile for your multi-module
programs. You can change the options specified by the macros AFLAGS and LFLAGS to those
you desire. The modules that make up your program replace those specified in the OBJS
macro. You can use different makefiles, having different names, to process your program
source modules differently. You can create makefiles to build different versions of the same
target program, one for debugging under Paradigm debugger, one for debugging under
Turbo Debugger, one for placement in ROM.

If the makefile in Fig. 20.3-2 is given the name makefl2, MAKE is invoked to use this
makefile with the command line:

        make   -fmakefl2

MAKE's -f option tells it to use the filename specified after the -f as the makefile. In
this case, makefile makefl2 is used. If the -f option is not used, MAKE looks for a file with
the name makefile by default.

A makefile's macros and rules can be made conditional so a command line macro
definition (using the -D option) can enable or disable sections of a makefile. This allows a
single makefile with one or more -D options to build different versions of your program,
instead of using different makefiles.

With its implicit rules, built-in macros, and conditional execution directives, makefiles can be very powerful, but very cryptic. However, once created and debugged, a makefile builds your target in a consistent manner every time, and with all the correct switches
and commands.

To check that your makefile does what you want it to do, you can invoke MAKE with the -B and -n options. For example,

make -B -n -fmakefl2

Make options are case sensitive. The -B option builds all targets regardless of file dates. The -n option tells MAKE to print the commands, but not to actually perform them. As a result of these options, MAKE prints all of the commands it would execute in the order it would execute them. You can examine this printout to verify that the commands you expect, with the appropriate switches or options, would be executed in the desired order. The output from executing this command is given in Fig. 20.3-3.

```
MAKE Version 3.7  Copyright (c) 1987, 1993 Borland International
       tasm /c /l /zi main.ASM
       tasm /c /l /zi module2.ASM
       tasm /c /l /zi module3.ASM
       tlink /s /v main.obj module2.obj module3.obj
       c:\locate -ccds.cfg myprog.EXE
```

Figure 20.3-3   Output from executing command make -B -n -fmakefl2 to print commands that would be generated by makefile without their execution.

20.4   Segment Groups

As stated in Section 20.2, the linker automatically combines segments with the same name and PUBLIC combine-type. Sometimes it is desirable to combine segments that have different names. For example, the data in an application may be logically partitioned into several differently named segments, each segment name reflecting the nature of its data.

The linker does not automatically combine logical segments with different names. This makes referencing objects in the different logical segments cumbersome. For example, consider two data segments, data1 and data2:

```
data1          segment public 'RAM'
buff1          db 10dup(?)
var1           db ?
var2           dw ?
data1          ends

data2          segment public 'RAM'
buff2          db 8 dup(?)
var3           dw ?
var4           db ?
data2          ends
```

If your program has just referenced a variable in data1, then before it can reference a variable in data2, DS must be loaded with data2's segment address. In addition, an ASSUME using data2 must be used:

```
assume ds:data2
mov     ax,data2
mov     ds,ax
mov     cx,var3
```

In this situation, it is preferable to combine these two logical segments, which have different names, into a single physical segment. This would allow variables or labels in either segment to be accessed using the same segment address. The GROUP directive allows this to be done.

The **GROUP** directive combines several logical segments into one physical segment. This makes all variables and labels in the segments grouped together addressable using the same segment address. GROUP has the form:

name group *segpart* [,...]

where *segpart* specifies a segment. The size of the group in bytes is the sum of the size of the segments that are grouped together. The group size must be less than or equal to 64K. The linker combines the segments into a single physical segment with all data in the grouped segments addressable relative to the same segment address.

Using the GROUP directive, the segments data1 and data2 can be combined into the group datgrp:

```
datgrp              group data1,data2
```

Figure 20.4-1 shows the two logical segments grouped as a single physical segment and the offsets of the variables relative to their segments and to the group. The offset of var3 relative to its segment is 8 and relative to the group is 21.

The name of the group is used in an ASSUME and is used to load the segment register:

```
assume          cs:code, ds:datgrp
mov     ax,datgrp
mov     ds,ax
```

Variables in either logical segment can then be referenced by their variable name alone and are addressable from the segment register loaded with the group address:

```
mov     dx,var2        ;addressable through DS
mov     cx,var3        ;addressable through DS
```

When a variable name or label that is in a group is used in an instruction, the assembler uses the offset relative to the group in creating the instruction. *However, when the OFFSET operator is used with a variable or label that is in a group, the group name must be used as a segment override in order to obtain the offset relative to the group.* Since the seg-

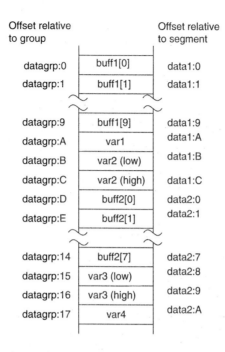

Figure 20.4-1   Two data segments combined into a single segment group.

ment register has been loaded with the group's segment address, it is the variable's offset relative to the group that is needed.

```
mov     bx,offset datgrp:var3
mov     cx,[bx]
```

The offset loaded into BX is 21, the required offset. If the group override is not used,

```
mov     bx,offset var3
```

BX is loaded with 8, which is incorrect.

Groups can consist of combinations of segments containing different kinds of information, for example, code segments and data segments. Some examples of such groups will be encountered in Section 20.6.

20.5   Mixed Language Programs

Programming in a high-level language relieves you from having to consider the architectural details of the microprocessor that will execute your program. As a result, you can focus at a more abstract level on the functions your system should accomplish. Because of their architectural independence, programs written in a high-level language are, in theory, portable to different microprocessors. A high-level language program written for one microprocessor can be recompiled and run on a different microprocessor. All that is required is a compiler that generates object code for the target microprocessor.

Using a high-level language has other advantages when compared to assembly language with regard to programming productivity, reliability, and maintainability.

The primary disadvantage of a high-level language in embedded system design is the inefficiency of the object code produced by the compiler. However, compiler efficiency has improved over the years. In addition, the relative inefficiency of a high-level language is diminished for a large program, because it is more difficult to write efficient large assembly language programs.

For complex applications, it is often desirable to create programs composed of modules written in more than one language. This approach allows you to use each language for those tasks where it is most effective. Usually multilanguage programs involve modules written in a single high-level language and modules written in assembly language. However, programs can also consist of modules written in different high-level languages and modules written in assembly language.

The single high-level language and assembly language approach often uses a high-level language module to control the program's overall execution flow. Tasks are then implemented by either functions in the high-level language or procedures in assembly language. The functions and procedures are contained in other modules. The assembly language procedures are called from the high-level language.

Assembly language procedures are typically used for tasks that involve low-level detailed control of peripheral hardware. Code that is hardware dependent can be isolated by putting it in assembly language modules. The resultant program is more portable, because only the assembly language modules need to be rewritten to port the program to a different target microprocessor. Assembly language procedures are also used to implement optimized high speed tasks.

Tasks that implement complex algorithms or use complex data types are often written as high-level functions. Many useful prewritten functions are available in libraries provided with a high-level language. For example, the 80C188EB, unlike the 80C186EB, does not provide support for a hardware floating point coprocessor. However, a high-level language provides floating point data types and a library with floating point functions.

High-level languages that are combined with assembly language must be compiled languages. In addition, the object files produced by the high-level languages' compiler and the assembler must be compatible. Or alternatively, translators must be available to translate object files into compatible formats. Once translated into compatible object files, the object files can be linked, as described in Section 2.2.

Intel's ASM86, C, Fortran, and PLM languages use a common object file format called **OMF86.** Assemblers and compilers from other manufacturers can usually create object files is this format. Languages from Borland, such as TASM, C++, C, Fortran, and Pascal use Intel's OMF. Microsoft's C tools produce a different object file format called **COFF.** You must be sure that the languages that you intend to use to create a multilanguage program have compatible object file formats, or can be translated to a compatible format.

20.6 Memory Models

A prerequisite for understanding the interface between C and assembly language is an understanding of memory models. A **memory model** for a high-level language specifies how segments that comprise a program are to be managed. Early C compilers for DOS required that all the code fit into a single 64 Kbyte segment and all of the data fit into a separate 64 Kbyte segment. This arrangement has come to be known as the **small model.** For greater flexibility, current C compilers provide several memory models.

Some common memory models are: tiny, small, medium, compact, and large. These models are listed in Table 20.6-1, along with the number of code and data segments each model allows. If a model allows only one code segment, then pointers to code are NEAR. If many segments are allowed, the code pointers are FAR. The same holds true for data segments and their data pointers.

Table 20.6-1   Memory model segment management.

Model	Code Segments	Data Segments
Tiny	one, includes data	one, shared with code
Small	one	one
Medium	many	one
Compact	one	many
Large	many	many

The most commonly used memory models are the small and large models. The small model has the advantage that it produces faster code. This occurs because pointers to code and data in the small model are NEAR pointers and pointers to code and data in the large model are FAR pointers. Since it takes more time to load two registers for a FAR pointer than one register for a NEAR pointer, small model code executes faster.

For command line compilers, the desired model is selected by an option switch. Integrated Development Environments (IDEs) available for most computers allow the model to be selected from a menu.

Names of segments and their attributes are predefined for each memory model. Table 20.6-2 provides this information for the Borland C compiler's small and large models.

For the small model, the name of the code segment is **_TEXT**, and the name of the initialized data segment is **_DATA.** Uninitialized data is distinguished from initialized data and is given its own segment. The segment name for uninitialized data is **_BSS.** The name of the stack segment is **STACK**. The data segment and stack segment belong to a group named **DGROUP.**

With the exception of its code segments, the large model's segment names are similar to those of the small model. Since the large model allows more than one code segment, each code segment is given a unique name corresponding to its module name and has the suffix _TEXT.

Segment names are important because assembly language modules that are to be combined with C modules must use the same segment names as the C modules. The C

Table 20.6-2   Default segment names and types for SMALL and LARGE memory models.

Model	Simplified Directive	Segment Name	Align Type	Combine Type	Class-name	Group
Small	.CODE	_TEXT	WORD	PUBLIC	'CODE'	
	.FAR.DATA	FAR_DATA	PARA	private	'FAR_DATA'	
	.FARDATA?	FAR_BSS	PARA	private	'FAR_BSS'	
	.DATA	_DATA	WORD	PUBLIC	'DATA'	DGROUP
	.CONST	CONST	WORD	PUBLIC	'CONST'	DGROUP
	.DATA?	_BSS	WORD	PUBLIC	'BSS'	DGROUP
	.STACK[a]	STACK	PARA	STACK	'STACK'	DGROUP
Large	.CODE	name_TEXT	WORD	PUBLIC	'CODE'	
	.FAR.DATA	FAR_DATA	PARA	private	'FAR_DATA'	
	.FARDATA?	FAR_BSS	PARA	private	'FAR_BSS'	
	.DATA	_DATA	WORD	PUBLIC	'DATA'	DGROUP
	.CONST	CONST	WORD	PUBLIC	'CONST'	DGROUP
	.DATA?	_BSS	WORD	PUBLIC	'BSS'	DGROUP
	.STACK[b]	STACK	PARA	STACK	'STACK'	DGROUP

a. STACK is not assumed to be in DGROUP if FARSTACK is specified in the MODEL directive.
b. STACK is not assumed to be in DGROUP if FARSTACK is specified in the MODEL directive.

modules' segment names are predefined based on the model selected when the C modules are compiled.

One method for determining the default segment names used by a compiler is to find the tables like Table 20.6-2 in the compiler's documentation. Another way is to compile a simple C program so that the corresponding assembly language source code is generated. You can then examine this code to see what default segment names were generated. For example, with Borland's command line C compiler, the -S option switch produces assembly language output. For Borland's IDE, a tool named C++ to Assembler is available that generates assembly language from C or C++.

20.7   Interfacing C and Assembly Language Modules

Currently the most popular high-level language for embedded systems design is C. C++, which is an evolutionary extension of C, is also finding increased use in embedded systems. C++ adds the flexibility of objects to the C language. Even though a program can be written entirely in C or C++, it is usually desirable to mix C and assembly language to take advantage of each language's strengths.

Since the interface between C++ and assembly language is the same as that between C and assembly language, the latter is used to illustrate the general concepts of interfacing between multi-language modules. In particular, Borland's C and TASM are used. Versions of Borland's C++ compiler can compile both C++ and C programs. While the examples in this text are C programs, they are compiled using a Borland C++ compiler.

The discussion of multi-language programs in the following sections assumes that you have some familiarity with C. Several introductory texts on C that are particularly appropriate for engineers, as well as some more advanced C texts that are particularly appropriate for embedded systems programming, are listed in the bibliography.

One method for mixing C and assembly language is to use **in-line assembly language.** In this approach, assembly language instructions are included directly in your C program. However, since the in-line assembly language instructions are microprocessor specific, this makes porting the program to another microprocessor difficult. You would have to find these in-line assembly language instructions wherever they appear throughout your C code and replace them with equivalent instructions for the new target microprocessor. In effect, using in-line assembly language eliminates C's portability advantage as a high-level language.

The preferred way of mixing C and assembly language, one which enhances a program's portability and modularity, is to write some modules in C and others in assembly language. Since C is a compiled high-level language, C modules can be separately compiled and their object code linked with assembly language object code.

A program comprised of C and assembly language modules can be written as an assembly language main program that calls some functions that are written in C or uses some prewritten C library functions. Alternatively, a program can be written as a C program that invokes some functions that are realized as assembly language procedures.

In the first approach, the program's overall architecture is created in assembly language with some of its procedures coded in C. The assembly language program calls functions written in C. This approach is often used for small programs where it is desirable to take advantage of functions that exist in the C library, such as floating point routines.

In the second approach, the program's overall high-level architecture and execution flow is built with one or more C modules. Functions that deal with low-level hardware details, or that require extremely fast execution, are coded as assembly language procedures. These procedures are contained in assembly language modules. This is the approach more commonly used for large programs and is the approach described in the remainder of this section.

The C program views assembly language procedures as C functions. When a C program needs to execute an assembly language procedure, it simply calls the procedure as a C function. Procedures called by a C program must be written to accommodate the C compiler's conventions for passing parameters to and receiving results from functions.

There are a number of details that must be considered and conventions that must be followed when mixing C and assembly language. Once you are familiar with these requirements you will find that using the two languages together is not difficult. The following subsections focus on these requirements. The last subsection provides a simple example that brings the concepts and requirements together.

20.7.1   C and Assembly Language Interface Requirements

To interface assembly language procedures contained in an assembly language module to a C module requires strict adherence to certain compiler conventions. The details of these conventions differ depending on the specific compiler, but the general guidelines are the same:

1. The assembly language module must use segment names that correspond to those of the memory model used by the C compiler.

2. Assembly language procedure names and variable names that are public must begin with an underscore and must be case sensitive.

3. Assembly language procedures must follow the C compiler's parameter passing and result returning conventions.

4. The size in bytes of each parameter passed to a procedure must be consistent with its type as defined by the C compiler.

5. Assembly language procedures called by a C program must preserve, save, and restore those registers that the C compiler requires be preserved by C functions.

6. Parameters passed to a procedure on the stack must be left on the stack by the procedure. It is the responsibility of the C program that calls a procedure to remove parameters from the stack after the return from the procedure occurs.

20.7.2   Assembly Language Segment, Label, and Variable Names

You are not free to choose the names of your module's segments when writing an assembly language module that contains C callable procedures. You must use the segment naming scheme defined by your C compiler for the chosen memory model. For the discussion and examples that follow, Borland's C compiler and Borland's Turbo Assembler (TASM) are used.

You must know what memory model is, or will be, used for your program's C modules. Once you know the model, you can consult your compiler's documentation to determine the segment names the compiler uses for that memory model. The segment names for Borland C's small and large memory models were given in Table 20.6-2. The name of the code segment is _TEXT. The name of the segment for initialized data is _DATA, and the name of the segment for uninitialized data is _BSS. Your assembly language modules must use these names.

Not only must you use the appropriate segment names, you must also use the specified combine type and classname in your SEGMENT/ENDS directives. If some of the segments are part of the group DGROUP, then the GROUP directive must be used at the beginning of your assembly language modules to assign those segments to DGROUP. An ASSUME directive is required at the beginning of your code segment. This directive associates the appropriate segment or group names with their corresponding segment register.

All external labels in C must start with an underscore character (_). The C compiler automatically prefixes an underscore to all function and variable names in C code. You must prefix each of your public procedure names and public variable names in your assembly language code with an underscore.

C code is case sensitive, so a distinction is made between upper and lower case letters in names. Therefore, procedure names and variable names in your assembly language program that are accessed by C code must exactly match their counterparts in your C code. Normally, TASM is case insensitive. All procedure and variable names in your source code are simply converted by TASM to upper case. To make TASM case sensitive for all symbols, you must include the /ml switch when assembling your program.

Your assembler procedures can read and write variables declared in C modules, and your C code can read and write variables declared in assembly language modules. A variable should be treated as having the same type in both your C and assembly language code. The correspondence between C data types and assembler data types is listed in Table 20.7-1.

Table 20.7-1   Correspondence between Borland C and TASM data types.

C data type	Assembler data type	C data type	Assembler data type
unsigned char	byte	unsigned long	dword
char	byte	long	dword
enum	word	float	dword
unsigned short	word	double	qword
short	word	long double	tbyte
unsigned int	word	near*	word
int	word	far*	dword

20.7.3   Passing Parameters from C to Assembler and Returning Results

EXTERN statements and C function prototypes in the C code define the assembly language procedures to be called as C functions. When a function is invoked in C, the compiler generates an assembly language calling sequence to pass parameters to the function and to save the return address. Borland C passes parameters to a function by pushing the parameters onto the stack in reverse order. C pushes the rightmost parameter in a function's parameter list onto the stack first. The remaining parameters are pushed onto the stack from right to left. Finally, a call instruction is generated that pushes the return address onto the stack.

The assembly language procedure that is called accesses parameters from the stack using based addressing relative to BP. This type of memory access was described in Section 8.5.5. The called procedure can return a result, just like a C function. Results are returned in registers, rather than on the stack. The register used depends on the data type returned. The correspondences between data types and the registers used to return a value are given in Table 20.7-2.

A parameter pushed onto the stack can be the actual value of a variable or constant or it can be a pointer to a variable. Pointers are particularly appropriate for passing strings or structures to a procedure.

20.7.4   Preserving Registers

When a function is returned from, the C program requires that registers BP, SP, CS, DS, and SS have the same values as when the function was invoked. Furthermore, if register variables are enabled in the C program, SI and DI must also be preserved. SI and DI are

Table 20.7-2   Location of return values expected by Borland C.

Return value data type	Return value location
unsigned char	AX
char	AX
enum	AX
unsigned short	AX
short	AX
unsigned int	AX
int	AX
unsigned long	DX:AX
long	DX:AX
float	8087 top-of-stack (TOS) register (ST(0))
double	8087 top-of-stack (TOS) register (ST(0))
long double	8087 top-of-stack (TOS) register (ST(0))
near*	AX
far*	DX:AX

used by Borland C for register variables. As long as your procedure preserves the values in these registers, Borland C does not care how you modify the contents of other registers.

Registers AX, BX, CX, and DX are considered to be volatile by a C program and do not have to be preserved.

When Borland C calls a function, the CS and DS registers have the values shown in Table 20.7-3. SS points to the stack and ES is undefined. You are free to use ES as you wish. DS points to the data group, which is normally what you want. If you choose to use DS to point to far data, you can load it with the segment address of the far data. However, if your procedure changes DS, it must restore DS before returning.

Table 20.7-3   Register settings when Borland C enters assembly language code.

Model	CS	DS
Tiny	_TEXT	DGROUP
Small	_TEXT	DGROUP
Compact	_TEXT	DGROUP
Medium	filename_TEXT	DGROUP
Large	filename_TEXT	DGROUP

An important difference between an assembly language procedure that is written to be called from assembly language code and one that is to be called from C code is how they should handle any parameters passed on the stack. If a procedure is written to be called from assembly language code, the procedure must remove the parameters from the stack before returning. This is normally accomplished by using a pop-value with the RET instruction.

If a procedure is written to be called from C code, the procedure must leave the parameters on the stack when it returns. The calling sequence generated by the C program is followed by instructions that remove the parameters from the stack. Since the C compiler knows how many words it pushed onto the stack before calling the procedure, it knows how many it should remove from the stack after the procedure is returned from. The compiler usually accomplishes this by adding to the stack pointer a number of bytes equal to twice the number of words it pushed onto the stack.

20.7.5   An Example C and Assembler Program

The C program mmin_out.c in Fig. 20.7-1 performs the same overall task as the program iorel.asm of Fig. 4.4-1. This program inputs a byte from the port SWITCHES, complements the byte, then outputs the complement of the byte to the port LEDS. This process is repeated indefinitely.

```
#define SWITCHES      0x8000
#define LEDS          0x8000

extern  "C" unsigned char inport_b(int portaddr);
extern  "C" unsigned char outport_b(int portaddr, unsigned char pdata);

void    main(void)
{
        unsigned char x;
        while (1) {
                x = inport_b(SWITCHES);
                x = ~x;
                outport_b(LEDS, x);
        }
}
```

Figure 20.7-1   A small model C program that inputs a byte from a port complements the byte and outputs it to another port.

The C program first equates the symbols representing the port names to the port addresses using the preprocessor directive #define.

Two function prototypes declare two functions inport_b and output_b as external. These functions are realized as procedures in a separate assembly language module. The "C" in the extern statement tells the C++ compiler to use C style names for the functions instead of the mangled names that the C++ compiler would generate by default. **Mangled**

function names have letters added to them to identify the number of and type of parameters the function requires. The C++ compiler uses this information for type checking.

In the function main, the automatic variable X is declared as an unsigned char. The unsigned char data type in C is equivalent to an unsigned byte in ASM86. Variable X is used to temporarily store the byte that is input from the port SWITCHES.

The statements in the body of the while (1) loop are repeated indefinitely. The statement

    x = inport_b(SWITCHES);

uses the external function inport_b to read the byte port SWITCHES. The function prototype for inport_b at the beginning of the program indicates that this function requires one parameter, a 16-bit port address. The port's address is passed to the function as a parameter. The byte read is assigned to the variable x.

The byte read from the input port is then complemented by the instruction

    x = ~x;

Finally, function outport_b is used to output x's value to the LEDS port.

    output_b(LEDS,x);

The function prototype for outport_b, at the beginning of the program, indicates that this function requires two parameters, a 16-bit port address and an 8-bit data value.

This program was compiled for the small model. When the program is compiled, the C compiler automatically prefixes underscores to the function names. The code generated by the compiler is shown in Fig. 20.7-2. This listing is obtained by compiling mmin_out.c using the -S switch. Header and trailer portions of the listing file, mmin_out.asm that deal primarily with segment names were deleted for clarity. We will return to this file while discussing the assembly language module.

The two external functions are written as assembly language procedures in the assembly language module port_io (Fig. 20.7-3).

Neither procedure needs to reserve memory for variables, so module port_io does not require a data segment. The stack segment is allocated in the startup code, which is in another module. Startup code is discussed in Section 20.9. Thus, the only segment required in this module is a code segment.

The code segment must have the name _TEXT because that is the name used by the small memory model for its code segment. An assume statement says that the segment address for _TEXT will be in CS when the instructions in this module are executed.

The segment/ends pair for the code segment uses the segment name _TEXT as required. Also, as required, the SEGMENT directive uses the PUBLIC combine type and CODE as the classname. This is the combine type and classname required by the small memory model.

Since the procedures in this module are called from outside of the module, they are declared as PUBLIC. The procedure's names must appear in this module with the underscore prefix.

The procedures use BP as a frame pointer to obtain their parameters. The first action of the _inport_b procedure is to save BP because C requires any function that it invokes to preserve BP.

```
_main  proc   near
       ?debug  C E8010C6D6D696E5F6F75742E6370705D9CD622
    ;
    ;   void   main(void)
    ;
       enter  2,0
@1@1:
    ;
    ;   {
    ;        unsigned char x;
    ;     while (1) {
    ;         x = inport_b(SWITCHES);
    ;
       push   -32768
       call   near ptr _inport_b
       pop    cx
       mov    byte ptr [bp-1],al

    ;
    ;      x = ~x;
    ;
       mov    al,byte ptr [bp-1]
       not    al
       mov    byte ptr [bp-1],al

    ;
    ;       outport_b(LEDS, x);
    ;
       mov    al,byte ptr [bp-1]
       push   ax
       push   -32768
       call   near ptr _outport_b
       add    sp,4
       jmp    short @1@1

    ;
    ;    }
    ;  }
    ;
       leave
       ret
_main  endp
       ?debug  C E9
       ?debug  C FA00000000
_TEXT  ends
```

Figure 20.7-2   Assembly language output produced by compiling the C program of Fig. 20.7-1.

```
_DATA   segment word public 'DATA'
s@      label  byte
_DATA   ends
_TEXT   segment byte public 'CODE'
_TEXT   ends
        extrn   _inport_b:near
        extrn   _outport_b:near
        public  _main
        end
```

Figure 20.7-2   Assembly language output produced by compiling the C program of Fig. 20.7-1. (Continued.)

When the C compiler compiles the statement that invokes the inport_b function it generates a calling sequence for the function (Fig. 20.7-2). The calling sequence pushes the parameter SWITCHES onto the stack and calls the near procedure _inport_b. Following the call, the compiler uses a pop cx instruction to remove the address parameter from the stack.

```
push    -32768              ;address parameter = 8000h
call    near ptr _inport_b  ;call procedure
pop     cx                  ;remove address parameter from stack
```

Procedure _inport_b (Fig. 20.7-3) after saving BP, then moves SP to BP, so that BP can be used as the frame pointer. The parameter must be accessed using based addressing relative to BP. Therefore, the parameter's position on the stack relative to BP must be determined. We know that the calling sequence pushes a word parameter onto the stack followed by the return address. The procedure then pushes BP onto the stack. Therefore, the word parameter's location on the stack relative to BP is BP+4. The procedure moves the parameter to DX using mov dx,[bp+4]. With the port address in DX, the byte is read from the input port.

The byte is now in AL. A C program expects an unsigned char data type to be returned in AX. Therefore, AH was zeroed. With the return value in AX, the procedure pops BP, restoring its original value, and then returns. The procedure does not use a pop-value on its RET instruction to remove the parameter from the stack. The C program removes this parameter from the stack using the pop cx instruction.

The compiler generated calling sequence for the procedure outport_b is:

```
push    ax                   ;push data byte parameter onto stack
push    -32768               ;push port address onto stack
call    near ptr _outport_b  ;call procedure
add     sp,4                 ;remove parameter from stack
```

Procedure _outport_b requires two parameters, a word port address and a byte data value to be written to that port address. Since the data byte is the rightmost parameter in the function's parameter list, it is pushed onto the stack first by the calling sequence. However, since all stack operations on the 80C188EB are word operations, a word is actually pushed onto the stack. The data byte parameter is the low byte of the word.

```
name    port_io
.186


    assume  cs:_TEXT
_TEXT       segment public 'CODE'
public      _inport_b, _outport_b

_inport_b   proc
   push   bp
   mov    bp,sp
   xor    ah,ah
   mov    dx,[bp+4]
   in         al,dx
   pop    bp
   ret
_inport_b   endp


 _outport_b      proc
   push   bp
   mov    bp,sp
   mov    dx,[bp+4]
   mov    ax,[bp+6]
   out    dx,al
   pop    bp
   ret
_outport_b  endp

_TEXT       ends
   end
```

Figure 20.7-3   Functions in assembly language to input a byte from a port and to output a byte to a port.

The word output port address is pushed onto the stack next. As a result of the order in which the parameters are pushed onto the stack, the word port address parameter is at BP+4 and the word that contains the data byte is at BP+6. The procedure uses these addresses to access the parameters.

After outputting the byte to the port, the procedure returns. The procedure _outport_b does not return a value. The calling C program removes the two parameters from the stack using the add sp,4 instruction.

20.7.6   I/O Functions in the C Library

All C compilers provide a library of useful functions that you can use in your programs. ANSI C compatible compilers provide the C standard library. This library is automatically searched at compile time to find any functions whose definitions are missing from the source modules. A copy of the executable code for these functions is automatically included in the compiled code.

The ANSI C library does not define functions for I/O port access. Port I/O functions are architecture specific. These types of low-level architecture specific function are implemented in assembly language as was done in Fig. 20.7-3. Since port I/O is fundamental, C compilers provide the functions in assembly language in their libraries. The functions are provided either as procedures or macros. Function prototypes for the four port I/O functions for Borland C, inport(), inportb(), outport(), and outportb(), are listed in Table 20.7-4. The prototypes for these functions are in the header file dos.h, which you should include at the beginning of any C program that uses these functions.

```
#include          <dos.h>
```

Driver functions for most IC I/O peripherals are most efficiently implemented as assembly language procedures.

Table 20.7-4   Borland C I/O port functions.

Function prototype	Purpose of function
int inport(int portid);	Inputs data from a word outport port
unsigned char inportb(int portid);	Inputs a byte from a byte input port
void outport(int portid, int value);	Outputs a word to a word output port
void outputb(int portid, unsigned char value);	Outputs a byte to a byte output port

20.8   Simplified Segment Directives

The **standard segment directives**, used throughout this book and discussed in detail in Section 20.1, allow complete control over segment naming, alignment, combination, and relative placement in memory. TASM and similar DOS assemblers provide an additional set of directives that can be used alternatively. These **simplified segment directives** are easier to write, but do not provide the full control over segment definition provided by the standard segment directives.

The advantage of using the simplified segment directives is that they take care of the segment naming and memory model details required for mixed assembly and high-level language programs.

For most assembly language modules that are to be linked with C, the simplified segment directives .186, .MODEL, .DATA, .DATA?, and .CODE are sufficient to define the program's segments. The program in Fig. 20.8-1 uses simplified segment directives and is equivalent to the program in Fig. 20.7-3.

```
.MODEL          small, c
.186


                public  inport_b, outport_b

.CODE
inport_b                proc
                push    bp
                mov     bp,sp
                xor     ah,ah
                mov     dx,[bp+4]
                in      al,dx
                pop     bp
                ret
inport_b                endp

outport_b               proc
                push    bp
                mov     bp,sp
                mov     dx,[bp+4]
                mov     ax,[bp+6]
                out     dx,al
                pop     bp
                ret
outport_b               endp

                end
```

Figure 20.8-1   Program from Fig. 20.7-3 rewritten using simplified segment directives.

The .MODEL directive specifies the memory model for the simplified segment directives. This determines exactly what segments the simplified directives create and how these segments are grouped. The .MODEL directive insures that the assembler's segment names correspond to those used by the C compiler. .MODEL also insures that labels established by PROC directives default to the type, NEAR or FAR, appropriate for the model. .MODEL also performs the group definition for DGROUP as defined for the particular memory model.

In Fig. 20.8-1, the directive .MODEL small, C tells the assembler to use the names defined for the small memory model for segments defined by the simplified segment directives. Furthermore, the C language specification in the .MODEL directive causes the assembler to automatically prefix all public and external symbol names with an underscore. Therefore, the procedure names that actually appear in the source code don't have underscore prefixes.

The .186 directive instructs the assembler to accept instructions from the 80186 instruction set.

The beginning of the code segment is indicated by the .CODE directive. No assume directive is required. No end segment directive is used with the simplified directives.

20.9   Startup Code

Every C program contains a function named main(). This function is considered to be the first function executed in the program. Whether a C program is run on a PC or an embedded system, the code in main() is not actually the first code executed. Code in the **startup module** is executed first. The startup module then calls main(). When main() is exited, execution returns to the startup code. In a system with an operating system, the startup code then returns execution to the operating system. In effect, the **startup code** takes the system from the bootstrap instruction to the first instruction in main().

The startup module is normally written in the assembly language of the target microprocessor. The purpose of the startup module is to handle microprocessor and system specific tasks required before main() can be executed. Placing all the microprocessor and architecture specific startup tasks in a single module makes C more portable. The compiler manufacturer can provide different startup modules for different operating systems. For systems without an operating system, you can write your own startup module in assembly language.

C compilers supply specific startup modules for each of the different system configurations the compiler supports. For Borland C, the startup code module for DOS is named co.asm and is in the compiler's library subdirectory. When compiling and executing C programs in DOS environments, the existence of the startup code is not readily apparent. For example, with Borland C you can compile a multi-module program containing two C modules and two assembly language modules with the command:

```
bcc mod1.c mod2.c mod3.asm mod4.asm
```

The C compiler compiles mod1.c, which contains the function main(). The C compiler then compiles mod2.c. The C compiler then invokes the assembler and assembles mod3.asm and mod4.asm. Next, the C compiler automatically invokes the linker. The linker automatically links the startup code and these four modules to create the module mod1.exe.

If you want to compile or assemble modules separately using a makefile, then your makefile has to explicitly include the startup module in its list of object modules to link together. Because the startup code defines the order and alignment of segments, it must be first in the list of object files linked.

Compiler supplied startup code is usually not appropriate for systems that do not execute under an operating system. For such systems you must either:

1. Write your own startup module.
2. Use a startup module supplied with a locator designed for embedded system code.

The complexity of a startup module varies depending on the complexity of the hardware on which it is executed and the C program. Some of the startup code's tasks for an 80C188EB system are:

1. Provide the bootstrap instruction that jumps to the beginning of the startup code.

2. Program the chip-select unit, specifically the upper and lower chip selects, to allow the system's ROM and RAM to be addressed.

3. Load the segment registers and initialize the stack.

4. Initialize RAM memory locations to zero.

5. If the C or assembly code uses initialized variables, the initial values of the variables must be copied from the code segment (ROM) to the appropriate variable locations in the data segment (RAM).

6. Call the function main().

The startup module contains a separately located segment for power-on reset. This segment contains instructions to configure the UCS (upper chip-select), so that execution can be transferred to the start of the ROM. This segment also contains the bootstrap instruction to transfer execution to the other code segment in the startup module, _TEXT.

In the _TEXT segment, the LCS (lower chip-select) and any other chip-selects required in the CSU are programmed. After this, all of the memory in the system is accessible. The segment registers are then loaded and the stack is initialized.

All RAM locations are initialized to zero. If any initialized variables are used in any of the C or assembly modules, their initial values must be stored in ROM. These initial values cannot be stored in the actual RAM locations corresponding to the variables because these locations have random values after power-on. The initial values of the variables must be copied from ROM to RAM.

The loading of interrupt vectors and the programming of other peripherals can either be done in the startup module or in main(). If these tasks are done in main(), they can be done by C functions or assembly languages procedures. If all peripherals that cause interrupts and all interrupt vectors are handled in the startup module, then interrupts can also be globally and locally enabled in the startup module. However, it will probably be desirable to enable and disable interrupts during your program's execution, so procedures will be required for enabling and disabling interrupts. As a result, it is probably better to enable and disable interrupts by invoking these procedures from main() or other C functions.

With these preliminary tasks completed, execution is transferred to main(). Calling main() from the startup code is an example of calling a C function from assembler. A simple startup module is given in Fig. 20.9-1.

Paradigm supplies a startup module for use with its LOCATE locator for the 80C188EB. This startup code uses a macro to allow you to configure it for your specific system hardware. There are also provisions that allow you to extend the startup code without modifying any of the Paradigm supplied code.

20.10   Summary

Large programs are constructed as multi-module programs. The modularity provided by using multiple modules simplifies the software development process. Multi-module programs can consist of a mix of both assembly language and high-level language modules.

Each module is separately written, assembled or compiled, and tested. The object code files from the separate assemblies and compilations are linked together to form the complete program.

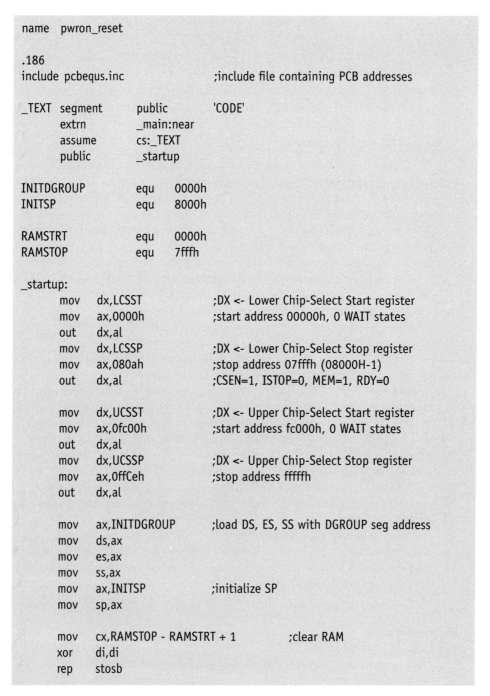

```
name    pwron_reset

.186
include pcbequs.inc                      ;include file containing PCB addresses

_TEXT   segment         public          'CODE'
        extrn           _main:near
        assume          cs:_TEXT
        public          _startup

INITDGROUP              equ     0000h
INITSP                  equ     8000h

RAMSTRT                 equ     0000h
RAMSTOP                 equ     7fffh

_startup:
        mov     dx,LCSST                ;DX <- Lower Chip-Select Start register
        mov     ax,0000h                ;start address 00000h, 0 WAIT states
        out     dx,al
        mov     dx,LCSSP                ;DX <- Lower Chip-Select Stop register
        mov     ax,080ah                ;stop address 07fffh (08000H-1)
        out     dx,al                   ;CSEN=1, ISTOP=0, MEM=1, RDY=0

        mov     dx,UCSST                ;DX <- Upper Chip-Select Start register
        mov     ax,0fc00h               ;start address fc000h, 0 WAIT states
        out     dx,al
        mov     dx,UCSSP                ;DX <- Upper Chip-Select Stop register
        mov     ax,0ffCeh               ;stop address fffffh
        out     dx,al

        mov     ax,INITDGROUP           ;load DS, ES, SS with DGROUP seg address
        mov     ds,ax
        mov     es,ax
        mov     ss,ax
        mov     ax,INITSP               ;initialize SP
        mov     sp,ax

        mov     cx,RAMSTOP - RAMSTRT + 1          ;clear RAM
        xor     di,di
        rep     stosb
```

Figure 20.9-1   Simple startup module for a C program.

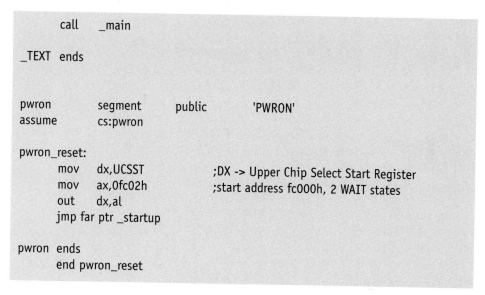

```
        call     _main

_TEXT  ends


pwron          segment       public         'PWRON'
assume         cs:pwron

pwron_reset:
        mov      dx,UCSST              ;DX -> Upper Chip Select Start Register
        mov      ax,0fc02h             ;start address fc000h, 2 WAIT states
        out      dx,al
        jmp far ptr _startup

pwron  ends
        end pwron_reset
```

Figure 20.9-1   Simple startup module for a C program. (Continued.)

A MAKE utility and a makefile are used to automate the building of a complete program. Once the makefile is created, management of the reassembly and recompilation of source modules that have been modified is handled automatically.

C is the high-level language most often used in mixed language embedded systems programs. For large programs, the main part of the program, the function main(), that controls the program's overall execution flow is written in C. main() calls functions that exist in other modules. Some of these functions are written in C and others are written, as procedures, in assembly language. Those functions that are most appropriate for implementation in assembly language are those that must deal with hardware at a detailed level. Assembly language is also used for functions that must be highly optimized for speed.

Assembly language procedures that are invoked as functions by C code must comply with the C compiler's conventions for functions. These conventions deal with matters such as segment names, underscore prefixes for procedure and variable names, parameter passing conventions, preservation of registers, and returning results. When these conventions are adhered to, it is easy to call assembly language procedures from C code.

Use of simplified segment directives, simplifies assembly language code that is interfaced to C code. These simplified segment directives handle segment naming conventions based on the memory model specified.

Every C program has at least one assembly language module, the startup module. This is the assembly language code that handles all the initializations required before main() can be called. When writing and executing programs on a system with an operating system, the linker automatically links in a prewritten startup module when your program is linked. For an embedded system without an operating system, you must write your own startup code or modify a prewritten startup module provided with linkers that can link object modules to create ROMable code.

APPENDIX A: ASCII CODES

Seven-bit ASCII code, with the high-order eighth bit (parity bit) always reset.

GRAPHIC OR CONTROL	ASCII (HEXADECIMAL)	GRAPHIC OR CONTROL	ASCII (HEXADECIMAL)	GRAPHIC OR CONTROL	ASCII (HEXADECIMAL)
NUL	00	+	2B	V	56
SOH	01	,	2C	W	57
STX	02	–	2D	X	58
ETX	03	.	2E	Y	59
EOT	04	/	2F	Z	5A
ENQ	05	0	30	[	5B
ACK	06	1	31	\	5C
BEL	07	2	32	]	5D
BS	08	3	33	∧(↑)	5E
HT	09	4	34	–(←)	5F
LF	0A	5	35	.	60
VT	0B	6	36	a	61
FF	0C	7	37	b	62
CR	0D	8	38	c	63
SO	0E	9	39	d	64
SI	0F	:	3A	e	65
DLE	10	;	3B	f	66
DC1 (X-ON)	11	<	3C	g	67
DC2	12	=	3D	h	68
DC3 (X-OFF)	13	>	3E	i	69
DC4	14	?	3F	j	6A
NAK	15	@	40	k	6B
SYN	16	A	41	l	6C
ETB	17	B	42	m	6D
CAN	18	C	43	n	6E
EM	19	D	44	o	6F
SUB	1A	E	45	p	70
ESC	1B	F	46	q	71
FS	1C	G	47	r	72
GS	1D	H	48	s	73
RS	1E	I	49	t	74
US	1F	J	4A	u	75
SP	20	K	4B	v	76
!	21	L	4C	w	77
"	22	M	4D	x	78
#	23	N	4E	y	79
$	24	O	4F	z	7A
%	25	P	50	{	7B
&	26	Q	51			7C
'	27	R	52	}(ALT MODE)	7D
(	28	S	53	~	7E
)	29	T	54	DEL (RUB OUT)	7F
*	2A	U	55		

APPENDIX B:
SOME USEFUL URLS

General

EE Times embedded systems special interest group includes list of links to embedded systems resources on the Internet.
http://techweb.cmp.com:80/eet/embedded/embedded.html

Embedded Systems Programming magazine and other information resources
http://www.embedded.com

List of Electronic Manufacturers with web pages on the internet.
http://www.webscope.com:80/elx

Integrated Circuit Manufacturers

Analog Devices
http://www.analog.com

Apex Microtechnology
http://www.teamapex.com

Dallas Semiconductor Corp
http://www.dalsemi.com

Hewlett - Packard
http://www.hp.com

Hitachi
http://www.hitachi.com

Integrated Device Technology, Inc.
http://www.idt.com

Intel Corporation
http://www.intel.com

Maxim Integrated Products
http://mxim.com

National Semiconductor Corporation
http://www.national.com

Texas Instruments
http://www.ti.com

USAR Systems
http://www.usar.com

Software and Software Debuggers

Borland International Inc.
http://www.borland.com

Concurrent Sciences, Inc.
http://www.debugger.com

Paradigm Systems
http://www.devtools.com

Systems & Software Inc.
http://www.beacontools.com

Hardware

Diamond Systems Corporation
http://www.diamondsys.com

Micro/sys
http://www.embeddedsys.com

R.L.C. Enterprises Inc.
http://www.rlc.com

Hardware Debuggers

Applied Microsystems Corporation
http://www.amc.com

Grammar Engine Inc.
http://www.gei.com

Device Programmers

Data I/O
http://www.data-io.com

APPENDIX C: INSTRUCTION
SET DESCRIPTIONS

intel®

This appendix provides reference information for the 80C186 Modular Core family instruction set. Tables C-1 through C-3 define the variables used in Table C-4, which lists the instructions with their descriptions and operations.

Table C-1. Instruction Format Variables

Variable	Description
dest	A register or memory location that may contain data operated on by the instruction, and which receives (is replaced by) the result of the operation.
src	A register, memory location or immediate value that is used in the operation, but is not altered by the instruction
target	A label to which control is to be transferred directly, or a register or memory location whose content is the address of the location to which control is to be transferred indirectly.
disp8	A label to which control is to be conditionally transferred; must lie within −128 to +127 bytes of the first byte of the next instruction.
accum	Register AX for word transfers, AL for bytes.
port	An I/O port number; specified as an immediate value of 0–255, or register DX (which contains port number in range 0–64K).
src-string	Name of a string in memory that is addressed by register SI; used only to identify string as byte or word and specify segment override, if any. This string is used in the operation, but is not altered.
dest-string	Name of string in memory that is addressed by register DI; used only to identify string as byte or word. This string receives (is replaced by) the result of the operation.
count	Specifies number of bits to shift or rotate; written as immediate value 1 or register CL (which contains the count in the range 0–255).
interrupt-type	Immediate value of 0–255 identifying interrupt pointer number.
optional-pop-value	Number of bytes (0–64K, ordinarily an even number) to discard from the stack.
external-opcode	Immediate value (0–63) that is encoded in the instruction for use by an external processor.

INSTRUCTION SET DESCRIPTIONS

intel®

Table C-2. Instruction Operands

Operand	Description
reg	An 8- or 16-bit general register.
reg16	An 16-bit general register.
seg-reg	A segment register.
accum	Register AX or AL
immed	A constant in the range 0–FFFFH.
immed8	A constant in the range 0–FFH.
mem	An 8- or 16-bit memory location.
mem16	A 16-bit memory location.
mem32	A 32-bit memory location.
src-table	Name of 256-byte translate table.
src-string	Name of string addressed by register SI.
dest-string	Name of string addressed by register DI.
short-label	A label within the −128 to +127 bytes of the end of the instruction.
near-label	A label in current code segment.
far-label	A label in another code segment.
near-proc	A procedure in current code segment.
far-proc	A procedure in another code segment.
memptr16	A word containing the offset of the location in the current code segment to which control is to be transferred.
memptr32	A doubleword containing the offset and the segment base address of the location in another code segment to which control is to be transferred.
regptr16	A 16-bit general register containing the offset of the location in the current code segment to which control is to be transferred.
repeat	A string instruction repeat prefix.

Table C-3. Flag Bit Functions

Name	Function
AF	Auxiliary Flag: Set on carry from or borrow to the low order four bits of AL; cleared otherwise.
CF	Carry Flag: Set on high-order bit carry or borrow; cleared otherwise.
DF	Direction Flag: Causes string instructions to auto decrement the appropriate index register when set. Clearing DF causes auto increment.
IF	Interrupt-enable Flag: When set, maskable interrupts will cause the CPU to transfer control to an interrupt vector specified location.
OF	Overflow Flag: Set if the signed result cannot be expressed within the number of bits in the destination operand; cleared otherwise.
PF	Parity Flag: Set if low-order 8 bits of result contain an even number of 1 bits; cleared otherwise.
SF	Sign Flag: Set equal to high-order bit of result (0 if positive, 1 if negative).
TF	Single Step Flag: Once set, a single step interrupt occurs after the next instruction executes. TF is cleared by the single step interrupt.
ZF	Zero Flag: Set if result is zero; cleared otherwise.

INSTRUCTION SET DESCRIPTIONS

intel.

Table C-4. Instruction Set

Name	Description	Operation	Flags Affected
AAA	**ASCII Adjust for Addition**: AAA Changes the contents of register AL to a valid unpacked decimal number; the high-order half-byte is zeroed. **Instruction Operands**: none	if ((AL) and 0FH) > 9 or (AF) = 1 then (AL) ← (AL) + 6 (AH) ← (AH) + 1 (AF) ← 1 (CF) ← (AF) (AL) ← (AL) and 0FH	AF ✓ CF ✓ DF − IF − OF ? PF ? SF ? TF − ZF ?
AAD	**ASCII Adjust for Division**: AAD Modifies the numerator in AL before dividing two valid unpacked decimal operands so that the quotient produced by the division will be a valid unpacked decimal number. AH must be zero for the subsequent DIV to produce the correct result. The quotient is returned in AL, and the remainder is returned in AH; both high-order half-bytes are zeroed. **Instruction Operands**: none	(AL) ← (AH) × 0AH + (AL) (AH) ← 0	AF ? CF ? DF − IF − OF ? PF ✓ SF ✓ TF − ZF ✓
AAM	**ASCII Adjust for Multiply**: AAM Corrects the result of a previous multiplication of two valid unpacked decimal operands. A valid 2-digit unpacked decimal number is derived from the content of AH and AL and is returned to AH and AL. The high-order half-bytes of the multiplied operands must have been 0H for AAM to produce a correct result. **Instruction Operands**: none	(AH) ← (AL) / 0AH (AL) ← (AL) % 0AH	AF ? CF ? DF − IF − OF ? PF ✓ SF ✓ TF − ZF ✓

NOTE: The three symbols used in the Flags Affected column are defined as follows:
      − the contents of the flag remain unchanged after the instruction is executed
      ? the contents of the flag is undefined after the instruction is executed
      ✓the flag is updated after the instruction is executed

INSTRUCTION SET DESCRIPTIONS

Table C-4. Instruction Set (Continued)

Name	Description	Operation	Flags Affected
AAS	**ASCII Adjust for Subtraction**: AAS Corrects the result of a previous subtraction of two valid unpacked decimal operands (the destination operand must have been specified as register AL). Changes the content of AL to a valid unpacked decimal number; the high-order half-byte is zeroed. **Instruction Operands**: none	if ((AL) and 0FH) > 9 or (AF) = 1 then (AL) ← (AL) − 6 (AH) ← (AH) − 1 (AF) ← 1 (CF) ← (AF) (AL) ← (AL) and 0FH	AF ✓ CF ✓ DF − IF − OF ? PF ? SF ? TF − ZF ?
ADC	**Add with Carry**: ADC *dest, src* Sums the operands, which may be bytes or words, adds one if CF is set and replaces the destination operand with the result. Both operands may be signed or unsigned binary numbers (see AAA and DAA). Since ADC incorporates a carry from a previous operation, it can be used to write routines to add numbers longer than 16 bits. **Instruction Operands**: ADC reg, reg ADC reg, mem ADC mem, reg ADC reg, immed ADC mem, immed ADC accum, immed	if (CF) = 1 then (dest) ← (dest) + (src) + 1 else (dest) ← (dest) + (src)	AF ✓ CF ✓ DF − IF − OF ✓ PF ✓ SF ✓ TF − ZF ✓

NOTE: The three symbols used in the Flags Affected column are defined as follows:
    − the contents of the flag remain unchanged after the instruction is executed
    ? the contents of the flag is undefined after the instruction is executed
    ✓ the flag is updated after the instruction is executed

C-5

INSTRUCTION SET DESCRIPTIONS

intel®

Table C-4. Instruction Set (Continued)

Name	Description	Operation	Flags Affected

ADD	**Addition:**
	
	ADD *dest*, *src*
	
	Sums two operands, which may be bytes or words, replaces the destination operand. Both operands may be signed or unsigned binary numbers (see AAA and DAA).
	
	Instruction Operands:
	
	ADD reg, reg
	ADD reg, mem
	ADD mem, reg
	ADD reg, immed
	ADD mem, immed
	ADD accum, immed
		(dest) ← (dest) + (src)	AF ✓
			CF ✓
			DF –
			IF –
			OF ✓
			PF ✓
			SF ✓
			TF –
			ZF ✓

AND	**And Logical:** AND *dest*, *src* Performs the logical "and" of the two operands (byte or word) and returns the result to the destination operand. A bit in the result is set if both corresponding bits of the original operands are set; otherwise the bit is cleared. **Instruction Operands:** AND reg, reg AND reg, mem AND mem, reg AND reg, immed AND mem, immed AND accum, immed	(dest) ← (dest) and (src) (CF) ← 0 (OF) ← 0	AF ? CF ✓ DF – IF – OF ✓ PF ✓ SF ✓ TF – ZF ✓

NOTE: The three symbols used in the Flags Affected column are defined as follows:
– the contents of the flag remain unchanged after the instruction is executed
? the contents of the flag is undefined after the instruction is executed
✓ the flag is updated after the instruction is executed

Table C-4. Instruction Set (Continued)

Name	Description	Operation	Flags Affected
BOUND	**Detect Value Out of Range**: BOUND *dest*, *src* Provides array bounds checking in hardware. The calculated array index is placed in one of the general purpose registers, and the upper and lower bounds of the array are placed in two consecutive memory locations. The contents of the register are compared with the memory location values, and if the register value is less than the first location or greater than the second memory location, a trap type 5 is generated. **Instruction Operands**: BOUND reg, mem	if ((dest) < (src) or (dest) > ((src) + 2) then (SP) ← (SP) − 2 ((SP) + 1 : (SP)) ← FLAGS (IF) ← 0 (TF) ← 0 (SP) ← (SP) − 2 ((SP) + 1 : (SP)) ← (CS) (CS) ← (1EH) (SP) ← (SP) − 2 ((SP) + 1 : (SP)) ← (IP) (IP) ← (1CH)	AF − CF − DF − IF − OF − PF − SF − TF − ZF −
CALL	**Call Procedure**: CALL *procedure-name* Activates an out-of-line procedure, saving information on the stack to permit a RET (return) instruction in the procedure to transfer control back to the instruction following the CALL. The assembler generates a different type of CALL instruction depending on whether the programmer has defined the procedure name as NEAR or FAR. **Instruction Operands**: CALL near-proc CALL far-proc CALL memptr16 CALL regptr16 CALL memptr32	if Inter-segment then (SP) ← (SP) − 2 ((SP) +1:(SP)) ← (CS) (CS) ← SEG (SP) ← (SP) − 2 ((SP) +1:(SP)) ← (IP) (IP) ← dest	AF − CF − DF − IF − OF − PF − SF − TF − ZF −

NOTE: The three symbols used in the Flags Affected column are defined as follows:
– the contents of the flag remain unchanged after the instruction is executed
? the contents of the flag is undefined after the instruction is executed
✓ the flag is updated after the instruction is executed

INSTRUCTION SET DESCRIPTIONS

intel®

Table C-4. Instruction Set (Continued)

Name	Description	Operation	Flags Affected
CBW	**Convert Byte to Word**: CBW Extends the sign of the byte in register AL throughout register AH. Use to produce a double-length (word) dividend from a byte prior to performing byte division. **Instruction Operands**: none	if $\quad$ (AL) < 80H then $\quad$ (AH) ← 0 else $\quad$ (AH) ← FFH	AF − CF − DF − IF − OF − PF − SF − TF − ZF −
CLC	**Clear Carry flag**: CLC Zeroes the carry flag (CF) and affects no other flags. Useful in conjunction with the rotate through carry left (RCL) and the rotate through carry right (RCR) instructions. **Instruction Operands**: none	(CF) ←0	AF − CF ✓ DF − IF − OF − PF − SF − TF − ZF −
CLD	**Clear Direction flag**: CLD Zeroes the direction flag (DF) causing the string instructions to auto-increment the source index (SI) and/or destination index (DI) registers. **Instruction Operands**: none	(DF) ←0	AF − CF − DF ✓ IF − OF − PF − SF − TF − ZF −

NOTE: The three symbols used in the Flags Affected column are defined as follows:
  − the contents of the flag remain unchanged after the instruction is executed
  ? the contents of the flag is undefined after the instruction is executed
  ✓ the flag is updated after the instruction is executed

Table C-4. Instruction Set (Continued)

Name	Description	Operation	Flags Affected
CLI	**Clear Interrupt-enable Flag**: CLI Zeroes the interrupt-enable flag (IF). When the interrupt-enable flag is cleared, the 8086 and 8088 do not recognize an external interrupt request that appears on the INTR line; in other words maskable interrupts are disabled. A non-maskable interrupt appearing on NMI line, however, is honored, as is a software interrupt. **Instruction Operands**: none	$(IF) \leftarrow 0$	AF − CF − DF − IF ✓ OF − PF − SF − TF − ZF −

CMC	**Complement Carry Flag**:
	
	 CMC
	
	 Toggles complement carry flag (CF) to its opposite state and affects no other flags.
	
	 Instruction Operands:
	
	 none
		if
		   $(CF) = 0$
		 then
		   $(CF) \leftarrow 1$
		 else
		   $(CF) \leftarrow 0$
			AF −
			 CF ✓
			 DF −
			 IF −
			 OF −
			 PF −
			 SF −
			 TF −
			 ZF −

NOTE: The three symbols used in the Flags Affected column are defined as follows:
− the contents of the flag remain unchanged after the instruction is executed
? the contents of the flag is undefined after the instruction is executed
✓ the flag is updated after the instruction is executed

intel.

Table C-4. Instruction Set (Continued)

Name	Description	Operation	Flags Affected

CMP	**Compare**:
	
	CMP *dest, src*
	
	Subtracts the source from the destination, which may be bytes or words, but does not return the result. The operands are unchanged, but the flags are updated and can be tested by a subsequent conditional jump instruction. The comparison reflected in the flags is that of the destination to the source. If a CMP instruction is followed by a JG (jump if greater) instruction, for example, the jump is taken if the destination operand is greater than the source operand.
	
	Instruction Operands:
	
	CMP reg, reg
	CMP reg, mem
	CMP mem, reg
	CMP reg, immed
	CMP mem, immed
	CMP accum, immed
		(dest) − (src)	AF ✓
			CF ✓
			DF −
			IF −
			OF ✓
			PF ✓
			SF ✓
			TF −
			ZF ✓

CMPS	**Compare String**:
	
	CMPS *dest-string, src-string*
	
	Subtracts the destination byte or word from the source byte or word. The destination byte or word is addressed by the destination index (DI) register and the source byte or word is addresses by the source index (SI) register. CMPS updates the flags to reflect the relationship of the destination element to the source element but does not alter either operand and updates SI and DI to point to the next string element.
	
	Instruction Operands:
	
	CMP dest-string, src-string
	CMP (repeat) dest-string, src-string
		(dest-string) − (src-string)
		if
		  (DF) = 0
		then
		  (SI) ← (SI) + DELTA
		  (DI) ← (DI) + DELTA
		else
		  (SI) ← (SI) − DELTA
		  (DI) ← (DI) − DELTA
			AF ✓
			CF ✓
			DF −
			IF −
			OF ✓
			PF ✓
			SF ✓
			TF −
			ZF ✓

NOTE: The three symbols used in the Flags Affected column are defined as follows:
  − the contents of the flag remain unchanged after the instruction is executed
  ? the contents of the flag is undefined after the instruction is executed
  ✓ the flag is updated after the instruction is executed

Table C-4. Instruction Set (Continued)

Name	Description	Operation	Flags Affected
CWD	**Convert Word to Doubleword**: CWD Extends the sign of the word in register AX throughout register DX. Use to produce a double-length (doubleword) dividend from a word prior to performing word division. **Instruction Operands**: none	if (AX) < 8000H then (DX) ← 0 else (DX) ← FFFFH	AF — CF — DF — IF — OF — PF — SF — TF — ZF —
DAA	**Decimal Adjust for Addition**: DAA Corrects the result of previously adding two valid packed decimal operands (the destination operand must have been register AL). Changes the content of AL to a pair of valid packed decimal digits. **Instruction Operands**: none	if ((AL) and 0FH) > 9 or (AF) = 1 then (AL) ← (AL) + 6 (AF) ← 1 if (AL) > 9FH or (CF) = 1 then (AL) ← (AL) + 60H (CF) ← 1	AF ✓ CF ✓ DF — IF — OF ? PF ✓ SF ✓ TF — ZF ✓
DAS	**Decimal Adjust for Subtraction**: DAS Corrects the result of a previous subtraction of two valid packed decimal operands (the destination operand must have been specified as register AL). Changes the content of AL to a pair of valid packed decimal digits. **Instruction Operands**: none	if ((AL) and 0FH) > 9 or (AF) = 1 then (AL) ← (AL) − 6 (AF) ← 1 if (AL) > 9FH or (CF) = 1 then (AL) ← (AL) − 60H (CF) ← 1	AF ✓ CF ✓ DF — IF — OF ? PF ✓ SF ✓ TF — ZF ✓

NOTE: The three symbols used in the Flags Affected column are defined as follows:
— the contents of the flag remain unchanged after the instruction is executed
? the contents of the flag is undefined after the instruction is executed
✓ the flag is updated after the instruction is executed

INSTRUCTION SET DESCRIPTIONS

intel®

Table C-4. Instruction Set (Continued)

Name	Description	Operation	Flags Affected
DEC	**Decrement**: DEC *dest* Subtracts one from the destination operand. The operand may be a byte or a word and is treated as an unsigned binary number (see AAA and DAA). **Instruction Operands:** DEC reg DEC mem	(dest) ← (dest) − 1	AF ✓ CF − DF − IF − OF ✓ PF ✓ SF ✓ TF − ZF ✓

NOTE: The three symbols used in the Flags Affected column are defined as follows:
− the contents of the flag remain unchanged after the instruction is executed
? the contents of the flag is undefined after the instruction is executed
✓ the flag is updated after the instruction is executed

Table C-4. Instruction Set (Continued)

Name	Description	Operation	Flags Affected
DIV	**Divide**: DIV *src* Performs an unsigned division of the accumulator (and its extension) by the source operand. If the source operand is a byte, it is divided into the two-byte dividend assumed to be in registers AL and AH. The byte quotient is returned in AL, and the byte remainder is returned in AH. If the source operand is a word, it is divided into the two-word dividend in registers AX and DX. The word quotient is returned in AX, and the word remainder is returned in DX. If the quotient exceeds the capacity of its destination register (FFH for byte source, FFFFH for word source), as when division by zero is attempted, a type 0 interrupt is generated, and the quotient and remainder are undefined. Nonintegral quotients are truncated to integers. **Instruction Operands**: DIV reg DIV mem	**When Source Operand is a Byte**: (temp) ← (byte-src) if (temp) / (AX) > FFH then (type 0 interrupt is generated) (SP) ← (SP) − 2 ((SP) + 1:(SP)) ← FLAGS (IF) ← 0 (TF) ← 0 (SP) ← (SP) − 2 ((SP) + 1:(SP)) ← (CS) (CS) ← (2) (SP) ← (SP) − 2 ((SP) + 1:(SP)) ← (IP) (IP) ← (0) else (AL) ← (temp) / (AX) (AH) ← (temp) % (AX) **When Source Operand is a Word**: (temp) ← (word-src) if (temp) / (DX:AX) > FFFFH then (type 0 interrupt is generated) (SP) ← (SP) − 2 ((SP) + 1:(SP)) ← FLAGS (IF) ← 0 (TF) ← 0 (SP) ← (SP) − 2 ((SP) + 1:(SP)) ← (CS) (CS) ← (2) (SP) ← (SP) − 2 ((SP) + 1:(SP)) ← (IP) (IP) ← (0) else (AX) ← (temp) / (DX:AX) (DX) ← (temp) % (DX:AX)	AF ? CF ? DF − IF − OF ? PF ? SF ? TF − ZF ?

NOTE: The three symbols used in the Flags Affected column are defined as follows:
− the contents of the flag remain unchanged after the instruction is executed
? the contents of the flag is undefined after the instruction is executed
✓ the flag is updated after the instruction is executed

INSTRUCTION SET DESCRIPTIONS

intel.

Table C-4. Instruction Set (Continued)

Name	Description	Operation	Flags Affected
ENTER	**Procedure Entry**: ENTER *locals, levels* Executes the calling sequence for a high-level language. It saves the current frame pointer in BP, copies the frame pointers from procedures below the current call (to allow access to local variables in these procedures) and allocates space on the stack for the local variables of the current procedure invocation. **Instruction Operands**: ENTER locals, level	(SP) ← (SP) − 2 ((SP) + 1:(SP)) ← (BP) (FP) ← (SP) if level > 0 then repeat (level − 1) times (BP) ← (BP) − 2 (SP) ← (SP) − 2 ((SP) + 1:(SP)) ← (BP) end repeat (SP) ← (SP) − 2 ((SP) + 1:(SP)) ← (FP) end if (BP) ← (FP) (SP) ← (SP) − (locals)	AF − CF − DF − IF − OF − PF − SF − TF − ZF −
ESC	**Escape**: ESC Provides a mechanism by which other processors (coprocessors) may receive their instructions from the 8086 or 8088 instruction stream and make use of the 8086 or 8088 addressing modes. The CPU (8086 or 8088) does a no operation (NOP) for the ESC instruction other than to access a memory operand and place it on the bus. **Instruction Operands**: ESC immed, mem ESC immed, reg	if mod ≠ 11 then data bus ← (EA)	AF − CF − DF − IF − OF − PF − SF − TF − ZF −

NOTE: The three symbols used in the Flags Affected column are defined as follows:
− the contents of the flag remain unchanged after the instruction is executed
? the contents of the flag is undefined after the instruction is executed
√the flag is updated after the instruction is executed

INSTRUCTION SET DESCRIPTIONS

Table C-4. Instruction Set (Continued)

Name	Description	Operation	Flags Affected
HLT	**Halt:** HLT Causes the CPU to enter the halt state. The processor leaves the halt state upon activation of the RESET line, upon receipt of a non-maskable interrupt request on NMI, or upon receipt of a maskable interrupt request on INTR (if interrupts are enabled). **Instruction Operands:** none	None	AF − CF − DF − IF − OF − PF − SF − TF − ZF −

NOTE: The three symbols used in the Flags Affected column are defined as follows:
− the contents of the flag remain unchanged after the instruction is executed
? the contents of the flag is undefined after the instruction is executed
✓ the flag is updated after the instruction is executed

INSTRUCTION SET DESCRIPTIONS

Table C-4. Instruction Set (Continued)

Name	Description	Operation	Flags Affected
IDIV	**Integer Divide:** IDIV *src* Performs a signed division of the accumulator (and its extension) by the source operand. If the source operand is a byte, it is divided into the double-length dividend assumed to be in registers AL and AH; the single-length quotient is returned in AL, and the single-length remainder is returned in AH. For byte integer division, the maximum positive quotient is +127 (7FH) and the minimum negative quotient is −127 (81H). If the source operand is a word, it is divided into the double-length dividend in registers AX and DX; the single-length quotient is returned in AX, and the single-length remainder is returned in DX. For word integer division, the maximum positive quotient is +32,767 (7FFFH) and the minimum negative quotient is −32,767 (8001H). If the quotient is positive and exceeds the maximum, or is negative and is less than the minimum, the quotient and remainder are undefined, and a type 0 interrupt is generated. In particular, this occurs if division by 0 is attempted. Nonintegral quotients are truncated (toward 0) to integers, and the remainder has the same sign as the dividend. **Instruction Operands:** IDIV reg IDIV mem	**When Source Operand is a Byte:** (temp) ← (byte-src) if (temp) / (AX) > 0 and (temp) / (AX) > 7FH or (temp) / (AX) < 0 and (temp) / (AX) < 0 − 7FH − 1 then (type 0 interrupt is generated) (SP) ← (SP) − 2 ((SP) + 1:(SP)) ← FLAGS (IF) ← 0 (TF) ← 0 (SP) ← (SP) − 2 ((SP) + 1:(SP)) ← (CS) (CS) ← (2) (SP) ← (SP) − 2 ((SP) + 1:(SP)) ← (IP) (IP) ← (0) else (AL) ← (temp) / (AX) (AH) ← (temp) % (AX) **When Source Operand is a Word:** (temp) ← (word-src) if (temp) / (DX:AX) > 0 and (temp) / (DX:AX) > 7FFFH or (temp) / (DX:AX) < 0 and (temp) / (DX:AX) < 0 − 7FFFH − 1 then (type 0 interrupt is generated) (SP) ← (SP) − 2 ((SP) + 1:(SP)) ← FLAGS (IF) ← 0 (TF) ← 0 (SP) ← (SP) − 2 ((SP) + 1:(SP)) ← (CS) (CS) ← (2) (SP) ← (SP) − 2 ((SP) + 1:(SP)) ← (IP) (IP) ← (0) else (AX) ← (temp) / (DX:AX) (DX) ← (temp) % (DX:AX)	AF ? CF ? DF − IF − OF ? PF ? SF ? TF − ZF ?

NOTE: The three symbols used in the Flags Affected column are defined as follows:
− the contents of the flag remain unchanged after the instruction is executed
? the contents of the flag is undefined after the instruction is executed
✓ the flag is updated after the instruction is executed

Table C-4. Instruction Set (Continued)

Name	Description	Operation	Flags Affected
IMUL	**Integer Multiply:** IMUL *src* Performs a signed multiplication of the source operand and the accumulator. If the source is a byte, then it is multiplied by register AL, and the double-length result is returned in AH and AL. If the source is a word, then it is multiplied by register AX, and the double-length result is returned in registers DX and AX. If the upper half of the result (AH for byte source, DX for word source) is not the sign extension of the lower half of the result, CF and OF are set; otherwise they are cleared. When CF and OF are set, they indicate that AH or DX contains significant digits of the result. **Instruction Operands:** IMUL reg IMUL mem IMUL immed	**When Source Operand is a Byte:** (AX) ← (byte-src) × (AL) if (AH) = sign-extension of (AL) then (CF) ← 0 else (CF) ← 1 (OF) ← (CF) **When Source Operand is a Word:** (DX:AX) ← (word-src) × (AX) if (DX) = sign-extension of (AX) then (CF) ← 0 else (CF) ← 1 (OF) ← (CF)	AF ? CF ✓ DF – IF – OF ✓ PF ? SF ? TF – ZF ?
IN	**Input Byte or Word:** IN *accum, port* Transfers a byte or a word from an input port to the AL register or the AX register, respectively. The port number may be specified either with an immediate byte constant, allowing access to ports numbered 0 through 255, or with a number previously placed in the DX register, allowing variable access (by changing the value in DX) to ports numbered from 0 through 65,535. **Instruction Operands:** IN AL, immed8 IN AX, DX	**When Source Operand is a Byte:** (AL) ← (port) **When Source Operand is a Word:** (AX) ← (port)	AF – CF – DF – IF – OF – PF – SF – TF – ZF –

NOTE: The three symbols used in the Flags Affected column are defined as follows:
– the contents of the flag remain unchanged after the instruction is executed
? the contents of the flag is undefined after the instruction is executed
✓ the flag is updated after the instruction is executed

intel.

INSTRUCTION SET DESCRIPTIONS

Table C-4. Instruction Set (Continued)

Name	Description	Operation	Flags Affected
INC	**Increment:** INC *dest* Adds one to the destination operand. The operand may be byte or a word and is treated as an unsigned binary number (see AAA and DAA). **Instruction Operands:** INC reg INC mem	(dest) ← (dest) + 1	AF ✓ CF − DF − IF − OF ✓ PF ✓ SF ✓ TF − ZF ✓
INS	**In String:** INS *dest-string, port* Performs block input from an I/O port to memory. The port address is placed in the DX register. The memory address is placed in the DI register. This instruction uses the ES register (which cannot be overridden). After the data transfer takes place, the DI register increments or decrements, depending on the value of the direction flag (DF). The DI register changes by 1 for byte transfers or 2 for word transfers. **Instruction Operands:** INS dest-string, port INS (repeat) dest-string, port	(dest) ← (src)	AF − CF − DF − IF − OF − PF − SF − TF − ZF −

NOTE: The three symbols used in the Flags Affected column are defined as follows:
− the contents of the flag remain unchanged after the instruction is executed
? the contents of the flag is undefined after the instruction is executed
✓ the flag is updated after the instruction is executed

Table C-4. Instruction Set (Continued)

Name	Description	Operation	Flags Affected
INT	**Interrupt**: INT *interrupt-type* Activates the interrupt procedure specified by the interrupt-type operand. Decrements the stack pointer by two, pushes the flags onto the stack, and clears the trap (TF) and interrupt-enable (IF) flags to disable single-step and maskable interrupts. The flags are stored in the format used by the PUSHF instruction. SP is decremented again by two, and the CS register is pushed onto the stack. The address of the interrupt pointer is calculated by multiplying interrupt-type by four; the second word of the interrupt pointer replaces CS. SP again is decremented by two, and IP is pushed onto the stack and is replaced by the first word of the interrupt pointer. If interrupt-type = 3, the assembler generates a short (1 byte) form of the instruction, known as the breakpoint interrupt. **Instruction Operands**: INT immed8	$(SP) \leftarrow (SP) - 2$ $((SP) + 1{:}(SP)) \leftarrow$ FLAGS $(IF) \leftarrow 0$ $(TF) \leftarrow 0$ $(SP) \leftarrow (SP) - 2$ $((SP) + 1{:}(SP)) \leftarrow (CS)$ $(CS) \leftarrow (\text{interrupt-type} \times 4 + 2)$ $(SP) \leftarrow (SP) - 2$ $((SP) + 1{:}(SP)) \leftarrow (IP)$ $(IP) \leftarrow (\text{interrupt-type} \times 4)$	AF – CF – DF – IF ✓ OF – PF – SF – TF ✓ ZF –

NOTE: The three symbols used in the Flags Affected column are defined as follows:
– the contents of the flag remain unchanged after the instruction is executed
? the contents of the flag is undefined after the instruction is executed
✓ the flag is updated after the instruction is executed

INSTRUCTION SET DESCRIPTIONS

Table C-4. Instruction Set (Continued)

Name	Description	Operation	Flags Affected
INTO	**Interrupt on Overflow:** INTO Generates a software interrupt if the overflow flag (OF) is set; otherwise control proceeds to the following instruction without activating an interrupt procedure. INTO addresses the target interrupt procedure (its type is 4) through the interrupt pointer at location 10H; it clears the TF and IF flags and otherwise operates like INT. INTO may be written following an arithmetic or logical operation to activate an interrupt procedure if overflow occurs. **Instruction Operands:** none	if $\quad$(OF) = 1 then $\quad$(SP) ← (SP) − 2 $\quad$((SP) + 1:(SP)) ← FLAGS $\quad$(IF) ← 0 $\quad$(TF) ← 0 $\quad$(SP) ← (SP) − 2 $\quad$((SP) + 1:(SP)) ← (CS) $\quad$(CS) ← (12H) $\quad$(SP) ← (SP) − 2 $\quad$((SP) + 1:(SP)) ← (IP) $\quad$(IP) ← (10H)	AF − CF − DF − IF − OF − PF − SF − TF − ZF −
IRET	**Interrupt Return:** IRET Transfers control back to the point of interruption by popping IP, CS, and the flags from the stack. IRET thus affects all flags by restoring them to previously saved values. IRET is used to exit any interrupt procedure, whether activated by hardware or software. **Instruction Operands:** none	(IP) ← ((SP) + 1:(SP)) (SP) ← (SP) + 2 (CS) ← ((SP) + 1:(SP)) (SP) ← (SP) + 2 FLAGS ← ((SP) + 1:(SP)) (SP) ← (SP) + 2	AF ✓ CF ✓ DF ✓ IF ✓ OF ✓ PF ✓ SF ✓ TF ✓ ZF ✓
JA JNBE	**Jump on Above:** **Jump on Not Below or Equal:** JA *disp8* JNBE *disp8* Transfers control to the target location if the tested condition ((CF=0) or (ZF=0)) is true. **Instruction Operands:** JA short-label JNBE short-label	if $\quad$((CF) = 0) or ((ZF) = 0) then $\quad$(IP) ← (IP) + disp8 (sign-ext to 16 bits)	AF − CF − DF − IF − OF − PF − SF − TF − ZF −

NOTE: The three symbols used in the Flags Affected column are defined as follows:
  − the contents of the flag remain unchanged after the instruction is executed
  ? the contents of the flag is undefined after the instruction is executed
  ✓ the flag is updated after the instruction is executed

Table C-4. Instruction Set (Continued)

Name	Description	Operation	Flags Affected

JAE
JNB
	Jump on Above or Equal:
	Jump on Not Below:
	
	JAE *disp8*
	JNB *disp8*
	
	Transfers control to the target location if the tested condition (CF = 0) is true.
	
	Instruction Operands:
	
	JAE short-label
	JNB short-label
		if
		  (CF) = 0
		then
		  (IP) ← (IP) + disp8 (sign-ext to 16 bits)
			AF –
			CF –
			DF –
			IF –
			OF –
			PF –
			SF –
			TF –
			ZF –

JB
JNAE
	Jump on Below:
	Jump on Not Above or Equal:
	
	JB *disp8*
	JNAE *disp8*
	
	Transfers control to the target location if the tested condition (CF = 1) is true.
	
	Instruction Operands:
	
	JB short-label
	JNAE short-label
		if
		  (CF) = 1
		then
		  (IP) ← (IP) + disp8 (sign-ext to 16 bits)
			AF –
			CF –
			DF –
			IF –
			OF –
			PF –
			SF –
			TF –
			ZF –

JBE
JNA
	Jump on Below or Equal:
	Jump on Not Above:
	
	JBE *disp8*
	JNA *disp8*
	
	Transfers control to the target location if the tested condition ((C =1) or (ZF=1)) is true.
	
	Instruction Operands:
	
	JBE short-label
	JNA short-label
		if
		  ((CF) = 1) or ((ZF) = 1)
		then
		  (IP) ← (IP) + disp8 (sign-ext to 16 bits)
			AF –
			CF –
			DF –
			IF –
			OF –
			PF –
			SF –
			TF –
			ZF –

JC	**Jump on Carry:**
	
	JC *disp8*
	
	Transfers control to the target location if the tested condition (CF=1) is true.
	
	Instruction Operands:
	
	JC short-label
		if
		  (CF) = 1
		then
		  (IP) ← (IP) + disp8 (sign-ext to 16 bits)
			AF –
			CF –
			DF –
			IF –
			OF –
			PF –
			SF –
			TF –
			ZF –

NOTE: The three symbols used in the Flags Affected column are defined as follows:
– the contents of the flag remain unchanged after the instruction is executed
? the contents of the flag is undefined after the instruction is executed
✓the flag is updated after the instruction is executed

INSTRUCTION SET DESCRIPTIONS

intel.

Table C-4. Instruction Set (Continued)

Name	Description	Operation	Flags Affected
JCXZ	**Jump if CX Zero:** JCXZ *disp8* Transfers control to the target location if CX is 0. Useful at the beginning of a loop to bypass the loop if CX has a zero value, i.e., to execute the loop zero times. **Instruction Operands:** JCXZ short-label	if (CX) = 0 then (IP) ← (IP) + disp8 (sign-ext to 16 bits)	AF – CF – DF – IF – OF – PF – SF – TF – ZF –
JE JZ	**Jump on Equal:** **Jump on Zero:** JE *disp8* JZ *disp8* Transfers control to the target location if the condition tested (ZF = 1) is true. **Instruction Operands:** JE short-label JZ short-label	if (ZF) = 1 then (IP) ← (IP) + disp8 (sign-ext to 16 bits)	AF – CF – DF – IF – OF – PF – SF – TF – ZF –
JG JNLE	**Jump on Greater Than:** **Jump on Not Less Than or Equal:** JG *disp8* JNLE *disp8* Transfers control to the target location if the condition tested (SF = OF) and (ZF=0) is true. **Instruction Operands:** JG short-label JNLE short-label	if ((SF) = (OF)) and ((ZF) = 0) then (IP) ← (IP) + disp8 (sign-ext to 16 bits)	AF – CF – DF – IF – OF – PF – SF – TF – ZF –
JGE JNL	**Jump on Greater Than or Equal:** **Jump on Not Less Than:** JGE *disp8* JNL *disp8* Transfers control to the target location if the condition tested (SF=OF) is true. **Instruction Operands:** JGE short-label JNL short-label	if (SF) = (OF) then (IP) ← (IP) + disp8 (sign-ext to 16 bits)	AF – CF – DF – IF – OF – PF – SF – TF – ZF –

NOTE: The three symbols used in the Flags Affected column are defined as follows:
– the contents of the flag remain unchanged after the instruction is executed
? the contents of the flag is undefined after the instruction is executed
✓the flag is updated after the instruction is executed

INSTRUCTION SET DESCRIPTIONS

Table C-4. Instruction Set (Continued)

Name	Description	Operation	Flags Affected
JL JNGE	**Jump on Less Than:** **Jump on Not Greater Than or Equal:** JL *disp8* JNGE *disp8* Transfers control to the target location if the condition tested (SF≠OF) is true. **Instruction Operands:** JL short-label JNGE short-label	if $\quad$ (SF) ≠ (OF) then $\quad$ (IP) ← (IP) + disp8 (sign-ext to 16 bits)	AF – CF – DF – IF – OF – PF – SF – TF – ZF –
JLE JNG	**Jump on Less Than or Equal:** **Jump on Not Greater Than:** JGE *disp8* JNL *disp8* Transfers control to the target location If the condition tested ((SF≠OF) or (ZF=0)) is true. **Instruction Operands:** JGE short-label JNL short-label	if $\quad$ ((SF) ≠ (OF)) or ((ZF) = 1) then $\quad$ (IP) ← (IP) + disp8 (sign-ext to 16 bits)	AF – CF – DF – IF – OF – PF – SF – TF – ZF –
JMP	**Jump Unconditionally:** JMP *target* Transfers control to the target location. **Instruction Operands:** JMP short-label JMP near-label JMP far-label JMP memptr JMP regptr	if $\quad$ Inter-segment then $\quad$ (CS) ← SEG $\quad$ (IP) ← dest	AF – CF – DF – IF – OF – PF – SF – TF – ZF –
JNC	**Jump on Not Carry:** JNC *disp8* Transfers control to the target location if the tested condition (CF=0) is true. **Instruction Operands:** JNC short-label	if $\quad$ (CF) = 0 then $\quad$ (IP) ← (IP) + disp8 (sign-ext to 16 bits)	AF – CF – DF – IF – OF – PF – SF – TF – ZF –

NOTE: The three symbols used in the Flags Affected column are defined as follows:
– the contents of the flag remain unchanged after the instruction is executed
? the contents of the flag is undefined after the instruction is executed
✓ the flag is updated after the instruction is executed

intel®

INSTRUCTION SET DESCRIPTIONS

Table C-4. Instruction Set (Continued)

Name	Description	Operation	Flags Affected
JNE JNZ	**Jump on Not Equal:** **Jump on Not Zero:** JNE *disp8* JNZ *disp8* Transfers control to the target location if the tested condition (ZF = 0) is true. **Instruction Operands:** JNE short-label JNZ short-label	if (ZF) = 0 then (IP) ← (IP) + disp8 (sign-ext to 16 bits)	AF − CF − DF − IF − OF − PF − SF − TF − ZF −
JNO	**Jump on Not Overflow:** JNO *disp8* Transfers control to the target location if the tested condition (OF = 0) is true. **Instruction Operands:** JNO short-label	if (OF) = 0 then (IP) ← (IP) + disp8 (sign-ext to 16 bits)	AF − CF − DF − IF − OF − PF − SF − TF − ZF −
JNS	**Jump on Not Sign:** JNS *disp8* Transfers control to the target location if the tested condition (SF = 0) is true. **Instruction Operands:** JNS short-label	if (SF) = 0 then (IP) ← (IP) + disp8 (sign-ext to 16 bits)	AF − CF − DF − IF − OF − PF − SF − TF − ZF −
JNP JPO	**Jump on Not Parity:** **Jump on Parity Odd:** JNO *disp8* JPO *disp8* Transfers control to the target location if the tested condition (PF=0) is true. **Instruction Operands:** JNO short-label JPO short-label	if (PF) = 0 then (IP) ← (IP) + disp8 (sign-ext to 16 bits)	AF − CF − DF − IF − OF − PF − SF − TF − ZF −

NOTE: The three symbols used in the Flags Affected column are defined as follows:
  − the contents of the flag remain unchanged after the instruction is executed
  ? the contents of the flag is undefined after the instruction is executed
  ✓ the flag is updated after the instruction is executed

Table C-4. Instruction Set (Continued)

Name	Description	Operation	Flags Affected
JO	**Jump on Overflow:** JO *disp8* Transfers control to the target location if the tested condition (OF = 1) is true. **Instruction Operands:** JO short-label	if (OF) = 1 then (IP) ← (IP) + disp8 (sign-ext to 16 bits)	AF – CF – DF – IF – OF – PF – SF – TF – ZF –
JP JPE	**Jump on Parity:** **Jump on Parity Equal:** JP *disp8* JPE *disp8* Transfers control to the target location if the tested condition (PF = 1) is true. **Instruction Format:** JP short-label JPE short-label	if (PF) = 1 then (IP) ← (IP) + disp8 (sign-ext to 16 bits)	AF – CF – DF – IF – OF – PF – SF – TF – ZF –
JS	**Jump on Sign:** JS *disp8* Transfers control to the target location if the tested condition (SF = 1) is true. **Instruction Format:** JS short-label	if (SF) = 1 then (IP) ← (IP) + disp8 (sign-ext to 16 bits)	AF – CF – DF – IF – OF – PF – SF – TF – ZF –
LAHF	**Load Register AH From Flags:** LAHF Copies SF, ZF, AF, PF and CF (the 8080/8085 flags) into bits 7, 6, 4, 2 and 0, respectively, of register AH. The content of bits 5, 3, and 1 are undefined. LAHF is provided primarily for converting 8080/8085 assembly language programs to run on an 8086 or 8088. **Instruction Operands:** none	(AH) ← (SF):(ZF):X:(AF):X:(PF):X:(CF)	AF – CF – DF – IF – OF – PF – SF – TF – ZF –

NOTE: The three symbols used in the Flags Affected column are defined as follows:
– the contents of the flag remain unchanged after the instruction is executed
? the contents of the flag is undefined after the instruction is executed
✓the flag is updated after the instruction is executed

C-25

INSTRUCTION SET DESCRIPTIONS

Table C-4. Instruction Set (Continued)

Name	Description	Operation	Flags Affected

LDS	**Load Pointer Using DS:**
	
	LDS *dest, src*
	
	Transfers a 32-bit pointer variable from the source operand, which must be a memory operand, to the destination operand and register DS. The offset word of the pointer is transferred to the destination operand, which may be any 16-bit general register. The segment word of the pointer is transferred to register DS.
	
	Instruction Operands:
	
	LDS reg16, mem32
		(dest) ← (EA)
		(DS) ← (EA + 2)
			AF −
			CF −
			DF −
			IF −
			OF −
			PF −
			SF −
			TF −
			ZF −

LEA	**Load Effective Address:** LEA *dest, src* Transfers the offset of the source operand (rather than its value) to the destination operand. **Instruction Operands:** LEA reg16, mem16	(dest) ← EA	AF − CF − DF − IF − OF − PF − SF − TF − ZF −
LEAVE	**Leave:** LEAVE Reverses the action of the most recent ENTER instruction. Collapses the last stack frame created. First, LEAVE copies the current BP to the stack pointer releasing the stack space allocated to the current procedure. Second, LEAVE pops the old value of BP from the stack, to return to the calling procedure's stack frame. A return (RET) instruction will remove arguments stacked by the calling procedure for use by the called procedure. **Instruction Operands:** none	(SP) ← (BP) (BP) ← ((SP) + 1:(SP)) (SP) ← (SP) + 2	AF − CF − DF − IF − OF − PF − SF − TF − ZF −

NOTE: The three symbols used in the Flags Affected column are defined as follows:
− the contents of the flag remain unchanged after the instruction is executed
? the contents of the flag is undefined after the instruction is executed
✓ the flag is updated after the instruction is executed

INSTRUCTION SET DESCRIPTIONS

Table C-4. Instruction Set (Continued)

Name	Description	Operation	Flags Affected
LES	**Load Pointer Using ES:** LES *dest, src* Transfers a 32-bit pointer variable from the source operand to the destination operand and register ES. The offset word of the pointer is transferred to the destination operand. The segment word of the pointer is transferred to register ES. **Instruction Operands:** LES reg16, mem32	(dest) ← (EA) (ES) ← (EA + 2)	AF – CF – DF – IF – OF – PF – SF – TF – ZF –
LOCK	**Lock the Bus:** LOCK Causes the 8088 (configured in maximum mode) to assert its bus LOCK signal while the following instruction executes. The instruction most useful in this context is an exchange register with memory. The LOCK prefix may be combined with the segment override and/or REP prefixes. **Instruction Operands:** none	none	AF – CF – DF – IF – OF – PF – SF – TF – ZF –

NOTE: The three symbols used in the Flags Affected column are defined as follows:
– the contents of the flag remain unchanged after the instruction is executed
? the contents of the flag is undefined after the instruction is executed
✓the flag is updated after the instruction is executed

INSTRUCTION SET DESCRIPTIONS

intel.

Table C-4. Instruction Set (Continued)

Name	Description	Operation	Flags Affected
LODS	**Load String (Byte or Word):** LODS *src-string* Transfers the byte or word string element addressed by SI to register AL or AX and updates SI to point to the next element in the string. This instruction is not ordinarily repeated since the accumulator would be overwritten by each repetition, and only the last element would be retained. **Instruction Operands:** LODS src-string LODS (repeat) src-string	**When Source Operand is a Byte:** $(AL) \leftarrow$ (src-string) if $(DF) = 0$ then $(SI) \leftarrow (SI) + $ DELTA else $(SI) \leftarrow (SI) - $ DELTA **When Source Operand is a Word:** $(AX) \leftarrow$ (src-string) if $(DF) = 0$ then $(SI) \leftarrow (SI) + $ DELTA else $(SI) \leftarrow (SI) - $ DELTA	AF − CF − DF − IF − OF − PF − SF − TF − ZF −
LOOP	**Loop:** LOOP *disp8* Decrements CX by 1 and transfers control to the target location if CX is not 0; otherwise the instruction following LOOP is executed. **Instruction Operands:** LOOP short-label	$(CX) \leftarrow (CX) - 1$ if $(CX) \neq 0$ then $(IP) \leftarrow (IP) + $ disp8 (sign-ext to 16 bits)	AF − CF − DF − IF − OF − PF − SF − TF − ZF −
LOOPE LOOPZ	**Loop While Equal:** **Loop While Zero:** LOOPE *disp8* LOOPZ *disp8* Decrements CX by 1 and transfers control is to the target location if CX is not 0 and if ZF is set; otherwise the next sequential instruction is executed. **Instruction Operands:** LOOPE short-label LOOPZ short-label	$(CX) \leftarrow (CX) - 1$ if $(ZF) = 1$ and $(CX) \neq 0$ then $(IP) \leftarrow (IP) + $ disp8 (sign-ext to 16 bits)	AF − CF − DF − IF − OF − PF − SF − TF − ZF −

NOTE: The three symbols used in the Flags Affected column are defined as follows:
  − the contents of the flag remain unchanged after the instruction is executed
  ? the contents of the flag is undefined after the instruction is executed
  ✓ the flag is updated after the instruction is executed

Table C-4. Instruction Set (Continued)

Name	Description	Operation	Flags Affected
LOOPNE LOOPNZ	**Loop While Not Equal:** **Loop While Not Zero:** LOOPNE *disp8* LOOPNZ *disp8* Decrements CX by 1 and transfers control to the target location if CX is not 0 and if ZF is clear; otherwise the next sequential instruction is executed. **Instruction Operands:** LOOPNE short-label LOOPNZ short-label	$(CX) \leftarrow (CX) - 1$ if $(ZF) = 0$ and $(CX) \neq 0$ then $(IP) \leftarrow (IP) + disp8$ (sign-ext to 16 bits)	AF – CF – DF – IF – OF – PF – SF – TF – ZF –

MOV	**Move (Byte or Word):**
	
	MOV *dest, src*
	
	Transfers a byte or a word from the source operand to the destination operand.
	
	Instruction Operands:
	
	MOV mem, accum
	MOV accum, mem
	MOV reg, reg
	MOV reg, mem
	MOV mem, reg
	MOV reg, immed
	MOV mem, immed
	MOV seg-reg, reg16
	MOV seg-reg, mem16
	MOV reg16, seg-reg
	MOV mem16, seg-reg
		$(dest) \leftarrow (src)$	AF –
			CF –
			DF –
			IF –
			OF –
			PF –
			SF –
			TF –
			ZF –

NOTE: The three symbols used in the Flags Affected column are defined as follows:
– the contents of the flag remain unchanged after the instruction is executed
? the contents of the flag is undefined after the instruction is executed
✓the flag is updated after the instruction is executed

INSTRUCTION SET DESCRIPTIONS

Table C-4. Instruction Set (Continued)

Name	Description	Operation	Flags Affected

MOVS	**Move String:**
	
	MOVS *dest-string, src-string*
	
	Transfers a byte or a word from the source string (addressed by SI) to the destination string (addressed by DI) and updates SI and DI to point to the next string element. When used in conjunction with REP, MOVS performs a memory-to-memory block transfer.
	
	Instruction Operands:
	
	MOVS dest-string, src-string
	MOVS (repeat) dest-string, src-string
		(dest-string) ← (src-string)	AF −
			CF −
			DF −
			IF −
			OF −
			PF −
			SF −
			TF −
			ZF −

MUL	**Multiply:** MUL *src* Performs an unsigned multiplication of the source operand and the accumulator. If the source is a byte, then it is multiplied by register AL, and the double-length result is returned in AH and AL. If the source operand is a word, then it is multiplied by register AX, and the double-length result is returned in registers DX and AX. The operands are treated as unsigned binary numbers (see AAM). If the upper half of the result (AH for byte source, DX for word source) is non-zero, CF and OF are set; otherwise they are cleared. **Instruction Operands:** MUL reg MUL mem	**When Source Operand is a Byte:** $(AX) \leftarrow (AL) \times (src)$ if $\quad (AH) = 0$ then $\quad (CF) \leftarrow 0$ else $\quad (CF) \leftarrow 1$ $\quad (OF) \leftarrow (CF)$ **When Source Operand is a Word:** $(DX{:}AX) \leftarrow (AX) \times (src)$ if $\quad (DX) = 0$ then $\quad (CF) \leftarrow 0$ else $\quad (CF) \leftarrow 1$ $\quad (OF) \leftarrow (CF)$	AF ? CF ✓ DF − IF − OF ✓ PF ? SF ? TF − ZF ?

NOTE: The three symbols used in the Flags Affected column are defined as follows:
  − the contents of the flag remain unchanged after the instruction is executed
  ? the contents of the flag is undefined after the instruction is executed
  ✓the flag is updated after the instruction is executed

Table C-4. Instruction Set (Continued)

Name	Description	Operation	Flags Affected
NEG	**Negate:** NEG *dest* Subtracts the destination operand, which may be a byte or a word, from 0 and returns the result to the destination. This forms the two's complement of the number, effectively reversing the sign of an integer. If the operand is zero, its sign is not changed. Attempting to negate a byte containing −128 or a word containing −32,768 causes no change to the operand and sets OF. **Instruction Operands:** NEG reg NEG mem	**When Source Operand is a Byte:** (dest) ← FFH − (dest) (dest) ← (dest) + 1 (affecting flags) **When Source Operand is a Word:** (dest) ← FFFFH − (dest) (dest) ← (dest) + 1 (affecting flags)	AF ✓ CF ✓ DF − IF − OF ✓ PF ✓ SF ✓ TF − ZF ✓
NOP	**No Operation:** NOP Causes the CPU to do nothing. **Instruction Operands:** none	None	AF − CF − DF − IF − OF − PF − SF − TF − ZF −
NOT	**Logical Not:** NOT *dest* Inverts the bits (forms the one's complement) of the byte or word operand. **Instruction Operands:** NOT reg NOT mem	**When Source Operand is a Byte:** (dest) ← FFH − (dest) **When Source Operand is a Word:** (dest) ← FFFFH − (dest)	AF − CF − DF − IF − OF − PF − SF − TF − ZF −

NOTE: The three symbols used in the Flags Affected column are defined as follows:
− the contents of the flag remain unchanged after the instruction is executed
? the contents of the flag is undefined after the instruction is executed
✓ the flag is updated after the instruction is executed

intel®

INSTRUCTION SET DESCRIPTIONS

Table C-4. Instruction Set (Continued)

Name	Description	Operation	Flags Affected
OR	**Logical OR:** OR *dest,src* Performs the logical "inclusive or" of the two operands (bytes or words) and returns the result to the destination operand. A bit in the result is set if either or both corresponding bits in the original operands are set; otherwise the result bit is cleared. **Instruction Operands:** OR reg, reg OR reg, mem OR mem, reg OR accum, immed OR reg, immed OR mem, immed	(dest) ← (dest) or (src) (CF) ← 0 (OF) ← 0	AF ? CF ✓ DF – IF – OF ✓ PF ✓ SF ✓ TF – ZF ✓
OUT	**Output:** OUT *port, accumulator* Transfers a byte or a word from the AL register or the AX register, respectively, to an output port. The port number may be specified either with an immediate byte constant, allowing access to ports numbered 0 through 255, or with a number previously placed in register DX, allowing variable access (by changing the value in DX) to ports numbered from 0 through 65,535. **Instruction Operands:** OUT immed8, AL OUT DX, AX	(dest) ← (src)	AF – CF – DF – IF – OF – PF – SF – TF – ZF –

NOTE: The three symbols used in the Flags Affected column are defined as follows:
– the contents of the flag remain unchanged after the instruction is executed
? the contents of the flag is undefined after the instruction is executed
✓the flag is updated after the instruction is executed

Table C-4. Instruction Set (Continued)

Name	Description	Operation	Flags Affected
OUTS	**Out String**: OUTS *port, src_string* Performs block output from memory to an I/O port. The port address is placed in the DX register. The memory address is placed in the SI register. This instruction uses the DS segment register, but this may be changed with a segment override instruction. After the data transfer takes place, the pointer register (SI) increments or decrements, depending on the value of the direction flag (DF). The pointer register changes by 1 for byte transfers or 2 for word transfers. **Instruction Operands**: OUTS port, src_string OUTS (repeat) port, src_string	(dst) ← (src)	AF – CF – DF – IF – OF – PF – SF – TF – ZF –
POP	**Pop**: POP *dest* Transfers the word at the current top of stack (pointed to by SP) to the destination operand and then increments SP by two to point to the new top of stack. **Instruction Operands**: POP reg POP seg-reg (CS illegal) POP mem	(dest) ← ((SP) + 1:(SP)) (SP) ← (SP) + 2	AF – CF – DF – IF – OF – PF – SF – TF – ZF –

NOTE: The three symbols used in the Flags Affected column are defined as follows:
– the contents of the flag remain unchanged after the instruction is executed
? the contents of the flag is undefined after the instruction is executed
✓the flag is updated after the instruction is executed

intel.

Table C-4. Instruction Set (Continued)

Name	Description	Operation	Flags Affected
POPA	**Pop All:** POPA Pops all data, pointer, and index registers off of the stack. The SP value popped is discarded. **Instruction Operands:** none	(DI) ← ((SP) + 1:(SP)) (SP) ← (SP) + 2 (SI) ← ((SP) + 1:(SP)) (SP) ← (SP) + 2 (BP) ← ((SP) + 1:(SP)) (SP) ← (SP) + 2 (BX) ← ((SP) + 1:(SP)) (SP) ← (SP) + 2 (DX) ← ((SP) + 1:(SP)) (SP) ← (SP) + 2 (CX) ← ((SP) + 1:(SP)) (SP) ← (SP) + 2 (AX) ← ((SP) + 1:(SP)) (SP) ← (SP) + 2	AF – CF – DF – IF – OF – PF – SF – TF – ZF –
POPF	**Pop Flags:** POPF Transfers specific bits from the word at the current top of stack (pointed to by register SP) into the 8086/8088 flags, replacing whatever values the flags previously contained. SP is then incremented by two to point to the new top of stack. **Instruction Operands:** none	Flags ← ((SP) + 1:(SP)) (SP) ← (SP) + 2	AF ✓ CF ✓ DF ✓ IF ✓ OF ✓ PF ✓ SF ✓ TF ✓ ZF ✓
PUSH	**Push:** PUSH *src* Decrements SP by two and then transfers a word from the source operand to the top of stack now pointed to by SP. **Instruction Operands:** PUSH reg PUSH seg-reg (CS legal) PUSH mem	(SP) ← (SP) – 2 ((SP) + 1:(SP)) ← (src)	AF – CF – DF – IF – OF – PF – SF – TF – ZF –

NOTE: The three symbols used in the Flags Affected column are defined as follows:
– the contents of the flag remain unchanged after the instruction is executed
? the contents of the flag is undefined after the instruction is executed
✓the flag is updated after the instruction is executed

Table C-4. Instruction Set (Continued)

Name	Description	Operation	Flags Affected
PUSHA	**Push All**: PUSHA Pushes all data, pointer, and index registers onto the stack . The order in which the registers are saved is: AX, CX, DX, BX, SP, BP, SI, and DI. The SP value pushed is the SP value before the first register (AX) is pushed. **Instruction Operands**: none	temp ← (SP) (SP) ← (SP) − 2 ((SP) + 1:(SP)) ← (AX) (SP) ← (SP) − 2 ((SP) + 1:(SP)) ← (CX) (SP) ← (SP) − 2 ((SP) + 1:(SP)) ← (DX) (SP) ← (SP) − 2 ((SP) + 1:(SP)) ← (BX) (SP) ← (SP) − 2 ((SP) + 1:(SP)) ← (temp) (SP) ← (SP) − 2 ((SP) + 1:(SP)) ← (BP) (SP) ← (SP) − 2 ((SP) + 1:(SP)) ← (SI) (SP) ← (SP) − 2 ((SP) + 1:(SP)) ← (DI)	AF − CF − DF − IF − OF − PF − SF − TF − ZF −
PUSHF	**Push Flags**: PUSHF Decrements SP by two and then transfers all flags to the word at the top of stack pointed to by SP. **Instruction Operands**: none	(SP) ← (SP) − 2 ((SP) + 1:(SP)) ← Flags	AF − CF − DF − IF − OF − PF − SF − TF − ZF −

NOTE: The three symbols used in the Flags Affected column are defined as follows:
− the contents of the flag remain unchanged after the instruction is executed
? the contents of the flag is undefined after the instruction is executed
✓ the flag is updated after the instruction is executed

INSTRUCTION SET DESCRIPTIONS

Table C-4. Instruction Set (Continued)

Name	Description	Operation	Flags Affected

RCL	**Rotate Through Carry Left:**
	
	RCL *dest, count*
	
	Rotates the bits in the byte or word destination operand to the left by the number of bits specified in the count operand. The carry flag (CF) is treated as "part of" the destination operand; that is, its value is rotated into the low-order bit of the destination, and itself is replaced by the high-order bit of the destination.
	
	Instruction Operands:
	
	RCL reg, n
	RCL mem, n
	RCL reg, CL
	RCL mem, CL
		(temp) ← count
		do while (temp) ≠ 0
		  (tmpcf) ← (CF)
		  (CF) ← high-order bit of (dest)
		  (dest) ← (dest) × 2 + (tmpcf)
		  (temp) ← (temp) − 1
		if
		  count = 1
		then
		  if
		    high-order bit of (dest) ≠ (CF)
		  then
		    (OF) ← 1
		  else
		    (OF) ← 0
		else
		  (OF) undefined
			AF −
			CF ✓
			DF −
			IF −
			OF ✓
			PF −
			SF −
			TF −
			ZF −

RCR	**Rotate Through Carry Right:**
	
	RCR *dest, count*
	
	Operates exactly like RCL except that the bits are rotated right instead of left.
	
	Instruction Operands:
	
	RCR reg, n
	RCR mem, n
	RCR reg, CL
	RCR mem, CL
		(temp) ← count
		do while (temp) ≠ 0
		  (tmpcf) ← (CF)
		  (CF) ← low-order bit of (dest)
		  (dest) ← (dest) / 2
		  high-order bit of (dest) ← (tmpcf)
		  (temp) ← (temp) − 1
		if
		  count = 1
		then
		  if
		    high-order bit of (dest) ≠
		    next-to-high-order bit of (dest)
		  then
		    (OF) ← 1
		  else
		    (OF) ← 0
		else
		  (OF) undefined
			AF −
			CF ✓
			DF −
			IF −
			OF ✓
			PF −
			SF −
			TF −
			ZF −

NOTE: The three symbols used in the Flags Affected column are defined as follows:
− the contents of the flag remain unchanged after the instruction is executed
? the contents of the flag is undefined after the instruction is executed
✓ the flag is updated after the instruction is executed

Table C-4. Instruction Set (Continued)

Name	Description	Operation	Flags Affected
REP REPE REPZ REPNE REPNZ	**Repeat**: **Repeat While Equal**: **Repeat While Zero**: **Repeat While Not Equal**: **Repeat While Not Zero**: Controls subsequent string instruction repetition. The different mnemonics are provided to improve program clarity. REP is used in conjunction with the MOVS (Move String) and STOS (Store String) instructions and is interpreted as "repeat while not end-of-string" (CX not 0). REPE and REPZ operate identically and are physically the same prefix byte as REP. These instructions are used with the CMPS (Compare String) and SCAS (Scan String) instructions and require ZF (posted by these instructions) to be set before initiating the next repetition. REPNE and REPNZ are mnemonics for the same prefix byte. These instructions function the same as REPE and REPZ except that the zero flag must be cleared or the repetition is terminated. ZF does not need to be initialized before executing the repeated string instruction. **Instruction Operands**: none	do while (CX) $\neq$ 0 service pending interrupts (if any) execute primitive string Operation in succeeding byte (CX) $\leftarrow$ (CX) $-$ 1 if primitive operation is CMPB, CMPW, SCAB, or SCAW and (ZF) $\neq$ 0 then exit from while loop	AF $-$ CF $-$ DF $-$ IF $-$ OF $-$ PF $-$ SF $-$ TF $-$ ZF $-$

NOTE: The three symbols used in the Flags Affected column are defined as follows:
      $-$ the contents of the flag remain unchanged after the instruction is executed
      ? the contents of the flag is undefined after the instruction is executed
      ✓the flag is updated after the instruction is executed

INSTRUCTION SET DESCRIPTIONS

intel®

Table C-4. Instruction Set (Continued)

Name	Description	Operation	Flags Affected
RET	**Return**: RET *optional-pop-value* Transfers control from a procedure back to the instruction following the CALL that activated the procedure. The assembler generates an intra-segment RET if the programmer has defined the procedure near, or an intersegment RET if the procedure has been defined as far. RET pops the word at the top of the stack (pointed to by register SP) into the instruction pointer and increments SP by two. If RET is intersegment, the word at the new top of stack is popped into the CS register, and SP is again incremented by two. If an optional pop value has been specified, RET adds that value to SP. **Instruction Operands**: RET immed8	$(IP) \leftarrow ((SP) = 1:(SP))$ $(SP) \leftarrow (SP) + 2$ if inter-segment then $(CS) \leftarrow ((SP) + 1:(SP))$ $(SP) \leftarrow (SP) + 2$ if add immed8 to SP then $(SP) \leftarrow (SP) + $ data	AF − CF − DF − IF − OF − PF − SF − TF − ZF −
ROL	**Rotate Left**: ROL *dest, count* Rotates the destination byte or word left by the number of bits specified in the count operand. **Instruction Operands**: ROL reg, n ROL mem, n ROL reg, CL ROL mem CL	$(temp) \leftarrow count$ do while $(temp) \neq 0$ $(CF) \leftarrow$ high-order bit of (dest) $(dest) \leftarrow (dest) \times 2 + (CF)$ $(temp) \leftarrow (temp) - 1$ if count = 1 then if high-order bit of (dest) $\neq$ (CF) then $(OF) \leftarrow 1$ else $(OF) \leftarrow 0$ else (OF) undefined	AF − CF ✓ DF − IF − OF ✓ PF − SF − TF − ZF −

NOTE: The three symbols used in the Flags Affected column are defined as follows:
− the contents of the flag remain unchanged after the instruction is executed
? the contents of the flag is undefined after the instruction is executed
✓ the flag is updated after the instruction is executed

Table C-4. Instruction Set (Continued)

Name	Description	Operation	Flags Affected
ROR	**Rotate Right**: ROR *dest, count* Operates similar to ROL except that the bits in the destination byte or word are rotated right instead of left. **Instruction Operands**: ROR reg, n ROR mem, n ROR reg, CL ROR mem, CL	(temp) ← count do while (temp) ≠ 0 (CF) ← low-order bit of (dest) (dest) ← (dest) / 2 high-order bit of (dest) ← (CF) (temp) ← (temp) − 1 if count = 1 then if high-order bit of (dest) ≠ next-to-high-order bit of (dest) then (OF) ← 1 else (OF) ← 0 else (OF) undefined	AF − CF ✓ DF − IF − OF ✓ PF − SF − TF − ZF −
SAHF	**Store Register AH Into Flags**: SAHF Transfers bits 7, 6, 4, 2, and 0 from register AH into SF, ZF, AF, PF, and CF, respectively, replacing whatever values these flags previously had. **Instruction Operands**: none	(SF):(ZF):X:(AF):X:(PF):X:(CF) ← (AH)	AF ✓ CF ✓ DF − IF − OF − PF ✓ SF ✓ TF − ZF ✓

NOTE: The three symbols used in the Flags Affected column are defined as follows:
  − the contents of the flag remain unchanged after the instruction is executed
  ? the contents of the flag is undefined after the instruction is executed
  ✓ the flag is updated after the instruction is executed

INSTRUCTION SET DESCRIPTIONS

Table C-4. Instruction Set (Continued)

Name	Description	Operation	Flags Affected

SHL
SAL
	Shift Logical Left:
	Shift Arithmetic Left:
	
	SHL *dest, count*
	SAL *dest, count*
	
	Shifts the destination byte or word left by the number of bits specified in the count operand. Zeros are shifted in on the right. If the sign bit retains its original value, then OF is cleared.
	
	Instruction Operands:
	
	SHL reg, n SAL reg, n
	SHL mem, n SAL mem, n
	SHL reg, CL SAL reg, CL
	SHL mem, CL SAL mem, CL
		(temp) ← count
		do while (temp) ≠ 0
		  (CF) ← high-order bit of (dest)
		  (dest) ← (dest) × 2
		  (temp) ← (temp) − 1
		if
		  count = 1
		then
		  if
		    high-order bit of (dest) ≠ (CE)
		  then
		    (OF) ← 1
		  else
		    (OF) ← 0
		else
		  (OF) undefined
			AF ?
			CF ✓
			DF −
			IF −
			OF ✓
			PF ✓
			SF ✓
			TF −
			ZF ✓

SAR	**Shift Arithmetic Right:**
	
	SAR *dest, count*
	
	Shifts the bits in the destination operand (byte or word) to the right by the number of bits specified in the count operand. Bits equal to the original high-order (sign) bit are shifted in on the left, preserving the sign of the original value. Note that SAR does not produce the same result as the dividend of an "equivalent" IDIV instruction if the destination operand is negative and 1 bits are shifted out. For example, shifting −5 right by one bit yields −3, while integer division −5 by 2 yields −2. The difference in the instructions is that IDIV truncates all numbers toward zero, while SAR truncates positive numbers toward zero and negative numbers toward negative infinity.
	
	Instruction Operands:
	
	SAR reg, n
	SAR mem, n
	SAR reg, CL
	SAR mem, CL
		(temp) ← count
		do while (temp) ≠ 0
		  (CF) ← low-order bit of (dest)
		  (dest) ← (dest) / 2
		  (temp) ← (temp) − 1
		if
		  count = 1
		then
		  if
		    high-order bit of (dest) ≠
		    next-to-high-order bit of (dest)
		  then
		    (OF) ← 1
		  else
		    (OF) ← 0
		else
		  (OF) ← 0
			AF ?
			CF ✓
			DF −
			IF −
			OF ✓
			PF ✓
			SF ✓
			TF −
			ZF ✓

NOTE: The three symbols used in the Flags Affected column are defined as follows:
− the contents of the flag remain unchanged after the instruction is executed
? the contents of the flag is undefined after the instruction is executed
✓ the flag is updated after the instruction is executed

Table C-4. Instruction Set (Continued)

Name	Description	Operation	Flags Affected
SBB	**Subtract With Borrow:** SBB *dest, src* Subtracts the source from the destination, subtracts one if CF is set, and returns the result to the destination operand. Both operands may be bytes or words. Both operands may be signed or unsigned binary numbers (see AAS and DAS) **Instruction Operands:** SBB reg, reg SBB reg, mem SBB mem, reg SBB accum, immed SBB reg, immed SBB mem, immed	if (CF) = 1 then (dest) = (dest) − (src) − 1 else (dest) ← (dest) − (src)	AF ✓ CF ✓ DF − IF − OF ✓ PF ✓ SF ✓ TF − ZF ✓

NOTE: The three symbols used in the Flags Affected column are defined as follows:
− the contents of the flag remain unchanged after the instruction is executed
? the contents of the flag is undefined after the instruction is executed
✓ the flag is updated after the instruction is executed

INSTRUCTION SET DESCRIPTIONS

Table C-4. Instruction Set (Continued)

Name	Description	Operation	Flags Affected
SCAS	**Scan String:** SCAS *dest-string* Subtracts the destination string element (byte or word) addressed by DI from the content of AL (byte string) or AX (word string) and updates the flags, but does not alter the destination string or the accumulator. SCAS also updates DI to point to the next string element and AF, CF, OF, PF, SF and ZF to reflect the relationship of the scan value in AL/AX to the string element. If SCAS is prefixed with REPE or REPZ, the operation is interpreted as "scan while not end-of-string (CX not 0) and string-element = scan-value (ZF = 1)." This form may be used to scan for departure from a given value. If SCAS is prefixed with REPNE or REPNZ, the operation is interpreted as "scan while not end-of-string (CX not 0) and string-element is not equal to scan-value (ZF = 0)." **Instruction Operands:** SCAS dest-string SCAS (repeat) dest-string	**When Source Operand is a Byte:** (AL) − (byte-string) if (DF) = 0 then (DI) ← (DI) + DELTA else (DI) ← (DI) − DELTA **When Source Operand is a Word:** (AX) − (word-string) if (DF) = 0 then (DI) ← (DI) + DELTA else (DI) ← (DI) − DELTA	AF ✓ CF ✓ DF − IF − OF ✓ PF ✓ SF ✓ TF − ZF ✓

NOTE: The three symbols used in the Flags Affected column are defined as follows:
− the contents of the flag remain unchanged after the instruction is executed
? the contents of the flag is undefined after the instruction is executed
✓ the flag is updated after the instruction is executed

INSTRUCTION SET DESCRIPTIONS

Table C-4. Instruction Set (Continued)

Name	Description	Operation	Flags Affected
SHR	**Shift Logical Right**: SHR *dest, src* Shifts the bits in the destination operand (byte or word) to the right by the number of bits specified in the count operand. Zeros are shifted in on the left. If the sign bit retains its original value, then OF is cleared. **Instruction Operands**: SHR reg, n SHR mem, n SHR reg, CL SHR mem, CL	(temp) ← count do while (temp) ≠ 0 (CF) ← low-order bit of (dest) (dest) ← (dest) / 2 (temp) ← (temp) − 1 if count = 1 then if high-order bit of (dest) ≠ next-to-high-order bit of (dest) then (OF) ← 1 else (OF) ← 0 else (OF) undefined	AF ? CF ✓ DF − IF − OF ✓ PF ✓ SF ✓ TF − ZF ✓
STC	**Set Carry Flag**: STC Sets CF to 1. **Instruction Operands**: none	(CF) ← 1	AF − CF ✓ DF − IF − OF − PF − SF − TF − ZF −
STD	**Set Direction Flag**: STD Sets DF to 1 causing the string instructions to auto-decrement the SI and/or DI index registers. **Instruction Operands**: none	(DF) ← 1	AF − CF − DF ✓ IF − OF − PF − SF − TF − ZF −

NOTE: The three symbols used in the Flags Affected column are defined as follows:
− the contents of the flag remain unchanged after the instruction is executed
? the contents of the flag is undefined after the instruction is executed
✓ the flag is updated after the instruction is executed

INSTRUCTION SET DESCRIPTIONS

Table C-4. Instruction Set (Continued)

Name	Description	Operation	Flags Affected
STI	**Set Interrupt-enable Flag:** STI Sets IF to 1, enabling processor recognition of maskable interrupt requests appearing on the INTR line. Note however, that a pending interrupt will not actually be recognized until the instruction following STI has executed. **Instruction Operands:** none	$(IF) \leftarrow 1$	AF – CF – DF – IF OF – PF – SF – TF – ZF –
STOS	**Store (Byte or Word) String:** STOS *dest-string* Transfers a byte or word from register AL or AX to the string element addressed by DI and updates DI to point to the next location in the string. As a repeated operation. **Instruction Operands:** STOS dest-string STOS (repeat) dest-string	**When Source Operand is a Byte:** $(DEST) \leftarrow (AL)$ if $(DF) = 0$ then $(DI) \leftarrow (DI) + DELTA$ else $(DI) \leftarrow (DI) - DELTA$ **When Source Operand is a Word:** $(DEST) \leftarrow (AX)$ if $(DF) = 0$ then $(DI) \leftarrow (DI) + DELTA$ else $(DI) \leftarrow (DI) - DELTA$	AF – CF – DF – IF – OF – PF – SF – TF – ZF –

NOTE: The three symbols used in the Flags Affected column are defined as follows:
– the contents of the flag remain unchanged after the instruction is executed
? the contents of the flag is undefined after the instruction is executed
✓the flag is updated after the instruction is executed

Table C-4. Instruction Set (Continued)

Name	Description	Operation	Flags Affected

SUB	**Subtract**:
	
	SUB *dest, src*
	
	The source operand is subtracted from the destination operand, and the result replaces the destination operand. The operands may be bytes or words. Both operands may be signed or unsigned binary numbers (see AAS and DAS).
	
	Instruction Operands:
	
	SUB reg, reg
	SUB reg, mem
	SUB mem, reg
	SUB accum, immed
	SUB reg, immed
	SUB mem, immed
		(dest) ← (dest) – (src)	AF ✓
			CF ✓
			DF –
			IF –
			OF ✓
			PF ✓
			SF ✓
			TF –
			ZF ✓

TEST	**Test**: TEST dest, src Performs the logical "and" of the two operands (bytes or words), updates the flags, but does not return the result, i.e., neither operand is changed. If a TEST instruction is followed by a JNZ (jump if not zero) instruction, the jump will be taken if there are any corresponding one bits in both operands. **Instruction Operands**: TEST reg, reg TEST reg, mem TEST accum, immed TEST reg, immed TEST mem, immed	(dest) and (src) (CF) ← 0 (OF) ← 0	AF ? CF ✓ DF – IF – OF ✓ PF ✓ SF ✓ TF – ZF ✓

NOTE: The three symbols used in the Flags Affected column are defined as follows:
– the contents of the flag remain unchanged after the instruction is executed
? the contents of the flag is undefined after the instruction is executed
✓ the flag is updated after the instruction is executed

intel®

INSTRUCTION SET DESCRIPTIONS

Table C-4. Instruction Set (Continued)

Name	Description	Operation	Flags Affected
WAIT	**Wait**: WAIT Causes the CPU to enter the wait state while its test line is not active. **Instruction Operands**: none	None	AF − CF − DF − IF − OF − PF − SF − TF − ZF −
XCHG	**Exchange**: XCHG *dest, src* Switches the contents of the source and destination operands (bytes or words). When used in conjunction with the LOCK prefix, XCHG can test and set a semaphore that controls access to a resource shared by multiple processors. **Instruction Operands**: XCHG accum, reg XCHG mem, reg XCHG reg, reg	(temp) ← (dest) (dest) ← (src) (src) ← (temp)	AF − CF − DF − IF − OF − PF − SF − TF − ZF −

NOTE: The three symbols used in the Flags Affected column are defined as follows:
− the contents of the flag remain unchanged after the instruction is executed
? the contents of the flag is undefined after the instruction is executed
✓ the flag is updated after the instruction is executed

Table C-4. Instruction Set (Continued)

Name	Description	Operation	Flags Affected
XLAT	**Translate:** XLAT *translate-table* Replaces a byte in the AL register with a byte from a 256-byte, user-coded translation table. Register BX is assumed to point to the beginning of the table. The byte in AL is used as an index into the table and is replaced by the byte at the offset in the table corresponding to AL's binary value. The first byte in the table has an offset of 0. For example, if AL contains 5H, and the sixth element of the translation table contains 33H, then AL will contain 33H following the instruction. XLAT is useful for translating characters from one code to another, the classic example being ASCII to EBCDIC or the reverse. **Instruction Operands:** XLAT src-table	AL ← ((BX) + (AL))	AF – CF – DF – IF – OF – PF – SF – TF – ZF –
XOR	**Exclusive Or:** XOR *dest, src* Performs the logical "exclusive or" of the two operands and returns the result to the destination operand. A bit in the result is set if the corresponding bits of the original operands contain opposite values (one is set, the other is cleared); otherwise the result bit is cleared. **Instruction Operands:** XOR reg, reg XOR reg, mem XOR mem, reg XOR accum, immed XOR reg, immed XOR mem, immed	(dest) ← (dest) xor (src) (CF) ← 0 (OF) ← 0	AF ? CF ✓ DF – IF – OF ✓ PF ✓ SF ✓ TF – ZF ✓

NOTE: The three symbols used in the Flags Affected column are defined as follows:
– the contents of the flag remain unchanged after the instruction is executed
? the contents of the flag is undefined after the instruction is executed
✓ the flag is updated after the instruction is executed

APPENDIX D: INSTRUCTION SET OPCODES AND CLOCK CYCLES

This appendix provides reference information for the 80C186 Modular Core family instruction set. Table D-1 defines the variables used in Table D-2, which lists the instructions with their formats and execution times. Table D-3, a guide for decoding machine instructions, has been omitted from this appendix and can be found in Intel's 80C186EB/80C188EB Microprocessors User's Manual, from which this information is reprinted. Table D-4 is a guide for encoding instruction mnemonics, and Table D-5 defines Table D-4 abbreviations.

Table D-1. Operand Variables

Variable	Description
mod	*mod* and *r/m* determine the Effective Address (EA).
r/m	*r/m* and *mod* determine the Effective Address (EA).
reg	*reg* represents a register.
MMM	*MMM* and *PPP* are opcodes to the math coprocessor.
PPP	*PPP* and *MMM* are opcodes to the math coprocessor.
TTT	*TTT* defines which shift or rotate instruction is executed.

r/m	EA Calculation
0 0 0	(BX) + (SI) + DISP
0 0 1	(BX) + (DI) + DISP
0 1 0	(BP) + (SI) + DISP
0 1 1	(BP) + (DI) + DISP
1 0 0	(SI) + DISP
1 0 1	(DI) + DISP
1 1 0	(BP) + DISP, if mod ≠ 00 disp-high:disp-low, if mod =00
1 1 1	(BX) + DISP

mod	Effect on EA Calculation
0 0	if r/m ≠ 110, DISP = 0; disp-low and disp-high are absent
0 0	if r/m = 110, EA = disp-high:disp-low
0 1	DISP = disp-low, sign-extended to 16 bits; disp-high is absent
1 0	DISP = disp-high:disp-low
1 1	r/m is treated as a reg field

DISP follows the second byte of the instruction (before any required data).

Physical addresses of operands addressed by the BP register are computed using the SS segment register. Physical addresses of destination operands of string primitives (addressed by the DI register) are computed using the ES segment register, which cannot be overridden.

reg	16-bit (w=1)	8-bit (w=0)
0 0 0	AX	AL
0 0 1	CX	CL
0 1 0	DX	DL
0 1 1	BP	BL
1 0 0	SP	AH
1 0 1	BP	CH
1 1 0	SI	DH
1 1 1	DI	BH

TTT	Instruction
0 0 0	ROL
0 0 1	ROR
0 1 0	RCL
0 1 1	RCR
1 0 0	SHL/SAL
1 0 1	SHR
1 1 0	—
1 1 1	SAR

INSTRUCTION SET OPCODES AND CLOCK CYCLES

Table D-2: INSTRUCTION SET SUMMARY

Function	Format				80C186EB Clock Cycles	80C188EB Clock Cycles	Comments
DATA TRANSFER							
MOV = Move:							
Register to Register/Memory	1 0 0 0 1 0 0 w	mod reg r/m			2/12	2/12 *	
Register/memory to register	1 0 0 0 1 0 1 w	mod reg r/m			2/9	2/9 *	
Immediate to register/memory	1 1 0 0 0 1 1 w	mod 000 r/m	data	data if w= 1	12/13	12/13	8/16-bit
Immediate to register	1 0 1 1 w reg	data	data if w= 1		3/4	3/4	8/16-bit
Memory to accumulator	1 0 1 0 0 0 0 w	addr-low	addr-high		8	8*	
Accumulator to memory	1 0 1 0 0 0 1 w	addr-low	addr-high		9	9*	
Register/memory to segment register	1 0 0 0 1 1 1 0	mod 0 reg r/m			2/9	2/13	
Segment register to register/memory	1 0 0 0 1 1 0 0	mod 0 reg r/m			2/11	2/15	
PUSH = Push:							
Memory	1 1 1 1 1 1 1 1	mod 1 1 0 r/m			16	20	
Register	0 1 0 1 0 reg				10	14	
Segment register	0 0 0 reg 1 1 0				9	13	
Immediate	0 1 1 0 1 0 s 0	data	data if s= 0		10	14	
PUSHA = Push All	0 1 1 0 0 0 0 0				36	68	
POP = Pop:							
Memory	1 0 0 0 1 1 1 1	mod 0 0 0 r/m			20	24	
Register	0 1 0 1 1 reg				10	14	
Segment register	0 0 0 reg 1 1 1	(reg≠ 01)			8	12	
POPA = Pop All	0 1 1 0 0 0 0 1				51	83	
XCHG = Exchange:							
Register/memory with register	1 0 0 0 0 1 1 w	mod reg r/m			4/17	4/17 *	
Register with accumulator	1 0 0 1 0 reg				3	3	
IN = Input from:							
Fixed port	1 1 1 0 0 1 0 w	port			10	10*	
Variable port	1 1 1 0 1 1 0 w				8	8*	
OUT = Output to:							
Fixed port	1 1 1 0 0 1 1 w	port			9	9*	
Variable port	1 1 1 0 1 1 1 w				7	7*	
XLAT = Translate byte to AL	1 1 0 1 0 1 1 1				11	15	
LEA = Load EA to register	1 0 0 0 1 1 0 1	mod reg r/m			6	6	
LDS = Load pointer to DS	1 1 0 0 0 1 0 1	mod reg r/m	(mod≠ 11)		18	26	
LES = Load pointer to ES	1 1 0 0 0 1 0 0	mod reg r/m	(mod≠ 11)		18	26	
LAHF = Load AH with flags	1 0 0 1 1 1 1 1				2	2	
SAHF = Store AH into flags	1 0 0 1 1 1 1 0				3	3	
PUSHF = Push flags	1 0 0 1 1 1 0 0				9	13	
POPF = Pop flags	1 0 0 1 1 1 0 1				8	12	

Shaded areas indicate instructions not available in 8086/8088 microsystems.

NOTE:
*Clock cycles shown for byte transfers. For word operations, add 4 clock cycles for all memory transfers.

INSTRUCTION SET OPCODES AND CLOCK CYCLES

Table D-2: INSTRUCTION SET SUMMARY (Continued)

Function	Format					80C186EB Clock Cycles	80C188EB Clock Cycles	Comments
DATA TRANSFER (Continued)								
SEGMENT = Segment Override:								
CS	00101110					2	2	
SS	00110110					2	2	
DS	00111110					2	2	
ES	00100110					2	2	
ARITHMETIC								
ADD = Add:								
Reg/memory with register to either	000000dw	mod reg r/m				3/10	3/10 *	
Immediate to register/memory	100000sw	mod 000 r/m	data	data if s w= 01		4/16	4/16 *	
Immediate to accumulator	0000010w	data	data if w= 1			3/4	3/4	8/16-bit
ADC = Add with carry:								
Reg/memory with register to either	000100dw	mod reg r/m				3/10	3/10 *	
Immediate to register/memory	100000sw	mod 010 r/m	data	data if s w= 01		4/16	4/16 *	
Immediate to accumulator	0001010w	data	data if w= 1			3/4	3/4	8/16-bit
INC = Increment:								
Register/memory	1111111w	mod 000 r/m				3/15	3/15 *	
Register	01000 reg					3	3	
SUB = Subtract:								
Reg/memory and register to either	001010dw	mod reg r/m				3/10	3/10 *	
Immediate from register/memory	100000sw	mod 101 r/m	data	data if s w= 01		4/16	4/16 *	
Immediate from accumulator	0010110w	data	data if w= 1			3/4	3/4	8/16-bit
SBB = Subtract with borrow:								
Reg/memory and register to either	000110dw	mod reg r/m				3/10	3/10 *	
Immediate from register/memory	100000sw	mod 011 r/m	data	data if s w= 01		4/16	4/16 *	
Immediate from accumulator	0001110w	data	data if w= 1			3/4	3/4 *	8/16-bit
DEC = Decrement								
Register/memory	1111111w	mod 001 r/m				3/15	3/15 *	
Register	01001 reg					3	3	
CMP = Compare:								
Register/memory with register	0011101w	mod reg r/m				3/10	3/10 *	
Register with register/memory	0011100w	mod reg r/m				3/10	3/10 *	
Immediate with register/memory	100000sw	mod 111 r/m	data	data if s w= 01		3/10	3/10 *	
Immediate with accumulator	0011110w	data	data if w= 1			3/4	3/4	8/16-bit
NEG = Change sign register/memory	1111011w	mod 011 r/m				3/10	3/10 *	
AAA = ASCII adjust for add	00110111					8	8	
DAA = Decimal adjust for add	00100111					4	4	
AAS = ASCII adjust for subtract	00111111					7	7	
DAS = Decimal adjust for subtract	00101111					4	4	
MUL = Multiply (unsigned):	1111011w	mod 100 r/m						
Register-Byte						26–28	26–28	
Register-Word						35–37	35–37	
Memory-Byte						32–34	32–34	
Memory-Word						41–43	41–43*	

Shaded areas indicate instructions not available in 8086/8088 microsystems.

NOTE:

*Clock cycles shown for byte transfers. For word operations, add 4 clock cycles for all memory transfers.

intel®

INSTRUCTION SET OPCODES AND CLOCK CYCLES

Table D-2: INSTRUCTION SET SUMMARY (Continued)

Function	Format	80C186EB Clock Cycles	80C188EB Clock Cycles	Comments
ARITHMETIC (Continued)				
IMUL = Integer multiply (signed):	`1 1 1 1 0 1 1 w` `mod 1 0 1 r/m`			
Register-Byte		25–28	25–28	
Register-Word		34–37	34–37	
Memory-Byte		31–34	31–34	
Memory-Word		40–43	40–43*	
IMUL = Integer Immediate multiply (signed)	`0 1 1 0 1 0 s 1` `mod reg r/m` `data` `data if s= 0`	22–25 29–32	22–2 29–32	
DIV = Divide (unsigned):	`1 1 1 1 0 1 1 w` `mod 1 1 0 r/m`			
Register-Byte		29	29	
Register-Word		38	38	
Memory-Byte		35	35	
Memory-Word		44	44*	
IDIV = Integer divide (signed):	`1 1 1 1 0 1 1 w` `mod 1 1 1 r/m`			
Register-Byte		44–52	44–52	
Register-Word		53–61	53–61	
Memory-Byte		50–58	50–58	
Memory-Word		59–67	59–67*	
AAM = ASCII adjust for multiply	`1 1 0 1 0 1 0 0` `0 0 0 0 1 0 1 0`	19	19	
AAD = ASCII adjust for divide	`1 1 0 1 0 1 0 1` `0 0 0 0 1 0 1 0`	15	15	
CBW = Convert byte to word	`1 0 0 1 1 0 0 0`	2	2	
CWD = Convert word to double word	`1 0 0 1 1 0 0 1`	4	4	
LOGIC				
Shift/Rotate Instructions:				
Register/Memory by 1	`1 1 0 1 0 0 0 w` `mod TTT r/m`	2/15	2/15	
Register/Memory by CL	`1 1 0 1 0 0 1 w` `mod TTT r/m`	5+ n/17 + n	5+ n/17 + n	
Register/Memory by Count	`1 1 0 0 0 0 0 w` `mod TTT r/m` `count`	5+ n/17 + n	5+ n/17 + n	

TTT Instruction
```
0 0 0   ROL
0 0 1   ROR
0 1 0   RCL
0 1 1   RCR
1 0 0   SHL/SAL
1 0 1   SHR
1 1 1   SAR
```

Function	Format	80C186EB Clock Cycles	80C188EB Clock Cycles	Comments
AND = **And:**				
Reg/memory and register to either	`0 0 1 0 0 0 d w` `mod reg r/m`	3/10	3/10 *	
Immediate to register/memory	`1 0 0 0 0 0 0 w` `mod 1 0 0 r/m` `data` `data if w= 1`	4/16	4/16 *	
Immediate to accumulator	`0 0 1 0 0 1 0 w` `data` `data if w= 1`	3/4	3/4 *	8/16-bit
TEST= **And function to flags, no result:**				
Register/memory and register	`1 0 0 0 0 1 0 w` `mod reg r/m`	3/10	3/10 *	
Immediate data and register/memory	`1 1 1 1 0 1 1 w` `mod 0 0 0 r/m` `data` `data if w= 1`	4/10	4/10 *	
Immediate data and accumulator	`1 0 1 0 1 0 0 w` `data` `data if w= 1`	3/4	3/4	8/16-bit
OR= **Or:**				
Reg/memory and register to either	`0 0 0 0 1 0 d w` `mod reg r/m`	3/10	3/10 *	
Immediate to register/memory	`1 0 0 0 0 0 0 w` `mod 0 0 1 r/m` `data` `data if w= 1`	4/16	4/16 *	
Immediate to accumulator	`0 0 0 0 1 1 0 w` `data` `data if w= 1`	3/4	3/4 *	8/16-bit

Shaded areas indicate instructions not available in 8086/8088 microsystems.

NOTE:
*Clock cycles shown for byte transfers. For word operations, add 4 clock cycles for all memory transfers.

INSTRUCTION SET OPCODES AND CLOCK CYCLES
Table D-2: INSTRUCTION SET SUMMARY (Continued)

Function	Format						80C186EB Clock Cycles	80C188EB Clock Cycles	Comments
LOGIC (Continued)									
XOR = Exclusive or:									
Reg/memory and register to either	0 0 1 1 0 0 d w	mod reg r/m					3/10	3/10 *	
Immediate to register/memory	1 0 0 0 0 0 0 w	mod 1 1 0 r/m	data	data if w= 1			4/16	4/16 *	
Immediate to accumulator	0 0 1 1 0 1 0 w	data	data if w= 1				3/4	3/4	8/16-bit
NOT = Invert register/memory	1 1 1 1 0 1 1 w	mod 0 1 0 r/m					3/10	3/10 *	
STRING MANIPULATION									
MOVS = Move byte/word	1 0 1 0 0 1 0 w						14	14*	
CMPS = Compare byte/word	1 0 1 0 0 1 1 w						22	22*	
SCAS = Scan byte/word	1 0 1 0 1 1 1 w						15	15*	
LODS = Load byte/wd to AL/AX	1 0 1 0 1 1 0 w						12	12*	
STOS = Store byte/wd from AL/AX	1 0 1 0 1 0 1 w						10	10*	
INS = Input byte/wd from DX port	0 1 1 0 1 1 0 w						14	14	
OUTS = Output byte/wd to DX port	0 1 1 0 1 1 1 w						14	14	
Repeated by count in CX (REP/REPE/REPZ/REPNE/REPNZ)									
MOVS = Move string	1 1 1 1 0 0 1 0	1 0 1 0 0 1 0 w					8+ 8n	8+ 8n*	
CMPS = Compare string	1 1 1 1 0 0 1 z	1 0 1 0 0 1 1 w					5+ 22n	5+ 22n*	
SCAS = Scan string	1 1 1 1 0 0 1 z	1 0 1 0 1 1 1 w					5+ 15n	5+ 15n*	
LODS = Load string	1 1 1 1 0 0 1 0	1 0 1 0 1 1 0 w					6+ 11n	6+ 11n*	
STOS = Store string	1 1 1 1 0 0 1 0	1 0 1 0 1 0 1 w					6+ 9n	6+ 9n*	
INS = Input string	1 1 1 1 0 0 1 0	0 1 1 0 1 1 0 w					8+ 8n	8+ 8n*	
OUTS = Output string	1 1 1 1 0 0 1 0	0 1 1 0 1 1 1 w					8+ 8n	8+ 8n*	
CONTROL TRANSFER									
CALL = Call:									
Direct within segment	1 1 1 0 1 0 0 0	disp-low	disp-high				15	19	
Register/memory indirect within segment	1 1 1 1 1 1 1 1	mod 0 1 0 r/m					13/19	17/27	
Direct intersegment	1 0 0 1 1 0 1 0	segment offset					23	31	
		segment selector							
Indirect intersegment	1 1 1 1 1 1 1 1	mod 0 1 1 r/m	(mod ≠ 11)				38	54	
JMP = Unconditional jump:									
Short/long	1 1 1 0 1 0 1 1	disp-low					14	14	
Direct within segment	1 1 1 0 1 0 0 1	disp-low	disp-high				14	14	
Register/memory indirect within segment	1 1 1 1 1 1 1 1	mod 1 0 0 r/m					11/17	11/21	
Direct intersegment	1 1 1 0 1 0 1 0	segment offset					14	14	
		segment selector							
Indirect intersegment	1 1 1 1 1 1 1 1	mod 1 0 1 r/m	(mod ≠ 11)				26	34	

Shaded areas indicate instructions not available in 8086/8088 microsystems.

NOTE:
*Clock cycles shown for byte transfers. For word operations, add 4 clock cycles for all memory transfers.

intel®

INSTRUCTION SET OPCODES AND CLOCK CYCLES

Table D-2: INSTRUCTION SET SUMMARY (Continued)

Function	Format				80C186EB Clock Cycles	80C188EB Clock Cycles	Comments
CONTROL TRANSFER (Continued)							
RET = Return from CALL:							
Within segment	`1 1 0 0 0 0 1 1`				16	20	
Within seg adding immed to SP	`1 1 0 0 0 0 1 0`	data-low	data-high		18	22	
Intersegment	`1 1 0 0 1 0 1 1`				22	30	
Intersegment adding immediate to SP	`1 1 0 0 1 0 1 0`	data-low	data-high		25	33	
JE/JZ = Jump on equal/zero	`0 1 1 1 0 1 0 0`	disp			4/13	4/13	JMP not taken/JMP taken
JL/JNGE = Jump on less/not greater or equal	`0 1 1 1 1 1 0 0`	disp			4/13	4/13	
JLE/JNG = Jump on less or equal/not greater	`0 1 1 1 1 1 1 0`	disp			4/13	4/13	
JB/JNAE = Jump on below/not above or equal	`0 1 1 1 0 0 1 0`	disp			4/13	4/13	
JBE/JNA = Jump on below or equal/not above	`0 1 1 1 0 1 1 0`	disp			4/13	4/13	
JP/JPE = Jump on parity/parity even	`0 1 1 1 1 0 1 0`	disp			4/13	4/13	
JO = Jump on overflow	`0 1 1 1 0 0 0 0`	disp			4/13	4/13	
JS = Jump on sign	`0 1 1 1 1 0 0 0`	disp			4/13	4/13	
JNE/JNZ = Jump on not equal/not zero	`0 1 1 1 0 1 0 1`	disp			4/13	4/13	
JNL/JGE = Jump on not less/greater or equal	`0 1 1 1 1 1 0 1`	disp			4/13	4/13	
JNLE/JG = Jump on not less or equal/greater	`0 1 1 1 1 1 1 1`	disp			4/13	4/13	
JNB/JAE = Jump on not below/above or equal	`0 1 1 1 0 0 1 1`	disp			4/13	4/13	
JNBE/JA = Jump on not below or equal/above	`0 1 1 1 0 1 1 1`	disp			4/13	4/13	
JNP/JPO = Jump on not par/par odd	`0 1 1 1 1 0 1 1`	disp			4/13	4/13	
JNO = Jump on not overflow	`0 1 1 1 0 0 0 1`	disp			4/13	4/13	
JNS = Jump on not sign	`0 1 1 1 1 0 0 1`	disp			4/13	4/13	
JCXZ = Jump on CX zero	`1 1 1 0 0 0 1 1`	disp			5/15	5/15	
LOOP = Loop CX times	`1 1 1 0 0 0 1 0`	disp			6/16	6/16	LOOP not taken/LOOP taken
LOOPZ/LOOPE = Loop while zero/equal	`1 1 1 0 0 0 0 1`	disp			6/16	6/16	
LOOPNZ/LOOPNE = Loop while not zero/equal	`1 1 1 0 0 0 0 0`	disp			6/16	6/16	
ENTER = Enter Procedure	`1 1 0 0 1 0 0 0`	data-low	data-high	L			
L = 0					15	19	
L = 1					25	29	
L > 1					22+ 16(n− 1)	26+ 20(n− 1)	
LEAVE = Leave Procedure	`1 1 0 0 1 0 0 1`				8	8	
INT = Interrupt:							
Type specified	`1 1 0 0 1 1 0 1`	type			47	47	
Type 3	`1 1 0 0 1 1 0 0`				45	45	if INT. taken/ if INT. not taken
INTO = Interrupt on overflow	`1 1 0 0 1 1 1 0`				48/4	48/4	
IRET = Interrupt return	`1 1 0 0 1 1 1 1`				28	28	
BOUND = Detect value out of range	`0 1 1 0 0 0 1 0`	mod reg r/m			33 − 35	33 − 35	

Shaded areas indicate instructions not available in 8086/8088 microsystems.

NOTE:
*Clock cycles shown for byte transfers. For word operations, add 4 clock cycles for all memory transfers.

INSTRUCTION SET OPCODES AND CLOCK CYCLES
Table D-2: INSTRUCTION SET SUMMARY (Continued)

Function	Format	80C186EB Clock Cycles	80C188EB Clock Cycles	Comments
PROCESSOR CONTROL				
CLC = Clear carry	11111000	2	2	
CMC = Complement carry	11110101	2	2	
STC = Set carry	11111001	2	2	
CLD = Clear direction	11111100	2	2	
STD = Set direction	11111101	2	2	
CLI = Clear interrupt	11111010	2	2	
STI = Set interrupt	11111011	2	2	
HLT = Halt	11110100	2	2	
WAIT = Wait	10011011	6	6	if TEST = 0
LOCK = Bus lock prefix	11110000	2	2	
NOP = No Operation	10010000	3	3	
	(TTT LLL are opcode to processor extension)			

Shaded areas indicate instructions not available in 8086/8088 microsystems.

NOTE:
*Clock cycles shown for byte transfers. For word operations, add 4 clock cycles for all memory transfers.

FOOTNOTES

The Effective Address (EA) of the memory operand is computed according to the mod and r/m fields:

if mod	=	11 then r/m is treated as a REG field
if mod	=	00 then DISP = 0*, disp-low and disp-high are absent
if mod	=	01 then DISP = disp-low sign-extended to 16-bits, disp-high is absent
if mod	=	10 then DISP = disp-high: disp-low
if r/m	=	000 then EA = (BX) + (SI) + DISP
if r/m	=	001 then EA = (BX) + (DI) + DISP
if r/m	=	010 then EA = (BP) + (SI) + DISP
if r/m	=	011 then EA = (BP) + (DI) + DISP
if r/m	=	100 then EA = (SI) + DISP
if r/m	=	101 then EA = (DI) + DISP
if r/m	=	110 then EA = (BP) + DISP*
if r/m	=	111 then EA = (BX) + DISP

DISP follows 2nd byte of instruction (before data if required)

*except if mod = 00 and r/m = 110 then EA = disp-high: disp-low.

EA calculation time is 4 clock cycles for all modes, and is included in the execution times given whenever appropriate.

Segment Override Prefix

0	0	1	reg	1	1	0

reg is assigned according to the following:

reg	Segment Register
00	ES
01	CS
10	SS
11	DS

REG is assigned according to the following table:

16-Bit (w = 1)	8-Bit (w = 0)
000 AX	000 AL
001 CX	001 CL
010 DX	010 DL
011 BX	011 BL
100 SP	100 AH
101 BP	101 CH
110 SI	110 DH
111 DI	111 BH

The physical addresses of all operands addressed by the BP register are computed using the SS segment register. The physical addresses of the destination operands of the string primitive operations (those addressed by the DI register) are computed using the ES segment, which may not be overridden.

Table D-4. Mnemonic Encoding Matrix (Left Half)

	x0	x1	x2	x3	x4	x5	x6	x7
0x	ADD b,f,r/m	ADD w,f,r/m	ADD b,t,r/m	ADD w,t,r/m	ADD b,ia	ADD w,ia	PUSH ES	POP ES
1x	ADC b,f,r/m	ADC w,f,r/m	ADC b,t,r/m	ADC w,t,r/m	ADC b,i	ADC w,i	PUSH SS	POP SS
2x	AND b,f,r/m	AND w,f,r/m	AND b,t,r/m	AND w,t,r/m	AND b,i	AND w,i	SEG =ES	DAA
3x	XOR b,f,r/m	XOR w,f,r/m	XOR b,t,r/m	XOR w,t,r/m	XOR b,i	XOR w,i	SEG =SS	AAA
4x	INC AX	INC CX	INC DX	INC BX	INC SP	INC BP	INC SI	INC DI
5x	PUSH AX	PUSH CX	PUSH DX	PUSH BX	PUSH SP	PUSH BP	PUSH SI	PUSH DI
6x	PUSHA	POPA	BOUND w,f,r/m	▨	▨	▨	▨	▨
7x	JO	JNO	JB/ JNAE/ JC	JNB/ JAE/ JNC	JE/ JZ	JNE/ JNZ	JBE/ JNA	JNBE/ JA
8x	Immed b,r/m	Immed w,r/m	Immed b,r/m	Immed is,r/m	TEST b,r/m	TEST w,r/m	XCHG b,r/m	XCHG w,r/m
9x	NOP (XCHG) AX	XCHG CX	XCHG DX	XCHG BX	XCHG SP	XCHG BP	XCHG SI	XCHG DI
Ax	MOV m→AL	MOV m→AX	MOV AL→m	MOV AX→m	MOVS	MOVS	CMPS	CMPS
Bx	MOV i→AL	MOV i→CL	MOV i→DL	MOV i→BL	MOV i→AH	MOV i→CH	MOV i→DH	MOV i→BH
Cx	Shift b,i	Shift w,i	RET (i+SP)	RET	LES	LDS	MOV b,i,r/m	MOV w,i,r/m
Dx	Shift b	Shift w	Shift b,v	Shift w,v	AAM	AAD	▨	XLAT
Ex	LOOPNZ/ LOOPNE	LOOPZ/ LOOPE	LOOP	JCXZ	IN	IN	OUT	OUT
Fx	LOCK	▨	REP	REP z	HLT	CMC	Grp1 b,r/m	Grp1 w,r/m

NOTE: Table D-5 defines abbreviations used in this matrix. Shading indicates reserved opcodes.

INSTRUCTION SET OPCODES AND CLOCK CYCLES

Table D-4. Mnemonic Encoding Matrix (Right Half)

x8	x9	xA	xB	xC	xD	xE	xF	
OR b,f,r/m	OR w,f,r/m	OR b,t,r/m	OR w,t,r/m	OR b,i	OR w,i	PUSH CS		0x
SBB b,f,r/m	SBB w,f,r/m	SBB b,t,r/m	SBB w,t,r/m	SBB b,i	SBB w,i	PUSH DS	POP DS	1x
SUB b,f,r/m	SUB w,f,r/m	SUB b,t,r/m	SUB w,t,r/m	SUB b,i	SUB w,i	SEG =CS	DAS	2x
CMP b,f,r/m	CMP w,f,r/m	CMP b,t,r/m	CMP w,t,r/m	CMP b,i	CMP w,i	SEG =DS	AAS	3x
DEC AX	DEC CX	DEC DX	DEC BX	DEC SP	DEC BP	DEC SI	DEC DI	4x
POP AX	POP CX	POP DX	POP BX	POP SP	POP BP	POP SI	POP DI	5x
PUSH w,i	IMUL w,i	PUSH b,i	IMUL w,i	INS b	INS w	OUTS b	OUTS w	6x
JS	JNS	JP/ JPE	JNP/ JPO	JL/ JNGE	JNL/ JGE	JLE/ JNG	JNLE/ JG	7x
MOV b,f,r/m	MOV w,f,r/m	MOV b,t,r/m	MOV w,t,r/m	MOV sr,f,r/m	LEA	MOV sr,t,r/m	POP r/m	8x
CBW	CWD	CALL L,D	WAIT	PUSHF	POPF	SAHF	LAHF	9x
TEST b,ia	TEST w,ia	STOS	STOS	LODS	LODS	SCAS	SCAS	Ax
MOV i→AX	MOV i→CX	MOV i→DX	MOV i→BX	MOV i→SP	MOV i→BP	MOV i→SI	MOV i→DI	Bx
ENTER	LEAVE	RET I(i+SP)	RET I	INT type 3	INT (any)	INTO	IRET	Cx
ESC 0	ESC 1	ESC 2	ESC 3	ESC 4	ESC 5	ESC 6	ESC 7	Dx
CALL	JMP	JMP	JMP	IN	IN	OUT	OUT	Ex
CLC	STC	CLI	STI	CLS	STD	Grp2 b,r/m	Grp2 w,r/m	Fx

NOTE: Table D-5 defines abbreviations used in this matrix. Shading indicates reserved opcodes.

INSTRUCTION SET OPCODES AND CLOCK CYCLES

Table D-5. Abbreviations for Mnemonic Encoding Matrix

Abbr	Definition	Abbr	Definition	Abbr	Definition	Abbr	Definition
b	byte operation	ia	immediate to accumulator	m	memory	t	to CPU register
d	direct	id	indirect	r/m	EA is second byte	v	variable
f	from CPU register	is	immediate byte, sign extended	si	short intrasegment	w	word operation
i	immediate	l	long (intersegment)	sr	segment register	z	zero

Byte 2	Immed	Shift	Grp1	Grp2
mod 000 r/m	ADD	ROL	TEST	INC
mod 001 r/m	OR	ROR	—	DEC
mod 010 r/m	ADC	RCL	NOT	CALL id
mod 011 r/m	SBB	RCR	NEG	CALL l, id
mod 100 r/m	AND	SHL/SAL	MUL	JMP id
mod 101 r/m	SUB	SHR	IMUL	JMP i, id
mod 110 r/m	XOR	—	DIV	PUSH
mod 111 r/m	CMP	SAR	IDIV	—

mod and *r/m* determine the Effective Address (EA) calculation. See Table D-1 for definitions.

BIBLIOGRAPHY

Chapter 1

Bar Codes

C. K. Harmon and R. Adams, *Reading Between the Lines: An Introduction to Bar Code Technology*, Peterborough, NH: Helmers Publishing Inc., 1984.

Digital Logic Design

D. L. Dietmeyer, *Logic Design of Digital Systems*, 3rd Ed., Allyn & Bacon, 1988, ISBN 0205112943.

J. P. Hayes, *Introduction to Digital Logic Design*. Reading, MA: Addison-Wesley, 1993.

J. F. Wakerly, *Digital Design Principles and Practices*. Englewood Cliffs, NJ: Prentice Hall, 1990.

Microprocessors and Embedded Systems

R. Cook, "Embedded systems in control," *Byte*, pp. 153–160, June 1991.

P. P. Gelsinger, P. A. Gargini, G. H. Parker, and A. Y. C. Yu, "Microprocessors circa 2000," *IEEE Spectrum*, pp. 43–47, Oct. 1989.

R. H. Katz and J. L. Hennessy, "High performance microprocessor architectures," *International Journal of High Speed Electronics*, vol. 1, no. 1, pp. 1–17, 1990.

M. S. Malone, *The Microprocessor: a Biography*. New York, NY: Springer-Verlag, 1995. ISBN 0-387-94342

G. J. Myers, A. Y. C. Yu, and D. L. House, "Microprocessor technology trends," Proc. of the IEEE, vol. 74, no. 12, pp. 1605–1622, Dec. 1986.

R. N. Noyce and M. E. Hoff, Jr., "A history of microprocessor development at Intel," *IEEE Micro*, pp. 8–21, Feb. 1981.

I. Peterson, *Fatal Defect: Chasing Killer Computer Bugs*. New York, NY: Times Books, 1995. ISBN 0-8129-2023-6

Chapter 3

S. P. Morse, B. W. Ravenel, S. Maxor, and W. B. Pohlman, "Intel Microprocessor 8008 to 8086." IEEE Computer, 1980.

Chapter 4

ASM86 Assembly Language

ASM86 Language Reference Manual. Santa Clara, CA: Intel Corporation, 1983.

ASM86 Assembler

iAPX 86,88 Family Utilities User's Guide. Santa Clara, CA: Intel Corporation, 1985.

TASM Assembler

T. Swan, *Mastering Turbo Assembler,* 2nd ed. Indianapolis IN: Sams Publishing, 1995.

User's Guide Borland Turbo Assembler, Version 4.0. Scott's Valley, CA: Borland International Inc., 1993.

Embedded Assembler Tool Sets

Organon Development Tools, CAD-UL GMBH, Einsteinstrasse 37, D-89077 Ulm, Germany. e-mail sales@cadul.de

Locators for EXE files

CSi Locate. Concurrent Sciences Inc.: Moscow, ID.

Paradigm LOCATE, Version 4.10 Reference Manual. Endwell, NY: Paradigm Systems, 1994.

DOS

T. Dettmann, *DOS Programmer's Reference,* 2nd ed. Carmel, IN: Que Corporation, 1989.

M. Podanoffsky, *Dissecting DOS: A Code-Level Look at the DOS Operating System.* Reading, MA: Addison-Wesley, 1995.

Integrated Circuits

LM34 Precision Fahrenheit Temperature Sensor Data Sheets. National Semiconductor, 1984.

"MAX165/MAX166 CMOS uP compatible 5 µs, 8-bit A/D converters," in *Maxim New Releases Data Book.* Sunnyvale, CA: Maxim Integrated Products, Inc, 1990.

Chapter 5

Debugging

M. Stitt, *Debugging: Creative Techniques and Tools for Software Repair.* New York, NY: Wiley and Sons, Inc, 1992.

T. Swain, *Mastering Turbo Debugger.* Carmel, IN: Hayden Books, 1990.

Chapter 8

D. L. Parnas and P. C. Clements, "On the criteria to be used in decomposing systems into modules," *Communications of the ACM,* pps. 1053–1058, 1972.

B. Witt, F. T. Baker, E. Merritt. *Software Architecture and Design.* New York, NY: Van Nostrand Reinhold, 1994.

Chapter 9

D. E. Knuth, *The Art of Computer Programming, Seminumerical Algorithms*, Vol. 2. Reading, MA: Addison-Wesley, 1981.

J. J. Labrosse, Using scaled arithmetic, *Embedded Systems Programming*. March, 1995.

D. Morgan, *Numerical Methods, Real-Time and Embedded Systems Programming*. San Mateo, CA: M&T Publishing, 1992.

Chapter 10

80C188EB/80C188EB Microprocessor

ApBUILDER: Interactive Application Programming Tool. (This is an interactive application programming tool that will generate the bit patterns and code to program the registers in the PCB.) Santa Clara, CA: Intel Corporation.

80C186EB/80C188EB and 80L186EB and 80L188EB 16-bit High-Integration Embedded Processors Data Sheet. Santa Clara, CA: Intel Corporation.

80C188EB/80C188EB Microprocessor User's Manual. Santa Clara, CA: Intel Corporation, 1994.

Embedded Microprocessors. Santa Clara, CA: Intel Corporation, 1994.

Microprocessor Clocks

T. Williamson, "AP–155 Oscillators for microcontrollers," in Intel Embedded Applications. Santa Clara, CA: Intel Corporation, 1993–1994.

Logic Families

J. F. Wakerly, *Digital Design Principles and Practices*. 2nd Ed. Englewood Cliffs, NJ: Prentice Hall, 1994.

FACT Advanced CMOS Logic Databook, Santa Clara, CA: National Semiconductor Corporation, 1993.

HCMOS Design Considerations, SCLA007, Dallas, TX: Texas Instruments, April 1996.

High-Speed CMOS Logic Data Book, 1988, Dallas, TX: Texas Instruments, 1988.

SN54/74HCT CMOS Logic Family Applications and Restrictions, SCLA011. Dallas, TX: Texas Instruments, May 1996.

Programmable Peripherals

PSD Programmable Peripherals Design and Applications Handbook. Fremont, CA: WaferScale Integration Inc., 1994.

Microprocessor Supervisory Circuits

"A guide for providing reliable microprocessor supervision, application note AN-5," in *Maxim 1992 New Releases Data Book*. Sunnyvale, CA: Maxim Integrated Products, 1992.

L. Shorthill, "Power supply voltage monitors maintain microprocessor data integrity," *PCIM Magazine*, June 1990.

Single Board 80C188EB Microcomputers

R.L.C. Enterprises, Inc. 5425 El Camino Real, Atascadero, CA 93422. Tel. (805) 466-9717.

Micro/sys. 3447 Ocean View Blvd. Glendale, CA 91208. Tel. (818) 244-4600.

Bus Standards

T. Shanley, and D. Anderson. *ISA System Architecture*. Richardson, TX: Mindshare Press, 1993. ISBN 1-881609-05-7.

Chapter 11

Programmable Logic Devices

M. Bolton, *Digital Systems Design with Programmable Logic*. Reading, MA: Addison-Wesley, 1990.

D. Pellerin and M. Holley, *Practical Design Using Programmable Logic*. Englewood Cliffs, NJ: Prentice Hall, 1991.

Programmable Read-only Memory

B. Dipert and M. Levey, *Designing with Flash Memory*. San Diego, CA: Annabooks. ISBN 0-929392-17-5

Flash Memory Products. Sunnyvale, CA: Advanced Micro Devices Inc., 1992–1993.

S. H. Leibson, "Nonvolatile, in-circuit-reprogrammable memories," *EDN*, pp. 89–102, Jan. 3, 1991.

Memory Products. Mt. Prospect, IL: Intel Corporation, 1993.

Semiconductor Memory

B. Prince, *Semiconductor Memory: A Handbook of Design, Manufacture, and Application,* 2nd ed., New York, NY: John Wiley, 1991. (An extensive overview of the design, manufacture, and application of semiconductor memory.) ISBN 0-471-94295-2.

Memory System Design

J. Cupal. A Technique for the "Design of microprocessor memory systems," *IEEE Transactions on Education,* vol. 37. no. 3., Aug. 1994.

P. Hazen, Intel's "Flash memory boot block architecture for safe firmware updates," Intel Application Brief AB-57, Dec. 1997.

Standards

JEDEC, JEDEC Standard Number 21-C *Configurations for Solid-State Memories*. Available from Global Engineering Documents, Englewood, CO.

JEDEC, JEDEC Standard JESD3-C *Standard Data Transfer Format Between Data Preparation System and Programmable Logic Device Programmer,* 1994. Available from Global Engineering Documents, Englewood, CO.

High Energy Density Capacitors

Cesiwid Inc. Maxcap Double Later Capacitors, Product Information and Application Data, Niagara Falls, NY.

Chapter 12

A. Ebright. "82C55 programmable peripheral interface applications," Application Note AP-15. Santa Clara, CA: Intel Corporation, 1976.

Chapter 14

80C188EB/80C188EB Microprocessor User's Manual. Santa Clara, CA: Intel, 1995.

J.G. Ganssle, *The Art of Programming Embedded Systems.* San Diego, CA: Academic Press, Inc., 1992.

S. Kohler et al. *AP-730 Application Note, Interfacing the 82C59A to Intel 186 Family Processors.* Santa Clara, CA: Intel, Mar. 1996.

Yu-cheng Liu and G.A. Gibson. *Microcomputer Systems: The 8086/8088 Family.* Englewood Cliffs, NJ: Prentice Hall, 1984.

Chapter 16

Interface Between Data Terminal Equipment and Data Communications Equipment Employing Serial Binary Data Interchange. Washington, D.C.: Electronic Industries Association, 1969.

MAX232 RS-232 Dual Transmitter-Receiver data sheet. Sunnyvale, CA: Maxim Integrated Products, Inc., 1985.

J. E. McNamara. *Technical Aspects of Data Communication,* 2nd ed. Bedford, MA: Digital Press, 1982.

Serial Communications Standards

Electronic Industries Association. *Recommended Standard 232, revision C—Interface Between Data Terminal Equipment and Data Communication Equipment Employing Serial Binary Data Interchange.*

Chapter 17

Sensor and Transducers

Motorola Pressure Sensor Device Data, Motorola Semiconductor Products, Phoenix, AZ, 1994.

Digital-to-Analog Converters

Analog Devices, *Design-in Reference Manual,* Analog Devices, Norwood, MA, 1994.

D. F. Hoeschele Jr., *Analog-to-Digital and Digital-to-Analog Conversion Techniques,* New York, NY: John Wiley, 1968.

R. C. Jaeger, "Tutorial: analog data acquisition technology, part I—digital-to-analog conversion," *IEEE Micro,* May 1982.

Applications Handbook. Sunnyvale, CA: Maxim Integrated Products, Inc., 1990.

R. Behzad. *Principles of Data Conversion System Design.* Piscataway, NJ: IEEE Press, 1995. ISBN 0-7803-1093-4.

Maxim, "Don't guess about A/D converter needs," *Application Note AN-7,* Sunnyvale, CA: Maxim
 Integrated Products, Inc.

National Data Acquisition Databook 1995, Santa Clara, CA: National Semiconductor Corporation,
 1995.

Operational Amplifiers

R. Coughlin and F. Driscoll Jr., *Operational Amplifiers and Linear Integrated Circuits,* Englewood
 Cliffs, NJ: Prentice Hall, 1991. ISBN 0-13-639923-1.

R. A. Gayakwad, *Op-Amps and Linear Integrated Circuits.* Englewood Cliffs, NJ: Prentice Hall, 1993.
 ISBN 0-13-630328-5

J. K. Roberge, *Operational Amplifiers: Theory and Practice.* New York, NY: John Wiley, 1975.

Apex Power Integrated Circuits Data Book, 7th ed., Tucson, AZ: Apex Microtechnology Corporation.

Digital Potentiometers

Dallas Semiconductor, Data Book

Xicor, E^2PROMs, E^2POTs, *NOVRAMs Data Book,* Milpitas, CA: Xicor Inc., 1990.

Chapter 18

Sensors

J. R. Carstens. *Electrical Sensors and Transducers.* Englewood Cliffs, NJ: Prentice Hall, 1993. ISBN 0-
 13-249632-1.

E. A. H. Hall. *Biosensors,* Englewood Cliffs, NJ: Prentice Hall, 1991. ISBN 0-13-084526-4.

P. Hauptman. *Sensors: Principles and Applications.* Englewood Cliffs, NJ: Prentice Hall. ISBN 0-13-
 805789-3.

A. J. Wheeler and A. R. Ganji. *Introduction to Engineering Experimentation.* Englewood Cliffs, NJ:
 Prentice Hall, 1996. ISBN 0-13-337411-4.

Filters

L. Huelsman, *Active and Passive Analog Filter Design, An Introduction,* New York, NY: McGraw-Hill.
 ISBN 0070308608.

L. P. Huelsman and P. L. Allen, *Introduction to the Theory and Design of Active Filters,* New York, NY:
 McGraw-Hill. ISBN 0070308543.

Filter Pro, Burr-Brown Filter Design Programs. Software available free from Burr-Brown. (Software
 computes the R and C values for filter circuits described in Burr-Brown Application Bulletins
 AB-034 and AB-035.)

L. D. Thede. *Analog and Digital Filter Design Using C.* Upper Saddle River, NJ: Prentice Hall, 1996.
 ISBN 0-13-352627-5.

A. Waters. *Active Filter Design.* New York, NY: McGraw-Hill, ISBN 0070684537.

Chapter 20

Introductory C Texts

P. Davies. *The Indispensable Guide to C With Engineering Applications.* Reading, MA: Addison-Wesley, 1995. ISBN 0-201-62438-9.

Embedded Systems Specific C Texts

J. Campbell. *C Programmer's Guide to Serial Communications.* Carmel, IN: SAMS, 1987. ISBN 0-672-22584-0.

J. J. Labrosse, *Embedded Systems Building Blocks, Complete and Ready-to-Use Modules in C.* Lawrence, KS: R & D Publications, 1995.

J. F. Brown, *Embedded Systems Programming in C and Assembly.* New York, NY: Van Nostrand Reinhold, 1994. ISBN 0-442-01817-7.

Other C Texts

A. Koenig. *C Traps and Pitfalls.* Reading, MA: Addison-Wesley, 1989. ISBN 0-201-17928-8.

L. Reznick, *Tools for Code Management,* Lawrence, KS: R & D Books, 1996. ISBN 0-87930-435-9.

S. Oualline. *C Elements of Style,* San Mateo, CA: M&T Books. ISBN 1-55851-291-8.

R. Sedgewick. *Algorithms in C.* Addison-Wesley, 1990. ISBN 0-201-51425-7.

M. A. Weiss. *Data Structures and Algorithm Analysis in C.* Redwood City, CA: Benjamin/Cumming, 1993. ISBN 0-8053-5440-9

General Programming Texts

S. McConnell. *Code Complete: A Practical Handbook of Software Construction.* Redmond, WA: Microsoft Press, 1993. ISBN 1-55615-484-4.

INDEX

Symbols

/, slash 29
/BHE 320, 353
/CS 329
/DEN 299
/OE 330
/RD 27, 283
/RESIN 289
/RP, Flash memory power
     down 344
/S1 296
/S2 283, 296
/WE 330
/WR 25, 283
_BSS 721
_DATA 721
_TEXT 721

Numerics

3 598
74AC 303
74ACT 304
74ACT541 384
74ACT573 385
74ALS 304
74ALS874 Dual 4-Bit D-type
     Edge-Triggered Flip-
     Flop 527
74HC 303
74HC148 priority encoder 525
74HC245, octal transceiver 299
74HC372 299
74HC540 384
74HC573 299
74HC573, octal latch 297
74HC574 385 to 386
74HCT 303
80186 microprocessor 17
80188 microprocessor 17
80286 microprocessor 17
8086 microprocessor 17, 72
8088
     interrupt sequence 467
8088 microprocessor 17
80C186EB 319 to 320
80C186EB microprocessor 18
80C188EB
     chip select unit, CSU 358
     crystal network 288

data registers 70
drive capability 299
fully buffered 299
general purpose registers 70
ground 287
IC 285 to 287
logic levels 287
packaging options 286
peripheral functions 285
Port 1 59, 401
Port 2 59, 402
power 287
programmer's view 71 to 72
read bus cycle 291
reset 289
Serial Communications Unit,
     SCU 576
speed versions 287
system bus 282
system clock 287
time-multiplexed pins 286
write bus cycle 291
80C188EB instructions 209
AAA, ASCII adjust for
     addition 270
AAD, ASCII adjust for
     division 271
AAM, ASCII adjust for
     multiply 271
AAS, ASCII adjust for
     subtraction 271
ADC, add with carry 261
ADD, addition 260
AND, logical AND 182
CALL 224
CBW, convert byte to word 268
CLC, clear carry flag 180
CLD, clear direction flag 206
CLI 473
CMC, complement carry 180
CMP, compare 198, 262
CMPS, compare string 209
CWD, convert word to
     doubleword 268
DAA, decimal adjust for
     addition 272
DAS, decimal adjust for
     subtraction 272
DEC, decrement 199, 262

DIV, divide 263
ENTER, procedure entry 243
HLT 479
IDIV, integer divide 269
IMUL, integer multiply 268
IN 145
INC, increment 199, 261
INS 147
INT 498
INTO 500
INTO, interrupt on
     overflow 268
IRET 470
JCXZ, jump while CX is
     zero 201
JPE 572
JPO 572
LDS 171
LEA 170
LEAVE, leave 244
LES 172
LOCK 692
LODS 164
LOOP, loop 200
LOOPE, loop while equal 200
LOOPNE, loop while not
     equal 201
LOOPNZ, loop while not
     zero 201
LOOPZ, loop while zero 200
MOV 148
MOVS 164
MUL 262
NEG, negate 267
NOT, logical NOT 182
OR, logical OR 182
OUT 145
OUTS 147
POP, pop 222
POPA, pop all 223
POPF 223
POPF, pop flags 223
PUSH, push 221
PUSHA, push all 223
PUSHF, push flags 223
RCL, rotate through carry
     left 188
RCR rotate through carry
     right 188

REP, repeat 206
RET 230
RET, return 224
ROL, rotate left 188
ROR, rotate right 188
SAL, shift arithmetic left 187
SAR, shift arithmetic right 187
SBB, subtract with borrow 262
SHL, shift logical left 186
SHR, shift logical right 187
STC, set carry flag 180
STD, set direction flag 206
STI 473
STOS 164
SUB, subtract 262
TEST, test 197
XCHG 148
XLAT 170
XOR, exclusive OR 182
80C188EB microprocessor 16, 18
80x86 microprocessor family 16
8254
     mode 0, interrupt on terminal
          count 454
     mode 1, hardware retriggerable
          one-shot 454
     mode 2, rate generator 455
     mode 3, square wave mode 456
     mode 4, software triggered
          strobe 456
     mode 5, hardware triggered
          strobe 456
8259A priority interrupt control-
     ler, PIC 503
82C55 Programmable Peripheral
     Interface 409

A

ABS, absolute type attribute 707
absolute objedct module 93
absolute segment 91
accumulator 38, 42
     extension 260
     register 42
accuracy
     of a DAC 614
acquisition time, track-hold 637
active
     high 24
     level 24
     low 24
active address range 361
actuator 609
AD620 Instrumentation
     Amplifier 654
AD7243 12-bit serial input
     DAC 621 to 623
AD7248A parallel 12-bit (8+4)
     DAC 620 to 621
AD7248A, Parallel 12-bit
     DAC 620

addition
     packed BCD 272
     unpacked BCD 270
     unsigned binary 260
addition, signed binary 268
address 29
     bus 9
     effective 68
     logical 142
     offset 62
     physical 55
     relocation 64
     return 228
     segment 62
address access time 427
address bit map 352
address bus 9
address decoder
     external PLD 366 to 372
address decoding
     external SSI and MSI 364 to 366
     fully decoded 356
     memory 356 to 358
     nonexhaustive 358, 365
     using PLDs 392
address latch enable, ALE 298
address register 41
address valid to end of write 429
address valid to start of write 429
address/data bus
     demultiplexing 296
addressability 167 to 170
addressable 167
ADDRESSES control 96
addressing
     fixed port 145
     I/O port 145 to 147
     immediate 148 to 150
     register 148
     variable port 146
addressing mode 142 to 144
addressing modes 142
ALE 298
aligned 320
aligned word 355
align-type 712
ALU 70
ALU-Data Bus 61
American Standard Code for
     Information Interchange,
     ASCII 570
analog 609
     data 608
     data acquisition 648
     data distribution system 610
     demultiplexer 610
     high level signal 648
     input device 608
     input subsystem 608
     low level signal 648
     multiplexer 633

output subsystem 609
     DAC per channel 610
     multichannel 610
     single channel 610
signal 608
signals
     clamping 656
Analog Devices AD775 8-bit 20
     MSPS ADC 687
analog-to-digital converter 648
     ADC 658
     coding 658
     counting converter 663
     decision levels 658
     delta-sigma converter 671
     differential nonlinearity 659
     direct conversion 661 to 668
     dual slope integrating
          converter 669
     flash converter 662
     gain error 659
     half-flash converter 663
     indirect conversion 662
     indirect conversion
          techniques 668 to 672
     linearity error 659
     nonexhaustive 358, 365
     offset error 659
     quanta 658
     quantization 658
     ramp converter 663
     successive approximation 665
     transition points 658
anonymous reference 160
ApBUILDER 317
aperture time, track-hold 637
applications 5 to 7
architecture 39
argument 234
arithmetic
     packed BCD 272
arithmetic and logic unit, ALU 70
arithmetic comparisions 197
arithmetic expression
     operator 149
arithmetic operands
     packed binary coded
          decimal 258
     signed binary 258
     unpacked binary coded
          decimal 258
     unsigned binary 258
arithmetic overflow 260
arithmetic shift 186
arithmetic underflow 262
array 153
ASCII 269
ASCII decimal digit 183
ASCII, See American Standard
     Code for Information Inter-
     change

ASCIIZ strings 168
ASM86 88 to 91
ASM86 directives
    LABEL 220
    PROC/ENDP 224
assembler 88 to 91
    cross 88
    errors 94
    native 88
    warnings 94
assembler operator
    FAR PTR 192
    SHORT 192
assembly
    relocatable 91
assembly language 80
    instructions 80 to 84
assembly time 88
asserted 25
ASSUME directive 89, 167
asymmetrically blocked Flash 343
asynchronous event 464
asynchronous transmission 570
auxiliary flag 270

B
backplane 15, 312
backward reference 191
balanced line 592
bar code symbol 7
base pointer, BP 70
based addressing 162
based indexed addressing 163
batch file 713
baud rate 570
baud rate clock 574
Baud Rate Compare 579
Baud Rate Counter 579
bidirectional 26
binary integer 259
binary operation 42
binary to BCD conversions 273
binding 96
BIOS, basic input/output
    system 100
bit 24
    complementing 184
    isolation 184
    setting 184
bit capacity 30
bit organized memory 335
bit time 571
bits per second 570
bitwise operations 183
BIU
    bus cycle
        address/status phase 296
        data phase 296
    state diagram 292
block data 682
block erase. 341

bond-out chip 122
boostrap instruction 69
BOOTSTRAP control 96
bootstrap instruction 96
borrow flag 262
BOUND 500
BP 70
BP as a frame pointer 239
bps 570
branch instructions 9
break-before-make, analog
        switch 635
breakpoint 499
breakpoint command 114
brownout 290
buffer/driver
    octal inverting 384
    octal non-inverting 384
buffered bus 301
buffering 302 to 306
bug 112
bulk erase 341
burst data 682
bus
    address 9
    control 9
    data 9
    system 3, 9
bus contention 33
bus cycle 34, 283
    Halt 293
    Idle 293
    interrupt acknowledge,
        INTA 503
bus drive capability 299
bus interface unit 60 to 62
bus latency 692
bus master 689
bus signals
    Intel-style control signals 554
    Motorola-style control
        signals 554
busy wait loop 397
byte 27
byte high enable, /BHE 320, 353
byte port 145
byte-wide memory 333

C
CALL 224
call
    intersegment 229
    intersegment direct 229
    intersegment indirect 229
    intrasegment 228
    IP relative 228
    table 229
calling a procedure 227
calling sequence 234
capacitive loading 306
capacity 570

carry flag 180
causality 27
cell 24, 326
center sampling 571
central processing unit, CPU 3,
        285
CF, carry flag 180
checksum 99
chip select 329
    access time 427
    active address range 361
Chip Select Start Register 359
Chip Select Stop Register 359
chip select to end of write 429
chip select to output high Z 427
Chip-Select Unit 330
circular memory buffer, 585
circular queue 585
clamp amp 657
clamping analog signals 656
class name 106, 712
CLI 473
CLKIN 288
CLKOUT 288
clock calendar 456
clocked sequential machine 287
closed loop control 608
code segment 66
code wheel 533
coding 14
COFF object code format 720
coincident selection 334
cold start 289
column decoder 334
combine-type 711
    PUBLIC 711
    STACK 711
command line
    options 103
    switches 103
command mode 113
common I/O 329
common mode voltage 652
communications channel 569
comparator 660
compatibility
    current drive 304
    voltage level 302
conditional data transfer 397
    polling, handshaking 196
conditional jump 189, 194
    far 198
conditional task execution 202
constant 168
consumer 585
contact bounce 514
context 468
control bus 9
control flag 180
    DF, direction flag 180
    IF, interrupt flag 180

TF, trap flag 180
control register 388
control section 41
control signals
    /RD 283
    /WR 283
controlled timeout 397
count-then-execute 205
CPU subsystem 3, 282 to 284
    fully buffered 299 to 301
CPU, central processing unit 3
critical section 465
cross assembler 88
crystal
    parallel resonant fundamental
        mode 288
    third-overtone mode 288
crystal frequency 287
crystal network 288
CS 66
CSU
    I/O chip select 391
CU20025ECPB-U1J VFD
        module 562
current drive
    compatibility 304
current reference direction 304
current steering mode R-2R
        DAC 625
currently addressable 66
current-to-voltage converter 633

D
DAC
    calibration 615
    relative accuracy 614
DAC circuit 611
DAC. See digital-to-analog con-
        verter
data
    reading from registers 27
    transfer between registers 31 to
        35
data acquisition system 648
    converter per channel 649
    multichannel 649, 675
data allocation directive 151
data bus 9
    buffering 299
data communications 568
data definition directive 151
data distribution system,
        analog 610
data entry
    manual 512
data hold time 428
data line 24
data register 388
data segment 66
data set 588
data setup time 428

data structure 153
    bit encoded 209
data transfer 142 to 144
    on 80C188EB system bus 283
    serial 568
daughter boards 311
DB 152
DCE 588
DD 152
deasserted 25
debouncing 514
debugging 112
decay, track-hold 638
decision element 202
decoding
    conventional 396
    linear selection 395
    port address 388, 391
decomposition of functions 244
dedicated memory locations 56
default segment register 66
define byte 152
define double-word 152
define word 152
demultiplexer
    analog 610
demultiplexing
    address/data bus 296
    local 297
design 14
destination 31
    index, DI 70
    register 31, 142
development cycle 11
device controller 387
device select pulse 390
DF, direction flag 206
DG528 multiplexer 673
DG528, 8-Channel Single-ended
        Latchable Multiplexer 633
DGROUP 721
DI 70
differential
    amplifier 653
    input voltage, op-amp 630
    line 592
    nonlinearity, DNL 615
    signals 651
digital Potentiometer 532
digital-to-analog converter 610 to
        614
    basic circuit 624
    current steering mode R-
        2R 625
    end-point linearity 615
    ideal 612
    ideal transfer function 612
    input codes 618
    latency 616
    microprocessor
        compatible 618

multiplying 612, 627
    parallel input 618
    R-2R ladder circuit 625
    reference voltage 626
    system bus interface 618 to 620
    with bipolar output 618
digital-to-analog converter,
        DAC 610
direct addressing 159
Direct memory access, DMA 689
direction flag, DF 206
directive 88
    ASSUME 89
    END 90
    EQU 89
    EVEN 320
    NAME 89
    SEGMENT/ENDS 89
displacement 68, 190
display
    common anode 543
    common cathode 543
    duty factor 545
    ghosting 549
    interdigit blanking time 549
    multiplexed 543
    passive 549
    referesh rate 545
    refresh 545
display command 114
displays 540 to 541
    directly driven 543
division
    divide by zero error 263
    error, interrupt type 0 263
    packed BCD 272
    signed binary 269
    unpacked BCD 271
    unsigned binary 263
DMA
    controller 689
    demand transfer DMA 692
DNL, differential
        nonlinearity 615
DOS
    assemblers 93
    running assembly language
        program 100 to 102
    system service 100
DOS, disk operating system 100
double buffering 574, 619
double jumping 198
double-word 150
DP8572A Real Time Clock 457
DRAM
    refreshing 328
drive 24
droop rate 638
DS 66
DS1867 Dual Digital
        Potentiometer 641

DT/R 299
DTE 588
dual maximum count mode 445
dual rank 574
DUP 153
duty factor 545
DW 152

E
EA 157
effective address, EA 68, 157
embedded assemblers 93
embedded system 1, 4
END directive 90
End-of-Interrupt command 483
ENDP, end of procedure 225
end-point linearity 615
EPROM 337 to 338
   one time programmable,
      OTP 338
EQU directive 89
ES 66
EVEN directive 172
even parity 572
event 464
exception 497
execute-then-count 206
execution
   breakpoint 115
   mode 113
   unit 61 to 62, 70 to 71
exhaustive decoding 356
extended accumulator 263
external references 710, 712
external register 142
externally clocked 601
extra segment 66
EXTRN, external directive 707

F
F 70
false start bit detection 571
fanout 305
FAR label 189
FAR procedure 225
FAR PTR, assembler operator 192
Fault 498
F-Bus 315
feedthrough 638
fetch-execute cycle 41
field, in a record 209
FIFO 575
FIFO interrupt trigger level 597
filter
   active 655
   first-order 655
   order 655
   passive low-pass 655
finite state machine 247
First/Last Flip-Flop 694
first-in first-out 575

fixed port addressing 145
flag 180
flag register 42
flags register, F 70
Flash
   asymmetrically blocked 343
Flash memory 339 to 349
Flash memory programming
      supply 344
flow control 592
flow through 386
foldback 365
font 540
foreground/background 497
frame 570
frame pointer 239
FS, nominal full scale 613
FSM 247
FSR, full-scale range 613
full duplex 569
full scale range, FSR 613
fully buffered 301
function decomposition 244
functional specification 13
fuse map 372

G
gain drift 615
Gain error 615
general purpose
      microcomputer 11
ghosting 549
glitch 617, 619
   impulse 618
global interrupt mask 473
go command 115
granularity 357, 391
GROUP directive 718

H
half duplex 569
handshaking 397
   82C55A 412
   for serial data transfer 592
hard real-time system 5
hardware architecture
      specification 13
hardware block diagram 13
hardware debugger 112
hardware design 13, 15
   board level 15
   component level 15
   system level 15
hardware implementation 13
hardware subsystems 13
hardware testing 14
hardware/software tradeoff
   accurate time intervals 423
   arithemtic computations 257
   BCD to seven segment
      decoder 168

counting ADCs 663
counting/timing 442
display multiplexing 543
general concept 13
keyboard scanning 527
quadrature shaft encoding 535
real time clocks, calendars 456
serial data transfer 572
successive approximation
      ADC 665
switch debouncing 514
table lookup 169
head pointer 585
HEX-ASCII 98
high-impedance state, Z 27
HLDA 692
HOLD 692
hold settling time 638
hold step 638
hold time 27
holdoff 592
hos 117

I
I/O
   basic 378 to 383
   interrupt driven 465
   isolated 388 to 389
   isolated address space 57
   memory mapped 59, 389
   MSI ports 384
   parallel 397 to 401
   ports 378 to 386
   serial 568 to 573
I/O chip select 390
I/O mapped chip select 361
I/O overhead 397
I/O port addressing 145 to 147
I/O ports
   8086 408
I/O read 37
I/O space 57
I/O subsystem 57 to 59
I/O subsystems 378
I2CON 484
I3CON 484
I4CON 484
IC technology 287
ICE, in-circuit emulator 122
ICM7218B eight digit multi-
      plexed LED display
      driver 547 to 549
ICU 480
IDE 124
Ideal DAC 612
ideal op-amp 630
Identifier 152
idle 571
Idle states 291
IDSP 390
IIHmax 304

IILmax 304
immediate addressing 148 to 150
implicit rules, makefile 715
IMSK 480
IN 145
in-circuit emulator, ICE 122
INCLUDE 127
index register 70
indexed addressing 161
information hiding 246
INL, integral nonlinearity 615
in-line assembly language 723
input
   subsystem 3
input device
   analog 608
input device-select pulses 38, 390
input port 31, 37, 378
input subsystem 3
Input/Output Unit 58
INS 147
INS8250 594
INSERV 483
In-Service Register 483
instruction
   assembly language 80 to 84
   breakpoint 499
   encoding 78
   interrupted 468
   machine language 78
   mnemonic 80
   overlapped fetch and
      execution 61
   prefetch 61
   register 41
   set 9, 43
   statement 88
   stream queue 61
   transfer 60
instruction mnemonic 81
   general purpose 80
instruction pointer 67
   relative addressing 190
instruction's boundary 502
instructions
   branch 9
   execution time 420
instrumentation amplifier 654
INSTS 488
INT 498
INT 3 128
INT0 486
INT1 486
integral nonlinearity 615
integral nonlinearity, INL 615
Integrated Development
   Environment 124
Integrated Device Technology's
   IDT7203/6 FIFO 686
integrated peripherals 18
interdigit blanking time 549

internal register 142
internally clocked 601
interrupt 464 to 467
   acknowledge bus cycle,
      INTA 503
   acknowledge signal 465
   control registers 484
   Control Unit 480
   divide error, type 0 498
   driven I/O 465
   driven systems 496 to 497
   edge-triggered 466
   external 473
   handler 465
   internal 497
   latency 500
   level-sensitive input 466
   lockout feature 466
   Mask Register, IMASK 480
   maskable 465
   maskable, INTR 473
   non-maskable 465
   nonmaskable interrupt,
      NMI 478
   nonspecific end of interrupt
      mode 506
   overflow, Type 4 500
   pending 483
   priority 467, 500
   priority controller 503
   processing sequence 468
   request 465 to 466
   request flip-flop 464
   Request Register 483
   response time 501
   service procedure, ISP 465, 491
      to 495
   service routine 465
   single step, type 1 499
   source 465
   Status Register 488
   type code 470
   vector 470
   vector table 470 to 473
Intersegment call 229
intersegment jump 189
interval timer 453
INTO 500
INTR 473
intrasegment jump 189
IO/M 55
IOHmax 304
IOLmax 304
IOZH 306
IOZL 306
IP 67
IRET 470
isolated I/O 388
isolated I/O space 57
ISR 465
iteration control 199

J
JEDEC, Joint Electronic Devices
   Engineering Council 339
Joint Electronic Devices Engineering Council, see JEDEC
jump
   conditional 189
   intersegment 189
   intrasegment 189
   table 192
   unconditional 189

K
keyboard 525 to 532
keyboard encoder 528
keypad 525 to 532
keys 525

L
LABEL 220
label 81, 189
   defined by a PROC 224
   FAR 189
   NEAR 189
latency
   of a DAC 616
LDS 171
LEA 170
LED display 541 to 547
LES 172
LIB86, library manager 94
librarian utility 712
library 92
life cycle model 14
LIFO 218
light-emitting diode, LED 541
line driver 590
line receiver 590
linear selection 395
linked dependency, makefile 715
linker 91
liquid crystal display module,
   LCD 549
list file 90
LM34 Fahrenheit temperature
   sensor 650
LM34 temperature
   transducer 648
load command 113
loading 302 to 306
loading object code 98 to 99
load-time locatable 101
LOC86, locator 96
local bus 301
local variable 240
locator 93 to 97
lockout feature 466
LODS 164
logic error 112
logic family
   compatibility analysis 302

logic level 302 to 306
logical address 62
logical execution flow structure
  DO WHILE 205
  IF/ELSE 202
  SEQUENCE 202
  SWITCH 204
  WHILE 204
logical segment
  in a program 89
logical shift 186
loop control variable 199
looping 199
LS8120 bar code symbol
  scanner 7, 11

M
machine code 78
machine language 78
macro 127
  expansion 127
macrocell 368
main module 91, 706
MAKE
  macro 715
make utility 713
makefile 713
  explicit rule 714
  implicit rules 715
  linked dependency 715
  rule 714
mangled function names 727
manual reset 290
map file 96
marking 571
mask 183
MASK operator 210
maskable interrupt 465
masking 183
master micorprocessor 598
MAX166 387, 390
MAX182 4-channel 12-bit
  ADC 676
MAX662A, Flash memory programming supply 344
MAX807, micprorocessor supervisory circuit 290
maximum information
  transfer 629
maximum power transfer 629
measurand 607
mechanical switches 512
memory 29
  allocation for data 150 to 157
  banks 351
  block address 357
  buffer 585
  dedicated locations 56
  depth 329
  generic classes 35
  locations 35

map 36, 55
model 721
organization 55 to 57
reserved locations 56
segmentation 62 to 70
subsystem 3, 326 to 328
unpopulated 57
width 329
memory addressing mode 157 to
  164
memory cell 24 to 27, 326
  dynamic 328
  static 328
memory IC
  logical organization 328
  logical structure and
    operation 328 to 333
  logical word 334
  three control inputs
    scheme 330
  timing parameters 425 to 429
  two-level decoding 334
memory mapped I/O 59, 389
memory subsystem design 349 to
  356
  8086 353
  8088 351
  steps 350
memory-mapped chip select 361
microcomputer 4
  single-chip 4
microcontroller 4
microprocessor 3
  architecture 39
  simple 39
  supervisory circuit 290
  three fundamental
    operations 282
  wordlength 39
microprocessor compatible
  IC 387
microprocessor selection 16
microprocessor supervisory
  circuit 290
minimum component system 309
  to 311
MM74C923 20-Key Encoder 528
mnemonic 80
mnemonic synonyms 187
modem 588
modified IP 190
modular
  core CPU 17
  software 244
  tasks 245
modulator 588
module 91
monitor 119
monotonic 616
MOV 148
MOVS 164

multi-board system 311 to 313
multidrop 600
multi-module program 706
multiple bus masters 312
multiplexer
  analog 633
  cross-coupling 674
  differential inputs 673
multiplication
  packed BCD 272
  unpacked BCD 271
  unsigned binary 262
multiplying DAC 612, 627
multiprecision number 260
multipurpose pins 286
mutual exclusion 495

N
NAME directive 89
named variable 151
native assembler 88
native debugger 118
n-bit register 27
NEAR label 189
NEAR procedure 225
negated 25
negative feedback 632
negative logic convention 590
nested interrupt 474
nesting, procedures 230
next state 247
nibble 27
N-key rollover 528
NMI 478
noise margin, DC 302
nominal full scale 613
nominal full scale, FS 613
nonmaskable interrupt 465, 478
NOR Flash memory 341
normally not ready 423
normally ready 424

O
object code 88
object code format
  COFF 720
  OMF86 720
object-hex translator 98
offset address 62
offset binary 618
offset drift 615
Offset error 614
OFFSET operator 160, 718
OH86, object-hex translator 98
OMF86 object code format 720
ON Circuit Emulation 122
ONCE 122
op-amp
  closed loop operation 632
  current-to-voltage
    converter 633

ideal 630
open loop gain 630
regions of operation 630
unity gain buffer
  unity gain buffer 633
op-amp. see operational
  amplifier 630
op-amps
  power 633
opcode 41
open loop control 607
operand 82
  transfer 60
operand addressing mode 143
operands
  numeric representations 258
operating system
  real-time 5
operation code 41
operational amplifier
  differential
    input voltage 630
optical encoder 532
optical shaft encoder 532
order 655
ORG directive 363
OSCOUT 288
OUT 145
output
  subsystem 3
output device select pulses 38
output device-select pulses 390
output enable 330
output enable input 27
output enable to output high
  Z 427
output enable to valid data 427
output hold time 427
output port 31, 38, 382
output subsystem 3, 609
output transducer 609
OUTS 147
overlay memory 123, 135
overrun error 401
oversampling 671

P
P25C8 Keyboard Encoder 531
packed BCD 272
pairing or balancing PUSHes and
  POPs 223
PAL 368
PALCE22V10 369
Paradigm Debugger
  Step Over 252
  Trace Into 252
Paradigm's LOCATE 105
parallel I/O 397 to 401
parameter 234
  pass by address 234
  pass by reference 234

passed by value 234
passing 234
parsing 248
partial decoding 358
passing parameters 234
  using a stack frame 239
PC/104
  bus 313
  Consortium 313
PCB base address 315
pedestal error 638
pending interrupt 465
period operator 166
peripheral 3
Peripheral Control Block,
  PCB 315 to 319
  relocating 317
  writing 80C188EB registers 315
peripheral IC 387
personal computer 11
PGA 655
phantom key 528
physical address 55, 63, 143
physical measurands, classes 650
physical organization 328
physical word 334
physical-level standards 586
pipeline 61
PLA 368
PLCC package 286
PLD. See programmable logic
  device
pointer 234
pointer register 70
POLL 489
Poll Register 489
Poll Status Register 489
polling 397
POLLSTS 489
POP 222
POPF 223
port 378
  input 378
    programmable LSI 409 to 415
  word 145
positive feedback 632
power op-amps 633
power-on reset 289
preempted 482
prefetch 61
prescalar 449
present state 247
PRIMSK 482
priority 400, 467
  interrupt controller, PIC 503
  mask bits 482
PROC 224
PROC/ENDP 224
procedure 224
  calling a procedure 227
  FAR 225

in a single module
  program 232
in modular software design 244
interrupt service 491 to 495
NEAR 225
nesting 230
pure 495
reentrant 240, 495
saving registers 231
shared 494
testing and debugging 252
procedures
  nested 230
processor status word, PSW 70,
  180
producer 585
product line 367
production prototyp 116
program 3, 9
  multimodule 706
program counter, PC 41
program structure
  sequential tasks 84 to 88
Programmable Array Logic 368
programmable gain
  amplifiers 655
programmable high-voltage
  power supply 633
programmable logic device 366,
  392
programmable microperipheral
  with memory 309
programmer's model 71
programmer's register view 43
programmer's view 71
prototype 116
PSD311 309
PSW, Processsor Status Word 70,
  180
PTR operator 161
PUBLIC, public directive 707
pure procedure 495
PUSH 221
PUSHA 223
PUSHes and POPs, pairing or
  balancing 223
PUSHF 223

Q
Q Bus 61
quantization 658
  error 659
  size 658

R
R-2R DAC ciruit 625
RAM 35
read cycle 332
read cycle timing 428
read pointer 585
read strobe 27

real time clock 453, 456
real-time operating system, RTOS 5
real-time system 5
  hard 5
  soft 5
record 209
record definition 210
RECORD directive 210
reentrant procedure 240
reference voltage, DAC 626
refresh 545
refresh rate 545
refreshing
  a DRAM 328
register 27
  address 41
  clearing 185
  destination 31, 142
  external 142
  flag 42
  internal 142
  operational 38 to 39
  saving in a procedure 231
  source 31, 142
  storage 38
  view of a simple
    microprocessor 43
register addressing 148
register file 29
register indirect addressing 160
register transfer expression 43
register view
  of a memory subsystem 35 to 36
  of a microprocessor 39 to 42
  of an I/O subsystem 36 to 38
  of system operation 43
registered PAL 368
relative 190
relative accuracy 615
relative displacement 190
release character 592
relocatable
  assembler 91
  object file 91
  object module 91
  segment 91
relocation 64
  register 317
RELREG, relocation register 317
remote debugger 120
remote demultiplexing 297
REPE, repeat while equal 209
repeated string instructions 206
REPNE, repeat while not
  equal 209
REQST 483
requirements analysis 13
requirements definition 13
reserved memory locations 56

reserved word 153
reset 289
resident monitor 119
resistor divider DAC circuit 624
resolution 613
RESOUT 289
RET 224, 230
return
  intersegment 230
  intrasegment 230
reuse of software 91
ring buffe 585
rollover 528
ROM 35
ROM emulator 129
ROMable 101
ROM-BIOS 35
RON modulation 674
row decoder 334
run time 88

S
sample-hold 636
  amplifier, SHA. see also track-
    hold 610, 638
sampling ADC 666
sampling rate 675
scale error 615
SCAS, scan string 209
schematic diagram 13
SCU 488
  mode 0—synchronous
    mode 602
  mode 1—8 bit asynchronous
    mode 577
  mode 2—master/slave
    mode 598
  mode 3—master slave
    mode 598
SCUCON 486
segment 62
  address 62
  align-type 712
  attribute 152
  base address 65
  override 167 to 170
  register 62 to 70
  register initialization 69
  wrap around 190
segment override 167
SEGMENT/ENDS directive 711
  pair 89
segmentation 335
segmented memory 62
self-clocked 601
self-generating 650
semaphore 495
sensor 609, 650
  electrical 650
separate I/O 36
serial channel 569

Serial Communication Unit,
  SCU 488
Serial Communications Unit, SCU
  80C188EB 576
Serial Control 579
serial data transfer 568
serial I/O 568 to 573
Serial Status 581
service request flag 397
setup time 27
seven segment display 543
SHA, sample-hold amplifier, see
  also track-hold 638
shared data bus 31
shared variable 706
shift count operator 210
SHORT, assembler operator 192
short-label 194
SI 70
sign bit 264
sign extension 268
signal
  analog 608
signal naming convention 24
signal to noise ratio 653
signed number
  two's complement 265
signed overflow 268
simple microprocessor 39
simplex 569
simplified segment directives 732
simulator 117
single board system 311 to 313
single channel analog output 610
single maximum count mode 442
single-board microcomputer 4
single-chip microcomputer 4
single-end 592
single-ended signal 651
single-pole/double-throw 512
Single-pole/single-throw 512
single-stepping 114
sink 304
slash, / 29
slave microprocessor 598
small model 721
SMP18 Octal Sample-and-hold
  with Multiplexed Input 638
sneak path 528
soft real-time system 5
software
  reuse 91
software architecture
  specification 13
software debouncing 514
software debugger 112
software design 14 to 15
  assembly language 16
  high-level language 16
  mixed assembly and high-level
    languages 16

software implementation 14
software module 13
software testing 14, 112
SoftwareBuilder 346
source 31, 304
source index, SI 70
source program 88
source register 31, 142
SP 70
SP, stack pointer register 220
Specially Fully Nested mode 486
specification 13
SRAM 333 to 336
    /CS controlled 428
    /WE controlled 428
SS 66
SS, stack segment register 220
STACK 721
stack 218
    balance 223
    empty stack 219
    full stack 219
    initialization 221
    length 218
    pointer, SP 70, 219
    pop 218
    push 218
stack frame 239
stack pointer register, SP 220
stack segment 66
    register, SS 220
standard bus system 312
standard segment directives 732
start bit 571
startup code 734
startup module 734
state table 248
statement 88
static random access memory 333
    to 336
    internal organization 333
static random access memory, see
    SRAM
status flag 180
    AF, auxiliary flag 180
    CF, carry flag 180
    OF, overflow flag 180
    PF, parity flag 180
    SF, sign flag 180
    ZF, zero flag 180
status register 388
step 613
step command 114
STI 473
stop bit 572
storage register 27 to 30
STOS 164
string 163
string addressing 163
string constants 149
STRUC/ENDS 165

structure 162, 164 to 167
structure template 164
structured programming 202
subroutine 224
subsystem
    CPU 3
    input 3
    memory 3
    output 3
subtraction
    packed BCD 272
    signed binary 268
    unpacked BCD 271
    unsigned binary 262
successive approximation register,
    SAR 666
sum line 367
Supersmart Card, VISA 6, 10
supervisory circuit 290
switch
    break-before-make, analog 635
symbolic debugging 115
symmetrically blocked. 348
synchronous transfer 570
synchronous transmission. self
    clocking 601
syntax error 112
system 5
    architecture 13
    common structure of 9 to 11
    evolution of 14
    integration 14
    maintenance of 14
    operation of 14
    physical subdivision of 3
    register view of a simple
        microprocessor 43
    validation of 14
system bus 3, 9, 282
    partially buffered 301
    read bus cycle 283 to 284
    write bus cycle 284
system clock 287
system clock frequency 287
system context 492
system state 492

T
T state 289
    phase 1 296
    phase 2 296
T0CON 486
T1CON 486
T2CON 486
table lookup 168
tables, call 229
tail pointer 585
target 88
target access probe 121
target addressing modes
    intrasegment direct 190

target file 714
target microprocessor 88, 117
target system 88
task 84
    behavioral specification 246
    cohesion 246
    interface specification 246
    specification 246
tasks
    loose coupling 245
    sequential 84 to 88
TASM 102
TCUCON 486
termination character 168
testing 112
THA. see track-hold 638
thermistor 650
thermocouple 650
thermometer code 662
three-wire 602
TI, idle state 291
Timer Control Register 442
Timer Count Register 442
timer cycle 446
timer event 445
Timer Maxcount Compare
    Register 442
timing
    compatibility calculations 429
        to 441
    general considerations 420
    impact on system
        architecture 420
timing compatibility calculation
    for EPROM 433, 441
    for SRAM 439
timing diagram 13
TLINK 712
track mode 610
track-hold 610
    acquisition time 637
    amplifier 638
    aperture time 637
    decay 638
    practical circuit 636
transceiver 299
    octal 299
transducer
    input 609
    matching output to ADC 648
    non-self-generating 650
    transduction principle 650
transduction principle 650
transfer function, ideal DAC 612
Trap 498
trouble shooting 112
true outputs 386
TTL
    open collector output 308
    totem-pole output 308
Turbo Assembler 102

two's complement number 264 to 265
two-key rollover 528
two-wire scheme 601
type 150
type code 470
typematic 532

U

UAF42 Universal Active Filter 656
unaligned word 320, 356
unary operation 42
unasserted 25
unbalanced 592
unconditional jump 189
unconditional transfer 397
universal asynchronous/receiver transmitter, UART 573
unpacked BCD 269
unpopulated 57
unsatisfied module 711
unsigned binary integer 259
USART. See universal synchronous/asynchronous receiver transmitter
utility usage 102

V

variable 151
    local 240
variable port addressing 146
vector 470
VIHmin 302
VILmax 302
VOHmin 302
volatile 35, 333
VOLmax 303
voltage level compatibility 302
voltage switching mode R-2R circuit 626

W

wait loop 197
WAIT states 292, 423 to 425
    for I/O Ports 390
warm start 289
watchdog timer 459
wear leveling 348
width of a register 27
WIDTH operator 211
word 27, 150
word aligned 320

word port 145, 390
word-wide memory 333
wrap around 190
write
    cycle 330
    cycle time 429
    endurance 338
    pointer 585
    pulse width 428
    release time 429
    strobe 25
write enable 330
    input 25

X

X9MME Digitally Controlled Potentiometer 641
XCHG 148
XLAT 170
XOFF 592
XON 592
XON/XOFF protocol 592

Z

Z state 27